Educating Students with Behavior Disorders

Second Edition

Educating Students with Behavior Disorders

Michael S. Rosenberg
Johns Hopkins University

Rich Wilson
Bowling Green State University

Larry Maheady
SUNY–Fredonia

Paul T. Sindelar
University of Florida

Allyn and Bacon
Boston • London • Toronto • Sydney • Tokyo • Singapore

Senior Editor: Ray Short
Editorial Assistant: Christine Svitila
Editorial-Production Administrator: Rob Lawson
Editorial-Production Service: Walsh & Associates, Inc.
Composition Buyer: Linda Cox
Manufacturing Buyer: Suzanne Lareau
Cover Administrator: Suzanne Harbison

Library of Congress Cataloging-in-Publication Data

Educating students with behavior disorders / Michael S. Rosenberg . . .
  [et al.] — 2nd ed.
     p.   cm.
  Includes bibliographical references and indexes.
  ISBN 0-205-26467-0
    1. Problem children—Education—United States.   2. Behavior disorders in children—United States.   3. Special education—United States.   I. Rosenberg, Michael S.
LC4802.E38   1996
371.93'0973—dc20
                                          96-36354
                                            CIP

For our wives and children,
Irene and Daniel
Maggie and Beth
Bethany, Jason, Joshua, and Connor
Robin and Daisy

Contents

Preface

Students with behavior disorders (BD) continue to be among the most neglected and underserved populations in our educational system. At both the national and local levels, we are presented with chilling data that verify what many educators have suspected for some time: Students with BD are isolated, extremely deficient in academic skills, and unprepared socially for the critical transition to the world of work. Moreover, many of the programs that serve these students are housed in segregated settings where containment often takes a higher priority than education. Not surprisingly, a disproportionately large number of these students drop out of school prior to the completion of their educational programs. The implication of these facts is clear: Many challenges must be met directly if we are to provide appropriate and meaningful services to this disturbed and disturbing group of exceptional students.

The nature, range, and severity of behaviors exhibited by students with behavior disorders require the talents and dedication of many individuals. To influence the lives of students positively, the efforts of medical, social work, and mental health professionals must supplement the practices of special educators. Still, a necessary prerequisite for any successful collaboration is that individuals involved in the collaborative effort be knowledgeable and effective in their own profesional areas.

The purpose of this second edition is to enhance the professional development of preservice and inservice teachers who plan to work with students identified as having BD. As it was with our first edition, our emphasis is on classroom-based strategies that have been successful in the assessment, management, and resolution of problem behaviors. Our primary goal is to provide a balanced data-based prresentation of what is currently regarded as best practices in the education of students with behavior disorders. One critical assumption guides the development of each chapter: An effective educational program is the most important sevice that teachers can deliver. Therefore, the majority of content focuses on teacher-directed educational activities that occur in instructional environments. Active and dedicated teachers aware of alternative strategies for assessing, managing, and resolving problem behavior should be able to successfully meet the challenging and unpredictable behaviors presented by these students.

The text is divided into three specific areas: definitional matters; assessing and classifying disordered behavior; and managing and teaching students with behavior disorders. In each part, the focus and primary referent are on the patterns of problem behavior exhibited by students. In the first section, a number of key concepts involving the definition and description of behavior disorders are provided. In particular, Chapter 1, Defining Behavior Disorders, covers the definition of BD, the variety of problems associated with defining behavior disorders, and the major theoretical explanations of this behavior. In Chapter 2, High-Incidence Behavior Disorders, the primary and secondary characteristics of hyperactivity, aggression, rule breaking/delinquency, and social withdrawal are provided. Prevalence rates and theories of causation for each of the patterns are also provided. Chapter 3 uses a similar format to address Low-Incidence Behavior Disorders. Highlighted are the primary and secondary characteristics of the pervasive developmental disorders such as autism and Asperger's syndrome as well as the sometimes fascinating theories of what are believed to be their respective etiologies.

The second area, assessing and classifying disordered behavior, contains three chapters that provide alternative ways to observe and identify disordered behavior systematically. Chapter 4, Standardized Instruments for Assessment and Classification, begins with a discussion and analysis of different measurement systems as they relate to disordered behavior and concludes with descriptions of available instrumentation for the screening and identification of disordered behavior. Chapter 5, Direct and Systematic Observation, provides a step-by-step guide for collecting meaningful classroom data through systematic observational techniques. Illustrations, forms, and case studies are provided for each step in the process. Chapter 6, Developing Individual Educational Programs for Students with BD, discusses ways to develop meaningful plans and how to involve parents in the IEP process.

In the third area, managing and teaching students with behavior disorders, management strategies are provided for each pattern of disordered behavior: hyperactivity, aggression, social withdrawal, and rule breaking/delinquency. The organization of these chapters reflects our philosophy that behaviors exhibited by students with BD should be the primary determinant in the consideration and selection of an intervention. Two additional chapters focus on (1) teaching academic skills to students with BD and (2) teaching and managing students with severe behavior disorders. The text concludes with a chapter on issues facing professionals involved in the education of students with BD and suggests several alternative directions for the future.

We wish to express our gratitude to many individuals who devoted a great deal of personal and professional time to the task of helping us complete this second edition. The faculty and staff in the Department of Special Education at Johns Hopkins University, The College of Education and Allied Professions at Bowling Green State University, The Department of Special Education at The University of Florida, and The School of Education at SUNY–Fredonia provided much support and encouragement throughout all phases of this project. In particular, we acknowledge Sharon Lampkin, Cathy Wagner, Peggy Card, Kay Gazarek, Larkin Misplay, Julie Buchness, Liz Spector, Ben Washburn, and Stacey Newbern. We also gratefully acknowledge the many contributions of the teachers we work with who continually remind us that there is a vast number of active and dedicated master teachers of students with BD. We also wish to express our appreciation to those professionals at Allyn and Bacon, Ray Short, and to Kathy Whittier of Walsh & Associates, Inc., as well as to the reviewers of this second edition including Jack Scott, Florida Atlantic University, and Stephen Smith, University of Florida. Finally, we express our love and appreciation to our families.

MSR
RW
LM
PTS

$$C \quad h \quad a \quad p \quad t \quad e \quad r \quad \mathbf{1}$$

Defining Behavior Disorders

Advance Organizer

As you read this chapter, prepare to identify and discuss:

- Terminology that refers to behavior disorders.
- A definition of behavior disorders.
- Problems associated with defining behavior disorders.
- The six major theoretical explanations of behavior disorders and their utility to special education.
- An alternative orientation to approach the management of behavior disorders based on specific patterns of deviance.
- Issues related to the prevalence of behavior disorders.

In "The Blind Men and the Elephant," poet J. G. Saxe described how six blind men set out to understand the great beast. The first man fell against its side, which convinced him that the elephant was "very like a wall." Another, grabbing a tusk, thought it "very like a spear." "Very like a snake," concluded the third blind man, as he cradled the trunk. "Very like a tree," reasoned the fourth, as he hugged the animal's knee. The fifth man, who grasped the elephant's ear, found it "very like a fan." The sixth man, holding the elephant's tail, thought it "very like a rope."

> *And so these men of Hindostan*
> *Disputed loud and long.*
> *Each in his own opinion*
> *Exceeding stiff and strong.*
> *Though each was partly in the right*
> *And all were in the wrong!*

1

The concept of behavior disorders is as complex, multifaceted, and difficult for us to understand as the elephant was for the blind men. Behavior disorders comprise many types, some bearing little resemblance to others. A disruptive, acting-out boy is no more like his withdrawn, preoccupied classmate than an elephant's tusks are like its tail. Yet both children may be described as having behavior disorders. The complexity of the concept has contributed to the problem of naming and defining it.

In this chapter, we first discuss the problems inherent in defining behavior disorders and present what has become its most widely accepted definition. Then we consider different views of behavior disorders and how their diversity adds to the difficulty of definition. Finally, because a phenomenon that is so hard to define will most assuredly be hard to measure as well, we present estimates of the prevalence of behavioral disturbance. Indeed, they do range widely.

Many terms are used to refer to what we will call behavior disorders: mental illness, emotional disturbance, emotional disorder, emotional handicap, social maladjustment, and serious emotional disturbance, to name a few. Some professionals use these terms precisely to distinguish subtle differences in the nature or severity of the problems. Others use the terms interchangeably. For the sake of simplicity, no distinctions are implied by the use of various terms in this text.

To a certain extent, the choice of terminology may reflect an individual's point of view about the nature of the problem. For example, someone who believes that deviant behavior itself constitutes the problem is likely to use the term *behavior disorders*, whereas someone who views problem behavior as the product of underlying emotional conflict might be more satisfied with *emotional disturbance*. Although the use of *behavior disorders* does reflect our point of view about the nature of these phenomena, there is a second and more important reason for choosing the term. In a sense, all other terms may be subsumed under the heading of behavior disorders: Unless an emotional disorder manifests itself in the overt actions of individuals, the existence of the disorder would not be known. Consequently, whatever we choose to call a problem or however we choose to perceive its nature, we experience it through the observable behavior of individuals. Thus, behavior disorders seems appropriate.

Definition

The Rules and Regulations governing Public Law 94-142, the Individuals with Disabilities Education Act (IDEA) (1975), include the following definition of emotional disturbance:

"Seriously emotionally disturbed" is defined as follows: (i) The term means a condition exhibiting one or more of the following characteristics over a long period of time and to a marked degree, which adversely affects educational performance: (A) An inability to learn which cannot be explained by intellectual, sensory, or health factors; (B) An inability to build or maintain satisfactory interpersonal relationships with peers and teachers; (C) Inappropriate types of behavior or feelings under normal circumstances; (D) A general pervasive mood of unhappiness or depression; (E) A tendency to develop physical symptoms or fears associated with personal or school problems. (ii)

The term includes children who are schizophrenic or autistic. The term does not include children who are socially maladjusted, unless it is determined that they are seriously emotionally disturbed. (Federal Register, Tuesday, August 23, 1977.)

The IDEA definition is not new to the field of behavior disorders; in fact, Bower published its original version in 1960. The few changes that were made in the original are not recognized by everyone as improvements. Kauffman (1981), for example, has taken issue with the addition of three statements to the original Bower definition: the two sentences under heading (ii) and the clause "which adversely affects educational performance" under heading (i). Kauffman has argued that points (B) and (C) make the separate inclusion of children with autism or schizophrenia unnecessary; that the exclusion of the socially maladjusted is inconsistent with point (B); and that the educational performance clause under heading (i) is redundant since it appears later as point (A), and it is unlikely that the other problems would exist in the absence of significant academic retardation. The inclusion of these points in the Rules and Regulations may serve a regulatory function, but only at the expense of definitional clarity.

Bower's definition and the adaptation of it in the Rules and Regulations have the advantage of being descriptive. The definition does not explain the causes of serious emotional disturbance; instead, it describes the likely manifestations of whatever the problem might be. Consequently, the definition is not bound to any single theoretical point of view. Although it will not satisfy strict adherents to a theoretical perspective, it does not alienate any particular group because of an implied theoretical perspective either. A second advantage derives from the codification of the definition. It now appears in law and allows for a common, albeit general, under- standing of serious emotional disturbance.

There are disadvantages to the Bower definition as well. Given the array of behavior that must be subsumed under any definition of behavioral disorders, a satisfactory all-encompassing definition may be all but impossible to write. The Bower definition is quite general. Many of its terms are not operationalized and are open to varying interpretations. For example, how long is "a long period of time'? What is "a marked degree"? Educators are especially likely to take issue with the use of the word *inability* in the phrase "inability to learn." Children with behavior disorders do learn, although they often have more difficulty learning because of the problems they experience. The phrase "inappropriate types of behavior or feelings," too, is ill-defined and open to interpretation. Finally, other authors (Algozzine, Schmid, & Connors, 1978; Kauffman, 1977) have begun to address the need to operationalize criteria for defining behavior disorders. The fact that a definition that includes undefined and nonoperational terms was adopted by the (then) Office of Education seems unfortunate indeed.

Measurement

The definition of certain disabilities involves the assessment of behaviors that can be reliably and validly measured. For example, mental retardation is defined, in part, in the Rules and Regulations as "subaverage general intellectual functioning." Although not explicitly stated in the definition, that intellectual functioning will be operationalized as a score on an intelligence test is understood. Thus, this particular disability is defined in part by a test score from an instrument that is understood to measure intellectual functioning. Similarly, the measurement of academic achievement is central to the definition of learning disabilities. Achievement also can be measured reliably and validly; discrepancies between expected and actual achievement serve as one defining characteristic of this disorder.

There are numerous other examples of disabilities that are, at least in part, defined by some measure of ability or performance. It should be noted, however, that seldom is the score from a single measure sufficient to define them. More commonly, these measures are used with other indices for the purposes of definition, and the contributions of these other indices are significant.

In defining behavioral disorders, on the other hand, no single measure of social or emotional functioning is sufficiently reliable and valid to serve in the way that intelligence tests do in defining mental retardation or achievement tests do in defining learning disabilities. As a result, in defining behavior disorders, it is impossible to rely, even in part, on a test score. The limitations of measuring social and emotional behaviors are discussed in Chapter 4; suffice it to say here that there is no equivalent of intelligence or achievement testing in the social and emotional domains.

Do not read into these arguments support for the use of standardized instruments in identifying students with emotional disorders. By standards of technical adequacy, measurement in the social and emotional domains lags far behind measurement in the intellectual and achievement domains (and even there, standardized testing is highly controversial). Decades may pass before researchers develop standardized processes for assessment in these domains that meet standards of technical adequacy for decision making.

Nowhere are the inadequacies of identifying and testing more detrimental than in the case of culturally diverse students (Executive Committee, 1989). Language or cultural differences may lead to social and academic failure (or to teachers' perceptions of failure) and trigger the referral/assessment process. And once students are referred, the probability is great that they will be found eligible (Graden, Casey, & Christenson, 1985). Thus, being different in language or culture increase a student's probability of being placed in special education programs.

School professionals must guard against unnecessary referrals of culturally different students. The Executive Committee of the Council for Children with Behavioral Disorders (1989) recommended the use of functional assessment in the identification of students with behavior disorders. Functional assessment involves relating student learning and comportment to teaching and classroom management practices and to monitoring changes over time. The use of direct observations of this sort should benefit all students, including those who are culturally diverse. The misperceptions of teachers that arise from misunderstanding or intolerance of cultural differences and lead to unnecessary referral may be dispelled by comparisons of culturally different children with their classmates.

Forness and Knitzer (1992) recently proposed an alternative on behalf of the Workgroup on Definition of the National Mental Health and Special Education

Coalition, an association of mental health and special education organizations. They used the term *emotional or behavioral disorders* (EBD) and defined it as "a disability characterized by behavioral or emotional responses in school so different from appropriate age, cultural, or ethnic norms that they adversely affect education performance" (p. 13). The authors defined educational performance broadly and went on to specify that such a disability

1. is more than a temporary, expected response to stressful events in the environment
2. is consistently exhibited in two different settings, at least one of which is school-related
3. is unresponsive to direct intervention in general education or the child's condition is such that general education interventions would be insufficient (p. 13)

Furthermore, EBD can occur contemporaneously with other disabilities and may include "children or youth with schizophrenic disorders, affective disorders, anxiety disorders, or other sustained disorders of conduct or adjustment when they adversely affect educational performance" (p. 13).

Although it has garnered a broad base of professional support, this definition has not yet been adopted in federal rule. Forness and Knitzer argued that it rectifies many of the shortcomings of the original federal definition of serious emotional disturbance and addresses many of the general problems involved in defining behavioral disorders. These include the lack of a widely accepted measuring device; the lack of a clear distinction between normal and deviant behavior in the social and emotional domains; and the abundance and diversity of explanations of behavior disorders. These difficult and perplexing problems will be discussed in detail in the following sections of this chapter.

We will return to the topic of assessment in later chapters. It is enough to say here that the problems associated with assessment in the social and emotional domains are exaggerated for language or culturally different students, and we recommend that care be taken to understand their behavior in terms of the social and linguistic environments in which they grew up and now live.

Deviant Behavior of Normal Individuals

One frightening aspect of working with children with behavioral disorders is the realization that their behavior is not totally unlike our own (Rhodes, 1967). Research has demonstrated repeatedly the surprisingly high frequency of deviant behavior in populations that are otherwise considered normal. Moreover, the range of behavior within disordered populations is vast, and its overlap with the range of acceptable behavior is considerable.

The research on which these generalizations are based has a long history. In one early longitudinal study (MacFarlane, Allen, & Honzik, 1954), researchers followed a sample of children through their childhood years during the 1930s. They interviewed the mothers periodically from the time their children were 21 months old until they were 14 years old. At least one-third of the mothers reported five or six problem behaviors at each age level between 21 months and 11 years. The most commonly identified problem behaviors among boys were overactivity, oversensitiveness, fears, and tantrums, and among girls, oversensitiveness, fears, tantrums, and excessive reserve. The frequency with which most problem behaviors were identified decreased as the children grew older, and some reliable differences between boys and girls were found.

The finding that many normally developing children exhibit sometimes serious emotional problems was confirmed in another early study (LaPouse & Monk, 1958). These researchers interviewed mothers of children 6 to 12 years old and asked them to identify the common problems their children exhibited. Their responses, like those of the mothers in the longitudinal study, revealed the common occurrence of problems among these normally developing children. For example, nearly half of the mothers identified fears and worries, temper loss, and overactivity as problems for their children. More than one-fourth noted that their children had nightmares, were restless, bit their nails, and picked their noses. Many of these behaviors are commonly associated with maladjustment and behavior deviance; the frequency with which they appear among normally developing children highlights the difficulty of defining behavior problems.

These early findings have been replicated in more recent studies (cf. Glavin, 1972; Rubin & Balow, 1978; Werry & Quay, 1971). Perhaps the most interesting, and surely the most extensive, of these studies was the longitudinal work of Rubin and Balow (1971, 1978). These researchers followed a sample of children born between 1960 and 1964 through their elementary school years. The sample did not differ from the general population on a number of critical variables such as IQ, socioeconomic status, and developmental measures. Each year, teachers were asked to indicate whether they considered the children to be behavior problems, although the term *behavior problem* was not defined. Rubin and Balow analyzed the data on children for whom two or more ratings were received in order to determine the prevalence and consistency of behavior problems. Approximately 35 percent of the boys at all grade levels were thought by their teachers to be problems; the percentage of girls so identified decreased from 26 percent at first grade to 13 percent at sixth. Among the children for whom six ratings were received, only 40 percent were never identified as problems. Although the percentages of consistent problems were not great (3 percent for both boys and girls), behavior thought to be a problem by at least one teacher was the rule rather than the exception among the children in the study. Because by definition emotional disturbance is a prolonged and marked phenomenon, these children could not be called disturbed, even though their behavior was disturbing to at least one of their teachers. A definition must differentiate between chronic and temporary problems that, on the surface, may not be distinguishable. Clearly, such distinctions are not easily drawn.

Compounding this problem is an effort to equate conduct disorders, a psychiatric classification, with social maladjustment, and to differentiate these two from severe emotional disturbance (Slenkovich, 1983). To do so would allow schools to deny conduct-disordered students special education services because in the federal definition students who are socially maladjusted are excluded from the protections of PL 94-142 (unless they are also severely emotionally disturbed). It would also allow districts to expel them (*Honig v. Doe*, 1988). Excluding students who are socially maladjusted presumes that they (and conduct-disordered students) may be differentiated reliably from students with emotional disturbances and that to draw this distinction was the intention of Congress when it passed the IDEA in 1975.

The Council for Children with Behavior Disorders (CCBD, 1990) has voiced serious opposition to the practice of excluding conduct-disordered students and has called for the removal from federal regulation of the social maladjustment exclusion. Their argument is based on many points and is only summarized here. The CCBD makes the point that currently there is no reliable method for differentiating social maladjustment from other disorders. If this distinction cannot be made accurately, then students may be excluded arbitrarily from special education services by being diagnosed as conduct disordered. Furthermore, there is no evidence to suggest that the socially maladjusted and emotionally disturbed are separate populations in the first place.

A cornerstone of the CCBD position is the belief that the IDEA was intended to be inclusionary, not exclusionary, and that efforts to exclude students with conduct disorders violate the spirit of the law. Cline (1990) traced the intent of Congress in adopting the IDEA definition of severe emotional disturbance by reviewing original testimony and concluded that "authorization to exclude students who are troublesome to school officials and expensive to serve can neither be inferred nor found anywhere in legislative history" (p. 170). The CCBD also noted that in arguments advanced for exclusion, administrative and financial factors are given precedence over educational ones. Yet not only are cost and convenience irrelevant to educational decisions, the notion that excluding conduct-disordered students from special education will result in savings is illusory because the costs of treating these people as adults may far exceed the costs of admitting them to special education. Furthermore, the prevalence of students classified as SED is not substantially or significantly greater in states whose definitions include social maladjustment than in those whose definitions do not (Skiba, Grizzle, & Minke, 1994).

This controversy attests to the difficulty involved in differentiating disturbed and normal individuals. Although there are clear instances of normal behavior and clear instances of disturbed behavior, between them is a large gray area of behavior in which this distinction cannot be reliably drawn. Conduct disorders seem to lie in this gray area. Simply because we cannot say with certainty that children with conduct disorders differ from children with emotional disturbance, can we justify excluding them from the protections of the IDEA?

The Diversity of Theoretical Explanations of Behavior Disorders

The number and variety of theoretical explanations of the development of behavior disorders are remarkable. Each explanation derives from a distinct set of assumptions, constructs, and principles about human behavior and personality.

Constructs differ from principles in that they cannot be proved or disproved; they are hypothetical. Empirical principles are facts established through the methods of scientific inquiry. Explanations that rely upon hypothetical constructs are believable when their internal logic is consistent and they correspond to human experience. Explanations that involve empirical principles are believable whether or not they are consistent with our own experiences because of the scientific methodology used to establish them. Moreover, each perspective has its own adherents who, more or less ardently, subscribe to a definition of behavior disorders that is consistent with the perspective's underlying theory. Although these points of view will be presented later in some detail, it may be illustrative here to describe how incompatible definitions may be.

Certain professionals adhere to what may be called a *biological* perspective. At the risk of oversimplification, it may be stated that behavioral disorders are understood from this point of view as the manifestations of some underlying physical disturbance or disorder. The identification of an underlying physical cause of a disorder leads to treatment that corrects both the biological dysfunction and its behavioral manifestations. Quite distinct from the biological perspective is the *behavioral* point of view, in which a behavior disorder is understood to be a learned pattern of responding. Individuals learn behaviors as they interact with their environments and come into contact with reinforcement contingencies. To correct the problems associated with behavior disorders, behavior therapists modify contingencies so that deviant behaviors are weakened, and competing, socially acceptable behaviors are learned. Clearly, no single definition that attempts to account for the development of behavior disorders could possibly satisfy adherents of these two divergent views.

From a *psychodynamic* point of view, behavior disorders arise from faulty psychosocial development. Critical components of personality fail to develop or they develop inadequately because of stressful experiences during developmental stages. As a result, individuals are limited in the control they can exert over their instinctual and sometimes primitive drives and desires. According to this perspective, deviant behaviors are the product of an incompletely developed personality; the therapist seeks amelioration by working to strengthen the faulty personality. Again, it is clear that any definition that is acceptable to adherents of this point of view would be incompatible with other points of view.

These and three other theoretical points of view are described in some detail in the following paragraphs. In presenting six, we have added a conceptual model to the five originally presented in the classic and frequently cited Child Variance Project publications (e.g., Rhodes & Tracey, 1974). The addition of the cognitive-behavioral model was necessitated by recent work in the areas of modeling, self-instruction, problem solving, and self-control.

Biophysical Explanations of Disturbed Behavior
The biophysical model accounts for disturbed behavior through a disease or medical model orientation (Sagor, 1974); some type of pathology is believed to lie within the individual. This belief can be traced back to Hippocrates (460–370 B.C.),

who taught that proper mentality was dependent on a healthy brain. Deviant thinking or behavior was seen as resulting from brain pathology (Wicks-Nelson & Israel, 1984).

In any event, what we are calling the biophysical model should not be conceptualized as a single theory of human behavior; rather, it comprises theories that vary greatly on a number of dimensions. They are, however, tied together by one common theme—the belief that behavior disorders have biophysical etiologies (Bootzin, 1980). What follows is a brief discussion of the major biophysical theories that have been used to explain disordered behavior in children and adolescents: genetic transmission, brain injury and neurological dysfunction, biochemical abnormalities, and temperament.

Genetic Transmission.   Some behavioral disorders are believed to occur through the process of genetic transmission. Because the extent to which genes influence behavior is not known, and because of the complexity of human behavior (relative to other attributes that are known to be genetically transmitted), genetic theories have generated more than their share of controversy. Genetic transmission theories have been put forward to explain the psychotic behavior patterns of autism and schizophrenia, as well as the less severe problems of hyperactivity, aggression, and rule breaking.

The most convincing findings have been reported in studies of schizophrenia. In general, twin and adoption studies have indicated that the closer the biological relationship of an individual to a clinically diagnosed schizophrenic, the greater the probability that the individual will develop schizophrenia (Buss, 1966; Kallman & Roth, 1956). Compared to the 1 percent incidence in the general population, the incidence among children with one schizophrenic parent ranges from 12 to 16 percent; with two schizophrenic parents, the probability range increases to 39 to 68 percent (Kety, 1973).

Genetic explanations of hyperactivity, aggression, and rule breaking have not been as commonly accepted, perhaps because they are less convincing. Reviews of family, twin, and adoption studies (e.g., Ross & Ross, 1981) offer at best tentative support for a genetic basis for hyperactivity. Most of the available research suffers from imperfect methodology and inadequate design.

Concerning aggression and rule breaking, interest has focused on the XYY sex-chromosome aberration found in approximately 0.2 percent of males. Speculation that there is a link between the extra Y gonosome and excessive aggressiveness grew as a result of studies indicating that the genetic abnormality occurred at higher rates among prison populations than in the general public. Furthermore, incarcerated men who possessed the extra Y gonosome were below average in intelligence, had extremely unstable personalities, and had a history of school problems during childhood and adolescence (Jacobs, Brunton, & Melville, 1965). Caution must be exercised when interpreting data appearing to link aggression to the extra Y gonosome, however. The overall proportion of XYY males who are incarcerated is low and, in general, their crimes are not excessively aggressive (Achenbach, 1974). In addition, many aggressive criminals and delinquents do not possess an extra Y gonosome. Thus, the link between chromosomal deviation and aggressive behavior and rule breaking may be more speculative than explanatory.

Brain Injury and Neurological Dysfunction.   Brain damage, injury, and dysfunction have long been thought to be causes of disordered behavior. Professionals dealing with behavior problems agree that any type of intensity of damage to the central nervous system (CNS) can result in abnormal behavior patterns (Chess & Gordon, 1984), yet correspondences between damage to a particular area of the CNS and specific problem behavior are at best imprecise (Werry, 1979). There is also controversy over whether a diagnosis of brain injury is valid in the absence of hard neurological data, as in the case of minimal brain dysfunction (MBD). MBD is a term frequently used to explain hyperactivity, impulsivity, and many other learning problems. Because there is no medical evidence of CNS irregularities with MBD, clinicians rely heavily on soft neurological signs—clumsiness in gross and fine motor skills, abnormal eye movements, tics, directionality problems, and deficient visual–motor integration.

The concept of MBD has been repeatedly and soundly criticized in the professional literature (e.g., Kauffman, 1985) for the following reasons: (1) soft neurological signs include many behaviors observed in large numbers of children who do not have learning and behavior problems; (2) there is a lack of intervention strategies related to the diagnosis; and (3) the diagnosis involves a circular logic, meaning the existence of the disorder is inferred from the presence of behaviors that the disorder is intended to explain. Nonetheless, the criticisms of MBD do not discredit all neuropsychological approaches, some of which have proved useful in explaining and eventually treating inappropriate behaviors resulting from clear-cut instances of brain damage (Thies, 1985).

Severe behavior problems are believed to occur because of neurological etiologies. For example, it has been estimated that up to 50 percent of all children with autism suffer some type of CNS dysfunction (Kolvin, Ounsted, & Roth, 1971). Both autism and childhood schizophrenia may be caused by perceptual inconsistencies resulting from deficient CNS functioning (Ornitz & Ritvo, 1968). Perceptual inconsistencies occur because past experiences cannot be integrated with present events.

Biochemical Abnormalities.   Biochemical explanations of disordered behavior stem from the belief that body chemistry is linked to behavior. Although it is widely believed that chemistry affects behavior, there is little agreement as to which specific processes, when disrupted, cause disordered behavior. Speculation has centered primarily on the role of neurotransmitters and diet.

Neurotransmitters are substances released by neurons to relay impulses to receptors on adjacent cells. For example, the behavior of children with pervasive developmental disorders (PDD) may be related to the overproduction of two such neurotransmitters, dopamine and serotonin. Treatment with neuroleptic drugs such as Thorazine, Haldol, Prolixin, and Stelazine is believed to control aggressiveness, bizarre behavior, and impulsivity because these drugs act as dopamine blockers.

That diet, inadequate nutrition, and food allergies may cause disordered behavior is a recurring theme in both the professional literature and the popular press. The most notable proponent of this view is Benjamin Feingold, a pediatric allergist. According to Feingold (1975), symptoms of hyperactivity, aggression, and impulsivity in some children are caused by naturally occurring substances in foods (salicylates, salt compounds found in many foods, that have chemical compositions similar to aspirin) and by artificial coloring and flavoring agents, and the strict elimination of these substances can significantly reduce the frequency of learning and behavior problems in a number of children and adolescents. Some children have been shown to be positive responders to the elimination diet (e.g., Rose, 1978); their problem behaviors are alleviated when food coloring (as in the Rose study) is eliminated from their diets. However, in the majority of studies (e.g., Harley et al., 1978), elimination diets of this sort have proved less successful in reducing hyperactivity-related learning and behavior problems.

Other researchers have focused on the effects of sugar consumption and megavitamin therapy on disordered behavior, and promising (albeit inconclusive) findings have been reported. For example, sugar consumption has been related to the quality of playroom behavior of hyperactive and normal children (Prinz, Roberts, & Hartman, 1980), and the behavior of autistic children was improved after they were given vitamin B6 (Rimland, Callaway, & Dreyfus, 1978).

Temperament. *Temperament* is a general term that refers to an inborn behavioral style. This style may be influenced by developmental and environmental events. An individual's temperament comprises a number of categories of behavior, including activity level, regularity of eating and sleeping, adaptability to new stimuli, mood quality, and attention span (Thomas, Chess, & Birch, 1969). Examples of early temperamental problems are colic, easy irritability, excessive activity, and irregular rhythmicity of function. Although most babies with difficult temperaments do not develop later learning and behavior problems, difficult babies do run the risk of straining parent–child relationships and setting the stage for inconsistent nurturing and high rates of conflict (Levine, Brooks, & Shonkoff, 1980).

Utility to Special Education. The major criticism of all these models is that they may create negative expectations for individuals with disabilities that result from biophysical etiologies. Professionals working with students with known biophysical impairment have in such etiology a convenient and powerful rationale for setting low expectations. For example, we've all heard such comments as "I can't get Sally to pay attention to her seatwork, but of course she's brain damaged, so what can you expect?"

Perhaps the most tenable view regarding biophysical models is that biological variables do contribute to certain behavioral disabilities, almost always in interaction with events in the environment (Kauffman, 1985), and that some disorders are amendable to treatment with approaches that derive from these models. Yet we educators must bear in mind that our responsibility to teach students does not end with the diagnosis of a biophysical anomaly or the prescription of a medical intervention.

Psychodynamic Explanations of Disturbed Behavior

The psychodynamic model encompasses a number of theories that seek to explain the motivation or driving forces behind human behavior and emotion. Central to psychodynamic theory is the belief that behavior is a function of internal (or intrapsychic) events and that it can be understood only in terms of those events (Bootzin, 1980). The essence of behavior disorders is not behavior per se, but an imbalance among the components of the personality that produces inappropriate behavior. The lexicon of psychodynamic thought pervades our language; seldom does a day pass when we do not hear such terms as *ego*, *subconscious*, and *defense mechanisms*.

Psychoanalytic Theory.   Freud's psychoanalytic theory, the best-known perspective of the psychodynamic model, posits that the human psyche or personality consists of three interacting forces: the id, ego, and superego. The id is the reservoir of the drives and impulses that constitute psychic energy and activate the personality; it influences us to seek the immediate maximization of pleasure and avoidance of pain. The ego is the organizer or regulator of the personality and serves to satisfy the instinctual drives of the id, within the limits imposed by the superego. The superego is our conscience and ego ideal; it tells us what we should do and infuses us with guilt feelings when we do wrong. At birth, we possess only the id; the ego and superego are differentiated as we progress through the stages of psychological development.

Development consists of five stages. The ego begins to develop during the oral period, at approximately 6 months, when infants start to differentiate themselves from their external worlds. The superego emerges during the phallic period, at 5 or 6 years, with the resolution of psychological conflicts (the Oedipal conflict for boys and the Electra conflict for girls) resulting from the close attachment that children feel toward their mothers and the competing need they feel to establish an independent identity. Although the content of these conflicts differs for boys and girls, resolution produces similar outcomes: the incorporation of the values, standards, and sexual orientation of the same-sex parent.

The ego develops and adopts defense mechanisms to cope with the stresses associated with these (and all other) stages of development. In this sense, defense mechanisms serve a valuable adaptive function and their use is normative. However, the failure to develop adequate defense mechanisms or the overreliance on one or two particular defenses can be pathological because distortions of reality easily result from perpetual self-protection. A brief description of the ego's major defense mechanisms can be found in Table 1.1.

The structure of the personality that emerges through development is the major determinant of normal and abnormal behavior patterns. Abnormal patterns of behavior result when development is incomplete or unbalanced. For example, aggressive behavior is believed to result from the individual's failure to develop ad-

TABLE 1.1   Defense Mechanisms

Repression	Forcing unacceptable impulses back into the unconscious.
Projection	Transferring one's own feared impulses onto an external agent.
Displacement	Venting emotions on a substitute object, out of fear of directing them toward the original object.
Denial	Refusing to acknowledge an anxiety-producing fact or feeling.
Reaction formation	Expressing or acting out the opposite of one's unacceptable feelings.
Rationalization	Offering plausible and socially acceptable reasons for behavior that in fact was motivated by unconscious and unacceptable impulses.
Regression	Returning mentally to an earlier stage of development in order to avoid conflict at the actual stage of development.
Sublimation	Redirecting libidinal or aggressive impulses away from unacceptable objects and toward acceptable substitute objects.

Source: Adapted from Bootzin, 1980, p. 36.

equate controls over aggressive impulses. Because these controls normally develop during conflict resolution, it is conjectured that aggression results when the individual's resolution is unsuccessful or incomplete. This outcome has been characterized as the *deficient superego* (Redl & Wineman, 1957). Because their egos have developed adequately, superego-deficient children can benefit from the imposition of external controls.

Redl and Wineman (1957) also described how disruptions at other stages of development can produce delinquent behavior. The *deficient ego* is rooted in a problem with earlier developmental roots: The individual has failed to develop mechanisms to cope with the impulses of the id and therefore expresses the antisocial desires of the id impulsively and without guilt or remorse. The *delinquent ego* is believed to have developed adequately, but serves the wrong master: It can defend against the impulsive desires of the id, but frequently uses its skills to rationalize misconduct and supersede any superego controls. Redl and Wineman have identified twenty-two such deficiencies; see Table 1.2 for examples.

Other Psychodynamic Conceptualizations.   Freud's psychoanalytic theory provided the foundation for most subsequent psychodynamic thought. Although later theories are varied and numerous, they follow two general trends (Bootzin, 1980). The first involves a stronger concentration on ego functioning and less emphasis on the id than Freud's theory. Ego psychologists such as Jung, Adler, and Erikson stressed the energy and autonomy of the ego. In fact, Erikson described a process of *psychosocial development* through which ego identity is established. Like Freud's theory of psychosexual development, psychosocial development proceeds through a series of chronological stages (described in Table 1.3) that extend from birth through adulthood and have a pronounced social emphasis. Development is

TABLE 1.2   Redl's Twenty-two Ego Deficiencies

According to Redl, the egos of many children exhibiting disordered behaviors can be considered deficient—that is, their egos are unable to control impulses generated by their ids. In order to illustrate the distinctive types of ego deficiencies, Redl and his colleagues (e.g., Redl & Wineman, 1957) have described twenty-two jobs that a healthy ego performs in life situations. What follows is a sampling of healthy ego functions and a brief description of how deficiencies in such functions may appear to a classroom teacher of behavior-disordered students.

1. Frustration tolerance	Low frustration tolerance; student requires immediate gratification and cannot control "impulse breakthrough."
2. Coping with insecurity anger, and fear	Extreme measures of behavior taken to escape feared situations.
3. Temptation resistance	Unable to summon the emergency energy to resist items of immediate gratification that often lead to danger or guilt (e.g., gadgetorial seduction).
4. Excitement and group psychological intoxication	Group of students picks up on the inappropriate behaviors that one student starts.
5. Newness panic	Unable to deal with changes in the environment or temporary changes in schedule.
6. Controlling the flood-gates of the past	Sudden onrush of past life events when frustrated in a current circumstance.
7. Evaporation of self-contributed links in the causal chain	Unable to see self as a participant in the chain of events that led to a classroom problem.

mediated by social agents—parents, siblings, peers, teachers, and spouses, to name only a few. At each stage of psychosocial development, there is conflict between the individual and socializing agents. Through the successful resolution of these conflicts, ego identity is developed and strengthened. If the ego fails to resolve any of these conflicts, the ongoing process of building ego identity is hampered and psychological problems will develop (Bootzin, 1980).

The second trend in post-Freudian thought is the belief that development—normal and abnormal alike—is highly dependent on the type and quality of the individual's social relationships. This concern with interpersonal dynamics is a central tenet of Karen Horney and Harry Stack Sullivan, both of whom are associated with the neo-Freudian movement. In this perspective, relationships with others define present psychological stability and serve to predict future psychological events. Difficult interactions between parents and children are one of the major sources of behavior disturbance. When children's needs for security, warmth, and affection are not met, anxiety-induced character patterns may result. These patterns include oversubmissiveness, withdrawal, and rigidity.

Utility to Special Education.   In the broadest sense, psychodynamic theory has contributed to the treatment of disordered behavior by providing alterna-

TABLE 1.3   Erikson's Stages of Psychosocial Development

Stages	Description	Age
Basic Trust vs. Mistrust	Consistent caregiver responses to needs of infant vs. negligence or irregular attention to needs.	Birth–18 mos.
Autonomy vs. Shame or Doubt	Physical self-control (e.g., toilet training, locomotion) and assertiveness vs. dependence on caregiver.	18 mos.–3½ yrs.
Initiative vs. Guilt	Increased language, exploration, and curiosity vs. feelings of self-doubt and fear.	3½ yrs.–6½ yrs.
Industry vs. Inferiority	Competence and self-confidence about one's skill vs. fear of failing and sense of inadequacy.	6 yrs.–12 yrs.
Identity vs. Role Confusion	Learning one's vocation and developing a healthy identity vs. role diffusion and a lack of a positive identity.	Adolescence
Intimacy vs. Isolation	Ability to form a stable love relationship vs. fear of commitment.	Early adulthood
Generativity vs. Stagnation	Desire to produce and contribute to the common good vs. self-absorption.	Middle adulthood
Integrity vs. Despair	Acceptance of one's life and the human life cycle vs. regret for past life and a strong fear of death.	Older adulthood

tives through which we can understand our actions and emotions. It is through such understanding that we ultimately achieve greater control over our lives. Proponents of psychodynamic theory believe that educators can promote such understanding by encouraging the expression of emotion in their classrooms and by developing greater sensitivity to the crises that children and youth experience.

At the same time, the model has been criticized for the apparent lack of scientific evidence to support its intrapsychic hypotheses. Psychodynamic theorists often cite as evidence of their beliefs subjective, case study data, even though such data are of limited scientific value. Also, psychodynamic explanations rely heavily on hypothetical constructs, such as the three components of personality—id, ego, and superego. These constructs have no referent in the physical world and cannot be observed or tested empirically.

From an educational perspective, psychodynamic theories can be criticized for providing little in the way of useful strategies for managing inappropriate classroom behavior. Treatment is based primarily on unconscious desires and conflicts that are discussed, interpreted, and resolved in the therapeutic process. Such activities are usually too impractical and time-consuming for educators working in busy special education settings.

Behavioral Explanations of Disturbed Behavior

Proponents of the behavioral model believe that human behavior, both normal and disordered, is learned. Although behavioral theorists recognize the roles of genetic constitution and reinforcement history in determining behavior, their primary concern is with current environmental conditions. In the behavioral model, emphasis is placed on the identification of external events responsible for *maintaining* behavior and on planning appropriate ameliorative procedures. Events that may have led to the acquisition of maladaptive behavior are not especially relevant to remediation because such events can no longer be observed or changed (Alberto & Troutman, 1986).

Four basic assumptions constitute the pillars of classical behaviorism (Bootzin, 1980). First, the behavioral model is concerned with only those responses that are observable. The hypothetical constructs of the psychodynamic model have no place in behavior analysis because they cannot be observed. Second, behaviorists treat both environmental stimuli and human responses as empirical entities that are observable and measurable. In effect, behaviors and their antecedents and consequences can be formally quantified through measures of magnitude, frequency, or intensity. Third, behaviorists maintain that human behavior, like other natural phenomena, can be predicted and eventually controlled. Despite the complexity of human activity, they believe that behavior relates functionally to environmental events. Responses interfering with the development of adaptive behaviors can be modified through careful and responsible changes in the environment. The final assumption of the behavioral model is that learning is the major determinant of behavior and that both normal and abnormal behavior can be explained in terms of learning theory.

Respondent conditioning and *operant conditioning* are key processes in the behavioral model. Respondent behaviors are unconditioned, reflexive responses. Learning occurs when a new stimulus is paired with the stimulus that initially elicited the respondent action. Pavlov's experiments in which dogs' salivation was conditioned are classic illustrations of respondent conditioning: An unconditioned stimulus (meat powder) that produces salivation is paired with a stimulus (a tone) so that the sounding of the tone alone will elicit salivation.

Respondent behaviors are completely controlled by antecedent events, but operant behaviors are controlled by both antecedent and consequent conditions. In regard to antecedent influences on behavior, the reflexive quality of respondent conditioning is absent in operant conditioning. Antecedent control of operant behavior is acquired through the process of discrimination learning in which certain stimuli set the occasion for specific responses. Behaviors under such stimulus control can continue to occur even when desirable consequences are infrequent (Alberto & Troutman, 1986). Most applications of operant conditioning, however, have focused on consequences or stimuli that follow an individual's behavior. If a behavior is followed by a desirable consequence, the response is strengthened and more apt to occur in the future; a behavior followed by a negative consequence is less likely to recur. Although we can do little to change the past circumstances that resulted in the acquisition of inappropriate behavior, current environmental consequences can be altered to promote the development of appropriate academic and social repertories of behavior. The operant and respondent paradigms are illustrated in Figure 1.1.

A great majority of behavioral programs for treating inappropriate behavior involve the simultaneous strengthening and weakening of different behaviors. When we refer to the strengthening of behavior, we are speaking of reinforcement. Positive reinforcement is the presentation of a consequence that results in an increase in the targeted behavior; negative reinforcement is the removal of an aversive or unpleasant event that results in an increase in the behavior that accomplished the removal. Several alternatives exist to decrease or weaken the strength of a target behavior. The most powerful is punishment, but its use in schools, and even its lasting effectiveness, are debatable issues. Extinction and differential reinforcement can also serve to weaken or reduce the strength of a targeted behavior. In Table 1.4, we list and briefly describe the more common methods by which behavior is strengthened and weakened.

Utility to Special Education.   Behaviorism's contribution to the field of special education has been documented in a large number of studies involving both academic and social behaviors. For one thing, the behavioral model has proved useful to special educators as a diagnostic system for analyzing behavior and for identifying potential causal variables. Second, the behavioral model provides teachers with a system of accountability: Instructional effectiveness can be measured against attainment of educational objectives through the regular monitoring of student performance. Finally, behavioral researchers have demonstrated effec-

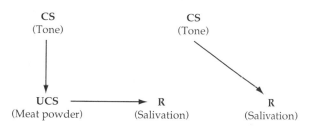

Respondent Behavior Paradigm

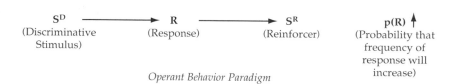

Operant Behavior Paradigm

**FIGURE 1.1   The Respondent Behavior and Operant Behavior
Paradigms**

TABLE 1.4 Common Methods for Strengthening and Weakening Behavior

	Definition	Examples
Positive reinforcement	Increasing the frequency or intensity of a behavior through the contingent presentation of a stimulus following a desired response.	Praise; activities; edibles; tokens.
Negative reinforcement	Increasing the frequency or intensity of a behavior through the contingent removal of an aversive stimulus following a response.	Parents giving in to a tantrumming child find that the tantrums increase.
Extinction	Decreasing the frequency or intensity of a behavior by withholding reinforcement for a previously reinforced behavior.	Teacher's planned ignoring of inappropriate behaviors that have previously received attention.
Punishment	Decreasing the frequency or intensity of a behavior through the presentation of a consequent, usually aversive, stimulus.	Time-out; overcorrection; corporal punishment.

tive means for managing and remediating a wide range of behavior problems in students of all ages and have provided a number of directive teaching strategies that effectively and efficiently increase academic achievement. In fact, no other theoretical model has as substantial a foundation of empirical support.

Cognitive-Behavioral Explanations of Disturbed Behavior

Over the last decades, behavioral and cognitive strategies have been combined in creative ways and used with individuals who exhibit academic and social problems. The cognitive influence on traditional behavioral approaches centers on the role of verbal mediation in learning and how these internal processes affect behavior. Deficiencies in verbal mediation have been viewed as explanations for a variety of academic and behavioral problems. It is believed that the development of verbal mediation is associated with the inhibitory function of language (Bash & Camp, 1985). Mediation allows individuals to block impulsive responses, to think before they act. Those who do not develop verbal mediation tend to respond impulsively rather than reflectively. As a result of their impulsivity, they fail to consider the range of alternative actions available to solve problems.

Cognitive-behaviorism has defied definition (Kendall & Hollon, 1979), partly because of the variability of cognitive-behavior modification (CBM) interventions. What distinguishes CBM is its emphasis on thinking and on how behavioral contingencies can facilitate and maintain changes in thinking and behavior. Cognitive-behavioral interventions build upon the success of traditional behavior modification by incorporating cognitive strategies (Kendall & Hollon, 1979). Cognitive-behavioral theorists have asserted that this expansion of the behavioral model gives professionals who work with disturbed individuals a more comprehensive account of learning and behavior problems. Still, this mix of cognitive psychology and traditional behaviorism has not rested well with many of the more radical behaviorists; mediation, as in covert self-instruction and internal self-monitoring, is difficult to operationalize and therefore suspect in the eyes of strict behaviorists (Rosenberg, 1985).

Nevertheless, many professionals who once espoused a behavioral orientation to special education are drifting toward the cognitive-behavior model because of several limitations that they have observed in operant procedures with students with disabilities. In particular, the failure of basic operant techniques to produce generalized and durable behavior change has been cited as a major reason for "going cognitive" (Meichenbaum, 1980). Proponents of the model consider CBM to hold greater promise in promoting generalization than traditional behavior modification because the intervention techniques include components for guiding the learner toward durable and generalized behavior change (Rooney & Hallahan, 1985).

The rise in popularity of CBM has also been attributed to an improved understanding of the role of language in controlling behavior. Many special educators, drawing upon the early work of Soviet psychologists Luria (1961) and Vygotsky (1962), have begun to recognize that children's behavior may come under verbal control through a formal three-stage process: (1) the speech of others, most often adults, directs behavior; (2) children's own overt speech regulates their behavior; and (3) subvocal speech is believed to assume the governing role.

A final impetus for the move toward the cognitive-behavioral approach has come from recent work indicating that many subgroups of exceptional children have deficits in metacognition or metaprocesses (Meichenbaum, 1980)—that is, thinking about thinking or reflecting on one's own behavior. Strengthening their covert self-regulatory mechanisms is believed to lead students deficient in metacognitive processes to become more successful and reflective problem solvers in both academic and social situations.

Cognitive-behavioral intervention in the form of self-instruction is most commonly applied to issues of self-control and problem solving (Rosenberg, 1985). Most self-instructional programs have either used or adapted the original techniques developed by Meichenbaum and Goodman (1971), in which impulsive children were taught to control their behavior through a combination of rehearsal, prompts, and feedback. In the original study, experimenters modeled self-statements to guide performance on complex tasks. Students were required first to say the statements out loud, then to whisper them, then to say them to themselves. The effects of these procedures were impressive, and applications of self-instructional procedures have abounded. A variety of problem behaviors typical of special education students, including aggression, rule breaking, and inattention to tasks as well as academic problems have been studied.

Most special educators and clinicians are optimistic about the utility of cognitive-behavioral strategies. The number of professionals embracing this orientation is large and growing. For example, it has been reported (Klesges, Sanchez, & Stanton, 1982) that 40 percent of new faculty in American Psychological Association (APA) programs described their theoretical orientation as cognitive-behavioral compared to only 18 percent who described themselves as behavioral. Perhaps a more relevant indicator of the impact of the cognitive-behavioral approach on special education is the number of research efforts that have applied CBM procedures to problems of students with disabilities; rarely does an issue of a special education journal fail to feature a data-based CBM article.

Utility to Special Education.   Since CBM has come into widespread use only recently, its utility to special educators is difficult to assess fully. Specific CBM procedures have been successful in improving a range of behaviors found in students with mild disabilities (Rooney & Hallahan, 1985), and researchers have begun to apply cognitive-behavioral procedures to more severely impaired populations (Kendall & Morrison, 1984; Litrownik, 1984).

As noted earlier, however, the major goal in using CBM is to teach children to use metacognitive processes to handle a host of self-control and problem-solving situations. To date, most CBM efforts, like traditional behavior modification studies, have resulted in only limited changes in a restricted range of targeted behaviors. The hoped-for success in fundamental cognitive change (e.g., metacognitive processes, generalization, maintenance) has not materialized, leaving more than a few special educators wondering if the theoretical claims regarding the benefits of CBM are more imaginary than real (Rooney & Hallahan, 1985). Like any new approach, cognitive behavior modification requires more refinement before a full assessment of its utility can be offered.

Sociological Explanations of Disturbed Behavior

Sociological models of deviance focus on how an individual's behavior is perceived in a particular social context. Although these models do not provide explanations for instances of behavior or concrete guidelines for intervention, they do give us valuable insight into how social factors influence the way we think about individuals who are different. In identifying inappropriate behaviors and teaching prosocial behaviors, we often overlook the fact that the distinction between appropriate and inappropriate behavior is rooted in an ever-changing social context. One need look no further than changing attitudes toward teacher-directed learning and classroom structure for an example. In the late 1960s and early 1970s, instructional practice centered on student-directed learning and minimal teacher control. Today, however, we are immersed in teacher-directed learning and controlled learning environments. This recent concern with structure and control in schools is a symptom of a "radical new political ethos that has emerged which has serious implications for the way we think about deviance in our society and the provisions we make" (Paul, 1985, p. 67).

Thus, sociological points of view allow us to step back from our workaday perspective on behavior disorders and view our treatment of individuals with problems in its full social and cultural context. Four major sociological perspectives that relate directly to disordered behavior have been identified (Des Jarlais, 1974): rule breaking, anomie, socialization failure, and labeling.

Rule Breaking.   Disordered behavior may be understood as the violation of societal rules. Some rules are explicit, like the formally stated codes, statues, and laws by which members of a society agree to abide. When such rules are broken, official consequences from formal societal institutions are sanctioned. Other rules are implicit and involve the unwritten and shared expectations we bring to social interactions. For example, although there are no explicit rules governing how much (or how little) eye contact an individual should make during conversation, anyone who deviates in either direction from what is considered normal is considered an implicit rule breaker. We feel uncomfortable in discussions with people who either don't look us in the eye or who stare at us, and we act to end the discussion (and our own discomfort).

If a society is to maintain a social structure, violations of both implicit and explicit rules must be met with negative evaluation and punishment. Such practices ensure the continuation of a particular way of life and promote conformity to shared social expectations. It can be argued that all those who deviate from normative expectations, be they behaviorally disordered or criminal, share the fate of degradation and ostracism from society.

Anomie.   Anomie results when a social system is unable to accommodate rapid change by adapting social norms (Durkheim, 1964). The gap between rapid change and norm adaptation is believed to create in members of a society a state of frustration and stress. Although there is little supporting evidence for a relationship between instances of anomie and measures of mental health, it is possible that the uncertainty created when normative expectations are upset within a social system is related to increased rates of disordered behavior.

Socialization Failure.   Socialization is the process by which children learn to follow societal rules and the value of doing so (Apter & Conoley, 1984). Socialization is a critical process; it ensures the survival and continuity of a chosen way of life. Ten influences on socialization have been identified (Lippitt, 1968): schools, churches, recreational agencies, therapeutic agencies, the legal system, the media, political leaders, employers, peers, and parents. Parents have the greatest influence on socialization in that they continually model and reward socially accepted behavior and attitudes and transmit cultural goals and values to their children.

Several factors contribute to socialization failure. First, biological deficiencies may render children unable to master the social skills emphasized by their parents. Regardless of the time and effort invested, biophysical limitations can preclude acquisition of some social skills. Second, socialization failure may result from inadequate parental modeling and teaching, outright neglect of parental responsibility, or lack of understanding or acceptance of cultural expectations. Finally, socialization failure may result from confusion created by conflicting definitions of appropriate behavior among different socialization agents. Inconsistent demands from one socialization agent to another place children in stressful situations, impeding their acculturation to societal norms.

Labeling.   Labeling of students with different patterns of academic and social behavior has been both a common practice and a serious concern of special educators. Despite the lack of conclusive findings linking labeling to poor self-concept (e.g., MacMillan, Jones, & Aloia, 1974), there is considerable evidence (e.g., Foster, Ysseldyke, & Reese, 1975) that people perceive nonlabeled and labeled individuals differently.

According to labeling theory, individuals are not considered deviant merely because they break social rules; they must be labeled deviant before social expectations are activated. Labels may be attached to individuals who commit crimes, are placed in residential facilities, or are assigned to special education classrooms. Like the behavioral view, labeling theory posits that the deviant persona develops in much the same fashion as the nondeviant one: through conformity to the expectations of others. Individuals labeled in a certain fashion begin to behave in the ways people expect them to act. Not everyone who breaks social rules receives a deviant label. Factors that determine whether the label is conferred include the extent to which society needs to have a deviant role identified and filled, the frequency and visibility of the rules being broken, societal tolerance of the rules being broken, the social distance between the rule violator and those with the authority to confer deviant labels, the relative power of the rule breaker, and whether special interests are being met by labeling the rule breaker (Des Jarlais, 1974).

Utility to Special Education.   The sociological model offers little to special education teachers mired in the complexity of managing and remediating problem behavior every day. However, it does broaden our understanding of deviance by encompassing all segments of our society and culture, and it does affect how educational services are delivered to students with disordered behavior.

First, this model highlights the socially defined nature of disordered behavior by proposing that problem behaviors are deviations from arbitrarily determined social rules. Second, the sociological model, particularly labeling theory, has sensitized participants in the referral, assessment, and placement processes to the dangers of labeling and classification systems, and out of such sensitivity may come new, minimally deleterious educational classification systems for students with behavior problems. For example, the Council for Children with Behavior Disorders has advocated that professionals serving children with behavior disorders refrain from using the term *emotional disturbance* because it promotes stigmatization in academic and social situations. Also, many states and local education agencies have adopted referral and placement procedures (e.g., noncategorical classes and generic certification for special education teachers) based on specific educational needs rather than on the traditional categorical labels.

Finally, the sociological model gives educators important guidelines for organizing classrooms. Although teachers may have little impact on how social institutions affect students, they do have considerable influence on how the classroom "microsociety" is organized (Paul & Epanchin, 1982). By emphasizing that much of the variation among individuals is more difference than deviance, teachers can minimize the stigma of special class placements.

Ecological Explanations of Disturbed Behavior

Ecological theory focuses on interactions between individuals and their environments. Consequently, disturbed behavior from the ecological perspective cannot be narrowly defined or attributed to a single cause. Rather, ecological explanations of disturbed behavior shift the focus to the mutual adaptation of individuals and community settings (Rhodes & Paul, 1978). Individuals are perceived as normal when they and the social elements of their ecosystems work together in a balanced fashion; then there is a match between an individual's behavior and the demands of the environment. When balance is not established, a mismatch results, and individuals are labeled either deviant or incompetent (Apter & Conoley, 1984).

Five major assumptions form the foundation of the ecological view of problem behavior in children (Apter, 1977): (1) children are inseparable parts of many different social systems; (2) disturbed behavior does not arise solely from children, but rather from a mismatch between behaviors and expectations; (3) interventions are designed to make systems work and to do so without the need for future intervention; (4) improvement in any part of the system benefits the entire system; and (5) intervention must involve the child, the environment, and the attitudes and expectations of all those in the ecosystem.

Several features distinguish the ecological perspective from other approaches to the treatment of disturbed behavior. First, children are not the sole focus of assessment or treatment procedures. Attention is given to the ecosystems in which problem behaviors occur. In contrast, traditional psychological and educational interventions focus on children exhibiting problem behavior, and most therapeutic efforts are designed to coerce them into conforming to the demands and expectations of the ecosystem. Consequently, little attention is paid to disturbing elements within the environment that contribute to the problem behavior.

Second, by virtue of its emphasis on solving problems in environmental contexts, the ecological perspective promotes generalization and maintenance of behavioral change. A major criticism of traditional therapeutic approaches is that treatment takes place in restrictive settings rather than in normal settings in which problem behaviors usually occur. Thus, treatment may be successful in the therapeutic environment but the change may not transfer to other environments. That is why individuals returning to their home environments so often revert to high rates of inappropriate behaviors. Because the ecological perspective refuses to make an arbitrary separation between individuals in need of treatment and the surrounding ecosystems and encourages community-based intervention, maintenance and generalization of behavior changes are greatly facilitated.

Finally, this perspective differs from the others in that there are no purely ecological interventions. Instead, the ecological perspective is a broad and inclusive umbrella that accommodates techniques from all theoretical perspectives—provided that the scope of intervention is ecosystem-wide (Apter & Conoley, 1984).

The distinctive feature of successful ecological interventions for children with problem behaviors is the coordination of efforts among the many professionals involved. As will be detailed in later chapters, the now historic Project ReED (Hobbs, 1966) involved teacher-counselors, social workers, and liaison teachers working in tandem with psychiatrists, psychologists, and mental health workers. Each group of professionals worked with students and others in the community to promote durable treatment effects and successful transitions from therapeutic environments to more normative settings. More recently, Project Aftercare (Harding, Bellew, & Penwell, 1980) employed a similarly coordinated approach in providing follow-up care to students whose behavioral problems had required residential placement. The program, which served as a bridge between the restrictiveness of residential placement and the demands of home and community living, used the services of educators, family workers, and community service workers.

Utility to Special Education.   Like the sociological model, the ecological perspective provides educators with a view of disordered behavior in its full social context. In particular, the ecological perspective stresses the importance of viewing disturbed behavior as a function of events occurring in the ecosystems in which children function. Children identified as disturbed are seldom, if ever, the sole cause of their problem behavior (Apter & Conoley, 1984). Unlike the sociological perspective, however, the ecological perspective suggests programmatic techniques and procedures for improving special education services. The perspective has spawned methods for promoting durable and generalized behavior change, including involvement in students' home environments, parent training, and advocacy groups.

The ecological perspective has also encouraged many teachers of disordered youngsters to view themselves as school-based consultants. As such, teachers work to change both the behaviors of students with problem behaviors and the activities of other individuals who may contribute to the maintenance of problem behaviors. Through collaborative consultation with parents, community officials, and fellow teachers, ecologically minded special educators can provide information, guidance, and encouragement to significant persons in the environments of disordered students. The transdisciplinary nature of the ecological perspective also requires special educators to make use of a wider range and different quality of information on their students, information from social workers, psychologists, and community service workers.

An Alternative Approach

The preceding section described the variety of models and theoretical orientations associated with the study of disordered behavior. Given these very different ways of thinking about disturbance and the strength of the attachments that many professionals feel toward them, it is not surprising that no consensus has developed about the definition of these complex phenomena. Because of the difficulties of defining behavior disorders, an alternative approach could be helpful.

Instead of considering behavioral disorders in any general sense, we will consider specific patterns of deviance and strategies for managing the problem behaviors associated with them. The five patterns we have chosen to use—hyperactivity, aggression, social withdrawal (and its concomitants, inadequacy, and immaturity), juvenile delinquency (and other manifestations of rule-breaking behavior), and severe behavior disorders (e.g., autism, PDD, etc.)—will be defined in specific behavioral terms. These patterns are derived from observations of the behavior of children and adolescents conducted by Quay and his colleagues (Peterson, 1961; Quay, 1966; Quay, Morse, & Cutler, 1966; Quay & Quay, 1965), using the *Behavior Problem Checklist* (*BPC*) (Peterson, 1961), a standardized behavioral assessment instrument. These patterns emerge as factors in statistical analyses that reliably have appeared repeatedly in research with the *BPC* and other instruments (Quay, 1979). The patterns have proved consistent across a wide variety of samples: elementary (Peterson, 1961) and junior high school students (Quay & Quay, 1965); students in public school classes for the emotionally disturbed (Quay, Morse, & Cutler, 1966); juvenile delinquents (Quay, 1966); and others.

The five patterns used to organize this text bear a closer relationship to patterns derived from factor analytic research than to more traditional and medically oriented approaches. In chapters that follow, each pattern will be presented in detail along with some consideration of their etiologies and methods for treatment. However, one additional topic must be considered before we move on to individual patterns: the prevalence of behavior disorders.

Prevalence of Behavior Disorders

Prevalence refers to frequency of occurrence, and the current prevalence of students classified with severe emotional disturbance is 0.89 percent (U. S. Department of Education, 1994). However, estimates of the number of students who *need* services far surpass the number who *receive* them, and because of our inability to agree upon a common definition, these estimates have varied dramatically. Still, there seems to be some consistency and reason to this variability and a plausible explanation for its occurrence.

A review of the studies in which estimates of the prevalence of behavior disorders have been made suggests that they fall into two clusters: low estimates of approximately 2 to 3 percent and high estimates of 25 percent or more (Wood & Zabel, 1978). Thus, although there is a significant discrepancy between these clusters, the fact that the estimates of prevalence do cluster suggests that there is some explanation for the discrepancy.

Low-prevalence estimates were obtained in two early surveys of school superintendents (Mackie, 1969) and state directors of special education (Shultz et al., 1971). Mackie surveyed the superintendents of public and private schools and institutions and reported that approximately 2 percent of the school-aged population was estimated to be emotionally disturbed or socially maladjusted. Her sample was extensive; responses were received from all fifty states and the District of Columbia. Furthermore, her report, in which estimates of the prevalence of all disabilities were made, has had a substantial impact upon federal and state policy, as illustrated by the findings of Shultz and his colleagues. These researchers surveyed state directors of special education from all fifty states and the District of Columbia in an effort to assess the status of special education programs for emotionally disturbed children. They reported that, among the states that reported prevalence figures, nearly two-thirds of the reporting states used either 2 or 3 percent, although the estimates did range from as low as 0.05 percent to as high as 15 percent. In later years, Morsink, Thomas, and Smith-Davis (1987) reported that the range had narrowed considerably, to 0.1 percent to 3.1 percent.

Illustrative of studies in which high-prevalence estimates have been reported is the work of Spivack, Swift, and Prewitt (1971). These researchers asked the teachers of roughly 800 elementary school children to rate their behavior using the *Devereaux Elementary School Behavior Rating Scales*, an instrument they had developed in previous research (Spivack & Swift, 1966). From these ratings they identified profiles of deviant behaviors, many of which occurred across grade levels. The prevalence of these deviant profiles was reported to be as high as 40 percent at some grade levels.

The results of studies in which estimates of the prevalence of both mild and severe problems have been made lend some clarity to the situation. For example, in a study of the prevalence and persistence of emotional disturbances among children residing in Onondaga County, New York, (McCaffrey & Cummings, 1969) teachers were asked to designate children who either presented problem behavior in the classroom or were considered emotionally disturbed. Nominations were obtained in this way for over 6,000 second and fourth graders. Approximately 21 percent of the boys in this sample and 9 percent of the girls were identified by their teachers as presenting problem classroom behavior. However, the percentages of children identified as emotionally disturbed were considerably lower: 4.5 percent of the boys and 2 percent of the girls. These results suggest that the discrepancy in estimates of prevalence might result from the definitions used in the studies. High estimates may occur when teachers are asked to identify children who present problem behavior; low estimates may be made when they are asked to identify more seriously disturbed children. This interpretation is also consistent with the results of subsequent studies (Kelly, Bullock, & Dykes, 1977; Rubin & Balow, 1978) that have addressed the same question.

Furthermore the two clusters of prevalence estimates can be differentiated by the persons asked to make the estimates (Wood & Zabel, 1978). Teachers and others with day-to-day contact tend to make high estimates, and administrators and other experts in the field tend to make low estimates. Teachers make low estimates when asked about serious and persistent problems. Both high and low estimates are important. High estimates are useful for teachers when they attempt to determine the number of children who may present management problems in their classrooms. We can say with some authority that teachers should expect as many as 25 percent of their children to present such problems. On the other hand, low-prevalence estimates are useful in planning special services for children with severe and persistent problem behaviors. Here, a 2 or 3 percent estimate would prove useful and accurate.

Summary

This chapter examined how behavior disorders are defined in educational settings. First, we introduced terminology typically used to refer to disturbed behavior and described how IDEA defines specifically the category of emotional disturbance. Then we discussed the difficulties inherent in defining problem behaviors, chief among them (1) a lack of sufficiently reliable measures of behavioral functioning, (2) a surprisingly high frequency of deviant behavior in populations considered normal, and (3) the diversity of theoretical explanations of disturbed behavior. Finally, we described six of the more prominent theoretical models—biophysical, psychodynamic, behavioral, cognitive-behavioral, sociological, and ecological—and critiqued them in terms of their utility to special educators.

Discussion Questions

1. Identify and provide a rationale for using the various terms that refer to "behavior disorders."

2. Compare the IDEA definition of emotional disturbance with Bower's (1960) definition. What are the major components, advantages, and disadvantages of each?

3. Discuss the factors that contribute to the difficulty of defining behavior disorders.

4. Identify and describe the six major theoretical explanations of behavior disorders.

5. Discuss the usefulness of the theoretical perspectives for providing special education services.

6. List specific patterns of deviance that may be used to approach the management of behavior disorders.

7. Discuss factors associated with prevalence estimates of behavior disorders and the utility of variable prevalence estimates.

References

Achenbach, T. M. (1974). *Developmental psychopathology.* New York: Ronald Press.

Alberto, P. A., & Troutman, A. C. (1986). *Applied behavior analysis for teachers,* 2nd ed. Columbus, OH: Merrill.

Algozzine, B., Schmid, R., & Connors, B. (1978). Toward an acceptable definition of emotional disturbance. *Behavioral Disorders, 4,* 58– 52.

Apter, S. J. (1977). Applications of ecological theory: Toward a community special education model for troubled children. *Exceptional Children, 43,* 366–373.

Apter, S. J., & Conoley, J. C. (1984). *Childhood behavior disorders and emotional disturbance.* Englewood Cliffs, NJ: Prentice-Hall.

Bash, M. S., & Camp, B. W. (1985). *Think aloud: Increasing social and cognitive skills.* Champaign, IL: Research Press.

Bootzin, R. R. (1980). *Abnormal psychology: Current perspectives.* New York: Random House.

Bower, E. M. (1960). *Early identification of emotionally handicapped children in school.* Springfield, IL: Charles C. Thomas.

Buss, A. H. (1966). *Psychopathology.* New York: Wiley.

Chess, S., & Gordon, S. G. (1984). Psychosocial development and human variance. In E. W. Gordon (Ed.), *Review of research in education*, Vol. 11 (pp. 3–62). Washington, DC: American Educational Research Association.

Cline, D. H. (1990). A legal analysis of policy initiatives to exclude handicapped/disruptive students from special education. *Behavioral Disorders, 15*, 159–173.

Council for Children with Behavioral Disorders. (1990). Position paper on the provision of service to children with conduct disorders. *Behavioral Disorders, 15*, 180–189.

Des Jarlais, D. C. (1974). Mental illness as social deviance. In W. C. Rhodes & M. L. Tracey (Eds.), *A study of child variance*, Vol. 1. *Conceptual models* (pp. 259–321). Ann Arbor: University of Michigan Press.

Durkheim, E. (1964). *The division of labor in society.* New York: Free Press.

Executive Committee of the Council for Children with Behavioral Disorders. (1989). White paper on best assessment practices for students with behavioral disorders: Accommodation to cultural diversity and individual differences. *Behavioral Disorders, 14*, 263–278.

Feingold, B. (1975). *Why your child is hyperactive.* New York: Random House.

Forness, S. R., & Knitzer, J. (1992). A new proposed definition and terminology to replace "Serious Emotional Disturbance" in the Individuals with Disabilities Education Act. *School Psychology Review, 12*, 12–20.

Foster, G. G., Ysseldyke, J. E., & Reese, J. H. (1975). "I wouldn't have seen it if I hadn't believed it." *Exceptional Children, 41*, 469–473.

Glavin, J. P. (1972). Persistence of behavior disorders in children. *Exceptional Children, 38*, 367–376.

Graden, J. E., Casey, A., & Christenson, S. L. (1985). Implementing a prereferral intervention system. I: The model. *Exceptional Children, 51*, 377–384.

Harding, E., Bellew, J., & Penwell, L. W. (1980). Project Aftercare: Follow-up to residential treatment. In N. Long, W. Morse, & R. Newman (Eds.), *Conflict in the classroom.* 4th ed. Pp. 200–205. Belmont, CA: Wadsworth.

Harley, J. P., Ray, R. S., Tomasi, L., Eichman, P. L., Mathews, G. G., Chan, R., Clelland, C. S., & Traisman, E. (1978). Hyperkinesis and food additives: Testing the Feingold hypothesis. *Pediatrics, 61*, 818–828.

Hobbs, N. (1966). Helping disabled children: Ecological and psychological strategies. *American Psychologist, 21*, 1105–1115.

Honig v. Doe, 108 S. Ct. 592 (1988).

Jacobs, P. A., Brunton, M., & Melville, M. M. (1965). Aggressive behavior, mental subnormality, and the XYY male. *Nature, 208*, 1351–1352.

Kallman, F. J., & Roth, B. (1956). Genetic aspects of preadolescent schizophrenia. *American Journal of Psychiatry, 112*, 599–606.

Kauffman, J. M. (1977). *Characteristics of children's behavior disorders*, 1st ed. Columbus, OH: Merrill.

Kauffman, J. M. (1981). *Characteristics of children's behavior disorders*, 2nd ed. Columbus, OH: Merrill.

Kauffman, J. M. (1985). *Characteristics of children's behavior disorders*, 3rd ed. Columbus, OH: Merrill.

Kelly, T. J., Bullock, L. M., & Dykes, M. K. (1977). Behavioral disorders: Teachers' perceptions. *Exceptional Children, 43*, 316–318.

Kendall, P. C., & Hollon, S. D. (1979). *Cognitive behavioral interventions: Theory, research, and procedures.* New York: Academy Press.

Kendall, P. C., & Morrison, P. (1984). Integrating cognitive and behavioral procedures for the treatment of socially isolated children. In A. W. Meyers & W. E. Craighead (Eds.), *Cognitive behavior therapy with children* (pp. 261–288). New York: Plenum.

Kety, S. S. (1973). Biochemical hypothesis in schizophrenia. In T. Million (Ed.), *Theories of psy-*

chopathology and personality: Essays and critiques, 2nd ed. (pp. 120–145). Philadelphia: Saunders.

Klesges, R. C., Sanchez, V. C., & Stanton, A. L. (1982). Obtaining employment in academia: The hiring process and characteristics of successful applicants. *Professional Psychology, 45,* 469–474.

Kolvin, I., Ounsted, C., & Roth, M. (1971). Studies in the childhood psychoses. V: Cerebral dysfunction and childhood psychoses. *British Journal of Psychiatry, 118,* 407–414.

LaPouse, R., & Monk, M. A. (1958). An epidemiologic study of behavior characteristics in children. *American Journal of Public Health, 48,* 1134–1144.

Levine, M. D., Brooks, R., & Shonkoff, J. P. (1980). *A pediatric approach to learning disorders.* New York: Wiley.

Lippitt, R. (1968). Improving the socialization process. In J. Clausen (Ed.), *Socialization and society* (pp. 321–374). Boston: Little, Brown.

Litrownik, A. (1984). Cognitive behavior modification with psychotic children: A beginning. In A. W. Meyers & W. E. Craighead (Eds.), *Cognitive behavior therapy with children* (pp. 229–260). New York: Plenum.

Luria, A. (1961). *The role of speech in the regulation of normal and abnormal behaviors.* New York: Liveright.

MacFarlane, J. W., Allen, L., & Honzik, M. P. (1954). *A developmental study of the behavior problems of normal children.* Berkeley: University of California Press.

Mackie, R. P. (1969). *Special education in the United States: Statistics 1948–1966.* New York: Teachers College Press.

MacMillan, D. L., Jones, R. J., & Aloia, G. F. (1974). The mentally retarded label: A theoretical analysis and review of the research. *American Journal of Mental Deficiency, 79,* 241–162.

McCaffrey, I., & Cummings, J. (1969). Persistence of emotional disturbances reported among second- and fourth-grade children. In H. Dupont (Ed.), *Educating emotionally disturbed children* (pp. 19–31). New York: Holt, Rinehart, & Winston.

Meichenbaum, D. (1980). Cognitive behavior modification: A promise yet unfulfilled. *Exceptional Education Quarterly, 1,* 83–88.

Meichenbaum, D., & Goodman, J. (1971). Training impulsive children to talk to themselves: A means of developing self-control. *Journal of Abnormal Psychology, 77,* 115–126.

Morsink, C. V., Thomas, C. C., & Smith-Davis, J. (1987). Noncategorical special education programs: Process and outcomes. In M. C. Wang, M. C. Reynolds, & H. J. Walberg (Eds.), *Handbook of special education: Research and practice.* Vol. 1: *Learner characteristics and adaptive education* (pp. 287–311). Oxford, England: Pergamon.

Ornitz, E. M., & Ritvo, E. R. (1968). Neurophysiological mechanisms underlying perceptual inconsistency in autistic and schizophrenic children. *American Journal of Psychiatry, 19,* 22–27.

Paul, J. L. (1985). Behavioral disorders in the 1980s: Ethical and ideological issues. *Behavioral Disorders, 11,* 66–72.

Paul, J. L., & Epanchin, B. L. (1982). *Emotional disturbance in children.* Columbus, OH: Merrill.

Peterson, D. R. (1961). Behavior problems of middle childhood. *Journal of Consulting Psychology, 25,* 205–209.

Prinz, R. J., Roberts, W. A., & Hartman, C. (1980). Dietary correlates of hyperactive behavior in children. *Journal of Consulting and Clinical Psychology, 48,* 760–769.

Public Law 94-142. (November 29, 1975). *Education for All Handicapped Children Act.*

Quay, H. C. (1979). Classification. In H. C. Quay & J. S. Werry (Eds.), *Psychopathological disorders in childhood,* 2nd ed. (pp. 1–42). New York: Wiley.

Quay, H. C. (1966). Personality patterns in preadolescent boys. *Educational and Psychological Measurement, 16,* 99–110.

Quay, H. C., Morse, W. C., & Cutler, R. L. (1966). Personality patterns of pupils in special classes for the emotionally disturbed. *Exceptional Children, 32,* 297–301.

Quay, H. C., & Quay, L. C. (1965). Behavior problems in early adolescence. *Child Development, 36,* 215–220.

Redl, F., & Wineman, D. (1957). *The aggressive child.* New York: Free Press.

Rhodes, W. C. (1967). The disturbing child: A problem in ecological management. *Exceptional Children, 33,* 449–455.

Rhodes, W. C., & Paul, J. L. (1978). *Emotionally disturbed and deviant children: New views and approaches.* Englewood Cliffs, NJ: Prentice-Hall.

Rhodes, W. C., & Tracey, M. L. (Eds.). (1974). *A study of child variance*, Vols. 1-2. Ann Arbor: University of Michigan Press.

Rimland, B., Callaway, E., & Dreyfus, P. (1978). The effect of high doses of vitamin B-6 on autistic children: A double-blind crossover study. *American Journal of Psychiatry, 135,* 472–475.

Rooney, K. J., & Hallahan, D. P. (1985). Future directions for cognitive behavior modification research: The quest for cognitive change. *Remedial and Special Education, 6,* 46–51.

Rose, T. L. (1978). The functional relationship between food colors and hyperactivity. *Journal of Applied Behavior Analysis, 11,* 438–449.

Rosenberg, M. S. (1985). Advances in educating students with special educational needs: A view from the United States. *Westminster Studies in Education, 8,* 77–96.

Ross, D. M., & Ross, S. A. (1981). *Hyperactivity: Research, theory, and action,* 2nd ed. New York: Wiley.

Rubin, R. A., & Balow, B. (1971). Learning behavior disorders: A longitudinal study. *Exceptional Children, 38,* 293–299.

Rubin, R. A., & Balow, B. (1978). Prevalence of teacher identified behavior problems: A longitudinal study. *Exceptional Children, 45,* 102–111.

Sagor, M. (1974). Biological bases of childhood behavior disorders. In W. C. Rhodes & M. L. Tracey (Eds.), *A study of child variance.* Vol. 1: *Conceptual models* (pp. 37–94). Ann Arbor: University of Michigan Press.

Shultz, E. W., Hirshoren, A., Manton, A., & Henderson, R. A. (1971). Special education for the emotionally disturbed. *Exceptional Children, 38,* 313–320.

Skiba, R., Grizzle, K., & Minke, K. M. (1994). Opening the floodgates? The social maladjustment exclusion and state SED prevalence rates. *Journal of School Psychology, 32,* 267–282.

Slenkovich, J. E. (1983). *PL 94-142 as applied to DSM III diagnoses: An analysis of DSM III diagnoses vis-à-vis special education law.* Cupertino, CA: Kinghorn Press.

Spivack, G., & Swift, M. S. (1966). The Devereaux Elementary School Behavior Rating Scale: A study of the nature and organization of achievement-related disturbed classroom behavior. *Journal of Special Education, 1,* 71–91.

Spivack, G., Swift, M. S., & Prewitt, J. (1971). Syndromes of disturbed classroom behavior: A behavioral diagnostic system for elementary schools. *Journal of Special Education, 5,* 269–292.

Thies, A. P. (1985). Neuropsychological approaches to learning disorders. In E. W. Gordon (Ed.), *Review of research in education.* Vol. 12. Washington, DC: American Educational Research Association.

Thomas, A., Chess, S., & Birch, H. (1969). *Temperament and behavior disorders in children.* New York: New York University Press.

U.S. Department of Education. (1994). *Sixteenth annual report to Congress on the Individuals with Disabilities Education Act.* Washington, DC: Author.

Vygotsky, L. (1962). *Thought and language.* New York: Wiley.

Werry, J. S. (1979). The childhood psychoses. In H. C. Quay & J. S. Werry (Eds.), *Psychopathological disorders of childhood* (pp. 43–89). New York: Wiley.

Werry, J. S., & Quay, H. C. (1971). The prevalence of behavior symptoms in younger elementary school children. *American Journal of Orthopsychiatry, 41,* 136–143.

Wicks-Nelson, R., & Israel, A. C. (1984). *Behavior disorders of childhood.* Englewood Cliffs, NJ: Prentice-Hall.

Wilson, J. E., & Sherrets, S. D. (1979). A review of past and current pharmacological interventions in the treatment of emotionally disturbed children and adolescents. *Behavioral Disorders, 5,* 60–69.

Wood, F. H., & Zabel, R. H. (1978). Making sense of reports on the incidence of behavior disorders/emotional disturbance in school-aged populations. *Psychology in the Schools, 15,* 45–51.

C h a p t e r 2

High-Incidence Behavior Disorders

Advance Organizer

As you read this chapter, prepare to identify and discuss:

- The primary characteristics of hyperactive behavior.
- The secondary characteristics of hyperactive behavior.
- The causes of hyperactivity, especially brain injury and conditioning.
- The primary characteristics of aggression.
- The secondary characteristics of aggression.
- Causes of aggression, especially psychodynamic and behavioral explanations.
- The primary characteristics of rule-breaking behavior.
- The secondary correlates of delinquency.
- The theories of causation of delinquency.
- The primary characteristics of social withdrawal.
- The secondary characteristics of social withdrawal.
- Theories of causation of social withdrawal.

This chapter was co-authored by Elana Esterson Rock.

Hyperactive, aggressive, rule-breaking, and socially withdrawn behaviors are often referred to as *high-incidence behaviors*. Note that incidence rate is a separate behavioral dimension from severity; all of the high-incidence behaviors may be exhibited in mild, moderate, or severe forms.

Each of the four high-incidence behaviors has been associated with students who receive special education services: Hyperactive behavior is frequently observed in students with learning disabilities, attention deficits, and conduct disorders. Aggressive behavior is the primary maladaptive behavior responsible for referral and placement in programs for students with behavior disorders. High rates of learning disabilities have been found among students in correctional facilities. Even certain social withdrawal behaviors (e.g., depression) have been observed in students with learning disabilities and severe emotional disturbance.

This chapter summarizes the patterns and characteristics of each high-incidence behavior. Generally, both primary and secondary characteristics are presented, followed by a brief overview of causation and prognosis. Although each of these behavior patterns is presented separately, readers should *not* infer either that these behaviors are discrete (i.e., that there is no overlap between hyperactive and aggressive behaviors, for example) or that students always exhibit just one of the behavior patterns. Both of these inferences are false: Students frequently exhibit multiple types of maladaptive behaviors, and it is often difficult for teachers and parents to differentiate between behaviors. Many rule-breaking behaviors, for instance, involve disruptive, hyperactive, or aggressive acts (e.g., criminal assault, arson, robbery).

Characteristics of Hyperactive Behavior

Some of the characteristics associated with hyperactivity are considered primary to the disorder; others are secondary because they result from the interaction of the primary characteristics with environmental events. The primary characteristics are overactivity or fidgetiness, distractibility or inattention, impulsiveness or judgment deficits, and excitability or negative affect. Among the secondary characteristics are learning problems or deficiencies in academic achievement, aggressive and antisocial behaviors, and poor self-concept and lack of self-esteem. These behaviors are described in the following sections.

Primary Behavioral Characteristics

Cantwell (1975), and most other authors, cite *overactivity* as one of the primary behavioral characteristics of hyperactivity. These individuals move around most frequently, more rapidly, and with less purpose than normally developing children. In school, they are often out of their seats, and when seated, they are likely to engage in foot or finger tapping. Paternite and Loney (1980) add *fidgetiness* to the list of primary characteristics originally reported by Cantwell.

Interestingly, even though hyperactivity is often identified on the basis of over-activity, there is not universal agreement about the specific nature of the differences between normal children and children with hyperactivity. For example, Schliefer and colleagues (1975) compared the behavior of children with true hyperactivity, children with situational hyperactivity (differentiated on the basis of teacher ratings), and normal children during free play and structured play settings. During free play, no differences among the three groups were observed, even though in the structured play setting, each hyperactive group could be differentiated from the controls on a number of behaviors. Kaspar, Millichap, Backus, Child, and Schulman (1971) reported similar findings for their samples of 5- to 8-year-olds with and without neurological impairments. Thus, the overactivity of children with hyperactivity may be partly a function of the environment in which they are observed. When little structure is imposed, separating them from normal children on the basis of their activity levels may not be possible.

Cantwell (1975) lists *distractibility* as the second defining characteristic of hyperactivity; Paternite and Loney (1980) and Taylor, Sandberg, Thorley, and Giles (1991) use the term *inattention* to refer to the same phenomenon. Specifically, students with hyperactivity have short attention spans and their attention is not held by activities that most students find engaging (e.g., games, stories, and television). Furthermore, their focus of attention changes rapidly, seemingly without regard for the relative importance of the stimuli. Thus, the student with hyperactivity is as likely to attend to a barking dog as to requests from his mother. Attending is a critical behavior in schools; it is felt that little learning can occur without it. The relationship between this primary behavioral characteristic and the secondary characteristic of the poor school performance is clear: Students who have difficulty sustaining attention and directing it to essential stimuli are likely to find it hard to master school subjects. It should be noted here that reaction time, a concept similar to attention, has *not* been found to be slower or faster for students with hyperactivity (van der Meer & Sergeant, 1988).

Cantwell (1975) lists *impulsivity* as the third primary characteristic of hyperactivity; Paternite and Loney (1980) refer to *judgment deficits*. Both terms imply a tendency on the part of students with hyperactivity to engage in behavior hurriedly or unsystematically, without regard for the potential consequences (Schworm & Birnbaum, 1989). Thus, students with hyperactivity are more likely to find themselves in predicaments: climbing a tree that can't be easily descended, running between parked cars to retrieve a lost ball, or offending someone with an unkind and needless remark.

The fourth and final defining characteristic that Cantwell (1975) lists is *excitability*; Paternite and Loney (1980) speak of *negative affect*. Both suggest that these students are easily excited by everyday events that create no great excitement for most students. Excitability, it is important to note, has two sides, one of which is partly positive: seemingly uncontrolled excitement in anticipation of everyday school events such as recess. Less easy to understand and tolerate is the other side of excitability: irritability, low frustration tolerance, and dramatic and rapid changes in mood. The unpredictability of the behavior of students with hyperactivity undoubtedly contributes to the difficulty they experience interacting with peers and adults.

Secondary Behavioral Characteristics

It is not surprising that *deficiencies in academic achievement* are frequently cited as a secondary characteristic of hyperactivity, because so much of the behavior associated with hyperactivity is incompatible with classroom learning. However, although there is general agreement about the prevalence of *learning problems* among students with hyperactivity, there is some question about whether these deficiencies are out of line with expectations for achievement based on intelligence test scores. Minde and colleagues (1971) found that students with hyperactivity had poorer performance than predicted by their intelligence scores, but Palkes and Stewart (1972) adjusted achievement test scores for differences in intelligence and found no significant differences between hyperactive and control groups on achievement in reading, spelling, and arithmetic.

In clinical descriptions of students with hyperactivity, *aggressive and antisocial behaviors* have appeared in small subgroups. For example, in an early and detailed clinical description, Stewart, Pitts, Craig, and Dieruf (1966) found that roughly half of their sample of students with hyperactivity were reported to fight, to be unresponsive to discipline, and to behave defiantly. That a disproportionate percentage of students with hyperactivity also engage in aggressive and antisocial behavior has been demonstrated repeatedly. For example, Weiss, Minde, Werry, Douglas, and Nemeth (1971) reported that fully one-fourth of the mothers of the students in their hyperactive sample noted antisocial behavior and that these maternal reports were corroborated by teachers, who also noted high rates of antisocial and aggressive behaviors. Mendelson, Johnson, and Stewart (1971), in a follow-up study in which they investigated teenagers who had been diagnosed as hyperactive in childhood, found that serious antisocial behaviors such as incorrigibility, fighting, stealing, and run-ins with police were reported by more than half of the mothers of subjects in their hyperactive sample. Clearly, aggression and other antisocial behaviors are common among youth with hyperactivity, although not as common as among students with emotional and behavior disorders (Margalit, 1989).

A third commonly cited secondary factor associated with hyperactivity is *poor self-concept and low self-esteem* (Loney, 1974). As with the other secondary characteristics, it is easy to understand how poor self-concept can develop as a function of the interaction between primary characteristics and the environment. Any student who is ill-equipped to function effectively in school, and who is likely to be punished by teachers and peers alike for this failure, will probably think poorly of herself or himself. For example, Weiss and associates (1971), in the follow-up study described above, reported that 70 percent of the mothers of children who were hyperactive described their children as being emotionally immature and 30 percent claimed that their children lacked ambition and exhibited little goal-oriented behavior. Psychiatrists who interviewed the children at follow-up noted an unusually high frequency of sadness and lack of self-esteem. In the follow-up by Mendelson, Johnson, and Steward (1971), over half of the mothers reported low self-concept in their teenagers. Finally, Loney, Comly, and Simon (1975) reported that self-concept was lower among poorly managed students with hyperactivity than among well managed students with hyperactivity. As we shall see later in this chapter, these findings have significance for prognosis and outcome.

Prevalence of Hyperactive Behavior

Historically, estimates of prevalence have ranged from 5 to 20 percent of the school-aged population, with boy–girl ratios ranging from 4:1 to 9:1 (Cantwell, 1975). Lambert, Sandoval, and Sassone (1978) analyzed estimates of the prevalence of hyperactivity made by teachers, parents, and physicians with a large sample (>5,000) of elementary students, and found that when hyperactivity was defined in its most restrictive sense (i.e., students identified by teacher, parent, *and* physician as hyperactive), estimates of prevalence were quite low (1.2 percent overall: 2.0 percent for boys and 0.3 percent for girls). However, the prevalence of students identified by at least one of these three agents was 4.9 percent, and students with comparable behavioral ratings who were not identified by any agent was 7.8 percent. Interestingly, Lambert and associates also reported that the highest estimates of prevalence were made by school personnel (7.6 percent of boys and 1.1 percent of girls). This is consistent with the findings of Schleifer and colleagues (1975) and Kaspar and colleagues (1971) (i.e., that hyperactive behavior is more readily apparent in highly structured environments, like school, where students face greater demands for quiet, attention, and immobility). Thus, variability in the estimates of prevalence may be a function of the environments in which ratings are made.

Etiology of Hyperactive Behavior

To date, hyperactivity cannot be attributed to a single cause or combination of causes. In fact, it may have many causes and distinct subgroups with a common etiology (Silver, 1992; Taylor et al., 1991). In the following review, minimal brain dysfunction, genetic transmission, complications of birth and pregnancy, biochemical factors, and environmental factors are considered.

Minimal Brain Dysfunction

Hyperactivity has long been conceptualized as the product of some (usually unspecified) brain damage or dysfunction. The association between hyperactivity and brain damage was more firmly established following the outbreak of encephalitis in the United States shortly after World War I (Stewart, 1970). Encephalitis is an inflammation of the brain, and many children who were afflicted during this epidemic demonstrated hyperactive behavior patterns. Consequently, the presence of the behavioral symptomatology came to imply to many the existence of brain damage, even in the absence of other, more reliable indicators (Ross & Ross, 1976). However, because we have become more sophisticated at diagnosing and detecting brain damage, and because we still cannot find evidence of brain damage for most individuals with hyperactivity, the term has been softened, so that we now speak of *brain dysfunction* rather than of *brain damage* (Ross, 1980).

Brain dysfunction of students who are hyperactive has been studied through electroencephalographic readings (EEG) and neurological soft signs. However, studies of EEG abnormalities among hyperactive and comparison groups have not shown clear and consistent differences, so there is some question as to whether the prevalence of EEG abnormalities is greater among students with hyperactivity than among other groups with behavior disorders or even among nonhyperactive controls. Dubey (1976), for example, reported EEG abnormalities for 20 to 50 percent of children who were hyperactive, but Werry and co-workers (1972) compared the EEG records of twenty normal children, twenty children with hyperactivity, and twenty children who were neurotic and found no differences among the groups in the frequency of major signs of abnormality. Satterfield, Cantwell, Lesser, and Podosin (1972) reported similar results in their study of children with hyperactivity and age- and IQ-matched controls.

A second difficulty with EEG research on hyperactivity is the fact that EEG abnormalities are not associated with more serious forms of hyperactivity (Dubey, 1976). If brain damage or dysfunction were truly central to the development of hyperactivity, we would expect the behavioral disturbance to grow progressively worse with increasingly severe evidence of brain damage. However, Satterfield and his colleagues (1972) reported that the presence of abnormalities was associated with positive response to stimulant medication and, in a subsequent study (Satterfield, Cantwell, Saul, & Yusin, 1974), with superior performance on measures of intelligence and visual-motor functioning.

The research with soft signs of neurological impairment (i.e., behavioral characteristics like immature reflexes and poor motor coordination not specifically associated with CNS damage) is even less definitive than EEG research. For one thing, not all researchers have found differences between children with hyperactivity and other children with behavior disorders on the frequency or severity of soft signs (Wilker, Dixon, & Parker, 1970), although some have (Werry et al., 1972). Furthermore, Dubey (1976) noted that the frequency of soft signs in all such research was typically low and that the number of soft signs bore no relationship to the number of more reliable signs of neurological dysfunction, such as EEG abnormalities.

On the basis of findings from these two areas of research, it can be concluded that not all children who are hyperactive have brain injury, and that this generalization holds whether we assess brain damage with EEG readings or more subjective soft signs. Further, when neurological impairment is present and detected, its presence does not seem to be related to the severity of the disorder. Finally, not all children with traumatic brain injury are hyperactive, and there is apparently little homogeneity in specific location of the damage among children who both have brain injury and hyperactivity (Houlilhan & Van Houten, 1989).

Genetic Transmission

Some researchers have argued that hyperactivity is transmitted genetically from generation to generation within families. Willerman (1973) investigated sets of same-sexed twins to determine the extent to which activity level was inherited by asking mothers of twins to rate their children on behavioral descriptors. She found that the correspondence of ratings of activity level was greater for the monozygotic twins than for the dizygotic twins, suggesting that activity level may have an inherited component—a finding consistent with earlier research (Scarr, 1966; Vandenberg, 1962). Wellerman's estimate of the heritability of activity level was .77 (with perfect heritability being 1.00), but it was considerably higher for boys (.83) than for girls (.58).

In a study of twins with hyperactivity, Lopez (1965) also found greater concordance among monozygotic than among dizygotic twins—that is, when one member of a monozygotic twin pair was considered to be hyperactive, the second was also hyperactive in a greater proportion of pairs than for dizygotic twins. However, boys were overrepresented among Lopez's monozygotic twin pairs, limiting (in light of Wellerman's finding of different estimates of heritability for boys and girls) the usefulness of his findings.

Morrison and Stewart (1971) and Cantwell (1972) each interviewed parents of children with hyperactivity and nonhyperactive controls to determine psychiatric status and developmental histories. The results of these two studies were remarkably similar. For children with hyperactivity, the researchers reported higher rates of alcoholism among mothers and fathers, sociopathy among fathers, and hysteria among mothers. The researchers also made retroactive diagnoses of hyperactivity in childhood for both groups of parents. Nearly all of the parents diagnosed as hyperactive in this way had children who were hyperactive.

Although alcoholism, sociopathy, and hysteria were more prevalent among the parents of children with hyperactivity than among the parents of nonhyperactive children, the proportions of parents who exhibited these disorders were nonetheless low. Simply because more parents of children with hyperactivity exhibited alcoholism, sociopathy, or hysteria does not imply that all parents of children with hyperactivity exhibit these disorders. Taken together, these two studies demonstrate a familial relationship between hyperactivity and certain adulthood disorders, but they provide little information about why these disorders occur together within families. At this point it is accurate to state that children with hyperactivity behave inappropriately and their parents respond more negatively than do parents of children without hyperactivity. However, it is not yet possible to prove whether hyperactivity is transmitted genetically or environmentally. It is just as likely that children with hyperactivity produce parental distress or psychiatric disorder as it is that disturbed parents produce children who are overactive, inattentive, and impulsive.

In order to separate environmental from genetic factors more clearly, Morrison and Stewart (1973) conducted a second study, this time using adoptive parents of children with hyperactivity as the subjects for investigation. They found that the prevalence of parental disorders was lower among adoptive than natural parents, suggesting that genetic transmission, at least for this population, contributed to the development of hyperactivity.

Pregnancy and Birth Complications

Pasamanick, Rogers, and Lilienfeld (1956) were the first to demonstrate a relationship between complications of pregnancy and learning and behavioral problems in later life. However, the information available on the prenatal and perinatal problems of mothers of children with hyperactivity is limited. Werry, Weiss, and Douglas (1964) found that mothers of children with hyperactivity experienced more complications during pregnancy and at birth than mothers of nonhyperactive controls, but others (e.g., Minde, Webb, & Sykes, 1968; Stewart et al., 1966) have reported few significant differences.

Waldrop and her associates (Waldrop & Haverson, 1971; Waldrop, Pederson, & Bell, 1968) documented an increased incidence of minor physical anomalies among preschool children with hyperactivity. Waldrop argued that such anomalies are indicative of subtle developmental deviations that are not readily detected during pregnancy or at birth, but that nonetheless are related to behavioral deviation. Waldrop, Bell, McLaughlin, and Halverson (1978) found that physical anomalies among newborns were predictive of distractibility and impulsivity at age 3. Quinn and Rapoport (1974) reported that the number of physical anomalies was related positively to the severity of hyperactivity and negatively to the age of onset. Thus, the more anomalies a child showed, the more likely that child was to exhibit severe behavioral disturbance and early onset of the behavioral symptomatology.

Biochemical Factors

In general, researchers have had little success relating biochemical factors to specific behavioral manifestations, with the notable exception of a few disorders such as phenylketonuria (PKU). However, David and his colleagues (David, Clark, & Voeller, 1972; David, Hoffman, Sverd, Clark, & Voeller, 1976) tested the hypothesis that chronically elevated levels of lead in the body led to hyperactivity. David and associates (1972) reported elevated lead levels in the blood and urine of children with hyperactivity, both those with known histories of lead exposure and those for whom a cause was unknown. In a subsequent study, David and co-workers (1976) treated children with hyperactivity with a heavy metal-chelating agent (i.e., a medication that removed lead from the body). The children with high initial levels of blood lead exhibited greater decreases in blood lead levels following treatment than the children for whose hyperactivity a probable cause other than lead poisoning was suspected. Behavioral ratings showed consistent and widespread improvement among the high-blood-lead-level group.

A second biochemical cause has been offered by Feingold (1975a, 1975b), who conceptualized hyperactivity as a reaction by genetically predisposed children to artificial food flavoring and coloring and to naturally occurring salicylates common in our diets. Although Feingold's work has found little support in the scientific community, because of the perceived success of the diet that he developed, his work is widely known and popular among the general population. The efficacy of the Feingold diet will be addressed in a subsequent chapter; suffice it to say at this point that it was once a popular treatment.

Home Environment Factors

Loney and her associates (Loney, 1974; Loney, Comly, & Simon, 1975; Prinz & Loney, 1974) tested the assumption that the primary characteristics of hyperactivity interacted with environmental variables to produce secondary problems. Loney and colleagues (1975) contrasted well-managed and poorly managed children with minimal brain dysfunction on measures of self-concept, impulsiveness, and drug response, hypothesizing that on the measure of self-concept (a secondary characteristic of hyperactivity) the well-managed group would score higher than the poorly managed group. The researchers also hypothesized that on the measure of impulsiveness (a primary characteristic), the two hyperactive groups would score significantly lower than the controls. However, only one of the three questions measuring self-concept differentiated between the well- and poorly managed groups, and only one of the three questions measuring impulsiveness differentiated between the two MBD groups and the controls.

In an initial analysis, Paternite, Loney, and Langhorne (1976) found that parenting variables were more predictive of the severity of secondary symptoms than socioeconomic status. High socioeconomic status students with hyperactivity were rated as having significantly less severe secondary symptoms, and low-socioeconomic status parents were rated as more hostile and less consistent than their high-socioeconomic counterparts. The researchers concluded that parenting variables contributed more to the prediction of secondary symptoms than socioeconomic status did. However, neither socioeconomic status nor parenting variables contributed to the prediction of the primary characteristics of hyperactivity.

Paternite and Loney (1980) also investigated the relationship between hyperactivity and home environment by comparing the symptomatology and home environments of 94 boys with hyperactivity. They determined that at referral, parent–child relationship was negatively related to aggression and behavior problems (i.e., the worse the relationship, the greater the likelihood of aggression and behavior problems) and positively related to prosocial behavior (i.e., the better the relationship, the greater the likelihood of prosocial behavior). Given these findings, it seems reasonable to conclude that the home environment's effect on hyperactivity is related to secondary symptomatology.

Course, Prognosis, and Outcome of Hyperactive Behavior

It was originally and widely believed that hyperactivity is a disorder of childhood that is outgrown in adolescence and early adulthood. This belief that the problem disappears has stood the test of empirical inquiry only to a limited extent in many ways, it has been disproved (Silver, 1992). Before considering the prognosis and outcome of the disorder, let us look closely at its developmental course.

Children with hyperactivity are remembered by their parents as difficult infants, both physiologically and behaviorally. Many infants with hyperactivity are described as demanding, irritable, not easily satisfied, and unpredictable. Overactivity is often apparent in the earliest months of life. In general, then, the picture is one of an infant whose behavior may seriously disrupt and perhaps damage a parent–child relationship.

Preschoolers with hyperactivity present a more serious management problem for parents because they are mobile and highly active. Stewart (1970) noted that preschool children with hyperactivity are more accident prone than their nonhyperactive agemates. He based this assertion on the overrepresentation of children with hyperactivity on hospital lists of accidental poisonings. In addition, evidence of attention deficits first becomes apparent at this age, and some preschoolers exhibit speech delay. Still, hyperactivity is difficult to diagnose during preschool years because the differences between normal children and children with hyperactivity are a matter of degree (Kaspar, 1971; Schleifer et al., 1975).

Although most of the professional literature involving hyperactivity relates to school-age children, some researchers followed students with hyperactivity as they grew up (Laufer, 1962). Weiss and colleagues (1971) and Mendelson and colleagues (1971) conducted follow-up studies of adolescents who had been diagnosed as hyperactive in childhood. Weiss and colleagues found that although the severity of the primary symptoms was reduced at follow-up, adolescents with hyperactivity were still rated as different from their nonhyperactive peers; and Mendelson and colleagues reported that adolescents with hyperactivity were less overactive, distractible, impulsive, and excitable at follow-up than at initial referral, but that these problems persisted into adolescence. Both researchers also found that severity of secondary symptomatology (i.e., antisocial behavior, aggression, school failure, and poor self-concept and low self-esteem) worsened or remained the same.

Finally, it should be noted that Mendelson and colleagues (1971) asked mothers to rate their adolescents on degree of improvement since childhood. More than half felt that their children had improved, but nearly one-third reported that their children were either the same or worse. Thus, hyperactivity is not a disorder that necessarily disappears with maturity. Apparently, the primary symptoms abate in severity, but school failure, antisocial behavior, and poor self-concept often worsen.

Definitive data on the adult adjustment of children with hyperactivity are limited. Morrison and Stewart (1971) and Cantwell (1972) found that the prevalence of alcoholism, sociopathy, and hysteria was greater among parents of children with hyperactivity than among parents of nonhyperactive controls, and that the parents of children with hyperactivity described themselves as hyperactive in childhood more frequently than did the parents of controls. Cantwell reported that four of five parents of children with hyperactivity who described themselves as hyperactive in their own childhood were diagnosed as psychiatrically ill in adulthood. Morrison and Stewart reported that nine of twelve parents with self-reported hyperactivity had definite psychiatric illness. These data lend some support to the notion that hyperactivity in childhood is associated with serious adult dysfunction.

Characteristics of Aggressive Behavior

Aggressive behaviors can be distinguished from other maladaptive, inappropriate, or disordered behavior by applying two criteria (Baron, 1977):

1. Antecedent events suggest that the behavior is intended to cause harm.
2. The behavior is directed at a victim.

Thus, aggressive behavior has three elements: an observable behavior, an intent to harm, and an identifiable victim.

Aggressive behaviors are typically divided into two discrete categories or clusters: verbal aggression and physical aggression. In addition, aggressive behaviors can also be considered as primary or secondary to the disorder. Among the primary characteristics are the following overt behaviors: biting, kicking, throwing objects, cursing, and threatening others. Among the many secondary characteristics are juvenile delinquency, temper tantrums, anger, lack of verbal mediation, and stealing.

Primary Behavioral Characteristics

The primary characteristics of aggressive behavior are those violent, abusive, threatening, and destructive actions that cause teachers and parents to rate these behaviors as number one among nonacademic classroom concerns (Mullen & Wood, 1986; Ruhl & Hughes, 1985). One of the most extensive studies of childhood aggression was conducted by Gerald R. Patterson and his colleagues at the Oregon Research Institute (Patterson, Reid, Jones, & Conger, 1975). Patterson and colleagues identified the following important information about aggressive behaviors: an extensive list of "noxious" behaviors exhibited by students who are aggressive; the frequency of noxious behaviors exhibited by students who are aggressive, and the frequency of noxious behaviors exhibited by nonaggressive peers. This research was important because the extensive descriptive findings that detailed patterns of childhood aggression were followed by the development of a comprehensive treatment plan (Patterson, 1975; Patterson et al., 1975).

Detailed descriptions of aggressive behavior were gathered by videotaping thousands of instances of family interactions (Patterson & Cobb, 1973). Analysis of the behavior patterns exhibited by the family members indicated that aggressive and related behaviors could be clustered into fourteen categories of "noxious" behaviors. These behaviors are listed in Table 2.1, where they are defined by typical home or classroom examples.

TABLE 2.1 Noxious Behaviors Associated with Aggression

Behavior	Definition
1. Disapproval	Disapproving of another's behavior with words or gestures.
2. Negativism	Using a negative tone of voice to state neutral content.
3. Noncompliance	Failing to do what is requested.
4. Yelling	Shouting.
5. Teasing	Verbally mocking another's actions.
6. High-rate activity	Extended aversive or annoying activities.
7. Negative physical actions	Abusive or violent actions, intended or completed physical attack behavior (e.g., kicking, biting, hitting).
8. Whining	High-pitched, nasal remarks or sounds.
9. Destructiveness	Attempting to or actually damaging objects or property.
10. Humiliation	Embarrassing, shaming, or ridiculing another.
11. Crying	Any crying.
12. Negative commands	Issuing demanding or threatening orders.
13. Dependency	Asking for assistance when none is needed.
14. Ignoring	Not responding to the behavior of another.

Source: Adapted from Patterson et al. (1975).

Secondary Behavioral Characteristics

Several related behavioral characteristics are associated with aggression. The noxious behaviors described in Patterson's research are all exhibited more frequently by students who are aggressive than by nonaggressive students, yet not all of these behaviors can be considered aggressive. Several are most likely to be called disruptive or noncompliant by classroom teachers, because they are more irritating than aggressive.

The behaviors in Table 2.1 are not the only secondary characteristics associated with children and youths who are aggressive. Others found to be prevalent include disruptive behaviors, juvenile delinquency, lying and stealing, lack of verbal mediation, anger and temper tantrums (Einon & Potegal, 1994), and hyperactive or impulsive behaviors (which were described earlier).

Disruptive Behaviors

Disruptive behaviors are maladaptive but less intense than aggressive behaviors. Typical classroom disruptions are talking out, getting out of seat, making noise, gesturing inappropriately, touching others' property, and playing. Many of these behaviors have been defined and measured in educational settings (viz. Turkewitz, O'Leary, & Ironsmith, 1975). Table 2.2 contains a list, with operationalized definitions, of eight related maladaptive classroom behaviors. Direct-observation

TABLE 2.2   Definitions of Disruptive Behavior Used in Direct Observation

1. *Out of chair:* Moving from own chair when not permitted or requested to do so by teacher. No part of the child's body is to be touching the chair.
2. *Modified out-of-chair:* Moving from own chair with some part of the body still touching the chair (excludes sitting on feet).
3. *Touching others' property:* Coming into contact with another student's property without permission to do so (includes grabbing, rearranging, and destroying the property of another, and touching the desk of another).
4. *Vocalization:* Any unpermitted audible behavior emanating from the mouth.
5. *Playing:* Using the hands to play with the student's own or community property in a manner incompatible with learning.
6. *Orienting:* The turning or orienting response necessary to get up or down, using the desk as a reference point.
7. *Noise:* Creating any audible noise other than vocalization without permission.
8. *Time off-task:* Not doing assigned work (e.g., student does not write or read when so assigned).

measurements of these behaviors in classrooms for students described as "disturbed" has demonstrated not only that they are exhibited at a high frequency by some students but also that carefully administered treatment programs can dramatically decrease their occurrence (Drabman, Spitalnik, & O'Leary, 1973).

It is important to distinguish disruptive from more serious aggressive behaviors for several reasons. First, if these behaviors are combined in a direct-observation measurement system, the exact nature of the student's presenting problem will be obscured. For example, if a referral for special education services states that a student exhibits twelve disturbing acts each day, the diagnostic team will not know whether the student gets into twelve fights a day or merely talks out twelve times daily. Second, the selected treatment must be carefully matched to the maladaptive behavior. Some highly intrusive treatment procedures, like seclusion time-out, are appropriate for reducing hitting or kicking, but inappropriate for reducing off-task or noisemaking behaviors.

Juvenile Delinquency

In everyday language, the term *delinquent* often refers to any unruly or disobedient child or youth. The term *juvenile delinquent*, however, should be reserved for youthful offenders who have been duly adjudicated for committing a crime (Kvaraceus, 1971). The association between juvenile delinquency and aggression appears to be a function of the type of crime committed. Many of the crimes committed by juvenile delinquents—like assault, rape, homicide, and battery—involve violent or aggressive acts. In fact, recent FBI reports indicate increasing rates of violent crimes for youths under 18. The most common offenses committed by this age group, in order of highest frequency, are auto theft, burglary, robbery, larceny, forcible rape, aggravated assault, and murder (Clarizio & McCoy, 1976).

Lying and Stealing

Lying and stealing have been found to be more prevalent among children who are aggressive than among nonaggressive children (Patterson et al., 1975). While there are logical explanations for the connection between aggressive behaviors and lying and stealing (e.g., a student blamed for hitting a classmate lies to avoid punishment), perhaps the more important consideration here is the implication for successful treatment. There is some evidence that response classes (i.e., clusters of related behaviors) are affected concurrently by various treatment techniques (Wahler, 1975). Specifically, the treatment of students who are aggressive has proved less than effective if the students also steal (Patterson et al., 1975). It is, therefore, likely that there is some connection between aggression and stealing and that successful treatment must target both maladaptive behaviors.

Verbal Mediation

There is also evidence that students who are aggressive employ less verbal mediation to control overt behavior. Theoretically, a reflective, self-controlled individual stops to think before acting in many situations. Camp (1977), however, found that students who are aggressive employ a cognitive functioning pattern that includes a rapid response style deficient in verbal mediation. The implication for treatment is that training a student who is aggressive in verbal mediation may reduce aggressive behavior.

Anger and Temper Tantrums

Teachers and parents who work with students who are aggressive know that these students often display anger and temper tantrums. Temper tantrums frequently occur when students who are aggressive are confronted or restrained by adults (Einon & Potegal, 1994). Teachers who attempt to restrain fighting youths may be attacked for their efforts. Those who physically restrain students to prevent them from harming themselves or others can expect prolonged and violent tantrums, consisting of screaming, crying, cursing, hitting, kicking, and other abusive behaviors (Schloss & Smith, 1987). Whenever teachers use treatments that involve physical confrontation with students who are disruptive (e.g., positive practice overcorrection or physical guidance to a time-out center), the result can be violent student behavior. Teachers must, therefore, decide between enforcing treatment rules, which may lead to a violent confrontation, and permitting students to escape the consequences of their acts, which may undermine the behavior management program.

Other Characteristics

There is convincing evidence that students with behavior disorders in general, as well as students who exhibit aggressive behaviors, experience other school-related problems. Researchers have found, for example, that both elementary and secondary student with behavior disorders, on average, perform significantly below the mean on intelligence and achievement tests (Coutinho, 1986; Scruggs & Mastropieri, 1986). These achievement deficits appear to exist across all academic areas

(Epstein, Kinder, & Bursuck, 1989) and to generate an intellectual and educational performance profile similar to that of students with learning disabilities. However, these findings must be interpreted with caution. There is no conclusive evidence, for example, that low achievement causes behavior disorders, or vice versa. While it is conceivable that one condition may precede and lead to the other, the results of current research merely support the conclusion that the presence of behavior disorders is *associated with* the presence of below-average achievement. Moreover, the distribution of all students with behavior disorders overlaps to a considerable extent the distribution of students without disabilities. Therefore, it is possible to state only that, *on the average*, the achievement and intellectual levels of students with emotional and behavior disorders are below those of students without disabilities. It is not possible, using only achievement or IQ data, to identify, with any degree of accuracy, a specific student with behavior disorders.

Prevalence of Aggressive Behavior

Exact estimates of the number of students who are aggressive are not available. Elementary teachers report that about 10 percent of their students exhibit behavior problems that are serious enough to warrant clinical attention and that the most common behavior problems are conduct disorders. If only *major* conduct problems are considered, approximately 6 percent of all students are rated by teachers as exhibiting persistent and serious difficulties (Rubin & Balow, 1978). The public schools alone serve between 350,000 and 400,000 children identified with a severe emotional disturbance. The best recent estimate (Oxford, Boyle, & Racine, 1991) is that approximately 5.5 percent of children exhibit behavior disorders that involve aggression.

Etiology of Aggressive Behavior

There is a consensus among professionals in education and psychology that aggressive behaviors constitute "surface" behavior that can be explained by underlying psychological and environmental influences (Long & Newman, 1971), but there is wide disagreement about etiology between theorists of the two psychological models (psychodynamic and behavioral) that are used most frequently in treating children and youth who are aggressive.

In brief, psychodynamic theorists state that aggression is caused by faulty resolution of underlying psychological conflicts (e.g., the Oedipus complex) that were precipitated or caused by pathological child-rearing practices. Behavioral theorists, in contrast, place little importance on nonobservable intrapsychic phenomena and view aggressive behavior as a learned, maladaptive response that results from the influence of specific environmental events on human behavior. Although many of these environmental events may be the same child-rearing practices deemed important by psychodynamic theorists, the psychological mechanisms that behaviorists believe explain aggressive behavior are quite distinct from those hypothesized by psychodynamic theorists.

The problem is compounded by the position that aggression is theorized to occupy in relation to pathology. Neither psychodynamic nor behavioral theory holds that aggression is directly related to a specific psychopathology or that aggressive behaviors constitute a unique set of symptoms. Even theorists who believe that aggression is symptomatic of an underlying psychological state agree that there is not one aggressive patient type or one common psychological element (Lion & Penna, 1974). In fact, a wide range of potential agents, including toxic psychosis, amphetamines, paranoid schizophrenia, learned responses, underlying drives, and the death wish, have been associated with the causes of aggression.

The Psychodynamic Model

The diverse group of clinicians, researchers, and theorists who subscribe to the psychodynamic model share certain definable and related characteristics. One primary consideration is the acceptance of unconscious forces as behavior determinants. The evolution of this view as it relates to aggression began with Freud's interpretation of intrapsychic phenomena. Freud viewed aggression as an instinctual drive toward death and one of two drives present in all humans, the other being sexual (Knutson, 1973). Later in life, Freud's own theory evolved away from the death instinct aspect of aggression, but he continued to view aggression as a primary innate drive (Baron, 1977).

Freud's contribution to present and past understanding of aggressive disorders has been important, but represents just one of three widely held explanations for aggression. The other two theoretical positions are the aggression–frustration hypothesis suggested by Dollard and colleagues and the social-learning hypothesis of Bandura (Bandura, 1973). The central elements in each of these theories are presented in simplified form in Table 2.3.

The psychodynamic explanation for aggressive behavior is very complex, but aggressive behavior is interpreted as having either a direct or an indirect relationship to intrapsychic dynamics. In Freudian terms, *intrapsychic dynamics* refers to the resolution or lack of resolution of conflicts among the intrapsychic phenomena (id, ego, and superego) caused by the presence of instinctual drives (psychosexual and aggressive). The aggressive instinct is a product of the id, the mechanism used to gain goal satisfaction. The most important intrapsychic conflict vis-à-vis the development of aggressive behavior is the Oedipal conflict. Psychodynamic theory holds that at the end of the phallic stage of psychosexual development (about 5 years of age), a male child directs hostility toward his father because he is in competition for his mother's affection. This conflict is resolved as, over time, a boy becomes disappointed by his mother while continuing to fear his father's retaliation. Eventually, he identifies with his father—a process that enables a male child to keep his mother as a love object, but to do so safely through his father.

TABLE 2.3 **Psychodynamic, Aggression–Frustration, and Social–Learning Theories of Aggression**

Theory	Casual Mechanism	Simplified Explanation
Psychodynamic	Aggressive instinct	Pathologic child-rearing habits contribute to a failure to resolve intrapsychic conflicts that impede development of adaptive controls (the ego and superego functions) on the amoral, self-satisfying instinctual force (the id).
Aggression–frustration	Drive reduction	Aggressive behavior is an adaptive response triggered by frustration when the organism, in an effort to satisfy basic needs (e.g., hunger, safety, pleasure), is denied fulfillment.
Social–learning	Environmental determinism	Aggressive behavior is learned primarily through observational learning, stimulus control, and reinforcement.

Resolution of the Oedipal conflict can be delayed or halted by a number of environmental factors because resolution is dependent upon the parents' reactions to the child's behavior. If the mother is overly seductive, for example, a boy will not need to identify with his father in order to receive maternal love; theoretically, this pattern can lead to specific psychological problems. If a father is overly punitive or inconsistent in disciplining his son, this, too, will have negative consequences. Failure to resolve the Oedipal conflict leads to the development of an Oedipus complex, characterized by a lack of control of the id's aggressive instinct (Pervin, 1980).

Although the Oedipus complex is typically associated with males, in at least one case the causes of aggressive behavior for a little girl have been interpreted as instinctual aggressive drives channeled by Oedipal processes (Bender, 1953). In this instance, the girl expressed impulses to destroy the inside of her mother's body.

How aggression is expressed as behavior is a function of whichever intrapsychic process is occurring within the individual (i.e., the content and focus of the aggression are determined by the current psychosexual phase or intrapsychic conflict). This process is a complex one and may involve either fixation at one psychosexual phase or regression to a lower phase (Buxbaum, 1970). A child nearing the end of the phallic stage who fails to resole the Oedipal conflict, for example, would be expected to direct aggression toward parent or other authority figures who frustrate the satisfaction of basic drives. Thus, the overt manifestation of aggressive behavior reflects both psychosexual development and psychological defense that a particular developmental phase places at the individual's disposal.

Because aggression typically involves the intrapsychic mechanism aroused during the resolution of the Oedipal conflict, it is often associated with the development, or lack of development, of the superego (Bender, 1953). This association leads to the interpretation that aggression is a defense mechanism created to deal with anxiety aroused by unresolved Oedipal wishes occurring at a stage in development when superego restraints are lacking (Kaufman, 1967). Because superego functions are viewed as controls over the id (the superego is often equated with the term *conscience* in the popular literature), the individual will behave aggressively because of the failure to develop internal controls over overt behavior. Acting out is thus seen as a substitute for reflective behavior and an attempt to resolve unconscious conflicts, which often result in the domination by the id of the superego (Ekstein, 1966).

The environmental causes of the intrapsychic conflicts that give rise to aggression are postulated to reside within the family, particularly in mother–child interactions (Bender, 1953). Conflicts can result from a number of pathological child-rearing patterns, including maternal deprivation, overindulgence, overprotection, and overauthority (Bakwin & Bakwin, 1967). Accordingly, parents can generate aggression in their children by behaving inconsistently, by developing overly close alliances with them, by fostering dependence in them, and by contributing to their separation anxiety. Ramsey and Walker (1988), for example, found that parents of antisocial students were deficient in important parenting skills, including disciplining and problem solving. Investigations into the relationship between separation anxiety and aggressive behavior have uncovered significant, but unreplicated, support for this position. McIntyre and Wolf (1973) found that highly anxious children, during separation from their mothers, demonstrated significantly less aggression as a response to a frustrating stimulus than their less anxious peers did. According to psychoanalytic theory, less aggression occurred because its expression was inhibited by the children's high levels of anxiety.

Superego deficits in parents are frequently associated with aggressive behavior in children (Johnson, 1972). This family interaction pattern results in a "superego lacunae" effect. Theoretically, children are unconsciously encouraged by their parents to act out forbidden parental impulses and are rewarded for doing so. Children often have a limited perception of this process, and when asked why they aggress, will reply that they realize they will be punished, but that they believe their fathers prefer them to be aggressive (Buxbaum, 1970). In this case, the family interaction pattern is one in which poorly psychologically integrated parents allow or encourage numerous continued small aggressive transgressions, and then react massively, often violently, to a single aggressive act (Johnson, 1972). A short case report will illustrate this process (Aichhorn, 1972):

> *A 17-year-old boy's father was periodically severely punishing of his son's behavior. The infrequent punishment accompanied by more frequent encouragement of fighting and other manly behavior produced both guilt and anxiety in the son. Since the boy was confused as to the cause or resolution of his guilt and anxiety, he continued to exhibit aggressive behavior which in turn led to repeated beatings.*

Frustration–Aggression Hypothesis

The second theoretical explanation was an effort to use emerging learning theory concepts to explain aggressive behavior within the psychodynamic framework (Dollard, Miller, Doob, Mowrer, & Sears, 1939). These theorists postulated that aggressive acts could be traced to the frustration of organisms in their attempts to satisfy basic needs. When an organism is kept in some way from attaining its goals, the resulting frustration leads directly to aggressive behavior. Because aggressive behavior is directed at removing the obstacle in order to attain the desired outcome, the intent to harm others becomes a central element in this explanation.

Contemporary views of the frustration–aggression hypothesis accept elements but not all of the theory. There is support for the premise that environmental frustrations can and do cause aggressive behavior in humans and laboratory animals. However, it is also believed that frustration is not the sole cause of aggression and that frustration does not inevitably produce an aggressive response (Mischel, 1971). Thus, the frustration–aggression hypothesis is currently accepted as one, but not the only, likely cause of aggressive behavior.

Learning Theory

The early work of Albert Bandura stands as an important contribution to understanding the causes of aggressive behavior. His investigations led to the development of *social-learning theory*, an expansion of traditional learning theory that incorporated modeling or observational learning as an operating principle to account for behavior change in human beings.

Learning theorists before Bandura focused primarily on behavioral principles that postulated that obviously contiguous environmental events affect behavior according to well-defined laws. Pavlov's experiments with respondent conditioning of salivating dogs and Skinner's work with operant conditioning of rats and pigeons are classic examples. Bandura's research, however, demonstrated that children who merely observed aggressive acts committed by live or filmed actors would later be more likely to exhibit aggressive behaviors than peers who had not observed aggressive behavior (Bandura, Ross, & Ross, 1963). Because there were no contiguous environmental events either immediately before or after the children's aggression to account for the behavior change, social–learning theorists maintained that the children had learned to act aggressively through observation, imitation, and modeling of another's behavior.

The Acquisition of Aggressive Behavior

Learning theorists often distinguish between processes that operate when an organism acquires new behaviors and processes that enhance the maintenance of already acquired behaviors. Early support for the operation of learning principles in the acquisition of new behaviors was provided by John Watson's classical conditioning experiments, performed shortly after World War I, which demonstrated that emotional and fear reactions could be conditioned in a young child (Watson &

Raynor, 1972). Recent behavioral theorists have also stressed the importance of considering environmental events that contribute to the long-term maintenance of maladaptive behaviors (Borkovec, 1976). The distinction between acquisition and maintenance is especially important for understanding aggressive behavior patterns because often the factors present when children first learn aggressive behaviors are quite different from those that maintain aggression.

Social-learning theorists propose that aggression is acquired primarily through two learning processes: first, and most typical, *modeling*; and second, *reinforcement* (Bandura, 1976). Early behavioral researchers who studied aggression focused on controlled experiments with laboratory animals. The results of these experiments indicated that aggressive behaviors could be acquired through both respondent and operant conditioning (Ulrich, Dulaney, Arnett, & Mueller, 1973). Aggression was produced operantly in animals by heating cage floors, pinching tails, and withdrawing morphine and positive reinforcement. Aggression was classically conditioned by pairing a tone with a shock so that in future trials an animal would attack a target even if the tone were presented alone. As a result of these findings, traditional behaviorists concluded that because aggression can be classically and operantly conditioned and elicited by observable environmental events, the need for explanative intervening variables commonly ascribed to the arousal of aggression (e.g., hate, fear, or frustration) is eliminated (Ulrich et al., 1973).

Modern behaviorists and social-learning theorists, however, believe that explanations of overt behavior that fail to include mediation by the individual are insufficient to explain human aggression. Early modeling experiments demonstrated that children imitated aggressive behavior in the absence of frustration, instigating environmental events, or reinforcement (Bandura et al., 1963), and numerous experiments have replicated and supported the modeling hypothesis for different age and intelligence levels (Talkington & Altman, 1973). Social-learning theorists believe that two environmental influences are most likely to cause imitated aggression: family members who exhibit aggression; and a subculture, such as gang violence, that considers aggression to be a positive attribute (Bandura, 1976).

Behavioral theorists also believe that reinforcement is central to the acquisition of aggression. It is frequently observed, especially in classroom and recess settings, that aggression has a payoff for the aggressor (Buss, 1971). Typically, when students exhibit violent behaviors, they are immediately rewarded. Teachers who have witnessed hitting and terrorizing behaviors resulting in victims' crying or cowering are also observing environmental reinforcement for aggression. In addition, robbery and battery often produce rewards for the violent criminal. The fact that aggressive behaviors are almost immediately reinforced by environmental events—before teachers, parents, or police can intervene—is one of the factors that makes aggression so difficult to treat.

The Maintenance of Aggressive Behavior

Two additional behavioral principles are postulated to contribute to the maintenance of aggressive behaviors: stimulus control and negative reinforcement. Stimulus control, the tendency of antecedent environmental events to set the occasion for the emission of a given behavior, has been closely associated with aggression.

The most extensive analysis of antecedent behaviors was conducted by Patterson and his colleagues at the Oregon Research Institute (Patterson & Cobb, 1973). These researchers videotaped 57,000 family interactions and found that one or more of the noxious behaviors listed in Table 2-1 preceded the emission of an aggressive response nearly 70 percent of the time. The conclusion that aggression is under stimulus control appears to be well supported in recent research by Ninness, Fuerst, and Rutherford (1995), who found that maladaptive behavior occurred following provocation from peers and continued in an escalating cycle.

When classroom teachers are asked to recall what occurred immediately prior to aggressive behavior, the answer is often a specific, though nonaggressive, event. Students have been physically or verbally attacked for bumping a desk, stepping on a foot, spilling water, or in some way accidentally disturbing an aggressive classmate. More often, however, the emission of aggressive acts can be viewed as an escalation of behavior, begun when one student misses an answer, a second student laughs, the first responds with a threatening gesture, the second follows with "Your mother" or some other verbal taunt, and then the fists fly.

The final process contributing to the maintenance of aggression is also the most complex. It has been called the *coercion hypothesis* (Patterson, 1975) and the *negative reinforcement trap* (Wahler, 1975). Consider the following behavior sequence:

1. Steven is yelling in the department store, complaining that his mother and father won't buy a toy he desires.
2. His mother (or father) yells at Steven, threatens punishment, and tells him to be quiet.
3. Steven begins to rage. He throws himself on the floor, screams as loudly as he can, sobs real tears, strikes out at his parents, and says he hates both of them.
4. His father (or mother) either gives in and buys him the toy or promises to do something else for him if he'll settle down.
5. Steven stops his temper tantrum.

It is quite possible that two or more behavioral principles are operating in this sequence. The coercion hypothesis states that children apply aversive acts either to accelerate or to decelerate some behavior exhibited by another family member. In this case, the child's temper tantrum (event number 3) results in the delivery of a reward. In effect, Steven's parents have rewarded tantrum behavior (event number 4), and in all likelihood they will witness more temper outbursts in similar situations in the future.

It is possible that negative reinforcement (a procedure whereby a behavior is emitted that removes an aversive stimulus, resulting in increased rates of the behavior) is also occurring. Because Steven's tantrum stopped the aversive parental scolding (event number 2), it is likely that Steven will tantrum more frequently in similar situations in the future.

In summary, behaviorists have postulated that there are several learning processes that contribute to the acquisition and maintenance of aggressive behavior. The explanations are all based on evidence gathered from direct observation of children's behavior at home or in school. The operational definitions and causative explanations that are a central part of the behavioral analysis of aggression lead directly to treatment. In general, behavioral treatment strategies are geared toward relearning appropriate behaviors or decreasing existing aggressive patterns. On a positive note, there is evidence that observing models who are coping with aggressive impulses decelerates aggressive behaviors (Rosenthal & Bandura, 1978; Goodwin & Mahoney, 1975).

Prognosis of Aggressive Behavior

Even though aggression is regarded as surface behavior that has several hypothesized causes, there is strong evidence that the presence of aggression in childhood is associated with both aggression and other mental health problems in later life (Cairns, et al., 1994; Farrington, 1991; Levitt, 1971; Morris, Escoll, & Wexler, 1956). The results of a ten-year longitudinal study that followed third-graders until they were out of high school indicated that the presence of aggression at age 9 was an excellent predictor of aggression at 18 (Eron, Huesmann, Lefkowitz, & Walder, 1974). Cairns, Santoyo, and Holly (1994) found similar results after following students from the fourth grade through post-high school graduation.

Aggression in childhood has also been associated with other adult adjustment problems, including alcoholism, criminal behavior, and psychoses (Eron, Huesmann, & Zelli, 1991; Robins, 1979). Thus, the treatment of childhood aggression deserves special focus for three reasons: (1) the behavior pattern, if untreated, is likely to remain stable; (2) childhood aggression is closely associated with serious adult problems; and (3) parents who are aggressive tend to raise children who are aggressive, increasing the likelihood of antisocial behavior in the next generation. On a positive note, Kellam, Rebok, Ialongo, and Mayer (1994) found that, with treatment, aggressive behavior was reduced from first grade to middle school.

In addition to the negative consequences of aggression for both the victim and the aggressor, there is a cost to society in the form of considerable community mental health, legal, and educational expense. Conduct disorders are the most frequent cause of referral to publicly funded community mental health centers, constituting from one-third to one-half of the referrals (Gilbert, 1957; Kazdin, 1987; Robins, 1981). The cost to the legal and educational system is also high. Private residential treatment centers for youths who exhibit severely disturbed, criminal, or antisocial behavior can cost from $25,000 to $50,000 per youngster per year (Linton & Russell, 1982). Even the cost of public school programs can exceed $10,000 per youth per year—a figure two to four times the average expenditure for nonaggressive students. Although the exact cost of educating students who are aggressive is unknown, the enormity of it is evident, because the public schools alone currently serve almost 400,000 students with emotional and behavior disorders, of which an estimated 20 percent were identified as having severe conduct disorders (Grosenick, 1981).

Rule Breaking and Juvenile Delinquency

Children and adolescents who violate rules that govern social interaction often provoke fear in the adults who are responsible for providing educational services. This fear is experienced not only by teachers. In many cases, social workers, peers, siblings, parents, and even law enforcement and legal personnel share the same feelings of trepidation and exasperation. In the following section, we define and describe the multifaceted behavioral characteristics of students who engage in rule breaking—and, in many cases, delinquent behavior—and discuss the incidence, various etiological theories, and prognosis of delinquency.

Characteristics of Rule-Breaking Behavior

Children and youths who violate societal norms or break the rules of accepted social and legal functioning are frequently characterized as delinquent, conduct disordered, or antisocial. Regardless of the terminology employed, this category includes a large number of young people who are frequently at odds with the law, their parents, peers, and often themselves (Feldman, Caplinger, & Wodarski, 1983). Siegel and Senna (1981) have estimated that up to 95 percent of our nation's young people engage in misconduct that *could* bring them into contact with the juvenile legal authorities. This misconduct ranges from minor curfew violations to criminal acts of violence. Nonetheless, a great majority of these young people are not what we usually conceptualize as "official delinquents"; they are essentially normally developing children and adolescents who are learning the many complex and confusing roles of adulthood.

The Legal Definition of Delinquency

The legal definition of delinquency is somewhat arbitrary and ambiguous. In some geographic areas, the term *delinquency* is used to refer to any and all acts of juvenile misconduct or antisocial behavior. The label is placed on a young person whether or not he or she has been apprehended by legal authorities (Achenbach, 1974). Still, in the traditional legal sense, the official juvenile delinquent is only that rule breaker who has been adjudged so by a juvenile court. In essence, a child is not a delinquent unless a court has found him or her to be one (Tappan, 1949).

The legal definition of delinquency overlooks what Gibbons (1970) refers to as "hidden delinquency." Hidden delinquents are the large numbers of youths who engage in acts of misconduct and lawbreaking that remain undetected. While many of the inappropriate behaviors of this population are minor, some are quite serious and costly. For example, public transportation officials often complain about the excessive cost of repeated vandalism. Very few of the culprits are apprehended for their offenses, but most are believed to be middle-class youths who use the subways and buses to commute to and from school.

Many experts (e.g., Simonsen & Gordon, 1982; West, 1982) believe that a legal criterion for determining delinquency makes the assessment process relatively easy (i.e., count only those juveniles adjudged by juvenile courts), but that a strict legal definition of delinquency tells us little about how delinquents differ from nondelinquents. Achenbach (1974) noted that because the adjudication of delinquency is usually an advanced step in a long sequence of problem behaviors, a more appropriate conceptual starting place for defining delinquency might be a description and explanation of antisocial or rule-violating behavior.

Descriptive Classifications of Delinquency

The Extent of the Problem

Simonsen and Gordon (1982) have suggested three basic factors that should be observed and considered when describing rule breaking: (1) the frequency of the act, (2) the seriousness of the act, and (3) the attitude of the juvenile offender. The *frequency* of the act indicates whether there is a pattern of misbehavior—for example, whether a young person is just experimenting with illegal drugs or alcohol or is a consistent substance abuser. The *seriousness* of a misbehavior is a subjective indicator depending on how a local community views juvenile misconduct. Simonsen and Gordon noted that a community may pressure law enforcement personnel to arrest and convict a young rapist, but view juvenile public intoxication as merely part of growing up and require nothing more than a "slap on the wrist." Finally, the *attitude* of the youth should be investigated. For example, a single angry or impulsive act of vandalism is quite different from chronic and repetitive acts of destruction to public and private property.

Criminal Offenses Versus Status Offenses

Because the legal concept of delinquency is often ambiguous and complex, many states have differentially classified youths into two distinct and sometimes independent categories: criminal offenders and status offenders (Siegel & Senna, 1981).

Criminal offenders are juveniles who have violated laws that would have resulted in a trial and possible incarceration if they had been adults. The most serious crimes are murder, rape, assault, larceny, and drug abuse. The key element is that the criminal offender has violated an adult law. However, because of his or her age, the juvenile offender is often treated more leniently. Whereas adults are usually tried in court and punished with prison terms, youthful criminal offenders are adjudicated as official delinquents and sent to detention facilities for treatment.

In contrast, status offenses are behaviors that are illegal only for juveniles. Such offenses are considered noncriminal for adults. Status offenses vary from community to community, but usually include curfew violation, truancy, sexual promiscuity, alcohol and tobacco use, disobedience toward parents and school officials, and running away. Communities undertake to control status offenses in the belief that these behaviors are detrimental to the developing child and adolescent.

Psychological Dimensions

In many instances, psychological concepts are employed to define rule breaking and delinquency. Quay (1964), through a factor analytic study of institutionalized delinquents, identified three primary types of rule breakers: (1) the subcultural-socialized delinquent, (2) the unsocialized-psychopathic delinquent, and (3) the neurotic-disturbed delinquent. The *subcultural-socialized delinquent* is capable of developing meaningful relationships with others. He or she possesses normal feelings of guilt, concern, and remorse, but frequently encounters local norms that prompt, support, and reinforce behavior in conflict with acceptable standards. The *unsocialized-psychopathic delinquent* fails to develop meaningful peer relationships and does not feel guilt and remorse when misbehaving or manipulating others. These individuals are usually irritable, overly aggressive, and often complain that others are being unfair to them. The *disturbed-neurotic delinquent* is shy, sensitive, timid, worrisome, and tends to experience great anxiety over rule-breaking behavior. Achenbach (1974) has observed that delinquents classified as disturbed-neurotic seem to have little in common other than a general demeanor of unhappiness, so the rule breaking of this group may be only a small part of a larger picture of disturbance (e.g., retardation, environmental deprivation, brain injury). Not surprisingly, these youths are not generally regarded as "hard-core" delinquents; they are usually considered to be in need of mental health services rather than correctional facilities (Van Evra, 1983).

Behavioral Dimensions

The behavioral practice of describing specific behaviors rather than labeling individuals is an alternative method for classifying rule breaking. Ross (1980) advocated viewing the rule breaker or delinquent as "one who has either not learned to discriminate between acceptable and unacceptable behavior or who, having learned the discrimination, has not acquired adequate controls so that his or her behavior is not guided by this discrimination" (p. 126). Within this behavioral approach to describing delinquency, classification is based upon specific skills either present in or absent from an adolescent's behavioral repertoire. The benefit of this formulation of delinquency is that treatment can be viewed as the teaching of appropriate, socially approved responses to environmental stimuli. Two of the major skills found lacking in the behavioral repertoires of rule breakers are the ability to maintain appropriate behaviors under conditions of delayed reinforcement (Ross, 1980) and the ability to evaluate alternatives when faced with impulse-laden problem-solving situations.

Prevalence of Rule Breaking and Juvenile Delinquency

It is impossible to arrive at precise statistics regarding the incidence of juvenile rule breaking and delinquency. Still, most experts agree that delinquency peaked in the 1970s (in terms of the absolute number of crimes committed by juveniles and the percentage of all crimes that are committed by juveniles) but that serious juvenile crime is rising at an alarming rate and is becoming more destructive and violent

(Sautter, 1995). For example, in 1960 youth under 18 accounted for 633,720 arrests, which represented 17 percent of all arrests, but only 513 arrests were for homicide. In 1970 the figures were 1,660,643 arrests (1,346 for homicide), which represented 26 percent of all arrests. In 1980 the figures were 2,025,713 arrests (1,742 for homicide), which represented 20 percent of all arrests. By 1992 youth arrests had fallen to 1,943,138, 16 percent of all arrests, but homicide arrests had risen to 2,829.

When people use figures, graphs, or percentage to note that juvenile crime is "way out of line," they are usually employing data provided by the FBI's Uniform Crime Reports (Siegel & Senna, 1981). These are yearly reports of crime in the United States as measured by the nation's local law enforcement agencies. It must be remembered, however, that youth known to be juvenile offenders or delinquents through national statistics represent only the tip of the iceberg (Achenbach, 1974). Nevertheless, the national data concerning juvenile crime provide a broad indicator as to the nature, range, and age trends of juvenile misconduct.

Murder, rape, and assault, as well as certain property crimes, are considered Index Crimes by the FBI (Federal Bureau of Investigation, 1993). The Crime Index is a separate set of national statistics on serious and intense crimes. In a most glaring illustration of the extent of serious juvenile rule breaking, it is estimated that in 1992 people under the age of 18 accounted for 40,434 robberies, 63,777 assaults, and 73,981 offenses in addition to the 2,829 murders.

Correlates of Rule Breaking and Delinquency

Rule-breaking behavior that results in the determination of delinquency status often correlates with other physical, social, cognitive, and environmental factors. What follows is a discussion of the factors that have either an hypothesized or a documented association with delinquent behavior (Clarizio & McCoy, 1983; Siegel & Senna, 1981).

Gender

Juvenile delinquency is regarded as primarily a male problem. Boys are referred to juvenile courts four times as often as girls and are sent to treatment or detention facilities at a far greater rate. Haskell and Yablonski (1974) observed that delinquency may be predominantly a boy's problem for much the same reason that crime is a man's problem: Males are expected and perceived to be more aggressive. However, arrests and court cases involving girls have been rising at a much greater rate in recent years—38 percent as opposed to 12 percent for boys (FBI, 1993).

The official data indicate that girls are usually arrested and adjudged for different kinds of offenses than boys. Their most frequent offenses are status in nature, and include running away, disobedience, substance abuse, and sexual misconduct. Boys, for the most part, tend to be apprehended for vandalism, assault, and auto theft. Such rule-breaking differences have led many to believe that male delinquency is a much more serious problem than female delinquency (Williams & Gold, 1972).

Race and Ethnic Factors

There is considerable variation in the rates of delinquency for different racial and ethnic groups, and researchers have reached certain conclusions after investigating the effect of race and ethnic factors. Wolfgang, Figlio, and Sellin (1972), in a massive study involving approximately 10,000 youths in Philadelphia, concluded that race was a predominant factor in predicting contact with police and judicial agencies. However, Siegel and Senna (1981) observed that African American youths are apprehended more frequently for alleged misconduct because police tend to monitor African American neighborhoods with greater frequency and intensity, a policy that would lead to differential apprehension rates (Gibbons, 1970). In particular, Piliavin and Briar (1964) found that police officers were aware of their differential arrest records in regard to African American and white youths. In a study designed to investigate the validity of official statistics, Chambliss and Nagasawa (1969) found similar self-reported involvement rates or delinquency among groups of white, Japanese American, and African American students. Thus, the difference between official and self-reported rates of delinquency may be the result of the bias of enforcement officials, the visibility of the rule-breaking offenses, or the attitude of individuals when confronted by an adult in authority. Official statistical data involving racial and ethnic factors may be telling us more about the process of compiling official records than about real racial-ethnic criminality and rule violating.

Socioeconomic Status and Community Differences

Official delinquency data typically reflect high correlations between socioeconomic status and delinquency. Still, several researchers (e.g., Dentler & Monroe, 1961; short & Nye, 1958) did not find a direct relationship between social class and *self-reported* delinquency. Like minority youths (Wolfgang et al., 1972), lower-class youths, it appears, are more likely to *receive attention* from legal authorities (Dentler & Monroe, 1961). In contrast, Elliott and Ageton (1980), also using self-report data, found that lower-class youths were actually more likely to engage in more serious and numerous offenses than middle-class youths.

Family Structure

The stability and quality of home life have often been associated with delinquency. In terms of stability, early researchers (e.g., Nye, 1958; Shaw & McKay, 1942) found that children from "broken homes" tended to have higher delinquency rates than those from intact homes. For example, Gordon (1962) found that 30 to 60 percent of the young people identified by law enforcement agencies as delinquent came from broken, single-parent homes.

Nonetheless, caution must be exercised in interpreting the data. When "broken home" studies are controlled for variables such as quality of parent–child relationship and age of the child at the time of separation, it is often not the removal of one parent that correlates with delinquency (Haskell & Yablonski, 1974). McCord,

McCord, and Thurber (1962) found that the relationship between delinquency and "brokenness" was largely moderated by family instability rather than paternal absence. In effect, the quality of the relationship between the child and the single parent and the stability of the home appeared to be the factor most predictive of future delinquency. Thus, "a warm, stable single parent has a much better chance of raising a non-delinquent child than do two parents who are in conflict" (Haskell & Yablonski, 1974, p. 100). In addition, the age of the child at the time of the "break" in the home may be important. Monahan (1957) observed that preteen children were more adversely affected by parental separation than teenagers.

Intelligence and Achievement

Caplan (1965) observed that when socioeconomic status was controlled, there were only minor differences in intellectual status (i.e., 8 IQ points) between delinquents and nondelinquents. More recently, however, Hirschi and Hindelang (1977) concluded that IQ was more important than race and social class for predicting delinquent behavior. Controlling for racial and socioeconomic factors, they found significant differences between delinquents and nondelinquents *within* different race and socioeconomic groupings and implied that a low IQ began a chain of events that eventually led to delinquency.

The conflicting data regarding the relationship between IQ and delinquency may be related to controversies concerning intelligence testing per se, as well as to the definitional problems of delinquency. Nonetheless, Siegel and Senna (1981) observed that society generally perceives children with low IQs as potentially disruptive individuals who possess "neither the capability nor the opportunity to support the system" (p. 82).

Academic achievement has also been investigated as a correlate of delinquent behavior. Many theorists and researchers believe that chronic underachievement and a poor school record are highly predicative—even more so than IQ, race, ethnic, or socioeconomic status—of rule breaking and delinquency (Siegel & Senna, 1981). For example, Jerse and Fakouri (1978) compared the academic records of delinquents and nondelinquents and reported that delinquents were more academically deficient.

In terms of specific academic areas, reading has been linked with delinquency (Andrew, 1978; Mulligan, 1972). While data indicating that poor reading causes delinquency are lacking (Andrew, 1981), the need for remediating reading problems should not be underemphasized. Poor reading often starts the school failure cycle, which has been hypothesized to be highly predicative of delinquent and criminal behavior.

Learning Disabilities

Parents and teachers have frequently speculated that juvenile delinquency is a probable consequence of learning disabilities (Keilitz, Zaremba, & Broder, 1979). As a result of these informal speculations, increasing numbers of researchers have attempted to locate links between learning disabilities (LD) and juvenile delinquency (JD).

In 1976, the American Institutes for Research (AIR) was commissioned by the National Institute for Juvenile Justice and Delinquency Prevention to undertake a "dispassionate assessment" of the existing data base involving the relationship between LD and JD (Murray, 1976). In approaching the task, the AIR adopted a three-tiered procedure: (1) an extensive literature search, (2) interviews of experts in the fields of LD and JD, and (3) a review of existing demonstration projects that have attempted to remediate learning disabilities among delinquents.

The rationale for the LD/JD causal connection was the belief that LD produces intermediate effects that ultimately produce delinquent behavior (Murray, 1976, p. 5). It is hypothesized that delinquency occurs through one of two possible routes: (1) LD leads to failure in school, then to dropping out of school, and finally to delinquent behavior; or (2) certain types and combinations of learning problems are essentially behavioral tendencies that facilitate an increased susceptibility to delinquent or rule-breaking behavior.

As reported by Murray (1976), in reviewing the data under the headings "The Case for a Link" and "The Case Against a Link" the AIR concluded that the evidence supporting an LD/JD causal relationship is weakly documented. With few exceptions, the AIR noted, the empirical work undertaken by proponents of the link was "so poorly designed and presented that it cannot be used for even rough estimates of the strength of the link" (p. 65). Even more surprising was the complete lack of data regarding whether a higher prevalence of learning disabilities existed among delinquent youths than among nondelinquents. Most studies merely reported that delinquents had below-average school performance, which prompted speculation that a "specific learning disability" also existed.

More recent observational studies with greater rigor and experimental control have not shown a link between LD and JD—that is, the presence of LD did not predict a future likelihood of delinquency (Broder, Dunivant, Smith, & Sultan, 1981; Spreen, 1981). Interestingly, however, Broder and colleagues found that an adolescent with LD who was brought before a juvenile court was more likely to be adjudged an official delinquent than an adolescent without LD. In studying a related issue, Sindelar and co-workers (1985) found that rule-breaking behavior was exhibited more frequently by students with behavior disorders than by students with learning disabilities.

Etiology of Rule Breaking and Juvenile Delinquency

No one theory can explain what causes rule breaking and delinquent behavior. Like many of the other patterns of behavior disorders, delinquent behavior can be explained through several model views. In the following sections, the etiology of delinquency will be discussed in terms of biophysical orientation, two psychological models (psychodynamic and behavioral), and a variety of sociological and ecological theoretical approaches.

Biophysical Explanations

The biophysical model suggests that delinquent or criminal behavior can be explained by physical factors or biological processes within an individual. These factors or processes include genetic transmission or predisposition, soma or body type, and the relatively new speculations regarding chromosomal abnormality.

Early Conceptualizations

Early biophysical theorists posited that criminals could be differentiated from noncriminals on the basis of physical appearance. Lombroso (1918) believed that criminal rule breakers had low foreheads, protruding ears, and deep-set eyes, all of which resulted from abnormal brain development. According to Lombroso, the criminal personality type was determined at birth and only massive social intervention could preclude this individual from criminal behavior.

The obvious fallacy of Lombroso's view was empirically demonstrated by Charles Goring. In comparing the physical traits (e.g., head circumference, weight, hair, eye color, and distance between the eyes) of thousands of hard-core, recidivist criminals and noncriminals, Goring (1913) found that none of the traits differentiated the criminal group from the noncriminal group.

Body Type and Delinquency

While Goring dismissed the notion of the "criminal physique," many aspects of Lombroso's work were not forgotten. Sheldon (1949) investigated the relationship between body type and personality. Differentiating people on the basis of body measurements, he arrived at three major body classifications: *endomorphs*, *mesomorphs*, and *ectomorphs*. Endomorphs were rotund, mesomorphs muscular and athletic, and ectomorphs slender. Sheldon believed that each body type possessed a distinctive personality and temperament. The rotund endomorph tended to be jovial and outgoing, while the slight and slender ectomorph tended to be aloof and introverted. The mesomorph was characterized as aggressive, physically active, and competitive.

While investigating the body types of juvenile delinquents, Sheldon found that approximately 60 percent were mesomorphs. Similarly, Glueck and Glueck (1950) found that 60 percent of a delinquent sample were mesomorphs, as opposed to 31 percent of a nondelinquent population. Still, no causal relationship that links body type and delinquency has been demonstrated. As Haskell and Yablonski (1974) noted, most police officers, military personnel, athletes, and energetic leaders in our society are also mesomorphic.

Chromosomal Deviation and Heredity

The discovery of the XYY sex chromosome combination in the early 1960s prompted research attempting to link the extra male Y gonosome (XY is normal) to rule breaking or criminal misconduct. Early studies (e.g., Jacobs, Brunton, & Melville, 1965) found that XYY males tended to have severe acne, be taller than XY males, have below-average IQs, and exhibit unstable personalities. Still, there were no consistent data supporting the existence of a *distinctive* psychological profile for an XYY male.

In terms of criminal behavior, Achenbach (1974) noted that the overall proportion of XYY males who are incarcerated is low and that their crimes are not excessively aggressive. These data, together with the fact that most criminals and delinquents do not possess an extra Y gonosome, have convinced many people that speculation regarding a possible link between chromosomal abnormalities and delinquency is more provocative than productive.

Psychological Explanations

Psychological explanations of rule breaking and delinquency focus on motivational patterns. While there is no single psychological theory that explains delinquency and rule breaking (Trojanewicz, 1973), two major, often incompatible, theoretical orientations have dominated the delinquency literature: the psychodynamic and the behavioral.

The Psychodynamic Orientation

As noted earlier, the psychodynamic view of deviance is deeply rooted in Freudian theories of personality development. Like aggressive behavior, delinquent behavior has been explained as the result of a failure to develop adequate superego controls caused by disturbances between parents and children during the Oedipal phase. Redl and Wineman (1957) characterized the result of failed superego development as the *deficient superego*. In an individual whose superego does not develop sufficient strength to exert needed control over the id and ego, many antisocial desires of the id are expressed.

Behavioral Explanations

Behavioral theorists approach rule breaking and delinquency as a set of specific maladaptive behaviors that occur in response to discriminative stimuli an reinforcing consequences (Bootzin, 1980). Behavior, be it appropriate or inappropriate, is viewed as learned. Delinquency is viewed as the demonstration of learned illegal behavior, resulting from the continuous interplay between behavior and its controlling circumstances (Clarizio & McCoy, 1983).

Within the behavioral conceptualization, modeling and reinforcement are viewed as major agents in the development of rule breaking and delinquency (Bandura, 1976). In effect, the inappropriate, yet successful, behavior of someone in the child's environment serves as the learning stimulus for impressionable children. The most prominent models for children an adolescents are parents, siblings, and peers. Researchers have also given attention to role models presented in movies, television, and other media. Data from several of these studies have indicated a significant positive correlation between youthful aggressive behavior and high television viewing (Eron et al., 1974; Rubinstein, 1978).

Reinforcement, the second important component of the behavioral explanation, refers to an increase in rule-breaking behavior when it is followed by rewards (Kazdin, 1975). Snyder (1977) observed that parents of children with conduct disorders frequently reinforced their children's behavior noncontingently, meaning they attended to and rewarded their offspring whether or not their children's behavior was socially appropriate. As a result, children learned that there was no functional connection between their behavior and the feedback they received from their parents. Because they continually received noncontingent reinforcement, the children developed a generalized insensitivity to social stimuli such as laws and rules (Bootzin, 1980).

Snyder (1977) also reported that when parents of children with conduct disorders did respond to antisocial behavior, their responses tended to be punishing. Thus, they inadvertently served as models of aggression by employing coercive "pain control" (Patterson et al., 1975) to get their way. Such actions may be effective in the short run, but long-term observational studies suggest that youngsters who are aggressive are likely to come from families that demonstrate high rates of punishing, coercive, and aggressive behaviors (Patterson, 1975).

Sociological and Ecological Explanations

The sociological and ecological models greatly expand the scope of causes for rule breaking and delinquency. Both models look beyond the immediate delinquent individual and delve into how people, institutions, and social processes affect behavior. In the following sections, several of the more prominent sociological and ecological theories are discussed briefly.

Cultural Transmission

Theories involving cultural transmission assert that youths living in slums and ghettos break rules because they follow different value systems from mainstream society. Siegel and Senna (1981) observed that these different value systems exist independently within lower socioeconomic class areas and are often in conflict with society norms and standards.

In a classic study of the cultural transmission theory, Shaw and McKay (1942) attempted to explain delinquent behavior in the changing urban environment of Chicago. Utilizing an impressive collection of data, including the arrest records of over 25,000 delinquents, Shaw and McKay were able to identify distinctive geographic zones, all of which reflected differing, yet highly stable, rates of delinquency. The areas containing the highest concentration of delinquent behavior tended to be the transitional inner-city areas, where significant numbers of recent immigrants resided. Areas farthest from the inner city were less prone to delinquency problems. Shaw and McKay concluded that differential delinquency rates resulted from the socialization mechanisms found within different individual neighborhoods: Areas with unstable, transitional neighborhoods have a higher probability of delinquency than stable and settled neighborhoods.

In a similar cultural transmission theory, Miller (1958) identified a unique group of values that allegedly dominated life among "the lower class." These focal concerns—trouble, toughness, street smartness, excitement, fate, and autonomy— were thought to draw young people into a delinquent subculture. Each focal concern was conceived by Miller as a dimension in which a wide range of behaviors could be chosen by different individuals under varying situations. By adhering to the values of the lower class, youths found themselves frequently in conflict with representatives of the larger cultural values (i.e., the police and the courts).

Subcultural-Strain Theories

Strain theories view rule breaking and delinquency as a reaction to the anger or frustration young people experience when they are unable to garner legitimate prestige and success. Subcultural-strain theories assert that youths who live in lower-class areas reject socially approved goals either because they do not have access to legitimate means of opportunity (Siegel & Senna, 1981) or because they are protesting against the prevailing values (Cohen, 1955). Consequently, these youths adhere to an alternative set of values and standards, complete with methods of obtaining particular forms of reinforcement. Often, however, these alternative methods and values are viewed by the dominant culture bearers as norm violations or delinquency.

Cloward and Ohlin (1960) defined a delinquent subculture as "one in which certain forms of delinquent activity are essential requirements for the performance of the dominant roles supported by the subculture" (p. 7). They divided subculture roles into three dominant types: the *criminal*, the *conflict type*, and the *retreatist*. The criminal engages in illegal behaviors such as theft, extortion, and assault for profit; the conflict type engages in violent criminal activity because of a need for status; and the retreatist consumes and is frequently addicted to drugs. Haskell and Yablonski (1974) observed that this anomie (normlessness) and breakdown of social control emerged because individuals in lower-class areas had no legitimate method for attaining culturally prescribed goals. Because they were denied reasonable opportunities to achieve normal goals and aspirations, young people in lower-class areas experienced a greater motivation to commit delinquent and rule-breaking behavior. Thus, while members of a delinquent subculture frequently exhibit rule-breaking and norm-violating behavior, they are impelled to do so by "strain" resulting from their inability to gain access to the dominant culture (Siegel & Senna, 1981).

In effect, culturally transmitted strain theory illustrates the psychodynamic notion of reaction formation: repressing feelings that cause ill-feeling, and then behaving in an opposite way. In delinquents, this takes the form of overt and guileful rebellion against accepted rules and standards.

Middle-Class Rule Breaking and Delinquency

While cultural transmission and strain theories offer explanations of lower-class delinquency, they seem to overlook delinquency problems found in the middle class. Criminologists who associated high rates of delinquency only with the lower class were surprised by studies that found high delinquency rates in upper- and middle-class neighborhoods (Siegel & Senna, 1981). Vaz (1967) theorized that middle-class delinquency resulted when exploratory, norm-violating activities, originally regarded as adventurous, become normative. For example, shoplifting, a common act of delinquency among middle- and upper-class youths, is often explained as an activity that started as a "game played for excitement and novelty" (Trojanewicz, 1973).

Other theories purporting to explain middle-class rule breaking rely on one or a combination of the following concepts: adolescent rebellion against forced postponement of adult status, inadequate parent–child relationships, ineffective school performance, anxiety felt by boys about their masculinity, and the influence of deviant peers (Shanley, 1967). As Gibbons (1970) observed, the state of theory regarding middle-class delinquency provides an "embarrassment of riches"—too many theories and too little validating evidence.

Prognosis of Rule Breaking and Juvenile Delinquency

By definition, delinquency is an age-bound phenomenon. The percentage of young people involved in delinquent behavior increases steadily from age 10 to approximately 16, and then drops from just under 17 through young adulthood (Wolfgang et al., 1972). Surprisingly, some rule-breaking behavior begins earlier than 10. Glueck and Glueck (1950) found that 60 percent of delinquents surveyed engaged in a first offense prior to their tenth birthday. In 1981, the FBI reported that approximately 50,000 children under the age of 10 were apprehended by legal authorities, about 60 percent for burglary and larceny. Such data are indeed troublesome if we subscribe to Haskell and Yablonski's (1974) view that many young children do not get formally processed by the legal authorities because adults tend to deal with very young rule breakers informally.

Several theorists have emphasized that social situations and cultural roles (Cavan, 1968; Haskell & Yablonski, 1974) account for the relationship between age and delinquency. Offenses associated with the role of "child" (e.g., vandalism and petty larceny) usually decrease through early adolescence, while more aggressive violations tend to increase during middle adolescence. Haskell and Yablonski noted that these more daring and aggressive delinquent behaviors decline in later adolescence "as the youth's anxiety about supermasculine identity lessons" (p. 66).

A majority of juvenile delinquents become law-abiding adults. Clarizio and McCoy (1983) noted that a record of delinquency is not predicative of adult criminal behavior and that a majority of delinquents "eventually get along without serious difficulty" (p. 307). Monahan (1982), who reviewed longitudinal and predictive studies on delinquents, found that three specific clusters often predict the future course of delinquent and adult criminal behavior: parent factors, child factors, and school factors. Regarding parents, four influences are critical: (1) the criminality of the parents, (2) the amount of parental supervision, (3) the level of conflict and disharmony between the parents, and (4) the harshness and physical nature of the child rearing. In the child-factor cluster, Monahan found five key influences: sex, race, IQ, temperament, and age of onset. Boys, minorities, those with low IQs, those with aggressive and impulsive temperaments, and those who begin delinquent behavior at an early age are more likely to continue with such behavior as juveniles and with criminal behavior as adults. In terms of the school-factor cluster, delinquents who experience interpersonal and academic difficulties at school are most likely to commit later offenses.

Perhaps of greater importance is Monahan's (1982) conclusion that a large number of studies have found no reduction in future crime for high-risk children exposed to prevention programs. However, recent interventions that are implemented during early childhood have demonstrated that delinquency rates for high-risk students can be reduced (Zigler, Taussig, & Black, 1992). Many of these programs begin during preschool years and stress sound parenting skills, home–school cooperation, community outreach, and interagency collaboration. Mulvey, Arthur, and Reppucci (1993) provide an excellent summary of the huge professional literature base by reviewing the effects of primary prevention programs, secondary prevention programs, and various treatment options. In brief, primary prevention programs (e.g., parent training, preschool interventions, community organizing, recreation, and family-based interventions) have demonstrated promising results in some studies, but a lack of a focus on juvenile delinquency and a lack of long-term follow-up precludes greater confidence. The effects of secondary prevention programs vary a great deal. Diversion programs (i.e., those that divert offenders from the penal system) produced mixed success, with most showing little effect on rearrest rates, while intensive family therapy produced a 50 percent decline in recidivism if treatment included family systems and behavioral treatments. However, the lack of long-term follow-up and high drop out rates from treatment (often 50 percent) lower confidence in results. The effects of various treatment options also varies, with Positive Peer Culture inconclusive; institutionalization promising for intense, model projects; psychodynamic therapy ineffective; family therapy somewhat effective (if it includes behavioral treatments), wilderness experiences ineffective; and community-based interventions somewhat effective. In general, treatments that were most effective in reducing recidivism had large and more intense community-based interventions, behavioral therapy for families, and interventions designed to modify the social network of the juvenile delinquents.

Characteristics of Social Withdrawal

Social withdrawal is a term used to describe behaviors that result in physical and emotional separation. Children who are socially withdrawn or isolated are distinguished by their lack of appropriate social interaction, failure to get satisfaction from social reciprocity, and preference for solitary play over group activities. The fundamental problem of social isolation is dysfunction in social development and interpersonal relationships due to behavioral deficiencies or excesses. This dysfunction causes the individual who is isolated to avoid, or fail in, interactions with others and inhibits the growth of normal social relationships.

There are two categories of social withdrawal: noninteraction and rejection (Greenwood, Walker, & Hops, 1977; Strain, Cooke, & Apollini, 1976). Children who are noninteractive fail to initiate, maintain, or reinforce interactions with others; prefer solitary activities; and avoid social activities. Children who are rejected initiate social interaction, but their inappropriate behaviors and excesses cause them to be rejected by their peers.

The primary characteristic of children who are noninteractive is a deficient social repertoire, including inadequacies in approach behaviors, responsiveness to others' initiations of social contact, and methods of social reinforcement. Furthermore, these children may engage in behaviors that distance them from others or discourage social interaction. For example, they may prefer solitary play and/or "tune out" when alone (Gottman, 1977). Children who are rejected are primarily characterized by behaviors that "turn off" their peers, including bossiness, jealousy, immaturity, and aggression (Cullinan, Epstein, & Lloyd, 1983).

The Primary Characteristics

Kohn and Rosman (1972) used the following descriptors to characterize socially withdrawn behavior in a child: (1) keeps to him- or herself, remains aloof, distant; (2) fails to play with other children; (3) declines to take part in activities when urged; (4) has a mournful, downcast expression, looks solemn, seldom smiles; and (5) stares blankly into space. Other descriptors of withdrawn behavior found in the literature are isolation, preoccupation, daydreaming, drowsiness, shyness, fear, depression, bashfulness, overcompliance, passivity, apathy, hypersensitivity, unhappiness, anxiety, and introversion. Further, the child who is withdrawn is considered to (1) be difficult to get to know, (2) show little compassion for others, (3) prefer solitary work and play, (4) fail to show feelings, (5) avoid eye contact, (6) be disinterested in the work of others, and (7) demonstrate a low rate of social interactions with peers (Brulle & McIntyre, 1982).

The primary characteristics of social withdrawal are considered to be deficits in the specific prosocial behaviors necessary for the development of social skills, primarily those that promote or maintain interaction, such as conversation skills (Mathur & Rutherford, 1994). As we have noted, children who are isolated typically manifest deficits in approach behaviors, including a failure to look at, talk to, play with, or touch peers appropriately. Similarly, these children do not respond to the initiation of social contact by others. They exhibit a lack of social reciprocity, which is defined as the exchange of mutual and equitable reinforcement characteristic of normal social development (Kauffman, 1985). Additionally, children who are withdrawn and isolated have been found to have difficulty with the specific social skills needed to make and keep friends. To sum up, social isolation involves quantitatively fewer interactions, qualitatively inadequate interactions (Hughes & Hall, 1985), and a general failure to understand and participate in the reciprocal interplay among individuals.

Characteristics typical of many children who are rejected are behavioral excesses that discourage or preclude social interactions. These behaviors, such as daydreaming or self-stimulating activities, interfere with appropriate social exchanges, distract the child from attending to social cues, and/or limit social learning. Other problematic behaviors include standing too close to others, inappropriate eye contact (too much or too little), repeatedly touching peers, and inappropriate language or comments.

The Secondary Characteristics

Secondary characteristics typically manifested by both children who are noninteractive and children who are rejected are having few or no satisfying friendships, moodiness, self-consciousness, anxiety, low self-esteem, self-derogation, and in extreme cases, suicide (Miller, 1994). Additionally, these children often become the targets of ridicule or taunts by their peers.

It is believed that children who fail at social intercourse (or any other skill area) feel inadequate or incompetent. As a result, they may lose self-esteem, harbor feelings of worthlessness, and manifest other symptoms of depression (e.g., listlessness, loss of appetite, hopelessness). Learning problems have also been associated with children who are withdrawn or isolated, possibly owing to their failure to benefit from interactions with their teachers and peers in school. Despite these associations, it may not be possible to prove that secondary characteristics are *caused* by the interaction of the primary characteristics with the environment. Rather, some secondary characteristics may be correlates, not results, of the primary characteristics.

Prevalence of Social Withdrawal

Although a degree of shyness and social avoidance can be normal in certain situations (e.g., a child's first day in kindergarten), social withdrawal and isolation are much more serious. Social isolation is recognized by educators, psychologists, and other mental health professionals as a major problem behavior pattern, even though it is not as disturbing to educational programs or other students as aggression and other emotional and behavior disorders. Approximately 10 to 15 percent of children referred to psychological clinics display withdrawn or isolate behavior (Cass & Thomas, 1979).

Identification of Social Withdrawal

Children who are socially isolated/withdrawn are typically identified through the use of assessment instruments, including sociometric measures, teacher ratings, personality testing, and direct observation.

Sociometric measures use peer-acceptance surveys to identify students who are isolated. When classmates are asked with which other students they would most and least like to interact, students who are *rejected* are those with whom other students avoid social contact and students who are *noninteractive* are those with whom no other students wish to play or work.

Teacher ratings are considered to be a relatively accurate and effective method for identifying students who are isolated, especially when combined with other assessment methods (Bower & Lambert, 1971; Greenwood et al., 1977). Basically, this method requires teachers to complete a student behavior checklist or questionnaire, which is then analyzed. Some examples of these instruments are the Early School Personality Questionnaire (Harris, King, & Drummond, 1978), the Walker Problem Behavior Checklist (Walker, 1976), Burks' Behavior Rating Scales (Burks, 1977), and the Behavior Problem Checklist (Quay & Peterson, 1975).

Psychological testing usually involves the individual administration of projective personality tests such as the Rorschach ("inkblot") Method of Personality Diagnosis (Klopfer & Davidson, 1960), the Thematic Apperception Test (TAT) (Beliak, 1947), or word association/sentence completion tasks (Forer, 1971). These instruments rely on the subjective interpretation of the examiner and may not have adequate normative information for the accurate assessment of some students.

A final method for identifying social isolation is through direct daily observations of behavior. Because students who are withdrawn have significantly fewer and poorer interactions with peers, they can be identified through a tally of the frequency and duration of their interactions. Although it is fairly easy to assess a student's rate of interaction, it is often quite time-consuming. Further, it is extremely difficult to assess the quality of those interactions or others' perceptions of them.

Overall, the most accurate identification appears to be direct observation, although teacher ratings have been shown to be nearly as accurate and much less time-consuming and intrusive (Greenwood, Walher, Todd, & Hops, 1979).

Etiology of Social Withdrawal

Several causes of withdrawn behavior have been suggested, including (1) biological factors, (2) family relationships, and (3) school experiences.

The biological factors believed to predispose children to introversion or isolation, as well as to other emotional and behavior disorders, are derived primarily from studies of children who are severely or profoundly emotionally disturbed (Brulle & McIntyre, 1982). Current medical technology, however, cannot demonstrate chemical or biological deficits in the majority of children who are mildly to moderately disturbed. Eysenck (1956) suggested that children may have an internal predisposition for extroversion or introversion that may be inherited. Although studies of temperament in children also suggest a genetic predisposition to introversion (Chess & Thomas, 1977), it is believed that environmental factors such as family relationships and school experiences significantly affect biological predispositions (Brulle & McIntyre, 1982).

Family relationships are believed to be extremely important to the causation of isolation. Family dysfunctions thought to contribute to the development of withdrawn behavior include parents' rigidity, overprotectiveness, overpermissiveness, rejection, symbiosis, inconsistency, neglect, vicariousness, psychosis, and marital problems (Schulman, 1967). "Obtuseness," or parents' own social incompetence, is believed to contribute as well (Sherman & Farina, 1974). Other factors reported to cause or exacerbate withdrawn behavior in children are aversive early social experiences, lack of opportunity for learning social reciprocity, and reinforcement of solitary play (Kauffman, 1985).

School experiences suggested to affect social withdrawal include teacher rigidity, students' boredom, reinforcement of inappropriate/withdrawn behaviors, and unrealistic class expectations.

Although biological, familial, and environmental factors appear to be involved in the development of isolation in children, there remain many unanswered questions about the etiology of emotional disturbances in general, and social withdrawal in particular.

Prognosis of Social Withdrawal

Children who are perceived as social isolates in the primary years have significant difficulty with learning and later socialization. Further, interactions in infancy and early childhood are considered to be closely linked to the development of sensorimotor capacities, cognitive skills, and impulse control (Bijou, 1976). These findings seem to suggest a poor prognosis for children who are withdrawn and isolated, but, surprisingly, prognosis studies vary from "poor" to "excellent." For example, while Watt and colleagues (1970) found that extreme withdrawal and social isolation carried a poor prognosis for later psychiatric status, especially for girls, other researchers (Gersten et al., 1976; Robins, 1979) found that social withdrawal by itself does not put a child at risk for later maladjustment.

Early interventions to increase prosocial behavior or to modify withdrawn behavior (e.g., peer modeling, social skills training, and social reinforcement) have produced significant improvements in the quantity and quality of children's interactions, as well as in their skill generalization and overall peer acceptance (Bandura, 1973; Gottman, Gonso, & Schuler, 1976; Stein & Friedrich, 1975; Strain, 1977; Walker, Greenwood, Hops, & Todd, 1979). Recent treatment investigations have also demonstrated impressive results. McMahon, Wacker, Sassy, and Melloy (1994), for example, taught a structured social skills intervention to elementary students and found increases in peer interactions and nontargeted prosocial responses. Other researchers have successfully taught appropriate game behaviors (Moore, Cartledge, & Heckman, 1995) and trained paraprofessionals to implement social skill instruction to socially delayed preschoolers (Storey, Danke, Ashworth, & Strain, 1994).

In conclusion, the prognosis for children who are withdrawn who receive no intervention services is poor, but a better prognosis is indicated for children enrolled in one of several types of intervention programs.

Summary

This chapter reviewed the characteristics of students who exhibit the high-incidence behavioral disorders of hyperactivity, aggression, juvenile delinquency, and social withdrawal. For each of these areas, we presented information on primary and secondary characteristics, etiology, prevalence, and prognosis. Professionals in the field of behavior disorders have amassed a considerable amount of valid and useful information, but our knowledge in many areas is inconclusive or incomplete. The contributions of several psychological models, predominantly the psychodynamic and behavior models, were described as they related to causes and treatments. The role of theory and psychological orientation remains an important consideration for professionals working with students with behavior disorders. Finally, the purpose of presenting information on student characteristics is to enhance understanding both of the children and youths receiving special education services and of the interventions presented in subsequent chapters in this book.

Discussion Questions

1. How can a poor self-concept develop in a child who is hyperactive?

2. How can child-rearing methods contribute to the development of hyperactive behavior?

3. Do you believe that brain injury may cause hyperactivity?

4. Is the psychodynamic explanation for aggressive behavior believable? Verifiable?

5. Are the behavioral explanations for aggressive behavior believable?

6. What is the difference between status and criminal offenses and why is this an important distinction?

7. Should children and youths who commit illegal offenses, but are not caught, be considered delinquents?

8. What delinquent acts have been committed in your neighborhood in recent years? Discuss how these acts affected the victims and the perpetrators.

9. What do you think is the most likely cause of social withdrawal?

10. Why is it important to know what causes social withdrawal? What effect might this knowledge have on treatment?

References

Achenbach, T. M. (1974). *Developmental psychopathology.* New York: Ronald Press.

Aichhorn, A. (1972). Underlying causes of delinquency. In S. Harrison & J. McDermott (Eds.), *Childhood psychopathology.* New York: International Universities.

Andrew, J. M. (1978). Why can't delinquents read? *Perceptual and motor skills, 47,* 640.

Andrew, J. M. (1981). Reading and cerebral dysfunction among juvenile delinquents. *Criminal Justice and Behavior, 8,* 131–144.

Bakwin, H., & Bakwin, R. (1967). *Clinical management of behavior disorders in children.* Philadelphia: Saunders.

Bandura, A. (1973). Social learning theory of aggression. In J. Knutson (Ed.), *The control of aggression: Implications from basic research.* Chicago: Aldine.

Bandura, A. (1976). Social learning analysis of aggression. In E. Ribes-Inesta & A. Bandura (Eds.), *Analysis of delinquency and aggression.* Hillsdale, NJ: Erlbaum.

Bandura, A., Ross, D., & Ross, S. (1963). Imitation of film-mediated aggressive models. *Journal of Abnormal and Social Psychology, 6,* 3–11.

Baron, R. (1977). *Human aggression.* New York: Plenum.

Bellack, L. (1947). *Bellak thematic apperception test.* New York: Psychological Corp.

Bender, L. (1953). *Aggression, hostility and anxiety in children.* Springfield, IL: Charles C. Thomas.

Bijou, S. W. (1976). *Child development: The basic stage of early childhood.* Englewood Cliffs, NJ: Prentice-Hall.

Bootzin, R. R. (1980). *Abnormal psychology: Current perspectives.* New York: Random House.

Borkovec, T. (1976). Physiological and cognitive processes in the regulation of anxiety. In G. Schwartz & D. Shapiro (Eds.), *Consciousness and self-regulation: Advances in research,* Vol. 1. New York: Plenum.

Bower, E., & Lambert, N. (1971). In-school screening of children with emotional handicaps. In N. Long, W. Morse, & R. Newman (Eds.).

Conflict in the classroom, 2nd ed. Belmont, CA: Wadsworth.

Broder, P. K., Dunivant, N., Smith, E. C., & Sutton, L. P. (1981). Further observations in the link between learning disabilities and juvenile delinquency. *Journal of Educational Psychology, 73,* 838–850.

Brulle, A. R., & McIntyre, T. C. (1982). *Socially withdrawn children: A review.* Charleston, IL: Eastern Illinois University, Department of Special Education. ERIC Document Reproduction Service No. ED 228 831.

Burks, H. F. (1977). *Burks' behavior rating scales.* Los Angeles: Western Psychological.

Buss, A. (1971). Aggression pays. In J. Singer (Ed.), *The control of violence and aggression.* New York: Academic Press.

Buxbaum, E. (1970). *Troubled children in a troubled world.* New York: International Universities.

Cairns, R., Santoyo, C., & Holly, K. (1994). Aggressive escalation: Toward a developmental analysis. In M. Potegal & J. Knutson (Eds.), *The dynamics of aggression.* Hillsdale, NJ: Lawrence Erlbaum Associates.

Camp, B. (1977). Verbal mediation in young aggressive boys. *Journal of Abnormal Psychology, 86,* 145–153.

Cantwell, D. P. (1972). Psychiatric illness in the families of hyperactive children. *Archives of General Psychiatry, 27,* 414–417.

Cantwell, D. P. (1975). Epidemiology, clinical picture and classification of the hyperactive child syndrome. In D. P. Cantwell (Ed.), *The hyperactive child: Diagnosis, management, and current research.* New York: Spectrum Publication.

Caplan, N. S. (1965). Intellectual functioning. In H. C. Quay (Ed.), *Juvenile delinquency.* Princeton, NJ: Van Nostrand.

Capute, A. J. Niedermeyer, E. F., & Richardson, F. (1968). The electroencephalogram in children with minimal cerebral dysfunction. *Pediatrics, 41,* 1104–1114.

Cass, L. K., & Thomas, C. B. (1979). *Childhood pathology and later adjustment: The question prediction.* New York: Wiley.

Cavan, R. S. (1968). *Juvenile delinquency*. Philadelphia: Lippincott.

Chambliss, W. J., & Nagasawa, R. H. (1969). On the validity of official statistics: A comparative study of white, black, and Japanese high school boys. *Journal of Research in Crime and Delinquency, 6*, 71–77.

Chess, S., & Thomas, A. (1977). Temperamental individuality from childhood to adolescence. *Journal of American Academy of Child Psychiatry, 16*, 218–226.

Clarizio, H. F., & McCoy, G. F. (1976). *Behavior disorders in children*, 2nd ed. New York: Crowell.

Clarizio, H. F., & McCoy, G. F. (1983). *Behavior disorders in children*. 3rd ed. New York: Harper & Row.

Clark, J., & Wenninger, E. (1962). Socioeconomic class and area as correlates of illegal behavior among juveniles. *American Sociological Review, 27*, 826–834.

Cloward, R., & Ohlin, L. E. (1960). *Delinquency and opportunity*. Glencoe, IL: The Free Press.

Cohen, A. (1955). *Delinquent boys*. Glencoe, IL: The Free Press.

Coutinho, M. (1986). Reading achievement of students identified as behaviorally disordered at the secondary level. *Behavioral Disorders, 14*, 157–165.

Cullinan, D., Epstein, M. H., & Lloyd, J. W. (1983). *Behavior disorders of children and adolescents*. Englewood Cliffs, NJ: Prentice-Hall.

David, O. J., Clark, J., & Voeller, K. (1972). Lead and hyperactivity. *Lancet, 2*, 900–903.

David, O. J., Hoffman, S. P., Sverd, J., Clark, J., & Voeller, K. (1976). Lead and hyperactivity: Behavioral response to chelation: A pilot study. *American Journal of Psychiatry, 133*, 1155–1158.

Dentler, R., & Monroe, L. (1961). Early adolescent theft. *American Sociological Review, 26*, 733–743.

Dollard, J., Miller, N., Doob, L., Mowrer, O., & Sears, F. (1939). *Frustration and aggression*. New Haven, CT: Yale University Press.

Dubey, D. R. (1976). Organic factors in hyperkinesis: A critical evaluation. *American Journal of Orthopsychiatry, 46*, 353–366.

Drabman, R. S., Spitalnik, R., & O'Leary, K. D. (1973). Teaching self-control to disruptive children. *Journal of Abnormal Psychology, 82*, 10–16.

Einon, D., & Potegal, M. (1994). Temper tantrums in young children. In M. Potegal & J. Knutson (Eds.), *The dynamics of aggression*. Hillsdale, NJ: Lawrence Erlbaum Associates.

Ekstein, R. (1966). *Children of time and space with action and impulse: Clinical studies on the psychoanalytic treatment of severely disturbed children*. New York: Appleton.

Elliott, D., & Ageton, S. (1980). Reconciling race and class differences in self-reported and official estimates of delinquency. *American Sociological Review, 45*, 95–110.

Epstein, M., Kinder, D., & Bursuck, B. (1989). The academic status of adolescents with behavioral disorders. *Behavioral Disorders, 14*, 157–165.

Eron, L., Huesmann, R., Lefkowitz, M., & Walder, L. (1974). How learning conditions in early childhood, including mass media, relate to aggression in later adolescence. *American Journal of Orthopsychiatry, 44*, 412–423.

Eron, L. D., Huesmann, L. R., Lefkowitz, M. M., & Walder, L. O. (1972). Does television violence cause aggression? *American Psychologist, 27*, 253–263.

Eron, L., Huesmann, L., & Zelli, A. (1991). The role of parental variables in the learning of aggression. In D. Pepler & K. Rubin (Eds.), *The development and treatment of childhood aggression*. Hillsdale, NJ: Lawrence Erlbaum Associates.

Eysenck, H. J. (1956). The inheritance of extroversion-introversion. *Acta Psychologia, 12*, 95–110.

Farrington, D. (1991). Childhood aggression and adult violence: Early precursors and later life outcomes. In D. Pepler & K. Rubin (Eds.), *The development and treatment of childhood aggression*. Hillsdale, NJ: Lawrence Erlbaum Associates.

Federal Bureau of Investigation. (1993). *Crime in the United States: Uniform Crime Reports*. Washington, DC: U.S. Government Printing Office.

Feingold, B. F. (1975a). Hyperkinesis and learning disabilities linked to artificial food flavors and colors. *American Journal of Nursing, 75*, 797–803.

Feingold, B. F. (1975b). *Why your child is hyperactive*. New York: Random House.

Feldman, R. A., Caplinger, T. E., & Wodarski. (1983). *The St. Louis Conundrum: The effective treatment of antisocial youths*. Englewood Cliffs, NJ: Prentice-Hall.

Forer, B. (1971). Word association and sentence completion methods. In A. Rabin and M. Haworth (Eds.), *Projective techniques with children*. New York: Grune & Stratton.

Gersten, J., Longner, T., Eisenberg, L., Simcha-Fagan, O., & McCarthy, D. (1976). Stability and change in types of behavior disturbances of children and adolescents. *Journal of Abnormal Child Psychology, 4*, 111–127.

Gibbons, D. C. (1970). *Delinquent behavior*. Englewood Cliffs, NJ: Prentice-Hall.

Gilbert, G. (1957). A survey of referral problems in metropolitan child guidance centers. *Journal of Clinical Psychiatry, 13*, 37–42.

Glueck, S., & Glueck, E. (1950). *Unraveling juvenile delinquency*. New York: Commonwealth Fund.

Goodwin, S., & Mahoney, M. (1975). Modification of aggression through modeling: An experimental probe. *Journal of Behavior Therapy and Experimental Psychiatry, 5*, 200–202.

Gordon, I. J. (1962). *Human development: Birth to adolescence*. New York: Harper & Row.

Goring, C. (1913). *The English convict*. London: His Majesty's Stationary Office.

Gottman, J. M. (1977). Toward a definition of social isolation in children. *Child Development, 48*, 513–517.

Gottman, J. M., Gonso, J., & Schuler, P. (1976). Teaching social skills to isolated children. *Journal of Abnormal Child Psychiatry, 4*, 179–197.

Greenwood, C. R., Walker, H. M., & Hops, H. (1977). Issues in social interaction/withdrawal assessment. *Exceptional Children, 43*, 490–499.

Greenwood, C. R., Walker, H. M., Todd, N. M., & Hops, H. (1979). Selecting a cost-effective screening measure for the assessment of preschool social withdrawal. *Journal of Applied Behavior Analysis, 12*, 639–652.

Grosenick, J. (1981). Public school and mental health services to severely behavior disordered students. *Behavioral Disorders, 6*, 183–190.

Harris, W. J., King, D. R., & Drummond, R. J. (1978). Personality variables of children nominated as emotionally handicapped by classroom teachers. *Psychology in the Schools, 15*, 361–363.

Haskell, M. R., & Yablonski, L. (1974). *Juvenile delinquency*. Chicago: Rand McNally.

Hewett, F., & Taylor, F. (1980). *The emotionally disturbed child in the classroom: The orchestration of success*. 2nd ed. Boston: Allyn & Bacon.

Hirschi, T., & Hindelang, M. (1977). Intelligence and delinquency: A revisionist review. *American Sociological Review, 42*, 471–586.

Houlihan, M., & Van Houten, R. (1989). Behavioral treatment of hyperactivity: A review and overview. *Education and Treatment of Children, 12*, 265–275.

Hughes, J., & Hall, D. (1985). Performance of disturbed and nondisturbed boys on a role play test of social competence. *Behavior Disorders, 11*, 24–29.

Jacobs, P., Brunton, M., & Melville, M. M. (1965). Aggressive behavior, mental subnormality, and the XYZ male. *Nature, 208*, 1351–1352.

Jerse, F. W., & Fakouri, M. E. (1978). Juvenile delinquency and academic deficiency. *Contemporary Education, 49*, 108–109.

Johnson, A. (1972). Sanctions for superego lacunae of adolescents. In S. Harrison & J. McDermott (Eds.), *Childhood psychopathology*. New York: International Universities.

Kaspar, J. C., Millichap, J. G., Backus, R., Child, D., & Schulman, J. L. (1971). A study of the relationship between neurological evidence of brain damage in children and activity and distractibility. *Journal of Consulting and Clinical Psychology, 36*, 329–337.

Kauffman, J. M. (1985). *Characteristics of children's behavior disorders*. Columbus, OH: Merrill.

Kaufman, I. (1967). Psychotherapy of children with conduct and acting-out disorders. In M. Hammer & A. Kaplan (Eds.), *The practice of psychotherapy with children*. Homewood, IL: Dorsey.

Kazdin, A. (1987). Treatment of antisocial behavior in children: Current status and future directions. *Psychological Bulletin, 102*, 187–203.

Kazdin, A. E. (1975). *Behavior modification in applied settings*. Homewood, IL: Dorsey.

Keilitz, I., Zaremba, B. A., & Broder, P. K. (1979). The link between learning disabilities and juvenile delinquency: Some issues and answers. *Learning Disability Quarterly, 2*, 2–11.

Kellam, S., Rebok, G., Ialongo, N., & Mayer, L. (1994). The course and malleability of aggressive behavior from early first grade into middle school: Results of developmental epi- demio-logically-based preventive trial. *Journal of Child Psychology and Psychiatry, 35*(2), 259– 281.

Klopfer, B., & Davidson, H. (1960). *The Rorschach method of personality diagnosis.* New York: Harcourt, Brace, & World.

Knutson, J. (1973). Introduction. In J. Knutson (Ed.), *The control of aggression. Implications from basic research.* Chicago: Aldine.

Kohn, M., & Rosman, B. (1972). Relationship of preschool social emotional functioning to later intellectual achievement. *Developmental Psychology, 6,* 445–452.

Kvaraceus, W. (1971). *Prevention and control of delinquency: The school counselor's role.* Boston: Houghton Mifflin.

Lambert, M. N., Sandoval, J., & Sassone, D. (1978). Prevalence of hyperactivity in elementary school children as a function of social system definers. *American Journal of Orthopsychiatry, 48,* 446–463.

Laufer, M. W. (1962). Cerebral dysfunction and behavior disorders in adolescents. *American Journal of Orthopsychiatry, 32,* 501–506.

Lees, J. P., & Newson, L. J. (1954). Family or sibling position and some aspects of juvenile delinquency. *British Journal of Delinquency, 5,* 46–65.

Levitt, E. (1971). Research in psychotherapy with children. In A. Bergin & S. Garfield (Eds.), *Handbook of psychotherapy and behavior change: An empirical analysis.* New York: Wiley.

Linton, T., & Russell, W. (1982). PROVE: An innovative high school program for educating anti-social disturbed adolescents. *The High School Journal, 66,* 18–25.

Lion, J., & Penna, M. (1974). The study of human aggression. In R. Whalen (Ed.), *The neurophysiology of aggression.* New York: Plenum.

Lombroso, C. (1918). *Crime: Its causes and remedies.* Boston: Little, Brown.

Loney, J. (1974). The intellectual functioning of hyperactive elementary school boys: A cross-sectional investigation. *American Journal of Orthopsychiatry, 44,* 754–762.

Loney, J., Comly, H. H., & Simon, B. (1975). Parental management, self-concept, and drug response in minimal brain dysfunction. *Journal of Learning Disabilities, 8,* 187–190.

Long, N., & Newman, R. (1971). Managing surface behavior of children in school. In N. Long, W. Morse, & R. Newman (Eds.), *Conflict in the classroom.* 2nd ed. Belmont, MA: Wadsworth.

Lopez, R. E. (1965). Hyperactivity in twins. *Canadian Psychiatric Association Journal, 10,* 421– 426.

Margalit, M. (1989). Academic competence and social adjustment of boys with learning disabilities and boys with behavior disorders. *Journal of Learning Disabilities, 22,* 41–45.

Mathur, S., & Rutherford, R. (1994). Teaching conversation social skills to delinquent youth. *Behavioral Disorders, 19*(4), 294–305.

McCord, J., McCord, W., & Thurber, E. (1962). Some effects of paternal absence on male children. *Journal of Abnormal and Social Psychology, 64,* 361–369.

McIntyre, A., & Wolf, B. (1973). Separation anxiety and the inhibition of aggression in pre-school children. *Journal of Abnormal Child Psychology, 1,* 400–409.

McMahon, C., Wacker, D., Sasso, G., & Melloy, K. (1994). Evaluation of the multiple effects of social skill intervention. *Behavioral Disorders, 20*(1), 35–50.

Mendelson, W., Johnson, N., & Stewart, M. A. (1971). Hyperactive children as teenagers: A follow-up study. *Journal of Nervous and Mental Disease, 153,* 273–279.

Miller, D. (1994). Suicidal behavior of adolescents with behavior disorders and their peers without disabilities. *Behavioral Disorders, 20*(1), 61–68.

Miller, W. (1958). Lower class culture as a generating milieu of gang delinquency. *Journal of Social Issues, 14,* 5–19.

Minde, K., Lewin, D., Weiss, G., Lavigueur, H., Douglas, V., & Sykes, E. (1971). The hyperactive child in elementary school: A 5 year, controlled, follow-up. *Exceptional Children, 38,* 215–221.

Minde, K., Webb, G., & Sykes, D. (1968). Studies on the hyperactive child. VI: Prenatal and paranatal factors associated with hyperactivity. *Developmental Medicine and Child Neurology, 10,* 355–363.

Mischel, W. (1971). *Introduction to personality.* New York: Holt, Rinehart, & Winston.

Monahan, J. (1982). Childhood predictors of adult criminal behavior. In F. N. Dutile, C. H. Foust, & D. R. Webster (Eds.), *Early childhood intervention and juvenile delinquency*. Lexington, MA: Heath.

Monahan, T. P. (1957). Family status and the delinquent child: A re-appraisal and some new findings. *Social Forces, 35,* 250–297.

Moore, R., Cartledge, G., & Heckman, K. (1995). The effects of social skill instruction and self-monitoring on game-related behaviors of adolescents with EBD. *Behavioral Disorders, 20*(4), 253–266.

Morris, H., Escoll, P., & Wexler, R. (1956). Aggressive behavior disorders of childhood: A follow-up study. *American Journal of Psychiatry, 112,* 991–997.

Morrison, J. R., & Stewart, M. A. (1971). A family study of the hyperactive child syndrome. *Biological Psychiatry, 3,* 189–195.

Morrison, J. R., & Stewart, M. A. (1973). Intellectual ability and performance of hyperactive children. *Archives of General Psychiatry, 28,* 888–891.

Mullen, J., & Wood, F. (1986). Teacher and student ratings of the disturbingness of common problem behaviors. *Behavioral Disorders, 11,* 168–176.

Mulligan, W. (1972). Dyslexia, specific learning disability, and delinquency. *Juvenile Justice, 23,* 20–25.

Mulvey, E., Arthur, M., & Reppucci, N. (1993). The prevention and treatment of juvenile delinquency: A review of the research. *Clinical Psychology Review, 13,* 133–167.

Murray, C. A. (1976). *The link between learning disabilities and juvenile delinquency*. Washington, DC: American Institute for Research.

Ninness, H., Fuerst, J., & Rutherford, R. (1995). A descriptive analysis of disruptive behavior during pre- and post-unsupervised self-management by students with serious emotional disturbance: A within-study replication. *Journal of Emotional and Behavior Disorders, 3*(4), 230–240.

Nye, F. I. (1958). *Family relationships and delinquent behavior*. New York: Wiley.

O'Leary, K., & Becker, W. (1968). The effects of the intensity of a teacher's reprimands on children's behavior. *Journal of School Psychology, 7,* 8–11.

Oxford, D., Boyle, M., & Racine, Y. (1991). The epidemiology of antisocial behavior in childhood and adolescence. In D. Pepler & K. Rubin (Eds.), *The development and treatment of childhood aggression*. Hillsdale, NJ: Lawrence Erlbaum Associates.

Palkes, H., & Stewart, M. (1972). Intellectual ability and performance of hyperactive children. *American Journal of Orthopsychiatry, 42,* 35–39.

Paternite, C. E., & Loney, J. (1980). Childhood hyperkinesis: Relationships between symptomatology and home environment. In C. K. Whalen & B. Henker (Eds.), *Hyperactive children: The sociology of treatment and identification*. New York: Academic Press.

Paternite, C. E., Loney, J., & Langhorne, J. E. (1976). Relationships between symptomatology and SES-related factors in hyperkinetic/MBD boys. *American Journal of Orthopsychiatry, 46,* 291–301.

Patterson, G. R. (1975). The aggressive child: Victim or architect of a coercive system? In L. A. Hamerlynck, L. C. Handy, & E. J. Mash (Eds.), *Behavior modification and families*. New York: Brunner & Mazell.

Patterson, G. R., & Cobb, J. (1973). Stimulus control for classes of noxious behaviors. In J. Knutson (Ed.), *The control of aggression: Implications from basic research*. Chicago: Aldine.

Patterson, G. R., Reid, J., Jones, R., & Conger, R. (1975). *Families with aggressive children*. Eugene, OR: Castalia.

Pervin, L. (1980). *Personality: Theory, assessment, and research*. 3rd ed. New York: Wiley.

Piliavin, I., & Briar, S. (1964). Police encounters with juveniles. *The American Journal of Sociology, 20,* 206–214.

Quay, H. C. (1964). Dimensions of personality in delinquent boys as inferred from the factor analysis of case history data. *Child Development, 35,* 479–484.

Quay, H. C., & Peterson, D. R. (1975). Manual for the behavior problem checklist. Unpublished.

Quinn, P. O., & Rapoport, J. L. (1974). Minor physical anomalies and neurological status in hyperactive boys. *Pediatrics, 53,* 742–747.

Ramsey, E., & Walker, H. (1988). Family management correlates of antisocial behavior among middle school boys. *Behavioral Disorders, 13,* 187–201.

Redl, F., & Wineman, D. (1957). *The aggressive child.* New York: The Free Press.

Robins, L. (1979). Follow up studies. In H. Quay and J. Worry (Eds.), *Psychopathological disorders of childhood.* 2nd ed. New York: Wiley.

Robins, L. (1981). Epidemiological approaches to natural history research: Antisocial disorders in children. *Journal of the American Academy of Child Psychiatry, 20,* 566–580.

Rosenthal, T., & Bandura, A. (1978). Psychological modeling: Theory and practice. In S. Garfield & A. Bergin (Eds.), *Handbook of psychotherapy and behavior change,* 2nd ed. New York: Wiley.

Ross, A. O. (1980). *Psychological disorders of children: A behavioral approach to theory, research, and therapy.* New York: McGraw-Hill.

Ross, D. M., & Ross, S. A. (1976). *Hyperactivity: Research, theory, and action.* New York: Wiley.

Rubin, R., & Balow, B. (1978). Prevalence of teacher identified behavior problems: A longitudinal study. *Exceptional Children, 45,* 102–111.

Rubinstein, E. A. (1978). Television and the young viewer. *American Scientist, 66,* 685–693.

Ruhl, K., & Hughes, C. (1985). The nature and extent of aggression in special education settings serving behaviorally disordered students. *Behavioral Disorders, 10,* 95–104.

Satterfield, J. H., Cantwell, D. P., Lesser, L. I., & Podosin, R. L. (1972). Physiological studies of the hyperactive child: I. *American Journal of Psychiatry, 128,* 1418–1424.

Satterfield, J. H., Cantwell, D. P., Saul, R. E., & Yusin, A. (1974). Intelligence, academic achievement, and EEG abnormalities in hyperactive children. *American Journal of Psychiatry, 131,* 391–395.

Sautter, R. (1995). Standing up to violence. *Phi Delta Kappan,* Kappan Special Report, 1–12.

Scarr, S. (1966). Genetic factors in activity motivation. *Child Development, 37,* 663–673.

Schleifer, M., Weiss, G., Cohen, N., Elman, M., Cvejic, H., & Kruger, E. (1975). Hyperactivity in preschoolers and the effect of methylphenidate. *American Journal of Orthopsychiatry, 45,* 38–50.

Schloss, P., & Smith, M. (1987). Guidelines for the use of manual restraint in public school settings for behaviorally disordered students. *Behavioral Disorders, 12,* 207–213.

Schulman, J. L. (1967). *Management of emotional disorders in pediatric practice.* Chicago: Year Book Medical Publishers.

Schworm, R., & Birnbaum, R. (1989). Symptom expression in hyperactive children: An analysis of observations. *Journal of Learning Disabilities, 22,* 35–40.

Scruggs, T., & Mastropieri, M. (1986). Academic characteristics of behaviorally disordered and learning disabled students. *Behavioral Disorders, 11,* 200–207.

Shanley, F. J. (1967). Middle-class delinquency as a social problem. *Sociology and Social Research, 51,* 185–198.

Shaw, C., & McKay, H. D. (1942). *Juvenile delinquency and urban areas.* Chicago: University of Chicago Press.

Sheldon, W. H. (1949). *The varieties of delinquent youth.* New York: Harper.

Sherman, H., & Farina, A. (1974). Social inadequacy of parents and children. *Journal of Abnormal Psychology, 83,* 327–330.

Short, J., & Nye, F. I. (1958). Extent of unrecorded deliquency: Tentative conclusions. *Journal of Criminal Law, Criminology, and Police Science, 49,* 296–302.

Siegel, L. J., & Senna, J. J. (1981). *Juvenile delinquency: Theory, practice, and law.* New York: West.

Silver, A. (1992). *Attention-deficit hyperactivity disorder: A clinical guide to diagnosis and treatment.* Washington, DC: American Psychiatric Press.

Sindelar, P., King, M., Gartland, D., Wilson, R., & Meisel, C. (1985). Deviant behavior in learning disabled and behaviorally disordered students as a function of level and placement. *Behavioral Disorders, 10,* 105–112.

Simonsen, C. E., & Gordon, M. S. (1982). *Juvenile justice in America.* New York: Macmillan.

Snyder, J. J. (1977). Reinforcement and analysis of interaction in problem and non-problem families. *Journal of Abnormal Psychology, 86,* 528–535.

Stein, A. H., & Friedrich, L. K. (1975). Impact of television on children and youth. In E. M. Hetherington (Ed.), *Review of child development research*. Vol. 5. Chicago: University of Chicago Press.

Stewart, M. A. (1970). Hyperactive children. *Scientific American, 222*, 94–98.

Stewart, M. A., Pitts, F. N., Craig, A. G., & Dieruf, W. (1966). The hyperactive child syndrome. *American Journal of Orthopsychiatry, 36*, 861–867.

Storey, K., Danko, C., Ashworth, R., & Strain, P. (1994). Generalization of social skills intervention for preschoolers with social delays. *Education and Treatment of Children, 17*(1), 29–51.

Strain, P. S. (1977). An experimental analysis of peer social initiations on the behavior of withdrawn preschool children: Some training and generalization effects. *Journal of Abnormal Child Psychology, 5*, 445–455.

Strain, P. S., Cooke, T. P., & Apolloni, T. (1976). *Teaching exceptional children: Assessing and modifying social behavior*. New York: Academic Press.

Talkington, L., & Altman, R. (1973). Effects of film-mediated aggression and affectual models on behavior. *American Journal of Mental Deficiency, 77*, 420–425.

Tappan, P. (1949). *Juvenile delinquency*. New York: McGraw-Hill.

Taylor, E., Sandberg, S., Thorley, G., & Giles, S. (1991). *The epidemiology of childhood hyperactivity*. New York: Oxford University Press.

Trojanewicz, R. C. (1973). *Juvenile delinquency: Concepts and control*. Englewood Cliffs, NJ: Prentice-Hall.

Turkewitz, H., O'Leary, K. D., & Ironsmith, M. (1975). Generalizations and maintenance of appropriate behavior through self-control. *Journal of Consulting and Clinical Psychology, 43*, 577–583.

Ulrich, R., Dulaney, S., Arnett, M., & Mueller, K. (1973). An experimental analysis of nonhuman and human aggression. In J. Knutson (Ed.), *The control of aggression: Implications from basic research*. Chicago: Aldine.

Vandenberg, S. G. (1962). The hereditary abilities study: Hereditary components in a psychological test battery. *American Journal of Human Genetics, 14*, 220–237.

Van Evra, J. P. (1983). *Psychological disorders of children and adolescents*. Boston: Little, Brown

Vaz, E. (1967). *Middle-class juvenile delinquency*. New York: Harper & Row.

Wahler, R. (1975). Some structural aspects of deviant child behavior. *Journal of Applied Behavior Analysis, 8*, 27–42.

Waldrop, M. F., & Halverson, C. E. (1971). Minor physical anomalies and hyperactive behavior in young children. In J. Hellmuth (Ed.), *Exceptional infant: Studies in abnormalities*. Vol. 2. New York: Bruner/Mazel.

Waldrop, M. F., Bell, R. Q., McLaughlin, B., & Halverson, C. F. (1978). Newborn minor physical anomalies predict short attention span, peer aggression, and impulsivity at age 3. *Science, 199*, 563–565.

Waldrop, M. F., Pederson, F. A., & Bell, R. Q. (1968). Minor physical anomalies and behavior in preschool children. *Child Development, 39*, 391–400.

Walker, H. (1976). *Walker Problem Behavior Identification Checklist*. Los Angeles: Western Psychological.

Walker, H., Greenwood, C. R., Hops, H., & Todd, N. M. (1979). Differential effects of reinforcing topographic components of social interaction: Analysis and direct replication. *Behavior Modification, 3*, 291–321.

Watson, J., & Raynor, R. (1972). Conditioned emotional reaction. In S. Harrison & J. McDermott (Eds.), *Childhood psychopathology*. New York: International Universities.

Watt, N., Stolorow, R., Lobensky, A., & McClelland, D. (1970). School adjustment and behavior of children hospitalized for schizophrenia as adults. *American Journal of Orthopsychiatry, 40*, 637–657.

Weiss, G., Minde, K., Werry, J. S., Douglas, V., & Nemeth, E. (1971). Studies on the hyperactive child. VIII: Five-year follow-up. *Archives of General Psychiatry, 24*, 409–414.

Werry, J. S., Minde, K., Guzman, A., Weiss, G., Dogan, K., & Hoy, E. (1972). Studies on the hyperactive child. VIII: Neurological status compared with neurotic and normal children. *American Journal of Orthopsychiatry, 42*, 441–451.

Werry, J. S., Weiss, G., & Douglas, V. I. (1964). Studies on the hyperactive child. I: Some preliminary findings. *Canadian Psychiatric Association Journal, 9*, 120–130.

West, D. J. (1982). *Delinquency: Its roots, careers, and prospects.* Cambridge, MA: Harvard University Press.

Wilker, A., Dixon, J. F., & Parker, J. B. (1970). Brain function in problem children and controls: Psychometric, neurological and electroencephalographic comparisons. *American Journal of Psychiatry, 127*, 634–645.

Willerman, L. (1973). Activity level and hyperactivity in twins. *Child Development, 44*, 288–293.

Williams, J., & Gold, M. (1972). From delinquent behavior to official delinquency. *Social Problems, 20*, 209–229.

Wolfgang, M., Figlio, R., & Sellin, T. (1972). *Delinquency in a birth cohort.* Chicago: University of Chicago Press.

Zigler, E., Taussig, C. & Black, K. (1992). Early childhood intervention: A promising preventive for juvenile delinquency. *American Psychologist, 47*(8), 997–1006.

Chapter *3*

Low-Incidence Behavior Disorders

Advance Organizer

As you read this chapter, prepare to identify and discuss:

- What is meant by the term *low incidence* behavior disorder.
- The historical origins of the study of childhood and youth psychoses, including terminology and diagnostic criteria.
- The characteristics, prevalence, and etiology of autism.
- The behavioral correlates of autism.
- The course and prognosis of autism.
- The characteristics, prevalence, and course of (1) Asperger's disorder, (2) childhood degenerative disorder, and (3) pervasive developmental disorder not otherwise specified (PDDNOS).
- The characteristics, prevalence, and etiology of early-onset schizophrenia.
- Differences between pervasive developmental disorder and early-onset schizophrenia.

After two weeks of intensive assessment procedures that included formal testing, parent interviews, and systematic observation, all the members of the CASE Conference Committee (representatives of local educational authorities responsible for placing exceptional students in appropriate educational settings) agreed that Owen's specific educational needs would not be best served in any of the district's existing programs for with students with behavior disorders. Although Owen frequently displayed aggressive and antisocial behaviors, the severity of his inappropriate behaviors precluded placement in a regular school environment where the teacher-student ratio was 12 to 1. The committee unanimously agreed that Owen would be best served in an environment where a great amount of direct individual attention could be given to his wide range of behavioral excesses and deficiencies.

At 6 years of age, Owen already had a long history of adjustment difficulties. His parents reported a lack of social responses from early infancy; Owen showed little interest in family members and neither smiled nor cuddled in the typical manner of babies. Of further distress was his avoidance of eye contact and unwillingness to make friends or play with peers. Owen spent most of his time in a variety of self-stimulatory behaviors such as hand flapping, arm waving, and intently spinning an old toy around the living room floor. If the toy was taken away from him, he would usually hold his ears and scream in a high-pitched voice. Systematic observations by trained psychologists indicated that Owen was also prone to self-injurious behavior when tantrumming. His parents reported that on several occasions they were forced to use arm restraints because they feared for the child's safety during a tantrumming episode. Owen did possess some language, although his speech sounded peculiar. Unlike the language of other children his age, it lacked spontaneity and the gestures of normal conversation. His verbalizations were typically monotonous and flat, and on many occasions echolalic.

It was decided that Owen's severe behaviors should be treated in a self-contained day school where a variety of trained professionals could implement a comprehensive intervention effort. Although this would involve the extra expense of transporting Owen to the local special education cooperative, it was decided that such a placement was in his and his family's best interests.

The previous chapter elaborated on the characteristics of high-incidence patterns of behavior disorders. We defined hyperactivity, aggression, social withdrawal, juvenile delinquency, and rule breaking as high in incidence because of the frequency with which they are seen and treated by educators. Both regular and special educators typically deal with high-incidence behavior problems on a daily basis.

In our discussion of low-incidence behavior disorders in this chapter, we will focus on behaviors that are only rarely observed by most educators—the behaviors of children with pervasive developmental disorders and early-onset schizophrenia. This reduced visibility to most educators can be largely attributed to two major factors: the nature and severity of the behaviors exhibited by these youngsters and the relatively low prevalence of such children and adolescents in the general population.

The relatively low visibility of youngsters with pervasive developmental disorders and early-onset schizophrenia does not reflect the attention and concern these disorders have received from professionals. There is a voluminous literature concerning the many issues related to the identification and treatment of these youngsters. As Werry (1979) has noted, the ongoing attention paid to these disorders is a function of the severity and seemingly unyielding persistence of the symptomology rather than of the disorder's rate of occurrence.

Historically, children with pervasive developmental disorders and early-onset schizophrenia were characterized by the generic term *psychotic*, a term that is almost synonymous with the legal term *insanity*. The person considered to be psychotic was believed to possess poor reality testing and to suffer from frequent delusions and hallucinations. Descriptions such as "unusual" and "bizarre" were used to describe such people by both professionals and nonprofessionals. The disorder was viewed as so severe that it was believed that the psychotic was unable to differentiate the "self" from others or reality from fantasy. The psychoses of childhood and adolescence were regarded as profound disorders that interfered with almost all facets of normal functioning and development: The individual either failed to respond to the environment or responded in an inappropriate fashion.

Although the umbrella term of *psychosis* is rarely used, considerable confusion and controversy remains in the identification of the specific types of low-incidence behavior disorders. For many years, different labels have been employed, somewhat interchangeably, to refer to these debilitating disorders. For example, many clinicians and researchers have used the terms *childhood schizophrenia, autism,* and *atypical child* synonymously with childhood psychosis. In the early 1980s it was believed that the majority of the low-incidence severe behavior disorders were accounted for by two separate syndromes *autism* and *childhood-onset pervasive developmental disorder* (American Psychiatric Association, 1980). However, recent thinking is that childhood-onset pervasive developmental disorder was a confusing diagnostic category with little clinical utility and that in practice it was difficult to distinguish it from autism (Waterhouse, Wing, Spitzer, & Siegal, 1992). Currently, a number of subcategories of disorders, including a more comprehensive developmentally organized set of criteria for autism, Asperger's disorder, and pervasive developmental disorders not otherwise specified are classified under the broad category of *pervasive developmental disorder* (PDD). The use of this new umbrella category recognizes that autism, now referred to as autistic disorder (as well as the other subcategories) constitutes a disorder of development rather than a psychosis (Rutter & Schopler, 1992). Finally, methods for making a differential diagnosis of pervasive developmental disorder and early-onset schizophrenia have been refined and articulated.

First we will present a brief historical overview of the study of low-incidence behavior disorders. Then we will try to unravel the confusion surrounding the identification of children with low incidence behavior disorders by presenting the current nomenclature, characteristics, etiology, and behavioral correlates associated with this diverse and challenging group of students.

Early Perspectives on Severe Behavior Problems of Childhood and Youth

In the inaugural issue of the *Journal of Autism and Childhood Schizophrenia*, Kanner (1971) presented a brief overview of past efforts to identify and treat youngsters with psychoses. The rationale for his historical sketch was to provide a context for what was to be a central depository of research involving preadult populations with psychoses. In retrospect, it can be seen that the inception of the journal was in and of itself an important historical event, for until its publication, there was no true focal point for the dissemination of information specific to psychotic behavior in children.

In the historical sketch, Kanner first cited the work of Maudsley, a mid-nineteenth-century British psychiatrist who was among the first to acknowledge insanity in children. He was fiercely criticized for suggesting that something as "unnatural" as insanity in children could exist. Still, Maudsley's groundbreaking work, including a six-point classification scheme, spurred others to investigate insanity in preadult populations. By the 1890s, several textbooks had appeared that addressed the issue of childhood psychosis as a distinct diagnostic entity. At the beginning of this century, Sante de Sanctis described a group of children as possessing "dementia praecocissima," which was regarded as a form of psychosis in preadults. These observations and descriptions served as the standards against which other investigators compared and contrasted their own discoveries.

At the same time, Bleuler introduced the term *schizophrenia* to replace the previously used *dementia praecox*. The new term was designed to describe the cluster of symptoms exhibited by adults with psychoses without implying the hopeless prognosis of dementia praecox (Shaw & Lucas, 1970). While Bleuler indicated that schizophrenia might have etiological roots in later childhood, he said little about actual childhood schizophrenia. Two decades later, however, Potter (1933) applied Bleuler's diagnostic criteria of schizophrenia to preadult populations. Potter's landmark effort, one of the first papers on the study of children with psychoses to appear in English (Werry, 1979), stipulated six conditions that had to be demonstrated for an appropriate diagnosis of childhood schizophrenia to be made:

1. Generalized retraction of interest from the environment.
2. Dereistic (i.e., deviation from normal logic) thinking, feeling, and acting.
3. Disturbances of thought, manifested through blocking, perseveration, incoherence, and mutism.
4. Defects in emotional rapport.
5. Rigidity and distortion of affect.
6. Alterations of behavior, with either increases or decreases in motility or bizarre behavior with a tendency to persevere or engage in stereotypical acts.

While fault can now be found with Potter's diagnostic criteria (see Werry, 1979), his effort did heighten the awareness of childhood psychosis.

In the years that followed, there were several significant developments. Bradley and Bowen (1941) attempted to objectify or define operationally the overt symptomology of childhood schizophrenia. By comparing behaviors of psychotic and nonpsychotic children, they were able to arrive at eight symptoms that could characterize schizophrenia. Of these, four—seclusiveness, bizarre behavior, regressive interests, and sensitivity—were considered universal or primary; that is, all of them had to be observed in order to make an appropriate diagnosis of schizophrenia. The remaining four symptoms—irritability, daydreaming, diminution of interests, and physical inactivity—were believed to be secondary conditions. Others prominent in the 1940s were Bender and Kanner. Werry (1979) noted a strong neurological and cognitive emphasis in Bender's descriptions of childhood schizophrenia. Specifically, Bender (1942) posited that schizophrenia could be attributed to developmental irregularities in the central nervous system as well as to specific cognitive abnormalities relating to perception and body image. In addition, Bender is credited with emphasizing the importance of age of onset in the differential diagnosis of specific childhood schizophrenia subtypes (pseudodefective—first 3 years of life; pseudodefective—early and middle childhood; pseudopsychopathic—preadolescence). Concurrently, Kanner (1943) first reported what he believed to be a separate diagnostic entity: early infantile autism. This notion of qualitatively different syndrome from childhood schizophrenia is still debated by both researches and practitioners. While most (e.g., Kolvin, 1971; Rimland, 1964; Rutter, 1978a) accept Kanner's differentiation between autism and childhood schizophrenia, others (e.g., Bender, 1971; Kauffman, 1981; Treffert, 1970) believe that there are few systematic differences besides the age of onset of the disorder. More on this controversy will be presented in a later section of this chapter.

The confusion regarding syndrome differentiation was further fueled by Rank in the early 1950s with the development of a third diagnostic subcategory: the "atypical child." Kanner's (1971) history implied that Rank formulated this new concept to accommodate those children presenting symptoms of what was believed to be maternally-induced ego fragmentation. Other etiological factors were ignored within this diagnostic framework; mother–child interactions and resultant effects on the ego were deemed to be the prime feature for categorization. This rather limited diagnostic view has had little impact on the many recent empirical attempts to clarify diagnostic issues; it is more usual for many characteristics and etiological factors to be incorporated into diagnostic formulations.

Kanner's brief history of the study of childhood psychoses, while limited, highlighted several points of interest. First, it was recognized that we were merely in the infancy of our efforts: It had been less than a century since Maudsley first mentioned the "unnatural" syndrome of what was then referred to as childhood psychosis. Second, the history of the study of these disorders was replete with controversy surrounding identification and diagnosis. Finally, the education and treatment of children presenting these severe and often debilitating disorders would probably become more efficient and effective if teachers, clinicians, and researchers could agree upon a common terminology and be more precise and functional in their diagnosis. Since Kanner's history, a number of changes have occurred, foremost being the realization that many low-incidence behavior disorders (e.g., autism) are not psychoses, but rather a form of developmental disability. These changes have been codified in DSM-IV (APA, 1994) and form the basis of our discussion of low-incidence behavior disorders.

Pervasive Developmental Disorders

Generally speaking, pervasive developmental disorders are characterized by severe and pervasive impairments in a number of areas of development including (1) social interaction skills, (2) communication skills, and/or (3) the presence of stereotyped behaviors, interests, and activities (APA, 1994). Those specific disorders under the pervasive developmental disorder umbrella include autistic disorder, childhood disintegrative disorder, Asperger's disorder, and pervasive developmental disorder not otherwise specified.

Autistic Disorder

Autistic disorder, frequently referred to as autism, is currently viewed as a severe developmental disorder marked by a very early age of onset, impaired social development, disturbances in language development, and perseveration/rigidity of behavior (Phelps & Grabowski, 1991). The classification of autism within the special education arena possesses a nomadic past. As noted earlier, autism and many other low-incidence behavioral disorders were believed to be mental illnesses and were classified under PL 94-142 with physical impairments and other health impairments. In the most recent IDEA amendments, autism was given a category of its own. According to IDEA, autism is defined as:

> *a developmental disability significantly affecting verbal and nonverbal communication and social interaction, generally evident before age 3, that adversely affects a child's performance. Other characteristics often associated with autism are engagement in repetitive activities and stereotyped movements, resistance to environmental change or change in daily routines, and unusual responses to sensory experiences. The term does not apply if a child's educational performance is adversely affected primarily because the child has a serious emotional disturbance (34 C.F.R. Section 300.7(b) (1) (1992)).*

The Universal and Specific Characteristics of Autism

While many behavioral patterns, biological phenomena, and environmental events are frequently associated with autism, it is generally believed that there are three cardinal characteristics that are *universal* and *specific* to autism: (1) profound failure to develop social relationships, (2) failure to develop communicative language, and (3) ritualistic or compulsive behavior. By universal and specific characteristics, we are referring to symptoms that are present in nearly all autistic youngsters and are relatively infrequent in children who are not autistic (Rutter, 1978a). Of primary importance to a differential diagnosis of autism is that the three universal and specific symptoms be evidenced during infancy or before the child reaches 3 years of age. While many parents do report a child's lack of interest in social interaction soon after birth, manifestations of autism in infancy can be subtle and more difficult to define than those observed after 2 years of age (APA, 1994).

Failure to Develop Social Relationships

Many authors (e.g., APA, 1994; Paluszny, 1979; Rutter, 1978a; Wing, 1969) have investigated how children with autism differ from normal peers in terms of social development. The failure of the child with autism to develop social relationships begins in early infancy, with parents often reporting that their infant does not do what "normal babies" do. For instance, normal babies usually respond to familiar faces with a social smile by 2 months of age. In contrast, the smile of the child with autism is not a social smile or a warm response to the primary caretaker, but a response to some other type of stimuli. In addition, the infant with autism does not exhibit the anticipatory posture to being picked up the way that normal babies do (the anticipatory posture is the baby's parting of the arms that typically precedes being picked up and held). Especially troubling to parents is the lack of attachment behaviors of the child with autism. Children with autism do not turn to their parents when hurt, and they rarely develop reciprocal affection bonds such as the "good night cuddle and kiss" (Rutter, 1978a). In general, they exhibit little, if any, pleasure in the presence of their parents, though Sigman and Ungere (1984) suggest that some youngsters with autism who have increased representational ability (cognizance of object permanence) may exhibit greater levels of social behaviors toward their mothers than toward strangers.

Children with autism tend to avoid direct eye contact and often treat others in the environment as if they didn't exist. In fact, this gaze aversion is often central to the perception of children with autism by others in their immediate environment (Miranda, Donnellan, & Yoder, 1983). As the child with autism grows older, impairments in social functioning become evident in a number of other ways: Developmental benchmarks such as friendships, normative play patterns, toilet training, regular eating patterns, and expressions of empathy are not easily reached, and disruptive behaviors become common during instructional situations (Koegel, Koegel, & Surratt, 1992).

Failure to Develop Communicative Language

Children with autism develop and use language differently from normal children and, consequently, are deficient in communication skills (Koegel, Rincover, & Egel, 1982; Rumsey & Denckla, 1987). Research efforts centering on the language development of children with autism have focused on both expressive and receptive language.

In terms of expressive language, approximately 50 percent of youngsters with autism do not acquire useful (i.e., expressive) speech (Rimland, 1964), with complete speech loss appearing more frequently in girls than in boys (Kurita,

Identifying Autism: Major Sources of Diagnostic Confusion

While most professionals agree that children with pervasive developmental disorders suffer abnormalities requiring specialized intervention, there is considerable confusion involving the differential diagnoses of these low-incidence disability conditions. Schloper (1983) has traced the sources of confusion to three major factors: historical antecedents, syndrome complexity, and misunderstood differences in selection purposes. Concerning historical factors, he observed that the vast literature focusing on children with autism reflects a variety of "diagnostic muddles" (p. 108), including the diagnostic labeling of unsubstantiated theories, the use of identical diagnostic terms for different concepts, and the assignment of varying clinical characteristics to a unitary diagnostic label. The second source of confusion, syndrome complexity, centers upon the narrow and apparently mistaken notion that autism is a unitary disease or syndrome with a singular cause, treatment, and prognosis. The available empirical evidence sharply contrasts with this view: Autism seems to have multiple possible etiologies and a variety of effective subject-specific treatment approaches. The third major source of confusion is the selection process used in grouping children believed to be autistic for research, clinical, and administrative purposes. In most cases, individual selection procedures are directly related to the purposes and goals of the study or project; confusion arises when relationships between goals and selection procedures are neither recognized nor understood. An unfortunate result of this inconsistency in the selection of representative samples of children with autism is the inability to generalize the results of one particular program or study to the wide variety of behavioral characteristics exhibited by populations of youngsters with autism.

Schloper contends that clarification of the first two sources of diagnostic confusion are readily available in the professional literature. In addressing historical errors, he strongly recommends the adoption of Rutter's (1978a) definition of autism, since it is based on a comprehensive empirical synthesis of more than one hundred systematic research publications. The turmoil involving symptom complexity could be resolved by adopting a multiaxial approach to classifying autism—rather than being regarded as a unitary disease process, autism would be viewed as a series of behaviors existing on several DSM-IV factor-specific axes. Finally, confusion resulting from selection processes could be reduced if grouping purposes for autism were cataloged to reflect the multiaxial classification system. Such organization would enhance diagnostic efforts as well as assist in matching specific treatment approaches and programs to the presenting problems of the individual child with autism.

1985). Children with autism who do develop speech often display peculiarities. Perhaps the most common speech abnormality is *echolalia*, the parrotlike response in which all or part of what is heard is repeated. Echolalia can occur either immediately or after a delay: Some children with autism mimic the immediate requests of parents and teachers, while others repeat, verbatim, television programming after a significant delay.

Youngsters with autism typically do not use speech for social communication; the reciprocal interaction common to normal conversation is rarely present. Similarly, children with autism do not employ the gestures, body movement, or intonation frequently found in daily social conversations. The speech they do use is monotonous, generally noncommunicative, and often filled with pronominal reversals; it lacks abstract referents and metaphorical terms. In general, children with autism do not use syntactically complex language, and their linguistic competence is comparable to that of much younger or retarded children (Pierce & Bartolucci, 1977).

In terms of receptive language, youngsters with autism are believed to have difficulties understanding spoken language. Nonetheless, given gestural cues and a familiar environment, they can follow simple one-step instructions. If a task is without cues of possessing two or more steps, it is more than likely that a child with autism will not complete it (Rutter, 1978a). Many of these receptive language deficits have been attributed to deficiencies in information processing, such as the discrimination, categorization, and organization of environmental input. Specifically, Tager-Flusberg (1981) found that children with autism do not use semantically based comprehension strategies, a strategy common to higher level cognition. Similarly, O'Connor and Hermelin (1973) found that children with autism code visual input spatially rather than temporally, a significant departure from the processing of normal children.

Ritualistic and Compulsive Behavior

Children with autism frequently engage in bizarre and repetitive patterns of behavior (APA, 1994). Discussions of these patterns frequently characterize the child with autism as possessing an anxious desire for the maintenance of sameness (Kanner, 1943), but Rutter (1978a) has objected to this terminology because it relies too heavily on inference. What we can say from observation is that children with autism engage in behaviors that are both rigid and devoid of imagination. Individuals who work with youngsters with autism frequently encounter stereotypic behavior patterns such as self-stimulatory behavior (e.g., rocking or arm flapping) and self-injurious behavior. In addition, these youngsters compulsively adhere to schedules and routines; varying their schedules or altering their environment can result in violent tantrums. Consistent with the rigidity of the child with autism, intensive attachments to certain objects are frequently noted. Unlike normal children, who may have a favorite doll or blanket, youngsters with autism may cling to a piece of string, a spoon, or a drinking straw (Hinerman, 1983). Play patterns also appear abnormally regimented; Children with autism have been known to line up toys or make elaborate patterns out of everyday objects. Similarly, mechanical devices such as light switches and toilets are often the objects of their repetitive "play."

Prevalence

It is difficult to accurately estimate the prevalence of children with autism because the cardinal characteristics just discussed have only recently provided guidance in the differential diagnosis of autism. Years of inconsistency in the identification and classification of autism have left us with only gross estimates of the size of the autistic population. It is generally believed, though, that autism is a rare disorder that appears in only 2 to 5 cases per 10,000 children. Available data indicate that the disorder occurs throughout the world and is approximately four to five times more common in males than in females (Ritvo et al., 1989), although girls with autism tend to be more severely afflicted (Tsai, Stewart, & August, 1981). The course of the disorder is chronic, and only a small percentage of individuals with the disorder go on to live and work independently; in one-third of the population, some level of supported or partial independence is possible (APA, 1994). Specifically, autistic children with speech and nonverbal IQs above the range of mental retardation are those that have the greatest chance of achieving positive outcomes in academic, employment, and residential settings (Venter, Lord, & Schopler, 1992).

Behavioral Correlates

For a child to be diagnosed appropriately as autistic, each of the universal and specific characteristics should be systematically observed. It must be remembered, however, that factors secondary to the defining features of autism must be addressed in order to implement successful instructional and habilitative programs. Two such factors—intellectual functioning and self-injurious behavior—are of particular interest to teachers.

Variable Intellectual Functioning

Historically, the intellectual functioning of children with autism has been difficult to quantify. In Kanner's (1943) original documentation of the autistic syndrome, it was assumed that children with autism had good intellectual potential; normal intellectual functioning even appeared to be part of the differential diagnosis. This assumption of normal intelligence was fueled, in part, by the display of the child's rote memorization skills and frequent use of facial expressions during the performance of assigned tasks (Samuels, 1981). In fact, the measured intelligence of children with autism is variable, ranging from superior to profoundly retarded. However, the distribution is positively skewed, with only 25 percent of children with autism having IQs above 70; in most cases, intelligence falls in moderate range with IQs ranging from 35 to 50 (APA, 1994).

Those students with autism who function within the normal range of intelligence are often referred to as high-functioning individuals with autism (HFIA). In addition to having higher levels of measured intelligence, HFIA differ from low-functioning children with autism in that they are less likely to exhibit (1) gross deficits in social interaction and emotional expression, (2) inappropriate play, (3) self-injurious behavior, and (4) delays in motor and language development (Yirmiya & Sigman, 1991). Although HFIA do have normal IQs, they tend to score higher on performance subtests than on verbal subtests, and tasks that require verbal abstractions and social reasoning are problematic. Still, recent research (e.g., Myles, Simpson, & Becker, 1994–1995) has indicated that students identified as HFIA present such a myriad of diverse characteristics that additional epidemiological work is necessary if the label HFIA is to assist in the development of targeted academic, behavioral, and social interventions.

While intelligence testing of students with autism has been reported to be both valid and stable over time (DeMyer et al., 1974; Lord & Schopler, 1989), the issue of the untestability of certain students with autism remains a large concern to educators and psychologists. The available data involving such students suggest that most of those deemed untestable were *unable* rather than *unwilling* to perform the test items (Alpern, 1967; Rutter, 1978a) and that valid measures can be obtained if the tests are commensurate with the child's developmental level and not dependent on language (Morgan, 1986; Wolf Schcin, 1993).

Self-Injurious Behavior

Self-injurious behavior (SIB) is self-directed aggression; examples of such behavior are punching, scratching, biting, and severe head-banging. Some (e.g., Kauffman, 1985) have claimed that ordinary human decency demands that we find the cause and cure for such behavior. Certainly, from a clinical or educational perspective, the elimination of intense physically destructive behaviors is a prerequisite to serious and continuous treatment. SIB often precludes placement in the least restrictive environment and limits access to a range of learning, working, and leisure opportunities (Symons, 1995).

SIB is not specific to autism—many individuals with severe handicaps also engage in these shocking behaviors. It has been reported that up to 5 percent of the entire psychiatric population exhibits some form of SIB (Frankel & Simmons, 1976); these rates tend to be higher (10–17 percent) among individuals who are institutionalized (Schroeder, Schroeder, Smith, & Dalldorf, 1978).

Unfortunately, it is not clear why SIB occurs or how it is caused, though a number of hypotheses reflecting the physical, behavioral, and psychodynamic perspectives have been proposed.

From the biophysical perspective, SIB is thought to be a result of abnormal physiological development or impaired biological functioning. It may be caused by inadequate central nervous system growth or by an imbalance of the biochemicals necessary for appropriate brain functioning (Cataldo & Harris, 1982).

From the behavioral perspective, SIB is believed to be a learned response, acquired and maintained by positive and/or negative reinforcement—positive reinforcement in the form of others' attention to the aberrant behavior, and negative reinforcement in the form of escape from instructional demands or situations the individual with autism perceives as unpleasant (Iwata, Pace, Kalsher, Cowdery, Cataldo, 1990; Lerman & Iwata, 1993). There is considerable evidence supporting the notion that changes in reinforcement patterns can reduce many patterns of SIB, and many behaviorally based techniques and programs have been developed to do so (see Chapter 12 for specific strategies).

In sharp contrast to the behavioral view, the psychodynamic perspective views SIB as resulting from the unconscious experience of guilt or mental anguish derived from uncontrolled instinctual drives. The psychodynamic explanation of SIB is unverifiable, however, because of the assumed nature of the internal personality structures and the lack of scientific experimentation and documentation. The available research indicates that interventions based on psychodynamic theory have not been effective in treating SIB (Symons, 1995).

Etiology

Many etiological speculations have been put forward to explain autism, reflecting the often-conflicting conceptual models that are associated with the study of human behavior. In-depth reviews of how each conceptual model explains autism are available elsewhere (see Cammisa, 1993; Egel, Koegel, & Schriebman, 1980; Phelps & Grabowski, 1991; Rutter & Bartak, 1971; Werry, 1979). For our purposes, it is best to group the major theories of causation into three major categories: nature, nurture, and nature–nuture interaction.

Nature-Based Explanations

From the nature perspective, the behavioral abnormalities of children with autism are a function of biophysical impairments, genetic effects, biochemical abnormalities, and/or neurological dysfunction. That autism is observed so early in life suggests biological involvement (Paluszny, 1979), and most investigators accept the growing body of empirical evidence that autism is biologically determined (Phelps & Grabowski, 1991). Using familial aggregation and twin studies, a number of researchers (e.g., Ritvo et al., 1989) have suggested that inheritable factors resulting in central nervous system dysfunction may be responsible for autism.

Rimland (1964) has speculated that extreme sensitivity to oxygen during infancy may result in damage to the reticular formation of the brain stem, an area of the brain believed to be critical for integrating current perceptions with memory. For some genetically predisposed infants, even those oxygen levels typical of our atmosphere could cause the brain impairment. Reviewing biochemical and hemotologic research, Ritvo, Rabin, Yuwiler, Freeman, and Geller (1978) found preliminary evidence suggesting that certain disturbances in the blood stream involving seratonin and platelet counts may be related to autism. It has also been proposed that neurological abnormalities exist in populations with autism. Some studies (e.g., Kolvin, Ounsted, & Roth, 1971) have reported that up to 50 percent of children with autism suffer from some type of brain dysfunction. Exactly where the abnormality resides is unclear, but research continues. For example, Delong (1978) has reported that a subpopulation of children with autism may possess anatomic defects in the left medial temporal lobe structures, while others (e.g., Tsai & Stewart, 1982) have found evidence of bilateral brain abnormalities in both hemispheres of the brain. Thus, while it is believed that some neurological dysfunction is always present, it is unlikely that any specific cerebral dysfunction has a direct role in the etiology of autism. In general, much of the nature-based research has assumed that autism is the result of a unitary, but still unidentified, biological condition. At this point, there is little evidence to affirm this view. It appears likely that autism is biologically based, but without a single etiology; rather, it may result from any one of several different and diverse abnormalities or impairments (Cammisa, 1993; Phelps & Grabowski, 1991; Schopler & Mesibov, 1987).

Nurture-Based Explanations

The nurture-based etiological theories of autism provide a rare example of similarity between the usually diametrically opposed behavioral and psychodynamic models. Theorists from both models have offered explanations claiming that the parents of children with autism are primarily responsible for the development and maintenance of the problem behaviors.

From the traditional psychodynamic view, autism results from failed ego development, a condition caused by abnormal parent–child interactions. A major proponent of this perspective, Bruno Bettelheim (1967), has claimed that autism is a child's response to extreme parental rejection—specifically, the failure to provide sufficient stimulation and feedback during key developmental periods. As a result of parental unresponsiveness, the child never learns appropriate speech, motor, or social/emotional behaviors. Another detrimental product of parental unresponsiveness is the child's withdrawal from the threatening and seemingly uncontrollable external world. By retreating into a private fantasy world, the child is able to create order and consistency through self-initiated ritualistic and obsessive patterns of behavior.

The behavioral explanation of autism also relies heavily upon the unresponsiveness of parents. Ferster (1961) proposed a parsimonious, albeit highly controversial, stimulus-response social–learning explanation of autism. Simply stated, the child with autism fails to develop language and appropriate social and emotional responses because early instances of such behaviors are not responded to correctly. Rather than attending to or reinforcing early attempts at prosocial behavior, Ferster believed that parents either ignore or only intermittently attend to appropriate behavior. Consequently, early prosocial responses are extinguished and more complex skills never have the opportunity to develop adequately. The child eventually learns to acquire the attention of adults by engaging in bizarre behaviors, and the result of this differential attention or reinforcement is an autistic repertoire of behavior.

Both the psychodynamic and behavioral explanations of autism have received considerable criticism. Research findings involving the parents of children with autism have been equivocal. Early researchers (Kanner, 1954; Lowe, 1966; Lotter, 1967) characterized these parents as obsessive, humorless, emotionally cold, and socially removed. In addition, most were highly intelligent, achievement oriented, and of middle or upper socioeconomic status. But more recent research (Cox, Rutter, Newman, & Bartak, 1975) has not supported the view that parents of children with autism are humorless, cold, and unfeeling.

The interpretation of any data relating to parent or family characteristics must be guarded because studies dealing with such variables are subject to what Bootzin (1980) calls chicken-and-egg questions. Because none of the parents was observed until after their child had been identified as autistic, we have no index to what they were like before they were living with a daily dose of bizarre behaviors. Thus, as with any correlational or ex post facto research, we cannot know the direction of the relationship between parent and child behavior. It is just as possible that the child with autism caused the cold and aloof parent as it is that the cold and aloof parent caused the child's autistic behavior.

As for the education and socioeconomic variables attributed to the parents of autistic children, the reported data may be influenced by a selection bias. Ross (1980) has illustrated how such biases explain the data:

> *true cases of early infantile autism are exceedingly rare. This means that most family physicians and pediatricians and few psychiatrists and psychologists will have had experience with such children. Many may thus be misdiagnosed as deaf, brain-injured, or mentally retarded, thus never coming to the notice of those who study and write about early infantile autism. Who, then, are the children who do come to the attention of those relatively few specialists who know about early infantile autism? Might it not be the children of parents who are sophisticated enough not to accept the first professional diagnosis, who read about other possibilities, who have the knowledge and the financial resources to seek professional advice at one of the major medical centers in this country where the specialists who study and write about early infantile autism are located? If this were the case, then these specialists would be getting to see primarily those autistic children whose parents are intelligent, educated, and reasonably well-to-do. (pp. 171–172)*

Nature–Nurture Interaction Explanations

From the interactionist perspective, autism is caused by a combination of biological factors and environmental influences. Cantwell, Baker, and Rutter (1978) have outlined several ways that nature and nurture can combine to cause and maintain autism. First, it is possible that the development of autism requires some type of environmental influence or stressor to activate a biological deficit. Thus, an organic, biochemical, or neurological impairment may be a necessary but not sufficient cause of autism. A second possibility is that biophysical impairments of the child with autism can result in extreme vulnerability to the normal, yet stressful, family interactions that do not disable other children. Finally, it is possible that environmental events influence autism only after the disorder has developed. A persuasive case for this view can be made since many educational and behavioral interventions that have implemented environmental alterations have changed the course and development of the disorder. As noted by Morgan (1986), the most plausible conclusion regarding etiology is that autism is the behavioral end product of an underlying organic defect (or combination of defects) that may arise in a number of ways through a variety of possible causal agents. Accepting such a conclusion does not mean denying that the disorder can be exacerbated or improved by environmental influences. All that is rejected is the notion that such influences *caused* the disorder.

The Course and Prognosis of Autistic Disorder

Generally speaking, the prognosis for children suffering from autism is quite poor. The course of autism is chronic, with only one child in six developing an adequate social adjustment. Another one in six makes only a fair adjustment, and a full two-thirds remain severely disabled and fail to develop independent living skills. Reviewing a series of follow-up studies involving children with autism, Lotter (1978) classified possible adjustment levels according to a four-point scale of outcomes: good, fair, poor, and very poor. A good outcome was defined as a normal or near-normal social life, with satisfactory functioning at school or work. A fair outcome was determined if some social and educational progress was observed despite marked abnormalities in behavior or interpersonal relationships. A poor outcome was defined as one in which no independent social progress was observed, and the classification very poor outcome was used when the individual was unable to live any kind of independent existence.

Lotter's results for the seven studies reviewed are presented in Table 3.1. Good outcomes ranged from 5 to 17 percent, while poor and very poor outcomes ranged from 61 to 73 percent. In addition, only a few of the individuals studied were employed and approximately half were institutionalized.

While Lotter's data present a rather bleak picture of the prognosis for children with autism, a certain amount of promise may be extracted from the study of those subjects who *did* achieve appropriate levels of adjustment. A number of researchers (e.g., Rutter, 1978b; Szatmari, Bartolucci, Bremner, Bond, & Rich, 1989; Venter et al., 1992) have reported that the cognitive functioning of a child with autism is most predictive of later outcomes. Children whose autism is accompanied by severe mental retardation rarely acquire communicative language and typically require long-term institutionalization. In contrast, children with autism with higher IQs do make edu-

TABLE 3.1   Classification of Outcomes—Follow-up Studies of Autistic Children

Study	No. at Follow-up	Outcome			
		Good	Poor or Very Poor	Employed	Institution
1	63	5%	73%	—	—
2	100	17%	73%	5%	39%
3	26	—	—	0	74%
4	63	14%	61%	3%	44%
5	63	17%	64%	13%	54%
6	29	14%	62%	4%	48%
7	27	14%	—	—	—

Source: From Lotter (1978).

cational gains and become reasonably adept at receptive and expressive language. Up to one-half of this subgroup become productive members of the labor market.

In addition to IQ, spoken language tends to be highly predictive of social adjustment. Since language and intelligence are interrelated, it is generally believed that if a child with autism fails to develop useful speech by age 5, gross retardation and disturbed behavior will most likely follow in later life. Eisenberg (1956) found that if the child with autism was speaking by age 5, there was a 50 percent chance of good or fair adjustment; if no useful speech was demonstrated by that age, then the chance of adjustment was 1 in 31, or only about 3 percent. Recent studies (e.g., Rumsey & Hamburger, 1988) have suggested that even small differences in language comprehension and expressive abilities are important factors in the development of positive outcomes. Clearly, the ability to understand narrative without visual cues is an important mediator of social and communicative skills that serves as a predictor of adaptive behavior and achievement in children and adolescents with autism (Venter et al., 1992).

In short, the prognosis for children with autism is discouraging. Still, we must keep in mind that improved treatment interventions can make a difference by modifying the course of the disorders. For example, Rutter and Bartak (Rutter, 1978b; Bartak, 1978; Rutter & Bartak, 1973) as well as Sparrow & Cicchetti (1985) have found that systematic instruction in a structured environment with an appropriate task can result in higher educational performance and greater social proficiency. While empirical data are lacking, it appears that the earlier intervention begins, the more effective the treatment will be. Parental involvement can also positively affect outcomes. In short, appropriate treatment interventions can and will affect prognosis.

Asperger's Disorder

Children and adolescents with Asperger's disorder are characterized by severe and sustained impairments in social interaction and the development of restricted, repetitive patterns of behavior interests and activities (APA, 1994). Although the presenting behaviors resemble those of HFIA, those with autistic disorder do not have significant delays in (1) language development, (2) cognitive development, or (3) the development of age-appropriate self-help or adaptive behavior skills (other than social interaction skills). The disorder is much more common in boys than girls and is rarely recognized before the age of 3.

The most obvious characteristic of Asperger's disorder is an impairment in social interaction. The individual appears to have an inability to understand or make use of the implicit rules that govern social behavior. As noted by Wing (1981), these rules are "unwritten and unstated, complex, constantly changing, and affect speech, gesture, posture, movement, eye contact, choice of clothing, proximity to others, and many other aspects of behavior" (p. 116). When communicating, these children present minimal facial expression and their vocal intonation tends to be monotonous and exaggerated. Correspondingly, children with Asperger's disorder have difficulty comprehending the communications of others

Case Study: Asperger's Disorder

In her clinical account of Asperger's disorder, Wing (1981) presented several case histories of individuals identified as having the disorder. The following is a reprint of a case history of a boy whose presenting behaviors were first noticed in early childhood.

B.H. is aged 10. He was delivered by forceps and had difficulty with breathing and cyanosis after birth, remaining in special care for 2 weeks. He was a large, placid baby who would lie without moving for long periods. He was not eager to use gestures, to clap or wave good-bye. His mother was worried about him from the beginning, partly because of the difficult birth and partly because of his behavior.

His parents were certain that he replied "Yes" appropriately to questions at 11 months. At around 14 months he began to speak in a fluent, but incomprehensible "language" of his own.

He made no effort to crawl, but one day, aged 17 months, he stood up and walked. He learned to crawl after this.

He retained his own language until aged 3 years, when he started to copy clearly the words he heard, and then went on to develop understandable speech. His comprehension of language has always lagged behind his expression. By the age of 4 he could read. His parents said they did not teach him—he presumably learned from the television. At the age of 5 he had a reading age of 9 years, but his comprehension was poor.

In his early years, B. remained quiet and passive, showing little emotion of any kind. He seemed to prefer a regular routine, but did not react at all to changes. He was not demanding and gave no trouble.

B. did not develop imaginative pretend play at the usual age. At the age of about 6 years he became fascinated with means of transport, read all about them and learned all the technical terms. He enacts actions involving cars, airplanes, and so on, but never with other children.

He appears clumsy and ill-coordinated, has problems with buttons and laces, and is afraid of climbing.

B. attends a special school. When first admitted he ignored the other children and carried on with his usual preoccupations. He appeared astounded when the teacher indicated that he should obey her instructions and follow the rest of the class. Gradually he began to fit in and to make active social approaches, though in a naive and inappropriate fashion. He has difficulty in following the rules of any game.

He speaks in a pedantic style, in an account quite unlike that of his local environment. For example, he referred to a hole in his sock as "a temporary loss of knitting." Many of his phrases are, like this one, inappropriately adapted quotations from television or books.

B. is now aware of and sensitive to other people's criticism, but appears unable to learn the rules of social interaction.

When tested at age 7 years he had a word recognition age of 12 years, scored at his age level on performance tasks, but was well below this on tests needing recall and comprehension of language.

and often misinterpret or ignore the nonverbal signals projected by adults and peers. Finally, children with this disorder tend to have an absorbing and circumscribed interest or attachment to specific subject areas or possessions. There is often an inflexible adherence to nonfunctional routines or rituals, and there is an attempt to impose stereotyped routines and motor patterns across most aspects of life (Gillberg & Gillberg, 1989).

The course of Asperger's disorder is continuous and in a vast majority of cases, the duration is lifelong (APA, 1994). The disorder has a later onset than autistic disorder and is often recognized when the child enters school; it is then that the specific idiosyncracies of the disorder appear. Referral is often the result of school-related problems such as refusal, running away, temper outbursts, stealing, and mutism. As noted by Barker (1995), children with Asperger's syndrome tend to be a distinct group of children whose behaviors fall somewhere between that of children with autistic disorder and children without disabilities. Similar to children with autistic disorder, they (1) present stereotypic behaviors, (2) attempt to impose ritualistic patterns on their environment, and (3) lack perceptiveness in interpreting meaning in social situations. In contrast to children with autistic disorder, they do not present a general delay in language or cognitive development.

Childhood Degenerative Disorder

According to DSM-IV (APA, 1994) childhood degenerative disorder (sometimes referred to as Heller's syndrome or disintegrative psychosis), is a marked regression in multiple areas of functioning following a period of normal or near-normal development. Following age appropriate development in the areas of verbal and nonverbal communication, social relationships, play, and adaptive behavior for at least two years after birth, there is a significant loss of previously acquired skills. Abnormalities are observed in at least two of the three following areas: (1) qualitative impairments in social interaction defined as impairment in nonverbal behaviors, a failure to develop peer relationships, and a lack of social or emotional reciprocity; (2) qualitative impairments in communication as evidenced by a delay or lack of spoken language, an inability to sustain a conversation, stereotyped use of language, and a lack of varied imaginative play; and (3) restricted, repetitive, and stereotyped patterns of behavior, interests, and activities.

Childhood degenerative disorder is a very rare disorder that by definition can only be diagnosed if onset of symptoms are preceded by two years of normal development and prior to the age of 10. The loss of skills may be progressive, but functioning does stabilize after months of deterioration (Barker, 1995). Still the duration of the disorder is lifelong and social, behavioral, and social difficulties persist throughout the lifespan. Childhood degenerative disorder can be differentiated from autistic disorder in two key respects: The period of normal development is longer than is the case with autism, and the pattern of regression is different in that there is a loss of skills beyond the domains of communication and social relationships (Rutter & Schopler, 1992).

Pervasive Developmental Disorder Not Otherwise Specified

Pervasive developmental disorder not otherwise specified is a diagnostic category reserved for children who have a severe and pervasive impairment in the development of social interaction and communication skills but do not meet the criteria for a specific PDD or early-onset schizophrenia. The fact that DSM-IV (APA, 1994) specifies no diagnostic criteria for this category has raised concerns among a number of researchers (e.g., Klin, Mayes, Volkmar, & Cohen, 1995; Towbin, Dykens, Pearson, & Cohen, 1993) who claim that this "adds little more than a demarcation of uncharted territory of clinical complexity" (p. 87). These researchers also claim that many children typically included in this category do present a cluster of symptoms, and consequently, specific diagnostic criteria should be articulated under the category of "multiplex developmental disorder." The symptoms of this disorder, listed in Table 3.2, typically fall into three major categories: (1) regulation of affective state and anxiety is impaired, (2) consistently impaired social behavior, and (3) impaired cognitive processing.

Still, pervasive developmental disorder not otherwise specified can serve as a broad category that allows a diagnostician the leeway to make a determination of pervasive developmental disorder without being constrained by rigid diagnostic criteria. While occurrences are very rare, Knopf (1984) has reported and described two forms of possible pervasive developmental disorder not otherwise specified: symbiotic infantile psychosis and Blueberry syndrome.

TABLE 3.2 Multiplex Developmental Disorder

Multiplex developmental disorder is a serious, early-onset, and persistent disturbance affecting several major domains of functioning including the following three major areas:

1. Regulation of affective state and anxiety is impaired beyond that seen in children of comparable age, as exemplified by several of the following:
   - Intense generalized anxiety or tension.
   - Fears and phobias (often usual or peculiar).
   - Recurrent panic episodes or flooding with anxiety.
   - Episodes of behavioral disorganization punctuated by markedly immature or violent behaviors.
   - Significant and wide emotional variability with or without environmental precipitant.
   - Frequent idiosyncratic or bizarre anxiety reactions.

2. Consistently impaired social behavior/sensitivity, as exemplified by the following types of disturbances:
   - Social disinterest, detachment, avoidance, or withdrawal despite evident competence.
   - Severely impaired peer relationships.
   - Markedly disturbed attachments: high degrees of ambivalence to adults (especially parents/caretakers).
   - Profound limitations in the capacity for empathy or understanding others' affects accurately.

3. Impaired cognitive processing, as exemplified by some of the following difficulties:
   - Irrationality, sudden intrusions on normal thought process, or repetition of nonsense words, desultory thinking, blatantly illogical, bizarre ideas.
   - Confusion between reality and inner fantasy life.
   - Perplexity and easy confusability (trouble understanding social processes or keeping thoughts "straight").
   - Delusions including fantasies of omnipotence, paranoid preoccupations, overengagement with fantasy figures, and grandiose fantasies of special powers.
   - The syndrome appears during the first several years of life.
   - The child is not suffering from autism or schizophrenia.

Adapted from Klin et al., 1995.

Symbiotic infantile psychosis is a rare disorder in which a child displays intense anxiety and panic when faced with separation from the mother. The child clings to the mother and will tantrum at the mere threat of separation. Such a child rarely displays normative rates of exploratory behavior, self-guidance, or assertiveness. As the disturbance develops, secondary symptoms become evident. Because he or she lives a restricted life with limited experiences, the child is prone to withdrawal and disturbances in thinking. Ultimately, previously acquired adaptive skills such as eating, sleeping, and toileting regress to the point where the child resembles a child with autism.

According to Knopf, there are limited data on the etiology of the disorder, though several psychogenic or environmental hypotheses involving a "pathological mother" have been proposed. The pathological mother has been characterized as an overprotective, extremely jealous individual who prevents her child from breaking away from the traditional mother–infant relationship. Still, no data to support this "parent-at-fault" speculation have been reported.

The second pervasive developmental disorder not otherwise specified reported by Knopf is Blueberry syndrome. Blueberry syndrome, originally described by Levinson (1980), is a disorder characterized by the inability to speak, low frustration tolerance, and a violent reaction to any invasion of personal space. While mental retardation is present, it is regarded as a result of the language difficulties. Although no data regarding its cause have been reported, it is believed that the disorder is the result of a genetic mutation.

Early-Onset Schizophrenia

Early-onset schizophrenia is an umbrella term intended to reflect what has previously been referred to as childhood schizophrenia. Although DSM-IV (APA, 1994) does not employ a specific category for childhood schizophrenia, there is reason to believe that the appearance of schizophrenia at an early age presents a number of unique and critical issues (Werry, 1992). This rare disorder was once viewed as a profound disturbance in social relations and multiple oddities of behavior that developed between the ages of 30 months and 12 years. Instances of disturbed social relationships include asociality, lack of peer relationships, and excessive and inappropriate clinging, as well as little affective responsivity. Oddities of behavior have been characterized as sudden and excessive anxiety, inappropriate affect, resistance to change in the environment, bizarre motor responses, speech abnormalities, and excessive reactions to sensory stimuli. Still, making a diagnosis of early-onset schizophrenia is difficult because of the challenge in distinguishing between fantasy and delusion, and because children's limited verbal skills make it difficult for them to describe their subjective experiences (Barker, 1995).

It is generally conceded that there is no unitary definition, description, or set of characteristics for early-onset schizophrenia. However, when Werry (1979) and Wicks-Nelson and Israel (1984) organized the various clinical features of early-onset schizophrenia or childhood schizophrenia by investigator or research team (e.g., Bender, 1942, 1953, 1971; Bradley & Bowen, 1941; and Eggers, 1978), they found several primary characteristics that are common to most clinical descriptions, albeit marked heterogeneity in the descriptors used by the many researchers in the field.

The Primary Characteristics of Early-Onset Schizophrenia

The primary characteristics of early-onset schizophrenia fall into four major categories: (1) disorders in speech and language, (2) disorders of relationship, (3) disorders of emotion, and (4) delusional beliefs and hallucinations. These categories are particularly useful for educators in that they emphasize psychoeducational deficiencies in need of remediation.

Speech and Language Disorders

Like children with autism, children with early-onset schizophrenia commonly exhibit severe speech and language disorders. Mutism, a severe language disorder, is common. Children who do have some speech, do not always use it for the purpose of communication. Instead, they seem to have a private language that cannot be understood by others. These often bizarre vocalizations interfere with efforts to increase communication and result in the child's becoming even more removed from reality (Clarizio & McCoy, 1983). The language of these children is believed to be a verbal reflection of their inability to organize or integrate ideas into a logical pattern of thought. Their responses do not usually exceed short sentence, and often are just single words. Their oral expression is devoid of abstraction and rarely conveys a mood or emotion. In many instances, their facial and body gestures bear little relationship to the content of what they are saying, and sometimes they emphasize words and syllables that are not essential to the interpretation of the message (Goldfarb, Braunstein, & Lorgo, 1956). To the casual observer, the most striking feature of schizophrenic speech is the high pitch and rising inflection evident at the end of sentences, a quality often interpreted as uncertainty or confusion.

Relationship Disorders

Children with early-onset schizophrenia exhibit profound disturbances in forming interpersonal relationships. Like youngsters with autism, these children tend to be unresponsive to others in their immediate environment. Shaw and Lucas (1970) have reported that some mothers often complain that their child looks at them as if they not there and that they feel they cannot get close enough to show affection. In contrast, other children with early-onset schizophrenia get too close, physically attaching themselves to their parents in a symbiotic way. The clinging, however, is usually accompanied by an unexpressive facial expression and an absence of normal emotional bonding. Almost all children with early-onset schizophrenia display little interest in their external environment—other people or activities—and reveal an almost complete break with reality. Absorption in the self seems to take the place of interpersonal relationships (Knopf, 1984).

Emotion

Children with early-onset schizophrenia are frequently described as being in a state of intense anxiety. Shaw and Lucas (1970) have characterized these youngsters as being always on the edge of panic or rage. Unpredictable and violent mood shifts are common. It is not unusual for a child with early-onset schizophrenia to feel that their impulses and emotions are externally controlled and to suddenly shift from an extremely withdrawn state to an all-consuming and seemingly uncontrollable tantrum (Barker, 1995). These tantrums or outbreaks of rage are qualitatively different from topographically similar behaviors observed in other problem children in that they seem to lack purpose or direction. It is thought that the lack of perceptual stability and inability to control sensory input or thought in children with early-onset schizophrenia are major causes of their outbursts (Coleman, 1972). Thus, unreliable and disorganized interpretations of the environment lead to confusion, fear, and the appearance of anxiety.

Delusional Beliefs and Hallucinations

The delusions of children with early-onset schizophrenia may reflect feelings of persecution or the misguided belief that one's thoughts are being manipulated by an external force. When they occur, hallucinations are typically auditory and can consist of either singular or multiple voices that (1) repeat a child's thoughts out loud or (2) discuss, argue, or comment on the individual's behavior (Barker, 1995).

The Secondary Characteristics of Early-Onset Schizophrenia

In addition to the primary disturbances exhibited by youngsters with early-onset schizophrenia, there are several secondary characteristics that are particularly important to educators and clinicians. These characteristics are considered secondary because not all children with early-onset schizophrenia possess them, and of those who do, the severity of the problem varies from case to case.

In terms of *motility*, many children with early-onset schizophrenia have unusual body movements. Rather than walking in a normal fashion, they move from place to place in a manner ranging from a graceful whirling to a robotlike rigidity. Shaw and Lucas (1970) have reported that the touch of such children is light and delicate and that there is a certain fragility to their physical structure. When being held, it's as "if they would melt into the holder's body or evaporate into the air" (p. 115). The control of motor behavior is also problematic. Children with early-onset schizophrenia have deficient postural control as well as poor control of their facial muscles, a condition that often leads to facial grimaces and unusual vocal sounds. Problems with bladder and bowel control are not unusual, and bizarre body movements such as repetitive rocking and twitching are fairly common.

With regard to *measured intelligence*, anywhere from one-third to one-half of all children with early-onset schizophrenia have an IQ below 80 (Knopf, 1984). Nonetheless, the pattern of performance on such tests tends to be inconsistent. It is not unusual for children with early-onset schizophrenia to answer difficult questions correctly, while failing to respond to easier items. In terms of actual *classroom performance*, children with early-onset schizophrenia often appear similar to children with mental retardation. Because they lack perceptual stability and are unable to control and interpret sensory input, their attention, concentration, and learning efficiency are diminished. True, some students with early-onset schizophrenia do possess standardized achievement levels commensurate to their chronological ages, but their test performance is not usually reflective of their classroom behavior. While a few of these youngsters may perform classroom activities with little difficulty, none use their acquired academic skills for purposeful activities. In sum, even children with early-onset schizophrenia who have learned academic skills fail to make use of those skills and rarely display their knowledge in the classroom (Clarizio & McCoy, 1983).

Etiology

The cause or causes of early-onset schizophrenia are not fully understood. While much has been written on the etiology of this puzzling disorder, it is important to keep in mind that this material is, at best, highly speculative. As with autism, the possible causes of early-onset schizophrenia reflect often-incompatible conceptual models. Here again, we will organize the various etiological speculations into the traditional categories of nature and nurture.

Nature-Based Explanations

The current consensus of opinion is that the causes of schizophrenia are biologically based (Barker, 1995). As with adult-onset schizophrenia, genetics has been proposed as a possible cause of early-onset schizophrenia. In general, the closer the biological relationship to a known schizophrenic, the greater the possibility of developing schizophrenia. The rate of occurrence of schizophrenia for a child with one schizophrenic parent ranges from 12 to 16 percent; the two-parent rate is 39 to 68 percent (Erlenmeyer-Kimling, 1968; Kety, 1978). The incidence for the general population is 1 percent. More compelling evidence of genetic involvement in schizophrenia centers upon studies (e.g., Kallmann & Roth, 1956) comparing monozygotic and dizygotic twins. In a review of several such studies, Buss (1966) found that concordance rates for monozygotic or identical twins ranged from 38 to 88.2 percent, while rates of dizygotic or fraternal twins ranged from 10 to 22.9 percent. This discrepancy strongly indicates some type of genetic involvement. Still, there have been cases in which discordance between identical twins (i.e., only one twin was diagnosed as schizophrenic) has been reported (Sagor, 1974), which indicates that the genetic influence on schizophrenia is one of risk or predisposition rather than certainty.

Caution must be exercised when applying the above data to early-onset schizophrenia because almost all of the studies focused on adult schizophrenics and thus may not be directly relevant to the disorders of childhood. If, however, there is a link between early-onset schizophrenia and adult schizophrenia, we can conclude that there is probably an inherited component to childhood schizophrenia.

Organic factors involving the central nervous system (CNS) have also been considered as a cause of early-onset schizophrenia. As with autism, Ornitz and Ritvo (1968) have speculated that a deficient CNS causes a lack of perceptual consistency that makes it impossible for the child to reliably interpret the environment. Perceptual distortions resulting from an unreliable interpretation of the environment evolve into a state of confusion in which past experiences cannot be integrated with present events—in effect, meaning cannot be derived from experience. Other evidence of CNS disturbance has also been reported, including hard neurological signs (e.g., abnormal EEG, epilepsy) and impaired levels of arousal (Gittelman & Birch, 1967; Mednick & McNeil, 1968).

Nurture-Based Explanations

Nurture or environmentally based etiological theories have stressed abnormal family interactions, severe early trauma, and our "sick" society as possible causes of early-onset schizophrenia.

In terms of possible family influences, a significant amount of work has documented the personological variables of the parents of children with early-onset schizophrenia. While some studies (e.g., Goldfarb, Spitzer, & Endicott, 1976; Kaufman et al., 1960) have reported that parents themselves exhibit schizophrenic patterns of behavior, it is generally believed that parents do not engage in practices, or possess attitudes or traits, that cause their child's condition (Knopf, 1984). Most inappropriate parental attitudes and behavior can be regarded as responses to the child's bizarre behaviors.

Some theorists have hypothesized that severe early trauma, ranging from perinatal difficulties (Mednick, 1970) to the early death of a parent, causes early-onset schizophrenia, but, obviously, few difficult pregnancies, births, or untimely deaths of parents result in the schizophrenic behavior of children. Similarly, countertheorists (e.g., Laing & Esterson, 1970) have attempted to explain schizophrenic behavior as a meaningful response to our less-than-perfect society. Again, this view is deficient in that only a small number of individuals suffer these severe side effects of adapting to our world.

The Course and Prognosis for Early-Onset Schizophrenia

The prognosis for children with early-onset schizophrenia is believed to be chronic (Barker, 1995; Werry, 1979). Early studies (e.g., Bender, 1953), while being suspect because of childhood schizophrenia–autism diagnostic confusion, have reported that (1) approximately one-third of children with schizophrenia achieve some degree of adequate adjustment; (2) one-third remain poorly adjusted, yet are serviced in community-based facilities; and (3) the remaining third require institutionalization. More recently, Eggers (1978), employing a more rigorous definition of childhood schizophrenia (i.e., age of onset about 7 years), found that approximately 50 percent displayed improvement of some kind, with several being fully recovered. Approximately 33 percent had very poor levels of functioning and the remainder were in the fair-to-poor-outcome categories. Predictors of a good outcome were above-average intelligence, onset of the disorder after the age of 10, and the presence of appropriate adaptive behavior (e.g., kindness, friendship, outside interests) before the appearance of the disorder.

Summary

In our chapter on low-incidence behavior problems we began by exploring the early perspectives on these challenging patterns of behavior. Historically, autism and childhood schizophrenia were believed to be examples of psychotic behavior. Currently, autism is viewed as a pervasive developmental disorder (PDD). Following this historical review, we described the characteristics and etiologies of autism, Asperger's disorder, childhood degenerative disorder, pervasive developmental disorder not otherwise specified, and early-onset schizophrenia. In terms of autism, the universal and specific characteristics—failure to develop social relationships, failure to develop communicative language, and ritualistic or compulsive behavior—were discussed at length; this was followed by a brief discussion of prevalence, behavioral correlates, and the course of the disorder. The causes of autism were discussed in terms of nature, nurture, and interaction-based explanations. We concluded the section on the developmental disorders by examining the defining characteristics and features of the other PDDs.

We examined early-onset schizophrenia in terms of its primary and secondary characteristics. Primary characteristics included speech and language deficits, disorders of relationship, and disorders of emotion, and delusional beliefs and hallucinations. Secondary characteristics involved the areas of motility, intelligence, and classroom performance. As with autism, etiology was organized according to nature- and nurture-based explanations. This was followed by a generic discussion of the course and prognosis of early-onset schizophrenia. Although the prognosis for children with PDD and early-onset schizophrenia is generally bleak, appropriate treatment interventions can influence the course of the disorder.

Discussion Questions

1. What is meant by the term low-incidence behavior problems?
2. Trace the history of the study of low-incidence behavior problems in children and youth.
3. Identify major sources of diagnostic confusion in relation to autism.
4. Describe the three characteristics that are universal and specific to autism. What is the impact of each on the child and the family?
5. Discuss the prevalence estimates of autism.
6. Discuss the behavioral correlates of autism that are of particular interest to educators.
7. Compare and contrast nature- and nurture-based explanations of autism.

8. What are the behavioral characteristics of high-functioning individuals with autism?

9. What are the defining characteristics of Asperger's disorder and childhood degenerative disorder? How are they similar to and different from autism?

10. Describe the primary and secondary characteristics of early-onset schizophrenia.

11. Identify possible causes of early-onset schizophrenia.

12. What are the differences between the PDDs and early-onset schizophrenia?

References

3Y C.F.R. Section 300.7 (b) (1) 1992. Assistance to States for the Education of Children with Disabilities Program and Preschool Grants for Children with Disabilities.

Alpern, G. D. (1967). Measurement of "untestable" autistic children. *Journal of Abnormal Psychology, 72*, 478–496.

American Psychiatric Association. (1994). *Diagnostic and statistical manual of mental disorders (DSM-IV)*. Washington, DC: APA.

American Psychiatric Association. (1987). *Diagnostic and statistical manual of mental disorders (DSM-III-R)*. Washington, DC: APA.

American Psychiatric Association. (1980). *Diagnostic and statistical manual of mental disorders (DSM-III)*. Washington, DC: APA.

Barker, P. (1995). *Basic child psychiatry*. Cambridge, MA: Blackwell Science.

Bartak, L. (1978). Educational approaches. In M. Rutter & E. Schloper (Eds.), *Autism: A reappraisal of concepts and treatment* (pp. 423–438). New York: Plenum.

Bender, L. (1942). Schizophrenia in childhood. *The Nervous Child, 1*, 138–140.

Bender, L. (1953). Childhood schizophrenia. *Psychiatric Quarterly, 27*, 663–681.

Bender, L. (1971). Alpha and omega of childhood schizophrenia. *Journal of Autism and Childhood Schizophrenia, 1*, 115–118.

Bettelheim, B. (1967). *The empty fortress*. New York: The Free Press.

Bootzin, R. R. (1980). *Abnonnal psychology: Current perspectives*. New York: Random House.

Bradley, C., & Bowen, M. (1941). Behavior characteristics of schizophrenic children. *Psychiatric Quarterly, 15*, 298–315.

Buss, A. H. (1966). *Psychopathology*. New York: Wiley.

Cammisa, K. (1993). Etiology of autism: A review of recent biogenic theories and research. *Occupational Therapy in Mental Health, 12*, 39–67.

Cantwell, D. P., Baker, L., & Rutter, M. (1978). Family factors. In M. Rutter & E. Schloper (Eds.), *Autism: A reappraisal of concepts and treatment* (pp. 269–296). New York: Plenum.

Cataldo, M. F., & Harris, J. (1982). The biological basis for self-injury in the mentally retarded. *Analysis and Intervention in Developmental Disabilities, 2*, 21–40.

Clarizio, H. F., & McCoy, G. F. (1983). *Behavior disorders in children*, 3rd ed. New York: Harper & Row.

Coleman, J. (1972). *Abnormal psychology and modern life*. Glenview, IL: Scott Foresman.

Cox, A., Rutter, M., Newman, S., & Bartak, L. A. (1975). A comparative study of infantile autism and specific developmental receptive language disorder. II: Parental characteristics. *British Journal of Psychiatry, 126*, 146–159.

DeLong & G. R. (1978). A neuropsychologic interpretation of infantile autism. In M. Rutter & E. Schloper (Eds.), *Autism: A reappraisal of concepts and treatment* (pp. 207–228). New York: Plenum.

DeMyer, M. K., Barton, S., Alpern, G. D., Kimberlin, C., Allen, J., Yang, E., & Steele, R. (1974). The measured intelligence of autistic children. *Journal of Autism and Childhood Schizophrenia, 4*, 42–60.

Egel, A., Koegel, R. L., & Schreibman, L. (1980). A review of educational treatment procedures for autistic children. In L. Mann & D. Sabatino

(Eds.), *Fourth Review of Special Education* (pp. 109–149). New York: Grune & Stratton.

Eggers, C. (1978). Course and prognosis of childhood schizophrenia. *Journal of Autism and Childhood Schizophrenia, 8,* 21–36.

Eisenberg, L. (1956). The autistic child in adolescence. *American Journal of Psychiatry, 112,* 607–612.

Erlenmeyer-Kimling, L. (1968). Studies of the offspring of two schizophrenic parents. In D. Rosenthal & S. S. Kety (Eds.), *The transmission of schizophrenia.* New York: Pergamon.

Ferster, C. B. (1961). Positive reinforcement and behavioral deficits of autistic children. *Child Development, 32,* 437–456.

Frankel, F., & Simmons, J. Q. (1976). Self-injurious behavior in schizophrenic and retarded children. *American Journal of Mental Deficiency, 80,* 512–522.

Gillberg, C., & Gillberg, C. (1989). Asperger syndrome: Some epidemiological considerations: A research note. *Journal of Child Psychology and Psychiatry and Allied Disciplines, 30,* 631–688.

Gittelman, M., & Birch, G. (1967). Childhood schizophrenia, intellect, neurologic status, perinatal risk, prognosis, and family pathology. *Archives of General Psychiatry, 17,* 16–25.

Goldfarb, W., Braunstein, P., & Lorgo, I. (1956). A study of speech patterns in a group of schizophrenic children. *American Journal of Orthopsychiatry, 26,* 544–545.

Goldfarb, W., Spitzer, R. L., & Endicott, J. (1976). A study of psychopathology of parents of psychotic children by structured interview. *Journal of Autism and Childhood Schizophrenia, 6,* 327–338.

Hermelin, B., & O'Connor, N. (1971). Spatial coding in normal, autistic, and blind children. *Perceptual Motor Skills, 33,* 127–132.

Hinerman, P. S. (1983). *Teaching autistic children to communicate.* Rockville, MD: Aspen.

Iwata, B., Pace, G. M., Kalsher, M. J., Cowdery, G. E., & Cataldo, M. F. (1990). Experimental analysis and extinction of self-injurious escape behavior. *Journal of Applied Behavior Analysis, 23,* 11–27.

Kallmann, F. J., & Roth, B. (1956). Genetic aspects of preadolescent schizophrenia. *American Journal of Psychiatry, 112,* 599–606.

Kanner, L. (1943). Autistic disturbances of affective contact. *The Nervous Child, 2,* 217–250.

Kanner, L. (1954). To what extent is early infantile autism determined by constitutional inadequacies? *Proceedings of the Association for Research on Nervous and Mental Diseases, 33,* 378–385.

Kanner, L. (1971). Childhood psychosis: A historical overview. *Journal of Autism and Childhood Schizophrenia, 1,* 14–19.

Kaufman, I., Frank, I., Herms, L., Herrick, J., Reiser, D., & Willer, L. (1960). Treatment implications of a new classification of parents of schizophrenic children. *American Journal of Psychiatry, 116,* 920–924.

Kauffman, J. M. (1981). *Characteristics of children's behavior disorders,* 2nd ed. Columbus, OH: Merrill.

Kauffman, J. M. (1985). *Characteristics of children's behavior disorders,* 3rd ed. Columbus, OH: Merrill.

Kety, S. S. (1978). Genetic and biochemical aspects of schizophrenia. In A. M. Nichol (Ed.), *The Harvard guide to modern psychiatry.* Cambridge, MA: Harvard University Press.

Klin, A., Mayes, L. C., Volkmar, F. R., & Cohen, D. J. (1995). Multiplex development disorder. *Journal of Developmental and Behavioral Pediatrics, 16* (3), S7–S11.

Knopf, I. J. (1984). *Childhood psychopathology: A developmental approach,* 2nd ed. Englewood Cliffs, NJ: Prentice-Hall.

Koegel, R. L., Koegel, L. K., & Surratt, A. (1992). Language intervention and disruptive behavior in preschool children with autism. *Journal of Autism and Developmental Disorders, 22* (2), 141–153.

Koegel, R. L., Rincover, A., & Egel, A. L. (1982). *Educating and understanding autistic children.* San Diego, CA: College-Hill Press.

Kolvin, I. (1971). Studies in the childhood psychoses. I: Diagnostic criteria and classification. *British Journal of Psychiatry, 118,* 381–384.

Kolvin, I., Ounsted, C., & Roth, M. (1971). Studies in the childhood psychoses. V: Cerebral dysfunction and childhood psychoses. *British Journal of Psychiatry, 118,* 407–414.

Kurita, H. (1985). Infantile autism with speech loss before the age of thirty months. *Journal of the*

American Academy of Child Psychiatry, 24, 191–196.

Laing, R. D., Esterson, A. (1970). *Sanity, madness, and the family*. Middlesex, England: Penguin.

Lerman, D. C., & Iwata, B. A. (1993). Descriptive and experimental analyses of variables maintaining self-injurious behavior. *Journal of Applied Behavior Analysis, 26* (3), 293–319.

Levinson, B. M. (1980). The Blueberry syndrome. *Psychological Reports, 46*, 47–52.

Lord, C., & Schopler, E. (1989). Stability of assessment results of autistic and nonautistic language impaired children from preschool years to early school age. *Journal of Child Psychology and Psychiatry and Allied Disciplines, 30*, 575–590.

Lotter, V. (1967). Epidemiology of autistic conditions in young children. II: Some characteristics of the parents and children. *Social Psychology, 1*, 163–173.

Lotter, V. (1978). Follow-up studies. In M. Rutter & E. Schopler (Eds.), *Autism: A reappraisal of concepts and treatment* (pp. 475–596). New York: Plenum.

Lowe, L. H. (1966). Families of children with early childhood schizophrenia. *Archives of General Psychiatry, 14*, 26–30.

Mednick, S. A. (1970). Breakdown in individuals at high risk for schizophrenia: Possible predispositional factors. *Mental Hygiene, 54*, 50–63.

Mednick, S., & McNeil, T. (1968). Current methodology in research on the etiology of schizophrenia. *Psychological Bulletin, 70*, 681–693.

Mirenda, P. L., Donnellan, A. M., & Yoder, D. E. (1983). Gaze behavior: A new look at an old behavior. *Journal of Autism and Developmental Disorders, 13*, 397–409.

Morgan, S. B. (1986). Early childhood autism: Changing perspectives. *Journal of Child and Adolescent Psychotherapy, 3*, 3–9.

Myles, B. S., Simpson, R. L., & Becker, J. (1994–95). An analysis of characteristics of students diagnosed with higher-functioning autistic disorder. *Exceptionality, 5* (1), 19–30.

O'Connor, N., & Hermelin, B. (1973). The spatial or temporal organization of short-term memory. *Quarterly Journal of Experimental Psychology, 25*, 335.

Ornitz, E. M., & Ritvo, E. R. (1968). Neurophysiological mechanisms underlying perceptual inconsistency in autistic and schizophrenic children. *American Journal of Psychiatry, 19*, 22–27.

Paluszny, M. J. (1979). *Autism. A practical guide for parents and professionals*. Syracuse, NY: Syracuse University Press.

Phelps, L., & Grabowski, J. (1991). Autism: Etiology, differential diagnosis, and behavioral assessment update. *Journal of Psychopathology and Behavioral Assessment, 13* (2), 107–125.

Pierce, S., & Bartolucci, G. (1977). A syntactic investigation of verbal autistic, mentally retarded, and normal children. *Journal of Autism and Childhood Schizophrenia, 7*, 121–134.

Potter, H. (1933). Schizophrenia in children. *American Journal of Psychiatry, 12*, 1253–1268.

Rimland, B. (1964). *Infantile autism*. New York: Appleton-Century-Crofts.

Ritvo, E. R., Freeman, B. J., Pingree, M. S., Mason-Brothers, A., Jorde, L., Jenson, W. R., McMahon, W. M., Peterson, P. B., Mo, A., & Ritvo, A. (1989). The UCLA-University of Utah epidemiologic survey of autism: Prevalence. *American Journal of Psychiatry, 146* (2), 194–199.

Ritvo, E. R., Rabin, K., Yuwiler, A., Freeman, B. J., & Geller, E. (1978). Biochemical and hematologic studies: A critical review. In M. Rutter & E. Schopler (Eds.), *Autism: A reappraisal of concepts and treatment* (pp. 163–184). New York: Plenum.

Ross, A. O. (1980). *Psychological disorders of children: A behavioral approach to theory, research, and therapy*. New York: McGraw-Hill.

Rumsey, J. M., & Denckla, M. B. (1987). Neurobiological research priorities in autism. In E. Schopler & G. B. Mesibov (Eds.), *Neurobiological issues in autism* (pp. 43–62). New York: Plenum.

Rumsey, J. M., & Hamburger, A. D. (1988). Neuropsychological findings in high-functioning men with infantile autism, residual state. *Journal of Clinical and Experimental Neurology, 10*, 201–210.

Rutter, M. (1978a). Diagnosis and definition. In M. Rutter & E. Schopler (Eds.), *Autism: A reappraisal of concepts and treatment* (pp. 1–26). New York: Plenum.

Rutter, M. (1978b). Developmental issues and prognosis. In M. Rutter & E. Schopler (Eds.), *Autism: A reappraisal of concepts and treatment* (pp. 497–506). New York: Plenum.

Rutter, M., & Bartak, L. (1971). Causes of infantile autism: Some considerations from recent research. *Journal of Autism and Childhood Schizophrenia, 1,* 20–32.

Rutter, M., & Bartak, L. (1973). Special educational treatments of autistic children: A comparative study. 11: Follow-up findings and implications for services. *Journal of Child Psychology and Psychiatry, 14,* 241–270.

Rutter, M., & Schopler, E. (1992). Classification of pervasive developmental disorders: Some concepts and practical considerations. *Journal of Autism and Developmental Disorders, 22* (4), 459–482.

Samuels, S. C. (1981). *Disturbed exceptional children: An integrated approach.* New York: Human Science Press.

Schloper, E. (1983). New developments in the definition and diagnosis of autism. In B. B. Lahey & A. E. Kazdin (Eds.), *Advances in clinical child psychology.* Vol. 6 (pp. 93–127). New York: Plenum.

Schopler, E., & Mesibov, G. B. (1987). *Neurobiological issues in autism.* New York: Plenum.

Schroeder, S. R., Schroeder, C. S., Smith, B., & Dalldorf, J. (1978). Prevalence of self-injurious behaviors in a large state facility for the retarded: A three year follow-up. *Journal of Autism and Childhood Schizophrenia, 8,* 261–270.

Shaw, C. R., & Lucas, A. R. (1970). *The psychiatric disorders of childhood.* New York: Appleton-Century-Crofts.

Sigman, M., & Ungere, J. A. (1984). Attachment behaviors in autistic children. *Journal of Autism and Developmental Disorders, 14,* 231–244.

Sparrow, S., & Cicchetti, D. V. (1985). Diagnostic uses of the Vineland Adaptive Behavior Scales. *Journal of Pediatric Psychology, 10,* 215–225.

Symons, F. J. (1995). Self-injurious behavior: A brief review of theories and current treatment perspectives. *Developmental Disabilities Bulletin, 23,* 91–104.

Szatmari, P., Bartolucci, G., Bremner, R. S., Bond, S., & Rich, S. (1989). A follow-up study of high functioning autistic children. *Journal of Autism and Developmental Disorders, 19,* 213–226.

Tager-Flusberg, H. (1981). On the nature of linguistic functioning in early infantile autism. *Journal of Autism and Developmental Disorders, 11,* 45–56.

Towbin, K. E., Dykens, E. M., Pearson, G. S., & Cohen, D. J. (1993). Conceptualizing borderline syndrome of childhood and childhood schizophrenia as a developmental disorder. *American Academy of Child and Adolescent Psychiatry, 32* (4), 775–782.

Treffert, D. (1970). Epidemiology of infantile autism. *Archives of General Psychiatry, 22,* 431–438.

Tsai, L. Y., & Stewart, M. A. (1982). Handedness and EEG correlation in autistic children. *Biological Psychiatry, 17,* 595–598.

Tsai, L. Y., Stewart, M. A. & August, G. (1981). Implications of sex differences in the familial transmission of infantile autism. *Journal of Autism and Developmental Disorders, 11,* 165–173.

Venter, A., Lord, C., & Schopler, E. (1992). A follow-up study of high functioning autistic children. *Journal of Child Psychology and Psychiatry and Applied Disciplines, 33* (3), 489–507.

Waterhouse, L., Wing, L., Spitzer, R., & Siegel, B. (1992). Pervasive developmental disorders: From DSM-III to DSM-III-R. *Journal of Autism and Developmental Disorders, 22* (4), 525–549.

Werry, J. S. (1979). The childhood psychoses. In H. C. Quay & J. S. Werry (Eds.), *Psychopathological disorders of childhood* (pp. 43–89). New York: Wiley.

Werry, J. S. (1992). Child and adolescent (early onset) schizophrenia: A review in light of DSM-III-R *Journal of Autism and Developmental Disorders, 22* (4), 601–624.

Wicks-Nelson, R., & Israel, A. C. (1984). *Behavior disorders of childhood.* Englewood Cliffs, NJ: Prentice-Hall.

Wing, L. (1969). The handicaps of autistic children: A comparative study. *Journal of Child Psychology and Psychiatry, 10,* 1 4D.

Wing, L. (1981). Asperger's syndrome: A clinical account. *Psychological Medicine, 11,* 115–129.

Wolf-Schein, E. (1993). Assessing the "untestable" client: ADLO. *Developmental Disabilities Bulletin, 21,* 52–70.

Yirmiya, N. (1991). High functioning individuals with autism: Diagnosis, empirical findings, and theoretical issues. *Clinical Psychology Review, 11,* 669–683.

Chapter 4

Standardized Instruments for Assessment and Classification

Advance Organizer

As you read this chapter, prepare to identify and discuss:

- The purpose of assessment and the controversy about classification of students with disordered behavior.
- Premises and limitations of clinically derived classification systems.
- Advantages and disadvantages of statistically derived classification systems.
- The major theoretical perspectives for identifying and classifying disordered behavior.
- Methods used to screen students for behavioral disorders.
- Methods used to identify students with behavioral disorders for placement and to determine their diagnostic category.
- Instruments commonly used in the identification process of behavioral disorders.
- Important considerations for interpreting assessment outcomes.

Most educators are familiar with the process schools use to identify and classify children as exceptional. Typically, a referral is made by teachers or parents to an individual (e.g., a counselor or school psychologist) or a small group of specialists (e.g., child study team) when a student is experiencing academic and/or behavioral difficulties (Walker, 1987). These specialists collect assessment information regarding the child's problem through diagnostic interviews, behavior rating scales, standardized tests, and perhaps direct observations in instructional and free play settings. Then team meetings are held to determine (1) the student's eligibility for special services (i.e., eligibility decision), (2) the nature of the disabling condition (i.e., exceptionality decision), and (3) instructional implications (i.e., special learning needs decisions) (Salvia & Ysseldyke, 1991; Ysseldyke & Algozzine, 1995). If a student is deemed eligible for special education services, an individualized educational plan must be developed.

Recently, many school systems have inserted another step into their traditional referral-to-placement process (Carter & Sugai, 1989; Hardiman, Drew, & Egan, 1996; Waldon, 1996). This step, often called *prereferral intervention*, is designed to remediate students' difficulties by making changes in existing instructional practices. If the problems are ameliorated through such modifications, then no additional assessment is necessary. But if the problems persist, further evaluation is warranted (Heller, Holtzman, & Messick, 1982; Maheady, Algozzine, & Ysseldyke, 1984).

Although the assessment process just described has become rather commonplace in schools, it is not often clear that educators truly understand what is going on during this process, why it is important, and how it can affect their own teaching practice. Specifically, there appears to be considerable ambiguity among educators surrounding (1) the basic purposes and/or goals of assessment, (2) the procedures used for collecting assessment information (particularly standardized tests), and (3) the meaning and usefulness of assessment outcomes. As a result, assessment information is often underutilized or used in a less than optimal manner when important educational decisions are being made (Walker, 1995).

In this chapter, we will try to clarify some of the ambiguities that surround the assessment process. First, we will examine the major purposes for collecting assessment information. We will argue that while assessment data can be collected for many different purposes, it is essential that the type of information collected be related *directly* to the type of question or problem being addressed. Next, we discuss in more detail one particular purpose of assessment—the identification and classification of disordered behavior—describe two major approaches to classification (clinical and statistical), and discuss the relevant strengths and weaknesses of each. Third, we will review some general procedures used for identifying and classifying behavior disorders, focusing particularly on standardized assessment measures. In addition, we will describe a few diagnostic instruments for identifying *specific* behavioral patterns such as hyperactivity, aggression, social withdrawal, and chronic rule violation. Finally, we will examine the meaningfulness and utility of assessment outcomes, in particular, what specific assessment information means and how it might assist practitioners in instructional programming for youths with behavioral disorders.

Purposes of Assessment

Salvia and Ysseldyke (1991) have defined assessment as a process of collecting information for the purpose of making educational decisions. They have suggested further that there are at least five distinct decisions that educators must routinely make concerning children with learning/behavior problems. First, they must collect assessment information for making *screening* decisions. That is, school personnel often administer standardized tests, usually to large groups, in order to identify those students who may be "at risk" of encountering academic and/or behavioral difficulties. Identified deficits might include physical limitations (e.g., poor visual acuity, hearing loss, or motor impairment) or acquired learning problems. The intent here is to detect problems that are not immediately obvious and to provide assistance as soon as possible in order to prevent subsequent learning difficulties.

The second major purpose of assessment is to identify those students who deviate significantly enough from the norm to qualify for special education services and to assign them a distinctive, diagnostic classification (e.g., learning disabled, behavior disordered, educable mentally retarded). Essentially, this is a two-step process: Students are first deemed eligible, and then they are classified (Ysseldyke & Thurlow, 1984). Eligibility decisions can only be made by *comparing* a child's performance against that of a *similar* sample of peers. Thus, standardized norm-referenced measures are used routinely in such decision-making.

The third reason educators collect assessment information is to develop instructional programs for students with learning/behavioral problems. Typically, this process involves determining "what" specific skills must be taught and "how" such instruction should be provided (Zigmond & Miller, 1986). It is important to point out that instructional planning decisions do not necessarily require the use of norm-referenced tests. On the contrary, instructional decision-making is often based upon students' performance on informal and curriculum-specific measures (Hoy & Gregg, 1994; Ysseldyke & Algozzine, 1995).

The fourth major purpose of assessment is to measure pupil progress. Providing special services to failing students is not enough. Educators must also demonstrate that students are making sufficient progress as a result of their involvement with such services. In this sense, assessment information that leads to and documents substantial pupil progress essentially validates its usefulness for instructional decision-making (Gersten, Keating, & Irvin, 1995).

Finally, educators collect assessment information in order to evaluate program effectiveness. The intent here is to demonstrate if a particular type of setting (e.g., resource room or self-contained classroom), instructional approach (e.g., linguistic readers or process writing), and/or specific classroom intervention (e.g., time-out or response cost) is effective with a select group of students. Systematic program evaluation is required for most programs that receive state and federal funding.

Although educators should be aware of the many purposes for conducting an assessment and the multiple evaluation options at their disposal, it is even more important that they understand *when* a particular assessment strategy should be used. Witt, Elliot, Gresham, and Kramer (1988) suggested that assessment decisions be driven by the need to answer a specific question or solve a particular problem involving students. That is, assessment procedures should be dictated by what the referring agent wants to know. Different "assessment audiences" typically want to know different kinds of things from student assessments (Waldon, 1996). For example, a parent or guidance counselor may want to know if a child is performing above or below average grade expectations; therefore, some type of standardized norm-referenced comparison must be made. On the other hand, a general education teacher may simply want to know how to improve a particular student's behavior in school or at home. Thus, direct observations within the troublesome situation, along with some environmental modifications, would be the more appropriate assessment approach.

Unfortunately, existing assessment practice does not always reflect such conventional wisdom. As Salvia and Ysseldyke (1991) have pointed out, quite often standardized batteries of tests (e.g., intelligence, achievement, perceptual–motor, and personality scales) are administered regardless of why particular children are referred. Pupils who are referred for behavioral difficulties are often given the same test battery as other students experiencing specific academic problems. Similarly, pupil progress and program evaluation decisions are often made using standardized tests administered on a pre-/post-test basis (i.e., summative evaluation), when it would be more appropriate to use curriculum-specific measures that are administered repeatedly over time (i.e., formative evaluation) (Deno, 1985; Deno & Mirkin, 1977; Fuchs, Fuchs, Hamlett, & Stecker, 1991; Tindal, 1985). Finally, teachers often refer students to obtain useful suggestions for improving academic or behavioral performance, even though there are ample data indicating that traditional norm-referenced testing yields few relevant instructional recommendations (e.g., Chistenson, Ysseldyke, & Algozzine, 1982; Thurlow & Ysseldyke, 1982). The problem in these situations is a fundamental mismatch between assessment purpose and method. Until this discrepancy is resolved, most participants in the traditional referral-to-placement process will be frustrated by a seemingly unresponsive assessment system.

Having established that assessment should be problem-driven and that specific evaluation methods must be differentiated according to one's purpose, we now turn our attention to one particular purpose of assesssment: the identification and classification of disordered behavior.

Identification and Classification of Disordered Behavior

Ysseldyke and Algozzine (1995) noted that a report from the National Commission on Testing and Public Policy (1990), indicates that America's 44 million school-aged children take approximately 127 million separate tests each year as part of standardized test batteries mandated by states and school districts. An additional 125 million tests are given to these pupils annually above and beyond district or state mandates, often as part of existing psychoeducational assessment procedures. The result is that America's school children take more tests than any other youngsters in the world (Ysseldyke & Algozzine, 1995). Given the extensiveness of such assessment practice and the fact that it has become a routine part of most educational systems, one may ask why so much time and effort has been spent testing children and trying to classify them as disabled. A number of reasons have been advanced.

Perhaps the major reason so many children are classified is because state and federal laws require that students be deemed eligible (classified) *before* they can receive special education services. Such legal mandates have promoted a norm-referenced assessment approach that rests upon two assumptions: (1) that overt behavioral problems are only "symptomatic" of underlying causes, and (2) that the "real" cause of children's learning/behavior problems must be identified *before* an effective form of treatment can be provided (Sarason & Doris, 1979; Thurlow & Ysseldyke, 1982). According to such theorizing, children cannot be helped until their "true" disability is identified. Quay (1986) suggested that classifications may serve a second important function—to enhance our scientific understanding. He argued that if our ultimate goal is to describe precisely those functional relationships that exist between entities (e.g., disabilities), we must be able to set apart such entities from one another and describe their properties in terms of observable phenomena. In special education, such entities must be understood in terms of their causes (etiologies), their responsiveness to different types of treatment, and their progress (Quay, 1986).

Blashfield (1984) noted a third important function of classification: Classification systems provide a nomenclature, a basic set of terms, that facilitate communication among people working in the field. Fourth, classification may also improve our ability to make predictions about disabled children (Blashfield, 1984). For example, if we know that a child has a particular disorder, then we should be able to predict other concomitant behavioral features, perhaps as yet unobserved, as well as preferred forms of treatment. Finally, classification appears to serve a useful administrative function (Blackhurst, Bott, & Cross, 1987). Funding decisions, third-party payments, and prevalence estimates are often made on the basis of individuals' diagnostic classifications. Children cannot obtain special services until they are declared eligible by a multidisciplinary assessment team. Therefore, diagnostic classification is often the key to a child's access to special services.

Still, not all educators agree that is is either possible or useful to classify disorders (see e.g., Arter & Jenkins, 1979; Duncan, Forness, & Hartsough, 1995; Galagan, 1985; Glass, 1983; Heller et al., 1982; Kavale & Mattson, 1980; Reynolds & Lakin, 1987; Thurlow & Ysseldyke, 1982; Winikur & Wohle, 1984). Some critics argue that the complex and ever-changing nature of human behavior, particularly among children, as well as the crude state of existing evaluation tools, precludes the accurate identification and classification of distinct disorders. Others cite ambiguities in diagnostic categories themselves, especially learning disabilities and behavior disorders, that impede accurate, reliable, and differential diagnoses. Still others charge that the primary function of schools and other health-related professions is *not* to classify, sort, and make predictions about individuals, but rather to educate and treat them in the most effective and efficient way possible. These proponents argue further that diagnostic classifications provide little, if any, instructionally relevant information, and that children's difficulties can be ameliorated without any need to classify them as disordered. Finally, another group of critics (e.g., Thurman & Lewis, 1979) argues that classification may actually be harmful to children. They cite instances of lowered parent/teacher expectations, self-fulfilling prophecies, and overt social rejection as common outcomes of the classification process.

The ensuing debate among professionals has left practitioners in a rather precarious situation. On the one hand, they are mandated by the Individuals with Disabilities Education Act (IDEA) to follow a prescribed assessment model (referral-evaluation-classification-placement) when children encounter persistent learning/behavior problems in their classrooms. On the other hand, many leading professionals argue that this approach is not very likely to provide instructionally relevant information for solving learning problems. Since mandated assessment practices are likely to remain in effect, it would be irresponsible to recommend that practitioners ignore the existing assessment process. It would be equally irresponsible, however, to recommend that they follow prescribed procedures without question. Perhaps the most appropriate recommendation that can be made at this time is that practitioners participate in the classification process as *informed consumers*—that is, that they direct assessment activities by specifying what it is they want to know at the referral stage. Practitioners should also ensure that there is an adequate match between their assessment purpose and the methods used to obtain information about referred students. Finally, practitioners should utilize evaluation outcomes in an informed and appropriate manner.

Given that classification serves a useful albeit controversial function, the next important question becomes how to classify disordered behavior. Quay (1986) and Kaplan (1996) have described two major classification schemes currently in use: clinically derived and statistically derived systems.

Clinically Derived Classification Systems

Historically, diagnostic classification evolved out of the observations of clinicians working with disordered individuals on a daily basis. These clinicians noticed certain characteristics (behaviors) that apparently occurred together with some regularity among certain groups of individuals and hypothesized that these "sets of characteristics" made up a distinct entity. Other clinicians soon noticed similar sets of characteristics among their clients as well. Such observations brought a degree of consensual validation to the original observations, and eventually the diagnostic entity became codified into a classification system. It is important to recognize, however, that most diagnostic categories in clinically derived systems were never submitted to independent, empirical verification (Achenbach, 1983; Quay, 1986).

The most widely used system for classifying disordered behavior in North America is contained in the Diagnostic and Statistical Manual, fourth edition (DSM-IV), published by the American Psychiatric Association in 1994. The DSM-IV is the "official" system for reporting disorders to government health agencies, for categorizing mentally ill persons in various official reports, and for treatment and research purposes (Quay, 1986). It provides descriptions and diagnostic criteria for major and minor psychological disorders as well as listings of information for physical disabilities, associated stresses, and premorbid levels of functioning (Quay, 1986). The major categories of the DSM-IV are presented in Table 4.1

Although most disorders found within the Diagnostic and Statistical Manuals have only limited relevance to children and educational settings, the system is used extensively in diagnosing and classifying child behavior disorders (Walker & Fabre, 1987). Teachers of students with behavior disorders, in particular, should be aware of how the system operates and of its relative strengths and weaknesses.

Typically, clinicians begin the classification process by examining and reviewing existing assessment information. They start with the most general pattern of behavior (e.g., physical complaints) and then eliminate alternatives, using clinical judgment and diagnostic aids (e.g., decision trees). They derive a tentative classification and then confirm it by referring to diagnostic criteria provided in the appropriate section of the DSM-IV Manual. Diagnoses are based upon the presence and/or absence of a predetermined number of criteria.

In many respects, the DSM-IV is an improvement over previous editions (American Psychiatric Association, 1952, 1968, 1980, 1987). For example, Achenbach (1983) noted the following: (1) the use of explicit diagnostic criteria instead of narrative descriptions; (2) the inclusion of research diagnostic criteria for adult disorders; (3) the elimination of unsubstantiated inferences concerning psychodynamic mechanisms; and (4) a broadened diagnostic scope through the addition of axes for nonpsychiatric medical conditions, severity of psychosocial factors, and level of adaptive functioning. In addition, DSM-IV now has an empirical literature or available data sets directly related to most diagnostic categories (APA, 1994). Unfortu-

---

TABLE 4.1   Major Components of the DSM-IV System

Disorders Usually First Evident in Infancy, Childhood, or Adolescence

---

Delirium, dementia, and amnestic and other cognitive disorders
Mental disorders due to a general medical condition not elsewhere classified
Substance-related disorders
Schizophrenia and other psychotic disorders
Mood disorders
Anxiety disorders
Somatoform disorders
Factitious disorders
Dissociative disorders
Sexual and gender identity disorders
Eating disorders
Sleep disorders
Impulse control disorders not elsewhere classified
Adjustment disorders
Personality disorders
Other conditions that may be a focus of clinician attention
Additional codes
Multiaxial system

nately, these advances in the formal properties of the Diagnostic and Statistical Manual have not contributed much to the accurate and reliable classification of *children's* disorders (Achenbach, 1983; Quay, 1986; Walker & Fabre, 1987). On the contrary, Walker and Fabre (1987) noted that these systems: (1) still lack relevance for school situations; (2) are unable to identify homogeneous groupings of children with specific behavior disorders; (3) lack utility for comparing different interventions for the same behavior disorders; (4) fail to prescribe measurement strategies, other than clinical judgment, for assessing child status on specific disorders; and (5) are technically inadequate (i.e., lack sufficient reliability and validity). Additional limitations are a failure to include developmental perspectives and a general lack of consistency in applying classification criteria (Achenbach, 1978, 1979; Achenbach & Edelbrock, 1978; Fremont & Wallbrown, 1979; Reichler & Schloper, 1976). More recently, researchers have reported very little correspondence between psychiatric diagnoses based upon the Diagnostic and Statistical Manual and eligibility for special education in the category of serious emotional disturbance (SED) as determined under IDEA (e.g., Duncan, et al., 1995; Forness, 1988; Maag & Forness, 1991; McGinnis & Forness, 1988; Sinclair, Forness, & Alexson, 1985).

Statistically Derived Classification System

In response to the numerous criticisms leveled against the Diagnostic and Statistical Manuals and other clinically derived systems, a second major approach to classification emerged. Statistically derived classification systems, in contrast to their clinical predecessors, provided a more objective means of classifying disordered behavior. Essentially, this approach involved giving standardized assessment measures (e.g., behavior rating scales, life histories, and standardized questionnaires) to large numbers of teachers, parents, and clinicians, and asking them to indicate the extent to which certain behaviors characterized their children. Child behavior ratings were then analyzed statistically (i.e., factor analysis) to isolate homogeneous behavioral groupings as diagnostic entities. The number of factors identified over the years has ranged from two to thirteen (Peterson, 1965; Spivack & Swift, 1967). Such factors, in turn, have been classified into broadband and narrowband syndromes (Walker & Fabre, 1987).

Perhaps the most "recognized" statistically derived classification system was developed by Quay and his colleagues (Quay, 1966; Quay & Quay, 1965; Quay, Morse, & Cutler, 1966). Using the Behavior Problem Checklist (BPC), a fifty-five item checklist of problematic behaviors, these researchers identified four major factors with some consistency. These factors, termed conduct disorder, anxiety–withdrawal, inadequacy–immaturity, and socialized aggression, have appeared repeatedly in research with the Behavior Problem Checklist and other measures (Quay, 1986), as well as across a variety of age ranges and samples (e.g., Quay et al., 1966; Quay & Quay, 1965). More recently, Quay and Peterson (1987) developed an eighty-nine-item Revised Behavior Problem Checklist that reliably identifies and classifies children's behavior along two additional dimensions, that is, psychotic behavior and motor excess. Although Quay's system has proven to be quite reliable, it does not provide treatment information. Therefore, its usefulness for intervening with children with behavior disorders has remained quite limited (Heward, 1996).

Some potentially useful work also has been done toward the development of empirically based classification systems that may hold greater relevance for school-related behavior disorders. For example, Fremont and Wallbrown (1979) proposed a school-specific classification system that consists of seven behavior patterns: (1) personality problems, (2) conduct problems, (3) immature, inadequate behavior, (4) socialized delinquency, (5) emotional disturbance, (6) social misperception, and (7) learning disabilities. One particularly positive feature of this system is that the attempt to classify is based on observable child behavior that is specific to school settings (Walker & Fabre, 1987).

A second major advance in statistically derived classification has been the identification of behavioral clusters for school versus home settings (Edelbrock, 1979) and for sex and age levels (Achenbach & Edelbrock, 1978; Edelbrock, 1979). This work suggests that the context of specific behavior disorders is often quite different for males and females and that children's behavior problems may vary as a function of age and the demands of a particular environment.

A third interesting development has been the use of a *bipolar* conceptualization of disordered behavior in children (see Achenbach & Edelbrock, 1978; Edelbrock, 1979; Ross, 1980; Schaefer, 1982). For example, Ross (1980) argued that existing behavioral factors, clusters, or patterns can be reduced to a broadband bipolar dimension that characterizes the *direction* of the disordered behavior—that is, disordered behavior can be directed either toward or away from the social environment. Various conceptualizations of this dimension have included excessive approach (aggression) versus excessive avoidance (withdrawal), conduct versus personality problems, and internalizing (actions directed toward self) versus externalizing (actions directed toward others) (Walker & Fabre, 1987). This bipolar conceptualization holds great relevance for treating school-based child behavior disorders. Ross (1980) suggests that problematic behaviors may fall into two major classes—those that deviate from the norm by occurring too frequently and those that deviate by occurring too rarely. Thus, some children with behavior disorders may come to our attention because they are deficient in adaptive academic and/or social skills while others will be noticed for their excessive rates of maladaptive behaviors (too often). Walker and Fabre (1987) noted that the adoption of such a simple bipolar classification scheme will provide valuable direction for treatment efforts (e.g., accelerate infrequent, adaptive responding or decelerate excessive, maladaptive behaviors) as well as permit the establishment of normative performance levels on various behavioral profiles.

Because statistically derived classification systems (e.g., Achenbach, 1991; Achenbach & Edelbrock, 1981; Quay & Peterson, 1987) are based to a much greater extent on the direct observation of specific behaviors, they appear to be more reliable and valid than their clinically derived predecessors (Kauffman, 1985). However, these multivariate approaches have their own limitations. For example, Clarizio (1987) suggested that one weakness of multivariate classification is that the quality of the classification one gets out of the statistical process will only be as good as the information one puts into the analysis. If, for instance, one samples a very limited population of individuals and/or uses a rating instrument with an insufficient number of items, then the factors that emerge will be equally limited. Achenbach (1983) also noted that statistically derived classifications reveal only the associations among test items, not necessarily the *patterns* of behavior that distinguish individual children from one another. Moreover, he argued that statistical associations among items usually reflect only one informant's perspective, be it parent or teacher. Different informants might provide different perspectives. Indeed, empirical studies suggest generally low levels of agreement (i.e., interrater reliability) among different informants for the same children (Hogan, Quay, Vaughn, & Shapiro; 1989; Simpson, 1991). In such instances, whose view represents a more accurate picture of the child?

Two final criticisms of statistically derived classifications are that they rely too heavily on verbal report (Clarizio, 1987) and that they fail to provide definitive descriptions and measurement of specific behavior problems (Kauffman, 1985). Achenbach (1983) responded, however, that most weaknesses associated with multivariate classification result from subordinating statistical techniques to a categorical (clinical) conceptual paradigm and that when used appropriately, multivariate approaches have several advantages over clinically derived systems (see also Quay, 1986).

Procedures for Identifying and Classifying Disordered Behavior

Salvia and Ysseldyke (1991) suggested that assessment procedures for identifying and classifying disordered behavior will vary as a function of the theoretical orientations of assessment personnel. They noted further that two major theoretical perspectives—personality and behavioral—have been dominant in the assessment of behavior disorders and that these perspectives appear to be nearly polar opposites. Personality theorists, for example, routinely use personality tests and other measures of "emotional states" (e.g., projective tests and self-concept measures) as part of a larger assessment battery comprised of intelligence, achievement, perceptual–motor, and language scales. These theorists presume that (1) there are "internal" causes of behavior; (2) identification of these underlying causes will facilitate an understanding of overt behavior and behavior change; and (3) personality tests can help to pinpoint pathology (Salvia & Ysseldyke, 1991). Behaviorally oriented theorists, on the other hand, openly reject the use of personality scales and other measures of emotional states, arguing that such devices are conceptually flawed, technically inadequate (i.e., lack sufficient norms, reliability, and validity), and instructionally irrelevant (Salvia & Ysseldyke, 1991; Taylor, 1989; Witt et al., 1988). Instead, they rely more heavily on direct observation, behavioral interviewing, analogue assessments, and behavior rating scales.

In this section, we examine the major methods used by both personality and behaviorally oriented personnel. We begin by reviewing procedures used for screening children for possible behavior disorders and then discuss methods for identification, paying particular attention to commonly used assessment instruments.

Screening Methods

In a very general sense, classroom teachers "screen" children every day for possible behavior problems through their daily interactions in the schools. Some children are perceived as disruptive and overactive, others as hostile and aggressive, and still others as overly passive and unassertive. When these behavior patterns persist over time or escalate in intensity, students are often referred for a more in-depth examination. Screening studies indicate that teachers typically refer from 2 to 6 percent of the school-age population for special services (Hyde, 1975; Nicholson, 1967; Robbins, Mercer, & Meyers, 1967). Less than half of these referrals, however, are specifically for behavior problems (Kirschenbaum, Marsh, & Devage, 1977). Of those children referred for behavior problems, the great majority can be characterized as "externalizers"—that is, they exhibit maladaptive behavior patterns that disturb the classroom atmosphere (e.g., acting out, hyperactivity, disruptiveness, aggression) (Walker, 1995; Walker & Fabre, 1987). Herein lies one of the major problems associated with using *informal* teacher observations as a basis for identifying disordered behavior. It appears that only externalizing or disruptive behaviors are troublesome to classroom teachers. Children with potentially significant internalizing problems (i.e., excessive withdrawal) are rarely referred and/or identified. This is problematic in that ample research suggests that these children are equally at risk for subsequent adjustment problems (see Chapter 8 for a more complete discussion). Moreover, teachers vary greatly in their tolerance levels for particular types of behavior, and many students may be referred inappropriately by teachers who have excessively low tolerance levels (Walker & Fabre, 1987).

Given the difficulties associated with informal screening methods such as subjective teacher judgments, many educators (e.g., Kirschenbaum et al., 1977; Walker & Fabre, 1987) have argued for the routine screening of all children in regular classrooms using more formal screening methods. Kirschenbaum and colleagues (1977), for example, demonstrated the effectiveness and feasibility of a mass screening procedure for identifying behavior disorders that required only 10 to 40 minutes per classroom. Using a brief teacher rating form, the AML (Cowen et al., 1973), these researchers found that this device identified more children with maladaptive behavior than teachers naturally referred for special assistance. Walker and Fabre (1987) suggested that a simple and economical measure like the AML was valuable because it utilized teachers' knowledge of child behavior, yet structured their judgments in such a way that all behavior disorders had an equal chance of being identified. Other excellent screening systems have been developed for both school-age and preschool populations (see, e.g., Clarfield, 1974; Greenwood, Walker, Todd, & Hops, 1979).

A second method of screening for behavior disorders involves teacher ranking of pupils along particular dimensions such as social competence, appropriate classroom behavior, social withdrawal, and achievement. Walker and Fabre (1987) found teacher rankings to be extremely accurate and predictive of child status on criterion measures. Those children ranked at the extremes of the distributions might be evaluated more thoroughly using such methods as behavior rating scales and direct observation. Teacher rankings may have an advantage over mass screening procedures in that they require behavior ratings on only a portion of students attending regular classes. An excellent resource for screening and assessing school-related disorders is *The Iowa Assessment Model in Behavior Disorders: A Training Manual* (Wood, Smith, & Grimes, 1985).

Perhaps the most exciting screening systems developed to date are the Systematic Screening for Behavior Disorders (SSBD) (Walker & Severson, 1990) and the Early Screening Project (ESP) (Walker, Severson, & Feil, 1995). The SSBD and ESP are multiple-gating screening systems for behavior-disordered pupils ages 3 to 11. In these systems, students must pass through a series of gates (or stages) in order to "qualify" for educational services (Figure 4.1). At the first stage of the SSBD, teachers are asked to *rank* every pupil in their class according to the prevalence of externalizing and internalizing problems. Only the top three pupils on each list proceed to stage two, the Critical Events Index. Here, classroom teachers are asked to *rate* each pupil's behavior according to thirty-three items that reflect common teacher behavioral standards and expectations. Pupils who exceed normative criteria on the Critical Events Index proceed to stage three where direct and repeated observations are made of their behavior during independent and work times. Students who exceed cutoff criteria on either or both observational measures are referred for subsequent evaluation and possible classification. According to Walker and Fabre (1987), the SSBD relies

> upon structured teacher judgments of pupil behavioral characteristics in stages one and two and uses normatively referenced, observational data to provide independent, in vivo assessments of the pupils' behavioral status in stage three within academic and free play settings. The results of the screening decisions in each gate are cross-validated by increasingly more intensive and complex assessments within subsequent stages. (p. 42)

Initial evidence collected on the SSBD looks promising. For example, the instruments making up the SSBD have been found to have excellent psychometric properties. The system reliably identified pupils with certified behavior disorders in regular classrooms, consistently differentiated externalizing from internalizing students, and produced high levels of interrater agreement among teachers in terms of both ratings and rankings. Finally, a year-long study involving the SSBD demonstrated that the system correctly classified approximately 90 percent of the externalizing, internalizing, and nondisabled students enrolled in eighteen regular

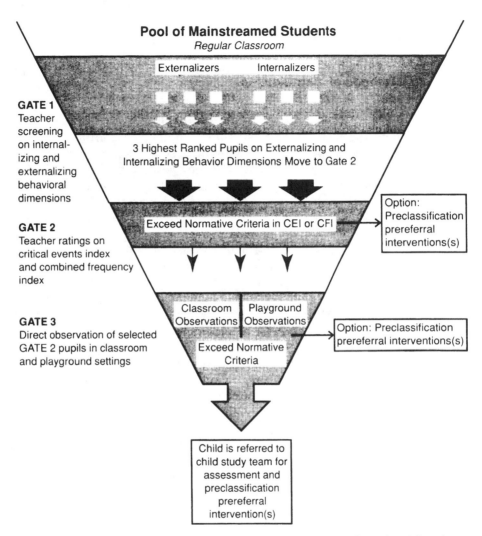

FIGURE 4–1 **Multiple-Gating Assessment Procedure for Identification of Behavior-Disordered Students**

Source: Walker, H. M., Severson, H., Stiller, B., Williams, G., Haring, N., Shinn, M., & Todis, B. (1988). Systematic screening of pupils in the elementary range at risk for behavior disorders: Development. . . . *Remedial and Special Education, 9*, 8–20.

classrooms (Walker & Fabre, 1987). According to Heward (1996), "the SSBD is the most systematic, fully developed instrument for screening children for possible emotional and behavioral disorders" (p. 262). More recently, several adaptations of the SSBD (e.g., ESP) have been developed, field-tested, and evaluated for their technical adequacy for use with preschool children (Feil & Becker, 1993; Sinclair, Del'Homme, & Gonzalez, 1993; Walker, 1995).

Methods of Identification

Once students have been screened for possible behavior disorders, they are referred for more intensive evaluation. It is at this stage that multidisciplinary or child study teams collect additional assessment information to determine if students are eligible for special education services (identification), and if so, under which diagnostic category (classification). It is also at this stage that assessing personnel differentiate their assessment methods according to the theoretical perspective they follow. First, we will describe some primary methods used by personality-oriented evaluators. Then we will proceed to procedures commonly used by behavioral assessment personnel. It should be noted, however, that the use of personality assessment has diminished substantially among school-based assessors during the past twenty-five years, while a concurrent increase has occurred in the use of more direct observational methods (Salvia & Ysseldyke, 1991). As such, our discussion of personality measures will be correspondingly shorter.

Personality-Oriented Assessment Methods

As noted earlier, the primary purpose of personality assessment is to find the underlying cause(s) of disordered behavior. Historically, personality theorists have relied upon a variety of assessment methods, the most significant of which are personality inventories and questionnaires, projective techniques, and measures of self-concept. Some of the most commonly used personality devices are listed in Table 4.2.

Personality Inventories

Personality inventories are designed to measure objectively the emotional characteristics of individuals. With the exception of the Personality Inventory for Children (Wirt et al, 1984), most personality measures are designed for adolescents and adults (Taylor, 1989). Some of the most widely used personality scales are described briefly below.

Minnesota Multiphasic Personality Inventory (MMPI) (Hathaway & McKinley, 1967). The MMPI, one of the most popular and widely used personality scales, is designed for individuals 16 years and older. The MMPI consists of 556 true–false items that are typically self-scored. The test yields scores for nine "clinical" and three validity scales. The clinical scales are hypochondriasis, hypomania, depression, hysteria, schizophrenia, paranoia, psychopathic deviate, psychoasthenia, and masculinity–feminity. The three validity scales, which are designed to determine if truthful responses are being given, are defensiveness, infrequency, and lie (Taylor, 1989).

Like most personality scales, the MMPI has been criticized for technical inadequacies, particularly insufficient validity data (Lanyon & Goodstein, 1971; Taylor, 1989). Moreover, this scale is quite time-consuming to administer and interpret, and its test items may be susceptible to social desirability effects (Taylor, 1989).

TABLE 4.2   Commonly Used Measures of Personality, Projection, and Self-Concept

General Personality and Emotional Development Scales

California Psychological Inventory (Gough, 1969)
California Test of Personality (Thorpe, Clark, & Tiegs, 1953)
Early School Personality Questionnaire (Coan & Cattell, 1970)
Edwards Personal Preference Schedule (Edwards, 1959)
Edwards Personality Inventory (Edwards, 1966)
Eysenck Personality Inventory (Eysenck & Eysenck, 1969)
Family Relations Test (Bene & Anthony, 1957)
Jr.–Sr. High School Personality Questionnaire (Cattell, Coan, & Belloff, 1969)
Minnesota Multiphasic Personality Inventory (Hathaway & McKinley, 1967)
Sixteen Personality Factor Questionnaire (Cattell, Eber, and Yatsuoka, 1970)

Projective Techniques

Bender Visual Motor Gestalt Test (Bender, 1938)
Blacky Pictures (Blum, 1967)
Children's Apperception Test (Bellak & Bellak, 1965)
Draw-A-Person (Urban, 1963)
Holtzman Ink Blot Test (Holtzman, 1966)
House-Tree-Person (Buck & Jolles, 1966)
Human Figures Drawing Test (Rorschach, 1966)
Rorschach Ink Blot Test (Rorschach, 1966)
School Apperception Test (Solomon & Starr, 1968)
Thematic Apperception Test (Murray, 1943)

Self-Concept Scales

Piers-Harris Children's Self-Concept Scale (Piers & Harris, 1969)
Tennessee Self-Concept Scale (Fitts, 1965)

Source: Adapted from Salvia, J., & Ysseldyke, J. E. (1991). Assessment in special and remedial education. 5th ed. Boston: Houghton Mifflin.

California Psychological Inventory (Gough, 1969).   Another popular personality scale is the California Psychological Inventory. The California Psychological Inventory consists of 480 true–false items that can be completed by individuals 13 years of age and older. Like the MMPI, the CPI yields scores on both personality and validity scales. The fifteen personality scales are Achievement via Conformity, Achievement via Independence, Capacity of Status, Dominance, Femininity, Intellectual Efficiency, Psychological-Mindedness, Responsibility, Self-Acceptance, Self-Control, Sense of Well-Being, Sociability, Socialization, Social Pressure, and Tolerance. The three validity scales are Community, Good Impression, and Well-Being. According to Taylor (1989), researchers have generally supported the use of California Psychological Inventory, even though there is some redundancy among the scales.

Personality Inventory for Children (Wirt, Lachar, Klinedinst, & Seat, 1984).   The Personality Inventory for Children is a 600-item personality scale designed for use with children between the ages of 3 and 16. The scale is completed by the referred child's parent, and scores are reported along thirteen "profile" and three validity scales. Unlike many personality scales, the Personality Inventory for Children reports substantial information regarding the test's technical properties. The Personality Inventory for Children appears to have adequate norms, except at the preschool level. However, it has been criticized for questionable validity and low interrater reliability (Taylor, 1989).

Projective Techniques
Projective techniques are the second major assessment method used by personality theorists. Theoretically, projective tests measure some underlying emotional characteristics of individuals, thought to be revealed by individuals' "projections" of their thoughts, feelings, needs, and/or motives onto ambiguous stimuli (Salvia & Ysseldyke, 1991). Typically, individuals are presented with particular stimuli, such as pictures of inkblots, word associations, partially completed sentences, and/or ambiguous drawings. They must then respond by describing what they see, supplying missing words, or saying the first thing that comes to mind. Their responses are interpreted by trained clinicians to ascertain the "real" cause of their difficulties.

    Although projective tests are still used in special education, particularly with youngsters with behavior disorders, their usefulness has been seriously questioned (e.g., Heward, 1996; O'Leary & Johnson, 1979; Salvia & Ysselyke, 1991). The major problems associated with projectives are their inadequate technical properties (norms, reliability, and validity), their instructional irrelevance, and the time-consuming nature of their administration and interpretation. Some of the most commonly used projective measures are described briefly in the following paragraphs.

Rorschach Ink Blot Test (Rorschach, 1932).   The Rorschach consists of ten inkblots that are presented one at a time to an individual, who simply reports what he or she sees in each inkblot. Responses are then scored according to content, location, and determinants of response (Beck, Beck, Levitt, & Molish, 1961; Taylor, 1989). Although a substantial amount of training and clinical experience is required to interpret the Rorschach, all interpretations remain suspect because of the technical inadequacies of this assessment method.

Human Figure Drawing Test (Koppitz, 1968).   A second popular projective is the Human Figure Drawing Test. This "test" is usually given at the beginning of an individual assessment session and is designed to "break the ice" or put the child at ease. Essentially, individuals are asked to draw a human figure. Their drawings are then scored for the presence or absence of thirty emotional "indicators" identified by Koppitz. Again, extreme caution should be used in interpreting outcomes from this assessment method because technical inadequacies seriously limit the validity and reliability of clinicians' interpretations.

Children's Apperception Test (Bellak, Bellak, & Haworth, 1974).   The Children's Apperception Test is another frequently used projective technique. The Children's Apperception Test consists of two sets of stimulus cards. The first set has ten cards that depict animals involved in a variety of situations, while the second set has ten "human" pictures. Children are asked to describe what's going on in each picture. Their responses are then "scored" and interpreted for particular emotional "themes." Although quantitative scoring systems have been developed, interpretation remains largely subjective (Taylor, 1989).

Self-Concept Measures
Self-concept measures are the third primary assesment method used by personality theorists. Typically, these devices rely upon self-evaluation and self-report (although some scales can be completed by parents or teachers). Individuals are presented with a particular statement, such as "I feel lonely at times," and they must either agree or disagree with the statement or indicate the degree (i.e., Likert-type scale) to which the item characterizes their own feelings. The logic underlying the measurement of self-concept is rather straightforward: The way individuals feel about themselves will affect how they behave. In the case of students with behavior disorders, it is assumed that a poor self-concept underlies their maladaptive behavior. In addition to the typical concerns about the technical adequacy of self-concept measures, these tests also face a social-desirability problem—that is, many individuals may answer self-concept items in the way they think others expect them to respond rather than in a way that reflects how they really feel. This, of course, further limits the validity of obtained responses. Only the most frequently used measure of self-concept is described here.

Piers-Harris Children's Self-Concept Scale (Piers & Harris, 1969).   The Piers-Harris is one of the most popular self-concept scales in educational settings. It is designed for children in grades 4 through 12, and measures individuals' feelings about their intellectual and school status, physical appearance and attributes, anxiety levels, popularity, happiness and satisfaction, and overt behavior (Taylor, 1989). Individuals are required to read eighty items and score each one "yes" or "no." Low scores in any particular area presumably reflect individuals' concerns about their ability in that domain. In general, the Piers-Harris appears to be a fairly reliable measure of self-concept, though validity data are limited (Taylor, 1989).

In sum, personality-oriented assessment personnel attempt to uncover the underlying causes for individuals' behavior problems by examining responses to questionnaires, ambiguous stimuli, and statements of self-worth. Traditionally, such evaluation has been conducted by clinical personnel during individual assessment sessions. In recent years, such assessment procedures have been criticized soundly because of the subjective nature of clinical interpretations and the lack of educational relevance of the findings obtained.

Behaviorally Oriented Assessment Methods

In contrast to their clinical counterparts, behavioral assessment personnel rarely, if ever, use personality scales, projectives, or measures of self-concept. Instead, they rely more heavily on direct measures of behavior, such as direct observation, behavioral interviews, analogue assessments, and behavior rating scales. Here we describe some of the major behavior rating scales currently being used in schools. (Direct observation procedures are discussed in Chapter 5.)

Behavior Rating Scales

A wide variety of behavior rating scales are currently being used with children who encounter interpersonal problems in schools. Some of the most commonly used scales are listed in Table 4.3.

Teacher and/or parent ratings of problem behavior are quite popular, partly because of their relative ease of administration. However, rating measures vary considerably, both in the domains assessed and in the responding format. For example, some measures, such as the Revised Problem Behavior Checklist (Quay & Peterson, 1987), the Walker Problem Behavior Identification Checklist (Walker, 1983), and the Child Behavior Checklist (Achenbach, 1991) are designed to tap several dimensions of problem behavior (e.g., attention problems, aggression, anxiety-withdrawal), while other scales, such as the Connors' Abbreviated Parent-Teacher Questionnaire (Connors, 1973), focus on a single type of problem behavior (e.g., hyperactivity). Similarly, some behavior rating scales require a simple yes/no rater response

---

TABLE 4.3   Commonly Used Behavior Rating Scales

Behavior Evaluation Scale (McCarney & Leigh, 1983)
Behavior Rating Scale (Brown & Hammill, 1978)
Burks' Behavior Rating Scale (Burks, 1969)
Child Behavior Checklist (Achenbach, 1991)
Connors' Abbreviated Parent-Teacher Questionnaire (Connors, 1973)
Devereux Adolescent Behavior Rating Scale (Spivack, Spotts, & Haimes, 1967)
Devereux Child Behavior Rating Scale (Spivack & Swift, 1966)
Devereux Elementary School Behavior Rating Scale (Spivack & Swift, 1967)
Revised Behavior Problem Checklist (Quay & Peterson, 1987)
Pupil Behavior Inventory (Vinter, Sarri, Vorwaller, & Schafer, 1966)
School Social Behavior Scales (Merrell, 1993)
Social Skills Rating System (Gresham & Elliot, 1990)
Walker-McConnell Scale of Social Competence and School Adjustment (Walker & McConnell, 1995)
Walker Problem Behavior Identification Checklist (Walker, 1983)

---

regarding the occurrence/nonoccurrence of particular behaviors, whereas others demand a more qualitative (e.g., "very true," "somewhat true," "not true") or quantitative (e.g., "never occurs" to "occurs very frequently") response (Witt et al., 1988). The particular rating scale selected should be determined primarily by the type of information one wants to know as well as by the technical adequacy of the instrument (Edelbrock, 1983; Mash & Terdal, 1981; Witt et al., 1988). Here we review some of the most frequently used behavior rating scales.

Walker Problem Behavior Identification Checklist (Walker, 1983).   The Walker Problem Behavior Identification Checklist is designed to identify the problem behavior of children in grades 4 through 6. It consists of fifty behaviors that are typically observed in school settings. Individuals familiar with the referred child mark whether they have observed the child display these particular behaviors. The Walker Problem Behavior Identification Checklist measures five categories of problem behavior: (1) acting out, (2) withdrawal, (3) distractibility, (4) disturbed peer relations, and (5) immaturity. A child receives a score on each factor, and these scores are then compared to the normative sample. It is important to note that the Walker Problem Behavior Identification Checklist is not designed to classify students. Rather, it is intended as a quick screening device for identifying those in need of more in-depth evaluation (Walker, 1983).

According to Witt and colleagues (1988), the Walker Problem Behavior Identification Checklist appears to be a relatively reliable and stable measure. It adequately differentiates behavior disordered from nondisabled students and incorporates problem behaviors that have direct relevance for instructional settings. The small number of items and relative ease of administration are additional advantages to this scale. However, the lack of a national, normative data base is a primary disadvantage (Walker, 1995).

Revised Behavior Problem Checklist (Quay & Peterson, 1987).   The Revised Behavior Problem Checklist (RPBC) is an eighty-nine-item scale designed to identify child and adolescent behavior problems. The scale can be completed by parents, teachers, or other individuals familiar with the child (e.g., child-care workers). The RPBC consists of six factors or dimensions of problem behaviors: (1) conduct disorders, (2) socialized aggression, (3) attention problems–immaturity, (4) anxiety–withdrawal, (5) psychotic behavior, and (6) motor excess. Children receive raw scores on each factor. These scores are then compared to data derived from empirical investigations of the scale. The RBPC Manual contains results of teacher and parent ratings for both "normal" and clinical samples of children between the ages of 5 to 18.

Witt and colleagues (1988) suggest that the RBPC is "a poorly standardized behavior rating scale that has limited evidence for reliability and validity" (p. 334). Although an earlier version of this instrument, the Behavior Problem Checklist (Quay & Peterson, 1967) possessed adequate technical properties, the newer version must still establish its own measure of reliability and validity. Similarly, the number of items and length of time required to complete the scale are additional disadvantages to the use of this measure. The RBPC may still be used, however, within a criterion-referenced framework and/or to compare several students' ratings within the same classroom (Witt et al., 1988).

Child Behavior Checklist (Achenbach, 1991).   The Child Behavior Checklist is considered to be the most comprehensive and technically robust rating scale for assessing child behavior (Walker, 1995). The Child Behavior Checklist consists of 113 problem behaviors that can be rated by either teachers or parents of children ages 4 to 16. Its manual provides separate norms for boys and girls in three age ranges: 4 to 5 years, 6 to 11 years, and 11 to 16 years. The CBC has two broadband factors: externalizing and internalizing syndromes. Each broadband factor, in turn, is comprised of several narrowband or specific factors. The specific factors vary both as a function of sex (boys versus girls) and age level. Examples of narrowband factors that make up the externalizing syndrome are aggressive, delinquent, hyperactive, and cruel. Children receive scores on each narrowband factor, and the scores are then visually displayed on the Revised Child Behavior Profile, which also provides norms for comparison.

According to Witt and colleagues (1988), the Child Behavior Checklist is "a well-designed, well-constructed, and well-researched parent rating scale that is useful in identifying clusters of behavior problems in children" (p. 332). It can be used to measure the cross-situationality of behavior (i.e., home and school) and to prioritize possible intervention targets. Its major strength is its careful attention to psychometric properties, although a more representative standardization sample is still needed (Witt et al., 1988). The primary disadvantage associated with its use is its length and excessive amount of time required for its completion (Walker, 1995).

In sum, behaviorally oriented assessment personnel typically use behavior rating scales to identify general domains of dysfunctional social behavior. They then conduct more in-depth analyses of specific problems through the use of behavioral interviews, analogue assessments, and direct observation in in vivo settings. Assessment data typically are collected over a number of days, as opposed to "one-shot" diagnostic sessions, and recommendations usually involve making specific changes in environmental variables and evaluating the subsequent effects upon children's behavior.

Interpreting Assessment Outcomes

Assessment information will be of little value unless the results are interpreted and communicated so that they are understood by those who make important instructional decisions (Salvia & Ysseldyke, 1991). Unfortunately, this is often not the case in traditional assessment practices in schools. As noted earlier, many educators are unsure of what is actually going on during the assessment process, and many others find assessment outcomes—specifically, standardized test scores—to be of limited instructional value. We believe that standardized test results *can be* of some value—particularly in making screening and eligibility decisions—but to be useful, they must be derived from technically sound assessment measures and be placed in an appropriate interpretive context. In this concluding section, we focus on the assessment needs of classroom teachers and describe how evaluation data may assist them in instructional programming for students with behavioral disorders.

Assessment Needs of Teachers

Classroom teachers generally want and need to know what to do instructionally for students (Salvia & Ysseldyke, 1991). In the case of youngsters with behavior disorders, teachers often want to know how to better manage their classroom behavior and improve their academic and social competence. Unfortunately, traditional norm-referenced assessment measures do not provide this type of information. After all, they were not designed to do so. Standardized tests were designed to compare a particular student's performance to that of a representative sample of peers upon whom the tests were normed. However, knowledge of the extent to which children deviate from the norm is rarely useful in designing interventions to reduce such discrepancies. Thus, standardized test results are typically too general to be useful in everyday teaching activities (Witt et al., 1988). Such test results can be useful, however, to identify which students are at risk for encountering future difficulties (screening decisions), which particular instructional domains may be most deficient (a student's strengths and weaknesses), and/or which pupils are more deficient overall (identification and classification).

To make such meaningful decisions, educators must be familiar with at least two facets of the assessment process: the technical adequacy of assessment instruments and the basic assumptions underlying all assessment practices. A working knowledge of this information will allow educators to evaluate the accuracy of test results and to place these outcomes into an appropriate context.

Technical Adequacy

Traditionally, a discussion of reliability, validity, and norming samples has elicited either yawns or anxiety from practitioners. Many educators either "don't care" how the test was developed, on whom it was normed, and how accurately or consistently it measures what it says it measures or they are confused by the complex array of correlation coefficients presented within test manuals. In fact, many practitioners often ignore the technical sections of test manuals. This is indeed unfortunate because many of the tests are still being employed to make important decisions about children. If the information used to make instructional decisions comes from tests with inadequate technical properties, then errors will be made in the subsequent decision-making. Here we provide only a cursory discussion of technical properties. Interested readers are referred to two excellent sources for additional information: Salvia and Ysseldyke, 1991 and Witt and colleagues, 1988.

Reliability refers to the consistency with which tests measure particular skills and/or traits. If a test is reliable and the tested behaviors are stable, then an individual will receive the same or at least a similar score on repeated testings. Reliability is important because test scores would be of little meaning if they fluctuated wildly from one occasion to the next. For example, how would our educational decisions be affected if a student earned a 20 percent higher or 20 percent lower score on an achievement measure when it was readministered one week later? Test reliability is often expressed in terms of a correlation coefficient. If there is relatively little error in a test, the coefficient will approach 1.00 (perfect reliability); if there is relatively large amount of error, the coefficient will approach .00 (total unreliability). Therefore, a test with a reliability coefficient of .90 will contain less error and be more reliable than a test with a reliability coefficient of .50. Salvia and Ysseldyke (1991) recommend that a minimum standard for reliability of .90 should be used whenever educators are making important educational decisions (e.g., identification and classification) about individual pupils.

Validity refers to the extent to which a test measures what its authors or users claim that it measures (Salvia & Ysseldyke, 1991). Generally, a test's validity is not measured directly. Instead, its validity for various uses is established on the basis of a wide array of information typically subsumed under the rubric of content-related, criterion-referenced, and/or construct validity. Although validity is a more complex construct to understand than reliability, a few general guidelines can be helpful. First, validity is the most important characteristic of a test. The other technical properties, reliability and norms, are subsumed under the issue of validity. Second, adequate norms, reliability, and a lack of bias are necessary characteristics for validity, but none alone is sufficient to guarantee validity. Third, a test is not valid simply because it sells well (has cash validity), clinicians claim that it is good, and/or it presents internal consistency data (Salvia & Ysseldyke, 1991). Information on a test's validity is often reported in terms of correlation coefficients (e.g., criterion- and predictive-validity coefficients), and educators are encouraged to only use tests with "high" (i.e., .90 and above) validity coefficients when making important decisions about individual pupils. More recently, Messick (1994) has argued convincingly that the validity of assessment efforts should not only be concerned about the technical and statistical properties of evaluation methods. In addition, one must be concerned about the use of assessment information and its subsequent effects upon student learning. That is, assessment information would be considered valid if it was actually used in instructional decision-making and if its use reliably produced improvements in student performance. This concept of "instructional validity" provides a potentially useful construct for examining the relationships between differing types of assessment information and subsequent differences in student performance.

The final technical characteristic of importance is the test's norming sample. *Norms* refer to the groups of individuals upon whom the test was standardized. It is very important for educators to be aware of this information because the norming population is the one against which their pupils' performance will be compared. Salvia and Ysseldyke (1991) suggest that the adequacy of a test's norms depends upon three factors: (1) the representativeness of the norm sample, (b) the number of cases in the sample, and (3) the relevance of the norm to the purpose of testing. In general, norms should be representative (in both number and proportion) of the population to whom comparisons are made. If test norms are not representative, scores will be inaccurate and interpretations may be faulty.

A discussion of technical characteristics might not be necessary if we could assume that all tests currently "on the market" are technically sound. Unfortunately, we cannot make such an assumption. Recent reviews suggest that the majority of standardized tests being used to make important educational decisions are technically inadequate (Galagan, 1985; Preliminary Report of the NASP/ NCAS Task Force, 1984; Salvia & Ysseldyke, 1991; Winikur & Wohle, 1984). In particular, measures of personality and emotional functioning (e.g., projectives, self-concept scales) have been cited as technically deficient. Salvia and Ysseldyke (1991), for instance, concluded that most personality assessment devices have inadequate norms and reliability coefficients that are generally too low for making important educational decisions. Moreover, since most major personality constructs or traits are rarely made operational, it is usually difficult to determine just what these tests were designed to measure (i.e., validity). In the absence of sound technical properties, educators must exercise extreme caution when interpreting and using test results.

Assumptions Underlying Psychoeducational Assessment

In addition to knowing whether test results were derived from technically adequate instruments, educators must be familiar with the basic assumptions that underlie valid assessment practice, because to the extent that these assumptions are not met, test results and subsequent interpretations may lack validity (Salvia & Ysseldyke, 1991). Newland (1971) identified five basic assumptions that underlie psychoeducational assessment: (1) the person giving the test is skilled; (2) error will be present in all tests; (3) acculturation of tested students is comparable to the norming sample; (4) behavior sampling is adequate; and (5) present behavior is observed and future behavior is inferred. Assumptions 2, 3, and 4 were discussed in the previous sections on technical properties. Here we will comment on assumptions 1 and 5.

To say that people giving standardized tests should be skilled appears to state the obvious. However, one may ask, Skilled at what? First, they must be skilled at establishing rapport. Students generally perform better when they are relaxed and comfortable. Failing to make them feel comfortable may result in depressed test performance, which, in turn, may be interpreted as ability deficits. Second, examiners must be skilled at administering, scoring, and interpreting the specific tests they are using. While many tests look easy to administer, score, and interpret, they are often complex to use (particularly to interpret). Too often, individuals with no special training administer intelligence tests or personality scales on a routine basis. Because these tests are used to make important educational decisions, the importance of examiner competence cannot be understated.

Assumption 5 underlying traditional, norm-referenced assessment practice is that whenever we "test" someone, we only observe their performance on one sampling of behavior (test items), at one point in time, and under one particular set of testing conditions. We observe what an individual does; we may not observe what he or she is capable of doing (Salvia & Ysseldyke, 1991). Essentially, we try to make predictions about how individuals will perform both within and outside school settings on the basis of a rather limited sampling of their behavior. We must never lose sight of the fact that test scores are simply aids in our decision-making process. They are not sufficient ends in and of themselves.

Recently, Walker (1995) offered a set of basic assumptions that he suggested should guide "best assessment practice" as it relates to student with behavior disorders. He argued that assessment procedures should primarily provide a roadmap or guide to the design and implementation of effective intervention strategies. In keeping with Messick's (1994) concept of instructional validity, assessors must strive to link their evaluation and intervention efforts. In addition, when possible, assessments should be multimethod, multisetting, and multiagent in nature. That is, they should incorporate more than one assessment approach (e.g., ratings, rankings, direct observations), occur in multiple settings (e.g., classroom, playground, at home), and involve more than one informant (e.g., teachers, parents, peers). Finally, Walker (1995) recommended that teacher-generated assessment information (e.g., ratings and rankings) should *always* be given high priority in student assessments.

Summary

This chapter attempted to clarify some of the ambiguities that surround existing assessment practices in schools. In particular, we examined the major purposes, procedures, and outcomes associated with the use of norm-referenced assessment practices. We argued that assessment methods must be differentiated according to the types of questions we want to answer about our students. Particular attention was paid to the identification and classification of disordered behavior. We described two major approaches to classification (clinical and statistical) and reviewed some of the major instruments used by personality and behaviorally oriented practitioners. The chapter concluded with the suggestion that all assessment outcomes be placed in the proper context—that is, that these findings are merely samples of children's behavior from which we must attempt to make generalizations. The accuracy of our generalizations, and ultimately the effectiveness of our decision-making, will be affected substantially by both the accuracy of the information we collect and the extent to which we meet the necessary assumptions underlying the use of our assessment methods.

Discussion Questions

1. Explain the four purposes of assessment.

2. What is the nature of the controversy about the classification of students with disordered behavior?

3. Differentiate between clinically derived and statistically derived classification systems.

4. Identify the limitations of clinically derived classification systems.

5. List the major components of the DSM-IV and describe the diagnostic process.

6. Discuss the advantages and disadvantages of statistically derived classification systems.

7. Describe and critique three methods often used to screen students for behavioral disorders.

8. Compare and contrast personality oriented and behaviorally oriented methods for identifying/classifying students with behavioral disorders.

9. List personality oriented and behaviorally oriented instruments commonly used in the identification process.

10. What factors should be considered in interpreting assessment outcomes?

References

Achenbach, T. M. (1978). Psychopathology of childhood: Research problems and issues. *Journal of Consulting and Clinical Psychology, 46*, 759–776.

Achenbach, T. M. (1979). The child behavior profile: An empirically based system for assessing children's behavioral problems and competencies. *International Journal of Mental Health, 7*, 24–40.

Achenbach, T. M. (1983). Behavior disorders of childhood: Diagnosis and assessment, taxonomy and taxometry. In R. J. McMahon & R. D. Peters (Eds.), *Childhood Disorders: Behavioral development approaches* (pp. 55–89). New York: Brunner & Mazel.

Achenbach, T. M. (1991). *The Child Behavior Checklist: Manual for the teacher's report form.* Burlington, VT: Department of Psychiatry, University of Vermont.

Achenbach, T. M., & Edelbrock, C. (1978). The classification of child psychopathology: A review and analysis of empirical efforts. *Psychological Bulletin, 85*, 1275–1301.

Achenbach, T. M., & Edelbrock, C. (1981). Behavioral problems and competencies reported by parents of normal and disturbed children 4 through 16. *Monographs of the Society for Research in Child Development, 46* (Serial No. 188).

American Psychiatric Association. (1994). *Diagnostic and statistical manual of mental disorders.* 4th ed. (DSM-IV). Washington, DC: Author.

Arter, J., & Jenkins, J. (1979). Differential diagnosis-prescriptive teaching: A critical appraisal. *Review of Educational Research, 49*, 517–555.

Beck, S., Beck, A., Levitt, E., & Molish, H. (1961). *Rorschach's test.* New York: Grune & Stratton.

Bellak, L., & Bellak, S. (1965). *Children's Apperception Test.* Cleveland: Modern Curriculum Press.

Bellak, L., Bellak, S., & Haworth, M. (1974). *Children's Apperception Test.* Larchmont, NY: C.P.S.

Bender, L. (1938). *A visual motor Gestaldt test and its clinical use* (Research Monograph No. 3). New York: American Orthopsychiatric Association.

Bene, E., & Anthony, J. (1957). *Family Relations TestL An objective technique for exploring emotional attitudes in children.* Windsor, England: NFER-Nelson.

Blackhurst, A. E., Bott, D. A., & Cross, D. P. (1987). Noncategorical special education personnel preparation. In M. C. Wang, M. C. Reynolds, & H. J. Walberg (Eds.), *Handbook of special education: Research and practice*, Vol. 1 (pp. 313–330).

Blashfield, R. K. (1984). *The classification of psychopathology: Neo-Kraeplinian and quantative approaches.* New York: Plenum.

Blum, G. (1967). *Blacky pictures: A technique for the exploration of personality dynamics.* Santa Barbara, CA: Psychodynamic Instruments.

Brown, L., & Hammill, D. (1978). *Behavior Rating Profile.* Austin, TX: Pro-Ed.

Buck, J., & Jolles, I. (1966). *House-Tree Person.* Los Angeles: Western Psychological Services.

Burks, H. (1969). *Burks' Behavior Rating Scale.* Los Angeles: Western Psychological Services.

Carter, J., & Sugai, G. (1989). Survey on prereferral practices: Response from State Departments of Education. *Exceptional Children, 55,* 298–302.

Cattell, R. B., Coan, R., & Belloff, H. (1969). *Jr.-Sr. High School Personality Questionnaire.* Indianapolis: Bobbs-Merrill.

Cattell, R. B., Eber, H., & Yatsuoka, M. (1970). *Sixteen Personality Factor Questionnaire.* Champaign, IL: Institute for Personality and Ability Testing.

Christenson, S., Ysseldyke, J. E., & Algozzine, B. (1982). Institutional constraints and external pressures influencing referral decisions. *Psychology in the Schools, 19,* 341–345.

Clarfield, S. (1974). The development of a teacher referral form for identifying early school maladaption. *American Journal of Community Psychology, 2,* 199–210.

Clarizio, H. (1987). *Strengths and weaknesses of four major diagnostic systems.* Unpublished manuscript, Department of Counseling, Educational Psychology, and Special Education, Michigan State University, East Lansing, Michigan.

Coan, R., & Cattell, R. B. (1970). *Early School Personality Questionnaire.* Champaign, IL: Institute for Personality and Ability Testing.

Connors, K. C. (1973). Rating scales for use in drug studies with children. *Psychopharmacology Bulletin, 24,* 24–84.

Cowen, E., Dorr, D., Clarfield, S., Kreling, B., McWilliams, S., Pokracki, F., Pratt, D., Terrel, D., & Wilson, A. (1973). The AML: A quick screening device for early detection of school maladaption. *American Journal of Community Psychology, 1,* 12–35.

Deno, S. L. (1985). Curriculum-based measurement: The emerging alternative. *Exceptional Children, 52,* 219–232.

Deno, S. L., & Mirkin, P. (1977). *Data-based program modification: A manual.* Minneapolis, MN: University of Minnesota, Leadership Training Institute/Special Education.

Duncan, B. B., Forness, S. R., & Hartsough, C. (1995). Students identified as seriously emotionally disturbed in school-based day treatment: Cognitive, psychiatric, and special education characteristics. *Behavioral Disorders, 20,* 238–252.

Edelbrock, C. (1979). Empirical classification of children's behavior disorders: Progress based on parent and teacher ratings. *School Psychology Review, 8,* 355–369.

Edelbrock, C. (1983). Problems and issues in using rating scales to assess child personality and psychopathology. *School Psychology Review, 12,* 253–299.

Edwards, A. (1959). *Edwards Personal Preference Schedule.* Cleveland: The Psychological Corporation.

Edwards, A. (1966). *Edwards Personality Inventory.* Chicago: Science Research Associates.

Eysenck, H., & Eysenck, S. (1969). *Eysenck Personality Inventory.* San Diego: Educational and Industrial Testing Service.

Feil, E. G., & Becker, W. C. (1993). Investigation of a multiple-gated screening system for preschool behavior problems. *Behavioral Disorders, 19,* 44–53.

Fitts, W. (1965). *Tennessee Self Concept Inventory.* Nashville: Counselor Recordings and Tests.

Forness, S. R. (1988). School characteristics of children and adolescents with depression.

Monographs in Behavioral Disorders, 10, 177–203.

Fremont, T., & Wallbrown, F. (1979, Spring). Types of behavior problems that may be encountered in the classroom. *Journal of Education,* 5–23.

Fuchs, L. S., Fuchs, D., Hamlett, C. L., & Stecker, P. M. (1991). Effects of curriculum-based measurement and consultation on teacher planning and student achievement. *American Educational Research Journal, 28,* 617–641.

Galagan, J. (1985). Psychoeducational testing: Turn out the lights, the party's over. *Exceptional Children, 52,* 288–299.

Gersten, R., Keating, T., & Irvin, L. K. (1995). The burden of proof: Validity as improvement of instructional practice. *Exceptional Children, 61,* 510–519.

Glass, G. (1983). Effectiveness of special education. *Policy Studies Review, 2,* 65–78.

Gough, H. (1969). *California Psychological Inventory.* Palo Alto, CA: Consulting Psychologists Press.

Greenwood, C. R., Walker, H. M., Todd, N., & Hops, H. (1979). *SAMPLE (School Assessment Manual for Preschool Level).* Eugene: Center at Oregon for Research in the Behavioral Education of the Handicapped (CORBEH), Clinical Services Building, University of Oregon.

Gresham, F. M., & Elliot, S. N. (1990). *The Social Skills Rating System (SSRS).* Circle Pines, MN: American Guidance Service.

Hardiman, M. I., Drew, C. J., & Egan, M. W. (1996). *Human exceptionality: Society, school, and family,* 5th ed. Needham Heights, MA: Allyn & Bacon.

Hathaway, S., & McKinley, J. (1967). *Minnesota Multiphasic Personality Inventory.* New York: Psychological Corporation.

Heller, K. A., Holtzman, W. H., & Messick, S. (1982). *Placing children in special education: A strategy for equity.* Washington, DC: National Academy Press.

Heward, W. L. (1996). *Exceptional children: An introduction to special education,* 5th ed. Columbus, OH: Merrill.

Hogan, A. E., Quay, H. C., Vaughn, S., & Shapiro, S. K. (1989). Revised behavior problem checklist: Stability, prevalence, and incidence of behavior problems in kindergarten and first-grade children. *Psychological Assessment, 1,* 103–111.

Holtzman, W. (1966). *Holtzman Inkblot Technique.* San Antonio, TX: The Psychological Corporation.

Hoy, C., & Gregg, N. (1994). *Assessment: The special educator's role.* Pacific Grove, CA: Brooks/ Cole Publishing Company.

Hyde, E. (1975). School psychological referral in an inner city school. *Psychology in the Schools, 12,* 412–420.

Kaplan, P. S. (1996). *Pathways for exceptional children: School, home, and culture.* Minneapolis, MN: West Publishing Company.

Kauffman, J. M. (1985). Characteristics of children with behavior disorders. 3rd ed. Coumbus, OH: Merrill.

Kavale, K., & Mattson, P. (1980). *One jumped off the balance: Meta-analysis of perceptual-motor training.* Unpublished manuscript, University of California at Riverside.

Kirschenbaum, D., Marsh, M., & Devage, J. (1977). The effectiveness of a mass screening procedure in an early intervention program. *Psychology in the Schools, 14,* 400–406.

Koppitz, E. (1968). *Human Figure Drawing Test.* New York: Grune & Stratton.

Lanyon, R., & Goodstein, L. (1971). *Personality assessment.* New York: Wiley.

Maag, J. W., & Forness, S. R. (1991). Depression in children and adolescents: Identification, assessment, and treatment. *Focus on Exceptional Children, 24* (1), 1–19.

Maheady, L., Algozzine, B., & Ysseldyke, J. E. (1984). Minorty overrepresentation in special education: A functional assessment perspective. *Special Services in the Schools, 1,* 5–19.

Mash, E., & Terdal, L. (1981). *Behavioral assessment of childhood disorders.* New York: Guilford.

McCarney, S. B., & Leigh, J. E. (1983). *Behavior Evaluation Scale (BES).* Austin, TX: Pro-Ed.

McGinnis, E., & Forness, S. R. (1988). Psychiatric diagnosis: A further test of the special education eligibility hypothesis. *Monographs in Behavioral Disorders, 11,* 3–10.

Merrell, K. W. (1993). *The School Social Behavior Scale (SSBS).* Brandon, VT: Clinical Psychology Publishing.

Messick, S. (1994). The interplay of evidence and consequences in the validation of performance assessments. *Educational Researcher, 23* (2), 13–23.

Murray, H. (1943). *Thematic Apperception Test.* Cambridge, MA: Harvard University Press.

Newland, T. E. (1971). Psychological assessment of exceptional children and youth. In W. Cruickshank (Ed.), *Psychology of exceptional children and youth.* Englewood Cliffs, NJ: Prentice-Hall.

Nicholson, C. (1967). A survey of referral problems in 59 Ohio school districts. *Journal of School Psychiatry, 5,* 280–286.

O'Leary, K. D., & Johnson, S. (1979). Psychological assessment. In H. Quay & J. Werry (Eds.), *Psychological disorders of childhood.* New York: Wiley.

Piers, E., & Harris, D. (1969). *The Piers-Harris Children's Self-Concept Scale.* Nashville, TN: Counselor Recordings and Tests.

Preliminary Report of the NASP/NCAS Task Force (1984). Report on school psychology and advocacy (third working draft). Cited in J. E. Galagan (1985).

Quay, H. C. (1966). Personality patterns in preadolescent delinquent boys. *Educational and Psychological Measurement, 16,* 99–110.

Quay, H. C. (1986). Classification. In H. C. Werry & J. S. Werry (Eds.), *Psychopathological disorders of children,* 3rd ed. (pp. 1–34). New York: Wiley.

Quay, H. C., Morse, W. C., & Cutler, R. L. (1966). Personality patterns of pupils in special classes for the emotionally disturbed. *Exceptional Children, 32,* 297–301.

Quay, H. C., & Peterson, D. R. (1967). Manual for the Revised Behavior Problem Checklist. Unpublished manuscript, University of Illinois.

Quay, H. C., & Peterson, D. R. (1987). *Manual for the Revised Behavior Problem Checklist.* (Available from H. C. Quay, P. O. Box 248185, University of Miami, Coral Gables, FL 33124-2070).

Quay, H. C., & Quay, L. C. (1965). Behavior problems in early adolescence. *Child Development, 36,* 215–220.

Reichler, R., & Schopler, E. (1976). Developmental therapy: A program model for providing individual services in the community. In E. Schopler & R. Reichler (Eds.), *Psychopathology and child development.* New York: Plenum.

Reynolds, M. C., & Lakin, K. C. (1987). Noncategorical special education: Models for research and practice. In M. C. Wang, M. C. Reynolds, & H. J. Walberg (Eds.), *Handbook of special education: Research and practice,* Vol. 1 (pp. 331–356). New York: Pergammon.

Robbins, R., Mercer, J., & Meyers, C. (1967). The school as a selecting-labeling system. *Journal of School Psychology, 5,* 270–279.

Rorschach, H. (1932). *Psychodiagnostik: Methodik un Ergenbisse eines Wahrnehmungs-diagnostischen Experiments.* 2nd ed. Bern, Switzerland: Huber.

Rorschach, H. (1966). *Rorschach Ink Blot Technique.* New York: Grune and Stratton.

Ross, A. (1980). *Psychological disorders of children: A behavioral approach to theory, research, and therapy,* 2nd ed. New York: General Learning Corporation.

Salvia, J., & Ysseldyke, J. E. (1991). *Assessment in special and remedial education,* 5th ed. Boston: Houghton Mifflin.

Sarason, S. B., & Doris, J. (1979). *Educational handicap, public policy, and social history.* New York: Macmillan.

Schaefer, E. (1982). Development of adaptive behavior: Conceptual models and family correlates. In M. Begab, H. Barber, & H. C. Haywood (Eds.), *Prevention of retarded development in psycho-socially disadvantaged children.* Baltimore: University Park Press.

Simpson, R. G. (1991). Agreement among teachers of secondary students in using the Revised Behavior Problem Checklist to identify deviant behavior. *Behavioral Disorders, 17,* 66–71.

Sinclair, E., Del'Homme, & Gonzalez, M. (1993). Systematic screening for preschool behavioral disorders. *Behavioral Disorders, 18,* 177–188.

Sinclair, E., Forness, S. R., & Alexson, J. (1985). Psychiatric diagnosis: A study of its relationship to school needs. *Journal of Special Education, 19,* 333–344.

Solomon, I., & Starr, B. (1968). *School Apperception Method.* New York: Springer.

Spivack, G., & Spotts, J. (1966). *Devereux Child Behavior Rating Scale.* Devon, PA: The Devereux Foundation Press.

Spivack, G., Spotts, J., & Haimes, P. (1967). *Devereux Adolescent Behavior Rating Scale.* Devon, PA: The Devereux Foundation.

Spivack, G., & Swift, M. (1967). *Devereux Elementary School Behavioral Rating Scale.* Devon, PA: The Devereux Foundation.

Taylor, R. L. (1989). *Assessment of exceptional students: Educational and psychological procedures.* 2nd ed. Englewood Cliffs, NJ: Prentice-Hall.

Thorpe, L., Clark, W., & Tiegs, E. (1953). *California Test of Personality.* Monterey, CA: CTB/McGraw-Hill.

Thurlow, M. L., & Ysseldyke, J. E. (1982). Instructional planning: Information collected by school psychologists vs. information considered useful by teachers. *Journal of School Psychology, 20,* 3–10.

Thurman, S. K., & Lewis, M. (1979). Children's response to differences: Some possible implications for mainstreaming. *Exceptional Children, 45,* 468–470.

Tindal, G. (1985). Investigating the effectiveness of special education: An analysis of methodology. *Journal od Learning Disabilities, 18,* 101–117.

Urban, W. (1963). *Draw-A-Person.* Los Angeles: Western Psychological Services.

Vinter, R., Sarri, R., Vorwaller, D., & Schafer, E. (1966). *Pupil Behavior Inventory.* Ann Arbor, MI: Campus Publishers.

Waldon, K. A. (1996). *Introduction to a special education: The inclusive classroom.* Albany, NY: Delmar Publishers.

Walker, H. M. (1983). *Walker Problem Behavior Identification Checklist.* Los Angeles, CA: Western Psychological Services.

Walker, H. M. (1995). *The acting out child: Coping with classroom disruption,* 2nd ed. Longmont, CO: Sopris West.

Walker, H. M., & Fabre, T. R. (1987). Assessment of behavior disorders in the school setting: Issues, problems, and strategies revisited. In N. Haring (Ed.), *Assessing and managing behavior disorders* (pp. 198–234). Seattle: University of Washington Press.

Walker, H. M., & McConnell, S. R. (1995). *The Walker-McConnell Scale of Social Competence and School Adjustment (SSCSA).* San Diego, CA: Singular Publishing Group.

Walker, H. M., & Severson, H. H. (1990). *Systematic Screening for Behavior Disorders (SSBD): User's guide and technical manual.* Longmont, CO: Sopris West.

Walker, H. M., Severson, H. H., & Feil, E. G. (1995). *The Early Screening Project: A proven child-find process.* Longmont, CO: Sopris West.

Walker, L. J. (1987). Procedural rights in the wrong system: Special education is not enough. In A. Gartner & T. Joe (Eds.), *Images of the disabled/disabling images* (pp. 98–102). New York: Praeger.

Winikur, D., & Wohle, R. (1984). Toward program based special education and school service delivery systems. Cited in J. Galagan (1985).

Wirt, R., Lachar, D., Klinedinst, J., & Seat, P. (1984). *Manual for the Personality Inventory for Children.* Los Angeles, CA: Western Psychological Services.

Witt, J. C., Elliot, S. N., Gresham, F. M., & Kramer, J. J. (1988). *Assessment of special children.* Glenview, IL: Scott Foresman.

Wood, F., Smith, C., & Grimes, T. (Eds.). (1985). *The Iowa assessment model in behavioral disorders: A training manual.* Des Moines: Department of Public Education, State of Iowa.

Ysseldyke, J. E., & Algozzine, B. (1995). *Special education: A practical approach for teachers,* 3rd ed. Boston: Houghton & Mifflin Company.

Ysseldyke, J. E., & Thurlow, M. L. (1984). Assessment practices in special education: Adequacy and appropriateness. *Educational Psychologist, 9,* 123–136.

Zigmond, N., & Miller, S. E. (1986). Assessment for instructional planning. *Exceptional Children, 52,* 501–509.

Chapter 5

Direct and Systematic Observation

Advance Organizer

As you read this chapter, prepare to identify and discuss:

- The steps in the direct-observation process.
- The purpose of each step using direct observation.
- Examples of pinpointing behaviors exhibited by students.
- Examples of classroom applications of each recording method.
- The basic graphing conventions for displaying direct-observation data.
- Examples of classroom use of each single-subject design.
- Examples of making data-reactive decisions.
- Examples and reasons for summarizing the effects of intervention.

Although norm-referenced standardized instruments are commercially available to teachers and parents of students with behavior disorders, often the most relevant information can be gathered through direct and systematic observation in the classroom or other applied setting. Using direct observation has several advantages for practitioners involved in the delivery of services to students with behavior disorders. First, the student's behavior is compared not to a nationwide, normative sample, as is the case with most standardized rating scales, but either to behavior the student has exhibited previously or to the behavior of well-adjusted peers in the same class, school, or community. Second, information that is gathered is immediately available in the setting where the student is currently functioning. Third, the assessment process, though informal and often conducted by the classroom teacher, can be rigorous and valid if specific guidelines are followed. Fourth, and perhaps most important, this type of assessment process is so closely tied to the student's daily environment that results are directly related to treatment. This last implication is especially relevant because the one goal of teachers for students with behavior disorders is to arrange an instructional and behavior management program that not only accepts and contains but also remedies maladaptive behaviors. Data gathered via direct observation can serve many purposes, including establishing a record of the current level of student performance and measuring the effect of a wide variety of treatments (e.g., token economics, counseling, and parent involvement).

Direct observation of student behavior can be both accurate and useful only if it is done systematically and with a deliberate purpose. Therefore, much of this chapter focuses on the delineation of specific procedural steps that must be taken to ensure that reliable and valid measures are obtained. Thus, regardless of the nature of the presenting problem, a careful, methodical plan of action should always be undertaken. The following case study from "Mrs. Haddit's Class," is an example of a classroom for students with emotional and behavior disorders where there is ample opportunity to use direct observation in the assessment and treatment of maladaptive behaviors.

The problem behaviors in Mrs. Haddit's classroom have all been treated successfully, and the use of direct observation is a key first step in the assessment–treatment process. Understanding the purpose and function of direct observation, however, is necessary before these procedures can be implemented in the classroom.

The Purposes and Steps in Direct and Systematic Observation

In general, the purpose of using direct observation in assessment is to determine the presence and magnitude of maladaptive behaviors in an applied setting. Teachers must know not only if a problem behavior exists but also the level of its severity. Each of the direct-observation steps in the assessment–treatment process listed below has a specific goal that is related to the overall purpose of providing teachers with accurate and meaningful information about problem behavior. Typically, the following steps are followed when direct observation of student behavior is the assessment method selected:

1. *Screening:* Screening involves determining which students or which behaviors are most in need of treatment. Thus, screening can have one of two purposes: either to identify the student with the most serious problem behavior from among a group of students, or to identify the most significant problem behavior from among several problem behaviors exhibited by one student.
2. *Functional Analysis:* Once the existence of a problem behavior is verified, a functional analysis is undertaken by observing the problem behavior in

Case Study: Mrs. Haddit's Class

Mrs. Iva Haddit is a teacher for elementary students with emotional and behavior disorders in the Premack School District, and from the evaluations done by her principal, she is very competent. This year, however, perhaps because of her superior past performance, she has found herself in a classroom with several students who demonstrate serious behavior problems. At a local teacher hangout, the following conversation took place between Iva Haddit and Les Able, a third-trade teacher.

"Les, I think this is the worst year I have ever had. It seems that my classroom has every problem student in the school. I've got two children who don't want to be in school, four with filthy minds, and at least ten who don't like me."

"Now, Iva," said Les, "don't take it so hard. I'm sure it can't be all that bad. My class is simply wonderful."

"Let me tell you, Les, about some of the things that go on in my class. Last week Bobby walked into the classroom ten minutes late, which was early for him. He stuck out his tongue at me, gave Ms. Dugood, our volunteer, the finger, cursed at Bill, and spit in the trash can. And he's one of my *better* students. Bill, not to be outdone, cursed back, threw his book at Bob, leered at me, and whispered something under his breath. All this time, Wanda is gazing out the doorway, moving her lips, never caring about what is happening in the classroom. Andy, who is the most immature boy I've had in years, winces every time Bill or Bob walks by, and they usually respond by hitting him. He cries, of course, but I've been told by John that Andy plays nasty tricks on Bill and Bob, like putting gum on their seats when they're not around. In addition to being immature, Andy has been certified as hyperactive by his physician, and I'm certain he can't concentrate on what I'm saying. Jill is another story. She steals anything that isn't nailed down. Searching her desk is like visiting the lost-and-found department. As bad as all this sounds, I think the child who worries me most is Wanda. She doesn't have any friends, seldom talks to other children, has a low-self-concept, and spends too much of her time thinking about all the terrible things that go on at home. Les, what am I to do?"

"Well, Iva, lemme buy you a beer."

relation to the setting and other environmental events. The purpose of this step is to analyze how the problem behavior operates relative to environmental events that either precede or follow it. Iva Haddit, concerned about Bill's hitting behavior, might observe when and where the hitting occurs as well as what happens immediately before and after. An informal functional analysis, verified through direct observation, often provides valuable information that can make treatment more likely to succeed.

3. *Pinpointing:* After the problem behavior is identified and its context observed, it is necessary to define the behavior in such a way that it can be observed readily and reliably. The purpose of pinpointing is to state the observable components of the problem behavior so that several individuals observing the same occurrence agree that the problem behavior took place. In the case of Bill's hitting, it is necessary to describe what action constitutes a hit and to differentiate hitting from other related, but different, behaviors such as pushing, back patting, or pulling. This step is also called *operationalizing* or *establishing a behavior definition.*

4. *Recording:* After the behavior is pinpointed, the teacher must record the level of the problem behavior. The purpose of this step is to develop and use an information-gathering system that most appropriately gauges the frequency, intensity, or duration of the problem behavior. Teachers can select one of the direct-observation recording systems described later in this chapter to quantify the occurrence of the problem behavior.

5. *Baseline Measurement:* The purpose of baseline measurement is to provide the teacher with information about the current level of the problem behavior. The teacher uses a recording system previously selected and gathers enough information, usually about one week's worth, to obtain an accurate and representative measure of a problem behavior. It should be noted, however, that there are cases where no baseline data need be gathered (e.g., violent behaviors such as head banging that cannot be left untreated) and cases in which one week's worth of data is not sufficient (e.g., highly variable rates of completing homework assignments).

6. *Goal Selection:* Once the problem behavior has been pinpointed and measured, it is necessary to select an appropriate goal for treatment. The purpose of this step is to choose goals that are both accomplishable in the classroom and important to the student. In the case of students placed in special classes, one important consideration is the selection of a treatment goal that will enhance the likelihood that the student will be able to return to and function in a general education classroom.

7. *Treatment Selection:* One of the advantages of direct observation is that the information gathered can be easily linked to treatment, and the same recording techniques used to gather baseline data can be employed to gather data during or after intervention. Although students in general and special education classrooms exhibit a seemingly endless assortment of problem behaviors, the professional literature contains successful interventions that are available to teachers.

8. *Measurement during Treatment:* Direct and frequent measurement should be gathered over the course of treatment. The purpose of gathering this information is to provide the teacher with objective, ongoing data on which to base behavior management decisions.

9. *Data-Reactive Decision Making:* Once a teacher has data from a behavior management program available for analysis, three decisions are possible. The teacher can decide either to *exit* the program if the treatment goal has been reached, to *continue* treatment if the student is making expected progress toward that goal, or to *change* the program if the student is not making expected progress. Whether the teacher uses a sophisticated decision-making model or visual inspection of graphed data, the purpose of this step is to ensure that the decision-making process is objective and accurate.

10. *Summative Treatment Evaluation:* The purpose of this last step is to evaluate the overall effect of the selected treatment. Assessment at this stage should include measurement of student performance on at least two occasions: at the end of the intervention, to determine short-term treatment effectiveness,

and several weeks or months later, to determine long-term maintenance of treatment gains.

Direct-Observation Methods

In order to satisfy the purpose and implement the steps of the direct-observation process, it is necessary to apply specific procedures during each stage of assessment. Typically, these procedures involve the teacher (and others) observing what the target student or students are doing in the classroom and then quantifying and analyzing the data.

Screening

For the most part, teachers are very aware when problem behaviors occur in the classroom. However, they need an objective means to begin the assessment-treatment process, one that provides information on both the presence and the severity level of maladaptive behaviors.

Whole-Class Screening of One Target Behavior

Teachers who want to identify which students in their classes exhibit inappropriate behaviors can use the informal screening scale in Table 5.1. Results from this instrument provide both relative levels of problem behavior (how each student compares to classroom peers) and individual information (how the problem behavior affects each student's academic achievement).

The procedure for administering the scale is straightforward. First, the teacher selects the most serious problem behavior exhibited in the class (e.g., a physically aggressive act such as hitting rather than a minor disruptive behavior such as talking out). The teacher then rates every child on every item and totals the scores. On items 1–13, higher scores reflect more serious problems. On items 14 16, scores on either the high or low extreme can indicate a concern, depending on the nature of the target behavior (e.g., high scores on verbal aggression or low scores on peer interactions both warrant teacher concern).

Whole-Class Screening of Many Behaviors

Rather than rating one behavior for all students in a class, a teacher might wish to screen many behaviors at once. The informal assessment scales in Tables 5.2, 5.3, and 5.4 are designed for this purpose and can be used to rate the student behaviors in three areas of social and emotional adjustment: self-adjustment, peer interactions, and adult relationships.

Note that each informal screening scale contains classroom concerns listed under two headings: behavior descriptors, which are general terms that describe student behavior; and specific behaviors, which are readily observable (once pinpointed) in the classroom. Neither of these categories is exhaustive, and teachers could enter other descriptors or specific behaviors that are of concern.

TABLE 5.1 Informal Screening Scale for Social Comparison of Problem Behaviors

Student _____

Target Behavior (e.g., Hitting) _____

	Not at All 1	Infrequently 2	Minor Problem 3	Moderate Problem 4	Severe Problem 5

Is the target behavior a problem expressed by:

1 - - - - - - - - - the student ·
2 - - - - - - - - - other students ·
3 - - - - - - - - - the parents ·
4 - - - - - - - - - other staff ·
5 - - - - - - - - - the teacher ·

Does the target behavior interfere with:

6 - - - - - - - - - the student's academic achievement ·
7 - - - - - - - - - the student's peer interactions· ·
8 - - - - - - - - - the student's authority relationships ·
9 - - - - - - - - - other students' academic achievement · · · · · · · · · · · · · · · · ·
10 - - - - - - - - - other students' social and emotional development · · · · · ·
11 - - - - - - - - - the teacher's instructional program ·
12 - - - - - - - - - the teacher's behavior management program · · · · · · · · · · ·
13 - - - - - - - - - the student's affective development ·

	Well Below Average	Below Average	About Average	Above Average	Well Above Average

How does the target behavior compare to the same behavior in same-age, well-adjusted peers in terms of:

14 - - - - - - - - - severity ·
15 - - - - - - - - - duration ·
16 - - - - - - - - - frequency ·

**TABLE 5.2   Informal Classroom Screening Scale
of Self-Adjustment Behaviors**

	Not a Problem 1	Minor Problem 2	Moderate Problem 3	Severe Problem 4
Behavior Descriptors:				
Low frustration level				
Daydreaming				
Distractibility				
Student energy level				
Immaturity				
Perfectionist				
Restlessness, hyperactivity				
Excitability				
Sadness				
Anxiety				
Specific Behaviors:				
Lying				
Stealing				
Crying				
Complaining of physical ailments				
Making facial or other tics				
Babbling				
Making negative self-statements				
Being unclean				
Threatening peers				

The teacher scores these three scales by rating each behavior descriptor and each specific behavior for every student using the 1–4 point scale. The higher the teacher rating, the more serious the behavior problem. Ratings for each student are then summed within each social and emotional area so that a student receives three scores: one for self-adjustment, one for peer interactions, and one for adult relationships.

Teachers can utilize the results in one of two ways: They can use the global scores to identify the student with the most serious problem behavior in their classes, or they can focus on specific behaviors (e.g., making negative statements to peers) and identify which students exhibit these behaviors. In either case, the step after screening is to determine the social and environmental context in which the problem behavior occurs—that is, to conduct a functional analysis.

**TABLE 5.3   Informal Classroom Screening Scale
of Peer Interaction Behaviors**

	Not a Problem 1	Minor Problem 2	Moderate Problem 3	Severe Problem 4
Behavior Descriptors:				
Aloofness, withdrawal				
Shyness				
Aggression				
Friendships				
Social inadequacy				
Cooperation				
Specific Behaviors:				
Time playing with peers				
Time talking with peers				
Teasing, name calling				
Hitting, pushing				
Cursing				
Making negative self-statements				

Functional Analysis

Teachers can conduct a functional analysis in either a structured or an unstructured fashion. The most systematic way to determine environmental context is to observe the problem behavior as it occurs in a real-life setting. If Mrs. Haddit is concerned about Bill's hitting during recess, for example, she could note exactly what happens immediately before and after he strikes another student. In this way, she will be gathering direct-observation information that leads to a better understanding of Bill's hitting. She may discover that Bob sets the occasion for Bill's hitting by teasing him, or that Andy runs away crying after being hit while the whole class laughs.

Writing down events that occur before, during, and after the target behavior is called *narrative recording*. Analysis of this type of written report enables teachers to get a good idea of when, where, and why a problem behavior occurs. An example of a segment from the form Mrs. Haddit used to observe Bill is depicted in Table 5.5.

Pinpointing

After teachers have identified the environmental context of the target behavior, it is necessary to provide an observable means of quantification. Pinpointing is important because it makes teacher concerns concrete and objective: With a

**TABLE 5.4   Informal Classroom Screening Scale
of Adult Relationship Behaviors**

	Not a Problem 1	Minor Problem 2	Moderate Problem 3	Severe Problem 4
Behavior Descriptors:				
Hates school				
Disrespectful of authority				
Rude, impolite				
Troublemaker				
Needs adult approval				
Specific Behaviors:				
Interrupting, talking out				
Out-of-seat				
Off-task				
Arguing and complaining				
Completing tasks				
Breaking class rules				
Complying with requests				
Participating in class				

well-pinpointed behavior, several observers who witness a classroom event can agree whether it has or has not occurred.

The pinpointing process involves going from the general to the specific. In everyday language, student behavior is often described in terms that give a listener an indication of the type of behavior the child exhibits (e.g., hyperactive, aggressive, impulsive, rude, disruptive, and withdrawn). These general terms are called *behavior descriptors*. Students described as physically aggressive, for example, often hit, push, or kick, while students described as withdrawn seldom engage in interpersonal contacts.

However, because the terms of everyday language are not specific enough to ensure reliable observation, it is necessary to attain additional objectivity through the pinpointing process. This is accomplished by identifying the *specific defining behaviors* that are the observable elements of the more general behavior descriptor. If a student's behavior is described as physically aggressive, for example, that student may exhibit one or more of the following specific behaviors in the classroom: hitting, kicking, spitting, tripping, pushing, or throwing objects at other persons. Listed in Table 5.6 are examples of behavior descriptors and specific defining behaviors in the areas of verbal aggression and disruptive behavior in the classroom.

TABLE 5.5   Narrative Recording Form

Student	Bill		Date	May 6, 1987

Target Behavior	Hitting		Class	Recess 2:00–2:30 p.m.

Time	Antecedent	Behavior	Consequences
2:07	The boys are playing kickball. Bob kicks a triple and is standing on third base close to Bill, the third baseman.	Bill hits Bob.	Bob chases Bill around the playground, yelling and screaming, while Bill laughs. Bob is caught by the recess aide and is sent back to the classroom for the rest of recess.

TABLE 5.6   Examples of Behavior Descriptors and Specific Behaviors

Behavior Descriptor:	Verbal aggression
Specific Observable Behaviors:	Cursing in the classroom Teasing classmates Threatening classmates Talking back to the teacher
Behavior Descriptor:	Disruptive behavior
Specific Observable Behaviors:	Getting out of seat Making noises Gesturing inappropriately Talking out

Even though these defining behaviors identify specific acts, unreliable observations can still occur if observers do not agree, for example, that the target student has actually hit another child. In these cases, the problem behavior needs to be defined with an even greater degree of specificity. Hitting can be more objectively defined by specifying the intensity of the hit in terms of the victim's reactions. *Hitting* might be reserved to label only those behaviors that cause the victim's body to move noticeably after being struck by the target student's hand and the victim to scream, complain, or cry, indicating the presence of some degree of pain. In this way, it is possible to differentiate hitting from back patting, shoving, and other related acts.

Although this additional level of specificity can be attained for many behaviors, and indeed is necessary in research studies, it is usually not required for informal classroom observation. Classroom noisemaking, for example, can be measured very accurately by specifying the decibel cut-off point between a disruptive noise and a nondisruptive noise. Out-of-seat behavior can be more objectively defined by specifying the number of inches a student's behind must be raised from the desk seat (Turkewitz, O'Leary, & Ironsmith, 1975). Nearly all target behaviors can be specified more rigorously, but teachers should only employ the degree of specificity necessary to ensure reliable observation in an efficient manner. The level of specificity obtainable in applied classroom settings is limited by the expense of observer training and measuring devices.

Pinpointing academic behaviors is usually easier than pinpointing nonacademic behaviors. Student responses to teacher questions, test items, or homework assignments can be scored as either correct or incorrect by comparing actual student performance to the correct answer. Thus, if a student's academic behavior descriptor is computational math, specific defining behaviors would include either the percent of correct problems or digits computed or the number of correct problems or digits computed per minute (Haring, Lovitt, Eaton, & Hansen, 1978). Oral reading fluency, also a behavior descriptor, can be specifically defined as the number of correct words read per minute, and reading comprehension as the percent of correct written or verbal answers to teacher questions about details or the main idea of a passage.

Recording

After the target behavior has been pinpointed, the teacher must select the most appropriate technique to record the behavior's intensity, frequency, or duration. Several recording techniques are available for classroom use, and the choice is typically made after an analysis of the target behavior.

Frequency Recording
The most commonly employed recording technique for classroom use is frequency or event recording, in which the observer makes a tally mark for each occurrence of the target behavior. This method of recording can provide an objective measure

---

Learn by Doing: Identifying and Pinpointing Target Behaviors

Directions

In the case study excerpt "Mrs. Haddit's Class," you are to identify all classroom behavior concerns and divide them into two categories: observable and unobservable. Observable behaviors are overt acts that you believe Mrs. Haddit and a second observer could watch independently and agree had occurred. Unobservable teacher concerns include behavioral descriptors, presumed underlying causes of student behavior, and other terms that do not describe a specific observable behavior. List ten concerns for each category.

In the second part of the activity, you are to select two students from the class and pinpoint one target behavior for each. For each target behavior selected, provide the descriptor and appropriate level of pinpointing. An example is provided below.

Observable Behaviors
(e.g., Bill hits Andy)

Unobservable Concerns
(e.g., Andy is immature)

Student   *(e.g., Bill)*
Behavior descriptor   *(e.g., physical aggression)*
Pinpointing level 1   *(e.g., Bill hits a classmate with his hand.)*

Pinpointing level 2   *(e.g., The victim's body moves noticeably after being struck, the victim cries, complains, winces, or yells after being struck by Bill.)*

of a large number of classroom behaviors, including hits, pushes, curses, threats, talk-outs, thrown objects, lies, noises, answers to teacher questions, smiles, tasks completed, arguments, and interruptions. Typically, the behaviors best measured with frequency recording are *discrete*—that is, each instance of the behavior has a definite and observable beginning and ending. The presence of a clear beginning and ending enables an observer to record one instance of the target behavior each time it occurs.

In addition to being discrete, behaviors best measured with frequency recording are those that are of approximately the same duration each time they occur. This qualification ensures that behaviors of widely varying durations will not be added together. For example, even though the beginning and ending of a temper tantrum may be discrete and observable, a student may tantrum for thirty minutes on one occasion and for forty-five seconds the next. For these behaviors, the frequency is far less important than the duration or intensity.

Frequency recording has been used successfully by teachers, parents, and applied researchers to measure disruptive and aggressive behavior (Carr, Newsom, & Blinkoff, 1980) as well as math facts (Farb & Thorne, 1978). Figure 5.1 depicts a tally sheet used to record the number of talk-outs by a student in math class.

When student behavior produces an outcome that remains after the behavior ceases to be emitted, it is possible to use the *permanent-product observational method*. This method of data collection is appropriate for quantifying many aspects of student achievement, especially those by which a student produces a written response. A written spelling test, a math worksheet, a spontaneous writing sample, and a test in history are examples of instances when a teacher can use the permanent products of a student's behavior to obtain a direct measure of that student's performance.

The permanent-product recording method is an accurate, easy, and convenient way to gather important classroom information, and this high degree of utility has made it a popular choice in data-based programs. Most permanent-product data represent a direct frequency count (e.g., the teacher counts the number of correct and incorrect spelling words, math facts, or history test items). In addition, by measuring the time it takes the student to respond, teachers can also easily gather rate-based data with permanent products (e.g., the number of correct and incorrect digits written per minute).

Permanent-product recording can be used to measure both academic and nonacademic behaviors. Researchers have employed this method to record spelling accuracy (Neef, Iwata, & Page, 1980), bed-wetting (Hansen, 1979), smoking (Lando, 1975), and room cleaning (Wood & Flynn, 1978). Audio and video taping devices, while less practical, also enable a teacher to make a permanent record of out-of-seat, off-task, and similar behaviors while teaching and then to analyze the data after class.

Duration Recording

A second commonly employed recording technique where the observer times how long a student is engaged in the target behavior is duration recording. Typically, behaviors best measured with duration recording are *continuous*—that is the

Frequency Recording

Student	Sam		Date	3/25/96–3/29/96
Behavior	Talking out		Time	1:30–2:15 P.M.
Teacher	Mrs. Natis		Setting	Math Class
Observer	Mrs. Natis			

Time

3/25/96 1:30–2:15 Math class	~~HHT~~ ~~HHT~~ ~~HHT~~ ////	– 19
3/26/96 1:30–2:15 Math class	~~HHT~~ ~~HHT~~ ~~HHT~~ /	= 16
3/27/96 1:30–2:15 Math class	~~HHT~~ ~~HHT~~ ~~HHT~~ ~~HHT~~ ///	= 23
3/28/96 1:30–2:15 Math class	~~HHT~~ ~~HHT~~ ~~HHT~~ /	= 16
3/29/96 1:30–2:15 Math class	~~HHT~~ ~~HHT~~ ~~HHT~~ ~~HHT~~ ~~HHT~~	= 25

FIGURE 5.1   A Frequency Recording of Sam's Talk-Outs during Math Class

emission of one behavior is followed closely and rapidly by the emission of more instances of the behavior.

Many maladaptive classroom behaviors can be measured accurately and efficiently with duration recording. This is the technique of choice if the length of time the student is emitting the behavior is the teacher's primary concern. Many of the stereotypic, repetitive behaviors of students with autism (e.g., hand flapping and rocking) are of concern to teachers because of the amount of time these behaviors take away from instruction. Similarly, the duration of temper tantrums is frequently the most important dimension of this maladaptive behavior. Less serious, but nonetheless disruptive, behaviors can also be measured with duration recording, including time out-of-seat and time off-task. Figure 5.2 is a recording sheet used to measure the duration of out-of-seat behavior during reading class.

Latency Recording

Latency recording is a variation of duration recording that measures the length of time between a teacher's request and the student's compliance. Typically, a teacher asks students to settle down and begin work, often after a transition

Duration Recording

Student	Sally	Date	5/6/96–5/10/96
Behavior	Out-of-seat	Time	9:30–10:00 A.M.
Teacher	Mrs. Patton	Setting	Reading Class
Observer	Mrs. Patton		

Time	Comments
Begin–End	
Monday	
9:10–9:12	At beginning of class
9:15–9:18	Sharpen pencil
9:25–9:31	
9:44–9:46	
9:52–9:56	
Tuesday	
9:10–9:14	At beginning of class
9:18–9:22	Sharpen pencil
9:24–9:25	Bathroom
9:48–9:56	
Wednesday	
9:10–9:12	At beginning of class
	Movie 9:15–9:45
9:50–9:58	Bathroom
Thursday	
9:10–9:13	At beginning of class
9:27–9:32	Sharpen pencil
9:41–9:43	
9:51–9:54	
Friday	
9:10–9:11	At beginning of class
9:17–9:21	Bathroom
9:30–9:45	Sharpen pencil
9:48–9:50	

Week's Summary

	Frequency	Duration
Monday	5	17
Tuesday	4	17
Wednesday	2	10
Thursday	4	13
Friday	4	12
TOTAL	19	69 minutes

FIGURE 5.2 A Duration Recording of Sally's Out-of-Seat Behavior during Reading Class

between activities. A teacher might be interested in recording how long it takes the class to get ready for English class after coming in from recess. Latency recording has also been used to measure the time a class took to get ready for spelling lessons (Fjellstedt & Sulzer-Azaroff, 1973) and writing assignments (Buisson, Murdock, Reynolds, & Cronin, 1995).

Accurate latency recording requires careful definition of two events: the antecedent stimulus (e.g., the teacher's instruction) and the target behavior that indicates student compliance. If instructions are explicit (e.g., "Take out your workbooks, open them to page 43, and complete problems 1 through 10"), latency measurement begins with the end of the instructions. If instructions are implied (e.g., students have been told previously that they are supposed to get ready for social studies class every day after coming in from recess), timing might begin after the last student has entered the room. The compliance target behavior also needs to be carefully operationalized. What does a teacher expect when students are asked to "get ready for social studies class"? In such a case, all students may be expected to clear their desks of everything except a notebook, pencil, and textbook. A latency recording form is depicted in Figure 5.3.

Interval Recording

The last major category of recording techniques includes three methods that use predetermined time intervals to quantify data. In each of these methods, total observation time is divided into smaller intervals (e.g., twenty seconds or five minutes) and a target behavior is recorded as it occurs either within or at the end of each interval. In *partial-interval recording*, a target behavior is recorded if it occurs at any time within an interval. If a teacher is using the recording sheet in Figure 5.4 to collect data on hand-flapping behavior, for example, she would record a "+" if hand flapping occurred during any part of a twenty-second interval. A "−" would be recorded if no hand flapping took place in the interval. In *whole-interval recording*, a "+" is recorded only if a target behavior is emitted throughout an entire interval. If a target behavior does not occur or if it is emitted for only part of the interval, a "−" is recorded for that interval.

The third interval recording technique is known as *momentary-time sampling* or *time-point sampling*. In this method, a target behavior is observed only at the end points of the interval. If a twenty-second interval is being used to observe on-task behavior, for example, an observer looks at a target student exactly as the twenty-second interval ends and records a "+" if the student is on-task and a "−" if the student is off-task at that precise moment. The student's behavior during the rest of the interval is not recorded by the observer.

Interval recording methods are often used because they provide an estimate of both the frequency and the duration of a target behavior and because it is possible, by selecting the appropriate interval technique, to record nearly all types of behaviors. However, there are disadvantages associated with interval recording. All three methods of interval recording provide only approximations of the actual record of a target behavior. In partial-interval recording, because even fleeting behaviors will cause the entire interval to be counted, there is a tendency to

Latency Recording

Student	Sol	Date	4/22/96–4/26/96
Behavior	Getting ready for class	Time	9:10–10:00 A.M.
Teacher	Mrs. Patton	Setting	Social Studies Class
Observer	Mrs. Patton		

Time	*Comments*
Begin–End 10:15–10:21 Monday	Begin = bell rings End = in seat, SS text, notebook, and pencil on desk Reminded Sol once
10:15–10:22 Tuesday	Reminded Sol twice
10:15–10:19 Wednesday	Reminded Sol once
10:15–10:22 Thursday	Out of room until 10:20
10:15–10:24 Friday	Began class anyway Reminded Sol twice

Week's Summary		*Duration*
	Monday	6
	Tuesday	7
	Wednesday	4
	Thursday	7
	Friday	9
	TOTAL	33 minutes

FIGURE 5.3   Latency Recording of Getting Ready for Social Studies Behavior

overestimate the occurrence of a target behavior. Conversely, in whole-interval recording, measurement of a target behavior is often underestimated because behaviors that do not continue throughout an entire interval are not counted. In addition, the accuracy of momentary-time sampling (as well as of whole- and partial-interval methods) depends on the length of interval chosen: The longer the interval, the lower the accuracy. On the other hand, if very short intervals are used (less than thirty seconds), it is often impossible for a teacher to deliver instruction while recording, so a trained, independent observer must be used.

Observation sheets for interval recording methods are often designed for specific target behaviors, but because all three methods use a timed interval, the generic recording form depicted in Figure 5.4 could be used for partial-interval, whole-interval or momentary-time sampling records. Figures 5.5, 5.6 and 5.7 are, respectively, examples of partial-interval recording of a number of disruptive

Direct Observation

Student	Date
Behavior	Time Start
Teacher	Time End
Observer	Setting

Observation method: Partial-interval, whole-interval, or momentary-time sampling at 20-second intervals.

Minutes	*1–20*	*21–40*	*41–60*
1			
2			
3			
4			
5			
6			
7			
8			
9			
10			
11			
12			
13			
14			
15			

FIGURE 5.4   A Generic Interval Recording Form

behaviors, whole-interval recording of staring out the window, and momentary-time sampling recording of on-task behavior.

Baseline Measurement

Purposes

After a teacher has decided which recording technique is most appropriate for collecting the direct-observation data desired, the next step is to gather sufficient data to provide an objective estimate of the current level of a target behavior in an applied setting. There are at least two purposes for gathering baseline data. The more important one is to obtain a representative sample of behavior (Kazdin, 1978). Because the next step in the assessment-treatment process involves selecting an intervention to change the target behavior in the desired direction, teachers need to know how serious the current problem has become before they intervene.

Interval Recording

Student _____   Date _____

Behavior _____   Time _____

Teacher _____   Setting _____

Observer _____

	Seconds		
Minutes	*1–20*	*21–40*	*41–60*
1	OS OT TO MN TN TS	OS OT TO MN TN TS	OS OT TO MN TN TS
2	OS OT TO MN TN TS	OS OT TO MN TN TS	OS OT TO MN TN TS
3	OS OT TO MN TN TS	OS OT TO MN TN TS	OS OT TO MN TN TS
4	OS OT TO MN TN TS	OS OT TO MN TN TS	OS OT TO MN TN TS
5	OS OT TO MN TN TS	OS OT TO MN TN TS	OS OT TO MN TN TS
6	OS OT TO MN TN TS	OS OT TO MN TN TS	OS OT TO MN TN TS
7	OS OT TO MN TN TS	OS OT TO MN TN TS	OS OT TO MN TN TS
8	OS OT TO MN TN TS	OS OT TO MN TN TS	OS OT TO MN TN TS
9	OS OT TO MN TN TS	OS OT TO MN TN TS	OS OT TO MN TN TS
10	OS OT TO MN TN TS	OS OT TO MN TN TS	OS OT TO MN TN TS
11	OS OT TO MN TN TS	OS OT TO MN TN TS	OS OT TO MN TN TS
12	OS OT TO MN TN TS	OS OT TO MN TN TS	OS OT TO MN TN TS
13	OS OT TO MN TN TS	OS OT TO MN TN TS	OS OT TO MN TN TS
14	OS OT TO MN TN TS	OS OT TO MN TN TS	OS OT TO MN TN TS
15	OS OT TO MN TN TS	OS OT TO MN TN TS	OS OT TO MN TN TS

Key: OS = Out-of-seat   MN = Make noise
OT = Off-task   TN = Touch neighbor
TO = Talk-out   TS = Throws something

FIGURE 5.5   Partial-Interval Recording for Disruptive Behaviors

The second purpose for gathering baseline data is to obtain a basis for predicting future student performance. Researchers have found that, on average, behaviors that are being successfully modified can be expected to change (i.e., increase in frequency, duration, or intensity if they are adaptive and decrease if they are maladaptive) about 25 percent each week (Haring et al., 1978).

Interval Recording Form

Student	Wanda	Date	4/15/96
Behavior	Staring out of window	Time Start	1:45
Teacher	Mrs. Leeds	Time End	2:00
Observer	Miss Floes	Setting	Math Class

Observation method: Whole-interval recording for 20-second intervals.

Minutes	1–20	21–40	41–60
1	+	+	0
2	0	0	+
3	0	0	0
4	0	0	0
5	+	+	+
6	0	0	0
7	0	+	+
8	+	+	0
9	0	0	0
10	0	0	0
11	0	0	0
12	0	+	0
13	0	+	+
14	0	+	0
15	0	0	0

Key: + = Staring
0 = Not Staring

FIGURE 5.6   Whole-Interval Recording of Staring Out the Window

Graphing

Baseline (and treatment) data are frequently presented on a graph so that a quick and accurate appraisal of progress can be made. Although graphing can be quite complex, most data can be displayed adequately by anyone who has mastered a few basic graphing conventions.

Momentary-Time Sampling

Student _____   Date _____

Behavior ___On-task___   Time _____

Teacher _____   Setting _____

Observer _____

Directions: Determine the context (e.g., reading or math) and the format of the activity (either seatwork [SW] or teacher-directed [TD]. At 10-second intervals, record a "+" if the student is on-task, a "−" if off-task. On-task means the student is watching an appropriate instructional object or person.

Activity 1: _____ SW TD   Activity 2: _____ SW TD

Time Begin _____ Time End _____   Time Begin _____ Time End _____

Total Time _____   Total Time _____

Minutes	*00*	*10*	*20*	*30*	*40*	*50*
1						
2						
3						
4						
5						
6						
7						
8						
9						
10						
11						
12						
13						
14						
15						

Minutes	*00*	*10*	*20*	*30*	*40*	*50*
1						
2						
3						
4						
5						
6						
7						
8						
9						
10						
11						
12						
13						
14						
15						

Totals for Activity #1:

$$\text{Time on task} = \frac{\text{total "+" 's}}{\text{total "+" 's and total "−" 's}} \times 100\% = _____$$

Totals for Activity #2:

$$\text{Time on task} = \frac{\text{total "+" 's}}{\text{total "+" 's and total "−" 's}} \times 100\% = _____$$

Comments: _____

FIGURE 5.7   Momentary-Time Sampling of On-Task Behavior

Figure 5.8 is an illustration of the components of a standard graph. The vertical line, or ordinate, contains a scale that provides a measure of the levels of a target behavior. This line is divided into units that will best present the data visually. If talk-outs during math class are being graphed, for example, the scale might resemble the one in Figure 5.9. If percents of time on-task during reading class are being graphed, the scale might resemble the one in Figure 5.10. Notice that the time-on-task scale has been truncated; there are no hashmarks representing on-task rates lower than 40 percent.

The horizontal line, or abscissa, contains a scale that represents the passage of time, quantified in units that reflect the time periods used in a classroom or research project. The abscissa scales in Figure 5.9 and 5.10 depict math and reading classes, respectively, but other labels are possible here, including days in school, therapy sessions, and learning trials.

The third basic component of graphing involves the visual display of data. In its simplest form, this process involves transcribing data from a recording sheet into points on a graph and connecting the points with solid lines. Sam's talking-out data from Figure 5.1 have been depicted in Figure 5.9. In some cases, data must be converted to different units before they can be graphed. This is true, for example, when the rate of behavior is important (e.g., the number of talk-outs per minute) or when percent data are desired (e.g., the percent of time spent off-task).

Goal Selection

Once teachers have measured the current level of maladaptive behavior by gathering baseline data, they must select a goal so that they can determine if progress is made. Although it is possible to proceed with intervention without first establishing

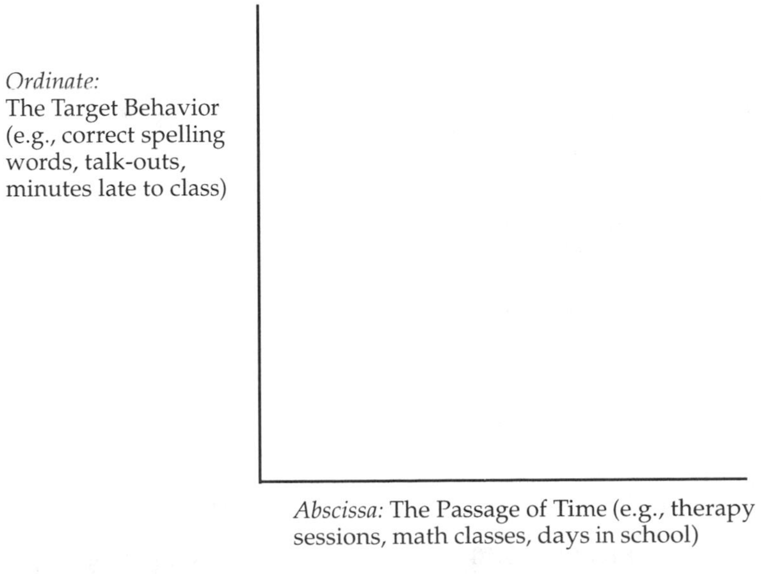

Ordinate:
The Target Behavior
(e.g., correct spelling
words, talk-outs,
minutes late to class)

Abscissa: The Passage of Time (e.g., therapy
sessions, math classes, days in school)

FIGURE 5.8   Basic Graphing Components

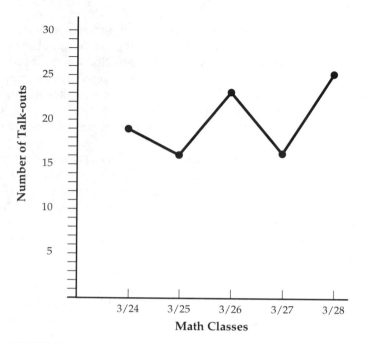

FIGURE 5.9   A Graph of Talk-Outs during Math Classes

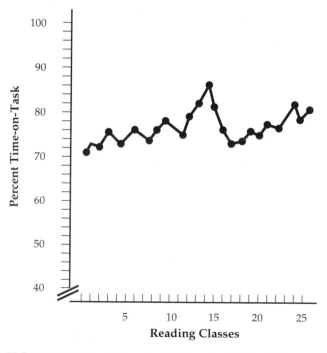

FIGURE 5.10   A Graph of Time On-Task during Reading Classes

an overall treatment goal, specifying a desired outcome by using one of the methods discussed below provides an added measure of objectivity that can be helpful when the success or failure of an intervention is being judged.

Social Validation

Kazdin (1977) provides teachers and practitioners with a means of setting treatment goals by comparing a target student's progress to that of a cross section of well-adjusted peers. Talking-out behavior serves as a good example. If a target student exhibits an average rate of fifteen inappropriate talk-outs during each ninety-minute reading class, a teacher could gather social-validation information by collecting talk-out data in a general education class of age peers who are considered to be average students. If an average student exhibits two talk-outs per class, then the teacher can set the treatment goal at two, knowing that if this level of behavior is achieved, the target student will be behaving in a fashion similar to other students for whom talking out is not considered to be a problem behavior.

Kendall and Wilcox (1980) used a variation of social validation in order to determine if their cognitive-behavioral treatment was effective for boys who were impulsive. The post-test scores of the students who received treatment were compared on measures of hyperactivity, self-control, response latency, and response errors to scores that represented the mean of one hundred randomly selected children. The purpose of using social-validation data was to demonstrate the degree

---

Learning by Doing: Graphing Frequency and Percent Baseline Data

Directions

Frequency Data. From the case study "Mrs. Haddit's Class," select one student's specific maladaptive behavior that is best measured using frequency or event recording. Write this information on a separate sheet of paper. Next, assume that data have already been gathered and that the numbers in the columns below represent the observed frequency during the baseline phase. Plot these data on graph paper, carefully following the required graphing conventions.

Target Student _____

Maladaptive Behavior _____

Baseline lasted two weeks and Mrs. Haddit gathered these data:

M	Tu	W	Th	F
8	6	14	*	12
7	14	13	9	11

* = absent

Percent Data. In addition to the student whose behavior was measured in the above section, Mrs. Haddit is worried about Wanda because she is off-task to such a degree that her academic performance is suffering. Mrs. Haddit arranges to have Wanda's off-task behavior observed during reading class using a ten-second momentary-time sampling procedure. The data below are from ten days of baseline. The top number represents the number of intervals judged off-task; the bottom number represents the total number of intervals observed that day. Convert the data to percent off-task and plot the data using the required graphing conventions.

M	Tu	W	Th	F
42/60	38/60	45/60	32/54	40/60
*	29/48	43/66	50/72	38/60

* = absent

of treatment success relative to a group of peers who did not exhibit problem behaviors. Once a target student's behavior has reached the level of peers' behavior, social-validation data can be used to support a recommendation that the student with behavior disorders is ready to be considered for mainstreaming.

Normative Data

Social-validation data may be gathered informally using only a few average students. If, however, large numbers of students have been observed, measures of central tendency can be used to set treatment goals (Haring et al., 1978). In some cases, local or community norms have been collected. In others, results from published research may be used. Fisher and colleagues (1980) found, for example, that general class second-grade students were on-task nearly 83 percent of the time during teacher-led instruction and 67 percent of the time during independent seatwork tasks. Unfortunately, national or local norms are not available for a wide range of behaviors, although gathering community norms remains an excellent idea for special education personnel.

Functional Level

The ideal way to set a treatment goal is to work toward that level of behavior that will enable a student to function adequately in an applied setting. In practice, these data levels are difficult to specify and often vary from setting to setting. If a teacher or counselor is working with a student who curses, for example, a reasonable treatment goal might be to reduce cursing to a level at which the student can function in class. In this case, the functional level is defined as the level of cursing a particular teacher can tolerate. The problems with setting functional levels in this example are twofold. First, it is difficult to specify objectively the level a teacher can tolerate. Second, it is quite likely that different teachers tolerate different levels of maladaptive behaviors.

Although there are often problems with subjectivity and setting variation, there are instances in which functional levels can be used effectively to set treatment goals. Bus-riding behavior—an area in which students with behavior disorders typically demonstrate significant problems—is often governed by rules that specify both the maladaptive behavior and the number of times the behavior can be exhibited before the student incurs bus suspension. In this case, the functional goal is that level of behavior that will permit a student to retain bus-riding privileges. Some teachers use classroom behavior management systems that specify exactly what happens when students commit a disruptive act. For teachers using assertive discipline (Canter & Canter, 1976), a sequence like the one below is typical:

Behavior	→	Consequence
1. First disruptive act	→	Name is written on board
2. Second disruptive act	→	Name is circled
3. Third disruptive act	→	Name is checked and student loses one recess period

Interim Goal Setting

Teachers often find that there are no readily available data to set goals based on social-validation, normative, or functional levels. In these instances, they can implement their own selected intervention and set interim goals as the student progresses through the program. Although this procedure can be done subjectively and the overall treatment goal left unspecified until it is determined that a behavior problem no longer exists, it is possible to set interim goals objectively. One method is to use the 1.25 rule (Haring et al., 1978), which predicts a 25 percent change in student behavior for each week of intervention. For a student who exhibits an average of twenty talk-outs per reading class during baseline, the first weekly goal would be determined by reducing the baseline rate by 25 percent (i.e., $20 \div 1.25 = 16$). If, however, the target behavior is adaptive—that is, one the teacher hopes to increase in frequency or duration (e.g., hand raising in class)—the weekly goal is set by increasing the base rate by 25 percent (i.e., $20 \times 1.25 = 25$).

Treatment Selection

After baseline data are gathered, a determination made that a problem exists, and an overall goal set, the teacher must select a treatment or intervention program that has some likelihood of changing a target behavior. Most teachers will have been exposed to successful treatment techniques during preservice or in-service training and past teaching experiences. In addition, the behavior management methods described in this text offer teachers some excellent ideas for intervention.

Using direct-observation techniques has at least two treatment-related advantages. First, although direct observation is the hallmark of applied behavior analysis, these techniques can be utilized to measure the success of interventions developed from *any* conceptual model as long as the target behavior can be described in observable terms. Thus, the success of life-space interviews, medication, diet, positive reinforcement, biofeedback, or psychoanalytic therapy can be determined as long as treatment goals can be specified in terms of child behaviors that are readily observable. The opposite side of this, of course, is that those components of treatment goals that are inherently unobservable (e.g., emotional stability, self-concept, or ego development) are not verifiable through direct observation.

Second, teachers can use the same direct-observation assessment methods to gather data before, during, and after intervention. This continuity is often not possible with other assessment methods. Teacher rating scales and sociometric devices, for example, have not proved sensitive enough to measure small increments of behavior change, and projective test results are often difficult to translate into observable target behaviors. Standardized tests (e.g., those that measure intelligence) cannot be readministered over the short time intervals needed to gauge small increments of behavior change.

Measurement during Treatment Using Single-Subject Designs

Gathering direct-observation data during treatment is accomplished in the same way as during baseline (i.e., the same recording techniques are used to measure the same target behaviors). The only difference between the baseline and the treatment phase is that the teacher has meanwhile implemented a program that, she hopes, has changed the target behavior in the desired direction. The purpose of gathering treatment data is to help the teacher determine the degree, type, and importance of the behavior change.

Treatment programs that use direct observation typically display the graphed data in one of several predetermined patterns. These patterns—or designs, as they are more commonly called—reflect different ways to present data in a visual form so that teachers can determine if the treatment has actually contributed to a change in the target behavior. Although a lengthy presentation of single-subject designs is beyond the scope of this chapter, and there are currently available several excellent sources of information (Alberto & Troutman, 1995; Barlow & Hersen, 1984; Tawney & Gast, 1984), a brief overview of the more popular teaching designs is presented here.

Comparison or AB Design

The simplest design has only two phases: baseline (A phase) and treatment (B phase). This design is commonly employed in teaching but is seldom seen in the research literature because it cannot be used to demonstrate experimental control (i.e., that implementation of treatment caused the change in the target behavior). Consider the results of a time-out treatment program designed to reduce aggressive acts during recess as depicted in Figure 5.11. Even though such dramatic

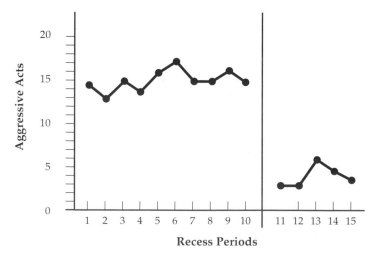

FIGURE 5.11   Comparison or AB Design

results cannot be used to prove that the time-out treatment caused the aggressive behavior to decrease (it is possible that some additional, outside factor occurred in the student's life at the same time the treatment began), teachers frequently use this design because they are more interested in controlling the problem behavior than in demonstrating experimental control.

Reversal Design

The reversal or withdrawal design is an extension of the comparison design that is created by adding a third phase, during which treatment is withdrawn, and often a fourth phase, during which treatment is reinstituted. Thus, the reversal design may be called an ABA or ABAB design. This design can be used to demonstrate experimental control, primarily by providing two or three instances when either the treatment was instituted and behavior improved or when the treatment was removed and behavior worsened. Examine the data graphed in Figure 5.12. These results would be considered sufficient proof that the time-out treatment caused a reduction in the aggressive recess acts of this student.

Though the reversal design commonly appears in the professional literature, it may be inappropriate for classroom use for two reasons. First, if a problem behavior has been successfully treated, teachers have little to gain by withdrawing treatment and causing the maladaptive behavior to increase (or causing the adaptive behavior to decrease). Second, many learned behaviors fail to reverse even when a treatment is removed. In fact, this failure to reverse is likely to be considered a desired result by teachers and often occurs either with academic target behaviors (e.g., number of sight words mastered), because students have remembered what they have been taught, or with adaptive responses (e.g., number of positive statements made to other students), because events outside the teacher's behavior

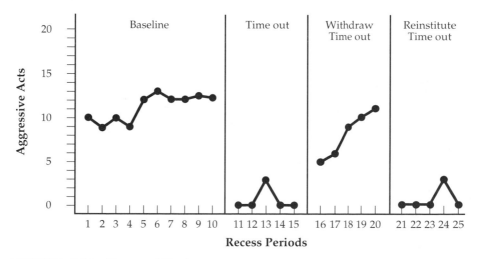

FIGURE 5.12 Reversal Design

change program continue to reinforce and maintain the student's new skills. This result is depicted in Figure 5.13. It would be considered an experimental failure but a treatment success.

Changing-Conditions Design

Like the comparison design, the changing-conditions design has many classroom applications but cannot demonstrate experimental control. A changing-conditions design would be used if a first treatment proved partly or totally unsuccessful and a teacher decided to implement a second treatment without programming a return to baseline phase. Because of the baseline–first treatment–second treatment order, this design is referred to as the ABC design. In practice, teachers may try one intervention after another until they find one that works, resulting in an ABCDE etc. design. Such a course of treatment is depicted in Figure 5.14.

Changing-Criterion Design

Like the previous two designs, the changing-criterion design is a variation of the basic comparison design. As in the comparison design, there are only two phases: baseline and treatment. However, in the changing-criterion design, the treatment phase is subdivided into segments that correspond to gradual changes in the treatment criterion. Treatment of inappropriate classroom interruptions, for example, may be displayed using this design, and the results of successful treatment are depicted in Figure 5.15. In this case, the baseline average was observed to be about forty interruptions per day. The first treatment goal was set at less than thirty interruptions per day, and the student successfully stayed below this criterion, perhaps earning a special privilege for doing so. As goals were met in the ensuing weeks, the criteria were gradually lowered until interruptions were reduced to

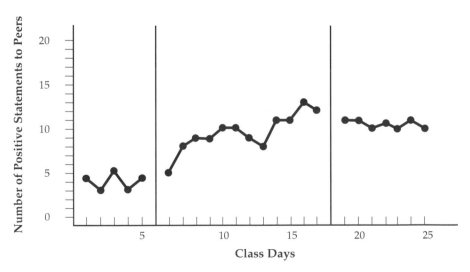

FIGURE 5.13   A Reversal Design That Didn't Reverse

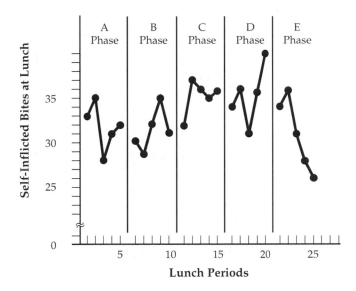

Phase A = Baseline
Phase B = Reminders to Stop Biting
Phase C = Ice Cream for Not Biting
Phase D = Remove Tray of Food for Biting
Phase E = Overcorrection Program

**FIGURE 5.14   Implementation of a Changing-
Conditions Design**

zero. The changing-criterion design is a natural selection whenever a gradual increase or decrease in the target behavior is desired. It has been used to display
treatments for smoking, weight loss, exercise, factory piecework (e.g., in sheltered
workshops), math problems, and reading fluency.

Multiple-Baseline Design
The multiple-baseline design permits the display of data from two or more related components of the dependent variable. Because there are three basic facets
that define the dependent variable—the target behavior, the target student, and
the applied setting—multiple-baseline designs come in the following three
varieties:

1. *Multiple baseline across behaviors:* Two or more target behaviors are observed for
   the same student in the same setting (e.g., Bill's hitting, cursing, and teasing
   behavior during recess).
2. *Multiple baseline across students:* Two or more students are observed for the
   same behavior in the same setting (e.g., talking out in math class by Sally, Tom,
   and Sam).

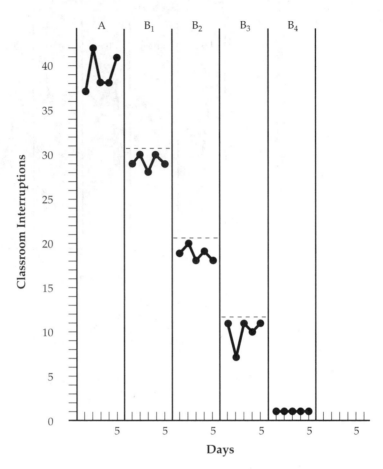

Phase A = Baseline
Phase B$_1$ = Treatment criterion, less than 30 interruptions per day
Phase B$_2$ = Treatment criterion, less than 20 interruptions per day
Phase B$_3$ = Treatment criterion, less than 10 interruptions per day
Phase B$_4$ = Treatment criterion, no interruptions per day

**FIGURE 5.15   A Changing-Criterion Design for
Classroom Interruptions**

   3. *Multiple baseline across settings:* The same behavior is observed in two or more
   settings for the same student (e.g., Julie's off-task behavior in math, English,
   social studies, and reading classes).

   The basic multiple-baseline graph appears in Figure 5.16; note that the ordi-
nates are aligned and the abscissas are parallel. After baseline data are gathered
for all students, behaviors, or settings, treatment is begun on one behavior (or one

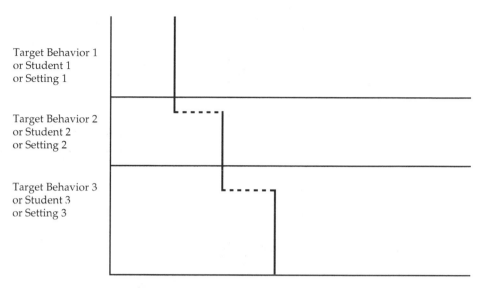

FIGURE 5.16   A Generic Multiple-Baseline Design

student or one setting) and the effect is observed on the untreated behaviors (or students or settings). If this treatment phase is successful and if there is no effect on the untreated behaviors (or students or settings), treatment is instituted on the second behavior (or student or setting). A similar procedure is followed for each additional behavior (or student or setting). The results of a successful program using self-monitoring to treat Julie's off-task behavior in several settings are displayed in Figure 5.17. The multiple-baseline design can be used to demonstrate experimental control if the results are similar to those depicted in Figure 5.17 (i.e., the desired change in the dependent variable occurs following treatment implementation *and* no change occurs in the other behaviors, students, or settings that received no treatment).

Alternating-Treatments Design
The alternating-treatments design is a relatively recent methodological development that teachers can use to evaluate the effectiveness of two or more instructional techniques (Kazdin & Hartman, 1978; Sindelar, Rosenberg, & Wilson, 1985). A typical classroom application of this design is depicted in Figure 5.18. In this case, after gathering a few baseline data points, a teacher decided to compare the effects of two interventions (losing recess versus earning extra recess) on Mike's noisemaking behavior. A third series of data points represents days when no treatment was implemented; these data can be used by the teacher to estimate how severe the problem behavior would have remained had intervention not been implemented.

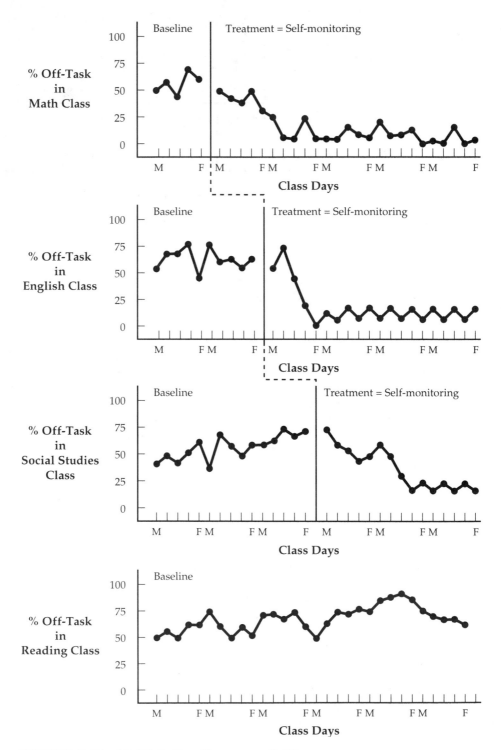

FIGURE 5.17   Multiple Baseline across Settings

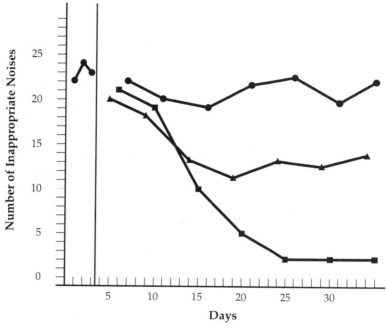

Key:
● = Baseline and no treatment
■ = Loss of 2 minutes of recess for each noise
▲ = Earn 2 minutes extra recess for 10 minutes without noise

FIGURE 5.18   An Alternating-Treatments Design

The advantages of this design are that it has many teaching applications. Teachers can, in effect, conduct classroom research to determine the relative effectiveness of a wide range of treatments on numerous target behaviors. The designs can also be used to display data from instructional programs when a teacher wants to compare the effect of two or more teaching techniques with an individual or group of students.

If objective results are desired, teachers must plan carefully before an alternating-treatments design is employed. One important consideration is that the scheduling of treatments must be counterbalanced to avoid scheduling all sessions of one of the treatments before lunch, for example, and all sessions of the other treatment after lunch. Counterbalancing can be used to control for the possible confounding effects of order, teacher, time of day, setting, or any other variable that may influence the outcome. An additional consideration is necessary if this design is used to compare instructional programs: The sets of problems taught in each of the different methods must be roughly equivalent (Sindelar et al., 1985). If, for example, the teacher wants to compare a VAKT spelling technique to a commercial program, the teacher must be able to demonstrate that the sets of words taught with each method are of roughly the same level of difficulty.

Data-Reactive Decision Making

Whichever design, graphing, or charting methods are chosen to display data, provision should always be made for evaluating success or failure during treatment. If treatment is successful, it should be continued; if unsuccessful, it should be modified. There are at least two data-based evaluation approaches that rely on direct observation methods: single-subject designs and data-reactive programs.

Single-Subject Designs

Several of the previously described designs have provisions for data-reactive decision making. The changing-conditions design is the most straightforward: If the treatment is contributing to a desired behavior change, it is continued; if not, it is stopped and a new treatment is implemented.

The changing-criterion design is also data reactive. If criterion performance is reached, the next phase of treatment begins to operate (e.g., if a student talks out less than fifteen times a day for an entire week, the goal for the second week becomes less than ten talk-outs per day). If the goal is not reached (e.g., if the student had three days with more than fifteen talk-outs), then the criterion for reinforcement remains the same during the second treatment week.

The alternating-treatments design can also be data reactive. If a teacher is trying to determine the best method to increase an adaptive behavior (e.g., smiling to peers) and has tried pep talks, stars, and smiles from classmates as rewards, and if smiles from classmates proves to be the most effective method, then the other two treatments are stopped.

Data-Reactive Programs

In addition to decision making based on single-subject designs, teachers can use highly structured data management systems that provide objective rules and criteria for implementing programs designed to change academic and nonacademic classroom behaviors. Two of the most widely used of these programs are Precision Teaching, developed from the work of O. R. Lindsley (Lovitt & Haring, 1979), and Data-Based Program Modification, developed at the University of Minnesota (Deno & Mirkin, 1977). Although these programs differ somewhat, each incorporates the following basic steps:

1. Pinpoint the target behavior (i.e., define the behavior in observable and measurable terms).
2. Gather base-rate data (i.e., define the current level of the target behavior).
3. Set a goal for behavior management or instruction.
4. Design the behavior change or academic instructional program.
5. Predict future rates of student performance by determining the minimum level of behavior change necessary to ensure that the target behavior changes from the base rate to the goal rate in the period of time allotted for the behavior management program.

6. Gather direct and frequent data during the course of the program.
7. Make program changes based on a comparison of the actual, obtained data with predicted or estimated progress.

Implementing the principles of Precision Teaching or Data-Based Program Modification involves substantial teacher training. Interested readers can find additional detailed material in the training manuals (Deno & Mirkin, 1977; Haring et al., 1978; White & Haring, 1980).

Summative Treatment Evaluation

After students have attained treatment goals, there are several important decisions teachers must make in order to ensure that long-term objectives are met and maintained. This process typically involves three considerations: fading out the artificial, externally controlled elements of the remedial program; measuring short- and long-term maintenance; and determining generalization to other applied settings.

Fading Out Treatment Programs

In general, the more artificial and external a remedial program, the less likely that gains made during treatment will be maintained once treatment is stopped. Teachers should never assume that students will continue to exhibit the appropriate behaviors that were acquired or not to exhibit the inappropriate behaviors that were decreased because of a successful treatment program. Rather, it is safer, and usually more accurate, to assume that unless special provisions are made, student behavior is likely to revert to preintervention levels.

The series of studies conducted by O'Leary and his colleagues on the effectiveness of a token economy illustrates this concern. In one study (Santogrossi et al., 1973), teachers awarded points backed up by tangible rewards, and successfully decreased disruptive behaviors of a group of teenage boys. However, when students began awarding their own points disruptive behaviors returned to near-baseline levels. In a later study (Turkewitz, O'Leary, & Ironsmith, 1975), the researchers implemented two procedures designed to change from teacher-awarded points to student-awarded points in a gradual, systematic fashion. The first procedure involved replacing teacher evaluation of student behavior with student evaluation. This was accomplished by comparing student evaluations to teacher evaluations at the end of the day. Initially, this was done every day for all students. Over time, fewer student self-ratings were double-checked and the checking was done at longer intervals. The second procedure involved gradually eliminating the backup reinforcers. Over time, backup reinforcers were provided first to all students, then to three-fourths, one-half, one-fourth, and finally no students. However, students did not know until the end of the day, when a lottery was conducted, who would receive the reinforcers. The implementation of these two fading techniques enabled the students to sustain most, though not all, of the treatment gains they had made initially under the teacher-awarded token economy.

Short- and Long-Term Maintenance

Even if treatment has caused a desired effect in a student's behavior, intervention cannot be considered successful unless gains are maintained after treatment is withdrawn. Short-term maintenance of a few weeks usually occurs naturally with learned academic behaviors. Thus, students who mastered a unit on fractions (Perkins & Cullinan, 1985) retained learned information in the short term. However, unless special provisions are made (e.g., fading teacher control while increasing student control), gains made with nonacademic behaviors are likely to be lost. Therefore, teachers and researchers must follow up students and measure the post-treatment level of behaviors. Graphed results of short-term and long-term follow-up data are illustrated in Figure 5.19. It is important to note that if student behavior reflects a significant loss of treatment gains, intervention must be reintroduced.

Generalization to Other Settings

Not only is maintenance across time important, teachers also need to know if treatment that is successful in one setting will generalize to other settings. One of the most common examples of this concern is generalization from the special education resource room to the mainstream classroom. A teacher of students with behavior disorders might, for example, teach a student how to use a self-monitoring technique (Kneedler, 1980) to reduce off-task behavior. In this intervention, the resource teacher would act as a consultant to the general-class teacher and train the student to monitor his or her own work behavior. After self-monitoring is mastered in the resource room, the student would then be expected to apply the same

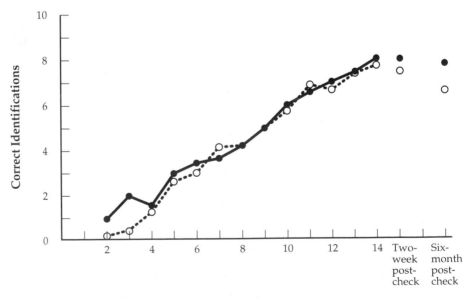

FIGURE 5.19   Short- and Long-Term Maintenance Postchecks

technique in a regular classroom. Researchers investigating this type of general-ization have noted that specific planning steps must be undertaken to ensure suc-cessful, and to avoid inappropriate, generalization (Rincover & Koegel, 1975).

Summary

This chapter described a series of comprehensive and systematic direct-observa-tion activities that can be used before, during, and after teachers have imple-mented any of a wide variety of treatments in the classroom. The advantages of using direct observation are that the information obtained is both current and rel-evant. As long as some element of the behavior management program can be spec-ified in observable and measurable terms, direct observation can be used to allow the teacher to monitor the relative levels of severity, frequency, or duration of the target behavior.

Discussion Questions

1. Give two practical examples of how a teacher might screen her class for problem behaviors.

2. Why bother gathering baseline data?

3. What would a teacher do with the results of whole-class screening (e.g., screening of so-cially withdrawn behaviors)?

4. What specific behaviors might a teacher be interested in identifying with events that oc-cur before or after the target behavior?

5. How would you pinpoint on-task behavior?

6. Which behaviors are best measured using duration recording? Why?

7. Why might social-validation data be especially important in a classroom for students with emotional or behavior disorders?

8. Give an example of a target behavior that should not be reversed. Why not?

9. How could an alternating-treatments design be used to display the results of several spelling programs?

10. Why must special-class teachers fade out extrinsic reinforcement programs before stu-dents return to general education classrooms?

References

Alberto, P.A., & Troutman, A. C. (1990). *Applied be-havior analysis for teachers*, 3rd ed. Columbus, OH: Merrill.

Barlow, D., & Hersen, M. (1984). *Single case experi-mental designs: Strategies for studying behavior change*. New York: Pergamon.

Buisson, G., Murdock, J., Reynolds, K., & Cronin, M. (1995). Effects of tokens on response latency of students with hearing impairments in a resource room. *Education and Treatment of Children, 18*(4), 408–421.

Canter, L., & Canter, M. (1976). *Assertive discipline.* Los Angeles: Canter

Carr, E. G., Newsom, C. D., & Blinkoff, J. A. (1980). Escape as a factor in the aggressive behavior of two retarded children. *Journal of Applied Behavior Analysis, 13,* 101–117.

Deno, S., & Mirkin, P. (1977). *Data-based program modification: A manual.* Reston, VA: The Council for Exceptional Children.

Farb, J., & Thorne, J. M. (1978). Improving the generalized mnemonic performance of a Down's syndrome child. *Journal of Applied Behavior Analysis, 11,* 413–419.

Fisher, C., Berliner, D., Filby, N., Marliave, R., Cahen, L., & Dishaw, M. (1980). Teaching behaviors, academic learning time, and student achievement: An overview. In C. Denham & A. Lieberman (Eds.), *Time to learn.* Washington, DC: National Institute of Education.

Fjellstedt, N., & Sulzer-Azaroff, B. (1973). Reducing latency of a child responding to instructions by means of a token system. *Journal of Applied Behavior Analysis, 6,* 125–130.

Hansen, G. D. (1979). Enuresis control through fading, escape and avoidance training. *Journal of Applied Behavior Analysis, 12,* 303–307.

Haring, N., Lovitt, T., Eaton, M., & Hansen, C. (1978). *The fourth R: Research in the classroom.* Columbus, OH: Merrill.

Kazdin, A. (1977). Assessing the clinical or applied significance of behavior change through social validation. *Behavior Modification, 1,* 427–452.

Kazdin, A. (1978). Methodological and interpretive problems of single-case experimental designs. *Journal of Consulting and Clinical Psychology, 46,* 629–642.

Kazdin, A., & Hartman, D. (1978). The simultaneous treatment design. *Behavior Therapy, 9,* 912–922.

Kendall, P., & Wilcox, L. (1980). Cognitive-behavioral treatment for impulsivity: Concrete versus conceptual training in nonself-controlled problem children. *Journal of Consulting and Clinical Psychology, 48,* 80–91.

Kneedler, R. (1980). The use of cognitive training to change social behaviors. *Exceptional Education Quarterly, 1,* 65–74.

Lando, H. (1975). An objective check upon self-reported smoking levels. *Behavior Therapy, 6,* 547–549.

Lovitt, T., & Haring, N. (1979). *Classroom application of precision teaching.* Seattle: Special Child Publications.

Neef, N. A., Iwata, B. A., & Page, T. J. (1980). The effects of interpersonal training versus high-density reinforcement on spelling acquisition and retention. *Journal of Applied Behavior Analysis, 13,* 153–158.

Perkins, V., & Cullinan, D. (1985). Effects of direct instruction intervention for fraction skills. *Education and Treatment of Children, 8,* 41–50.

Rincover, A., & Koegel, R. (1975). Setting generality and stimulus control in autistic children. *Journal of Applied Behavior Analysis, 8,* 235–246.

Santogrossi, D., O'Leary, K., Romanczyk, R., & Kaufman, K. (1973). Self-evaluation by adolescents in a psychiatric hospital school program. *Journal of Applied Behavior Analysis, 6,* 227–287.

Sindelar, P., Rosenberg, M., & Wilson, R. (1985). An adapted alternative treatments design for instructional research. *Education and Treatment of Children, 8,* 67–76.

Tawney, J. W., & Gast, D. L. (1984). *Single subject research in special education.* Columbus, OH: Merrill.

Turkewitz, H., O'Leary, K., & Ironsmith, M. (1975). Generalization and maintenance of appropriate behavior through self-control. *Journal of Consulting and Clinical Psychology, 43,* 577–583.

White, O. R., & Haring, N. G. (1980). *Exceptional teaching.* 2nd ed. Columbus, OH: Merrill.

Wood, R., & Flynn, J. M. (1978). A self-evaluation token system versus an external evaluation token system alone in a residential setting with predelinquent youth. *Journal of Applied Behavior Analysis, 11,* 503–512.

Chapter 6

Developing Individual Education Programs for Students with Behavior Disorders

Advance Organizer

As you read this chapter, prepare to identify and discuss:

- Each of the required elements of an Individualized Education Program (IEP).
- The most prevalent school placement for students with behavior disorders.
- The rationale for placing a student in an appropriate least restrictive educational setting.
- The *Lora* consent decree and its importance for students with behavior disorders.
- The relationship between student characteristics and IEP requirements.
- Due process rights for students, parents, and local education agencies.
- Typical statements of present educational levels.
- Typical statements of annual goals.
- Typical statements of short-term objectives.
- The *Honig v. Doe* case and its importance for students with behavior disorders.

Students exhibiting behavior disorders represent one group that is eligible to receive the special education services first required by Public Law 94-142 (1975) now Public Law 101-476, the Individuals with Disabilities Education Act (1990). In addition to special education services, IDEA mandates that every student with a disability (e.g., an emotional behavior disorder, learning disability, visual impairment) must have an Individualized Education Program (IEP). The IEP must be contained in a written document, and it is the legal responsibility of each local educational agency (LEA) to implement the educational plan described in the IEP document.

Legally Mandated IEP Requirements

In our daily educational jargon, the IEP has come to signify the document that describes the special education student's instructional plan. In reality, however, an IEP is much more. Each IEP must describe a comprehensive program that contains all of the legally mandated components described below (Fiscus & Mandell, 1983). Not only must each student with behavior disorders have an instructional program that meets academic and behavior management needs, but each IEP must also contain six other elements:

   1. *A Statement of the Extent to Which the Student Can Participate in General Education Programs*   This requirement incorporates the concepts of least restrictive environment and mainstreaming. It is the responsibility of the LEA to ensure that students with behavior disorders receive their education in the setting that is least restrictive (i.e., the setting that is most similar to the general educational program). Most states provide special education services in the settings listed in Figure 6.1.

   Students with behavior disorders are found in all of the placements illustrated in Figure 6.1. Ideally, students are placed in settings as a function of the severity level of their behavior disorders—the more severe the disorder, the more restrictive the placement. Students with mild behavior problems are most often educated in the general education classroom or resource room. Students with

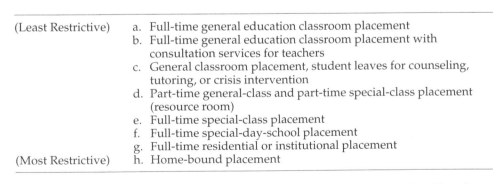

FIGURE 6.1   A Continuum of Services for Students with Behavior Disorders

moderate behavior disorders are frequently placed in full-time special classes or day schools, while those with severe emotional and behavior disorders (e.g., childhood schizophrenia or early infantile autism) and adjudicated offenders are often educated in residential settings.

There are, however, exceptions to the ideal practice of matching setting and severity. Early as well as recent evidence, for example, indicates that there is a substantial group of students with behavior disorders who receive no special services (i.e., they are placed in the general education class although they or their teachers could benefit from support services). Exceptions can also occur with positive results; for example, students with severe behavior disorders have been successfully educated in settings close to the mainstream. Peter Knoblock (1970) established two such programs: one providing for the education of students who are aggressive and emotionally disturbed in an "open education" program, and the other providing for the education of students with early infantile autism in a class with general education peers.

The intent of the framers of IDEA was that student characteristics and student needs determine placement, not that students be placed in the most appropriate settings available within a given LEA. If a student with severe behavior disorders requires a special placement (a decision made initially by the IEP team), the LEA must either provide or pay for the special placement.

2. *An Unbiased Comprehensive Evaluation* IDEA also mandates that each student with emotional and behavior disorders (EBD) receive an objective, complete, and unbiased educational and behavioral evaluation on which placement into services for emotional and behavior disorders rests. IDEA mandates that all tests, interviews, rating scales, and observation methods used to determine the presence of behavior disorders adhere to the following guidelines:

a. Assessment devices must be chosen, administered, and interpreted without cultural, racial, sexual, or other discrimination.
b. The student's native language must be used during the evaluation.
c. A multifaceted rather than a single test or assessment procedure must be administered.
d. Assessment devices must be reliable and valid and be administered and interpreted by appropriately trained personnel.

This provision of IDEA is particularly important for practitioners involved in an IEP process for students with behavior disorders (see Legal Issues: The Lora Case). In order for an IEP team to document the presence of one or more of the five characteristics in Table 6.1 that must be exhibited by students with behavior disorders, IQ and achievement tests, direct observation, medical evaluations, psychological evaluations, rating scales, and other tests must be used appropriately. The diverse nature of the characteristics of behavior disorders implies that a multifaceted evaluation is the required course of action.

TABLE 6.1 Psychological and Educational Variables Associated with Definitional Criteria

Student Characteristics	Variables to Be Measured
1. Inability to learn that cannot be explained by intellectual, sensory, or health factors.	1. Academic achievement, intelligence, vision, hearing, other medical factors.
2. Inability to make or keep interpersonal relationships.	2. Social skills, social patterns.
3. Inappropriate behavior or feelings in normal circumstances.	3. Classroom behavior, thoughts, attitudes, and emotions.
4. Pervasive unhappiness or depression.	4. Emotions, behavior.
5. Physical symptoms or fears.	5. Physical condition, phobias, neuroses.
Behavior Patterns	
1. Exhibits one or more of the above characteristics over a long period of time.	1. Duration of condition.
2. Exhibits one or more of the characteristics to a marked degree.	2. Relative frequency or intensity of condition.
3. One or more of the student's characteristics adversely affects educational performance.	3. Classroom behavior and academic achievement.

3. *The Right to Due Process* One of the basic provisions of IDEA is that parents, public schools, and prospective and current special education students have certain specified legal rights. These rights begin well before placement and include the right to be notified of, to give informed consent for, and to be involved in the psychoeducational evaluation of any student suspected of having behavior disorders. However, if parents ignore or refuse to grant a request to conduct an evaluation, a school district retains the option of pursuing permission through hearings and court proceedings.

Parents also have the right to attend the IEP conference during which labeling and placement decisions are made as well as to bring an advocate or legal counsel with them. In addition, if parents disagree with any IEP team decision, they have the right to appeal: first, in one or more hearings held before an impartial hearing officer (in some states, this must be a lawyer; in others, it may be a special education expert); and subsequently, to a court of law. The local school district enjoys the same rights.

Several due process rights are related to interventions that have been used with students with EBD. Educators who employ seclusionary time-out, for example, a punishment intervention with the potential for physical confrontations, are advised to secure parental consent and involve the IEP team (Yell, 1994). In fact, the

Legal Issues: The Lora Case

Lora v. The Board of Education of the City of New York (1984) was a class action suit filed in 1975 that resulted in a consent decree issued in 1984. *Lora* involved many concerns related to a student's right to receive an unbiased evaluation (Wood, Johnson, & Jenkins, 1986). Lawyers representing Isaac Lora and other New York City students placed in special day schools for students with severe emotional and behavior problems argued that the students' rights had been violated because of the discriminatory referral, assessment, and placement practices used by the public schools. These discriminatory practices were alleged to have resulted in a disproportionate number of minority students (specifically African and Hispanic Americans) being placed in special schools for students with emotional and behavior disorders. Experts who analyzed demographic data gathered during the case found that the general school population was 36 percent African American, 23 percent Hispanic American, and 41 percent other, but that the special school population was 68 percent African American, 27 percent Hispanic American, and only 5 percent other.

The 1984 consent decree that resolved the *Lora* case is important not only for the nondiscriminatory standards and procedures that resulted, but also because the practices that led to discriminatory evaluation and placement procedures were uncovered. The consent decree provides an excellent example of plaintiffs, defendants, a board of experts, and a court all working together successfully to change a flawed system. Some of the factors found to contribute to discriminatory placement were the use of non-native language tests and untrained evaluators, limited dissemination of due process information to parents, and a loophole in the regulations that permitted knowledgeable parents or those able to afford legal counsel to have their students placed either in a general education school or in a private day school at a public school's expense. Even before the case was settled, the Board of Education moved to implement nondiscriminatory practices, and the final consent decree was viewed as a negotiated and practical, but reasonable, compromise (Wood et al., 1986).

The nondiscriminatory standards specified in the *Lora* consent decree follow IDEA guidelines quite closely—placement in the least restrictive environment; informed consent for parents both for evaluation and placement, to be obtained in the parent's native language; evaluation in the student's native language; use of standard assessment procedures; a multifaceted evaluation; a structured observation in the general education class; use of extreme caution with self-reports and projective tests; elimination of ethnic or cultural causes for behavior; suggestions to try prereferral interventions; and placement based on student needs rather than availability of existing services.

Council for Children with Behavior Disorders, the largest professional organization representing educators of students with EBD recommends that the use of all behavior reduction techniques be written into the student's IEP (Council for Children with Behavior Disorders, 1990).

One of the most important due process issues for students with behavior disorders concerns suspension and expulsion. LEAs, teachers, and the courts have all been involved in the decisions that have, over time, formed the policies and practices that specify student and parent rights as well as LEA responsibilities. The most important recent court decision, *Honig v. Doe*, is the subject of the Legal Issues box presented below.

Legal Issues: *Honig v. Doe*

The Legal Question: When may students with disabilities be suspended or expelled from school?

Background information: IDEA is silent (i.e., lacks specific guidelines) on issues related to expulsion and suspension of students with disabilities. Thus, over the years, a body of *common law* has developed. Common law guidelines are based on court decisions and may be contrasted with *enacted law* guidelines, which are based on statutes passed by legislative bodies. Common law principles based on earlier court decisions (e.g., *Doe v. Koger* [1976], *Kaelin v. Grubbs* [1982] include.

1. Short-term suspensions are permissible.
2. Longer suspensions or expulsions represent changes in educational placements and involve due process rights.
3. A multidisciplinary team must answer the critical question: Is the misbehavior that resulted in suspension/expulsion caused by the student's disability?
4. Under certain circumstances, it is permissible to transfer students who exhibit violent or harmful behaviors.

In *Honig v. Doe* (1988), two students with emotional and behavior disorders enrolled in the San Francisco LEA were attending a special school placement. Both students, following assaultive and maladaptive behavior, were subsequently placed on indefinite suspension while expulsion proceedings were begun. The court's judgment extended and reaffirmed previous decisions and resulted in the following common law guidelines.

1. Expulsion of students with disabilities for maladaptive behavior *caused* by the disability is prohibited.

2. Expulsion is always a change in placement, and therefore involves due pro-cess protection.
3. If the misbehavior is not caused by the student's disability, then the student may be expelled.

Common law guidelines based on the *Honig v. Doe* decision have resulted in recommended practices for LEAs regarding the expulsion or suspension of students with disabilities. Because short-term suspensions have been permitted, LEAs may suspend students with disabilities for up to a total of ten days within any academic year. Suspensions and expulsions longer than ten days violate the *stay put* provision of IDEA (i.e., that a student must remain in his or her present placement until the IEP team decides that a change is needed). If a change in placement is desired (e.g., moving a violent student to a more restrictive setting), the LEA must reconvene the IEP team, consider the available evidence, and decide on the appropriate placement. If all parties agree, the change in placement will occur. If parents refuse to permit the change in placement to a more restrictive setting, the LEA may use the ten-day suspension period to seek judicial relief (i.e., to exercise the school's due process rights by asking the court to allow the change in placement).

Although *Honig v. Doe* answers some questions about suspension and expulsion of students with emotional and behavior disorders, other concerns remain (Yell, 1989): The complex issue of how to determine when misbehavior is caused by a student's disability is still open to interpretation, permitted disciplinary practices have yet to be specified, and the complicated issue of matching specific misbehaviors with various restrictive placements remains undetermined.

4. *The IEP Document Must Be Properly Completed*   After parents are informed and assessment data are gathered and interpreted, an IEP conference is held to determine eligibility for special education services and type of placement (Crandall, 1979). One of the responsibilities of the participants in the IEP conference is to create an IEP document that describes the evaluation and placement process. IDEA requires that each IEP document contain the following items:

   a. *A statement of present levels of educational performance.* Because the criteria for behavior disorders can involve intellectual, academic, medical, motor, self-help, social, emotional, and behavioral concerns, the student's present education level for each relevant factor must be determined. Typically, information on present educational levels falls into two categories: standardized, formal, and normative data; and informal, observational, criterion-referenced, and curriculum-based data. The first type of data is obtained by administering standardized tests; for example, academic data in the form of grade-equivalent scores can be obtained by administering group or individual achievement tests, such as the Woodcock-Johnson Psychoeducational Battery, that provide norm-referenced scores in reading, math, and written language. The second type of data is obtained by using direct observation methods or criterion-referenced tests—for example, an informal reading or math inventory to determine ratings of student performance on a specific set of academic tasks such as regrouping in addition or comprehending fourth-grade reading material.

   b. *A statement of annual goals.* On the basis of the student's present educational level, IEP members must set annual goals in those areas in which the student will receive special education services (e.g., social skills, reading, math, classroom behavior). Because present educational levels can be stated either in a standardized test or a criterion-referenced format, annual goals based on these present educational levels will follow the selected format. Thus, a criterion-referenced annual goal might be to master a set of instructional tasks such as multiplication facts, prosocial skills, or good grooming habits. Standardized annual goals might refer to raising grade-equivalent or standard scores on a formal reading test or to improving behavior rating scale scores.

   c. *A list of short-term objectives.* IEP members must also develop a number of short-term instructional objectives for each annual goal. The purpose of this procedure is to specify the tasks a student will be expected to master during an academic year. Students with annual goals in the area of addition might be expected to master these tasks: facts with sums to 10, facts with sums from 11 to 18, sums to 100 with no regrouping, and sums to 100 with regrouping. Students with annual goals in the area of prosocial skill development might be expected to master these skills: establishing and keeping eye contact during a conversation, making positive comments to peers, and smiling at teachers and peers.

   d. *A statement of specific educational services a student will receive following initial placement.* IEP members must list the time and subjects to be taken in the general education program; the time and content of special education services; the type and time of related services (e.g., adapted physical education or nursing services); and the specialized instructional media or materials needed (e.g., large print, Braille readers, talking books).

   e. *A reasonable timetable and justification for delivery of services.* IEP conference members must state in writing when a special education program will begin and approximately how long the special services will be needed.

f. *A statement of agreement or disagreement with the eligibility and placement decision.* Members of the IEP conference must sign the document indicating agreement or disagreement. Those who disagree are entitled to enter a statement describing the reasons for their disagreement.

5. *A Reevaluation Procedure Must Be Conducted* Reevaluations are of two types. First, an annual evaluation must be conducted, typically by the teacher delivering direct services to the student, to determine if annual and short-term goals are being met. In addition, at least once every three years a complete reevaluation must be undertaken to determine if the student still meets special education eligibility requirements.

6. *Other Requirements Must Be Met* IDEA mandates several additional IEP-related requirements, including confidentiality of all test, interview, and written results of referral, evaluation, and placement; appointment of a surrogate to serve *in loco parentis* for students without a parent or guardian; and continuation of staff development to implement the IEP mandates.

IEPs for Students with Behavior Disorders

Although the IEP procedure is mandated by IDEA for all students with disabilities, the differences in referral, evaluation, and placement practices across the disability conditions result in significantly different IEP documents for each student group. The specific requirements in IEP documents for students with behavior disorders are largely determined by the educational and psychological variables specified in the federal definition of severe emotional disturbance. The five student characteristics and three resulting behavior patterns derived from the federal definition are depicted in Table 6.1. The variables that must be measured in order to document the presence of behavior disorders are also provided. It may be necessary for IEP teams to measure and describe all the variables listed in Table 6.1 in each of the three major sections of the IEP document (i.e., present educational levels, annual goals, and short-term objectives).

Present Educational Levels

Because IDEA requires that each student's IEP document contain a statement of present educational levels, all state and many local special educational administrative districts have developed forms and procedures to measure performance and record results. Although data on all of the variables listed in Table 6.1 are not required for every potential student with behavior disorders, present educational levels may need to be provided on intelligence, academic achievement, sensory acuity, medical and physical health factors, social skills, classroom behavior, thoughts and attitudes, and emotional development. For each of these variables, data can be gathered using standardized, norm-referenced instruments or informal, criterion-referenced instruments. Accordingly, the forms used to report present educational levels should provide space for listing the various assessment devices and results. In addition, the present educational levels must include a statement describing how the student's disability affects the present levels of functioning (Federal Register, 1981). Blank and completed samples are contained in Figure 6.2.

Although either norm-referenced or criterion-referenced data will satisfy IDEA requirements, it is usually preferable to provide both types of information. The standardized test information can be used to compare a student's performance to a cross section of peers in the national sample of which the test was standardized. The results of Willy's formal tests, given in Figure 6.2, indicate that he tests mostly in the average range (plus or minus one standard deviation from the mean or 50th percentile) in academic areas. His standard scores in reading, math, and written language, however, are well below his standard intelligence scores, indicating that he is achieving significantly less than would be predicted on the basis of his ability. He also tested better in the basic skill areas within reading and math (i.e., decoding and computation) than in the higher-order skill areas (i.e., comprehension and applications). His test results reveal significant deficits in spoken language, classroom behavior, and home behavior.

The informal, criterion-referenced or curriculum-based data can be used to compare a student's performance on a number of selected tasks either to teacher-determined mastery levels or to the performance of a group of well-adjusted, normally functioning peers. This procedure is called *social validation* (Kazdin, 1977).

IDEA mandates that each IEP contain a statement describing how the student's present educational level is affected by his or her disability. For many students with behavior disorders, this statement will be similar to the one in Figure 6.2—namely, that maladaptive behaviors have interfered in some way with learning.

Note that not only data on social or emotional behavior are included in an IEP. Information on academics, intelligence, study skills, and other areas should also be incorporated, because this information will be used to determine the presence or absence of behavior disorders and also because the information will be used by the student's teachers. If a student is placed in a full-time program, for example, a teacher must provide academic instruction in addition to behavior management.

The academic, intelligence, and other information that must be entered on the IEP of a student with behavior disorders will not be unique to the student's disability condition. The IEPs of students with learning disabilities, mental retardation, and other developmental disabilities will contain similar types of data, plus, to a lesser degree, data on social and emotional behavior. So although data on social and emotional behavior will not be unique to the IEPs of students with behavior disorders, these students' IEPs will contain relatively more social and emotional goals and objectives. Table 6.2 contains examples of standardized and informal data typically gathered for students who exhibit aggressive, hyperactive, autistic, and socially withdrawn behaviors. It should be noted that if students are referred for aggressive behavior, this does not mean that they do not also exhibit hyperactive or other maladaptive behaviors.

Statement of Present Educational Levels

Student _____

DOB _____

Grade _____

Date _____

Standardized, Norm-Referenced Assessment

Tests   (Date)   *Administered by*   *Results*

_____

_____

_____

_____

_____

_____

Direct Observation, Criterion-Referenced, and Curriculum-Based Assessment

Tests or
Instruments   (Date)   *Administered by*   *Results*

_____

_____

_____

_____

_____

_____

Summary of Strengths   *Summary of Areas*
                                        Needing Strengthening

_____

_____

_____

_____

_____

Effect of Disability on Performance

_____

_____

_____

FIGURE 6.2   Willy's Present Educational Levels

Statement of Present Educational Levels

Student	Willy Paserfale
DOB	6/6/84
Grade	4th
Date	4/29/96

Standardized, Norm-Refrenced Assessment

Tests	(Date)	Administered by	Results
WISC-R	4/1/96	L. Jones	Verbal IQ = 128; Performance IQ = 115; Full Scale IQ = 121.
K-TEA	4/13/96	S. Smith	Math Comp = 107; Math Appl = 97; Read Comp = 98; Read Decod = 113.
TOWL	4/13/96	S. Smith	Written-Language Quotient = 95.
TOLD-I	4/21/96	J. Jopper	Spoken-Language Quotient = 79.
BRP	4/13/96	T. Trussman	Teacher Scale = 5 (X = 10, SD = 3). Parent Scale = 6 (mother).

Criterion-Referenced and Curriculum-Based Assessment

Tests or Instruments	(Date)	Administered by	Results
Informal Writing Inventory	4/21/96	J. Jopper	Deficits in capitalization and sentence structure.
Observation of On-Task Time	4/8/96 4/12/96 4/20/96	L. Jones	55 percent on-task during seatwork, 85 percent during teacher-led time.
Curriculum-Based Reading Inventory	4/19/96	S. Smith	100 percent comprehension, 85 correct words/min on 3rd-grade material; 50 percent comp, 55 wpm, on 4th-grade material.
Observation of Disruptive Behavior	4/8/96 4/12/96 4/20/96	L. Jones	.6 disruptions/min, class average = 0.4/min

Summary of Strengths

Higher-order skills in math application.

Reading decoding.

Written language and spelling.

Summary of Areas Needing Strengthening

Reading comprehension.

Spoken-language deficit.

Classroom behavior: Low in on-task, high in disruptive behavior.

Written language—mechanics and sentence structure.

Effect of Disability on Performance

Willy's low on-task rate and high level of disruptive behavior appear to be contributing to his academic, social, and spoken-language deficits.

FIGURE 6.2   *Continued*

TABLE 6.2   Types of Formal and Informal Data Gathered to Determine the Present Educational Level of Maladaptive Behaviors

Maladaptive Behavior	Formal Data	Informal Data
Aggressive behavior	1. Walker Behavior Checklist 2. Burke's Behavior Checklist 3. Quay Peterson Checklist	1. Number of acts of physical aggression per school day. 2. Number of acts of verbal aggression per school day.
Hyperactive/impulsive behavior	1. Conner's Rating Scale 2. Self-Control Rating Scale 3. Matching Familiar Figures Test	1 On-task rate. 2. Number of disruptive behaviors per class or school day. 3. Time taken to respond in problem situation.
Socially withdrawn behavior	1. Walker Behavior Checklist 2. Behavior Rating Profile	1. Percent of eye contact. 2. Number of initiations of conversations with peers. 3. Number of positive comments to and from peers.
Autism	1. Autistic Behavior Rating	1. Number or percent of intervals of self-injurious behavior in class period. 2. Number or percent of intervals of self-stimulating behaviors.

Annual Goals

The most important consideration for annual goals is that they must be logically derived from the previously stated present educational levels. Thus, teachers must develop at least one annual goal in any academic or behavior area that is pertinent to the identification of a student with behavior disorders (e.g., social skills or disruptive behavior). In some states it is accepted practice to develop annual goals for any academic objectives that will be pursued by the special education teacher. Thus, if a student is identified with behavior disorders because he or she exhibits numerous disruptive and aggressive classroom behaviors that have interfered with reading achievement, it is necessary to develop annual goals dealing with disruptive behavior (e.g., out-of-seat, off-task, or talking-out behavior), aggressive behavior (e.g., fistfights, temper tantrums, or hair pulling), and reading (e.g., word attack or reading comprehension). In addition, if an IEP team decides to place a student in a self-contained class, it is often advisable to develop annual goals in the remaining basic academic skill areas (i.e., math computation, math reasoning, and written language). Table 6.3 contains examples of annual goals that might be developed for Willy. Table 6.4 contains annual goals specific to various behavior disorders. In spite of the requirements for the reflection of relevant diagnostic information on the IEP document, recent research found that academic deficits were frequently not reported and that social and emotional, diagnostically relevant areas were often not included in Annual Goal statements (Reiher, 1992).

TABLE 6.3 Potential Annual Goals for Willy Paserfale

Willy will increase his on-task behavior.

Willy will decrease his disruptive classroom behaviors.

Willy will improve in the area of spoken language.

Willy will improve in the area of written language.

Willy will improve his reading comprehension.

TABLE 6.4 Selected Annual Goals for Different Maladaptive Behaviors

Maladaptive Behavior	Annual Goals
Aggressive behavior	decrease the frequency and intensity of physical aggression.
The student will . . .	decrease the frequency of verbal aggression.
	obtain a rating on the Walker Problem Behavior Checklist: Aggression Scale within one standard deviation of the mean.
Hyperactive behavior	improve on-task behavior.
The student will . . .	decrease disruptive classroom behaviors to the average rate of well-adjusted peers.
	obtain a rating on the Self-Control Rating Scale (SCRS) within one standard duration of the mean.
Autistic behavior	decrease self-injurious behaviors.
The student will . . .	obtain a rating on the Autistic Behavior Rating Scale within one standard deviation of the mean.

Short-Term Objectives

Each annual goal developed in the IEP must be broken down into units that define measurable and attainable educational objectives. An annual goal that states that the student will improve reading performance in the area of word attack skills might contain short-term objectives (STOs) that state that the student will master beginning and ending consonant sounds, short and long vowel sounds, pronunciation of consonant-vowel-consonant words, and a list of one hundred high-frequency but phonetically irregular sight words such as *the, once, two,* and *his.*

IDEA does not specify the number of short-term objectives to be included under each annual goal. The task of the person(s) responsible for developing the STOs (often special education teachers) is to develop objectives that can be easily translated into educational programming. To this end, the following guidelines should be followed when writing short-term objectives:

1. Each STO must fall logically under one of the annual goals.
2. Each STO must be observable.
3. Each STO must be attainable within one academic year.
4. Measurement methods must be specified.
5. The person responsible must be identified.

To meet these criteria, STOs often resemble instructional objectives (Mager, 1975) that have four components: student, condition, behavior, and criteria. However, STOs differ somewhat, in that their required components include student, behavior, criteria, measurement instrument (e.g., teacher-made test, direct observation), person responsible, and date mastered (see Table 6.5).

Often the most difficult aspect of writing relevant STOs is making them attainable individually and collectively. Individually, each STO must be reasonable for teacher and student to accomplish within one academic year. To state that a student will master comprehension of four grade levels of reading material may be unrealistic, especially if a student has in previous years made less than average progress. In addition, many maladaptive behaviors (e.g., aggressive, withdrawn, and autistic-like behaviors) have prognoses such that, even with successful treatment, several years may elapse before a student can be considered to be functioning within the average range. Thus, teachers should state STOs in units of behavior change that are possible to accomplish in one year.

Making STOs collectively attainable requires stating *only* the number of objectives that can be expected to be accomplished. Each teacher must strike a balance between listing too few or too many STOs. In the same respect, each teacher must decide how specific to be when developing STOs. Should every academic task (e.g., each beginning, ending, and medial consonant or vowel sound) and every behavior (e.g., out-of-seat, off-task, noisemaking, and talking out) be listed, or should tasks and behaviors be grouped (e.g., phonics tasks and disruptive behaviors)? There is no clear answer to this question. Although grouping across response classes is often expedient, there are times when specific academic tasks or behaviors should be stated. This decision is often based on the nature of treatment: If an intervention is designed to teach all letter sounds (e.g., an instructional phonics unit) or to decrease all disruptive classroom behaviors (e.g., an individually negotiated behavioral contract), then objectives are best grouped. But if one task or behavior is to be treated at a time, then individual and specific STOs are recommended. Table 6.5 contains a selected list of STOs related to several maladaptive behaviors.

Other IEP Requirements for Students with Behavior Disorders

Related and Extraordinary Services

Students with behavior disorders frequently exhibit problems or impairments in areas other than academic and classroom behavior or they exhibit specific maladaptive behaviors that require unique support services. In the first case, it is the responsibility of the LEA to provide special education services if the student suffers from one or more of the disabilities covered in IDEA. If a student also has a visual or hearing impairment, orthopedic disability, or physical health impairment, the LEA is responsible for providing a free appropriate public education that meets the needs created by each of these disabilities. If a student with behavior disorders exhibits conditions not covered by IDEA (e.g., a student is gifted or talented), an LEA has more discretion in decisions concerning services.

TABLE 6.5 Short-Term Objectives for Selected Target Behaviors

Target Behaviors	STOs			
	Student, behavior, criteria	Measurements	Person responsible	Date met
Physical aggression	Tom will decrease hitting, pinching, and pushing other students to less than five times per school day.	direct observation	Mrs. Jones (EBD teacher)	date _____ yes/no
Verbal aggression	Sally will decrease cursing, threatening, and teasing other students to less than five times per school day.	teacher observation	Mrs. Taft (paraprofessional)	date _____ yes/no
Self-injurious behaviors	Phillip will decrease hitting, pinching, and biting himself to zero times per school day.	teacher observation	Mr. Salter (psychologist)	date _____ yes/no
Social skills	Karen will decrease hitting, pinching, and pushing other students to less than five times per school day.	direct observation	Mrs. Jones (EBD teacher)	date _____ yes/no
Disruptive behavior	Arnie will decrease talk-outs, and out-of-seats to less than five times per math class.	direct observation	Mrs. Taft (paraprofessional)	date _____ yes/no

In the second case, where unique support services are required by the IEP team, it is often, though not always, the LEA's responsibility to secure and pay for those services. If, for example, an IEP team requests additional assessment by a clinical psychiatrist, specifies a residential treatment facility (even though there is none in the district or state), or recommends that a neurological evaluation be obtained, the LEA must pay for these services. But if the IEP team does not specify a need for such services, parents must either pay or take their case to a due process hearing. The most common extraordinary services for students with behavior disorders are residential or home-bound placements; psychiatric, medical, and physical evaluations; and drug or psychotherapy.

Placements

Although there are students with behavior disorders in every educational setting in the hierarchy of services, these students are distributed differently across available placements than students with other disabilities. Whereas, for example, most students with learning disabilities are placed in resource rooms in part-time special education programs, self-contained classrooms and special day schools remain the most prevalent service option for students with behavior disorders (Grosenick, George, & George, 1987); in fact, one of the most widely copied models for the self-contained class—the engineered classroom—was developed nearly thirty years ago specifically for students with behavior disorders (Hewett, 1968). However, because of the variety of emotional and behavior disorders, a significant number of these students are receiving educational services in other settings: Some students leave the general education classroom for individual or group counseling; some are placed in a resource room for one or two hours a day; some are educated in their homes; some with severe and debilitating conditions (e.g., early infantile autism) are placed in residential institutions; and those who are adjudicated can be placed in a wide variety of corrections facilities, detention institutions, or group homes.

The national movement toward inclusion of students with disabilities has also affected students with behavioral disorders, and many now receive services within their general education classroom. However, recent legal decisions involving inclusion and students with behavioral disorders, have supported the right of the local school district to place students with significant management problems out of the general education classroom (Yell, Clyde, & Puyallup, 1995). One central issue in recent court decisions is the negative effect of the behavior of the student with EBD on the other students.

Involving Parents in the IEP Process

IEP-Based Parent Involvement

Parents' involvement in special education programs for students with behavior disorders typically begins with the assessment phase associated with IEP developments. Prior to contact with special education personnel, however, parents of students with behavior problems usually have had frequent, often negative, contacts with the schools. Reports of misbehavior in general education classrooms, incidents in which students are sent to the principal's office, detention for breaking school rules, and even suspension or expulsion may be part of the histories of students with behavior disorders.

As previously mentioned, the IEP process requires mandatory contact with parents at several phases of the assessment-identification-placement process. For parents who have not referred their children for special education evaluation or services (classroom teachers make the majority of initial referrals), the first required contact usually comes as a request from the school to conduct a multifactored evaluation. LEAs are expected to document multiple, reasonable attempts to secure informed parental consent prior to commencing this evaluation. However, both parents and LEAs enjoy due process appeal rights should parents (or LEAs) request an evaluation and the LEA (or parents) refuse consent. A second mandated parent contact is at the IEP conference, in which case LEAs are expected to go to some length to secure parental participation (i.e., holding the IEP conference in the parent's home or conducting the meeting in the parent's native language).

A number of other types of parental involvement are recommended, though not mandated. If LEAs have instructional assistance teams (i.e., building or district level groups of educators, administrators, counselors, or school psychologists) who receive referrals from general classroom teachers asking for help with learning or behavior problems, then parents should be actively involved in the process. At a minimum, parents should be respondents who provide the team with pertinent suggestions for their child. This early parental involvement, well before labeling or a new placement occurs, is one of the best ways to involve and inform parents, to demonstrate meaningful home–school cooperation, and to avoid parent–school conflicts. Finally, parents should be continually and actively involved throughout the time that their student receives special education services. Selected examples of involving parents in their children's treatment are discussed below.

Parent Involvement in Treatment

The research on parent involvement has demonstrated that most (but not all) parents want to become involved, that parents can be trained to implement home-based treatments, that parents can work cooperatively with educators, and, most importantly, that treatments involving parents can be successful in reducing a range of maladaptive behaviors of their children. Some of the most successful treatments for juvenile delinquency, for example, include important parental components. The most effective programs involve parents in two ways: training parents in effective child rearing practices and training parents to use behavioral techniques such as individual contracting and reinforcement (Mulvey, Arthur, & Reppucci, 1993).

Aggression and conduct problems are areas of behavior disorders in which parent involvement has been well researched. Patterson and his colleagues at the Oregon Research Institute (ORI) have conducted numerous studies of parental involvement in the treatment of students who are aggressive (Patterson, Chamberlain, & Reid, 1982). A more thorough discussion of ORI activities may be found in the chapter on managing aggression. In addition, there is a significant body of professional literature that demonstrates that behavioral techniques can be mastered by parents and effectively implemented to reduce maladaptive behavior or increase prosocial behavior.

There are other areas in which parent involvement results in improved behavior or academic performance of students with disabilities. Homework is one of these areas. Researchers have found that among the many attributes of effective homework, involving parents and communicating regularly with parents are particularly important (Polloway, Bursuck, Jayanthi, & Epstein, 1996). Another area of recommended home–school communication involves parent–teacher conferences. Careful planning, knowledge of parent rights, and respect for the family's background and culture are important components of successful conferences (Olson & Platt, 1996). Finally, parents can be effective partners in the treatment of students with behavior disorders. For example, parents can reward students (Kozloff, 1994) for good school behavior (perhaps with TV time); be a party to individual contracts signed by students, parents, and teachers that specify adaptive home and school behaviors; and, arrange for community services (e.g., counseling at the community mental health center).

Summary

This chapter described the IEP-mandated requirements as they relate to the education of students with behavior disorders. IDEA provides comprehensive procedures for referral, identification, and placement of students with behavior disorders and other disability conditions. If special education personnel wish to fulfill both the letter and the spirit of IDEA, they will view the IEP document as more than bothersome paperwork; they will see it as a plan of action, a set of guidelines that defines and creates an individualized program that is specific to one student.

Discussion Questions

1. Name several likely similarities between IEP documents for students with learning disabilities and IEPs for students with behavior disorders.

2. Name several likely differences between IEP documents for students with learning disabilities and IEPs for students with behavior disorders.

3. Why are day schools and self-contained classes the most common placements for students with behavior disorders?

4. What types of circumstances could lead to home-bound instruction?

5. How could bias (e.g., racial or religious bias) affect the assessment or placement of students?

6. Why is criterion-referenced information so useful for teachers?

7. Why are the issues of expulsion and suspension so important for students with behavior disorders?

8. Approximately how many short-term objectives would you write for each annual goal?

9. When would a school district need to pay for a neurological exam for a student with behavior disorders?

10. Are teachers legally responsible for making certain that their students meet or master every short-term objective on the IEP? (*Hint:* The answer is in the 1981 *Federal Register.*)

References

Council for Children with Behavioral Disorders (1990). Position paper on use of behavior reduction strategies with children with behavioral disorders. *Behavioral Disorders, 15* (4), 243–260.

Crandall, E. (1979). *Implementation of the individualized education program: A teacher's perspective.* Dover, DE: Department of Public Instruction.

Federal Register. (January 19, 1981). Rules and regulations. Vol. 46, No. 12.

Fiscus, E., & Mandell, C. (1983). *Developing individualized education programs.* St. Paul, MN: West.

Grosenick, J., George, M., & George, N. (1987). A profile of school programs for the behaviorally disordered: Twenty years after Morse, Cutler, and Fink. *Behavioral Disorders, 12,* 159–168.

Hewett, F. (1968). *The emotionally disturbed child in the classroom.* Boston: Allyn & Bacon.

Kazdin, A. (1977). Assessing the clinical or applied importance of behavior change through social validation. *Behavior Modification, 1,* 427–437.

Kozloff, M. (1994). *Improving educational outcomes for children with disabilities: Principles for assessment, program planning, and evaluation.* Baltimore, MD: Paul H. Brookes Publishing.

Knoblock, P. (1970). Open education for emotionally disturbed children. *Exceptional Children, 39,* 358–365.

Lora v. Board of Education of City of New York (1984). 587 F. SUPP.1572, U.S. District Court, E.D. New York.

Mager, R. (1975). *Preparing instructional objectives.* 2nd ed. Belmont, CA: Pitman Learning.

Mulvey E., Arthur, M., & Reppucci, N. (1993). The prevention and treatment of juvenile delinquency: A review of the research. *Clinical Psychology Review, 13,* 133–167.

Olson, J., & Platt, J. (1996). *Teaching children and adolescents with special needs,* 2nd ed. Columbus, OH: Merrill.

Patterson, G., Chamberlain, P., & Reid, J. (1982). A comparative evaluation of a parent-training program. *Behavior Therapy, 13,* 638–650.

Polloway, E., Bursuck, W., Jayanthi, M., Epstein, M., & Nelson, J. (1996). Treatment acceptability: Determining appropriate interventions within inclusive classrooms. *Intervention in School and Clinic, 31*(8), 133–144.

Public Law 94-142. (1975). *Equal education for all handicapped children act.* Regulations, Section 121a.344.

Public Law 101-476. (1990). *Amendments to PL 94-142: Individuals with disabilities act.* Washington, DC: 101st Congress, October 30, 1990.

Reiher, T. (1992). Identified deficits and their congruence to the IEP for behaviorally disordered students. *Behavior Disorders, 17*(3) 167–177.

Wood, F., Johnson, J., & Jenkins, J. (1986). The *Lora* case: Nonbiased referral, assessment, and placement procedures. *Exceptional Children, 52,* 323–331.

Yell, M. (1989). *Honig v. Doe:* The suspension and expulsion of handicapped students. *Exceptional Children, 56,* 60–69.

Yell, M. (1994). Time-out and students with behavior disorders: A legal analysis. *Education and Treatment of Children, 17*(3), 293–301.

Yell, M., Clyde, K., & Puyallup, S. K. (1995). School district: The courts, inclusion, and students with behavioral disorders. *Behavioral Disorders, 20* (3), 179–189.

Chapter 7

Managing Hyperactive Behavior

Advance Organizer

As you read this chapter, prepare to identify and discuss:

- The variety of organizational frameworks used to categorize the explanations of hyperactivity.
- The types of stimulant medications (and their relative effects) typically prescribed for children with hyperactivity.
- The effects of stimulant medications on the primary characteristics of hyperactivity (overactivity, distractibility, and impulsivity) and on the academic performance of children with hyperactivity.
- The controversial issues surrounding the use of stimulant medications with children with hyperactivity.
- The role of educators in the maintenance of drug treatment regimens.
- The efficacy of dietary approaches in the management of hyperactive behavior.
- The various types of reinforcers and punishers typically used in behavioral programs designed to influence hyperactive behavior.
- Guidelines for the correct use of time-out procedures.
- The effects of behavioral techniques on hyperactive behaviors.
- How the use of cognitive-behavior modification (both self-instruction and self-control procedures) can serve to regulate hyperactive behaviors.

An assessment of the massive number of books, articles, and other educational media that have focused on the management of hyperactivity yields a most divergent and often confusing state of affairs. This confusion is especially disquieting if one assumes the role of parent or teacher of a child with hyperactivity. Obviously, most parents and teachers of youngsters with hyperactivity seek out the most effective methods of controlling inappropriate behavior. Yet, in attempting to discover the "best" method, they are faced with too much of a choice—a richness of theory and practice that is hard to decipher if not approached in an organized manner.

A variety of strategies have been used to organize the many explanations of and treatment alternatives for hyperactivity. This is partly because of the wide range of behaviors considered hyperactive. As noted in earlier chapters, the primary characteristics of hyperactivity are overactivity, distractibility, impulsiveness, excitability, and poor motor coordination. Secondary characteristics—secondary in the sense that they are often the result of interactions between the primary characteristics and environmental events—are learning problems, aggressiveness, antisocial behavior, and poor self-concept or self-esteem. A second reason for the existence of so many organizational strategies is that hyperactivity, like other manifestations of disturbed behavior, has been explained by a multitude of etiological and treatment models that are in many respects incompatible.

In one traditional organizational framework, the clinical views of hyperactivity are categorized into three major models: deficit, delay, and difference (Kinsbourne & Swanson, 1979). The *deficit model*, a direct descendant of early-brain-damage conceptualizations, posits that hyperactive behaviors result from neurological or central nervous system defects. The *delay model* includes those formulations that assert that children with hyperactivity suffer from a "developmental lag" in cognitive-skill development. This view interprets the behavior of a child with hyperactivity as immaturity and proposes that recovery, resulting from either treatment or a spontaneous developmental spurt, can occur throughout a child's developmental period. The *difference model* holds that hyperactive behavior is only quantitatively, not qualitatively, different from normal behavior. Thus, hyperactive behavior is regarded as a problem of degree rather than one of disease, and the child with hyperactivity is a child who responds to environmental stimuli at a greater frequency or intensity than normal youngsters. Similar organizational strategies (Barkley, 1981; Cullinan, Epstein, & Lloyd, 1983; Ross & Ross, 1982) differ in nomenclature, but not in concept.

Other organizational strategies used to categorize explanations of hyperactivity include specific differentiated subgroups of hyperactive children (Connors, 1979; Hastings & Barkley, 1978), differentiated components (e.g., impulsivity, overactivity, distractibility) of hyperactive behavior (Cantwell, 1975; Kauffman, 1985), and how those with hyperactivity function within diverse environments (Maag & Reid, 1994). A relatively nontraditional approach (Lahey et al., 1979) uses historical events and the concept of paradigm shift (see Kuhn, 1962) to organize the explanation and treatment of hyperactivity. In the first paradigm conceptualization (pre-1960), hyperactivity was viewed as the symptom of a medical disorder. Included in this category were theories and practices involving neuropsychology, perceptual-motor

Case Study: Hyperactivity

On Friday afternoon, while everyone else was winding down, David Hibner was still at it. His right foot kept up a rapid tattoo on the floor. Every now and then, he hurriedly and somewhat jerkily changed his position in his seat. He tightly clasped his thighs with his hands; his knuckles were white from the tension. His hand was the first raised following each of my questions, although I was sure that David did not know every answer. And with his hand rose a series of rapid and accelerating *oohs*—it seemed funny to me that David would think it necessary to make sounds to get my attention.

In my exasperation, I remember saying to David that he didn't have to do any more work that week, that he didn't have to participate or even attend to the lesson. All I wanted him to do was sit still and take it easy. Relax. Read a book if he wanted. Take out his crayons and color a picture. Anything, so long as he was quiet and still. At the time, I was amazed that David couldn't do it. He could not relax; he could not take it easy. But I was young and new in the profession. I didn't know a great deal about hyperactivity.

Looking back on my first classroom and David Hibner and the others, I wonder how my students and I survived. There was so much I didn't know. Had I known more about

hyperactivity at the time, I might have been more appreciative of how well balanced David was compared to most children with hyperactivity. He exhibited the overactivity, impulsiveness, and distractibility that characterize hyperactivity in childhood, and these were difficult problems for me, as a beginning teacher, to manage. On the other hand, David was friendly, hard-working, and sincere; he tried awfully hard to be good. He was friendly with the other children in the classroom, and I knew that many of them regarded him as their friend. He didn't seem any more aggressive than any of the other fourth-grade boys. So I missed the common problems that are so frequently related to hyperactivity: poor self-concept, aggressive behavior, antisocial behavior, and lack of strong friendships. David was behind in his schoolwork, but relative to the other kids in the class, he had some solid skills, and he made progress over the course of the year.

In spite of David's good side, I found him to be the most frustrating child to work with in my first class. It was difficult for me to understand the driven quality of his behavior and his inability to control it. And as I stood by him that Friday afternoon and implored him to sit still, I didn't realize the fruitlessness of my pleas.

training, and psycholinguistic processes. Then, in the early 1970s, a full paradigm shift took place in which disease formulations were replaced by a behavioral orientation. Hyperactive behaviors were no longer viewed as symptoms of underlying psychoneurological problems, but rather as specific problem behaviors that could be reduced in frequency and intensity. The third paradigm (in the later 1970s) was regarded as a further refinement of the behavioral orientation. Inappropriate or questionable targets for behavioral intervention (e.g., impulsivity, activity level, and perceptual/cognitive disorders) were replaced with appropriate targets for intervention (e.g., conduct problems and academic learning). Rather than merely decreasing teacher-determined behavioral targets, the third paradigm advocated increasing behaviors incompatible with hyperactive behavior.

No matter what the "paradigm" or "organizational structure" used to explain it, hyperactivity is one of the major childhood disorders of our time (Reid

& Katsiyannis, 1995). It is, in fact, the single most common disorder seen by child psychologists, psychiatrists, and educational specialists (Shaywitz & Shaywitz, 1991). Children exhibiting hyperactive behaviors are generally brought to professional attention before they begin school or early in their educational careers. Since there are many treatment alternatives, a particular intervention is usually the result of how the consulting professional views the problem. The remainder of this chapter highlights the rationale, program, and applied research of three model strategies for intervention: the biophysical, behavioral, and cognitive-behavioral model strategies. It also examines such less traditional therapies as biofeedback/progressive relaxation and stimuli reduction.

Biophysical Interventions

As it does for any form of deviance or disturbance, the biophysical explanation of hyperactivity focuses upon the concept of disease. The normal individual is regarded as physiologically intact and healthy, with a physiological development appropriate to his or her chronological age. Children with hyperactivity, it is believed, possess a certain pathology residing within their physiology that leads to hyperactive behavior. This pathology can be the result of genetic abnormalities, organic factors such as brain or central nervous system (CNS) damage, minimal brain dysfunction, or environmental factors (e.g., toxins, infectious diseases, or allergy-producing substances).

These biophysical explanations have generated interventions designed to treat the pathology of the hyperactive child directly. Treatment alternatives include drug therapy, dietary and/or food additive restriction, and megavitamin therapy.

Drug Therapy

Drug or pharmacological treatment is by far the most frequently used and most controversial method for managing hyperactivity. Over 750,000 children, or more than 2 percent of the school-age population, take medication for the management of their behavior (DuPaul & Stoner, 1994; Safer & Krager, 1988), and approximately 90 percent of these students are identified as being hyperactive (Gadow, 1986). The drugs typically used with children with hyperactivity are stimulants, major tranquilizers, and sedatives.

The Use of Stimulant Medication

Types of Stimulant Medication

The most commonly used drugs in the treatment of hyperactive children are CNS stimulants (Gomez & Cole, 1991), with methylphenidate (Ritalin), dextroamphetamine (Dexedrine), and pemoline (Cylert) the most widely prescribed. Methylphenidate and dextroamphetamine are easily ingested and are quickly absorbed from the gastrointestinal system. Both drugs take effect within a half hour, and peak between one and two hours after ingestion; effects dissipate within four to five hours (Barkley, 1981; Quay & Werry, 1979). Recently, a long-acting spansule has been made available for methylphenidate so that multiple administration of the drug may not be necessary. Pemoline, a slower-acting substance than the others, first shows its effects within an hour of ingestion. Peak effects occur within two to four hours, and the drug's effects dissipate after six to eight hours. Similar to the methylphenidate spansule, pemoline is usually administered once a day, most often at breakfast. The effects of all three types of stimulants are essentially the same, regardless of the number of administrations. Effects are neither cumulative nor permanent, and little tolerance to the drugs is believed to develop (Kinsbourne & Swanson, 1979). While many arguments can be cited for the use of one drug over another, methylphenidate appears to be the overwhelming treatment of choice, with over 90 percent of the children who receive stimulants using this medication (DuPaul, Barkley, & McMurray, 1991).

The Action of Stimulant Medication

Whatever the type of stimulant used, the effect on the hyperactive child is somewhat puzzling since prescribing a *stimulant* for *hyperactivity* is an apparent paradox. Nonetheless, the stimulant's calming effect on the child with hyperactivity can be explained.

As reported by Fish (1975), the true action of stimulant medication is by no means paradoxical; the notion of a paradox arises because "people slip from the behavioral description of quieting and decreased activity to the assumption that there is a pharmacological sedative action" (p. 113). In essence, it is believed that the CNS of the hyperactive child is *under*-aroused—that is, that the hyperactive child lacks adequate CNS inhibitory control over motor and sensory functions. Without inhibitory control, the child with hyperactivity is driven by impulses typically ignored or controlled by a normal child, and these impulses result in the frequently observed behaviors of overactivity, distractibility, and impulsivity.

Stimulant therapy, therefore, does exactly what we would expect it to do: The drug activates CNS inhibitory mechanisms to a normal level of functioning (Anastopoulos, DuPaul, & Barkley, 1991; Satterfield, 1975). Thus, stimulant medication does not "paradoxically" reduce or sedate overarousal; rather, it restores CNS inhibitory control so the child with hyperactivity can regulate sensory input, attend selectively, and control motor responses.

The Effects of Stimulant Medication on Specific Behaviors

The efficacy of stimulant medication has been assessed through a variety of methodologies and its use critiqued in a number of excellent reviews (see Adelman & Compas, 1977; Barkley, 1981; DuPaul & Stoner, 1994; Gadow, 1986; Sroufe, 1975). In general over 70 percent of children with hyperactivity respond favorably to these medications (Anastopoulos et al., 1991; Gomez & Cole, 1991). To assess outcomes, many researchers have used rating scales of parent or teacher opinion; others have sought to directly assess stimulant-induced changes in the syndrome's primary characteristics (overactivity, distractibility, and impulsivity). Research involving the direct assessment of hyperactive characteristics is often regarded as more methodologically rigorous since direct-measurement procedures necessitate the careful specification of what is to be measured. In contrast, rating scales that measure opinions are more readily disposed to bias and other threats to experimental validity (Sroufe, 1975).

Whatever the type of measure employed, the documented efficacy of stimulant medication in reducing overactivity is virtually indisputable: No other treatment produces such dramatic improvements in so short a time (Barkley, 1981). Efforts to assess the influence of stimulants on activity level have found the drug to be effective in reducing excessive task-irrelevant activity (Barkley, 1977; Barkley & Cunningham, 1978; Rie, Rie, Stewart, & Ambuel, 1976). Still, some data suggest that the stimulant's action on activity level may be situation specific.

In highly structured situations, stimulants were found to reduce levels of activity more consistently than they did in free-field or free-play situations. Several researchers (Ellis, Witt, Reynolds, & Sprague, 1974; Schleifer et al., 1975) have reported little stimulant-induced changes in activity levels when the child is placed in settings and situations where demands for compliance and structure are significantly lower. Still, these data are inconclusive; one review of eight drug studies (Barkley & Cunningham, 1979) conducted in free-play settings found that stimulants *did* reduce activity levels. In any event, the possibility that there is a setting-by-medication interaction tells us something important about the usefulness and appropriateness of medication in environments that vary in structure and demand.

A majority of studies (e.g., Barkley, 1977; DuPaul et al., 1991; Michael, Klorman, Saltzman, Borgstedt, & Dainer, 1981) have found that stimulants increase attention span and concentration with effects on sustained attention strongest at higher dosages. There is some evidence, however, that task demands influence the effects of the stimulants. For example, for tasks of low attentional demand, few differences in the rate of on-task behavior were found among normal students, students with hyperactivity receiving stimulant medication, and students with hyperactivity receiving a placebo (Prichep, Sutton, & Hakerem, 1978). However, with tasks that demanded a high degree of attention, significant differences in attention were found among the groups: Both the normal student group and the treated hyperactive group attended to a greater extent than did the placebo group. Such results indicate that stimulants may be necessary for only those tasks that require a high degree of attention.

Impulsivity is characterized as the rapid responding to environmental events without considering alternative, and possible more desirable, responses. In terms of cognitive style, the typical child with hyperactivity is considered to be impulsive rather than reflective. Cognitive style has been operationalized and assessed in a variety of ways: Kagan's Matching Familiar Figures Test (Mock, Swanson, & Kinsbourne, 1978), laboratory-based cognitive tasks (Swanson, Kinsbourne, Roberts, & Zucher, 1978; Weingartner, Rapoport, Ebert, & Caine, 1979), and motor-skill acquisition (Wade, 1978). The effects of stimulant medication on these tests of cognitive style have been inconclusive. Although drugs may improve performance on motor-skill acquisition, tests of verbal retrieval, and stimulus equivalence learning

(Brown & Sleator, 1979; DuPaul & Stoner, 1994), their effects may be influenced by subject variables such as aggression and entry-level cognitive ability (Mock et al., 1978; Weingartner et al., 1979). As expected, when subject variables are ignored, some subjects respond positively to stimulants on measures of cognitive performance while others do not (Swanson et al., 1978).

Effects on social interaction remain unclear. While some earlier studies have found that stimulant medication increases children's compliance to parent and/or teacher requests (e.g., Barkley, Karlsson, Strzelecki, & Murphy, 1984) and the ability to behave more appropriately with peers (e.g., Cunningham, Siegel, & Offord, 1985), recent investigations have reported undesirable social effects. For example, Buhrmester, Whalen, Henker, MacDonald, and Hinshaw (1992) found that stimulant medication resulted in reductions in social engagement with accompanying dysphonia (a lacking of positive affect).

In conclusion, stimulant medication appears to have its greatest effects in situations that require task attention and the restraint of task-irrelevant behavior. More complex cognitive skills and processes are not as clearly affected. Still, we would expect that significant increases in attention and decreases in activity level would result in collateral increases in classroom performance and academic achievement. However, stimulant drugs have not been found to enhance the long-term academic performance of most children with hyperactivity. Barkley and Cunningham (1978), in a summary of eighteen studies on the effects of stimulant medication on academic performance, found that the majority failed to report academic performance improvements. Of the fifty-five academic performances assessed in the studies, forty-six (or 83.6 percent) were not significantly improved as a result of drug therapy. In a more recent review, Gadow (1985) examined sixteen studies to better understand the relationship between stimulant drug therapy and behavioral interventions designed to enhance academic performance. The conclusion was that certain academically oriented behavioral interventions were superior to stimulant medication in facilitating academic performance in hyperactive, learning-disabled, and hyperactive learning-disabled children. While the drugs did serve to increase learning-related behaviors (i.e., reading short passages, attention span, productivity), they did not markedly facilitate the academically oriented behavioral interventions.

Barkley (1981) and DuPaul and Stoner (1994) have offered several possible explanations for the apparent failure of stimulant medication to improve academic performance: (1) children with hyperactivity are given medication too late to affect classroom learning; (2) the tests used to assess performance are not sensitive to the effects that stimulants have on classroom performance; or (3) stimulants do not affect the factors contributing to the academic problems of students with hyperactivity. With regard to the first explanation, students with hyperactivity are usually given medication by the first or second grade, early enough to produce academic change. The second explanation is more plausible because many achievement tests include too few items at any difficulty level to reflect actual changes in academic performance. Still, the lack of significant results in long-term follow-up studies (see Barkley & Cunningham, 1978), as well as those studies that used productivity as a primary dependent measure (e.g., Christensen, 1975), weighs against such a view.

The third explanation is considered the most viable: stimulant drugs do not alter all the variables that result in underachievement in hyperactive children. The components of appropriate academic achievement involve more than just normative levels of attention and acceptable rates of activity, so more than medication will be required to remediate the underachievement of hyperactive children. Ultimately,

---

Stimulant Drug Treatment for Preschool Children: Does It Work?

Little of the considerably large data base concerned with the treatment of hyperactivity has focused on preschool children; the majority of studies have been limited to children between the age of 6 and 12 years. Weiss (1975) has noted two major reasons for this age-related emphasis: (1) children believed to be hyperactive display their symptomology with greater uniformity and less variability during the elementary school years, and (2) the beginning of school automatically means a child is placed in an environment in which new limitations and demands bring previously unnoticed hyperactive behaviors to the surface. The paucity of research with children below the age of 5 years may also be the result of the many difficulties in determining normal versus abnormal rates of behavior during the various preschool stages of development.

Nevertheless, work centering on hyperactive symptomology has been spurred by the belief that the onset of hyperactivity typically occurs when children are between the ages of 3 and 5. While a formal diagnosis is usually made after a child enters school, several authors have made persuasive cases for early identification. For example, Ross and Ross (1982) and Barkley (1982) have reviewed considerable data and concluded that it is possible to identify preschoolers whose hyperactive behaviors will later restrict their appropriate functioning in school settings. The rationale for the early identification of hyperactive behaviors is that early intervention can either eliminate or reduce the severity of the presenting problem behaviors. Because of these early identification efforts and the fact that drug interventions tend to be the favored treatment of

many pediatricians, the issue of the efficacy and possible side effects of the medications on preschool children is one we can no longer neglect. Available survey data (Gadow, 1981) indicate that close to 5 percent of all children enrolled in early childhood special education programs already receive methylphenidate to control their hyperactivity.

In reviewing the literature, Rosenberg (1987) found only six studies that addressed the use of stimulant drug therapy with young hyperactive children. Although the stated purposes, experimental designs, and number and quality of dependent measures varied across the studies, several trends were clear. Rosenberg concluded that the limited data base does not justify the widespread use of stimulants with preschool populations. Five of the six studies reviewed contained a greater number of nonsignificant results and deleterious side effects than positive outcomes. Several of the side effects, including irritability, poor appetite, sadness, and difficulties in going to sleep, were so severe that many of the parents of medicated children discontinued drug use either during or soon after the studies were completed. In the one investigation that reported positive outcomes (Barkley et al., 1984), high dosages of stimulants were required to enhance mother–child interactions.

Rosenberg (1987) concluded that we need to compile more short-term and long-term data before we can adequately assess the relative costs and benefits of early stimulant drug treatment with preschool children. Until then, interventions other than medication should be used with this population.

specific educational techniques that directly address the child's academic problems will be necessary to produce increases in achievement (Barkley, 1981).

Thus, there is no clear evidence that stimulant medication has any direct effect on academic achievement. Stimulant medication alone does make children with hyperactivity more manageable and attentive in the short-term; however, the question of long-term academic benefits remains open (Swanson, Cantwell, Lerner, McBarrett & Hanns, 1991). Unfortunately, teachers have a tendency to perceive medicated students as improving in their work; when noting behavioral improvement, they mistakenly infer that students are making academic progress as well. This misperception may preclude educational efforts to increase achievement (Rie et al., 1976). The mere perception that the drug is working may only serve to increase underachievement and learning problems in medicated students with hyperactivity.

Dosage Levels

Dosage levels have also been found to influence the effects of stimulant medication. For example, Sprague and Sleator (1977) assessed the effects of two dosage levels—0.3 mg/kg (milligrams per kilogram of body weight) and 1.0 mg/kg of methylphenidate and a placebo—upon three dependent measures: teacher-rated social behavior in the classroom, performance on a short-term memory task, and heart rate. The results of the study are presented in Figure 7.1. Three target behaviors were affected differentially by different dosage levels. Performance on the memory task showed greatest improvement (over placebo performance) at the 0.3 mg/kg dosage, while teacher-rated classroom behavior showed peak improvement at 1.0 mg/kg. In terms of heart rate, no increase was noted at 0.3 mg/kg, while a substantial increase was noted at 1.0 mg/kg.

These outcomes have broad implications for the use of stimulants with children with hyperactivity. The dosage (1.0 mg/kg) that resulted in the best rating of classroom behavior failed to enhance academic performance, while the dosage (0.3 mg/kg) that resulted in the best performance on the academic task proved less effective in controlling classroom behavior. Since most physicians rely on parent and teacher reports to determine dosage levels (Barkley, 1981), overmedication to the point of endangering the primary goal of improved academic performance may be a common occurrence. Furthermore, since the 1.0 mg/kg dosage also produced effects on the cardiovascular system, overmedication presents some physical side-effects.

In a more recent effort to measure dose response effects, Tannock, Schachar, Carr, and Logan (1989) reported academic task results that are inconsistent with those of Sprague and Sleator. In their study, a dose of 1.0 mg/kg resulted in a leveling of academic performance rather than a decline. The lack of consistent data precludes any firm generalizations other than the individuality of children in their dose and response profiles (Rapport, DuPaul, & Kelly, 1989). Therefore, it is essential that physicians consider dose responses across a number of measures (e.g., behavioral, cognitive, physical) when determining an optimal dose for an individual child. Given what we already know, however, it is fortunate that most physicians prescribe conservatively and employ only low to moderate doses of stimulant medication (Gadow, 1981).

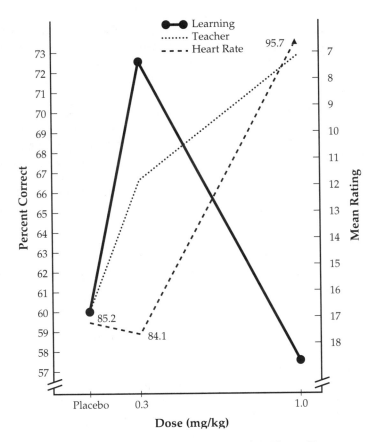

FIGURE 7.1 **Dose-Response Curves for Three Target Behaviors: Laboratory (Short-Term Memory) Learning Task, Teacher Rating of Social Behavior, and Heart Rate**

Source: Sprague & Sleator (1977).

Side Effects

The most common side effects when using stimulant drug treatment are insomnia and loss of appetite. Other, less common side effects are weight loss, irritability, Tourette syndrome (a disorder consisting of persistent motor tics and involuntary, compulsive obscene vocalizations), and, surprisingly, drowsiness (Barkley, McMurray, Edelbrock, & Robbins, 1990; Gadow, 1982). Not surprisingly, some children decrease their rate of social interaction under the influence of stimulants. Parents have been known to comment that their children are no longer "childlike" in their behavior and are *too* controlled (Barkley, 1981). Another reported effect that is understandably upsetting to parents is referred to as the "amphetamine look" (Ross & Ross, 1982). While this sunken-cheeked and sallow appearance is not considered to be a physiological concern, it may cause some harm to a young child's self-concept.

Unfortunately, less is known about the potential long-term side effects of stimulant medication. Although stimulants have been reported to suppress height and weight growth (Safer & Allen, 1973), the suppression occurs primarily during the first year of treatment and growth rebounds after the drug treatment is stopped (Safer, Allen, & Barr, 1975); in fact, growth has been observed to either return to or exceed its expected rate with little alteration in eventual adult height or weight. Any long-term side effects due to influences on the cardiovascular system remain to be conclusively determined (Cantwell & Carlson, 1978; Satterfield, Schell, & Barb, 1980). As for long-term social consequences, there is little support for a "later drug-use hypothesis" (Hechtman, Weiss, & Perlman, 1984). In a study of approximately 500 junior-high male students, for example, Whalen and Henker (1980) found only minor differences in attitudes and use patterns of licit and illicit drugs between those receiving stimulants and comparison peers. Boys who had received drug treatment were abstaining from illicit substances and exhibited low rates of drinking. Furthermore, when surveyed about their future plans, the treated boys planned to continue to abstain from illicit drugs, though not from legal substances such as alcohol and tobacco. However, the authors speculated that two small subgroups of drug-treated students may show higher-than-normal later drug use: children who demonstrate predelinquent patterns of antisocial aggressive behavior and children who may have a physiological predisposition toward psychoactive drug dependency.

Issues in Stimulant Therapy

No treatment or therapy has aroused as much controversy as the use of stimulants in the management of children with hyperactivity. While research has demonstrated positive and dramatic effects on some behaviors, many questions remain unanswered. The absence of methodologically sound evidence that stimulants have an effect on specific behaviors and academic achievement should dictate that more prominence be given to the issue of side effects (Adelman & Compas, 1977; Swanson et al., 1991). Also, the relative ease of a drug solution might allow parents and teachers to abdicate their child-rearing and behavior management responsibilities (Sroufe, 1975).

What, then, can we conclude about stimulant medication? On the one side, we are tempted to say that the demonstrated efficacy of stimulant medication should not be misjudged or impugned because of inadequacies in prescription (i.e., dosage) and monitoring. Moreover, stimulants are more cost-effective than their psychoeducational alternatives. But on the other side, we are concerned that the studies demonstrating efficacy are not methodologically rigorous enough to be judged satisfactory. In fact, stimulant medication may be "an overly simplistic solution to complex, social, educational, and intrafamilial problems" (Sroufe, 1975, p. 395). Even advocates of drug therapy acknowledge the gravity of using stimulant medication for children. Informed parents, in conjunction with physicians, educators, and psychologists, must weigh the potential benefits against possible risks

Drug Treatment with Hyperactive Children: Issues Worthy of Consideration

Whoever is involved in the process of drug treatment for hyperactive children should ask themselves a series of questions concerning the ethics and social impact of this most controversial procedure. This brief listing of issues adopted from Barkley (1981) should never "be too far from our thinking as we engage in the modification of children's social conduct through psychopharmacologic means" (p. 220).

How ethical is it to treat children with drugs of little-known long-term efficacy because their behavior is intolerable to their parents or teachers?

Have drugs simply become too easily available as a method of treatment? Have professionals abdicated their responsibilities to implement less convenient, but equally effective, nonmedical therapies?

Can society afford the apparent double standard of instructing children not to turn

to recreational drugs to solve their problems while using similar drugs to solve its own problems?

Are hyperactive children learning to view medicine as the solution to their social problems?

What are the implications of the politics of drug therapy? We seem to be more likely to use drugs with children of lower educational and socioeconomic backgrounds, whose parents may be less literate and may also be members of racial minorities.

Are the research findings clear enough to warrant medicating 600,000 or more children every year?

Should schools and physicians team up as they do to "coerce" parents into using drugs with their children? Are we simply patching up an obsolete educational system?

Source: Barkley (1981).

and make a decision that is appropriate for their particular child. Figure 7.2, provides a quick reference as to what should and should not be expected regarding the use of stimulant medication.

The Educator's Role in Drug Treatment Regimens

Surveys (Gadow, 1981, 1986) indicate that 42 to 60 percent of all special education teachers have some level of involvement with students receiving some kind of medication for behavior problems. Nonetheless, many special educators are either unaware of or confused about their roles and responsibilities in the drug therapy process. There is considerable evidence that a majority of special educators lack a basic familiarity with the how, when, or why of drug therapy. In fact, the typical special educator receives little or no substantive preservice or in-service training in this area.

Superficially, it may appear that educators have little to do with drug management of problem behaviors. After all, teachers cannot prescribe medication and few have been trained in the intricacies of central nervous system functioning. Upon closer scrutiny, however, it is clear that educators are critical to the success of drug therapy because they can ensure that drug treatments are appropriate, effective, and safe for students deemed in need of such therapy. We

What Should Be Expected

1. Temporary Management of Diagnostic Symptoms
    a. Overactivity (improved ability to modulate motor behavior)
    b. Inattention (increased concentration or effort on tasks)
    c. Impulsivity (improved self-regulation)

2. Temporary Improvement of Associated Features
    a. Deportment (increased compliance and effort)
    b. Aggression (decrease in physical and verbal hostility)
    c. Social interactions (decreased negative behaviors)
    d. Academic productivity (increased amount and accuracy of work)

What Should Not Be Expected

1. Paradoxical Response
    a. Responses of normal children are in same directions
    b. Responses of normal adults are in same directions
    c. Responses of affected adults and children are similar

2. Prediction of Response
    a. Not by neurological signs
    b. Not by physiological measures
    c. Not by biochemical markers

3. Absence of Side Effects
    a. Infrequent appearance or increase in tics
    b. Frequent problems with eating and sleeping
    c. Possible psychological effects on cognition and attribution

4. Large Effects on Skills or Higher Order Processes
    a. No significant improvement of reading skills
    b. No significant improvement of athletic or game skills
    c. No significant improvement of positive social skills
    d. Improvement on learning/achievement less than improvement in behavior/attention

5. Improvement in Long-Term Adjustment
    a. No improvement in academic achievement
    b. No reduction in antisocial behavior or arrest rate

FIGURE 7.2 **In Their Massive Review of Reviews, Swanson and Colleagues (1993) Integrated a Number of Generalizations on the Typical Expected Benefits of Stimulant Medication. These Are Reprinted Above.**

Source: Swanson et al. (1993). Effect of stimulant medication on children with attention deficit disorder: A "review of reviews." *Exceptional Children, 60,* 159. Copyright 1993 by The Council for Exceptional Children. Reprinted with permission.

can conceptualize the educator's role in drug treatment as twofold: the educator as informed source of current information and the educator as monitor of drug effects.

Informed Source

Information provided by educators is crucial in the initial diagnosis of hyperactivity. Their input is second only to parents' in terms of overall behavioral functioning and is most important when the primary problem is academic performance (Barkley, 1981). Consequently, responsible physicians will give considerable credence to the opinions of educators about the appropriateness of drug intervention in a particular child. Similarly, it is not unusual for families of children with hyperactivity to seek educators' advice regarding the severity of the hyperactive symptoms observed in school or to solicit their opinion about drug therapy. Although they are obviously not in a position to provide medical advice, special educators are generally regarded by parents as trustworthy advocates for their children. Thus, it is not uncommon for parents to ask special education personnel about drug treatment alternatives for social and academic problems.

Monitor of Drug Effects

Once an appropriate drug treatment plan is implemented, the educators' opinions on the child's responses to the drug will probably be used in determining proper dosage. If physicians do not request such information, Barkley (1981) recommends that school personnel take the initiative and contact them with their observations. Teachers are in the unique situation of being able to monitor the drug's effects on both classroom behavior and academic performance, as well as how varying dosage levels differentially affect each set of behaviors. Also, school personnel can provide input on what additional strategies (e.g., structured contingency management programs and social-skills training) to adopt to maximize the effects of the medication. More often than not, these educational interventions are necessary supplements to the medication. Finally, teachers assist in the last phase of the drug regimen—the follow-up. This is a continual activity in which those who come into contact with the student under treatment look for potential changes in response to the medications and note any possible side effects. Table 7.1, adapted from DuPaul and Stone (1994), lists a variety of methods that can be used to monitor and assess the effects of medication. Table 7.2 lists some important considerations related to medications.

Not everyone is in favor of involving teachers in the drug treatment regimen. For example, Ross and Ross (1976) advocate not even *informing* a teacher that a child is on medication, on the grounds that such a restriction of information is in the best interests of the child. Citing a series of studies, the authors state that most teachers are not well informed about these drugs, are uncertain about their desirability, frown upon the stereotypical notion of "teacher as pusher of drugs," and are generally comfortable with assuming a passive role in the treatment plan. In short, they have neither the necessary knowledge nor the desire to be involved in evaluating a drug treatment program, so it is best to keep the knowledge of such interventions between parents and their pediatricians. Sprague and Gadow (1976), in contrast, advocate a more facilitative role for the teacher. They assert that a properly trained educator can play an important role in a day treatment program by monitoring behavioral change and becoming the focal point in communications among the school, the home, and the physician's office.

TABLE 7.1   Measures to Assess Medication Response

1. Teacher rating scales
    a. Conners Teacher Rating Scale—Revised (Goyette et al., 1978).
    b. ADD+H Comprehensive Teacher Rating Scale (Ullmann et al., 1985).
    c. ADHD Rating Scale (DuPaul, 1991a).
    d. School Situations Questionnaire (Barkley, 1990) or Questionnaire—Revised (DuPaul & Barkley, 1992a).
    e. Academic Performance Rating Scale (DuPaul et al., 1991).
    f. Side Effects Rating Scale (Barkley, 1990).

2. Parent rating scales
    a. Conners Parent Rating Scale—Revised (Goyette et al., 1978).
    b. Home Situations Questionnaire (Barkley, 1990) and/or Questionnaire—Revised (DuPaul & Barkley, 1992).
    c. ADHD Rating Scale (DuPaul, 1991).
    d. Side Effects Rating Scale (Barkley, 1990).

3. Direct observations of school performance
    a. Classroom Observation Code (Abikoff et al., 1977).
    b. ADHD Behavior Coding System (Barkley et al., 1988).
    c. Classroom Observations of Conflict and Attention Deficit Disorders (Atkins et al., 1985).
    d. On-Task Behavior Code (Rapport et al., 1987).
    e. Code for Observing Social Activity (Sprafkin et al., 1986).

4. Academic performance measures
    a. Percentage of assigned work completed correctly.
    b. Curriculum-based measurement.

5. Self-report rating scales
    a. Piers-Harris Children's Self-Concept Scale (Piers, 1984).

Source: Adapted from DuPaul & Stoner (1994). By permission of The Guilford Press.

TABLE 7.2   Stimulant Medication: Important Considerations for Educators

1. How old is the student? Is he or she too young for psychotropic medication? How severe are the presenting symptoms?

2. Have alternative, less intrusive interventions been tried?

3. Are you informed as to how the medication that will be administered to the student works? Has a system to monitor the student for possible side effects been developed?

4. Is there an adequate network of communication so that parents, educators, and physicians can discuss aspects of a student's drug therapy?

5. Are parents strongly against the use of medication? Do parents have enough skill to monitor the administration and effects of the medication?

6. Has the drug therapy been discussed with the student in terms that he or she can comprehend? What is the student's attitude toward medication?

7. Are you aware of the school district policy regarding the administration of prescribed medications in the school setting?

8. Are you prepared to continue with an effective program of academic instruction after the medication is introduced?

9. Has a system to monitor the effects of the drugs been developed and field-tested?

Source: Adapted from Barkley (1981; 1990), Courtnage (1982), and Epstein & Olinger (1987).

To improve the delivery of services to students receiving medication in educational settings, Gadow (1981) advocates the following:

1. More information and training regarding drug therapy for educational personnel.
2. An increase in the quantity and quality of communication among parents, teachers, and physicians.
3. Greater teacher involvement in the drug treatment process.
4. The development of formal guidelines for the role of the school in the treatment regimen.

It is also suggested that educators develop contingency plans for dealing with possible parental mismanagement of the treatment procedures and that they lobby for improved physician practices in the prescription and monitoring of medications used during school hours.

The Use of Tranquilizers, Antidepressants, and Other Drugs Infrequently Used with Children

A number of tranquilizers, antidepressants, and other chemical agents have been used to treat hyperactivity. Major tranquilizers have been found to produce negative side effects in 60 percent of the children treated (Brundage-Aguar, Forehand, & Ciminero, 1976). Furthermore, these drugs showed no consistent effect on attention and the treated children's task performance was reported to decrease. In effect, tranquilizers have been judged to be inferior to stimulant medication in terms of behavioral and cognitive functioning (Werry, Aman, & Diamond, 1980).

Antidepressants (e.g., imipramine), which have been successful in the treatment of enuresis, have demonstrated some ability to decrease overactivity and increase attention span and sociability (Biederman, Baldessarini, Wright, Knee, & Harmatz, 1989). Nonetheless, relatively little is known about the long-term efficacy of these drugs, and deleterious side effects such as increases in blood pressure and electrocardiographic abnormalities have been observed (DuPaul & Stoner, 1994).

Other chemical agents such as lithium carbonate and caffeine have been employed to manage hyperactivity. Lithium carbonate treatments have proved no more effective than placebos with children with hyperactivity (Brundage-Aguar et al., 1976), and the results from several caffeine studies cannot be regarded as promising (Connors, 1979; Firestone, 1978; Gadow, 1986).

Dietary and Nutritional Approaches

While drug intervention may be the most *common* form of treatment for the child with hyperactivity, dietary and nutritional approaches appear to be the most *popular*. These approaches frequently receive exposure in mass-market outlets such as television, magazines, and newspapers. The dietary approach most often referred to is the Kaiser-Permanente (K-P) diet, which was described in 1975 by Benjamin Feingold. Briefly stated, Feingold's (1975) hypothesis was that symptoms of hyperactivity, aggression, and impulsiveness can be diminished through the strict K-P diet. The K-P diet is specifically designed to eliminate all foods that contain natural salicylates (a salt compound found in many fruits that is chemically similar to aspirin), artificial colors, and artificial flavors from the child's diet. According to Feingold, these sugars and additives are responsible for causing the learning and behavioral problems in as many as 50 percent of all children with hyperactivity. In essence, hyperactivity is an allergic reaction to salicylates and artificial colors and flavors.

It has been difficult to assess the efficacy of the K-P diet because Feingold's assertions about the success of his treatment are based on case studies that rely almost exclusively upon anecdotal data. Although a number of case studies attesting to the success of the diet have appeared in quasi-scientific publications (Barkley, 1981), there is little evidence from rigorously controlled studies to support the efficacy of the diet. A review of the more scientifically rigorous studies (e.g., Connors, Goyette, Southwick, Lees, Andrylonis, 1976; Harley et al., 1978; Pescara-Kovach & Alexander, 1994; Weiss et al., 1980) leads one to the conclusion that the Feingold diet cannot be considered a primary treatment for most children with hyperactivity. True, a few children have been found to be positive responders to the diet (Rose, 1978; Varley, 1984), but the majority require some other form of treatment.

Another popular approach to the management of hyperactivity has been to control sugar consumption. Sugar, because of its ability to produce quick energy, seems a logical element to examine in the management of problematic overactivity, distractibility, and impulsivity. Unfortunately, we have little well-controlled research to go on. In one study (Prinz, Roberts, & Hartman, 1980), the amount of sugar consumption was related to quality of playroom behavior for both hyperactive and normal children. For the hyperactive group, significant relationships were found between amount of sugar consumed and restlessness and destructive-aggressive behavior, but this relationship did not hold true for the normal children. Although no causal relationship should be inferred from these correlational data, the notion that sugar affects some children's behavior should not be dismissed without further study. It has been frequently observed that different levels of sugar in the blood stream can predispose certain groups of children to experience a range of problematic symptoms, some of which are remarkably similar to the characteristics generally referred to as hyperactivity (Baren, Liebl, & Smith, 1978).

Behavioral Interventions

The behavioral model focuses on the observable behavior of individuals. It is based on the assumption that *all* behavior—inappropriate as well as appropriate—is learned. Academic and social-emotional problems are not viewed as symptoms of underlying psychological or neurological disorders, but are treated as individual behavioral targets in need of modification through a system of empirically based behavior-change techniques. The behavioral model posits that antecedent environmental events immediately preceding and following an individual's behavior can greatly influence that individual's future behavior or learning. Through the modification of these environmental events (e.g., environmental design issues, daily schedules, class rules, and task demands) previously learned behaviors can be increased or decreased and new behaviors can be learned (Abramowitz & O'Leary, 1991).

Three types of learning have played a major role in conceptualizing the behavioral orientation: classical conditioning, operant conditioning, and observational learning (Craighead, Kazdin, & Mahoney, 1981). Specific behavioral programs designed to remediate hyperactivity, however, have relied primarily upon the principles of operant conditioning. Operant conditioning involves the relationship between an individual's voluntary behavior and the many environmental events that can potentially shape or influence it. While both antecedent and consequent events are responsible for behavior change, most applications of operant conditioning principles have focused on the consequences—the environmental stimuli that follow behavior (Kazdin, 1975). Consequences, whether positive or negative, can be systematically manipulated to change a number of inappropriate and undesirable behaviors. In essence, behavioral change can occur when planned consequences are delivered contingently upon the performance of a particular behavior. Many different types of contingencies have been employed to remediate problematic hyperactive behaviors. A catalog of these techniques and a discussion of their efficacy follow. Note that the effectiveness of the techniques discussed are not limited to the behavioral symptoms of hyperactivity; the behavioral approach is robust, and its techniques can be applied to a variety of problem behaviors, including aggression, social withdrawal, and rule breaking delinquency.

The Behavioral Control of Hyperactivity

Successful treatment of problematic behaviors such as hyperactivity typically involve strengthening or weakening different target behaviors. Programs designed simply to reduce or eliminate inappropriate behaviors may be lacking in that they do not necessarily result in the strengthening or teaching of desired behaviors. To illustrate this point, consider the total day of a child with hyperactivity as a pie (Ross, 1980). While specialized behavioral interventions and treatments can reduce these undesirable behaviors, some other behavior will have to fill the open space. In effect, a behavioral vacuum, or a time period without behavior, cannot exist. In order to ensure than an appropriate behavior substitutes for inappropriate behavior, the behavior modifier must plan to reinforce, strengthen, or teach a desired behavior as well. Without it, the vacant time might be inadvertently filled by still another inappropriate behavior.

Thus, while behavioral techniques that increase and decrease behavior are often presented and described in isolation, they are most effectively employed together. Following is a brief discussion of several behavior change strategies that increase and decrease behavior and how these techniques have been combined to remediate problematic hyperactive behavior.

Increasing Behavior

When we speak of increasing the frequency of a behavior, we are referring to the process of reinforcement. Positive reinforcement refers to an increase in the frequency (or strength) of a behavior that results from the contingent presentation of a positive consequence or positive reinforcer. Reinforcers can be either primary or secondary. Primary reinforcers are unconditioned in that their reinforcing properties are not dependent on any prior learning; food and water are examples. Secondary, or conditional reinforcers, acquire a reinforcing ability through learning and paired associations with other events that are already reinforcing to the individual. Negative reinforcement (often confused with punishment) involves the removal of an aversive or unpleasant event; like positive reinforcement, it results in an increase in the frequency of a behavior.

Critical to any discussion of reinforcement is the premise that reinforcement (both positive and negative) is a functional term. Reinforcement always refers to increases in the frequency or intensity of a behavior. Thus, praise or certain conditioned rewards are not necessarily reinforcers. In order for praise or a reward to be a positive reinforcer, it must serve to increase the strength of a particular target behavior. Consequently, one major task in using reinforcement effectively is the selection of potential reinforcers that have the greatest likelihood of increasing behavior. We turn now to the various types of reinforcers that are commonly used for remediating hyperactivity.

Edibles.   Edibles have been used as reinforcers with a variety of populations with handicaps because of their strength as a primary reinforcer. Although edibles are often necessary reinforcers for populations with more severe handicaps, there are several shortcomings to using them with children with hyperactivity in a classroom setting. First, assuming that desirable foods for individual students can be secured, the delivery and consumption of such items as candy, ice cream, gum, and soft drinks can disrupt important classroom activities. In addition, some edibles are too cumbersome for the active classroom teacher or behavior modifier to deliver. While staff can readily carry pockets of some candies, other foods such as beverages and ice cream are not easily transported (Kazdin, 1975). Furthermore, if we accept the *possibility* that hyperactive behaviors result from the ingestion of certain foods, we face the danger of inadvertently fueling hyperactivity by using desired, yet symptom-producing, edibles. Since children with hyperactivity are generally responsive to praise and other more convenient reinforcers, edibles should not be used until other types of reinforcers have proved ineffective.

Praise and Attention.   Praise and attention are examples of social reinforcers that can be quite powerful in treating hyperactive behaviors in both the classroom and home. These reinforcers can be easily and quickly administered by teachers and parents and are usually not obtrusive during classroom activities. There are, however, a number of guidelines that should be followed to maximize the effectiveness of praise and attention. First, these reinforcers should be delivered immediately after the target behavior has occurred (Walker, 1979). Second, statements of praise should be varied so that the delivery of praise does not become monotonous and appear insincere. Finally, praise or attention should be descriptive of, or reflect, the target behavior. Since descriptive praise facilitates the discrimination between appropriate and inappropriate behaviors, the child with hyperactivity should be told precisely those behaviors for which praise or attention is being given. One caution should be noted: Praise and attention are not always reinforcing; their reinforcement value is conditional and subject to prior learning.

High-Probability Behaviors.   A child's preferred activities—by definition, those behaviors that possess a high probability of occurring—serve to reinforce lower-probability behaviors. This differential use of a student's behavior, often referred to as the *Premack Principle*, is advantageous because of its powerful, yet mostly cost-free, ability to change behavior. High-probability behaviors frequently used in management programs for children with hyperactivity are free time, movie viewing, and magazine reading. Time for these activities is contingently awarded for lower-probability or less preferred behaviors such as academic work, attention to task, and compliance.

Performance Feedback.   Feedback, defined as information about one's progress toward the attainment of a goal (Kazdin, 1975), can be a powerful and convenient reinforcer. While feedback can be conveyed through a variety of modalities, it must always inform students of their present level of performance. Obviously, some feedback is an implicit component of any system of reinforcement deliver. Nonetheless, additional mechanisms of feedback can be employed to heighten reinforcer effects. Charted feedback, for example, has been reported to enhance the effects of behavioral programming (Jenkins, Mayhall, Reschke, & Townsend, 1974; Jen & Shores, 1969). Research documenting that feedback alone can improve behavior has, not surprisingly, raised the question of whether some management programs unnecessarily or prematurely utilize tangible rewards (Axelrod, 1983; Drabman & Lahey, 1974).

Tokens.   Tokens are conditioned-generalized reinforcers that are associated with a variety of other reinforcers. Tokens can take a variety of forms, ranging from poker chips and checkmarks to stickers and tickets. In and of themselves, tokens are not reinforcing; their strength derives from the times, activities, or consequences they represent.

Because of their versatility, tokens offer several advantages to teachers and parents of children with hyperactivity (Alberto & Troutman, 1986). First, they combat satiation in that they can purchase a variety of reinforcers. Second, they are conveniently delivered in most situations and serve to bridge the time period between the occurrence of an appropriate behavior and the delivery of a primary reinforcer. Finally, and perhaps of greatest value, tokens allow for graduations of reinforcement that reflect differing degrees of performance. Thus, when shaping appropriate nonhyperactive behaviors, approximations toward terminal goals can be reinforced.

The use of tokens also has several disadvantages. The major one involves the fading of the tokens once behavioral change has been accomplished. While it is usually recommended that teachers and parents transfer control to naturally occurring reinforcers, this process is sometimes neglected for fear that the inappropriate behaviors will reappear as soon as the token program is ended. Token procedures also present problems of record-keeping and often take up a large amount of teacher time (Axelrod, 1983), time that could be put to better use in instruction.

Contingency Contracting. Contingency contracting has been an effective method for delivering reinforcement to children displaying a wide range of problem behaviors, including hyperactivity. Contingency contracts are not reinforcers; rather, they are written agreements that specify relationships between appropriate child behaviors and certain positive consequences. Contracts can be used for any aspect of behavior, and can be of varying complexity, but the contingencies in the contract should be the result of negotiation between the child and the parent or teacher. Since contingency contracts specify in advance the positive and aversive consequences for behavior, children with hyperactivity know what behaviors are expected of them and do not regard teacher or parental responses as either arbitrary or unfair.

According to Hall and Hall (1982), contingency contracts should always be stated in positive terms, formatted to promote success (i.e., reward small gradients of change), allow for frequent and immediate reinforcement, and be the result of negotiation. A sample generic behavioral contract between student and teacher is provided in Figure 7.3 on page 218. Note that the physical body of the contract contains: (1) the date the contract is to begin, end, and/or be negotiated; (2) a clear specification of the behavior(s) pinpointed for intervention; (3) the consequences (i.e., rewards) for meeting the terms of the contract; (4) a listing of who is to provide the rewards; and (5) a signature of all parties involved in the contract.

Decreasing Behavior
Several alternatives are readily available to decrease the frequency of hyperactive behaviors. Extinction, punishment, and differential reinforcement will be described.

Extinction. Extinction is a decrease in the strength of a behavior that results from the withholding of rewards for previously reinforced behavior. The most common form of extinction is ignoring a behavior that was previously reinforced with attention (Craighead et al., 1981). The planned ignoring of inappropriate hyperactive behavior is often difficult for parents and teachers. The frustration of "just doing nothing" is compounded when they face initial increases in the frequency of the inappropriate behavior they are intent on ignoring. Parents and teachers who are not aware of this extinction-burst phenomenon often give up, although if they had persisted, the inappropriate behavior would have eventually decreased. Since extinction is a relatively slow process, parents and teachers who have difficulty accepting gradual change are advised to choose another procedure for decreasing behavior strength (Axelrod, 1983).

Extinction is best suited to behaviors that fall under the general heading of minor rule breaking. High-intensity behaviors that occur at a relatively low frequency, such as tantrumming, fighting, and defiance, require the application of stronger behavior-reducing techniques. In general, extinction should be used only

This is a contract between _____ and

student's name

_____ .

teacher's name

The student _____ agrees to work on the following behaviors:

1. _____

2. _____

3. _____

If I meet the above conditions, I will get from the teacher:

_____

_____

_____

as a special reward. If the terms of the contract are not met by the student, all rewards will be withheld.

Signatures and date

_____	_____
student	Date
_____	_____
teacher	Date
_____	_____
witness	Date

We will review this contract on _____ to reevaluate this contract.

Date

FIGURE 7.3   Sample Generic Behavioral Contract

for behaviors that are minimally disruptive to the classroom atmosphere and are believed to be the result of teacher attention. While extinction is not the best method of dealing with many of the behaviors associated with hyperactivity, it should be considered as a first-try method because it does not call for applying aversive consequences. The parent or teacher can always move on to more obtrusive punishment techniques if extinction fails to get results.

Punishment.   Punishment refers to the manipulation of a consequence to decrease the strength of a target behavior. Punishment takes one of two forms: the presentation of an aversive consequence or the removal of a reinforcer. Like reinforcement, punishment should be thought of as a functional term; punishers must reduce the future occurrence of the behaviors to which they are applied. Contrary to many popular misconceptions, punishment need not involve pain or physical coercion (Linn, 1983).

Four types of punishers have been used for the classroom management of students with hyperactivity: reprimands, response-cost, time-out, and overcorrection. A *reprimand* is an expression of disapproval directed toward a particular behavior.

Reprimands are easy to apply, require little planning, and are a common occurrence in the classroom and home. Nevertheless, the lack of consistent outcomes in the research investigating reprimands should signal caution in their use (Kazdin, 1975). In one classic study (Madsen, Becker, & Thomas, 1968), a teacher's use of "sit down" reprimand was found to increase rather than decrease out-of-seat behavior. Reprimands have proved effective (Hall et al., 1971; McAllister, Stachowiak, Baer, & Conderman, 1969) when combined with praise for appropriate behavior. There is also evidence that soft, private reprimands result in a greater reduction of inappropriate behaviors than loud, public reprimands (O'Leary, Kauffman, Kass, & Drabman, 1970).

Response-cost, a technique often used in conjunction with token systems, is a formal system of penalties applied in response to inappropriate behaviors. The strength of response-cost procedures is evident in many of our daily routines. If we are caught driving above the legal speed limit and assessed a fine, for example, we will most likely decrease the frequency of our speeding. Response-cost used in combination with reinforcement procedures is more effective in controlling undesirable behaviors than positive reinforcement is alone and has been demonstrated to increase levels of on-task behavior, seatwork productivity, and academic accuracy among students with hyperactivity (DuPaul, Guevremont, & Barkley, 1992). While the removal of points and/or tokens is the most commonly reported application of response-cost, loss of privileges such as free-time minutes and television viewing time can also be successful (Kazdin, 1972).

Whereas response-cost refers to the removal of all or part of a specific activity or valued item (tokens, points, etc.), *time-out* can be conceptualized as limiting access to all positive enforcers for a set amount of time. Time-out can be administered in a number of ways, but usually takes one of two forms: either removing the child to a (presumably) less reinforcing environment (seclusionary or exclusionary) or making the existing environment of the child less reinforcing (nonseclusionary). To achieve maximum effects with time-out, the child should have no access to reinforcing events. However, the removal of all possible reinforcers is an ideal that cannot always be attained in classrooms serving students with behavior problems such as hyperactivity. In fact, a survey by Zabel (1986) revealed that 63 percent of teachers who used time-out did not have access to a separate time-out room, but used an area of their classroom. Parents and teachers should be aware that many of the areas to which they remove a child possess reinforcers. For example, the teacher who sends a misbehaving student to the office may not realize that spending time in the office is an interesting experience; the child sees other teachers and watches the secretaries at work. Thus, a trip to the office may well service to *increase* inappropriate behavior. Similarly, parents who send their child to his or her room for misbehaving at the dinner table may be reinforcing misbehavior if the child has access to many toys and playthings in the room.

Regardless of the type of time-out used—seclusionary or nonseclusionary—it is the discrepancy between the time-in and time-out environments that influences the effectiveness of the procedure (Harris, 1985). Time-out applied for a misbehavior in a generally positive, rewarding environment is likely to be more effective than the removal of the child from an environment in which little praise or positive reinforcement is received. Children who are removed from nonreinforcing environments do not feel they are missing much and may actually desire removal over participation in class activities. In any event, the use of time-out should be carefully planned and administered with caution. It is quite easy to overuse this technique to the point of abuse, since the peace and quiet following the removal of a disruptive child may negatively reinforce the parent or teacher!

In general, the duration of a time-out should be brief; typically 1 to 5 minutes is sufficient (Gast & Nelson, 1977). The following sequence (Abramowitz & O'Leary, 1991; Alberto & Troutman, 1986) should be followed:

1. The behaviors that will result in a time-out should be clearly identified and the duration of the time-out for each of the pinpointed behaviors should be specified.
2. When the misbehavior occurs, the teacher should reidentify it and direct the student to the time-out area for the specified period of time. If the child puts up resistance, the teacher should be prepared to (a) gently but firmly lead the student to time-out; (b) add time to the time-out period for yelling, screaming, or getting aggressive; (c) require the student to clean up any mess or destruction resulting from the resistance to time-out; and (d) employ a backup consequence for students who adamantly refuse to go to the time-out area.
3. The teacher should see that the student returns to the activity he or she was engaged in prior to the time-out to avoid negatively reinforcing an escape from that activity. The teacher should not make any comments on how the student behaved during the time-out.
4. A written record of all time-outs should be maintained along with baseline and postintervention rates of the target behavior(s).

Overcorrection and corporal punishment are alternative punishments for reducing hyperactive behavior. The two components of *overcorrection* are restitution (the student is required to correct the effects of his or her inappropriate behavior) and positive practice (a procedure in which the student is required to extensively rehearse a correct form of behavior). Since overcorrection procedures have not been regularly used in classrooms, their efficacy as a technique for managing hyperactivity has not been evaluated (Axelrod, 1983).

There is a similar lack of information on the use of *corporal punishment* with children with hyperactivity. Although used commonly by some parents, corporal punishment has not been studied because of its "unethical nature in terms of standards for scientific research" (Barkley, 1981, p. 253).

Despite numerous reports indicating the beneficial effects of many punishment procedures, the use of punishment in classroom settings has been questioned because of a number of possible side effects. As noted by Craighead and colleagues (1981), these side effects are the avoidance of the individual administering the punisher, imitation of the use of punishment, and increased emotional responding. While some severe behavior may require the use of punishment, most behavioral problems should initially be approached with a less intrusive alternative. Often the differential reinforcement of behaviors incompatible with the problem behaviors is the recommended strategy.

Differential Reinforcement.   Undesirable hyperactive behaviors can be indirectly reduced or eliminated through the creative use of reinforcement contingencies. One method, differential reinforcement of low rate of response allows reinforcement of inappropriate behavior if the rate of the behavior is at, or below, a prespecified level. This technique is particularly useful if a parent or teacher does not wish to eliminate a behavior completely, but merely reduce its frequency. Another technique, differential reinforcement of other behavior, involves the reinforcement of any other behavior but the inappropriate target response. More stringent is the reinforcement of appropriate behavior incompatible with the targeted problem response. Since an appropriate behavior such as staying in one's seat cannot occur at the same time as inappropriate behavior such as running around the classroom, the reinforcement of the appropriate behavior would indirectly result in a decrease of the inappropriate behavior.

The Effects of Behavioral Techniques on Hyperactive Behaviors
Behavior Modification of Attention.   The apparent relationship between attention to task and academic achievement has spurred many educators to investigate direct approaches for increasing attention to task. Such attempts have demonstrated that attending can be strengthened by the contingent delivery of a variety of reinforcers. For example, increases in attention have resulted from teacher praise (Kazdin, 1975) and a token economy (Craig & Holland, 1970). Among the classic studies, Walker and Buckley (1968) found that an individual conditioning procedure in a controlled setting could increase attending and lead to generalization beyond the experimental setting. The procedure was oriented to developing successful, task-oriented classroom performance. During treatment, the child was told that when an interval of time had elapsed in which no inappropriate behavior had occurred, a click would sound. The click would represent the earning of a point, and the accumulation of points would eventually lead to buying an item of choice. The number of points necessary for the backup reinforcer was specified before the treatment began. Although this was a rather elaborate treatment not readily available to teachers, other, simpler treatments (e.g., Cossairt, Hall, & Hopkins, 1973; Novy, Burnett, Powers, & Sulzer-Azaroff, 1973) have yielded similar results.

The problem with this technique is that it can be used only when on-task behavior is defined as a physical orientation to task or teacher. Such overt on-task behavior, alas, may fail to improve a student's educational performance (see Hallahan & Kauffman, 1975; Shemberg, Keeley, Gill, & Garton, 1972), and thus be a short-sighted target. Some researchers (Winett & Winkler, 1972; Winett & Roach, 1973) have claimed that on-task behaviors constitute merely "attention and obedience" rather than something essential to the learning process. For that reason, behavioral intervention programs should shift away from targeting on-task behaviors to modifying contingencies involving academic performance. The direct manipulation of academic contingencies alone should result not only in desired performance gains but also in collateral gains in appropriate classroom attending. One study testing this hypothesis (Hay, Hay, & Nelson, 1977) assessed the relative efficacy of on-task and academic performance. It found that the reinforcement of appropriate on-task behavior resulted merely in increasing time on-task; there were no collateral gains in academic performance. In contrast, contingencies aimed at increasing academic performance produced increases in both performance and attention to task. The same effect was found in other studies (Ayllon, Layman, & Bruke, 1972; Ayllon & Roberts, 1974; Sulzer, Hunt, Ashby, Koniarsky, & Krams, 1968).

Still, the goal of reinforcing attention may be appropriate and necessary when designing instructional programs for severely distractible children whose attention deficits are so severe that academic performance contingencies alone would produce no changes in student behavior (Packard, 1970). Task variables also may signal the need for setting contingencies for attention. For example, for highly active boys working on difficult tasks, contingencies involving both attention and performance were necessary to maintain high rates of time on-task and increased academic achievement (Rosenberg, Sindelar, & Stedt, 1985). Students completing a difficult task with contingencies for only correct academic performance were off-task more and scored lower on three measures of academic performance than students who were operating under contingencies for both attention and performance. Under simple task conditions, no such differential effect was noted; all students, regardless of contingency condition, maintained high rates of time on-task and academic performance.

In summary, teachers can employ a variety of behavioral techniques to improve attention skills. If the child does not have severe attention deficits or if the task is not too difficult, it may be appropriate to reinforce correct academic responding and indirectly increase attending behaviors. However, with highly distractible students and tasks that require a considerable amount of attention, supplemental attention contingencies may be necessary to maximize program effectiveness.

Behavior Modification of Overactivity.   Since deficits in attending behavior are often associated with overactivity, many studies have focused on both attention and overactivity (Hallahan & Kauffman, 1975). Although the defining feature of overactivity is a high level of motor behavior, the distinction between high-activity levels per se and high-activity levels that elicit conflict is important (Lahey, Hobbs, Kupfer, & Delameter, 1979). Consequently, many teachers have sought to decrease only those inappropriate behaviors that frequently interfere with successful classroom functioning. Successful techniques have included the differential awarding of teacher attention (Madsen et al., 1968), soft, private reprimands (O'Leary et al., 1970), token systems (Ayllon, Layman, & Kandel, 1975), home-based reinforcement (Todd, Scott, Boston, & Alexander, 1976), and time-out (Ramp, Ulrich, & Dulaney, 1971).

Behavior Modification of Impulsivity. The simplest behavioral technique for controlling impulsivity is to program contingencies that reward students for spending more time considering their responses. Still, merely slowing down a student's response time does not ensure that the extra time will be used for problem solving, so many educators have designed programs to teach strategies for problem solving with contingencies for the application of the strategies. Since the teaching and maintenance of these cognitive strategies involve behavioral techniques, many educators place them under the rubric of "cognitive behavior modification." These cognitive influences are discussed in a later section. Traditional behavioral alternatives used to remediate impulsivity include forced delay (Heider, 1971), reinforcement and response-cost contingencies (Nelson, Finch, & Hooke, 1975), and modeling (Ridberg, Parke, & Hetherington, 1971). These traditional operant procedures alone do not result in making impulsive children more reflective (Messer, 1976; Finch & Spirito, 1980). Nonetheless, they have proved to be valuable when combined with cognitive training (Kendall & Finch, 1976, 1978).

Managing Hyperactivity through the Control of Antecedent Events

It has been conclusively shown that structured reinforcement and punishment strategies can successfully manage problematic hyperactive behaviors. Still, several researchers have cautioned against the acceptance of the notion that behavioral consequences can solve all classroom problems (Lahey & Drabman, 1981; Lloyd & Carnine, 1981). While programming contingencies for increasing and decreasing the various aspects of hyperactivity are essential, parents and teachers should not overlook the many antecedent events that can be manipulated to induce behavioral change. Antecedent modifications can range from the simple rearrangement of physical space to more difficult changes in parenting or teaching style. Although interest in antecedent control has taken a back seat to the manipulation of consequences, the effects of classroom structure and structured or direct instruction on the behavior of children with hyperactivity have been studied. These two areas will now be discussed.

Classroom Structure
Children who exhibit hyperactive behaviors require home and school environments that place firm limits on their inappropriate behaviors. Such structured environments are characterized by clear expectations of behavior, directions that lead to successful performance, and consistent follow-through from adults. In many cases, it is the lack of a definite structure that precipitates disruptive behavior in the first place. Some children exhibit disturbed patterns of behavior precisely because there is no order or structure in their home environments. Therefore, the school is an ideal environment in which to begin providing them with limits and structure.

The key to establishing structure in the classroom is the setting of reasonable rules and limits (O'Melia & Rosenberg, 1989; Sprick, & Nolet, 1991). Rules serve to delineate teacher instructions and expectations in language that children can understand. Walker (1979) has proposed several guidelines for the successful communication of rules. First, rules should be clearly and consistently defined; vague, inconsistent expectations relating to generally ambiguous definitions of behavior are not effective with children. Second, to combat ambiguity, the correct interpretation of a rule should involve both teachers and children, who are generally more committed to a system of rules when they have had input into their development. Third, the teacher must ensure that all students understand the classroom rules. Activities that can facilitate this understanding include class discussions, modeling, and role playing. Fourth, rules should be posted in areas where all students can view them. The high visibility of classroom rules can serve to prompt students to engage in appropriate classroom behavior. Finally, the effectiveness of rules is usually a function of the consequences that back them up. When rules are backed up with rewards for adherence and no rewards for nonadherence, they can be quite effective in managing classroom behavior. Still, rules alone may not curb the inappropriate behavior of acting-out children; it may take the effective use of consequences in conjunction with regular daily reminders of rules to increase appropriate behaviors (Rosenberg, 1986).

There is also evidence that the manipulation of time can promote appropriate behavior. Limiting the amount of time in which reinforcement is available encourages students to immediately engage in appropriate behavior in order to receive desired consequences. Employing this "limited hold" technique (Ferster & Skinner, 1957) makes it clear to students that they do not have the time to engage in both disruptive behavior *and* the appropriate behavior (e.g., task completion) necessary to receive reinforcement. Classroom applications of this technique have been favorable (Ayllon & Rosenbaum, 1977). One study (Garber, cited in Ayllon & Rosenbaum, 1977) found not only that decreases in disruptive behavior were related to reductions in the amount of time available for task completion but also that academic performance more than doubled in rate. These data illustrate the critical need for teachers to make effective use of their allotted instructional time. If they provide too much time for task completion, they may be inadvertently inviting inappropriate behavior. Effective instruction is less a function of how much time is available for instruction than of how time is used.

Structured or Direct Instruction.   Hyperactive behavior is usually targeted for intervention on the assumption that it is incompatible with academic achievement and, left untreated, will ultimately result in deficiencies in academic skills. As noted earlier, however, recent interventions have cast some doubt on these assumptions and have emphasized the desirability of focusing directly on academic goals. As we saw, there is evidence (Hay et al., 1977) that reduced hyperactivity does not automatically improve achievement, but academic interventions may indirectly improve measures of hyperactivity while increasing academic performance. Thus, in seeking the most effective methods for controlling hyperactivity, many educators have concentrated on the components of effective instruction and specific "good" teacher behaviors.

Teacher-Directed Verbal Strategies for Increasing Attention to Task

A major assumption of the structured or direct-instruction model is that a carefully organized alteration of teacher behavior can result in pre-planned changes in a learner's academic and social performance (Lloyd & Carnine, 1981). With such a belief in mind, George (1986) has identified several verbal strategies that special educators can readily use to increase attention to task in their students.

Speed up the pace of lessons to promote students' attention and decrease nondisruptive inattention.

Press for student responses persistently, repeatedly, and consistently. Ask as many questions and signal for as many answers as possible during a given activity.

Have students repeat correct responses many times.

When praising a student's correct response, provide only specific and descriptive verbal reinforcement. In particular, restate or specify what behavior the praise is directed toward.

If a student cannot answer a question quickly and correctly, provide a verbal cue to assist responding.

Direct or *structured instruction* refers to the carefully organized manipulation of environmental events designed to result in prespecified changes in a learner's performance (Lloyd & Carnine, 1981). Directive teaching is a highly structured activity in which appropriate teacher behaviors are often specified through scripted presentations (e.g., DISTAR). The purpose of these scripted presentations is to ensure that a teacher uses only those teaching methods whose efficacy has been documented. In any particular lesson, a teacher would follow specific procedures to prompt responses, demonstrate or model appropriate responding, provide opportunities for practice, and reinforce appropriate behavior. In essence, the teacher directs the lesson in an active fashion, focusing almost exclusively on academics (Stevens & Rosenshine, 1981). When learning is particularly troublesome, instruction and practice are repeated until students attain mastery. Large-scale studies, demonstration projects, and reviews (e.g., Anderson, Evertson, & Brophy, 1979; Barnes & Rosenberg, 1985; Christensen, Ysseldyke, & Thurlow, 1989; Epstein & Cullinan, 1981; Reith & Evertson, 1988) have documented the relative efficacy of the various components of structured or direct instruction. These components are explored in detail in Chapter 11.

Cognitive-Behavior Modification

A unique combination of cognitive psychology and behavior modification has recently been employed with hyperactive students. This cognitive influence on behavioral principles has centered on the role of mediation in learning and on how internal symbolic processes influence behavior (Craighead et al., 1981). Many educators have adopted cognitive-behavioral approaches because of deficiencies they perceive in the purely behavioral approach. One major deficiency is that traditional operant behavior management programs do not seem to generalize to non-experimental conditions nor be maintained over time (Meichenbaum, 1979).

Another perceived deficiency of the behavioral approach is its neglect of the influence of covert verbalization on observed behavior. Through the early work of the Soviet psychologists Luria (1961) and Vygotsky (1962) and the more recent work of many American researchers (e.g., Bornstein & Quevillan, 1976; Meichenbaum & Goodman, 1971), educators have become increasingly aware of the role that internal verbalization plays in the control of voluntary behavior. It is believed that a child's voluntary behavior comes under covert verbal control through a three-stage process: First, the speech of others directs the child's behavior. Then, the child's own overt speech regulates behavior. Finally, it is believed that inner speech assumes the governing role. While traditional operant researchers have successfully trained children to employ overt vocalizations in the control of certain behaviors (e.g., Lovitt & Curtiss, 1968), the major focus of current cognitive-behavior modification (CBM) research has been the design of treatments for increasing the internal-control function of language (Leon & Pepe, 1983) and the development of a strategic method of solving academic and social problems (e.g., Deshler, Ellis, & Lenz, 1995).

Data from recent cognitive-oriented research suggest that many students with mild disabilities are deficient in metaprocesses or metacognition (Swanson, 1989), that is, cognition about conditions or conscious reflection on ongoing cognitive activity (Meichenbaum, 1979). These functions are usually ignored by traditional operant behaviorists. By designing and implementing treatment programs to develop covert, verbal self-regulatory mechanisms, exceptional children could become better problem solvers in a variety of academic and social-emotional situations (Borkowski, Estrada, Milstead, & Hale, 1989).

Applications of Cognitive Self-Instructional Training with Hyperactive Children

Applications of CBM with children with hyperactivity frequently involve teaching them how to use self-instruction. Self-instruction, or internal speech, serves to verbally regulate both simple and complex motor behaviors. There are many self-instruction procedures designed to remediate a variety of problems relating to hyperactivity, but most use or adapt the now-classic package originally developed by Meichenbaum and Goodman (1971). This multifaceted package, designed to teach impulsive children to think before they act, included unique combinations of modeling, overt and covert rehearsal, prompts, feedback, and social reinforcement. The training program employed the following procedural steps:

1. Adult model performed task while talking out loud; student observed.
2. Student performed task under the direction of the adult's instructions.

3. Student performed task while instructing self out loud.
4. Student performed task while instructing self in a whisper.
5. Student performed task while instructing self covertly.

During the treatment program, self-instructional statements were modeled by the adult and rehearsed both overtly and covertly by the students. The statements were designed to highlight task-related skills that were judged to be important for the successful completion of an assigned writing task. These skills were problem definition, focused attention and response guidance, self-reinforcement, self-evaluative coping skills, and error-connection options. Here is an example of the kind of statements used:

> *Okay, what is it I have to do? You want me to copy the picture with the different lines. I have to go slowly and carefully. Okay, draw the line down, down, good; and then to the right, that's it; now down some more and to the left. Good, I'm doing fine so far. Remember, go slowly, now back up again. Just erase the line carefully. . . . Good. Even if I make an error I can go on slowly and carefully. I have to go down now. Finished. I did it! (Meichenbaum & Goodman, 1971, p. 117).*

Results from the Meichenbaum and Goodman self-instructional treatment regimen were impressive. Impulsive second-grade students from an "opportunity remedial class" who received the treatment improved significantly compared to students assigned to placebo control and traditional control conditions on several measures of impulsivity (latency but not errors) as well as on the performance portion of the WISC-R. Of even greater importance were the data indicating that latency effects of the self-instructional training maintained for one month after completion of the program. No effects were noted on classroom observations of behavior or teacher ratings, however. Nonetheless, these are powerful results considering that the experimental group received only four half-hour treatment sessions.

As we noted earlier, many researchers have adapted the Meichenbaum and Goodman procedure for a variety of target behaviors. In reviewing these efforts, Meichenbaum and Burland (1979) found that the cognitive-behavioral paradigm has been successful in establishing inner speech control over a variety of hyperactive behaviors, including disruptive classroom behavior (Bornstein & Quevellon, 1976; Douglas, Parry, Marton, & Garson, 1976), aggression (Camp, Bloom, Hebert, Van Doornick, 1977), and cheating (Monahan & O'Leary, 1971). More recently, the self-instructional methodology has been expanded to academic areas. Modifications of the Meichenbaum and Goodman (1971) training regimen have been responsible for improvements in handwriting skills (Kosiewicz, Hallahan, Lloyd, & Grues, 1979), expository writing (Harris & Graham, 1992), word attack skills (Lloyd, 1980), and arithmetic computations (Davis & Hajicek, 1985; Leon & Pepe, 1983; Miller, Miller, Wheeler, & Selinger, 1989; Wood, Rosenberg, & Carran, 1993).

While several studies of the self-instructional training regimen have been positive, others (e.g., Abikoff, 1985; Abikoff et al., 1988) have found little difference between training with and without self-produced verbalizations. For example, an assessment of the effects of self-instruction on the printing of kindergarten children (Robin, Armel, & O'Leary, 1975) found no relationship between the number of self-instructions and writing performance. While self-instruction produced a small effect over the no-verbalization condition, no differences were discovered on measures of generalization. In addition, the experimenters noted that it was difficult to shape and maintain the student's use of self-instruction. Similarly, Abikoff et al. (1988) found that an academically oriented cognitive self-instructional package did not enhance the academic performance of students receiving medication alone or with tutoring.

In noting these data, a number of reviewers (e.g., DuPaul & Stone, 1994; Fiore, Becker, & Nero, 1993) have suggested that cognitive behavioral interventions have not consistently demonstrated positive effects on a scale that would warrant its widespread use. Still, it is a major component in a number of applied programs. Clearly a persistent problem faced by CBM self-instructional researchers is the lack of consistent evidence on generalization and maintenance (Meichenbaum, 1980; Rooney & Hallhan, 1985). As with operant procedures, it may be that generalization and maintenance of self-instructional procedures must be programmed rather than just hoped for (cf. Stokes & Baer, 1977). Another problem in current CBM usage may be too great a reliance on the student alone to accomplish behavioral change. Although the student is necessarily responsible for the internal dialogue, teacher modeling, cooperative problem solving, and reinforcement are also necessary for successful performance (O'Leary, 1980).

To promote success in a CBM self-instructional program, Meichenbaum (1980) offered the following clinical and educational guidelines:

1. Guard against using self-statements in a mechanical noninvolved fashion.
2. Be animated when presenting the treatment components.
3. Supplement self-instruction training with imagery practice or role playing.
4. Back up self-instructional training with operant reinforcement procedures.
5. Use peers as cognitive models.

It is also advisable that educators considering the use of cognitive self-instructional procedures carefully consider such task variables as the level of difficulty, the entry-level characteristics of the learner, and what resources are available for teaching the cognitive skill. The decision to use a CBM procedure must not result in the neglect of other appropriate and effective teaching behaviors.

Self-Control Procedures

The eventual goal of all programs designed to increase students' attention to a particular task is that the attending occur at an acceptable rate absent artificial external consequences. To that end, a variety of self-control procedures have been taught to children with hyperactivity in the belief that such behavioral self-regulation can produce improvements in generalized rates of time on-task. Most self-control procedures have four components: self-assessment, self-recording, self-determination of reinforcement, and self-administration of reinforcement (Glynn, Thomas, & Shee, 1973).

Reviews of self-control programs have been favorable. Fowler (1986) reported that such interventions, when paired with adequate teacher supervision, can be as effective as teacher-managed programs and more time-efficient. Teachers can spend more time teaching and planning because their management functions are being shared with their students. Equally important, many self-control procedures can be easily and inexpensively administered by classroom teachers with little or no outside assistance. A study by McLaughlin, Krappman, and Welsh (1985) illustrates how a well-planned and systematic self-control procedure can augment existing classroom management programs.

Four behaviorally disordered students were chosen to receive self-control procedures because of their low rates of on-task behavior during academic instruction. A multiple-baseline design across students was used to measure the possible effects of the intervention. During the baseline phases of the program, students earned tokens according to their level of compliance with normal classroom rules and procedures. During the experimental self-control phases, students were given self-recording forms consisting of twenty squares and were instructed to record plus signs each time they thought they had done their work and minus signs if they were not working at that time (students were prompted by a prerecorded signal). To assess the effects of the self-recording procedure, students were observed by a teacher aid via an internal recording procedure during regularly scheduled math periods. Follow-up data were also collected 90, 110, and 130 days after the self-control procedure was terminated.

Results indicated that intervals of on-task behavior increased for all four of the students by an average of approximately 44 percent. Also, follow-up data indicated that the treatment results maintained at appropriately high rates. This present set of procedures, and others similar to it (e.g., Christie, Hiss, & Lozanoff, 1984; Rooney, Hallahan, & Lloyd, 1984; Varni & Henker, 1979), demonstrate that well-conceived, low-cost, minimally intrusive self-control procedures can assist in the management of inappropriate behaviors typically associated with youngsters with hyperactivity.

According to Hallahan, Lloyd, and Stoller (1982), materials needed for a self-control program include a self-monitoring tape, a self-monitoring card, and an assigned task that a student can complete while self-monitoring. The procedure is introduced by teaching an individual or small group to keep track of the occurrence or nonoccurrence of a target behavior (e.g., attention to task). The student or group is then taught the purposes of the cuing tape, tape recorder, and self-monitoring card. Every time a student hears the tone of the cueing tape, he or she is to ask covertly, "Was I engaging in the target behavior?" and to mark the monitoring card appropriately. These steps should be modeled by the teacher and practiced under direct supervision to ensure that students can reliably differentiate between the occurrence and nonoccurrence of the target behavior. Upon reaching an acceptable level of performance of the target behavior, the student must be weaned from the external aspects of the self-monitoring intervention. It is generally recommended that the fading process begin with the removal of the cueing tape or the self-monitoring card. If, however, student performance falters, there should be no delay in resuming the external prompts as part of a modified maintenance strategy (Hallahan et al., 1982).

Combined Approaches

From a purely intuitive perspective, it seems that a combination of approaches would work best in dealing with the many challenges presented by children who exhibit hyperactivity. A number of studies have investigated the effects of stimulant medication combined with either behavioral or cognitive behavioral interventions. For example Hinshaw, Buhrmester, and Heller (1989) found that boys with hyperactivity who received both a cognitive-behavioral anger management group training procedure along with methylphenidate decreased their responses to verbal provocation significantly more that those received the cognitive training alone. In contrast, Brown, Borden, Wynne, Schlesser, and Clingerman (1986) found that the combination of stimulant medication and cognitive training was not superior to any of the treatments alone on measures of attention, cognitive style, academic achievement, and behavior. In their "review of reviews," Swanson and colleagues (1993) found few empirical studies that support the notion that stimulant medication should always be used in combination with educational or behavioral interventions. Still, this conclusion should be viewed as a shortcoming in the existing data base, rather than a condemnation of multimodal treatment approaches. In spite of the massive amount written on interventions for hyperactivity, considerably more systematic, research-based answers need to be found before definitive treatment regiments can be determined.

Other Therapies for Hyperactivity

Progressive Relaxation and Biofeedback

The successful use of relaxation therapy and biofeedback with adults troubled by anxiety and muscular problems has prompted several researchers to test these techniques on children who exhibit hyperactive behaviors. The major goal of relaxation training is to reduce physiological arousal and produce a positive effect (Paul & Bernstein, 1973). *Progressive relaxation* involves the systematic tensing and releasing of various muscle groups within the body and the simultaneous attending to the feelings aroused by such actions (Borkovec & Sides, 1979). *Biofeedback* is a generic term applied to a variety of procedures that feature the continuous display of information regarding the physiological status of the body. It is speculated that instrumentation conveying immediate information about biological conditions (e.g., muscle tension, skin surface temperature, brain wave activity, galvanic skin response, blood pressure, heart rate) can enable an individual to become an active participant in controlling these seemingly involuntary processes (Fuller, 1977; Strider & Strider, 1979).

Biofeedback techniques have been used with students with hyperactivity in the belief that inappropriate hyperactive behaviors are the result of deficient CNS arousal systems. We noted earlier that several biophysical researchers (e.g., Fish, 1975) believe that hyperactivity results from insufficient inhibitory control over motor functions. As we saw, this belief has promoted the common use of stimulant medication because of its action on the arousal levels of the CNS. However, psychopharmacology is not the only treatment available for impaired CNS arousal levels. Biofeedback of sensorimotor rhythms (SMR) has also produced significant reductions in the overactivity and distractibility of children with hyperactivity (Lubar & Shouse, 1979). SMR is recorded from the sensorimotor cortical regions of the brain; increases in the rhythm activity are associated with the inhibition of motor activity and the onset of sleep.

Investigators who have focused on progressive relaxation assume that hyperactive characteristics are the result of high levels of muscle tension and stress. Students who repeatedly encounter academic learning problems are thought to experience an "emergency" or "fight or flight" reaction (Carter & Russell, 1981). Because it is usually impossible for students in classrooms to fight or run away, there is no way for the heightened level of tension to dissipate, and therefore, high levels of activity persist. Several programs of relaxation have been investigated for combating this arousal pattern. While positive outcomes for remediating hyperactive behaviors have been attributed to relaxation therapy (e.g., Lupin, Braud, Braud, & Daur, 1976), the literature on relaxation therapy for children with hyperactivity is sparse and characterized by confusion, contradictions, and methodological flaws (Bhatara, Arnold, Lorence, & Gupta, 1979).

Reducing Exposure to Fluorescent Lights

Ott has speculated that hyperactive behaviors may be a reaction to exposure to soft X rays from conventional fluorescent lighting and certain TV sets (Ott, 1976). While Ott's speculations were once thought to have enormous implications for children with hyperactivity (Ross & Ross, 1982), there is no solid empirical evidence linking soft X rays and hyperactivity. Most of the investigations in this area (Hartley, 1974; Mayron, Ott, Natrons, & Mayron, 1974; Ott, 1976) were uncontrolled single-case studies that suffered from a plethora of methodological problems. A well-controlled study (O'Leary, Rosenbaum, & Hughes, 1978) reported no differences in the disruptive behavior of first-grade children when lighting with and without soft x-rays was alternated.

Minimum Stimulation

Pioneer work by Strauss and Lehtinen (1947) prompted several researchers to adopt a stimulus-reduction strategy to increase the ability of children with hyperactivity to attend. This reduction strategy consisted of reducing or influencing almost all of the stimulus events in the student's learning environment by removing pictures and bulletin boards, painting rooms in neutral tones, and requiring adults in these rooms to wear inconspicuous clothing with no distracting ornaments.

Experimental classrooms were designed to test the effects of minimal stimulation on the learning and behavior problems of children (Cruickshank, Bentzen, Ratzeburg, & Tannhauser, 1961). Stimulation was reduced in these classrooms through the use of cubicles and the removal of nonessential visual and auditory events. In addition, attention-directing instructional materials were used within the context of a multisensory teaching curriculum. The results were not favorable when compared to control conditions. Both experimental and control conditions resulted in significant, yet generally similar, post-test gains—an outcome that led many (e.g., Ross & Ross, 1982) to believe that some variable other than reduced stimulation was responsible for the gains of both groups (perhaps, reduced teacher-student ratio).

Nonetheless, the mid-1960s and early 1970s saw a dramatic increase in the use of cubicles for students with hyperactivity and learning disabilities. Evaluation of the use of cubicles has been somewhat puzzling: While attention to task and productivity tended to be greater (Jenkins, Gorrafa, & Griffiths, 1972), no effects on general achievement tests were observed (Rost & Charles, 1967). These results suggest that although children may attend more and accomplish greater amounts of work in cubicles, they may be missing critical directive teaching as well as the many important instances of observational and incidental learning that occur in classrooms.

Summary

This chapter reviewed a variety of techniques that have been used in the management of hyperactive behaviors. Three major model orientations—biophysical, behavioral, and cognitive-behavioral—guided our review. Under the biophysical heading, the roles of stimulant medication and elimination diets were highlighted, and teacher-related concerns about these techniques were addressed. Under the behavioral perspective, both the traditional consequent techniques (e.g., token economics, response-cost) and antecedent factors were discussed. We stressed the need for dynamic interventions that provide for the reduction of inappropriate behavior and the development of appropriate prosocial behaviors. Finally, we discussed applications of cognitive-behavioral techniques, highlighting those strategies that focused on self-instructional regimens for children with hyperactivity. The chapter concluded with a brief discussion of several nontraditional approaches to the management of hyperactivity—relaxation, biofeedback, and minimum stimulation.

Discussion Questions

1. What are the salient differences among the three clinical views—that is, deficit, delay, and difference—of hyperactivity?

2. How common is the use of pharmacological intervention in the treatment of hyperactive children? What types of drugs are commonly prescribed and what are their effects on the primary characteristics of hyperactivity?

3. How would you characterize the effects of stimulant medications on the academic performance of students with hyperactivity?

4. What is currently known about the side effects of stimulant medications?

5. Describe two of the major controversies surrounding the use of stimulant medications.

6. Discuss the role of the educator in dealing with students who are receiving psychoactive medications.

7. What is currently known regarding the efficacy of dietary and nutritional approaches in the control of hyperactivity?

8. List and describe the relative strengths and weaknesses of the range of behavioral alternatives (i.e., reinforcers and punishers) used in the control of hyperactivity. Which of the alternatives are most conducive to improving behavior in a classroom setting?

9. Describe the appropriate sequence for administering time-out in the control of hyperactivity.

10. How can antecedent events like classroom structure and instructional format influence the rate and intensity of hyperactivity?

11. Describe how systematic training in self-instruction and self-control procedures can decrease the rate and intensity of some patterns of hyperactive behavior.

12. How effective are cognitive-behavioral interventions in the control of hyperactive behaviors?

References

Abikoff, H. (1985). Efficacy of cognitive training intervention in hyperactive children: A critical review. *Clinical Psychology Review, 5,* 479–512.

Abikoff, H., Ganeles, D., Reiter, G., Blum, C., Foley, C., & Klein, R. G. (1988). Cognitive training in academically deficient ADDH boys receiving stimulant medication. *Journal of Abnormal Child Psychology, 16*(4), 411–432.

Abikoff, H., Gittelman-Klein, R., & Klein, D. (1977). Validation of a classroom observation code for hyperactive children. *Journal of Consulting and Clinical Psychology, 60,* 881–892.

Abramowitz, A. J., & O'Leary, S. (1991). Behavioral interventions for the classroom: Implications for students with ADHD. *School Psychology Review, 20*(2), 220–234.

Adelman, H. S., & Compas, B. E. (1977). Stimulant drugs and learning problems. *Journal of Special Education, 11,* 377–416.

Alberto, P. A., & Troutman, A. C. (1986). *Applied behavior analysis for teachers,* 2nd ed. Columbus, OH: Merrill.

Anastopoulos, A. D., DuPaul, G. J., & Barkley, R. A. (1991). Stimulant medication and parent training therapies for attention deficit-hyperactivity disorder. *Journal of Learning Disabilities, 24*(4), 210–218.

Anderson, L. M., Evertson, C. M., & Brophy, J. E. (1979). An experimental study of effective teaching in first grade reading groups. *Elementary School Journal, 79,* 193–222.

Atkins, M. S., Pelham, W. E., & Licht, M. H. (1985). A comparison of objective classroom measures and teacher ratings of Attention Deficit Disorder. *Journal of Abnormal Child Psychology, 13,* 155–167.

Axelrod, S. (1983). *Behavior modification for the classroom teacher.* 2nd ed. New York: McGraw-Hill.

Ayllon, T., Layman, D., & Burke, S. (1972). Disruptive behavior and reinforcement of academic performance. *The Psychological Record, 22,* 315–323.

Ayllon, T., Layman, D., & Kandel, H. J. (1975). A behavioral-educational alternative to drug control of hyperactive children. *Journal of Applied Behavior Analysis, 8,* 137–146.

Ayllon, T., & Roberts, M. D. (1974). Eliminating discipline problems by strengthening academic performance. *Journal of Applied Behavior Analysis, 7,* 71–76.

Ayllon, T., & Rosenbaum, M. S. (1977). The behavioral treatment of disruption and hyperactivity in school settings. In B. B. Lahey & A. E. Kazdin (Eds.), *Advances in clinical child psychology.* Vol. 1. New York: Plenum.

Baren, M., Leibl, R., & Smith, L. (1978). *Overcoming learning disabilities: A team approach.* Reston, VA: Reston.

Barkley, R. A. (1977). The effects of methylphenidate on various measures of activity level and attention in hyperkinetic children. *Journal of Child Psychology, 5,* 351–369.

Barkley, R. A. (1981). *Hyperactive children: A handbook for diagnosis and treatment.* New York: Guilford.

Barkley, R. A. (1982). Guidelines for defining hyperactivity in children: Attention deficit disorder with hyperactivity. In B. B. Lahey & A. E. Kazdin (Eds.), *Advances in clinical child psychology.* Vol. 5 (pp. 137–175). New York: Plenum.

Barkley, R. A. (1990). Attention deficit hyperactivity disorder: A handbook for diagnosis and treatment. New York: Guilford.

Barkley, R. A., & Cunningham, C. E. (1978). Do stimulant drugs improve the academic performance of hyperactive children? *Clinical Pediatrics, 17,* 85–92.

Barkley, R. A., & Cunningham, C. E. (1979). Stimulant drugs and activity level in hyperactive children. *American Journal of Orthopsychiatry, 40,* 491–499.

Barkley, R. A., Fischer, M., Newby, R., & Breen, M. (1988). Development of a multi-method clinical protocol for assessing stimulant drug responses in ADHD children. *Journal of Clinical Child Psychology, 20,* 163–188.

Barkley, R. A., Karlsson, J., Stzelecki, E., & Murphy, J. V. (1984). Effects of age and Ritalin dosage on mother-child interactions of hyperactive children. *Journal of Consulting and Clinical Psychology, 52,* 750–758.

Barkley, R. A., McMurray, M. B., Edelbrock, C. S., & Robbins, K. (1990). The side effects of Ritalin in ADHD children: A systematic placebo-controlled evaluation of two doses. *Pediatrics, 86,* 184–192.

Barnes, D., & Rosenberg, M. (1985). Increasing pupil achievement: Good teachers make the difference. In R. Weaver (Ed.), *Toward excellence in education* (pp. 1–19). Muncie, IN: Ball State University.

Bhatara, V., Arnold, L. E., Lorence, T., & Gupta, D. (1979). Muscle relaxation in hyperkinesis: Is it effective? *Journal of Learning Disabilities, 12,* 182–186.

Biederman, J., Baldessarini, R. J., Wright, V., Knee, D., & Harmatz, J. S. (1989). A double-blind placebo-controlled study of desipramine in the treatment of ADHD: I. efficacy. *Journal of the American Academy of Child and Adolescent Psychiatry, 28,* 777–784.

Borkovec, T. D., & Sides, J. K. (1979). Critical procedure variables related to the physiological effects of progressive relaxation: A review. *Behavior Research and Therapy, 17,* 119–125.

Borkowski, J. G., Estrada, M. T., Milstead, M., & Hale, C. A. (1989). General problem-solving skills: Relations between metacognition and strategic processing. *Learning Disabilities Quarterly, 12,* 57–70.

Bornstein, P., & Quevillon, R. (1976). The effects of a self-instructional package on overactive preschool boys. *Journal of Applied Behavior Analysis, 9,* 176–188.

Brown, R. T., Borden, K. A., Wynne, M. E., Schleser, R., & Clingerman, S. R. (1986). Methylphenidate and cognitive therapy with ADD children: A methodological reconsideration. *Journal of Abnormal Child Psychology, 14*(4), 481–497.

Brown, R. T., & Sleator, E. K. (1979). Methylphenidate in hyperkinetic children: Differences in dose effects on impulsive behavior. *Pediatrics, 64,* 408–411.

Brundage-Aguar, D., Forehand, R., & Ciminero, A. R. (1976). A review of treatment approaches for hyperactive behavior. *Journal of Clinical Psychology, 6,* 3–10.

Buhrmester, D., Whalen, D. K., Henker, B., Mac-Donald, V., & Hinshaw, S. P. (1992). Prosocial behavior in hyperactive boys: Effects of stimulant medication and comparison with normal boys. *Journal of Abnormal Child Psychology, 20*(1), 103–121.

Camp, B., Bloom, G., Hebert, F., & Van Doornick, W. (1977). "Think aloud": A program for developing self-control in young aggressive boys. *Journal of Abnormal Child Psychology, 5,* 175–189.

Cantwell, D. P. (1975). *The hyperactive child: Diagnosis, management, and current research.* Holliswood, NJ: Spectrum.

Cantwell, D. P., & Carlson, G. A. (1978). Stimulants. In J. Werry (Ed.), *Pediatric psychopharmacology.* Pp. 171–207. New York: Brunner & Mazel.

Carter, J., & Russell, H. L. (1981). Use of biofeedback procedures with learning disabled children. Paper presented at the meetings of the International Council for Exceptional Children, New York.

Christensen, D. (1975). Effects of combining methylphenidate and a classroom token system in modifying hyperactive children. *American Journal of Mental Deficiency, 80,* 266–276.

Christensen, S. L., Ysseldyke, J. E., & Thurlow, M. L. (1989). Critical instructional factors for students with mild handicaps: An integrative review. *Remedial and Special Education, 10,* 21–31.

Christie, D. J., Hiss, M., & Lozanoff, E. (1984). Modification of inattentive classroom behavior: Hyperactive children's use of self-recording with teacher guidance. *Behavior Modification, 8,* 391–406.

Connors, C. K. (1979). Discussion of "models of hyperactivity." In R. Trites (Ed.), *Hyperactivity in children* (pp. 21–23). Baltimore: University Park Press.

Connors, C. K., Goyette, C. H., Southwick, D. A., Lees, J. M., & Andrylonis, P. A. (1976). Food additives and hyperkinesis: A controlled double-blind experiment. *Pediatrics, 58,* 154–166.

Cossairt, A., Hall, R. V., & Hopkins, B. L. (1973). The effects of experimenters, instructions, feedback, and praise on teacher praise and student attending behavior. *Journal of Applied Behavior Analysis, 6,* 89–100.

Courtnage, L. (1982). A survey of state policies in the use of medication in schools. *Exceptional Children, 49,* 75–77.

Craig, H. B., & Holland, A. L. (1970). Reinforcement of visual attending in classrooms for deaf children. *Journal of Applied Behavior Analysis, 3,* 97–109.

Craighead, W. E., Kazdin, A. E., & Mahoney, M. J. (1981). *Behavior modification: Principles, issues, and applications,* 2nd ed. Boston: Houghton Mifflin.

Cruickshank, W. M., Bentzen, F. A., Ratzeburg, F. H., & Tannhauser, M. T. (1961). *A teaching method for brain injured and hyperactive children.* Syracuse, NY: Syracuse University Press.

Cullinan, D., Epstein, M. H., Lloyd, J. W. (1983). *Behavior disorders of children and adolescents.* Englewood Cliffs, NJ: Prentice-Hall.

Cunningham, C. E., Siegel, L. S., & Offord, D. R. (1985). A developmental dose response analysis of the effects of methylphenidate on peer interactions of attention deficit boys. *Journal of Child Psychology and Psychiatry, 26,* 955–971.

Davis, R. W., & Hajicek, J. O. (1985). Effects of self-instructional training and strategy training on mathematics tasks with severely behaviorally disordered students. *Behavioral Disorders, 10,* 211–218.

Deshler, D. D., Ellis, E. S., & Lenz, B. K. (1995). *Teaching adolescents with learning disabilities: Strategies and method.* Denver: Love.

Douglas, V., Parry, P., Marton, P., & Garson, C. (1976). Assessment of a cognitive training program for hyperactive children. *Journal of Abnormal Child Psychology, 4,* 389–410.

Drabman, R. S., & Lahey, B. B. (1974). Feedback in classroom behavior modification: Effects of the target and her classmates. *Journal of Applied Behavior Analysis, 7,* 591–598.

DuPaul, G. J. (1991). Parent and teacher ratings of ADHD symptoms: Psychometric properties in a community-based sample. *Journal of Clinical Child Psychology, 20,* 245–253.

DuPaul, G. J., & Barkley, R. A. (1992). Situational variability of attention problems: Psychometric properties of the revised home and school situations questionnaires. *Journal of Clinical Child Psychology, 21,* 178–188.

DuPaul, G. J., Barkley, R. A., & McMurray, M. B. (1991). Therapeutic effects of medication on ADHD: Implications for school psychologists. *School Psychology Review, 20*(2), 203–219.

DuPaul, G. J., Guevremont, D. C., Barkley, R. A. (1992). Behavioral treatment of attention-deficit hyperactivity disorder in the classroom: The use of the attention training system. *Behavior Modification, 16*(2), 204–225.

DuPaul, G. J. & Stoner, G. (1994). *ADHD in the schools: Assessment and intervention strategies.* New York, NY: Guilford Press.

DuPaul, G. J., Stoner, G., Tilly, W. D., & Putnam, D. (1991) Interventions for attention problems. In G. Stoner, M. Shinn, & H. Walker (Eds.), *Interventions for achievement and behavior problems* (pp. 685–714). Silver Spring, MD: National Association of School Psychologists.

Ellis, M. J., Witt, P. A., Reynolds, R., & Sprague, R. L. (1974). Methylphenidate and the activity of hyperactives in the informal setting. *Child Development, 45,* 217–220.

Epstein, M. H., & Cullinan, D. (1981). Project EXCEL: A behaviorally-oriented educational program for learning disabled pupils. *Education and Treatment of Children, 4,* 357–373.

Epstein, M. H., & Olinger, E. (1987). Use of medication in school programs for behaviorally disordered pupils. *Behavioral Disorders, 12,* 138–145.

Feingold, B. (1975). *Why your child is hyperactive.* New York: Random House.

Ferster, C. B., & Skinner, B. F. (1957). *Schedules of reinforcement.* New York: Appleton-Century-Crofts.

Finch, A. J., & Spirito, A. (1980). Use of cognitive training to change cognitive processes. *Exceptional Education Quarterly, 1,* 31–39.

Fiore, T. A., Becker, E. A., & Nero, R. C. (1993). Education interventions for students with attention deficit disorder. *Exceptional Children, 60*(2), 163–173.

Firestone, P. (1978). The effects of caffeine on hyperactive children. *Journal of Learning Disabilities, 11,* 133–141.

Fish, B. (1975). Stimulant drug treatment of hyperactive children. In D. P. Cantwell (Ed.), *The hyperactive child* (pp. 109–128). New York: Spectrum.

Fowler, S. A. (1986). Peer-monitoring and self-monitoring: Alternatives to traditional teacher management. *Exceptional Children, 52,* 573–581.

Fuller, G. D. (1977). *Biofeedback: Methods and procedures in clinical practice.* San Francisco: Biofeedback Press.

Gadow, K. D. (1981). Prevalence of drug treatment for hyperactivity and other childhood behavior disorders. In K. D. Gadow & J. Loney (Eds.), *Psychosocial aspects of drug treatment for hyperactivity* (pp. 13–76). Boulder, CO: Westview Press.

Gadow, K. D. (1982). School involvement in pharmacotherapy for behavior disorders. *Journal of Special Education, 16,* 385–399.

Gadow, K. D. (1985). Relative efficacy of pharmacological, behavioral, and combination treatments for enhancing academic performance. *Clinical Psychology Review, 5,* 513–533.

Gadow, K. D. (1986). *Children on medication.* Vol. I. San Diego, CA: College Hill Press.

Gast, D. L., & Nelson, C. M. (1977). Legal and ethical considerations for use of timeout in special education settings. *Journal of Special Education, 11,* 457–467.

George, P. (1986). Teaching handicapped children with attention problems: Teacher verbal strategies make a difference. *Teaching Exceptional Children, 18,* 172–175.

Glynn, E. L., Thomas, J. D., & Shee, S. M. (1973). Behavioral self-control of on-task behavior in an elementary classroom. *Journal of Applied Behavior Analysis, 6,* 105–113.

Gomez, K. M. & Cole, C. L. (1991). Attention deficit hyperactivity disorder: A review of treatment alternatives. *Elementary School Guidance & Counseling, 26,* 106–114.

Goyette, C. H., Conners, C. K., & Ulrich, R. F. (1978). Normative data on Revised Conners and Parent and Teacher Rating Scales. *Journal of Abnormal Child Psychology, 6,* 221–236.

Hall, R. V., Axelrod, S., Foundopoulos, M., Shellman, J., Campbell, R. A., & Cranston, S. S. (1971). The effective use of punishment to modify behavior in the classroom. *Educational Technology, 11,* 24, 26.

Hall, R. V., & Hall, M. C. (1982). *How to negotiate a behavioral contract.* Austin, TX: PRO-ED.

Hallahan, D. P., & Kauffman, J. M. (1975). Research on the education of distractible and hyperactive children. In W. M. Cruickshank & D. P. Hallahan (Eds.), *Perceptual and learning disabilities in children: Research and theory.* Vol. 2 (pp. 221–258). Syracuse, NY: Syracuse University Press.

Hallahan, D. P., Lloyd, J., & Stoller, L. (1982). *Improving attention with self-monitoring: A manual for teachers.* Charlottesville: University of Virginia Learning Disabilities Research Institute.

Harley, J. P., Ray, R. S., Topmasi, L., Eichman, P. L., Matthews, G. G., Chan, R., Cleeland, C. S., & Traisman, E. (1978). Hyperkinesis and food additives: Testing the Feingold hypothesis. *Pediatrics, 61,* 818–828.

Harris, K. (1985). Definitional, parametric, and procedural considerations in time-out interventions and research. *Exceptional Children, 51,* 1–16.

Harris, K. R. & Graham, S. (1992). *Helping young writers master the craft.* Cambridge, MA: Brookline.

Hartley, E. R. (1974). Radiation that's good for you. *Science Digest, 76,* 39–45.

Hastings, J. E., & Barkley, R. A. (1978). A review of psychophysiological research with hyperactive children. *Journal of Abnormal Child Psychology, 7,* 413–447.

Hay, W. M., Hay, L. R., & Nelson, R. O. (1977). Direct and collateral changes in on-task and academic behavior resulting from on-task versus academic contingencies. *Behavior Therapy, 8,* 431–441.

Hechtman, L., Weiss, G., & Perlman, T. (1984). Hyperactives as young adults: Past and current substance abuse and antisocial behavior. *American Journal of Orthopsychiatry, 54,* 415–425.

Heider, E. R. (1971). Information processing and the modification of an impulsive conceptual tempo. *Child Development, 42,* 1276–1281.

Hinshaw, S. P., Buhrmester, D., & Heller, T. (1989). Anger control in response to verbal provocation: Effects of stimulant medication for boys with ADHD. *Journal of Abnormal Child Psychology, 17*(4), 393–407.

Jenkins, J. R., Gorrafa, S., & Griffiths, S. (1972). Another look at isolation effects. *American Journal of Mental Deficiency, 76,* 591–593.

Jenkins, J. R., Mayhall, W., Reschke, C. & Townsend, M. A. (1974). Using direct and daily measures to increase learning. *Journal of Learning Disabilities, 19,* 604–608.

Jens, K. E., & Shores, R. E. (1969). Behavioral graphs as reinforcers for work behavior of mentally retarded adolescents. *Education and Training of the Mentally Retarded, 4,* 21–28.

Kauffman, J. M. (1985). *Characteristics of children's behavior disorders.* 3rd ed. Columbus, OH: Merrill.

Kazdin, A. E. (1972). Response cost: The removal of conditioned reinforcers for therapeutic change. *Behavior Therapy, 3,* 533–546.

Kazdin, A. E. (1975). *Behavior modification in applied settings.* Homewood, IL: Dorsey.

Kendall, P. C., & Finch, A. J. (1976). A cognitive-behavioral treatment for impulse control: A case study. *Journal of Consulting and Clinical Psychology, 44,* 853–887.

Kendall, P. C., & Finch, A. J. (1978). A cognitive behavioral treatment of impulsivity. A group comparison study. *Journal of Consulting and Clinical Psychology, 45,* 330–338.

Kinsbourne, M., & Swanson, J. (1979). Models of hyperactivity: Implications for diagnosis and treatment. In R. Trites (Ed.), *Hyperactivity in children* (pp. 1–20). Baltimore: University Park Press.

Kosiewicz, M. M., Hallahan, D. P., Lloyd, J., & Grues, A. W. (1979). *The effects of self-instruction and self-correction procedures on handwriting performance.* Technical Report No. 5. Charlottesville: University of Virginia Learning Disability Research Institute.

Kuhn, T. S. (1962). *The structure of scientific revolutions.* Chicago: University of Chicago Press.

Lahey, B. B., & Drabman, R. S. (1981). Behavior modification in the classroom. In W. E. Craighead, A. E. Kazdin, & M. S. Mahoney (Eds.), *Behavior modification: Principles, issues, and applications,* 2nd ed. (pp. 418–433). Boston: Houghton Mifflin.

Lahey, B. B., Hobbs, S. A., Kupfer, D. L., & Delameter, A. (1979). Current perspectives on hyperactivity and learning disabilities. In B. B. Lahey (Ed.), *Behavior therapy with hyperactive and learning disabled children* (pp. 3–18). New York: Oxford University Press.

Leon, J. A., & Pepe, H. J. (1983). Self-instructional training: Cognitive behavior modification for remediating arithmetic deficits. *Exceptional Children, 50,* 54–60.

Linn, R. (1983). Behavior modification. In R. E. Schmid & L. M. Nagat (Eds.), *Contemporary issues in special education.* New York: McGraw-Hill.

Lloyd, J. (1980). Academic instruction and cognitive behavior modification: The need for attack strategy training. *Exceptional Education Quarterly, 1,* 53–64.

Lloyd, J., & Carnine, D. W. (1981). Foreword. *Exceptional Education Quarterly, 2,* viii–ix.

Lovitt, T. C., & Curtiss, K. A. (1968). Effects of manipulating an antecedent event on mathematics response rate. *Journal of Applied Behavior Analysis, 1,* 329–333.

Lubar, J. F., & Shouse, M. N. (1979). Use of biofeedback in the treatment of hyperactivity. In B. B. Lahey (Ed.), *Behavior therapy with hyperactive and learning disabled children.* New York: Oxford University Press.

Lupin, M., Braud, L. W., Braud, W. G., & Daur, W. F. (1976). Children, parents, and relaxation tapes. *Academic Therapy,* 105–113.

Luria, A. (1961). *The role of speech in the regulation of normal and abnormal behaviors.* New York: Liveright.

Maag, J. W., & Reid, R. (1994). Attention-deficit hyperactivity disorder: A functional approach to assessment and treatment. *Behavioral Disorders, 20*(1), 5–23.

Madsen, C. H., Becker, W. C., & Thomas, D. R. (1968). Rules, praise, and ignoring: Elements of elementary classroom control. *Journal of Applied Behavior Analysis, 1,* 139–150.

Madsen, C. H., Becker, W. C., Thomas, D. R., Koser, L., & Plager, E. (1968). An analysis of the reinforcing function of "sit down" commands. In R. K. Parker (Ed.), *Readings in educational psychology* (pp. 265–278). Boston: Allyn & Bacon.

Mayron, L. W., Ott, J., Natrons, R., & Mayron, E. (1974). Light, radiation, and academic behavior. *Academic Therapy, 10,* 33–47.

McAllister, L. W., Stachowiak, J. G., Baer, D. M., & Conderman, L. (1969). The application of operant conditioning techniques in a secondary school classroom. *Journal of Applied Behavior Analysis, 2,* 277–285.

McLaughlin, T. F., Krappman, V. F., & Welsh, J. M. (1985). The effects of self-recording for on-task behavior of behaviorally disordered special education students. *Remedial and Special Education, 6,* 42–45.

Meichenbaum, D. (1979). Teaching children self-control. In B. B. Lahey & A. E. Kazdin (Eds.), *Advances in clinical child psychology.* Vol. 2. New York: Plenum.

Meichenbaum, D. (1980). Cognitive behavior modification with exceptional children: A promise yet unfulfilled. *Exceptional Education Quarterly, 1,* 83–88.

Meichenbaum, D., & Burland, S. (1979). Cognitive behavior modification with children. *School Psychology Digest, 8,* 426–433.

Meichenbaum, D. H., & Goodman, J. (1971). Training impulsive children to talk to themselves: A means of developing self-control. *Journal of Abnormal Psychology, 77,* 115–126.

Messer, S. B. (1976). Reflection-impulsivity: A review. *Psychological Bulletin, 83,* 1026–1052.

Michael, R. L., Klorman, R., Saltzman, L. F., Borgstedt, A. D., & Dainer, K. (1981). Normalizing effects of methylphenidate on hyperactive children's vigilance performance and evoked potentials. *Psychophysiology, 18,* 665–667.

Miller, M., Miller, S., Wheeler, J., & Selinger, J. (1989). Can a single classroom treatment approach change academic performance and behavioral characteristics in severely behaviorally disordered adolescents: An experimental inquiry. *Behavioral Disorders, 14,* 215–225.

Mock, K., Swanson, J., & Kinsbourne, M. (1978). Stimulant effects on matching familiar figures: Changes in impulsive and distractible cognitive styles. Paper presented at the American Educational Research Association Meeting, Toronto, Canada.

Monahan, J., & O'Leary, D. (1971). Effects of self-instruction on rule-breaking behavior. *Psychological Reports, 29,* 1059–1066.

Nelson, W. M., Finch, A. J., & Hooke, J. F. (1975). Effects of reinforcement and response cost on the cognitive style of emotionally disturbed boys. *Journal of Abnormal Psychology, 84,* 426–428.

Novy, P., Burnett, J., Powers, M., & Sulzer-Azaroff, B. (1973). Modifying attending to work behavior of a learning disabled child. *Journal of Learning Disabilities, 6,* 20–24.

O'Leary, K. D., Kauffman, K. F., Kass, R., & Drabman, R. (1970). The effects of loud and soft reprimands on the behavior of disruptive students. *Exceptional Children, 37,* 145–155.

O'Leary, K. D., Rosenbaum, A., & Hughes, P. C. (1978). Fluorescent lighting: A purported source of hyperkinetic behavior. *Journal of Abnormal Psychology, 6,* 285–289.

O'Leary, S. G. (1980). A response to cognitive training. *Exceptional Education Quarterly, 1,* 89–94.

O'Melia, M. C., & Rosenberg, M. S. (1989). Classroom management: Preventing behavior problems in classrooms. *LD Forum, 15,* 23–26.

Ott, J. N. (1976). Influence of fluorescent lights on hyperactivity and learning disabilities. *Journal of Applied Behavior Analysis, 9,* 417–422.

Packard, R. G. (1980). The control of "classroom attention": A group contingency for complex behavior. *Journal of Applied Behavior Analysis, 3,* 13–28.

Paul, G. L., & Bernstein, D. (1973). *Anxiety and clinical problems: Systematic desensitization and related techniques.* Morristown, NJ: General Learning Press.

Pescara-Kovach, L. A., & Alexander, K. (1994). The link between food ingested and problem behavior: Fact or fallacy? *Behavioral Disorders, 19*(2), 142–148.

Piers, E. V. (1984). *Piers-Harris Children's Self-Concept Scale: Revised manual.* Los Angeles: Western Psychological Services.

Prichep, L. S., Sutton, S., & Hakerem, G. (1978). Evoked potentials in hyperkinetic and normal children under certainty and uncertainty: A placebo and methylphenidate study. *Psychophysiology, 13,* 419–428.

Prinz, R. J., Roberts, W. A., & Hartman, C. (1980). Dietary correlates of hyperactive behavior in children. *Journal of Consulting and Clinical Psychology, 48,* 760–769.

Quay, H. C., & Werry, J. (1979). *Psychopathological disorders of childhood,* 2nd ed. New York: Wiley.

Ramp, E., Ulrich, R., & Dulaney, S. (1971). Delayed time out as a procedure for reducing disruptive classroom behavior: A case study. *Journal of Applied Behavior Analysis, 4,* 235–239.

Rapport, M. D., DuPaul, G. J., & Kelly, K. L. (1989). Attention-deficit hyperactive disorder and methylphenidate: The relationship between gross body weight and drug response in children. *Psychopharmacology Bulletin, 25,* 285–290.

Rapport, M. D., Jones, J. T., DuPaul, G. J., Kelly, K. L., Gardner, M. J., Tucker, S. B., & Shea, M. S. (1987). Attention-deficit disorder and methyl-phenidate: Group and single subject analyses of dose effects on attention in clinic and classroom settings. *Journal of Clinical Child Psychology, 16,* 329–338.

Reid, R., & Katsiyannis, A. (1995). Attention-deficit/hyperactivity disorder and section 504. *Remedial and Special Education, 16*(1), 44–52.

Reith, H., & Evertson, C. (1988). Variables related to the effective instruction of difficult to teach children. *Focus on Exceptional Children, 20,* 1–8.

Ridberg, E. H., Parke, R. D., & Hetherington, E. M. (1971). Modification of impulsive and reflective cognitive styles through observation of film-mediated models. *Developmental Psychology, 5,* 366–377.

Rie, H. E., Rie, E. D., Stewart, S., & Ambuel, J. P. (1976). Effects of methylphenidate on underachieving children. *Journal of Consulting and Clinical Psychology, 44*, 250–260.

Robin, A., Armel, S., & O'Leary, K. D. (1975). The effects of self-instruction on writing deficiencies. *Behavior Therapy, 6*, 178–187.

Rooney, K. J., & Hallahan, D. P. (1985). Future directions for cognitive behavior modification research: The quest for cognitive change. *Remedial and Special Education, 6*, 46–51.

Rooney, K. J., Hallahan, D. P., & Lloyd, J. (1984). Self-recording of attention by learning disabled students in the regular classroom. *Journal of Learning Disabilities, 17*, 360–364.

Rose, T. L. (1978). The functional relationship between food colors and hyperactivity. *Journal of Applied Behavior Analysis, 11*, 439–449.

Rosenberg, M. S. (1986). Maximizing the effectiveness of structured classroom management programs: Implementing rule-review procedures with disruptive and distractible students. *Behavioral Disorders, 11*, 239–248.

Rosenberg, M. S. (1987). Psychopharmacological interventions with young hyperactive children. *Topics in Early Childhood Special Education, 6*, 62–74.

Rosenberg, M. S., Sindelar, P. T., & Stedt, J. (1985). The effects of supplemental on-task contingencies upon the acquisition of simple and difficult academic tasks. *Journal of Special Education, 19*, 189–203.

Ross, A. O. (1980). *Psychological disorders of children: A behavioral approach to theory, research and therapy.* 2nd ed. New York: McGraw-Hill.

Ross, D. M., & Ross, S. A. (1976). *Hyperactivity: Research, theory, and action.* New York: Wiley.

Ross, D. M., & Ross, S. A. (1982). *Hyperactivity: Research, theory, and action,* 2nd ed. New York: Wiley.

Rost, K. J., & Charles, D. C. (1967). Academic achievement of brain injured and hyperactive children in isolation. *Exceptional Children, 34*, 125–126.

Safer, D. S., Allen, R. P., & Barr, E. (1975). Growth rebound after termination of stimulant drugs. *Journal of Pediatrics, 86*, 113–116.

Safer, D. S., & Krager, J. M. (1988). A survey of medication treatment for hyperactive/inattentive students. *Journal of the American Medical Association, 260*, 2256–2258.

Safer, R. P., & Allen, D. J. (1973). Factors influencing the suppressant effects of two stimulants on the growth of hyperactive children. *Pediatrics, 51*, 660–667.

Satterfield, J. H. (1975). Neurophysiologic studies with hyperactive children. In D. P. Cantwell (Ed.), *The hyperactive child: Diagnosis, management, current research* (pp. 67–82). New York: Spectrum.

Satterfield, J. H., Schell, A. M., & Barb, S. D. (1980). Potential risk of prolonged administration of stimulant medication for hyperactive children. *Developmental and Behavioral Pediatrics, 1*, 102–107.

Schleifer, M., Weiss, G., Cohen, N., Elman, M., Cvejic, H., & Kruger, E. (1975). Hyperactivity in preschoolers and the effect of methylphenidate. *American Journal of Orthopsychiatry, 45*, 38–50.

Shaywitz, S. E., & Shaywitz, B. A. (1991). Introduction to the special series on Attention Deficit Disorder. *Journal of Learning Disabilities, 24*, 68–71.

Shemberg, K. M., Keeley, S. M., Gill, K., & Garton, A. (1972). A note on the inhibitory effects of the initiation of a behavioral program. *Behavior Therapy, 3*, 622–626.

Sprafkin, J., Grayson, P., Gadow, K. D., Nolan, E. E., & Paolicellu, L. M. (1986). *Code for Observing Social Activity (COSA).* Stony Brook, NY: State University.

Sprague, R. L., & Gadow, K. D. (1976). The role of the teacher in drug treatment. *School Review, 85*, 109–140.

Sprague, R. L., & Sleator, E. (1977). Methylphenidate in hyperactive children: Differences in dose effects on learning and social behavior. *Science, 198*, 1274–1276.

Sprick, R., & Nolet, V. (1991). Prevention and management of secondary-level behavior problems. In G. Stoner, M. Shinn, & H. M. Walker (Eds.), *Interventions for achievement and behavior problems* (pp. 519–537). Silver Spring, MD: NASP.

Sroufe, L. A. (1975). Drug treatment of children with behavior problems. In F. D. Horowitz

(Ed.), *Review of child development research*. Vol. 4. Chicago: University of Chicago Press.

Stevens, R., & Rosenshine, B. (1981). Advances in research on teaching. *Exceptional Education Quarterly, 2,* 1–10.

Stokes, T. F., & Baer, D. M. (1977). An implicit technology of generalization. *Journal of Applied Behavior Analysis, 10,* 349–367.

Strauss, A. A., & Lehtinen, L. E. (1947). *Psychopathology and education of the brain-injured child*. New York: Grune & Stratton.

Strider, M., & Strider, F. (1979). Current applications of biofeedback technology to the problems of youth and children. *Behavioral Disorders, 5,* 53–59.

Sulzer, B., Hunt, S., Ashby, E., Koniarsky, C., & Krams, K. (1968). Increasing rate and percent correct in reading and spelling in a fifth grade public school class of slow readers by means of a token system. In E. P. Ramp & B. L. Hopkins (Eds.), *New directions for education: Behavior analysis*. Lawrence: The University of Kansas, Department of Human Development.

Swanson, H. L. (1989). Strategy instruction: Overview of principles and procedures for effective use. *Learning Disability Quarterly, 12,* 3–15.

Swanson, J. M., Cantwell, D., Lerner, M., McBurnett, K., & Hanna, G. (1991). Effects of stimulant medication on learning in children with ADHD. *Journal of Learning Disabilities, 24*(4), 219–230.

Swanson, J. M., Kinsbourne, M., Roberts, W., & Zucher, K. (1978). Time response analysis of the effect of stimulant medication on the learning ability of children referred for hyperactivity. *Pediatrics, 61,* 21–29.

Swanson, J. M., McBurnett, K., Wigal, T., Pfiffner, L. J., Lerner, M. A., Williams, L., Christian, D. L., Tamm, L., Willcutt, E., Crowley, K., Clevenger, W., Khouzam, N., Woo, C., Crinella, F. M., & Fisher, T. (1993). Effect of stimulant medication on children with attention deficit disorder: A "review of reviews." *Exceptional Children, 60*(2), 154–162.

Tannock, R., Schachar, R. J., Carr, R. P., & Logan, G. D. (1989). Dose response effects of methyl-phenidate on academic performance and overt behavior in hyperactive behavior. *Pediatrics, 54,* 645–657.

Thiessen, I., & Mills, L. (1975). The use of mega-vitamin treatment in children with learning disabilities. *Journal of Orthomolecular Psychiatry, 4,* 288–296.

Todd, D. D., Scott, R. B., Boston, D. E., & Alexander, S. B. (1976). Modifications of the excessive inappropriate classroom behavior of two elementary school students using home-based consequences and daily report card procedures. *Journal of Applied Behavior Analysis, 9,* 106.

Ullman, R. K., Sleator, E. K., & Sprauge, R. L. (1985). Introduction to the use of the ACTeRS. *Psychopharmacology Bulletin, 21,* 915–920.

Varley, C. K. (1984). Diet and the behavior of children with attention deficit disorder. *Journal of the American Academy of Child Psychiatry, 23*(2), 182–185.

Varni, J. W., & Henker, B. (1979). A self-regulation approach to treatment of three hyperactive boys. *Child Behavior Therapy, 1,* 171–192.

Vygotsky, L. (1962). *Thought and language*. New York: Wiley.

Wade, G. M. (1978). The effects of methyl-phenidate on motor skill acquisition of hyperactive children. *Journal of Learning Disabilities, 9,* 443–447.

Walker, H. M. (1979). *The acting out child: Coping with classroom disruption*. Boston: Allyn & Bacon.

Walker, H. M., & Buckley, N. K. (1968). The use of positive reinforcement in conditioning attending behavior. *Journal of Applied Behavior Analysis, 1,* 245–250.

Weingartner, H., Rapoport, J., Ebert, M., & Caine, E. (1979). Cognitive processes in normal and hyperactive children in their response to amphetamine treatment. *Journal of Abnormal Psychology, 89,* 25–37.

Weiss, B., Williams, J. H., Margen, S., Abrams, B., Caan, B., Citron, L., Cox, C., McKibben, J., Ogar, D., & Schultz, S. (1980). Behavioral responses to artificial food colors. *Science, 207,* 1487–1488.

Weiss, G. (1975). The natural history of hyperactivity in childhood and treatment with stimulant medication at different ages: A summary of research findings. *International Journal of Mental Health, 4,* 213–226.

Werry, J. S., Aman, M. G., & Diamond, E. (1980). Imipramine and methylphenidate in hyperactive children. *Journal of Child Psychology and Psychiatry, 21,* 27–35.

Whalen, C. K., & Herker, B. (1980). *Hyperactive children: The social ecology of identification and treatment.* New York: Academic Press.

Winett, R. A., & Roach, A. M. (1973). The effects of reinforcing academic performance on social behavior: A brief report. *The Psychological Record, 23,* 391–396.

Winett, R. A., & Winkler, R. C. (1972). Current behavior modification in the classroom: Be still, be quiet, be docile. *Journal of Applied Behavior Analysis, 5,* 499–504.

Wood, D. A., Rosenberg, M. S., & Carran, D. (1993). The effects of tape-recorded self-instruction cues on the mathematics performance of students with learning disabilities. *Journal of Learning Disabilities, 26*(4), 250–258.

Zabel, M. K. (1986). Time-out use with behaviorally disordered students. *Behavioral Disorders, 12,* 15–21.

Chapter 8

Managing Aggressive Behavior

Advance Organizer

As you read this chapter, prepare to identify and discuss:

- The components and use of milieu therapy.
- How the presence or absence of anxiety affects psychodynamic treatment.
- The components and use of life-space interviewing.
- The contributions of Bruno Bettelheim to the treatment of aggression.
- The required components of a token economy.
- The use of differential reinforcement to reduce aggressive behavior.
- The use of punishment to reduce aggressive behavior.
- The use of time-out to reduce aggressive behavior.
- The use of self-reinforcement to reduce aggressive behavior.
- Self-instructional training.

Because of the violent nature of aggressive actions, these behaviors are a prime concern of teachers. Naturally, most educators are interested in finding a quick and effective treatment for students who are aggressive, but, unfortunately, in the majority of cases, treatment is a time- and energy-consuming process that is most effective when carefully planned, managed, and monitored.

Aggressive behaviors are distinguished from other maladaptive, inappropriate, or disordered behaviors by applying two criteria (Baron, 1977):

Case Study: The Great Finger-Paint Massacre: An Excerpt from the Diary of a Teacher for Students with Behavior Disorders

The first day of school is often uniquely memorable for both teachers and students, especially if it's also the teacher's first day on the job. I thought a nonthreatening finger-painting activity would enable me to get acquainted with my twelve students. After all, isn't finger painting supposed to be both soothing and revealing of a student's emotional development?

Things did not go according to plan. Alex became excited while painting; his war whoops should have warned me of the disaster to come. He squeezed the easy-flow plastic paint containers, and red paint soon covered Jason and Rick. Jason cowered in the corner, but Rick retaliated with blue. Before I could catch them, our room—which we shared with the music teacher—and my clothes had been decorated with gobs of blue and red paint.

I bent over Jason to see if he'd been hurt and looked up in time to see a file cabinet toppling toward me. It ripped the intercom off the wall and flattened me against the floor. Alex and Rick were laughing as they bolted out the door. It was going to be a long year.

In later years, I would come to recognize the factors that had ignited the "Great Finger-Paint Massacre" and similar episodes in my class for students with behavior disorders. At the time, I was concerned with protecting the other students from Alex and Rick, catching the escapees, restoring order to the class, cleaning the room for Mrs. Lewes, the music teacher, and controlling my own frustrations and rage. I

thought if I could make it through this first day, I'd be fine. By 4:30 P.M., I had nearly made it. I had cleaned the room and was asking myself if I really wanted to be a teacher, when the principal sent for me. It seems that Jason's mother wanted to know how her son had gotten blue paint in one ear and red in the other. This, of course, put everything in perspective.

I learned a lot that first day about my students and about myself. Among other things, I learned that my teacher training hadn't really prepared me for aggressive student behavior. I learned that children can be much more violent than I'd ever expected, and I found that the activities I planned actually contributed to my students' aggressive behaviors. I had to learn how to control the class soon or someone would be badly injured.

During that first year, Rick, Alex, and others exhibited many aggressive behaviors. Their physically aggressive acts—fighting, tripping, kicking, biting, and throwing objects—required immediate action on my part. But these same students were also verbally aggressive, and their taunting, threatening, name calling, and cursing were likely to cause different kinds of harm. The common element of their physical and verbal aggression was the intent to strike out in some way at a victim, and as teachers and parents of students who are aggressive know, student peers are not the only targets. As on my first day in class, I was often on the receiving end of violent and abusive behaviors.

1. Antecedent events suggest that the behavior is intended to cause harm, and
2. The behavior is directed at a victim.

Thus, aggressive behavior has three elements: an observable behavior, an intent to harm, and an identifiable victim. Of course, the primary types of aggressive behavior are those violent, abusive, threatening, and destructive actions that cause teachers and parents to rate aggression number one among their nonacademic classroom concerns.

Treatment of aggressive behaviors comes in many forms and can be tailored to most instructional and therapeutic settings. As with all behavior reduction techniques, treatments for aggression must follow the guidelines developed by our professional societies (CCBD, 1990). Comprehensive treatment programs have been developed within both the psychodynamic and behavioral models, while other, less numerous but still significant, interventions have been developed within other models. In actual practice, though, most treatment facilities that serve children and youths who are aggressive employ a wide variety of interventions that cut across psychological and medical orientations.

Psychodynamic Interventions

Historically, practitioners following the psychodynamic model have been a dominant force in the treatment of students who are aggressive. In their view, aggression is a defense mechanism created by the individual to deal with the anxiety aroused by unresolved intrapsychic conflicts. In addition, according to psychoanalytic theory, aggression is an ever-present instinctual drive; the best humanity can hope for is to rechannel, redirect, or sublimate it (Berkowitz, 1962).

The Role of Anxiety

The complex psychoanalytic view of causation points to two directions for treatment. The key is the presence or absence of anxiety. If a child or youth displays anxiety along with aggressive acts, this indicates that the individual's superego remains largely undeveloped. Because a high level of anxiety can lead to suicide attempts, treatment is conducted in a nonconfrontational manner, contained within a totally accepting atmosphere, and aimed at the establishment of one trusting relationship (Kaufman, 1967). If, on the other hand, the child displays a low anxiety level, this indicates that sufficient ego control has developed to permit the student to accept some limits on behavior. In this case, treatment is more confrontational and designed to enhance normal superego development, which will restrain the aggressive instincts of the id (Frankel, 1977).

Although psychodynamic theorists and practitioners have generated a considerable number of general techniques to deal with emotional disturbance and mental illness, those specifically designed for the treatment of aggression are surprisingly few in number. The most prevalent general practices are milieu therapy and individual psychotherapy.

Milieu Therapy

The most pervasive general treatment utilized by psychodynamic practitioners is milieu therapy, and one of the best descriptions of this therapy is provided by Fritz Redl (Redl & Wineman, 1952). Redl was associated with Pioneer House, a family-style group home in Detroit for children who were aggressive. During the years that Pioneer House existed, Redl developed important and far-reaching techniques for working with disturbed children in a residential setting, one of which was milieu therapy. A *milieu* is the sum of all influences that interact with a youngster while in an institution; and *milieu therapy* is a comprehensive, diffuse, encompassing treatment consisting of all the elements of therapeutic interaction with staff and environment that are not specified as other forms of treatment, such as play therapy (Redl, 1959b). Redl describes the milieu as a clinically elastic therapeutic environment that is highly structured and managed by a carefully selected and well-trained staff. The cooks, janitors, and teachers all react in psychodynamically therapeutic, nonpunitive ways to temper tantrums, rage, destructiveness, and other outbursts. The entire residential milieu is actively involved in therapeutically correct interactions. This is not a passive therapy; it is not live and let live. Rather, it is designed intervention with a treatment focus.

Milieu therapy is especially important because students who are aggressive often fail to respond to individual psychotherapy (Redl, 1959b). In the therapeutic milieu, their whole waking day becomes the therapy hour, and all the staff their therapists. The critical components of milieu therapy are a warm, friendly atmosphere, a minimum of unessential formality, maximum staff and patient participation and cohesion, group discussions of changes that will affect the group, and both the students and the staff's active involvement in determining the physical arrangements. Redl and Wineman (1952) listed the essential milieu elements at Pioneer House in the following descriptive phrases:

> *A house that smiles.*
> *Routines which relax.*
> *A program which satisfies.*
> *Symptom tolerance guaranteed.*
> *Rich flow of tax-free love.*
> *Leeway for regression and escape.*
> *Freedom from traumatic handling.*
> *Ample flexibility and emergency help.*
> *Cultivation of group emotional securities.*

Individual Psychotherapy

The most prevalent psychodynamic intervention is psychotherapy, which consists of individual or group sessions in which a patient talks to and interacts with a therapist. The course of successful treatment usually begins with assessment, continues with relationship building and ego and superego development, and ends with a patient's control and understanding of his or her own thoughts and behavior.

Assessment

The initial interview in a psychodynamic program of individual therapy provides important assessment information. Dynamic assessment is typically conducted in structured interviews that may involve role-playing, play, or questions and answers. Often projective tests are administered and interpreted, although for children who are aggressive projective tests frequently produce conflicting data. When Davids (1973) studied assessment results from the Rorschach, Thematic Apperception Test, and clinical psychologist interviews, he found that only the clinical interview findings were reliable predictors of overt behavior ratings. Researchers who evaluated the Hand Test, a projective measure in which the patient describes various pictures of hands, found unacceptably low test-retest reliability scores as well as low criterion validity when aggression was assessed (Breidenbaugh, Brozovich, & Matheson, 1974). In residential programs, after the usual in-depth case history interview, assessment often includes a short trial period in the institution (Wardle, 1974).

The goals of the psychodynamic assessment process are to describe and delineate the overt symptoms, note related physical conditions, establish the level of overt maturation and intrapsychic drive development, determine if there is fixation or regression of psychosexual development, estimate the level of ego development, and measure the presence of defense mechanisms (Henry & Sanford, 1969).

Therapeutic Intervention

The complex process of deciding how to proceed with individual or group psychotherapy is a difficult matter when treating students who are aggressive. Because aggression is viewed as surface behavior that may exist in conjunction with any of several underlying intrapsychic states, the focus of therapy cannot be solely on overt behavior. In fact, clinicians attempting psychotherapy with children who are aggressive often find that the overt symptoms preclude holding in-depth probing sessions (Kaufman, 1967). It is common for the child or youth who is aggressive to view talk therapy as antagonistic to his or her lifestyle (King, 1976). The trusting relationship that is essential to successful therapy just cannot be established with many of these students. They frequently have entrenched defenses against introspection, and the violent nature of their behavior can make talk therapy difficult or impossible (Lion & Penna, 1974). Further complicating the issue is the average therapist's reaction to aggression. Most therapists feel repugnance toward violence and physical abuse, which increases the potential for *countertransference* (i.e., forces working against rapport and identification of the patient with the therapist) during therapy (King, 1976). Accordingly, the decision in residential institutions for children and youth who are aggressive is frequently to defer individual therapy until milieu therapy has prepared a student for a trusting relationship or has decreased the frequency of destruction behavior (Wardle, 1974).

Another crucial question in the process of individual psychotherapy is whether to enforce limits or to tolerate aggressive behavior. It is not the overt aggressive behavior but rather the underlying dynamics that determine the restraint or use of limits. Frankel (1977) presented short case histories to illustrate this difficult decision. Limits were indicated with Ken, a child who exhibited a low anxiety level and showed regression to an earlier psychosexual stage, but also had sufficient ego development to enable him to accept limits on his behavior. For Ken, the imposition of limits was aimed at restoring normal superego development. Ed, however, displayed a great deal of underlying anxiety, and his explosive outbursts were hypothesized to be defenses against what he perceived as an overwhelming and disorganizing anxiety. His ego strength was determined to be seriously underdeveloped, so the therapeutic decision was to wait until his anxiety abated before imposing external limits on his behavior (Frankel, 1977). Early therapeutic goals for a child such as Ed would include stabilizing the environment to allow for the development of trust in one significant other (Kaufman, 1967).

Play Therapy
With young children who are aggressive, the individual therapy of choice is often play therapy (Bender, 1953). Play therapy is preferred, not only because the young child is often unable or unwilling to benefit from more traditional talk therapy, but also because play is seen as the road to the child's unconscious (Henry & Sanford, 1969). Play is the medium through which the child expresses fantasies and, in so doing, reveals unconscious drives, wishes, and conflicts to the therapist (Bender, 1953). The goal of play therapy is the release of hateful, jealous, and sexual concerns through play.

During the course of therapy, appropriate play action replaces impulsive and inappropriate aggression, which then permits normal development and rechanneling of aggressive impulses into thinking, fantasy, and redirection (Ekstein, 1966). The vehicle for this change is *transference*, a psychological process whereby the child first identifies his or her id with the therapist, and then, over time, gains insight and develops a superego of his or her own. Play therapy has been used successfully to treat children who are aggressive in clinics, day schools, and residential institutions (Bender, 1953; Buxbaum, 1970; Henry & Sanford, 1969).

Theraplay
A more recent psychodynamic therapeutic technique derives from the theories of Austin Des Lauriers. A combination of therapist intrusion and play therapy was developed by Jernberg (1979) in 1971 at the Theraplay Institute in Chicago. Theraplay was originally designed to treat children with autism but was later extended to the treatment of young children who are aggressive.

Each Theraplay session is highly structured, with the therapist directing, manipulating, and controlling the action from the start to finish. Unlike a traditional play therapist, a Theraplay therapist remains in command of all activities during the session and lets the child know who is setting the tempo and controlling the action.

Jernberg (1979) considers the four essential components of sound mothering (and therefore of sound therapy) to be nurturing, structuring, challenging, and intruding. Thus, during a Theraplay session, the therapist engages the child in activities carefully selected to meet each of these goals. A therapist might rub a child's tummy with powder as a nurturing activity, and examine the child's toes, ears, or hands as an intruding exercise. Structuring activities involve experimentation, identification, and control by the child of his or her environment and person. The therapist actively aiding the child in alternately flexing and relaxing muscles is an example of a structuring activity. Leg wrestling and other contact, competitive, or confrontational activities are examples of activities that challenge the child.

During a session, the therapist is the primary playroom object as well as the director of the action. The therapist focuses all play and talk in the present, making little effort to delve into the child's past. All activities are intended to be minimally frustrating, though for many children who are aggressive, even minimally intrusive and structuring activities can trigger temper tantrums. Outbursts are worked through by maintaining constant physical contact, during which the therapist restrains the child from striking either her or himself or the therapist. The therapeutic message is a simple, straightforward "I can't let you hurt me or yourself." There is no moralizing or lecturing.

The Life-Space Interview

The life-space interview was developed as a therapeutic tool to aid in the emotional rehabilitation of students who displayed severely disturbed, aggressive behavior. This strategic intervention was first conceptualized as the marginal interview in Detroit in the late 1940s by Fritz Redl and David Wineman. Several modifications in theory and technique were made in the 1950s on the premises of the National Institutes of Health, Child Research Branch, and the name was changed to the life-space interview.

Both settings for the development of the life-space interview technique were residential treatment programs (Redl, 1959a). At the National Institutes of Health there were six boys, all classified as extremely aggressive. They spent approximately five years in the treatment program—three years on a locked ward and two years in an open cabin, attending nearby public schools. The treatment program was intensive, structured, carefully controlled, and directed by Fritz Redl with the help of other professionals. Individual psychotherapy was made available to all the boys, but it was Redl's wish to supplement this treatment with a therapeutic intervention that could both deal with immediate crises in everyday living and generate insightful adaptive behavior for the future (Newman, 1963; Redl, 1959a).

Redl describes the nature of the life-space interview by contrasting it to the "pressurized cabin" of the therapy hour. He states that the life-space interview has its roots in the psychoanalytical process, but differs primarily in the depth of interpretation and transference and in the choice of a setting (Redl, 1959a). While the psychoanalyst schedules a weekly hour-long meeting, the setting and time of the life-space interview are often beyond the control of the interviewer because interviews are precipitated by crises, acting-out behaviors, or violent disturbances within the student's life space.

The goals of the life-space interview are drawn from the psychoanalytic assumption that life events influence behavior and that appropriate verbal mediation following an environmental event can make the experience a positive one in the long term. Therefore, in crisis situations or in cases where the students' perceptions of reality are markedly distorted, therapeutic adult intervention is an effective aid to the child or youth, both to increase accurate perception and to interpret experience. Morse (1963) labels the first of these two goals as "emotional first aid on the spot" that is designed to prevent traumatization caused by delusional perceptions and inadequate self-controls; and the second, a long-term goal, as "clinical exploitation of life events" that is designed to introduce the child to insight and coping skills for future reference.

The short-term procedures for giving emotional first aid on the spot include these activities:

1. *Drain-off of frustration acidity* (i.e., encouraging the child or youth to express anger and hostility).
2. *Support for the management of panic, fury, and guilt* (i.e., making certain that violent temper tantrums are handled with a minimum of harm to the child or youth, thus decreasing guilt and providing assistance for quicker integration following the temper outburst).
3. *Communication maintenance in moments of relationship decay* (i.e., preventing the child's or youth's withdrawal into a fantasy world).
4. *Regulation of behavioral and social traffic* (i.e., pointing out to the child or youth the rules that were broken and the consequences of breaking the rules).
5. *Provision of umpire services* (i.e., praising the child's or youth's current efforts at self-control even if they were unsuccessful and noting how self-control develops over time).

Fulfilling the long-term goal of the life-space interview—the clinical exploitation of life events—involves linking current aggressive behavior and its consequences to similar past experiences in an effort to assist the student in interpreting behavioral cause-and-effect patterns and developing new behaviors that might be used to avoid similar conflicts in the future. Several of the key techniques for clinically exploiting life events are:

1. *The reality rub-in* (i.e., reexamining factual events in an effort to circumvent the denial and distortion defenses erected by the child or youth).
2. *Symptom estrangement* (i.e., pointing out that the maintenance of aggressive behaviors has many negative side effects).
3. *Massaging numb value areas* (i.e., helping the child or youth to develop sensitivity to values that are important for successful integration into society).
4. *New-tool salesmanship* (i.e., helping the child or youth develop new coping skills to replace detrimental aggressive behaviors).
5. *Manipulation of the boundaries of the self* (i.e., helping the child or youth to see the effects aggression has on others and to develop an awareness of the effects others have on his or her aggression).

Morse (1971) cautions that knowing the goals of the life-space interview is insufficient; the successful interviewer must also know when and how to apply each life-space interview procedure. Morse suggests that the interviewer use the life-space interview only after considering each of these concerns: central theme relevance, ego proximity, role compatibility, mood manageability, timing, and the impact of terrain and props. Thus, the choice of a specific life-space interview strategy depends on the child or youth, treatment goals, setting, life-space event, and the current phase of therapy (Redl, 1959a).

The successful application of the life-space interview with children and youth who are aggressive generally follows these steps (Morse, 1971): First, there is an instigating condition (e.g., a fistfight over who was the first in line) that precipitates the interview and is carefully selected by the interviewer. Next, there is a a test for depth and spread of the meaning of the incident to the child or youth. A clarification of the reality of the issue by the interviewer follows. The interviewer then attempts to promote a feeling of acceptance and refrains from imposing value judgments. Together, the child or youth and the interviewer explore potential avenues for change. Finally, there is a resolution of the current situation that is accepted, understood, and believed by the child or youth.

Although the life-space interview was developed in residential settings, Newman (1963) observed that aggression often occurs in educational settings and the technique could be adapted for use there. Within a residential treatment facility classroom, Kitchener (1963) used the life-space interview to help students be maintained in school, to understand school rules, to complete assigned work, and to return to a public school placement. Within the public schools, the cooperation of the teacher and the principal is viewed as essential for the success of this technique (Bernstein, 1963).

The use of the life-space interview in a public school setting is not without pitfalls. Long (1963) found that teachers were initially impressed when they learned this new psychological tool, but once back in their classrooms, some of them became disillusioned. Although they were pleased at the students' response to the life-space interview, they didn't expect to uncover so many complex and difficult-to-solve problems—many of which they neither completely understood nor could sufficiently control. Without support or supervision, teachers became depressed, felt inadequate, and soon abandoned the technique (Long, 1963). On the other hand, clinicians and educators have utilized the life-space interview successfully in play therapy sessions and in camp settings.

Even though the life-space interview has existed for many years, empirical verification that it produces successful behavior change is lacking in the professional literature. The technique is intuitively appealing, however, and appears to hold potential for the treatment of aggression because it can be used to manage surface behavior and provide for future change.

Psychodynamic Programs That Treat Aggressive Children

The placement of choice for young children who suffer from childhood schizophrenia, autism, or violent aggression is often a residential one (Bettelheim, 1955). The major reason for residential placement is the need to remove the child from a family situation that is closely tied to the origins of the pathology. Bettelheim (1974) stated that the most comprehensive therapy is likely to be the most effective and that a therapeutically designed institution can achieve this goal far more efficiently than other types of settings.

The Orthogenic School of the University of Chicago

This school for children with serious emotional and behavior disturbances was established in 1944 with Bruno Bettelheim as its director. Over the next three years, Bettelheim molded the small residential institution into a model for the psychodynamic treatment of children with autism, schizophrenia, or aggression. Bettelheim (1974) sought to develop family-style living, with six to eight children per cottage and a total of less than fifty children. The grounds and buildings were remodeled to his specifications in order to create a completely therapeutic environment. The goals of the program were comprehensive and included the development of self-esteem and insight as necessary components for a restoration of full participation in life.

Bettelheim postulated that children who are aggressive have an underlying need for safety that is so overwhelming that they beat down or destroy in order to ensure that safety. In theory, the therapeutic solution is to create an institutional environment that is completely nonthreatening, thereby eliminating the need for violent defense on the part of the child. In practice, this means accepting, tolerating, and suffering through one or more years of daily outbursts, temper tantrums, physical destruction, verbal abuse, and violent behavior by the child who's aggressive (Bettelheim, 1955).

In a truly therapeutic program, the entire institution is mobilized to provide nurturance, safety, and protection for the aggressive child (Bettelheim, 1974). Physical restrain is not used, nor are children locked in their cottages. All doors are open for egress, even though they are locked against entrance from the outside. Bettelheim disdained the use of physical punishment and aversive consequences. His therapeutic milieu was organized to hold the patient in high esteem, to expect the child to act like a decent human being, to accept whatever symptoms were present, and to deal with the aggressive lapses that occurred. The treatment of Harry (see the case study below) is a notable example.

Highlights of Other Psychodynamic Treatment Programs

While the Orthogenic School may be considered a relatively pure example of the application of psychodynamic principles to the treatment of children and youth who are aggressive, other programs evidence only several of the defining criteria. The Mount Sinai Psychiatric Hospital, for example, is a psychodynamic facility designed for intensive screening and short-term treatment (Heacock, 1980). It is a three-week evaluation center that was established in 1962 as an in-patient facility. Though diagnosis follows the psychodynamic model by investigating intrapsychic conflicts, this is supplemented by extensive medical and clinical information. The educational program is viewed as a component of the total treatment plan, and the teacher is one of several members of a team that is led by the psychiatrist. The students attend school five days a week, six hours each day. The teacher must have a

Case Study: Harry

The case study of Harry highlights the treatment of extreme aggression at the Orthogenic School (Bettelheim, 1955). Harry was admitted when he was 7 years old. He was frequently truant from school and also stole, lied, and ran away from home. Harry had tried to kill himself, had exhibited frequent and violent aggressive acts against others, and had tried to stab his mother on several occasions. He was a threat to bite unsuspecting victims or to throw pots and pans out of windows at pedestrians on the sidewalk below. His mother was emotionally distant, a severe punisher who gave Harry lots of negative attention. Harry's father was an alcoholic who physically abused both Harry and Harry's mother. The father frequently told his son that he was proud of his bravado. On admission, Bettelheim observed that Harry exhibited a high level of anxiety and concluded that his anxiety stemmed from the deep insecurity of his relationship with his parents and that his aggression was a defense and relief from the potentially overwhelming anxiety.

Accordingly, treatment was aimed first at removing the underlying anxiety rather than at confronting Harry's overt behavior. The initial goal was to establish a rudimentary relationship between Harry and one enlightened adult. For the first several months, this adult was available to Harry 24 hours a day and followed Harry through an incredible series of aggressive rampages, including running naked across the rooftops; knifing other therapists; running away for days at a time; breaking store and institution windows; hurting, kicking, biting, and punching other residents; breaking furniture; urinating on children he didn't like; cursing frequently; and attempting self-injury. The staff and the environment were passive but protecting agents during this troubled phase, which lasted nearly 12 months, though they did deter Harry from hurting other children and attempted to keep him from harming himself. An excellent example of this passive, acceptant, and protective philosophy occurred after Harry had broken the cottage living room furniture

for the third time. Instead of punishing Harry, Bettelheim ordered that the new furniture be heavy, as indestructible as possible, and bolted to the wall to prevent Harry from throwing it through the window. As violent as his acts were, Harry was never punished with Bettelheim's approval. On two occasions, distraught staff paddled or physically beat Harry; Bettelheim fired both of these individuals in front of Harry and the other children.

By 11 months, the nurturant, acceptant therapeutic milieu was producing changes in Harry's behavior. Bettelheim cites two major breakthroughs. Once, upon returning to the institution at 4 A.M. after running away for two days, Harry received a stern talking to—the message not one of punishment, but rather that the staff were concerned about his safety and were worried. Harry replied, "I never knew you cared so much." The second breakthrough occurred two months later, when Harry was picked up by the local police and placed in a detention home until he could be identified. Usually, if the police knew a runaway child was a patient at the Orthogenic School, they entertained him until Bettelheim arrived. However, on this occasion, Harry had wandered so far from the institution that he was picked up in another precinct and placed in detention for two days before he was identified. He was visibly affected by the ordeal, especially the locked doors and the bad food, enough so that Bettelheim decided to tell Harry that if he ran away again, they were going to permit detention to happen again. Harry immediately tested this limit by running away that night and getting picked up by the police. Consequently, he was placed in the detention center for two days before being returned to the Orthogenic School. Bettelheim warned Harry that it could be even longer the next time, even though no one wanted him to leave or be picked up. Bettelheim reported that street-wise Harry, even though he continued to run away, was never again picked up by the police.

Continued

Case Study: *Continued*

Shortly thereafter, truancy and running away ceased completely and Harry became open to talk therapy, through which he demonstrated slow but steady improvement. He first identified his id with his counselor, and later developed a primitive superego of his own.

Harry improved more in his second year and, after staying at the Orthogenic School for five years, returned to live with his remarried mother. When this arrangement was terminated, he went to live with his reformed, remarried father.

strong emotional ability to withstand rejection, testing, anger, and attack, in addition to a basic understanding of the psychodynamic nature of behavior. The roles of the teacher include therapist, educator, and counselor. Heacock presents several case study vignettes demonstrating treatment success with a very aggressive population.

Evangelakis (1974), the director of a psychodynamic residential center in Florida designed to treat aggression and other disturbances in children and youth, describes an educational component that is far more structured than the one in the Orthogenic School. Here the school serves as the vehicle for establishing discipline and purpose in the student's life. Although the teachers must be aware of unconscious motivations, their primary concern is the development and administration of a sound academic curriculum. Evangelakis states that school should play a major role in the treatment process, but that teachers should not be expected to be therapists. They should, however, make an attempt to familiarize themselves with the underlying psychodynamics of aggression so that they are able to implement task-appropriate procedures and display calm acceptance of every student.

The Menninger Clinic Children's Division was established to assess and treat children with many types of serious disturbance, including aggressive behavior (Henry & Sanford, 1969). Opened in 1926, it follows a medical and psychodynamic model. An intense five-day diagnostic effort includes a complete medical and psychological workup, with special attention to assessment of the dynamics within the child (i.e., ego strengths, defense mechanisms, unconscious drives, and superego development). Treatment includes an array of milieu, group, and individual play therapies in addition to drug therapy.

Some programs have incorporated elements of psychodynamic and behavioral therapies into one intervention program for students with aggressive behaviors. Konstantareas and Homatidis (1984), for example, combined psychotherapy, counseling, and contingency management, and successfully reduced aggressive behavior and increased prosocial behavior for children in a day treatment clinic.

Empirical and Practical Considerations
Verification of outcome success for psychodynamically oriented practitioners generally takes the form of in-depth case studies. Empirical or statistical evaluation is usually not a major concern, although there have been several attempts to quantify

patient progress. Researchers at the Bellefaire Residential Institution, for example, assessed fifty boys at admission, discharge, and a two-year follow-up (Allerhand, Weber, & Haug, 1966). The outcome measure was a staff rating of how well each boy was functioning. The treatment variables included ratings of the patient's accessibility to casework, role fulfillment, intrapsychic index of observed behavior, adaptability, and situational stress. The researchers found that only the casework treatment plan successfully predicted who would be functioning well at discharge. They also found that over 80 percent of the students attended a full-time school (one-third were in the appropriate chronological grade) and that 64 percent had a rating of adequate or better on the level-of-adjustment scale.

As can be seen from the examples of treatment cited previously, most psychoanalytic interventions have been designed for residential settings. Teachers working in these settings typically function as members of treatment teams, and the goals of intervention are comprehensive, often encompassing return to normal functioning. Because many psychoanalytic techniques (e.g., milieu therapy, play therapy, Theraplay) are not available or appropriate for use in the public schools, teachers in these settings must rely on outside agencies (e.g., mental health clinics, private psychotherapists) to provide a wide range of treatment options. Although a few psychoanalytic treatments (e.g., life-space interviewing) may be applied in public school settings by teachers in resource or self-contained classrooms for students with emotional and behavior disorders, there is little evidence that such treatments are successful in these settings.

Behavioral Interventions

The other major psychological orientation followed by practitioners who treat children who are aggressive is the behavioral model. In comparison to psychodynamic practitioners, who assess intrapsychic phenomena and analyze outcomes with in-depth case study reports, behavioral practitioners focus on overt behavior and analyze treatments with empirically based methodology.

Behaviorists believe that aggression is learned primarily through modeling (observing others act aggressively) and reinforcement (being rewarded for aggressing) and is maintained by reinforcement and stimulus control (a process whereby antecedent events elicit or set the occasion for aggressive responses) (Bandura, 1976; Gardner, Cole, Davidson, & Karan, 1986; Mace, Poge, Ivancic, & O'Brien, 1986). Behavioral researchers have demonstrated that aggression can be conditioned as both a respondent and an operant behavior (Ulrich, Dulaney, Arnett, & Mueller, 1973); that normal children (Bandura, Ross, & Ross, 1963) and children with developmental delays (Talkington & Altman, 1973) who observe aggression performed by film models will behave aggressively; that aggressive behavior remains stable over at least a ten-year period (Eron, Huesman, Lefkowitz, & Walder, 1974); that patterns of aggressive behaviors are present in early and continuing family interactions (Bugenthal, Love, & Kaswan, 1972; Patterson, Reid, Jones, & Conger, 1975); that aggression leads to escape from aversive conditions

(Carr, Newsom, & Binkoff, 1980); that aggressive behavior is usually preceded (and, to an extent, controlled) by antecedent stimuli such as threatening, cursing, teasing (Patterson & Cobb, 1973); and that students who are aggressive frequently assign hostile intentions (and therefore react aggressively) to otherwise neutral social antecedent events (Nasby, Hayden, & De Paulo, 1980).

In addition to investigating theoretical questions, behavioral researchers have evaluated the effect of numerous interventions designed to decrease the frequency, intensity, or duration of aggressive behavior with students of average and below-average intelligence (Matson & Smith, 1986). One group of interventions can be classified as positive treatments because they rely on nonaversive techniques to reduce maladaptive behaviors such as aggression. The second group of behavioral interventions incorporate punishment and aversive techniques.

Positive Treatments to Reduce Aggression

The Token Economy

The behavioral equivalent of the psychodynamic therapeutic milieu is the token economy, a carefully and comprehensively designed structure aimed at managing the gamut of aggressive behaviors while providing a vehicle for behavior change. There are three basic requirements for setting up a token economy: tokens, backup reinforcers, and specified contingencies. Within these broad outlines, there is room for variation in the choice of tokens, in the type of contingencies (e.g., individual or group), and in the selection of backup reinforcers. Other behavioral techniques, such as response-cost or time-out, can be integrated into the token system. Today, token economies are an accepted, widespread, and effective all-purpose treatment in which control of aggressive behavior has been demonstrated in group homes (Yates, Haven, & Thorensen, 1979), self-contained classrooms (Hewett & Taylor, 1980), community youth centers (Stahl, Fuller, Lefebre, & Burchard, 1979), day schools (O'Leary & Schneider, 1977), psychiatric hospitals (Ayllon & Azrin, 1968), and residential placements (Pizzat, 1973).

The use of token economies as a technique to control aggressive behavior in educational settings has been widely investigated. O'Leary & Becker (1967) established a token economy for eight children who were disruptive by rewarding appropriate behavior and ignoring inappropriate behavior. They found that aggressive behavior decreased from 76 percent of the monitored time intervals during baseline to 10 percent of the intervals following treatment. Tokens, in the form of stars, have also been used effectively to reduce the aggressive behavior of students who were abused and neglected (Timmons-Mitchell, 1986). O'Leary and Drabman (1971) reviewed the use of token reinforcement and concluded that token reinforcement treatments have demonstrated repeated effectiveness in decreasing disruptive and aggressive classroom behavior.

Although token economies have been effective in changing behavior in applied settings, successful treatment frequently fails to maintain once treatment is stopped or to generalize to nontreatment settings (O'Leary & Drabman, 1971).

Turkewitz, O'Leary, and Ironsmith (1975) found that two techniques enhance generalization and maintenance: Following successful implementation of a teacher-directed token program, the students in their study rated their own behavior to determine the number of tokens earned, and later the backup reinforcers were gradually faded and eliminated.

Recent research and practice has extended token economy interventions into other promising areas. The fact that over 90 percent of teachers of students with behavior disorders use some form of token economy is convincing testimony to its acceptance and popularity. One procedure that is growing in use is the level system, a variation of the token economy where students move through a series of point-based systems as their behavior improves. Level I, for students just admitted to the emotional and behavior disorders setting, might consist of a list of expected and permitted behaviors tied to specific contingencies and privileges earned for good behavior. After the student has met Level I criteria for the required number of days or weeks, he or she moves to Level II, where expected behavior typically increases in difficulty or demands as earned privileges also increase. Progression through levels continues until the student demonstrates behaviors that suggest that a return to a less restrictive placement is in order. Although growing in popularity, the empirical support for level systems is just beginning to emerge (Smith & Farrell, 1993).

Positive Reinforcement Treatments

A group of positive behavioral interventions has been developed to decrease or eliminate maladaptive behaviors such as aggression without resorting to aversive or punishment procedures. The four most prevalent of these techniques are extinction, DRO (differential reinforcement of other behaviors), DRL (differential reinforcement of low-rate behaviors), and DRI (differential reinforcement of an incompatible response).

Although extinction procedures (those that remove reinforcement following aggression) can be successful they are usually not recommended for the treatment of harmful or violent behaviors because they work slowly and aggressive behaviors cause injuries that should not be ignored. To take one dismal example, a child

---

A Token Economy for Chimps

The classic early study by Wolfe (1936) that used tokens with chimps is the ancestor of current token economy research. Wolfe trained his chimps to perform tasks using secondary rewards (poker chips) that could be exchanged for primary reinforcers (grapes). Among his conclusions the one cited most frequently is equal performance for tokens or grapes. Several of his other findings, however, have impli-

cations for research on token economies today. He found that tokens given after a two-minute delay produced little behavior effect; that once the chimps accumulated several tokens, they stopped working; that the chimps could discriminate between chips worth one and those worth two grapes; and that a side effect often occurred—the chimps began to beg for poker chips.

hit himself over 10,000 times before his self-injurious behavior extinguished (Lovaas, 1969). Also not recommended are DRL procedures (delivering reinforcement to the student if less than a given number of maladaptive behaviors occur), primarily because the treatment goal is complete elimination rather than simply a low rate of aggression.

DRO procedures (delivering reinforcement if a student exhibits no aggressive behavior during a specified time period) have been used to reduce aggression, both alone and in combination with other treatments. Bostow and Bailey (1969) combined DRO and time-out treatments to reduce violent behavior in two institutionalized patients with mental retardation. In addition to using time-out as a punishment when aggression occurred, Bostow and Bailey rewarded the patients with tangible reinforcements such as juice, coffee, milk, or soda if they exhibited no aggressive behavior during specified time periods that ranged from two to ten minutes. The combined treatment effectively reduced aggressive behavior to near-zero levels.

DRI procedures (delivering reinforcement to students when they smile or make positive statements that are incompatible with aggression) have not only been successful in treating aggression (Smith, 1985), but may be faster than DRO interventions and are recommended for use with time-out and other treatments that have no positive focus (Tarpley & Schroeder, 1979). Such combined approaches are designed to reduce aggression *and* to increase positive, adaptive responses concurrently.

Self-Control and Cognitive-Behavioral Treatments

Treatment of acting-out and aggressive behaviors has also been investigated by researchers using self-control and cognitive-behavioral modification techniques. The aim of these interventions is to provide students with a means to control their own aggression. Self-control procedures typically involve self-administration of reinforcement or punishment, while cognitive-behavioral treatments are often designed to increase verbal mediation so that students will stop before they aggress, consider the consequences of violent behavior, and substitute a nonaggressive coping response.

Self-Reinforcement

A series of studies has been conducted on management of reinforcement within a token economy. In investigating the effect of self-evaluation on disruptive and aggressive behaviors, Santogrossi, O'Leary, Romanczyk, and Kaufman (1973) found that self-evaluation in the form of student monitoring and rating of their own behavior produced no behavioral change. However, a teacher-administered token economy did produce a sizable decline in maladaptive behavior—a gain that was maintained briefly when the students were trained to self-determine the number of points they had earned. Later in the student-determined reinforcement treatment, however, disruptive behaviors increased to near-baseline levels, apparently because self-rewarded lying occurred. These results suggest that self-management interventions must be carefully sequenced and implemented when working with older students with serious adjustment problems.

In a related study, Drabman, Spitalnik, and O'Leary (1973) evaluated the effect of two self-control procedures for eight disruptive boys in an after-school remedial reading class. Following the establishment of baseline, a teacher-determined token treatment successfully reduced disruptive and aggressive behaviors, and the gain was maintained during the ensuing phases when backup reinforcers were faded and student evaluation was substituted for teacher evaluation. The treatment effect also generalized to a fifteen-minute segment of the class during which no tokens were used. The authors reported honest, accurate self-evaluations by the boys.

In a third study in this series, Turkewitz and colleagues (1975) examined the effect of teacher-administered and self-control procedures on students who demonstrated disruptive classroom behavior and academic problems. By the end of the first treatment, a teacher-determined token economy, disruptive and aggressive behavior had decreased significantly. During the next treatment phase, in which student ratings gradually replaced teacher ratings of behavior, most treatment gains were maintained. Backup reinforcers were then eliminated in an attempt to imbue the students with self-control, and although disruptive behavior continued to increase, it remained well below initial baseline levels.

In summary, self-reinforcement treatments have demonstrated a limited utility with aggressive behaviors. As a component of a combined treatment, self-evaluation and self-reinforcement can successfully augment externally applied procedures. One promising use of self-reinforcement is as a maintenance procedure after teacher-managed contingencies have effectively reduced aggressive behavior.

Self-Instructional Training (SIT)

While antecedent and contingency variations of self-management have been investigated in only a few studies, self-instructional training, developed by Meichenbaum and Goodman (1971), has been well researched. SIT stresses the importance of control of overt behavior by private speech and verbal mediation. In two early studies, Meichenbaum and Goodman (1969, 1971) trained children to use verbal mediation in problem-solving situations. The students first observed the trainer using overt verbal mediation (i.e., talking aloud to solve problems), then learned to talk covertly to themselves as they solved problems. Meichenbaum and Goodman found that the SIT group performed better than a control group on the Matching Familiar Figures Test, Porteus Mazes, and three subtests of the Wechsler Intelligence Scale for Children (WISC). However, there was little change in observed classroom behavior.

A few early studies of SIT focused directly on aggressive behaviors. Camp (1977) developed a program entitled Think Aloud, which was based on the theory that children who are aggressive fail to develop verbal mediation to exert functional control over their behavior. Camp reasoned that SIT, a general problem-solving strategy, could be adapted to deal with aggressive behaviors because these students exhibit a rapid response style that is deficient in verbal mediation.

Subsequently, Camp, Bloom, Hebert, and van Doornick (1977) evaluated the effect of SIT on aggressive behavior. Their results were mixed: The group of students who received SIT improved significantly over two other groups on the Matching Familiar Figures Test, WISC-R subtests, and prosocial behaviors, but there were no differences between the groups on teacher ratings of aggressive behaviors.

Snyder and White (1979) investigated the effect of SIT on a group of teenage residential patients admitted for severe aggression, drug use, and criminal activities. The treatment group received SIT supplemented with discussion of the antecedents and consequences of aggression, rehearsal of appropriate verbalizations, and directions to apply these procedures to cottage and school situations. The SIT group improved significantly more than the control groups in staff ratings of truancy, self-care tasks, drug use, aggressive acts, stealing, and property destruction.

Forman (1980) compared the performance of three treatments: cognitive restructuring training similar to SIT, a response-cost punishment procedure, and a control. The dependent variables included a teacher rating scale and direct observation of specific aggressive behaviors. The results indicated that the cognitive restructuring group equaled the response-cost group on all measures, and both treatment groups demonstrated significantly less aggressive behavior than the control group. The response-coat treatment was slightly superior on the important measure of observed aggressive behavior. When Lochman, Curry, Burch, and Lampron (1984) investigated the effect of a cognitive-behavioral intervention that included an anger-coping strategy, they found that boys who were taught how to cope with their anger displayed fewer aggressive behaviors at school and at home, as well as a slight increase in self-esteem.

Effectiveness research on self-management treatment of aggression has increased in recent years. Etscheidt (1991) investigated the effect of a cognitive-behavioral treatment on the aggressive behavior of adolescents and found both increased self-control and fewer aggressive acts. Coleman, Pfeiffer, and Oakland (1992) investigated the effect of aggression replacement training with adolescents in a residential setting and found no change in aggressive behavior. On a positive note, Smith, Siegel, O'Conner, and Thomas (1994) found that their cognitive-behavioral treatment reduced the anger and aggressive behavior of elementary-aged students.

In summary, the ability of self-instructional programs to affect test and academic behavior has been shown by repeated replication of Meichenbaum and Goodman's early study, but effects on aggressive behavior have not been convincingly or repeatedly demonstrated (Wilson, 1984). Still, the results of a growing number of studies (e.g., Etscheidt, 1991; Smith et al., 1994) suggest considerable potential.

Multiple-Component Treatments
Several researchers have investigated multiple-component treatments of aggressive behavior. McCullough, Huntsinger, and Nay (1977) treated a 16-year-old boy with an 11-year history of temper outbursts and physical and verbal abuse. The treatment consisted of role-playing with video feedback, muscle relaxation, and behavioral contracting. During the final one hundred days of the school year, the youth exhibited no temper outbursts.

Two recent studies examined the use of videotapes on aggression. Knapczyk (1992) found that student videotape viewing of events that occurred prior to their aggressive acts resulted in both decreased aggression and increased acceptable, alternative responses. Lonnecker, Brady, McPherson, & Hawking (1994) found that videotape training resulted in an increase in cooperative classroom behaviors and decreases in inappropriate behavior.

Robin, Schneider, and Dolnick (1976) developed a four-part intervention called the Turtle Technique to reduce aggressive behavior. First, the "Turtle" response was taught: The student learned to fold his or her body into a turtlelike position following a verbal cue from the teacher or class. Muscle relaxation, problem solving, and peer praise were also implemented. In one classroom for primary-age students who were severely aggressive, the Turtle Technique reduced aggressive behavior from 20 to 12 percent of observed intervals. In a second class for children who were moderately disruptive, rates of aggressive behavior decreased from 5 to 3 percent. These 40 percent reductions in the frequency of aggressive behavior represent a substantial improvement for both groups.

Punishment Treatments to Reduce Aggression

Although positive approaches are preferred, aversive and punishment treatments have been developed to be used if positive treatments fail to reduce aggressive behavior. Probably the most widely used punishment technique is time-out from reinforcement, although other procedures have also demonstrated success.

Time-Out

Time-out, defined as removal of the individual's access to positive reinforcement, is a frequently used behavioral intervention for treating aggressive behavior. The use of time-out in the classroom involves removing or isolating the student from classroom activities immediately following aggressive behavior. The different levels of time-out, each determined by the setting to which the student is taken, are the following:

1. *Contingent observation:* The student is removed to a nearby chair and is able to observe the class, but is not permitted to participate in classroom activities.
2. *Exclusionary time-out:* The student is removed to another part of the classroom, often a corner behind a partition, and is able to hear but not observe classroom activities.
3. *Seclusionary time-out:* The student is removed to a setting, often called a time-out room, that is outside the classroom.

Time-out has been used successfully to reduce a variety of aggressive behaviors in several settings. O'Leary and Schneider (1977) employed time-out to diminish the aggressive behavior of students in a day school. Bostow and Bailey (1969) used a brief two-minute time-out period to decrease screaming and physical violence in institutionalized patients with mental retardation. Each time the patients emitted verbal or physically aggressive behavior, they were taken into a small time-out booth, where they remained at least two minutes; they had to be silent for at least fifteen seconds prior to release. Aggressive behavior by these patients was reduced to near-zero level following treatments. The success of time-out procedures in curtailing aggressive behavior has also been documented in residential institutions (Pizzat, 1973) and self-contained classes (Hewett & Taylor, 1980). Although time-out itself has no positive focus, this kind of intervention has been used to supplement and enhance the effects of prosocial skill instruction (Wahler & Fox, 1980). Time-out can also have positive side effects in that it discourages aggressive behaviors in nontargeted children in the class (Wilson, Robertson, Herlong, & Haynes, 1979). The use of warnings to students has also been investigated by Twyman, Johnson, Buie, and Nelson (1994) who found that warning students who were presently in contingent observation time-out that a more intrusive time-out punishment could occur, resulted in decreased appropriate behavior while in contingent observation but no increase in the use of exclusionary time-out.

Time-out is not a problem-free treatment, however. Usually, it is imposed only after violent outbursts, temper tantrums, or fights are in progress, necessitating the intervention of the teacher into a potentially dangerous situation. Also, whenever a student must be moved from one setting to another, there is a potential for physical confrontation. Moreover, placing a student in seclusionary time-out in a small room raises the issue of unlawful restraint. Because of these considerations, the following practical, ethical, and legal guidelines have been suggested for teachers who implement time-out treatment programs (Gast & Nelson, 1977; Nelson & Rutherford, 1983; Schloss & Smith, 1987; Wood & Braaten, 1983; Yell, 1994):

Practical Considerations

1. The student must be removed from a setting where reinforcement occurs.
2. The student must be taken to a setting where no reinforcement can occur.
3. A brief time-out (about two to five minutes) is just as effective as a longer one.
4. A short period of calm and quiet should be required of the student immediately before he or she is released from time-out to prevent reinforcement of maladaptive behavior.
5. Time-out must be used consistently with a minimum of teacher–student verbal exchange.

Ethical and Legal Considerations

1. A standardized, written procedure for implementing time-out punishment must be developed that includes:

    a. An explanation of and rationale for using the procedure
    b. A set of highly specific and objective rules that define the aggressive behaviors, length of time-out, and release conditions
    c. Involvement of the IEP team

2. Informed, written consent should be obtained from parents or guardians.
3. The student must be observed and monitored at all times, especially while in a seclusionary time-out room.
4. Although a student may be unable to open the door to the seclusionary time-out room from the inside, the door should not be locked and should allow for immediate access into the room by the observer.
5. The total time-out period should never exceed fifty minutes.
6. Students should first be given the option to enter the time-out setting on their own.
7. Seclusionary time-out should not be used unless the maladaptive behavior is serious enough to warrant an intervention that has the potential for physical confrontation. Aggressive and destructive behaviors are considered appropriate target behaviors for time-out; talk-outs and out-of-seat are not.
8. Because time-out has an entirely negative focus (it is a punishment for exhibiting aggressive behaviors), it should always be used in conjunction with interventions that teach positive, adaptive, or prosocial skills.
9. The frequency of aggressive behavior must be monitored and reviewed to determine if the time-out treatment is working and should be continued.
10. Procedures that are less intrusive and involve less likelihood of physical confrontation should be tried both before implementing time-out and after a successful time-out treatment—in the first case to avoid using time-out, and in the second to maintain treatment gains.

Other Punishment Procedures

Punishment procedures (i.e., applying an aversive stimulus immediately following the emission of aggressive behavior) have been shown to be effective, but are recommended as treatments of last resort, to be used only in cases involving extreme urgency, harm to self or others, or after protracted and demonstrated failure of positive treatments (e.g., Doke, Wolery, & Sumberg, 1983). Ironically, one type of aggressive behavior, self-inflicted violence, has been treated successfully with a variety of aversive techniques, including smelling salts, water mist, and, in extreme cases, electric shock.

Comprehensive Behavioral Programs

The Engineered Classroom

The classic early program that combined different behavioral strategies for managing and reducing aggressive behaviors in a classroom setting was designed by Frank Hewett (Hewett, 1968). His engineered classroom—a highly structured, comprehensive program for use in day school or self-contained classes—quickly became the model for the many classes for students with emotional and behavior disorders that were established during the 1970s. Hewett had specific recommendations for all facets of instruction, including a floor plan; number of students; arrangement of student desks, teacher desks, and learning stations; a token economy; a developmental task sequence; and the use of time-out. His token economy was a comprehensive management system that required the administration of fifteen checkmarks every 15 minutes for each student—10 for completing academic work and five for displaying appropriate behavior. Hewett created three instructional centers in each room, each one representing a different level of student performance. The *order center* contained puzzles, pegboards, and other tasks designed to keep the student attending and working on easy and motivating tasks. The *exploratory center* contained science activities designed to involve the student in exploring and manipulating the environment in a structured fashion. The *mastery center* consisted of rows of student desks and looked much like a regular class in miniature.

Three components of the engineered classroom were intended to decrease aggressive behaviors. First, the student was positively reinforced for engaging in appropriate classroom behaviors that were incompatible with aggression (a DRI procedure). Second, students were assigned to academic and preacademic tasks that they were capable of completing. Third, if preventive measures failed and aggression occurred, time-out was applied.

Group Homes: Achievement Place and Learning House

When token economies proved effective within institutions, the logical extension was to establish token economies in the community. The result was Achievement Place and similar teaching-family community-based group homes for youth who displayed aggression (Wolf, Braukmann, & Ramp, 1987). The first home, opened in 1967, was staffed with professional teaching parents and housed six to eight 12-to-16-year-old boys who lived at Achievement Place, but attended school in the community. The major behavior-change intervention was a comprehensive token economy that used snacks, hobby time, and monetary allowances as backup reinforcers (Phillips, Phillips, Wolfe, & Fixsen, 1975; Phillips, Wolfe, Fixsen, & Bailey, 1976). Research conducted at Achievement Place demonstrated the token economy's effectiveness in reducing violent behavior, both at the home and in school (Kirigin, Wolf, Brankmann, Fixsen, & Phillips, 1979).

Kirigin and colleagues (1979) reported that Achievement Place was as economical as it was effective: Group home placement cost approximately one-third what a nearby residential placement cost. In comparison to a control group, the boys who resided at Achievement Place demonstrated less repeat institutionalization, fewer police contacts, and higher attendance in public schools. Achievement Place and similar treatment programs (e.g., Learning House, a family-style group home [Thoresen et al., 1979; Yates et al., 1979]) have been widely replicated across the country (Wolf et al., 1987).

Oregon Research Institute

Another behavioral treatment and research program for children who are aggressive was established by Gerald Patterson at the Oregon Research Institute at the University of Oregon. Although Patterson's early research involved the successful use of operant conditioning to reduce one boy's specific aggressive behaviors

(Patterson, 1965), the primary focus at the Oregon Research Institute has been family intervention (Alexander & Parsons, 1975; Berkowitz & Graziano, 1975).

Patterson and Cobb (1973) first operationalized aggressive behavior and family interaction patterns through an exhaustive observation of over 57,000 instances of family talk and overt behavior. Fourteen behavior patterns that occurred immediately prior to a child's aggression were isolated. These antecedent events, referred to by Patterson as "noxious behaviors," were discussed with each family in treatment and the relevant aggressive behaviors were selected as targets for behavior change. Five weeks of intensive training followed (Wiltz & Patterson, 1974). The first step was to set up a contingency contract. Then the parents were taught to negotiate, collect data, and use time-out, tokens, and positive reinforcement.

When Patterson and colleagues (1975) investigated the effect of training, they found a 60 to 75 percent decline in aggressive behavior, a modest reduction in coercive family patterns, an increase in parent awareness of specific problem behaviors, less parental reinforcement of coercive or noxious child behavior, more effective use of negative reinforcement and punishment, larger roles in limit setting for fathers, and generally happier families. Interestingly, the dramatic decrease in specifically targeted aggressive behaviors did not extend to nontargeted maladaptive behaviors. Still, at a twelve-month follow-up, approximately two out of three families reported maintenance of improvement. Patterson suggested that the one-third failure rate was associated with parents who did not use time-out or who failed to implement contingencies consistently. High failure rates were also found among parents who had given serious consideration to institutionalizing their children because they believed them to be mentally ill. In recent extensions of the Oregon Research Institute parent training programs into the area of juvenile delinquency, aggression and other antisocial behaviors decreased during intervention, but once intervention was stopped, there was often little maintenance of treatment gains (Bank, Patterson, & Reid, 1987).

Other Treatments for Aggressive Behavior

Aggressive behavior has been treated with a variety of other interventions that cannot be clearly classified as either psychodynamic or behavioral. The effect of assertion training, for example, was investigated by Lee, Hallberg, and Hassard (1979), who found that junior high students trained in assertiveness improved in that area but showed no reduction in aggression. Osborne, Kibur, and Miller (1986) investigated the effect of videotaping self-injurious behavior and found that for one 15-year-old subject, the videotape intervention sharply reduced self-inflicted hitting. Goldstein and his associates (Goldstein, Sherman, Gershaw, Sprafkin, & Glich, 1978; Goldstein, Sprafkin, Gershaw, & Klein, 1983) investigated the effect of Structured Learning Therapy, a psychoeducational intervention designed to teach prosocial skills and to decrease aggressive behaviors. Adolescents were taught such social skills as listening, conversing, and complimenting in addition to alternative, nonaggressive responses. The authors claim to have achieved success with aggression and other behavior disorders, but there is little evidence in the research literature supporting the effectiveness of Structured Learning Therapy.

The treatments reviewed above were designed to decrease the *frequency* of aggressive behavior. Several other techniques have been developed to manage or control aggression *during* temper tantrums, fights, and other violent outbursts. The general thrust of these techniques is to protect the professional while restraining the student who is aggressive (Bullock, Donahue, Young, & Warner, 1985). Although little research has been conducted in this area, the consensus among professionals is that all practitioners working with aggressive persons should be trained in restraint techniques, but that manual restraint should be used sparingly—*only* when there is likely to be injury (Hughes, 1985; Ruhl, 1985), and only if rigorous, well-defined guidelines are followed (Schloss & Smith, 1987).

Summary

This chapter reviewed and evaluated treatments designed to manage aggressive behavior. Most such interventions follow either the psychodynamic or the behavioral model. We presented and discussed several of the most commonly used therapies based on the psychodynamic model, including the life-space interview, play therapy, and milieu therapy. The true purpose of psychodynamic interventions is not to manage aggression, which is viewed as "surface behavior" controlled by underlying intrapsychic causation factors, but to resolve intrapsychic conflicts and to promote ego and superego development, insight, and healthy emotional functioning of the whole person. Psychodynamic interventions are derived from a rich theoretical base and have been used in clinics, residential settings, and (to a lesser extent) schools; however, very few of them have demonstrated efficacy. We also presented and discussed a wide variety of behavioral interventions that have been developed for students who exhibit aggression. Behavioral interventions have two foci: to decrease aggressive behaviors and to increase prosocial behaviors. We described positive (reinforcement) and negative (punishment) techniques that have effected desired behavior changes. Both externally administered and self-administered strategies have been developed; in general, the external programs have proved more effective in reducing aggression, though long-term maintenance remains a concern.

Discussion Questions

1. Why would conventional talk therapy be unlikely to work with many students who are aggressive?

2. Should young children who are aggressive be confronted directly during treatment?

3. Why are changes caused by psychodynamic techniques difficult to observe and measure?

4. Why did Bruno Bettelheim tolerate twelve months of Harry's aggressive behavior? Would you?

5. How can medical treatments (e.g., drug therapy) be used in conjunction with psychodynamic treatments? With behavioral treatments?

6. Why are many psychodynamic treatments seldom used in the public schools?

7. How can positive reinforcement be employed to reduce aggressive behavior?

8. Why is punishment considered the treatment of last resort?

9. Why does time-out work with aggressive behaviors?

10. Why are self-applied treatments for aggression generally less effective than teacher-applied methods?

References

Alexander, J., & Parsons, B. (1975). Short-term behavioral intervention with delinquent families: Impact on family process and recidivism. In A. Graziano (Ed.), *Behavior therapy with children II*. Chicago: Aldine.

Allerhand, M., Weber, R., & Haug, M. (1966). *Adaptation and adaptability: The Bellefaire follow-up study*. New York: Child Welfare League.

Ayllon, T., & Azrin, N. (1968). *The token economy: A motivational system for therapy and rehabilitation*. New York: Meredith.

Bandura, A., Ross, D., & Ross, S. (1963). Imitation of film-mediated aggressive models. *Journal of Abnormal and Social Psychology, 6*, 3–11.

Bank, L., Patterson, G., & Reid, J. (1987). Delinquency prevention through parent training in family management. *The Behavior Analyst, 10*, 75–82.

Baron, R. (1977). *Human aggression*. New York: Plenum.

Bender, L. (1953). *Aggression, hostility and anxiety in children*. Springfield, IL: Charles C. Thomas.

Berkowitz, B., & Graziano, A. (1975). Training parents as behavior therapists: A review. In A. Graziano (Ed.), *Behavior therapy with children II*. Chicago: Aldine.

Berkowitz, L. (1962). *Aggression: A social psychology analysis*. New York: McGraw-Hill.

Bernstein, M. (1963). The life space interview in the school setting. *American Journal of Orthopsychiatry, 33*, 717–719.

Bettelheim, B. (1955). *Truants from life: The rehabilitation of emotionally disturbed children*. New York: Free Press.

Bettelheim, B. (1974). *A home for the heart*. New York: Knopf.

Bostow, D., & Bailey, J. (1969). Modification of severe disruptive and aggressive behavior using brief time-out and reinforcement procedures. *Journal of Applied Behavior Analysis, 2*, 31–37.

Breidenbaugh, B., Brozovich, R., & Matheson, L. (1974). The hand tests. *Journal of Personality Assessment, 79*, 285–290.

Bugenthal, D., Love, L., & Kaswan, J. (1972). Videotaped family interaction: Differences reflecting presence and type of child disturbance. *Journal of Abnormal Psychology, 79*, 285–290.

Bullock, L., Donahue, C., Young, J., Warner, M. (1985). Techniques for the management of physical aggression. *The Pointer, 29*, 38–44.

Buxbaum, E. (1970). *Troubled children in a troubled world*. New York: International Universities.

Camp, B. W. (1977). Verbal mediation in young aggressive boys. *Journal of Abnormal Psychology, 86*, 145–153.

Camp, B. W., Bloom, G. E., Hebert, F., & van Doornick, W. J. (1977). "Think aloud": A program for developing self-control in young aggressive boys. *Journal of Abnormal Child Psychology, 5*, 157–169.

Carr, E., Newsom, C., & Binkoff, J. (1980). Escape as a factor in the aggressive behavior of two retarded children. *Journal of Applied Behavior Analysis, 13,* 101–117.

Council for Children with Behavioral Disorders (CCBD) (1990). Position paper on use of behavior reduction strategies with children with behavioral disorders. *Behavioral Disorders, 15*(4), 243–260.

Coleman, M., Pfeiffer, S., & Oakland, T. (1992). Aggression replacement training with behaviorally disordered adolescents. *Behavioral Disorders, 18*(1), 54–66.

Davids, A. (1973). Aggression in thought and action of emotionally disturbed boys. *Journal of Consulting and Clinical Psychology, 40,* 322–327.

Doke, L., Wolery, M., & Sumberg, C. (1983). Treating chronic aggression: Effects of response-contingent ammonia spirits. *Behavior Modification, 7,* 531–556.

Drabman, R. S., Spitalnik, R., & O'Leary, K. D. (1973). Teaching self-control to disruptive children. *Journal of Abnormal Psychology, 82,* 10–16.

Ekstein, R. (1966). *Children of time and space with action and impulse: Clinical studies on the psychoanalytic treatment of severely disturbed children.* New York: Appleton.

Eron, L., Huesmann, R., Lefkowitz, M., & Walder, L. (1974). How learning conditions in early childhood, including mass media, relate to aggression in later adolescence. *American Journal of Orthopsychiatry, 44,* 412–423.

Etscheidt, S. (1991). Reducing aggressive behavior and improving self-control: A cognitive-behavioral training program for behaviorally disordered adolescents. *Behavioral Disorders, 16*(2), 107–115.

Evangelakis, M. (1974). *A manual for residential and day treatment of children.* Springfield, IL: Charles C. Thomas.

Forman, S. (1980). A comparison of cognitive training and response cost procedures in modifying aggressive behavior of elementary school children. *Behavior Therapy, 11,* 594–600.

Frankel, S. (1977). The management aspect of psychotherapy with aggressive children. *Child Psychiatry and Human Development, 7,* 169–185.

Gardner, W. I., Cole, C. L., Davidson, D. P., & Karan, O. C. (1986). Reducing aggression in individuals with developmental disabilities: An expanded stimulus control, assessment, and intervention model. *Education and Training of the Mentally Retarded, 21,* 3–12.

Gast, D., & Nelson, C. (1977). Legal and ethical considerations for the use of time-out in special education settings. *Journal of Special Education, 11,* 457–467.

Goldstein, A. P., Sherman, M., Gershaw, N. J., Sprafkin, R. P., & Glick, B. (1978). Training aggressive adolescents in prosocial behavior. *Journal of Youth and Adolescence, 7,* 73–92.

Goldstein, A. P., Sprafkin, R. P., Gershaw, J., & Klein, P. (1983). Structured learning: A psychoeducational approach for teaching social competencies. *Behavioral Disorders, 8,* 161–170.

Heacock, D. (1980). *A psychodynamic approach to adolescent psychiatry: The Mount Sinai experience.* New York: Marcel Dekker.

Henry, W., & Sanford, N. (1969). *Disturbed children, examination and assessment through team process: The Menninger Clinic Children's Division.* San Francisco: Jossey-Bass.

Hewett, F. (1968). *The emotionally disturbed child in the classroom.* Boston: Allyn & Bacon.

Hewett, F., & Taylor, F. (1980). *The emotionally disturbed child in the classroom: The orchestration of success,* 2nd ed. Boston: Allyn & Bacon.

Hughes, C. (1985). Physical intervention: Planning and control techniques. *The Pointer, 29,* 34–37.

Jernberg, A. (1979). *Theraplay.* San Francisco: Jossey-Bass.

Kaufmann, I. (1967). Psychotherapy of children with conduct and acting-out disorders. In M. Hammer & A. Kaplan (Eds.), *The practice of psychotherapy with children.* Homewood, IL: Dorsey.

King, C. H. (1976). Counter-transference and counter-experience in the treatment of violence prone youth. *American Journal of Orthopsychiatry, 46,* 43–52.

Kirigin, K., Wolf, M., Braukmann, C., Fixsen, D., & Phillips, E. (1979). Achievement Place: A preliminary outcome evaluation. In J. Stumphauzer (Ed.), *Progress in behavior therapy with delinquents.* Springfield, IL: Charles C. Thomas.

Kitchener, H. (1963). The lifespace interview in the differentiation of school in residential treatment. *American Journal of Orthopsychiatry, 33,* 720–723.

Kanpczyk, D. R. (1992). Effects of developing alternative responses on the aggressive behavior of adolescents. *Behavioral Disorders, 17*(4), 247–263.

Konstantareas, M. M., & Homatidis, S. (1984). Aggressive and prosocial behaviors before and after treatment in conduct-disordered children and in matched controls. *Journal of Child Psychology and Psychiatry and Allied Disciplines, 25,* 607–620.

Lee, D., Hallberg, E. T., & Hassard, H. (1979). Effects of assertion training on aggressive behavior of adolescents. *Journal of Counseling Psychology, 26,* 459–561.

Lion, J., & Penna, M. (1974). The study of human aggression. In R. Whalen (Ed.), *The neurophysiology of aggression.* New York: Plenum.

Lochman, J. E., Curry, J. F., Burch, P. R., & Lampron, L. B. (1984). Treatment and generalization effects of cognitive behavioral and goal-setting interventions with aggressive boys. *Journal of Consulting and Clinical Psychology, 52,* 915–916.

Long, N. (1963). Some problems in teaching LSI techniques to graduate students in education in a large class at Indiana University. *American Journal of Orthopsychiatry, 33,* 723–726.

Lonnecker, C., Brady, M. P., McPherson, R., & Hawking, J. (1994). Video self-modeling and cooperative classroom behavior in children with learning and behavior problems: Training and generalization effects. *Behavioral Disorders, 20*(1), 24–34.

Lovaas, O. (1969). Behavior modification: Teaching language to psychotic children (16 mm film). New York: Appleton-Century-Crofts.

Mace, F. C., Poge, T. J., Ivancic, M. T., & O'Brien, S. (1986). Analysis of environmental determinants of aggression and disruption in mentally retarded children. *Applied Research in Mental Retardation, 7,* 203–221.

Matson, J. L., & Smith, D. G. (1986). A review of treatment research for aggressive and disruptive behavior in the mentally retarded, *Applied Research in Mental Retardation, 7,* 95–103.

McCullough, J., Huntsinger, G., & Nay, R. (1977). Self-control treatment of aggression in a 16-year-old male. *Journal of Consulting and Clinical Psychology, 45,* 322–331.

Meichenbaum, D. H., & Goodman, J. (1969). The developmental control of operant motor responding by verbal operants. *Journal of Experimental Child Psychology, 7,* 553–565.

Meichenbaum, D. H., & Goodman, J. (1971). Training impulsive children to talk to themselves: A means of developing self-control. *Journal of Abnormal Psychology, 77,* 115–126.

Morse, W. (1963). Working paper: Training teachers in LSI. *American Journal of Orthopsychiatry, 33,* 727–730.

Morse, W. (1971). Workshop on LSI for teachers. In N. Long, W. Morse, & R. Newman (Eds.), *Conflict in the classroom,* 2nd ed. Belmont: Wadsworth.

Nasby, W., Hayden, B., & De Paulo, B. (1980). Attributional bias among aggressive boys to interpret unambiguous social stimuli as displays of hostility. *Journal of Abnormal Psychology, 89,* 459–468.

Nelson, C. M., & Rutherford, R. B. (1983). Timeout revisited: Guidelines for its use in special education: *Exceptional Education Quarterly, 3,* 56–67.

Newman, R. (1963). The school-centered LSI as illustrated by external threat of school issues. *American Journal of Orthopsychiatry, 33,* 730–733.

O'Leary, K., & Becker, W. (1967). Behavior modification of an adjustment class: A token reinforcement program. *Exceptional Children 9,* 637–642.

O'Leary, K., & Drabman, R. (1971). Token reinforcement programs in the classroom: A review. *Psychological Bulletin, 75,* 379–398.

O'Leary, S., & Schneider, M. (1977). Special class placement of conduct problem children. *Exceptional Children, 43,* 24–30.

Osborne, S., Kibur, C., & Miller, S. (1986). Treatment of self-injurious behavior using self-control techniques with a severe behaviorally disordered adolescent. *Behavioral Disorders, 12,* 60–67.

Patterson, G. (1965). An application of conditioning techniques to the control of a hyperactive child. In L. Ullman & L. Krasner (Eds.), *Case studies in behavior modification*. New York: Holt, Rinehart & Winston.

Patterson, G., & Cobb, J. (1973). Stimulus control for classes of noxious behaviors. In J. Knutson (Ed.), *The control of aggression: Implications from basic research*. Chicago: Aldine.

Patterson, G., Reid, J., Jones, R., & Conger, R. (1975). *Families with aggressive children*. Eugene, OR: Castalia.

Phillips, E., Phillips, E., Wolfe, M., & Fixsen, D. (1975). Achievement place: Development of the elected manager system. In A. Graziano (Ed.), *Behavior therapy with children II*. Chicago: Aldine.

Phillips, E., Wolfe, M., Fixsen, D., & Bailey, J. (1976). The achievement place model: A community based, family style, behavior modification program for predelinquents. In E. Ribes-Inesta & A. Bandura (Eds.), *Analysis of delinquency and aggression*. Hillsdale, NJ: Lawrence Erlbaum.

Pizzat, F. (1973). *Behavior modification in residential treatment for children*. New York: Behavioral Publications.

Redl, F. (1959a). Strategy and techniques of the life space interview. *American Journal of Orthopsychiatry, 29*, 1–18.

Redl, F. (1959b). The concept of a therapeutic milieu. *American Journal of Orthopsychiatry, 29*, 721–736.

Redl, F., & Wineman, D. (1952). *Controls from within: Techniques for the treatment of the aggressive child*. New York: Free Press.

Robin, A., Schneider, M., & Dolnick, M. (1976). The Turtle Technique: An extended case study of self-control in the classroom. *Psychology in the Schools, 13*, 449–453.

Ruhl, K. L. (1985). Handling aggression: Fourteen methods teachers use. *The Pointer, 29*, 30–33.

Santogrossi, D. A., O'Leary, K. D., Romanczyk, R. G., & Kaufman, K. F. (1973). Self-evaluation of adolescents in a psychiatric hospital school token program. *Journal of Applied Behavior Analysis, 6*, 227–287.

Schloss, P., & Smith, M. (1987). Guidelines for ethical use of manual restraint in public school settings for behaviorally disordered students. *Behavioral Disorders, 12*, 207–213.

Smith, M. D. (1985). Managing the aggressive and self-injurious behavior of adults disabled by autism. *Journal of the Association for Persons with Severe Handicaps, 10*, 228–232.

Smith, S. W. & Farrell, D. T. (1993). Level system use in special education: Classroom intervention with prima facie appeal. *Behavioral Disorders, 18*(4), 251–264.

Smith, S. W., Siegel, E. M., O'Conner, A. M., & Thomas, S. B. (1994). Effects of cognitive-behavioral training on angry behavior and aggression of three elementary-aged students. *Behavioral Disorders, 19*(2), 126–135.

Snyder, J., & White, M. (1979). The use of cognitive self-instruction in the treatment of behaviorally disordered adolescents. *Behavior Therapy, 10*, 227–235.

Stahl, J., Fuller, E., Lefebre, M., & Burchard, J. (1979). The token economy community youth center: A model for programming peer reinforcement. In J. Stumphauzer (Ed.), *Progress in behavior therapy with delinquents*. Springfield, IL: Charles C. Thomas.

Talkington, K., & Altman, R. (1973). Effects of film-mediated aggression and affectual models on behavior. *American Journal of Mental Deficiency, 77*, 420–425.

Tarpley, H., & Schroeder, S. (1979). Comparison of DRO and DRI on rate of suppression of self-injurious behavior. *American Journal of Mental Deficiency, 84*, 188–194.

Thoresen, K., Thoresen, C., Klein, S., Wilbur, C., Packer-Haven, J., & Haven, W. (1979). Learning House: Helping troubled children and their parents change themselves. In J. Stumphauzer (Ed.), *Progress in behavior therapy with delinquents*. Springfield, IL: Charles C. Thomas.

Timmons-Mitchell, J. (1986). Containing aggressive acting out in abused children. *Child Welfare, 65*, 459–468.

Turkewitz, H., O'Leary, K. D., & Ironsmith, M. (1975). Generalization and maintenance of appropriate behavior through self-control. *Journal of Consulting and Clinical Psychology, 43*, 577–583.

Twyman, J., Johnson, H., Buie, J., & Nelson, C. M. (1994). The use of a warning procedure to signal a more intrusive time-out contingency. *Behavioral Disorders, 19*(4), 243–253.

Ulrich, R., Dulaney, S., Arnett, M., & Mueller, K. (1973). An experimental analysis of nonhuman and human aggression. In J. Knutson (Ed.), *The control of aggression: Implications from basic research.* Chicago: Aldine.

Wahler, R. G., & Fox, J. J. (1980). Solitary toy play and time out: A family treatment package for children and aggressive and oppositional behavior. *Journal of Applied Behavior Analysis, 13,* 23–29.

Wardle, C. (1974). Residential care of children with conduct disorders. In P. Barker (Ed.), *The residential psychiatric treatment of children.* New York: Wiley.

Wilson, C., Robertson, S., Herlong, L., & Haynes, S. (1979). Vicarious effects of time-out in the modification of aggression in the classroom. *Behavior Modification, 3,* 97–111.

Wilson, R. (1984). A review of self-control treatments for aggressive behavior. *Behavior Disorders, 9,* 131–140.

Wiltz, N., & Patterson, G. (1974). An evaluation of parent training procedures designed to alter inappropriate aggressive behaviors of boys. *Behavior Therapy, 5,* 215–221.

Wolf, M., Braukmann, C., & Ramp, K. (1987). Serious delinquent behavior as part of a significantly handicapping condition: Cures and supportive environments. *Journal of Applied Behavior Analysis, 20,* 347–359.

Wolfe, J. (1936). Effectiveness of token-rewards for chimpanzees. *Comparative Psychological Monographs, 12,* 60–65.

Wood, F. H., & Braaten, S. (1983). Developing guidelines for the use of punishing interventions in the schools. *Exceptional Education Quarterly, 3,* 68–75.

Yates, B., Haven, W., & Thoresen, C. (1979). Cost effectiveness analysis at Learning House: How much charge for how much money? In J. Stumphauzer (Ed.), *Progress in behavior therapy with delinquents.* Springfield, IL: Charles C. Thomas.

Yell, M. (1994). Time-out and students with behavior disorders: A legal analysis. *Education and Treatment of Children, 17*(3), 293–301.

Managing Socially Withdrawn Behavior

Advance Organizer

As you read this chapter, prepare to identify and discuss:

- Three common characteristics among socially withdrawn youngsters.
- Reasons that social withdrawal is a problem.
- Three different procedures for assessing and identifying socially withdrawn children.
- At least three peer-assisted options for working with withdrawn youngsters.
- Student-managed procedures for teaching socially withdrawn pupils to get along with others.
- General guidelines for selecting intervention strategies for working with socially withdrawn students.

LaChandra is a 7-year old socially withdrawn child. She rarely speaks out in class, and when she does, her voice is almost imperceptible. LaChandra seldom makes eye contact when she speaks and often tries to move away from those who approach her. During recess, she can be found playing by herself, usually in an isolated corner of the playground. In the cafeteria, she will sit at the same table as her classmates, yet rarely, if ever, interact with them. Her peers speak to one another continuously, pass snacks both in front of and around her, but seldom address her directly. LaChandra comes to school daily, making only a minimal amount of social contact.

Like many of the children we have discussed, LaChandra's behavior is disordered. Unlike other children with behavior disorders, however, she rarely comes to our attention; primarily because she seldom "bothers" anyone. In fact, LaChandra's parents, teachers, and peers doubt that anything is wrong with her. She is seen simply as a "shy little girl who is just not very outgoing." The most frequently heard advice is, "Don't worry, she'll grow out of it." Unfortunately, an accumulating body of evidence suggests that children like LaChandra do not "grow out of it" (e.g., Kerr & Nelson, 1989; Odom & DeKlyen, 1986; Odom, McConnell, & McEvoy, 1992; Strain, Guralnik, & Walker, 1986; Walker, 1995). Rather, data indicate that excessive social withdrawal may place such children "at risk" for later adjustment problems.

In this chapter, we will examine the nature of social withdrawal in childhood and its educational implications. We will describe a multimethod approach for identifying socially withdrawn children and review a variety of intervention alternatives for working with these youngsters. We will propose intervention options in three broad domains: (1) teacher-directed, (2) peer-assisted, and (3) student-managed and provide some general guidelines for selecting and evaluating intervention strategies for socially withdrawn children.

The Nature of Social Withdrawal

Social withdrawal or isolation refers to a *cluster of behaviors* that result in an individual's escaping or avoiding social contact (Kerr & Nelson, 1989; Kauffman, 1989). Withdrawal may be intentional, as in the extreme case of elective mutism; it may reflect a broader lack of interpersonal competence, such as is found among many people who are mentally retarded, psychotic, and/or autistic; or it may be maintained through a process of negative reinforcement. In the first and last instances, individuals actually possess the requisite skills to perform satisfactorily, but they fail to do so under existing environmental conditions; these youngsters exhibit *performance deficits* (Gresham & Elliot, 1984; Sheridan, 1995). Individuals from the remaining group, on the other hand, may have not learned the requisite skills necessary to engage in meaningful social interactions; these individuals have *social-skills deficits* (Gresham & Elliot, 1984; Sheridan, 1995). This distinction is very important because in each case the individual's problem is being maintained by different contingencies and therefore warrants different types of intervention.

According to Odom and DeKlyen (1986), withdrawn children share at least three common characteristics: (1) they spend an inordinate amount of time in solitary play; (2) they rarely engage in positive social interactions with peers; and (3) they seldom verbalize. For the most part, others rarely notice that these children are even around. To some adults, withdrawn youngsters are "ideal" children who do their best and never bother anyone. Why, then, do we classify these children as behavior disordered? Why must we develop strategies to improve their social relationships, and how do we go about doing so? These, and many similar questions, have only recently been asked.

Historically, social withdrawal was not considered a serious problem; that is, until two data bases prompted interest in the impact of social isolation on child development (Odom & DeKlyen, 1986). The first was research findings indicating that the consequences of untreated social withdrawal can be quite serious. McConnell and Odom (1986) reported, for example, that a failure to establish appropriate peer relationships in childhood was a good predictor of social adjustment problems later on: Socially withdrawn children are at greater risk for both juvenile delinquency (Roff, Sells, & Golden, 1972) and adult mental health problems (Robins, 1966). Similarly, Cobb (1972) found that children who interacted very infrequently with their peers demonstrated major deficits in three academic-related behaviors: attending to task, talking with peers about assignments, and compliance with requests. Kohn (1977), in a longitudinal study, reported that socially isolated preschoolers remained withdrawn through the fourth grade and performed more poorly academically than a matched group of aggressive children. More recently, participation in meaningful peer relationships has been equated with the development of childhood friendships. These friendship patterns, in turn, have been linked to growth in a variety of cognitive and social domains (Hurley-Geffner, 1995). It should be noted here that not everyone is convinced that social withdrawal poses a serious problem. Coie and Kupersmidt (1983), for instance, argue that many problems associated with withdrawn behavior will disappear as children grow older and increase their social contacts. While this may be true for some children, there is certainly no evidence to suggest that such outcomes are experienced by all or even most withdrawn youngsters.

The second data base that gave rise to concern about social withdrawal centers on the developmental significance of peer social interactions. As early as 1926, Piaget suggested that peer interactions promoted cognitive development among children by providing them with alternative cognitive perspectives. More recently, Guralnick (1981) noted that social encounters among young children may also promote communication skills. Peer social interactions provide an opportunity for children to engage in coequal verbal exchanges. These daily exchanges, in turn, provide ample opportunities for children to try out, receive feedback, and refine a variety of linguistic and nonverbal communicative skills. Finally, Hartup and Sancilio (1986) suggested that peer social interactions may also facilitate the acquisition of important social skills. For example, children may learn to share and work cooperatively, display acceptable responses to aggression, and acquire appropriate sex-role behavior. Children may also enhance their group entry skills, strengthen impulse control, and improve their understandings of self and others (Hartup & Sancilio, 1986).

In sum, current thinking suggests that children learn much from their social interactions with one another and that failure to engage in such social exchanges may limit their opportunity to learn important cognitive, communicative, and social behaviors. Chronic failure to interact may also place children with social withdrawal at risk for subsequent academic and interpersonal problems. So social withdrawal is a legitimate problem for educators. The next logical questions are: How many children experience social withdrawal? What are the causes of their failure to interact? How do we go about identifying and helping these youngsters?

Prevalence and Etiology

Determining how many children are socially withdrawn is a difficult task. This difficulty stems, in part, from the absence of a standard definition of social isolation. Prevalence estimates vary considerably as a function of what one believes constitutes socially withdrawn behavior. For example, Strain, Cooke, and Apolloni (1976) estimated that at least 15 percent of all children referred for psychological services show signs of social withdrawal. Direct observations of general education classrooms indicated that withdrawn children were 12.5 to 13.7 percent of all children observed (Coie, Dodge, & Coppotelli, 1982; Dodge, 1983; Dodge, Coie & Brakke, 1982). These prevalence estimates drop sharply, however, when low rates of social interaction are compared to local class norms. For example, using one standard deviation below the class mean rate of interaction as a cutoff point, researchers (Hops & Greenwood, 1981; Weinrott, Corson, & Wilchesky, 1979) identified 1 to 3 percent of the student population as withdrawn. One suspects that the latter figures most closely approximate the "true" number of withdrawn youngsters.

Given the rather large number of withdrawn children, how does this isolated behavior develop in the first place? A variety of explanations have been offered. Some have argued that withdrawn children never achieved an adequate emotional separation from their parents and therefore have remained insecure and unable to form lasting interpersonal ties (e.g., Bowlby, 1969; Erickson, 1963). Others speculate that withdrawn children may have had a series of negative social encounters with peers during their formative years that caused them to turn inward and refrain from social contacts. Still other theorists (Gottman, Gonso, & Rasmussen, 1975; Renshaw & Asher, 1982) suggest that many socially withdrawn children simply lack the requisite knowledge and/or social skills to successfully engage others. Because they have not been exposed to appropriate role models or received insufficient opportunities to learn critical social behaviors, these children failed to acquire the necessary skills to initiate and maintain social contacts and/or the knowledge of when and where to use such skills. In all likelihood, social withdrawal has multiple etiologies. Many withdrawn children probably did have early negative social experiences with either parents or peers, and these aversive encounters may have substantially reduced their willingness to engage others in social interaction. This diminished interaction pattern, in turn, may have resulted in substantially fewer opportunities to learn appropriate social behaviors.

Regardless of what causes social withdrawal, it is clear that classroom teachers must be prepared to teach these youngsters more appropriate ways of interacting socially. The consequences of failing to do so have already been described. Therefore, classroom teachers must be able to identify children as socially withdrawn and then to select an appropriate and effective form of intervention.

Identification of Social Withdrawal

As we noted earlier, withdrawn children are seldom noticed or referred for "special" assistance, because they rarely bother anyone (Walker, 1995). Thus, it may be necessary for educators to actively seek out such youngsters. It appears there is no one standard way to identify withdrawn children. On the contrary, the field is split among at least three camps, each advocating its own assessment methodology. We believe that all three perspectives offer valuable assessment information and that this information can be combined effectively into a comprehensive, multilevel, multimethod assessment approach (e.g., Odom, & DeKlyen, 1986; Walker, 1995).

Sociometric Approach

One group of researchers (e.g., Asher & Hymel, 1981) advocates the use of sociometric methods for identifying socially withdrawn children, on the premise that peers are the best judges of their classmates' social behavior. The logic behind sociometric identification is rather straightforward: Social withdrawal disrupts peer relationships, and this disruption should be reflected in sociometric ratings of withdrawn children.

Sociometric assessment includes a number of different procedures. The most commonly used method is *peer nomination*. In this procedure, peers are asked to name classmates (typically three) with whom they would like to participate in a specific activity (like to work with, play with, sit near, etc.). They are also asked to name classmates with whom they would not like to work or play. The number of times a particular child is nominated as a "liked" or "not liked" classmate is then tallied and comparisons are made between those children receiving the most and the least nominations. Socially withdrawn children characteristically receive very few nominations, either positive or negative. Figure 9.1 shows an example of a peer nomination form (Gronlund, 1959).

A second popular sociometric method is called *peer ratings*. This assessment procedure provides children with a listing of all their classmates' names and instructs them to rate each peer, using a Likert-type scale, on one or more criteria (e.g., play, work, or sit by). Numeric values are attached to each rating (e.g., 5 = "like a lot," 3 = "OK," and 1 = "do not like at all"). When assigned ratings for each child are totaled, teachers have a measure of the general level of acceptance for every child. An example of a peer sociometric rating scale is provided in Figure 9.2.

As shown in Figure 9.2, a question mark is also provided occasionally as an option for student raters who may either not know a particular child or be unable to reach a decision about a rating. It is also possible to substitute children's pictures for names when working with younger children (Asher, Singleton, Tinsley, & Hymel, 1979; Odom et al., 1992).

A third form of sociometrics is *paired comparisons*. Unlike nomination and rating scales, paired comparisons are seldom used by practitioners and researchers, primarily because of the time-consuming nature of the task. With this procedure, each child in a class is shown the pictures (or given the names) of two of their classmates. They must then choose one of the two for a stated criterion (e.g., "With which of the two children would you most like to work?"). All possible pairs of children are shown and the total number of choices for each child is tallied. Although this assessment method may yield the most reliable sociometric data, it is not clear that this improved sensitivity offsets the arduous data collection requirements (McConnell & Odom, 1986).

Odom and DeKlyen (1986) suggest that peer nominations offer the best potential for identifying socially withdrawn children. Using this procedure, social isolates

Name _____   Date _____

During the next few weeks, we will be changing our seats around, working in small groups and playing some group games. Now that we all know each other by name, you can help me arrange groups that work and play best together. You can do this by writing the names of the children you would like to have sit near you, to have work with you, and to have play with you. You may choose anyone in this room you wish, including those pupils who are absent. Your choices will not be seen by anyone else. Give first name and initial of last name. Make your choices carefully so the groups will be the way you really want them. I will try to arrange the groups so that each pupil gets at least two of his choices. Sometimes it is hard to give everyone his first few choices, so be sure to make five choices for each question.

Remember!
1. Your choices must be from pupils in this room, including those who are absent.
2. You should give the first name and the initial of the last name.
3. You should make all five choices for each question.
4. You may choose a pupil for more than one group if you wish.
5. Your choices will not be seen by anyone else.

I would choose to sit near these children:

1. _____   3. _____   5. _____

2. _____   4. _____

I would choose to work with these children:

1. _____   3. _____   5. _____

2. _____   4. _____

I would choose to play with these children:

1. _____   3. _____   5. _____

2. _____   4. _____

FIGURE 9.1   Sample Peer Nomination Form for Upper Elementary School Children

Source: Gronlund, 1959, p. 50.

can be identified as those who receive very few, if any, nominations—they are the children who are simply not chosen for any particular activity by their classmates. It is important, however, to contrast these youngsters with other "unpopular" children. For example, some investigators (Green, Vosk, Forehand, & Beck, 1981) labeled children who received no nominations as "neglected," and those who received a high number of negative nominations as "rejected" (Peery, 1979; Sheridan, 1995). Subsequent direct observations have revealed significant behavioral differences between these two groups of youngsters.

Perhaps the most innovative analysis of peer nomination scores to date was developed by Coie and colleagues (1982). These researchers computed two dimensions

Please rate how much you like each of the following:

		Don't Know	Like a Lot	OK	Don't Like At All
A.	Dog	(?)	☺	😐	☹
B.	Tiger	(?)	☺	😐	☹
C.	Monkey	(?)	☺	😐	☹
D.	Capybara	(?)	☺	😐	☹
E.	Cow	(?)	☺	😐	☹

Examples (label at left spanning rows A–E)

		Don't Know	Like a Lot	OK	Don't Like At All
1.	Jon B.	(?)	☺	😐	☹
2.	LaChandra S.	(?)	☺	😐	☹
3.	Tiffany R.	(?)	☺	😐	☹
4.	Jason C.	(?)	☺	😐	☹
5.	Marcus L.	(?)	☺	😐	☹
6.		(?)	☺	😐	☹
7.		(?)	☺	😐	☹
8.		(?)	☺	😐	☹
9.		(?)	☺	😐	☹
10.		(?)	☺	😐	☹

FIGURE 9.2   Sample Peer Sociometric Rating Scale

of social status. The first, social preference, was a measure of "liking" for an individual child. Preference was determined by subtracting the total number of negative nominations the child received from the total number of positive nominations. Coie and colleagues (1982) categorized children as popular if they had a high social preference score (e.g., 22 positive – 3 negative nominations = +19), and rejected if they had a low preference score (e.g., 6 positive – 15 negative = –9). The second dimension, social impact, measured a child's "visibility." Impact scores were computed by adding the number of positive and negative nominations a particular child received. Children were categorized as neglected (withdrawn) if they had low social impact scores (e.g., 1 positive + 0 negative nominations = +1), and controversial if they had a high social impact and both high positive and negative nominations (e.g., 8 positive + 8 negative nominations = 16). This analysis of peer nomination scores is quite important because it provides a clearer identification of neglected (withdrawn) children and distinguishes these youngsters from their rejected classmates.

Rate-of-Interaction Approach

Another way to identify socially withdrawn children is to observe their rates of social interaction with peers. The logic of this assessment approach is equally straightforward: Children who engage in consistently low rates of social interactions with their peers are functionally withdrawn from social contact. Rate of interaction is measured primarily through direct observation, usually during unstructured play or work time. Social interaction data may be reported in terms of the (1) rate of social interactions per minute, (2) total frequency of social interaction per standard observation sample, or (3) percentage of intervals during which interactions occurred (Odom & DeKlyen, 1986; Sheridan, 1995). Typically, observation data are collected on particular children presumed to be at risk, as well as on a randomly selected group of nondisabled classmates. Comparisons are then made between these groups to see if the target child's interaction rates differ significantly from their classmates. In essence, the peer groups' social behavior provides a standard or "local" norm against which the socially withdrawn child's behavior is compared.

Unfortunately, daily classroom rates of social interaction have not been developed to date. One large-scale observational study of young children in free-play settings (Greenwood et al., 1981), however, did collect over six hours of data per child across twenty-seven classroom settings. The average social interaction rates per minute were .51 for 3-year olds, .64 for 4-year olds, .62 for 5-year olds, .63 for 6-year olds, and .68 for 7-year olds. Social interaction rates were consistently higher among boys than among girls across all age groups: Mean interaction rates of .68 and .58 were reported for boys and girls, respectively.

Greenwood, Todd, Hops, and Walker (1982) later examined the use of rate-of-interaction measures for identifying socially withdrawn preschoolers. First, they established a global interaction rate to identify high, middle, and low interactors (the mean rates of interaction were 1.00, .46, and .14, respectively). Next, they used a more fine-grained analysis to examine "qualitative" aspects of children's social behavior. They found that low interactors (1) initiated fewer positive interactions, (2) received fewer social initiations from peers, (3) responded less frequently to peers' initiations, and (4) verbalized significantly less often than their peers. Moreover, these youngsters spent more time in solitary play, observed but failed to join in group activities, and interacted more often with adults. Interestingly, the low interactors also engaged in fewer negative social interactions than either their middle- or high-interaction counterparts.

Psychometric Approach

The third major approach to identifying socially withdrawn children involves the use of parent and/or teacher behavior and/or social skills rating scales. There are presently a number of teacher and parent rating scales that include social withdrawal or some related categorization (e.g., anxious, nervous). Significant among these scales are the Child Behavior Checklist (Achenbach, 1991), the Social Skills Rating Scale (SSRS) (Gresham & Elliot, 1990), the School Social Behavior Scales (SSBS) (Merrell, 1993), and the Walker Problem Behavior Identification Checklist (Walker, 1983). Typically, rating scales are completed by significant others (i.e., parents and/or teachers), and scores are derived on particular factors or dimensions. If a student's score on a specific dimension lies significantly beyond established norms, pathology is indicated. Although the developers of all these rating scales have not collected observational data to substantiate child behavior in in vivo settings (e.g., at school or at home), the psychometric qualities (reliability, validity, and adequacy of the normative sample) of these scales are typically quite good (Odom & DeKlyen, 1986; Walker, 1995).

Collectively, the three diverse approaches for identifying socially withdrawn children provide teachers with a variety of good assessment options. Odom and DeKlyen (1986) argue, however, that no single approach is sufficient for identifying withdrawn pupils. Instead, they have proposed a multilevel, multimethod assessment approach.

Multilevel, Multimethod Assessment Approach

Odom and DeKlyen (1986) advanced a comprehensive assessment approach that is both multilevel and multimethod. This approach is multilevel in that it first conducts assessments at a screening level to identify at-risk youngsters and then provides more in-depth evaluations to confirm withdrawal as a major behavioral disorder. This system is multimethod in that it utilizes teacher and/or parent behavior rating scales, peer sociometric measures, and direct observations of students' interaction patterns. Similar assessment methods were described in some detail in Chapter 4 under the rubric of multi-gating evaluation procedures (e.g., Walker & Severson, 1990; Walker, Severson, & Feil, 1995). It should be noted, for example, that the Systematic Screening for Behavior Disorders (SSBD) is designed specifically for identifying children with internalizing types of behavior disorders. What follows, here, is a brief description of how a generalized multilevel, multimethod assessment approach would work.

Initially, a large number of students would be screened for possible behavior disorders. Since direct observation would be extremely time-consuming for either teachers or consultants, it would probably be more feasible to begin with teacher rating scales and/or rankings of social interaction rates. In addition to being cost-efficient, these measures appear to be quite accurate. For example, Greenwood, Walker and their colleagues (Feil & Becker, 1993; Greenwood, Walker & Hops, 1977; Greenwood et al., 1979; Walker, 1995) have found that teachers are quite good at identifying the most socially withdrawn children in their classrooms. These researchers first asked teachers to rank the students in their classes in terms of frequency of verbal interaction and popularity and then to rate their social behavior. In addition, direct observations and positive peer nominations were collected. Teachers' rankings and ratings of children's social behavior were correlated moderately with direct observations of children's social behavior. More importantly, teachers could identify reliably, by rating and rankings, the least socially interactive and verbal children in the class. Greenwood, Todd, Walker, & Hops (1978) subsequently developed an assessment measure, the Social Assessment Manual for Preschool Level (SAMPLE) that provides a useful screening technique for preschoolers.

Once a child has been identified as at risk, a more comprehensive evaluation is undertaken to confirm the presence of the problem. Many researchers (e.g., Hops & Greenwood, 1981; McConnell & Odom, 1986; Odom et al., 1992; Sheridan, 1995; Walker, 1995) have recommended that at least two or three independent sources of information be collected to confirm the presence of disordered behavior. Three possible sources of information are peer sociometric nominations, direct observational data on important social behavior (e.g., rates of social initiations, responses to peer initiations and verbalizations), and teacher rating scales that contain both negative and positive social behavior. For precise identification, Odom and DeKlyen (1986) recommend that agreement should occur across at least two of these three measures. That is, socially withdrawn children should exhibit low rates of positive and negative social interactions with peers, evidence very low social impact scores on peer nomination measures, and/or receive a low social interaction ranking or high "social withdrawal" rating from their classroom teachers. School personnel could also use instruments such as the SSBD to routinely screen for youngsters who fail to interact at appropriate rates with their peers.

Intervention Options

Despite the relative inattention paid to withdrawn children, a wide variety of intervention strategies have been developed to address their pervasive lack of social responsiveness. These strategies span a variety of theoretical perspectives (e.g., psychoeducational, social learning, and behavioral) and are available from diverse groups of professionals (educators, counselors, psychiatrists, school psychologists, and social workers). Moreover, these intervention approaches differ substantially in both the quantity and the quality of supporting data.

It is safe to say that no one treatment approach is universally effective with socially withdrawn children. Here we offer a set of potentially useful interventions as instructional options for educators who wish to improve the social competence of their withdrawn pupils. The ultimate effectiveness of any proposed intervention can only be determined by examining its effects upon targeted students' performance.

To facilitate our discussion, we have categorized intervention options into three broad domains: teacher-directed, peer-assisted, and student-managed (see Table 9.1). It should be recognized that all intervention approaches contain some elements of teacher or adult involvement; our categorization of these strategies is designed merely to highlight the primary individual(s) involved in carrying out the intervention. Finally, it is beyond the scope of this chapter to review all the available social-skills interventions. Interested readers are referred to other excellent reviews for additional information (e.g., Conger & Keane, 1981; Gresham & Elliot, 1989; Hops, 1982; Sheridan, 1995; Strain & Kerr, 1981).

Teacher-Directed Interventions

Most strategies designed to increase the social responsiveness of withdrawn children have incorporated a substantial role for classroom teachers or other adult caretakers. The logic of this approach is quite clear. Classroom teachers are in a unique position to structure learning environments in ways that increase social interaction. They are also in an excellent position to recognize and reward prosocial interactions when they occur. In this section, we examine four instructional options that require substantial teacher involvement: (1) structuring physical settings, (2) teacher prompting and reinforcement, (3) social-learning approaches (modeling and social coaching), and (4) "packaged" social-skills curricular approaches.

Structuring Physical Settings

Observational research suggests that how physical environments are structured will have a substantial effect on the quantity and quality of work that students produce and the frequency and nature of their social interactions (e.g., Paine, Radicchi, Rosellini, Deutchman, & Darch, 1983; Sainato & Carta, 1992; Schloss & Sedlack,

TABLE 9.1   Instructional Options for Working with Socially Withdrawn Students

Teacher-Directed Options	Peer-Assisted Options	Student-Managed Options
Structure and management of physical setting	Peer imitation training	Self-observation
Teacher prompting and reinforcement	Peer social initiation	Self-monitoring

Social-learning approaches
    Modeling
    Social coaching
	Peer prompting and reinforcement	Self-evaluation

Packaged social skills curricula	Group-oriented contingencies and cooperative learning	
	Peer tutoring	

1986; Wolery, Bailey, & Sugai, 1989). At the most basic level, learning environments may be structured in ways that promote both academic and social competence. Occasionally, we may have to decide which skills to emphasize at a particular time, but one thing is clear: Withdrawn children will not become more socially competent if we do not provide them with sufficient opportunities to learn appropriate interpersonal behavior.

Teachers have a number of options when structuring their classrooms to promote social interaction. First, the seating patterns and arrangement of classroom furniture will influence the amount and perhaps types of interaction that occur. Students tend to engage in more social interactions, for example, when they are grouped in close proximity and are facing one another. To ensure that such increased social interaction is both positive and constructive, teachers should use functional classroom rules that explicitly state the kinds and amounts of social interaction that are permissible. Second, teachers should schedule daily opportunities for students to work together. During academic periods, these may involve peer tutoring and/or cooperative learning tasks. Unstructured play and cleanup times also provide opportunities for increased interactions (Sainato & Carta, 1992). Cooperative and team-oriented games that involve all students may be beneficial here. Research also suggests that the types of toys and games that are made available will also influence children's interaction patterns. For example, Stoneman, Cantrell, and Hoover-Dempsey (1983) found that children were much more likely to play with others when certain toys (e.g., blocks, vehicles, water) were present than when more "solitary" toys were available. Increased social interactions were noted as well when toys were placed in close proximity to one another.

A third instructional option teachers may use to promote prosocial interaction involves "status" roles, that is, teachers place children in particular roles that increase either their "visibility" or their "status" within the classroom. For example, Sainato, Maheady, and Shook (1986) assigned three socially withdrawn children to the rotating role of "toy manager." The toy manager's primary "job" was to distribute toys to all classmates just before unstructured play time and to collect them at the end of each play session. Since all students were required to interact with the manager when requesting and returning toys, the sheer number of social contacts with the withdrawn children increased substantially. Moreover, toys were dispensed and collected in an orderly fashion. Data indicated that socially withdrawn children's social status and interaction patterns improved greatly while they were in the manager's role. Follow-up assessments revealed that these social gains dissipated somewhat when the children were no longer managers, but that they remained significantly higher than baseline levels.

Another status role that teachers may wish to examine is that of peer tutor. The notion here is that socially withdrawn children may improve their social status and interaction patterns if they get involved in an ongoing tutoring relationship. This may proceed in a number of ways. Children may be asked to tutor either a younger, less-skilled student (cross-age tutoring) or a less academically competent classmate (same-age tutoring). Similarly, a variety of classwide peer tutoring programs are now available to engage all pupils within a particular class in ongoing tutoring relationships. Moreover, these systems frequently involve reciprocal tutoring components and offer pupils the opportunity to work with most if not all of their classmates throughout the school year (see for example, King-Sears & Bradley, 1995; Maheady, Harper, & Mallette, 1991). Serving as a tutor not only carries some prestige, but also provides additional opportunities to engage in social interactions. Another possibility is pairing a socially withdrawn student with a social "star" for ongoing tutoring sessions. Maheady and Sainato (1985) found that the social status and interpersonal interactions of "rejected" students was enhanced substantially while they were working with high-status classmates. Peers' positive initiations, in particular, increased greatly during the tutoring sessions. If such social gains accrue for sociometrically rejected youngsters, one might reasonably expect comparable improvements among individuals who are socially isolated.

Teacher Prompting and Reinforcement
Providing verbal praise or adult attention (i.e., social reinforcement) after a social exchange occurs is another commonly used intervention for socially withdrawn children. In the first controlled study, Allen, Hart, Buell, Harris, and Wolf (1964) provided adult attention to a socially withdrawn preschooler whenever she interacted with her peers. The amount of time the young girl spent interacting with other children increased from 20 to 60 percent of observed intervals. In a later study, Hart, Reynolds, Baer, Brawley, and Harris (1968) demonstrated that the contingent nature of adults' attention to a child's cooperative play behavior was the controlling aspect of the intervention strategy. Subsequent replications involving both disabled and nondisabled withdrawn children have reaffirmed the powerful and immediate effects of contingent teacher attention (McEvoy, Odom, & McConnell, 1992). The primary implication for classroom teachers is that they should attempt to "catch withdrawn youngsters being good"; that is, recognize them when they are interacting in an appropriate social manner with their peers.

Other researchers (e.g., Cooke & Apolloni, 1976; Strain, Shores, & Kerr, 1976; Walker, Hops, Greenwood, & Todd, 1979) have attempted to increase specific qualitative behaviors (rather than the general interaction rate) of children. Cooke and Apolloni (1976), for example, used contingent social praise to teach four prosocial behaviors—verbal compliments, smiling, sharing, and positive physical contact—to socially withdrawn, learning-disabled students. Interestingly, they found that as they learned smiling, some children also increased their sharing and positive contact with peers without teacher prompting. Furthermore, other, nontrained withdrawn children in the same play sessions increased their sharing as well. These instances of response generalization and a "spillover" of treatment effects (i.e., increases in social interactions among nontrained children) were replicated in another study involving three socially withdrawn and behaviorally handicapped preschoolers (Strain et al., 1976). Walker and colleagues (1979) used adult praise and tokens to reinforce three types of social behavior: Starting (beginning interaction with a peer), Answering (responding to peers), and Continuing (extending the social interaction). Their intention was to evaluate the effects of reinforcing different behaviors upon the total amount of social interaction, but they found that the most effective way to increase total interaction was to reinforce all three target behaviors simultaneously. Finally, Lindeman, Fox, and Redelheim (1993) demonstrated the effectiveness of "double prompting" (i.e., prompting and reinforcing target children and peers) and of booster sessions as techniques for increasing and maintaining withdrawn preschoolers' peer interactions.

The preceding discussion is not meant to imply that adult prompting and reinforcement are without problems. On the contrary, Odom and DeKlyen (1986) have delineated three specific problems associated with such approaches. First, adult prompting and reinforcement techniques have not produced reliable social gains that generalize across settings or time, although some success has been noted when systematic fading procedures and/or booster training sessions are used (e.g., Timm, Strain, & Eller, 1979; Paine et al., 1982; Lindeman et al., 1993). Second, adult reinforcement often disrupts the natural reciprocity that occurs during social exchanges and therefore interferes with the development of extended social interactions. Finally, there has been a failure to assess the effects of reinforcement interventions on students' sociometric status or their satisfaction. In effect, although we know that these techniques lead withdrawn children to increase their rates of interaction, we have not documented consistently that such changes are socially important.

Social-Learning Approaches

According to social-learning theory, social skills instruction should contain at least three training objectives: (1) to enhance skill concepts (knowledge changes), (2) to promote skillful performance (behavior changes), and (3) to foster skill maintenance and generalization (Ladd & Mize, 1983). Although not all interventions grouped under the social-learning perspective incorporate these components, most treatments do reflect the convergence of cognitive and behavioral psychology. Social-learning approaches have been used quite extensively with socially withdrawn youngsters. The two broad treatment strategies employed most often are modeling and social coaching.

Modeling.   Observational learning (learning through observation and imitating the successful performance of other children) is a cornerstone of the social-learning approach (Odom & DeKlyen, 1986). O'Connor (1969) conducted one of the first modeling studies with socially withdrawn children. He showed socially withdrawn preschoolers a narrated videotape of children playing cooperatively with their peers and receiving reinforcement for doing so. In a later play period, the children who had watched the film interacted significantly more often with peers than a comparable group of children who had not seen the film. O'Connor (1972) later replicated these social improvements with another group of withdrawn preschoolers. In this investigation, increased social interaction rates were maintained across a three-week follow-up period.

Because modeling represented a cost-efficient mode of intervention and possessed such potentially powerful effects, O'Connor's studies prompted numerous replications and/or modifications. Odom and DeKlyen (1986) summarized a number of practical implications from this line of research. First, modeling appears to be most effective with children who are interested in playing with peers, that is, children responded well to modeling if peers had reinforcing value for them (Gresham & Nagle, 1980). Second, the effectiveness of modeling seemed to be independent of teachers' social reinforcement (attention) for the occurrence of social behavior (Evers & Schwartz, 1973). This finding is important because it shows that the reciprocal nature of the social exchanges may be reinforcing enough to maintain ongoing interactions and, therefore, substantial teacher involvement may not be necessary. Third, modeling effects where enhanced by using children as opposed to adults as narrators in the modeling films (Jakibchuk & Smeriglio, 1976). Finally, modeling could be used to train specific social behaviors as well as to increase general levels of interaction. Keller and Carlson (1974), for instance, found significant increases in behaviors that children had exhibited most frequently before treatment, suggesting that modeling may affect skill performance more than skill acquisition (Odom & DeKlyen, 1986). To take an example, children who already know how to play cooperatively, but fail to do so regularly (i.e., performance deficit), may be more likely to play cooperatively after watching a modeling film. However, if these same students do not know how to play cooperatively (i.e., skill deficit), they probably won't start doing so simply as a result of watching a film.

Modeling studies have been criticized on a number of grounds. The most relevant criticisms for practitioners are that modeling studies have been done primarily with mildly withdrawn children, have focused on a limited number of outcome measures, and have been conducted almost exclusively with preschool and primary grade-level children. It is significant that very few modeling studies have been carried out with children between the ages of 9 and 16.

Social Coaching.   The second major social-learning strategy is social coaching. Oden and Asher (1977) designed one of the first social-coaching interventions for withdrawn children. In it, children were taught behavioral strategies through verbal discussion and role-playing, given the opportunity to practice these skills with peers, and instructed to use these strategies in subsequent play sessions and then report verbally to the teacher on how their classmates responded to them. Oden and Asher found that socially withdrawn children's social status improved significantly after coaching, and that these status gains were maintained across a one-year time period. However, no detectable changes were noted in the children's overt social behavior.

Ladd (1981) later extended Oden and Asher's social-coaching intervention in another study with socially withdrawn youngsters. Here again, children were trained through verbal instruction and role-playing. But they then practiced their social interaction skills in a game format and were provided with feedback on their performance. Finally, they were instructed to use their newly acquired skills in natural settings with both familiar and unfamiliar peers, report back to the "coach," and generate alternative strategies for using these skills should failure occur. Once again, social coaching produced beneficial effects. Withdrawn children who had received the coaching improved significantly in two out of three social behaviors and received higher sociometric ratings than children in two comparison control groups.

Not all social-coaching experiments have been successful, however. For example, LaGreca and Santogrossi (1980) and Oden and Asher (1977) failed to find significant improvements in both sociometric status and overt social behavior. Moreover, social coaching has been used only with limited populations. The efficacy of these procedures with younger or older withdrawn children must still be documented.

Packaged Social-Skills Curricula

Although researchers have confirmed the effectiveness of a number of interventions for treating social withdrawal, it is highly unlikely that classroom teachers will use any of these strategies regularly unless they are packaged into a user-friendly format. Luckily, a number of treatment packages and social-skills curricula have become available commercially in recent years. Although these commercially available packages differ substantially in terms of their theoretical foundations, the specific social skills that are taught, and the empirical support underlying their use, they share a number of common elements:

1. They all use modeling to introduce new social skills.
2. They all provide ample practice opportunities via role-playing and behavioral rehearsal.
3. They all supply performance feedback.
4. They all require some "homework" component along with self-monitoring of performance in real-life situations.

Only those treatment packages that have applicability to socially withdrawn children will be reviewed here. Readers interested in other social-skills curricula are referred to the following excellent sources: Epstein & Cullinan (1987), Kerr & Nelson (1989), and Neel (1984). Specific information on target populations, social skills taught, and materials contained in each of the six treatment packages described can be found in Table 9.2.

The first three treatment packages listed on Table 9.2—PEERS, SCIPPY, and ACCEPTS—can be classified primarily as behaviorally oriented interventions, for these programs emerged from systematic lines of empirical research with behavior-disordered youth. The most relevant treatment package for socially withdrawn children is the PEERS program—Procedures for Establishing Relationships Skills (Hops et al., 1978)—which was designed for use by a classroom consultant and a teacher. PEERS contains assessment procedures for initially identifying withdrawn children, a series of social-skills tutoring sessions for teaching several target behaviors (e.g., Starting, Answering, Continuing), a set of joint practice activities with nondisabled peers, a recess point system, and a student self-report procedure. PEERS has been used effectively to increase the social interaction rates of withdrawn children (Hops, Walker, & Greenwood, 1979).

TABLE 9.2 Major Social-Skills Curricula

Name of Program	Target Population	Materials Description	Training Format	Evidence of Effectiveness
1. Procedures for Establishing Relationship Skills (PEERS) (Hops et al., 1978)	Socially withdrawn elementary-aged children.	Consultant-mediated program. Assessment procedures; training manual; teacher scripts for teaching three target behaviors (i.e., Starting, Answering, and Continuing); joint activities between withdrawn and nondisabled children; recess point system; self-report procedure.	Based on a direct-instruction model. Skills are clearly defined and sequenced; examples and nonexamples of target skills are provided. Structured opportunities for practice are given as well as a recess point system. Corrective feedback is available throughout the program.	PEERS has been used effectively to increase the rate of social interaction among socially withdrawn children (Hops et al., 1979).
2. Social Competence Intervention Package for Preschool Youngsters (SCIPPY) (Day, Powell & Stowitschek, 1980).	Preschool handicapped and nonhandicapped children who are socially withdrawn.	Teacher-directed, peer-mediated program. Training manual; procedures for identifying appropriate candidates for treatment; detailed training scripts for target students and peer confederates; detailed descriptions of a variety of play activities.	Based on a direct-instruction model. Primary focus on teaching Starting, Answering and Continuing social behaviors. Heavy use of prompting and reinforcement techniques. Social skills are practiced via a variety of play and classroom activities.	SCIPPY was used to significantly increase the frequency of specific social behaviors of socially withdrawn handicapped children (Day et al., 1982).
3. A Children's Curriculum for Effective Peer and Teacher Skills (ACCEPTS) (Walker et al., 1983)	Handicapped children in grades K–6.	Primary goal is to prepare students to enter and succeed in mainstream settings. Twenty-eight skills are taught within five content areas: classroom skills; basic interaction skills; getting along; making friends; and coping skills. Training manual, videotapes, teaching scripts, and behavior management procedures.	Based on a direct-instruction format. Instructional format permits one-to-one small- or large-group instruction. Program can be completed in five to ten weeks. Program includes pretest.	Evaluation study found handicapped children receiving ACCEPTS training were rated higher on peer-to-peer skills, increased appropriate social interactions, decreased isolate play and reduced inappropriate behaviors (Walker et al., 1983).

(Continued)

TABLE 9.2 *Continued*

Name of Program	Target Population	Materials Description	Training Format	Evidence of Effectiveness
4. Getting Along with Others (Jackson, Jackson & Monroe, 1982).	Geared primarily toward nondisabled elementary-aged pupils. Authors suggest that program can be adapted for other populations.	Two major components: program guide and skills lessons. Seventeen "core" social skills are taught. A five-tape video series is available. Program also includes scripted skill lessons, homework sheets, home notes, relaxation exercises, and sample role-play scenarios.	Individual skills lessons follow a similar format: labeling and defining skills to be taught, demonstrated instances and noninstances of skills, role-play practice exercises, rationale review for skill use, and trouble-shooting if problems arise.	Evaluation data suggest that program is successful with children referred to special education and mental health clinics for social-skills deficits (Epstein & Cullinan, 1987).
5a. Structured Learning: Skillstreaming the Elementary Aged Child (McGinnis, et al., 1984)	a. Nondisabled and disabled students in grades K–6.	a. Sixty social skills are taught in five skills groups; classroom survival skills; friendship making; skills for dealing with feelings; alternatives to aggression; and skills for dealing with stress.	Modeling, role-playing performance, feedback and transfer of training exercises are basic components of both programs. After skills are selected, all lessons follow the same seven-step format.	Goldstein, Sprafkin, Gershaw, & Klein (1980) reported that several evaluative studies conducted with structured learning have produced favorable social effects. Data on the "elementary" version were not located.
b. Skillstreaming the Adolescent (Goldstein et al., 1980)	b. Nondisabled students in grades 7–12.	b. Fifty social skills grouped into six categories: beginning social skills; advanced social skills; dealing with feelings; alternatives to aggression; dealing with stress; and planning skills.		

6. Asset: A Social-Skills Program for Adolescents (Hazel, Schumaker, Sherman, & Sheldon-Wildgen, 1982)	Designed for adolescents in grades 6–12. Program functions best with groups of 5–8 students.	An asset manual, nine lesson plans, skills sheets, home notes, checklists, consent forms, and questionnaires. Nine videotaped displays of targeted social skills. Eight areas of social skills are taught; giving positive and negative feedback, accepting negative feedback, resisting peer pressure, problem solving, negotiation, following instructions, and conversation.	Each session follows the same format: review of home notes; review or previously learned skills; presentation and discussion of targeted skills; work on skill sheets; verbal rehearsal; role-playing; feedback; criterion role plays; and assignment of home notes.	According to Epstein & Cullinan (1987), initial evaluation data on asset indicate that it has been used successfully.

SCIPPY—Social Competence Intervention Package for Preschool Youngsters—is a teacher-directed treatment package that was also developed for disabled and nondisabled withdrawn preschoolers. SCIPPY contains a number of components similar to those used in PEERS, but differs in that the teacher alone is responsible for implementation. Detailed instructional procedures describe prompting and reinforcement techniques. Additional training enlists the help of peers in carrying out practice activities. Evaluation studies conducted by the authors indicate that SCIPPY can be used effectively to increase specific social behaviors of withdrawn handicapped children (Day, Powell, & Stowitschek, 1980; Day et al., 1982).

The third behavioral treatment package, ACCEPTS—A Children's Curriculum for Effective Peer and Teacher Skills (Walker et al., 1983)—is perhaps the most widely known intervention. Although this program was designed primarily for mildly handicapped students enrolled in mainstream elementary classrooms, it can also be used with socially withdrawn children. ACCEPTS contains both classroom and peer-to-peer skill components. The peer-skills component, which has the most relevance for withdrawn youngsters, contains four major skill groups: (1) basic interactional skills (e.g., eye contact, audible voice); (2) getting along (e.g., sharing, using polite words); (3) making friends (e.g., smiling, complimenting); and (4) coping (e.g., when someone tries to hurt you). All social skills are taught through a direct-instruction format. An evaluation study conducted by Walker and his colleagues (1983) indicated that students trained with ACCEPTS interacted more appropriately in free–play settings, engaged in solitary play less often, and decreased the frequency of their inappropriate behavior.

The three remaining interventions—Getting Along with Others, Structured Learning, and Asset—are more accurately described as social-skills training curricula than as behavioral treatment packages. Although they share many of the data-based procedures inherent in the first three programs, they diverge somewhat from the strict behavioral model by incorporating a variety of "cognitive" components. (In this sense, these programs more closely resemble social-learning approaches.) Moreover, the latter three programs appear to focus more attention on the development of a wider range of social behaviors. Structured Learning, for example, focuses on dealing with feelings and stress; Asset concentrates on problem solving, following instructions, and negotiation; and Getting Along with Others addresses "joining a conversation," "ignoring-attending-praising others," and social problem solving. All three programs come neatly packaged with an assortment of training manuals, videotapes, structured practice activities, and strategies for teaching when and where to use specific skills. The findings of evaluation studies conducted to date, primarily by the developers of each system, have been quite favorable. It should be noted, however, that no systematic investigations with socially withdrawn youngsters have yet been undertaken. More recently, Sheridan (1995) described three different "levels" at which social skills training can occur; that is, small group, classwide, and schoolwide, and provided detailed instructions for implementing each variation within school settings.

Like other teacher-directed interventions, packaged social-skills training programs have their problems. Lovitt (1987) noted three that are particularly relevant for practitioners. First, efficacy data on social-skills training programs have not kept pace with the rapid proliferation of materials. Therefore, many treatment packages have been marketed in the absence of data showing that they work. Second, there is still some concern over *what* is being taught in social-skills training programs (i.e., content) and *how* it is being taught. At least two concerns emerge regarding which social skills to teach. One is that some social-skills training programs come without pretests and teachers are urged to instruct *all* skills. This approach fails to recognize that all students may not need to learn all, or perhaps even most, of the targeted social behaviors. Secondly, many of the instructed behaviors may not be socially important. Thus, students may improve in their use of these specific skills, but such skill usage may be unrelated to others' perceptions of their social competence.

Equally troublesome are concerns over how these programs teach social skills. On the theory that social skills cannot be taught in the same regimented fashion as academic skills, some critics have argued that establishing regular schedules for teaching social skills and engaging students in carefully sequenced role plays is artificial. They suggested, instead, that social behavior be infused throughout daily school experiences and that instruction capitalize on "naturally occurring" social interactions. The latter point is related closely to Lovitt's final concern: Where does social-skills training fit into an already crowded academic schedule? We cannot hope to develop improved social competence if social-skills training is perceived as another add-on instructional requirement.

Peer-Assisted Interventions

In addition to the adult-led instructional options we have just discussed, classroom teachers have a number of peer-mediated interventions from which to choose when working with withdrawn youngsters. Using peers as systematic behavior-change agents is a relatively recent development in behavioral psychology, yet one that has grown remarkably over the years. Entire volumes now offer suggestions for incorporating peers into social-skills training (e.g., Strain, Guralnick, & Walker, 1986). Here we will examine three peer-mediated strategies for young and/or more severely involved youngsters—peer imitation training, peer social initiation, and peer prompting and reinforcement—and two interventions for older and/or more mildly handicapped students—group-oriented contingencies and peer tutoring/cooperative learning.

Peer Imitation Training
In peer imitation training, a classmate of a socially withdrawn child is asked to help teach that child specific social behaviors. Typically, this classmate models selected social behaviors—for example, making requests, offering verbal comments and sharing—for the withdrawn peer. The target child is then asked by an adult trainer to imitate this behavior. If the withdrawn child does so upon request, he or she is reinforced with praise and affectionate pats from the adult trainer. If the target child fails to imitate the modeled behavior, the trainer physically prompts the

desired response. These procedures are repeated over a predetermined number of trials, with physical guidance gradually being faded and successive approximations continuing to be reinforced. When the target child successfully imitates the peer model without prompting, training is moved to a less structured setting (e.g., a playtime situation). Systematic prompting and reinforcement procedures are repeated here *if* the withdrawn child fails to imitate the peer model.

In one of the few studies conducted on peer imitation training, Cooke, Cooke, and Apolloni (1978) reported substantial increases in the verbal interactions of young children with mental retardation after exposure to nonretarded models. The authors suggested further that peer imitation training is most effective when used in the most natural setting possible, preferably an integrated classroom. Kerr and Nelson (1989) noted that it is very important to select an "effective" peer model. They recommended selecting students who attend school regularly, display frequent appropriate social skills with others, can imitate and follow verbal instructions well, and can concentrate on training tasks for *at least* ten minutes per training session.

Because peer imitation training requires the presence of an adult, it is rather labor intensive and therefore may need to be reserved for more severely withdrawn youngsters. Its advantage is that it appears to be quite flexible and can be used to teach a variety of social, preacademic, and/or self-help skills.

Peer Social Initiation

A second peer-mediated strategy is peer social initiation training (James & Egel, 1986; Odom & Strain, 1984; Strain, Shores, & Timm, 1977). When using this procedure, the teacher typically trains a nondisabled peer (although developmentally delayed children have been used) to direct social initiations to a socially withdrawn child. For example, the peer may make a play suggestion (e.g., "Let's play") or offer to share something with the withdrawn classmate (e.g., "Do you want to hold my truck?"). These initial social bids are designed to draw the withdrawn child into social interaction. During the intervention, adults do not prompt or reinforce the social behavior of the withdrawn child, though they do remain close by to prompt the peer trainer if necessary. According to Odom and DeKlyen (1986), peer initiations are used instead of adult reinforcement because this is a more "natural" way to acquire social skills, no disruption occurs in the ongoing social interaction pattern, and this strategy may promote generalization more readily.

In the initial study, Strain and co-workers (1977) taught peer "confederates" to make social initiations to six socially withdrawn preschoolers. The children were divided into two play groups (called "triads) and a different peer trainer was assigned to each group. When peer trainers began to make social initiations within their groups, the social initiation rates of five out of six withdrawn children increased substantially. These treatment effects have been replicated in a number of subsequent studies (e.g., Hendrickson, Strain, Tremblay, & Shores, 1982; Ragland, Kerr, & Strain, 1978).

Like peer imitation training, the social initiation intervention can be labor intensive. Although adults need not be present to prompt and reinforce withdrawn children, they may have to assist peer trainers (at least initially). Moreover, Kerr and Nelson (1989) found that the first few days of peer social initiation training may be particularly trying. They note, for example, that isolated children may ignore or overtly resist (e.g., by tantrumming) their peer's social bids. Both teacher and peer trainer must be prepared to handle this rejection. Kerr and Nelson recommend that the peer trainer continue initiating and that, if necessary, the teacher intervene by prompting and reinforcing the withdrawn child. Fortunately, the "difficult period" generally lasts no more than four or five sessions; after that, pupils usually cooperate and enjoy their interactions.

Peer Prompting and Reinforcement

A third, closely related strategy is peer prompting and reinforcement (Strain, Kerr, & Ragland, 1979; Strain & Timm, 1974). This strategy requires a peer trainer to assist withdrawn children in playing with one another. The peer trainer initially prompts one child to interact (beginning with a verbal prompt and escalating to physical guidance if necessary) and then verbally reinforces the withdrawn children for interacting. The procedure continues until the target children are interacting without prompts. Afterward, training is moved to less structured situations.

Only limited research has been conducted on peer prompting and reinforcement to date, but the initial evidence is quite promising (see, e.g., Strain et al., 1979; Strain & Timm, 1974). Kerr and Nelson (1989) recommend that this strategy be used as a follow-up to peer social initiation training and that different playmates be introduced gradually over time. They suggest further that at least four twenty-minute sessions are necessary to prepare peer trainers and that isolated children should be part of the training right from the start.

Two other peer-mediated options are available to classroom teachers. Group-oriented contingencies and peer tutoring/cooperative learning are designed for use with older students and those with more mild disabilities. Although neither of these general approaches were developed specifically for use with socially withdrawn students, both have been used successfully with this population. Certainly, more widespread applications are warranted.

Group-Oriented Contingencies

Group-oriented contingencies are really a form of teacher-directed intervention but since peers mediate the delivery of treatment via prompts and reinforcement, we are discussing such procedures as peer-assisted interventions. Three types of group-oriented contingencies are available. *Independent or standardized strategies* (Kazdin, 1977) establish a standard performance criterion for each member of a group (or class). Reinforcement is delivered *only* when an individual's performance meets the established criteria. In this strategy, individuals' reinforcement is tied directly to their own performance. For example, a teacher may establish an independent group contingency system by informing the class that all students who complete their academic seatwork with 85 percent accuracy (i.e. standard performance criterion) will be allowed to have free time in which to play (reinforcement).

Those who meet the criterion are reinforced, whereas those who do not must continue working.

The second option, a *dependent group-oriented system*, provides reinforcement for the entire group contingent upon one or more of the individual group members meeting their criterion. In this arrangement, all group members' reinforcement is linked or dependent on the performance of only one or a few individuals. Weinrott and colleagues (1979) demonstrated how dependent group contingencies can be used with students who are social isolates. In their study, a socially withdrawn boy could earn points for the group by engaging in a variety of social behaviors. When he earned a predetermined number of points, the entire group was reinforced. Walker and Hops (1973) conducted a similar study in which an entire class of first-graders was awarded points each day that a socially withdrawn girl made a specified number of social initiations toward others. Both studies resulted in significant improvements in the social behavior of targeted students.

In an *interdependent group-oriented* system, reinforcement is contingent upon the group's level of performance. Individual group members are reinforced only if the whole group reaches an established performance criterion. A teacher might establish an interdependent group contingency, for example, by informing the class that if they make a total of *x* initiations toward a socially withdrawn classmate during daily recess, everyone will be given ten minutes of free time. This makes it likely that students will encourage one another to seek out and initiate toward the target student. Walker and Hops (1973) demonstrated that this strategy can be successful in increasing a withdrawn child's level of peer social interaction. Similarly, a considerable data base on cooperative learning has established the powerful effects of interdependent group contingencies on student academic and social performance (e.g., Maheady et al., 1991).

Surely much more work must be done with group-oriented contingencies, particularly with regard to socially withdrawn children. Odom and DeKlyen (1986) have argued convincingly that these approaches may be especially relevant for increasing the social skills of withdrawn children because, by definition, social interaction requires the peer group. They caution, however, that negative side effects may arise when an individual's failure to reach a criterion prohibits the group from being reinforced. Therefore, practitioners must structure their initial efforts for success by targeting competence levels that are within the child's existing interpersonal repertoire. This may, in turn, bolster substantially the social status of withdrawn children when they are personally responsible for earning the group's reward.

Peer Tutoring/Cooperative Learning
A final peer-mediated option that teachers may consider when working with socially withdrawn children is peer tutoring/cooperative learning. In actuality, these are two distinct but overlapping types of intervention. Both peer tutoring and cooperative learning have established histories and data bases that cannot be

summarized here. Interested readers are referred to some extensive reviews (e.g., Greenwood, Maheady, & Carta, 1991; Slavin, 1980, 1990). These approaches are considered here primarily because they have produced consistent social as well as academic benefits among disabled and nondisabled students. Moreover, by their very nature, peer tutoring and cooperative learning increase students' opportunities to interact.

Although we were only able to locate a few peer tutoring or cooperative learning studies that involved socially withdrawn children specifically, we may be able to extrapolate findings from studies done with other pupils with behavior disorders. For example, Scruggs, Mastropieri, and Richter (1985) reviewed data from seventeen peer tutoring studies involving behavior-disordered students. They noted that some studies found more positive and less negative social interactions among tutors and tutees (Csapo, 1976; Franca, 1983); others reported "friendlier play" during tutoring sessions (Balmer, 1972); and another (Asper, 1973) noted an increase in the frequency of social contacts initiated by withdrawn tutees toward their peers. Scruggs and associates (1985) cautioned, however, that peer tutoring should be viewed as a supplementary social-skills training approach and that more direct interventions may be necessary to teach new social skills. In any event, peer tutoring appears to be a good medium for socially withdrawn children to practice taking turns, providing and receiving feedback, and working with another child.

Cooperative learning is equally appealing as a potential intervention strategy for withdrawn youngsters. Cooperative learning refers to a set of instructional methods in which small heterogeneous groups of students are encouraged or required to work together on academic tasks for their mutual benefit. These systems vary in their complexity as well as in the ways they have been applied (see Johnson & Johnson, 1986; Slavin, 1990 for reviews of various cooperative learning methods). In a recent cooperative learning study involving students with autism, Dugan, Kamps, Leonard, Watkins, Rheinberger, and Stackhaus (1995) demonstrated that these instructional methods substantially improved pupils' academic performance, increased their rates of academic engagement, and lengthened the duration of their social interactions during intervention. What was most impressive about this particular study was that it was conducted in a regular fourth grade classroom and instructional benefits were documented for *both* nondisabled youngsters and their peers with autism. Most reviews of the cooperative learning literature suggest that students who are involved in cooperative groups like one another better, improve their social interactions with others, develop better attitudes toward school in general and trained academic content in particular, and feel better about themselves. Given the rather extensive data base on cooperative learning it is somewhat surprising that these methods have not been used more frequently with socially withdrawn children. Nonetheless, it appears that such approaches are well-suited for engaging isolated children in social interactions and for reinforcing their cooperative efforts.

Student-Managed Interventions

The final set of instructional options available to teachers working with withdrawn children are student-managed strategies. Student management refers to a set of procedures whereby children control their own planned intervention (Kerr & Nelson, 1989). Admittedly, these methods have been investigated less extensively than the other techniques discussed in this chapter, but they seem to hold great promise for helping isolated children who are aware of their "problem" and wish to do something about it.

In a typical student-managed intervention, the withdrawn child is first involved in the selection of a target behavior that he or she wants to increase. For example, the child may want to increase the frequency of answering questions posed by peers or of asking someone to play with him or her during recess. After target behaviors are selected, the student is given a self-recording data sheet that contains a list of selected target behaviors with space to record the frequency with which the behaviors occurred (Sheridan, 1995). The target behaviors are reviewed with the student and put into the student's own words if necessary. Next, the student practices using the measurement system in real life situations. It is a good idea for the teacher to monitor the child's behavior independently, at least in the initial phases of intervention, in order to reinforce the child for matching these external evaluations. Once the student is self-monitoring accurately, occasional reliability checks should be done at random times to ensure continued accuracy. Criterion levels should be established for increased social interactions. When criteria are reached either the teacher or the child may select the reinforcer.

The purpose of self-recording is to make students aware of their positive interactions with others and how to increase them. Ultimately, students begin to manage their own interaction patterns. At this point, there may no longer be a need for either teacher-directed or peer-mediated interventions.

General Guidelines for Selecting Intervention Strategies

It is our sincere belief that withdrawn children should be helped and that assistance should be provided in integrated settings to the maximum extent possible. In this concluding section, we would like to provide a few guidelines to assist practitioners in selecting among the various intervention alternatives offered. These guidelines were proposed earlier by Odom and DeKlyen (1986) and still appear to reflect good instructional practice.

First, developmental factors must be considered when selecting particular interventions. Highly verbal or complex strategies, such as social coaching and group-oriented contingencies, may be more appropriate for elementary-aged and older students. Less verbal strategies, such as adult prompting and reinforcing and peer imitation training, will probably be more appropriate for younger children or those with limited verbal skills. It is significant that very few strategies have been developed specifically for or tested with socially withdrawn adolescents. Research in this domain is sorely needed.

Second, intervention strategies should be selected according to the nature of the child's problem. For example, some withdrawn children exhibit performance deficits—that is, they possess the requisite skills to interact successfully, but they fail to do so. For these children, strategies such as adult reinforcement and modeling as well as the use of group contingencies appear to be most useful. Withdrawn children with skill deficits, however, must be taught how to interact appropriately. For them, social coaching and/or social skills training may be the treatment of choice. Finally, it may be desirable to improve withdrawn children's academic and social behavior concurrently. In this instance, cooperative learning, peer tutoring, and/or group-oriented contingencies would be most appropriate.

Third, intervention procedures should be as least intrusive as possible and should be delivered in the most inclusive instructional settings available. If intervention can be carried out without singling out individual students, then this would be preferred. Similarly, efforts to build, maintain, and extend prosocial behavior would be preferred over those methods that are designed to simply reduce inappropriate responding. In the same vein, practitioners should apply their interventions within integrated academic settings as much as possible. Recent efforts to include students with severe and profound disabilities into general education classrooms, for example, have generated numerous mechanisms to support both students and teachers in their implementation efforts.

To reiterate the conviction we expressed at the beginning of this chapter; the one thing we *cannot* do is accept or ignore withdrawn children's social isolation. There are simply too many wonderful things to be learned from prosocial interactions. We should do all that we can to ensure that children like LaChandra are afforded the opportunity to learn these things.

Summary

This chapter introduced you to a "new" kind of child with a behavior disorder—the socially withdrawn child. We suggested that although such children do not bother anyone, they need our assistance if they are to lead productive and socially rewarding lives. To this end, we detailed procedures that may be used to identify withdrawn children and outlined a variety of teacher-directed, peer-mediated, and student-managed instructional options for assisting them in school settings. We noted that each of these strategies has been used with varying degrees of success with socially withdrawn children. The chapter concluded with some guidelines for choosing among interventions.

Discussion Questions

1. Is social withdrawal a legitimate behavior disorder? Cite empirical evidence to justify your response.

2. What are the common characteristics of socially withdrawn children?

3. Describe three general approaches for identifying socially withdrawn pupils.

4. What is meant by a multilevel, multimethod assessment approach? How would this approach be used to identify isolate children?

5. In what ways can classroom teachers structure their environments to increase social interactions among pupils?

6. Name two major social-learning strategies and describe how they might be used with withdrawn youngsters.

7. What are the common components of most packaged social-skills training programs? What criticisms have been raised about the use of such programs?

8. Briefly describe three peer-minded interventions that have been used effectively with social isolates.

9. What are the three primary types of group-oriented contingencies and how does each type operate?

10. What are three general guidelines to use when selecting classroom interventions for withdrawn youngsters?

References

Achenbach, T. M. (1991). *The Child Behavior Checklist: Manual for the teacher's report form.* Burlington, VT: Department of Psychiatry, University of Vermont.

Allen, K. E., Hart, B., Buell, J. S., Harris, F. R., & Wolf, M. M. (1964). Effects of social reinforcement on isolate behavior of a nursery school child. *Child Development, 35,* 511–518.

Asher, S. R., & Hymel, S. (1981). Children's social competence in peer relations: Sociometric and behavioral assessment. In J. Wine & M. Smye (Eds.), *Social competence* (pp. 125–137). New York: Guilford.

Asher, S. R., Singleton, L. C., Tinsley, B. R., & Hymel, S. (1979). A reliable sociometric measure for preschool children. *Developmental Psychology, 15,* 443–444.

Asper, A. L. (1973). The effects of cross-age tutoring on the frequency of social contacts initiated by withdrawn elementary school children. *Dissertation Abstracts International, 35*(02-A), 878.

Balmer, J. (1972). Project tutor—Look, I can do something good. *Teaching Exceptional Children, 4,* 166–175.

Bowlby, J. (1969). *Attachment and loss, Vol. I: Attachment.* New York: Basic Books.

Cobb, J. A. (1972). Relationship of discrete classroom behaviors to fourth grade academic achievement. *Journal of Educational Psychology, 63,* 74–80.

Coie, J. D., Dodge, K. A., & Coppotelli, H. (1982). Dimensions and types of social status: A cross-aged perspective. *Developmental Psychology, 18,* 557–570.

Coie, J. D., & Kupersmidt, J. B. (1983). A behavior analysis of emerging social status in boys' groups. *Child Development, 54,* 1400–1416.

Conger, J. C. & Keane, S. P. (1981). Social skills intervention in the treatment of isolated or withdrawn children. *Psychological Bulletin, 90,* 478–495.

Cooke, T. P. & Apolloni, T. (1976). Developing positive social-emotional behaviors: A study of training and generalization effects. *Journal of Applied Behavior Analysis, 9,* 65–78.

Cooke, S. A., Cooke, T. P., & Apolloni, T. (1978). Developing nonretarded toddlers as verbal models for retarded classmates. *Child Study Journal, 8,* 1–8.

Csapo, M. (1976). If you don't know it, teach it! *Clearing House, 12,* 365–367.

Day, R., Powell, T., Dy-Linn, E., & Stowitschek, J. (1982). An evaluation of the effects of a social interaction training package on mentally handicapped preschool children. *Education and Training of the Mentally Retarded, 17,* 125–130.

Day, R. M., Powell, T. H., & Stowitschek, J. J. (1980). *SCIPPY: Social Competence Intervention Package for Preschool Youngsters.* Nashville, TN: Vanderbilt University.

Dodge, K. A. (1983). Behavioral antecedent of peer social status. *Child Development, 54,* 1386–1399.

Dodge, K. A., Coie, J. D., & Brakke, N. P. (1982). Behavior patterns of socially rejected and neglected preadolescents: The role of social approach and aggression. *Journal of Abnormal Child Psychology, 10,* 389–410.

Dugan, E., Kamps, D., Leonard, B., Watkins, N., Rheinberger, A., & Stackhaus, J. (1995). Effects of cooperative learning groups during social studies for students with autism and fourth-grade peers. *Journal of Applied Behavior Analysis, 28,* 175–188.

Epstein, M. H., & Cullinan, D. (1987). Effective social skills curricula for behaviorally disordered students. *The Pointer, 31,* 21–24.

Erickson, E. (1963). *Childhood and society.* New York: Norton.

Evers, W., & Schwartz, J. (1973). Modifying social withdrawal in preschoolers: The effects of modeling and teacher praise. *Journal of Abnormal Child Psychology, 1,* 248–256.

Feil, E. G., & Becker, W. C. (1993). Investigation of a multiple-gated screening system for preschool behavior problems. *Behavioral Disorders, 10,* 177–203.

Franca, V. M. (1983). *Peer tutoring among behaviorally disordered students: Academic and social benefits to tutor and tutee.* Unpublished doctoral dissertation, George Peabody College of Vanderbilt University, Nashville, TN.

Goldstein, A. P., Sprafkin, R. P., Gershaw, N. J., & Klein, P. (1980). *Skillstreaming the adolescent.* Champaign, IL: Research Press.

Gottman, J., Gonso, J., & Rasmussen, B. (1975). Social interaction, social competence, and friendship in children. *Child Development, 46,* 709–718.

Green, K. D., Vosk, B., Forehand, R., & Beck, S. (1981). An examination of differences among sociometrically identified accepted, rejected, and neglected children. *Child Study Journal, 11,* 117–124.

Greenwood, C. R., Maheady, L., & Carta, J. J. (1991). Peer tutoring programs in the regular education classroom. In G. Stoner, M. R. Shinn, & H. M. Walker (Eds.), *Interventions for achievement and behavior problems* (pp. 179–200). Washington, DC: National Association for School Psychology.

Greenwood, C. R., Todd, N. M., Hops, H., & Walker, H. M. (1982). Behavior change targets in the assessment and treatment of socially withdrawn preschool children. *Behavioral Assessment, 4,* 273–297.

Greenwood, C. R., Todd, N. M., Walker, H. M., & Hops, H. (1978). *Social Assessment Manual for Preschool Level (SAMPLE).* Eugene, OR: Center at Oregon for Research in the Behavioral Education of the Handicapped.

Greenwood, C. R., Walker, H. M., & Hops, H. (1977). Issues in social interaction: Withdrawal assessment. *Exceptional Children, 43,* 490–499.

Greenwood, C. R., Walker, H. M., Todd, N. M., & Hops, H. (1979). Selecting a cost-effective screening measure for the assessment of preschool social withdrawal. *Journal of Applied Behavior Analysis, 12,* 639–652.

Greenwood, C. R., Walker, H. M., Todd, N. M., & Hops, H. (1981). Normative and descriptive analysis of preschool freeplay social interaction rates. *Journal of Pediatric Psychology, 4,* 343–367.

Gresham, F. M. (1983). Multitrait-multimethod approach to multifactored assessment: Theoretical rationales and practical application. *School Psychology Review, 12,* 26–34.

Gresham, F. M., & Elliot, S. N. (1984). Assessment and classification of children's social skills: A review of methods and issues. *School Psychology Review, 13,* 292–301.

Gresham, F. M., & Elliot, S. N. (1989). Social skills assessment technology for LD students. *Learning Disability Quarterly, 12,* 141–152.

Gresham, F. M., & Elliott, S. N. (1990). *The Social Skills Rating System (SSRS).* Circle Pines, MN: American Guidance Service.

Gresham, F. M., & Nagle, R. J. (1980). Social skills training with children: Responsiveness to modeling and coaching as a function of peer orientation. *Journal of Consulting and Clinical Psychology, 18,* 718–729.

Gronlund, N. E. (1959). *Sociometry in the classroom.* New York: Harper.

Guralnick, M. J. (1981). Peer influences on development of communicative competence. In P. Strain (Ed.), *The utilization of peers as behavior change agents* (pp. 31–68). New York: Plenum.

Hart, B. M., Reynolds, J. J., Baer, D. M., Brawley, E. R., & Harris, F. R. (1968). Effects of contingent and noncontingent social reinforcement on the cooperative play of a preschool child. *Journal of Applied Behavior Analysis, 1,* 73–76.

Hartup, W. W., & Sancilio, M. F. (1986). Children's friendships. In E. Schopler & G. B. Mesibov (Eds.), *Social behavior in autism* (pp. 61–79). New York: Plenum.

Hazel, J. S., Schumaker, J. B., Sheman, J. A., & Sheldon-Wildgen, J. (1982). *Asset: A social skills program for adolescents.* Champaign, IL: Research Press.

Hendrickson, J. M., Strain, P. S., Tremblay, A., & Shores, R. E. (1982). Interactions of behaviorally handicapped children: Functional effects of peer social initiations. *Behavior Modification, 6,* 323–353.

Hops, H. (1982). Social skills training for socially withdrawn/isolate children. In P. Karoly & J. Steffin (Eds.), *Improving children's competence: Advances in child behavior analysis and therapy.* Vol. 1. Pp. 39–101. Lexington, MA: Heath.

Hops, H., & Greenwood, C. R. (1981). Social skills deficits. In E. Mash and L. Terdal (Eds.), *Behavioral assessment of children's disorders.* Pp. 347–394. New York: Guilford.

Hops, H., Guild, J. J., Fleischman, D. H., Paine, S. C., Street, A., Walker, H. M., & Greenwood, C. R. (1978). *PEERS (Procedures for Establishing Relationships Skills).* Eugene, OR: CORBEH.

Hops, H., Walker, H. M., & Greenwood, C. R. (1979). PEERS: A program for remediating social withdrawal in school. In L. A. Hamerlynck (Ed.), *Behavioral systems for the developmentally disabled in school and home environments* (pp. 48–88). New York: Bruner & Mazel.

Hurley-Geffner, C. M. (1995). Friendships between children with and without developmental disabilities. In R. L. Koegel & L. K., Koegel, (Eds.), *Teaching children with autism: Strategies for initiating positive interactions and improving learning opportunities* (pp. 105–125). Baltimore: Paul Brookes Publishing.

Jackson, N. F., Jackson, D. A., & Monroe, C. (1983). *Getting along with others: Teaching social effectiveness to children.* Champaign, IL: Research Press.

Jakibchuk, Z., & Smeriglio, V. L. (1976). The influence of symbolic modeling on social behavior of preschool children with low levels of social responsiveness. *Child Development, 47,* 838–841.

James, S. D., & Egel, A. L. (1986). A direct prompting strategy for increasing reciprocal interactions between handicapped and nonhandicapped siblings. *Journal of Applied Behavior Analysis, 19,* 173–186.

Johnson, D. W., & Johnson, R. T. (1986). *Cooperation and competition: Theory and research.* Edina, MN: Interaction Book Co.

Kauffman, J. M. (1989). *Characteristics of behavior disorders of children and youth,* 4th ed. Columbus, OH: Merrill.

Kazdin, A. E. (1977). *The token economy: A review and evaluation.* New York: Plenum.

Keller, M. F., & Carlson, P. M. (1974). The use of symbolic modeling to promote social skills in children with low levels of social responsiveness. *Child Development, 45,* 912–919.

Kerr, M. M., & Nelson, C. M. (1989). *Strategies for managing behavior problems in the classroom.* 2nd ed. Columbus, OH: Merrill.

King-Sears, M. E., & Bradley, D. F. (1995). Class-Wide Peer Tutoring: Heterogeneous instruction in general education classrooms. *Preventing School Failure, 40,* 29–35.

Kohn, M. (1977). *Social competence, symptoms and underachievement in childhood: A longitudinal perspective.* Washington, DC: Winston.

Ladd, G. W. (1981). Effectiveness of a social learning method for enhancing children's social interactions and peer acceptance. *Child Development, 52,* 171–178.

Ladd, G. w., & Mize, J. (1983). A cognitive-social learning model of social skills training. *Psychological Review, 90,* 127–157.

LaGreca, A. M., & Santogrossi, A. A. (1980). Social skills training with elementary school students: A behavioral group approach. *Journal of Consulting and Clinical Psychology, 48,* 220–227.

Lindeman, D. P., Fox, J. J., & Redelheim, P. S. (1993). Increasing and maintaining withdrawn preschoolers' peer interactions: Effects of double prompting and booster session procedures. *Behavioral Disorders, 19,* 54–66.

Lovitt, T. C. (1987). Social skills training: Which ones and where to do it? *Journal of Reading, Writing, and Learning Disabilities International, 3,* 213–221.

Maheady, L., Harper, G. F., & Mallette, B. (1991). Peer mediated instruction: A review of potential applications for special educators. *Reading, Writing, and Learning Disabilities, 7,* 75–103.

Maheady, L., & Sainato, D. (1985). The effects of peer tutoring upon the social status and social interaction patterns of high and low status elementary school children. *Education and Treatment of Children, 8,* 51–65.

McConnell, S. R., & Odom, S. L. (1986). Sociometrics: Peer-referenced measures and the assessment of social competence. In P. Strain, M. Guralnick, & H. Walker (Eds.), *Children's social behavior: Development, assessment, and modification* (pp. 215–284). New York: Academic Press.

McEvoy, M. A., Odom, S. L., & McConnell, S. R. (1992). Peer social competence intervention for young children with disabilities. In S. L. Odom, S. R. McConnell, & M. S. McEvoy (Eds.), *Social competence of young children with disabilities* (pp. 113–133). Baltimore: Paul Brookes Publishing.

McGinnis, E., Goldstein, A. P., Sprafkin, R. P., & Gershaw, N. J. (1984). *Skillstreaming the elementary school child.* Champaign, IL: Research Press.

Merrell, K. W. (1993). *The School Social Behavior Scale (SSBS).* Brandon, VT: Clinical Psychology Publishing.

Neel, R. (1984). Teaching school routines to behaviorally disordered youth. In J. Grosenick, S. Hunter, E. McGinnis, & C. Smith (Eds.), *Social/affective interventions in behavioral disorders.* Washington, DC: U.S. Department of Education.

O'Connor, R. D. (1969). Modification of social withdrawal through symbolic modeling. *Journal of Applied Behavior Analysis, 2,* 15–22.

O'Connor, R. D. (1972). The relative efficacy of modeling, shaping, and the combined procedures for the modification of social withdrawal. *Journal of Abnormal Psychology, 79,* 327–334.

Oden, S, & Asher, S. (1977). Coaching children in social skills for friendship making. *Child Development, 48,* 496–506.

Odom, S. L., & DeKlyen, M. (1986). *Social withdrawal in childhood.* Unpublished manuscript, Department of Special Education, Vanderbilt University, Nashville, TN.

Odom, S. L., McConnell, S. R., & McEvoy, M. A. (1992). Peer-related social competence and its significance for young children with disabilities. In S. L., Odom, S. R., McConnell, & M. A., McEvoy, (Eds.)., *Social competence of young children with disabilities* (pp. 3–35). Baltimore: Paul Brookes Publishing.

Odom, S. L., & Strain, P. S. (1984). Peer-mediated approaches to promoting children's social interaction: A review. *American Journal of Orthopsychiatry, 54,* 544–557.

Paine, S. C., Hops, H., Walker, H. M., Greenwood, C. R., Fleishman, D. H., & Guild, J. J. (1982). Repeated treatment effects: A study of maintaining behavior change in socially withdrawn children. *Behavior Modification, 6,* 171–199.

Paine, S. C., Radicchi, J., Rosellini, L. C., Deutchman, L., & Darch, C. B. (1983). *Structuring your classroom for academic success.* Champaign, IL: Research Press.

Peery, J. C., (1979). Popular, amiable, isolated, rejected: A reconceptulization of sociometric status in preschool children. *Child Development, 50,* 1231–1234.

Piaget, J. (1926). *The language and thought of the child.* London: Routledge & Kegan Paul.

Ragland, E. U., Kerr, M. M., & Strain, P. S. (1978). Behavior of withdrawn autistic children. *Behavior Modification, 2,* 565–578.

Renshaw, P., & Asher, S. R. (1982). Social competence and peer status: The distinction between goals and strategies. In K. Rubin & H. Ross (Eds.), *Peer relationships and social skills in childhood* (pp. 374–395). New York: Springer-Verlag.

Robins, L. N. (1966). *Deviant children grow up.* Baltimore: Williams & Wilkins.

Roff, M., Sells, B., & Golden, M. M. (1972). *Social adjustment and personality development in children.* Minneapolis: University of Minnesota Press.

Sainato, D. M., & Carta, J. J. (1992). Classroom influences on the development of social competence in young children with disabilities. In S. L. Odom, S. R., McConnell, & M. A., McEvoy (Eds.), *Social competence of young children with disabilities* (pp. 93–109). Baltimore: Paul Brookes Publishing.

Sainato, D. M., Maheady, L., & Shook, G. G. (1986). The effects of a classroom manager role on the social interaction patterns and social status of withdrawn kindergarten students. *Journal of Applied Behavior Analysis, 19,* 187–195.

Schloss, P. J., & Sedlack, R. A. (1986). *Instructional methods for students with learning and behavior problems.* Boston: Allyn & Bacon.

Scruggs, T. E., Mastropieri, M. A., & Richter, L. (1985). Peer tutoring among behaviorally disordered students: Social and academic benefits. *Behavioral Disorders, 11,* 283–294.

Sheridan, S. M. (1995). *The tough kid social skills book.* Longmont, CO: Sopris West.

Slavin, R. E. (1980). Cooperative learning. *Review of Educational Research, 50,* 315–342.

Slavin, R. E. (1990). *Cooperative learning: Theory, research, and practice.* Englewood Cliffs, NJ: Prentice-Hall.

Stoneman, Z., Cantrell, M. L., & Hoover-Dempsey, K. (1983). The association between play materials and social behavior in a mainstreamed preschool: A naturalistic investigation. *Journal of Applied Developmental Psychology, 4,* 163–174.

Strain, P. S., Cooke, T. P., & Apolloni, T. A. (1976). *Teaching exceptional children: Assessing and modifying social behavior.* New York: Academic Press.

Strain, P. S., Guralnick, J. J., & Walker, H. (1986). *Children's social behavior: Development, assessment and modification.* New York: Academic Press.

Strain, P. S., & Kerr, M. M. (1981). Modifying children's social withdrawal: Issues in assessment and clinical intervention. *Progress in Behavior Modification, 11,* 203–248.

Strain, P. S., & Kerr, M. M., & Ragland, E. U. (1979). Effects of peer-mediated social initiations and prompt reinforcement procedures on the social behavior of autistic children. *Journal of Autism and Developmental Disorders, 9,* 41–54.

Strain, P. S., Shores, R. E., & Kerr, M. M. (1976). An experimental analysis of "spillover" effects on the social interaction of behaviorally handicapped preschool children. *Journal of Applied Behavior Analysis, 9,* 31–40.

Strain, P. S., Shores, R. E., & Timm, M. A. (1977). Effects of peer social initiations on the behavior of withdrawn preschool children. *Journal of Applied Behavior Analysis, 10,* 189–198.

Strain, P. S., & Timm, M. A. (1974). An experimental analysis of social interaction between a behaviorally disordered preschool child and her classroom peers. *Journal of Applied Behavior Analysis, 7,* 583–590.

Timm, M. A., Strain, P. S., & Eller, P. H. (1979). Effects of systematic, response dependent fading and thinning procedures on the maintenance of child-child interaction. *Journal of Applied Behavior analysis, 12,* 208.

Walker, H. M. (1983). *Walker Behavior Problem Identification Checklist Revised 1983.* Los Angeles, CA: Western Psychological Services.

Walker, H. M. (1995). *The acting out child: Coping with classroom disruption.* 2nd ed. Longmont, CO: Sopris West.

Walker, H. M., & Hops, H. (1973). The use of group and individual reinforcement contingencies in the modification of social withdrawal. In L. Hamerlynk, L. Handy, & E. Mash (Eds.), *Behav-*

ior change: Methodology, concepts, and practice (pp. 269–307). Champaign, IL: Research Press.

Walker, H. M., Hops, H., Greenwood, C. R., & Todd, N. (1979). Differential effects of reinforcing topographic components of free play social interaction: Analysis and direct replication. *Behavior Modification, 3,* 291–321.

Walker, H. M., McConnell, S. R., Holmes, D., Todis, B., Walker, J., & Golden, N. (1983). *ACCEPTS: A Children's Curriculum for Effective Peer and Teacher Skills.* Austin: Pro-Ed.

Walker, H. M., & Severson, H. H. (1990). *Systematic Screening for Behavior Disorders (SSBD): User's guide and technical manual.* Longmont, CO: Sopris West.

Walker, H. M., Severson, H. H., & Feil, E. G. (1995). *The Early Screening Project: A proven child-find process.* Longmont, CO: Sopris West.

Weinrott, M. R., Corson, L. A., & Wilchesky, M. (1979). Teacher mediated treatment of social withdrawal. *Behavior Therapy, 10,* 281–294.

Wolery, M., Bailey, D. B., Jr. & Sugai, G. M. (1989). *Effective teaching principles and procedures of applied behavior analysis with exceptional students.* Boston: Allyn & Bacon.

Chapter **10**

Managing Rule Breaking and Delinquency

Advance Organizer

As you read this chapter, prepare to identify and discuss:

- Why legal definitions of delinquency tend to be of little practical use to educators.
- The chief components of the four major theoretical approaches that have guided attempts to manage rule breaking and delinquency.
- Why rule breaking behaviors such as theft, vandalism, and substance abuse are difficult to modify.
- Guidelines that should be followed when designing intervention programs for theft reduction.
- Schoolwide efforts that can be used to reduce instances of school vandalism.
- Strategies that have been successful in preventing and remediating truancy.
- How in-school and out-of-school suspensions are to be administered for students with behavior problems.
- When day and residential school alternatives are appropriate for rule breaking and delinquent students.

This chapter contains contributions by Addison Watanabe.

In Chapter 2, on high-incidence behavior disorders, we observed that there is considerable variability in the way professionals define and explain rule breaking or delinquent behavior. From the legal perspective, rule breaking is commonly referred to as *juvenile delinquency.* Any rule breaker who has been apprehended by the authorities and adjudged by a juvenile court is considered a juvenile delinquent. Unfortunately, legal definitions of delinquency are of little practical use for educators seeking to reduce the instances of rule breaking in their schools and communities, for two reasons. First, juvenile courts tend to be vague and inconsistent on the subject of what rule violations constitute delinquency. Second, and more important, legal definitions of rule breaking do not accommodate those individuals believed to be "hidden delinquents" (Mulvey, Arthur, & Reppucci, 1993). School officials are frequently responsible for developing management programs for students who violate rules, yet never appear before a juvenile court. Descriptive classifications of rule breaking have differentiated juveniles by offense committed (e.g., criminal versus status) and by diagnosing norm violators according to particular psychological factors. In advocating even greater precision, proponents of the behavioral perspective have stressed the need to describe the specific behavioral excesses and deficiencies of the rule breaker rather than merely finding a correct label.

Etiological formulations of rule breaking and delinquency have reflected the wide variety of conceptual models typically associated with the study of deviance. Biophysical theorists have suggested that delinquent or criminal behavior can be explained by body type (e.g., Sheldon, 1949), chromosomal deviation, or heredity. The psychodynamic perspective, deeply rooted in the Freudian notion of personality development, views rule breaking or delinquency as a failure to develop adequate ego strength or superego controls. Behavioral theorists have approached juvenile rule violations as a set of maladaptive behaviors that are learned and maintained by specific discriminative stimuli and reinforcers in the environment. In addition, observational learning or modeling is believed to play a central role in the development of rule-breaking behavior. Finally, a variety of sociological and ecological theories have been proposed as possible causes of delinquent behavior. These diverse theories share the view that the breaking of socially accepted rules is a result of institutional and socialization deficiencies within an ecosystem.

While there is considerable diversity in how to define and explain rule breaking and delinquency, almost all agree that something must be done to remediate or prevent the rising tide of juvenile misconduct in this country. Both the frequency and intensity of serious juvenile rule breaking and crime are rising at an alarming rate. For example, individuals under the age of 18 accounted for 17 percent of all arrests (Uniform Crime Report, 1994). Moreover, the percentages are increasing; between 1989 and 1993, the total number of juvenile arrests increased by 13 percent. Unfortunately, rule breaking and delinquency are not strangers to school environments. A number of observers (e.g., Lantieri, 1995; Sautter, 1995; Zirkel, 1980) have reported that schools are the scene of major discipline problems including robbery, drug and alcohol abuse, disorderly conduct, and possession of weapons. This is a far cry from the kinds of misbehaviors—running in the hall, chewing

---

Case Study: Rule Breaking

I'll always remember the Friday afternoon Dale Frazier's permanent educational records were delivered to my school. The amplified voice of the school secretary invaded my secondary behavior disorders classroom, requesting that I promptly pick up the large packages. To my chagrin, the secretary suggested that I bring two students to assist with the transporting of the data. Being a conscientious first-year teacher, I quickly selected two helpers and proceeded to the office.

Viewing the two boxes of student data, I was paralyzed for a moment by disbelief. How could one boy, a mere 15-year-old, have occasioned such an immense amount of written documentation? Upon reading the contents of

the boxes, my disbelief was replaced by mortal terror. This young man, who would be attending my class the following Monday, was characterized by the authors of the paperwork as a cross between J. R. Ewing of *Dallas* fame and Charles Manson. He was a frequent drug and alcohol abuser and was once arrested for robbing a few dollars from a senior citizen. He had run away from home on three separate occasions and had even hit an elementary school principal. His frequent truancy was the only good news in the boxes. The bottom line was that, at 15 years of age, Dale Frazier had managed to break every rule in the book—and he was coming to my classroom. My weekend was ruined!

---

gum, wearing improper clothes—listed as major disruptors by educators prior to World War II (Sabatino, Sabatino, & Mann, 1983). Even more frightening is the knowledge that the available data on rule breaking represent merely the tip of the iceberg of total behavior.

What follows is a catalog of strategies and procedures for managing, remediating, and preventing those behaviors typical of students who violate societal norms and break the rules of accepted legal and moral functioning. First, we will survey several of the major approaches traditionally used in the management of delinquency. We will follow this with a survey of model programs and procedural guidelines designed to prevent, manage, and remediate the rule violations educators typically encounter. Specific problem areas addressed are theft, vandalism, substance abuse, and truancy. Finally, we will discuss several systemwide interventions that have been successfully employed by both local schools and residential settings to remediate rule breaking and delinquency.

Major Approaches to Managing Rule Breaking and Delinquency

Traditional Medical Model/Psychodynamic Approaches

The traditional psychodynamic perspective views rule breaking and delinquency as it does most instances of deviant behavior, as symptoms of an underlying pathology. According to advocates of this point of view, the surface behavior—offenses such as truancy, theft, and substance abuse—are indications of some underlying pathology. Specifically, the underlying pathology is a defect in the structure of personality (id, ego, and superego), and thus the focal point of treatment is the repair of the ill-formed components of the personality.

Redl's Pioneer House Program
The most frequently cited practitioner of the psychodynamic approach with delinquents is Fritz Redl. Working primarily with aggressive delinquents, Redl and his associates (Redl & Wineman, 1957) translated the complex structural hypothesis into an educational and therapeutic regimen.

As was fully explored in Chapter 8, Redl's therapeutic program consisted of two major components: the management of surface behavior and the life-space interview. While not designed for long-term therapeutic gain, the surface behavior management techniques of the Redl program do provide teachers with alternatives for handling daily instances of inappropriate behavior. To influence the surface behavior of rule breakers, educators are to find the proper combination of the following options: permitting behavior, tolerating behavior, interfering with behavior, and preventative planning. In sharp contrast, the life-space interview is a technique for attaining some measure of long-term therapeutic growth. The life-space interview is to be conducted immediately at the time of a crisis situation and administered by a trained individual from the student's natural environment. These two major components of the life-space interview—*emotional first aid on the spot and clinical exploitation of life events*—are designed to provide emotional support for the developing youngster and to use the crisis as a viable therapeutic learning situation.

While the Redl Program is a comprehensive regimen for managing and eventually remediating disturbed behavior, the procedures are not symptom- or behavior-specific. Therefore, anyone attempting to deal with rule breaking would be unable to find a strategy or particular approach in this program for treating a specific problem behavior such as stealing or substance abuse. This is not an accident. The psychodynamic perspective views the rule breaking behavior as merely superficial and long-term intervention as necessary to the resolution of the underlying conflicts that are causing the rule violations. Unfortunately for the advocates of this theory, there is little evidence that the modification of underlying structures affects overt behavior. Thus, while Redl's techniques embody a great deal of common sense and bear an appealing nomenclature, the lack of well-controlled studies concerning specific rule breaking activities leaves much to be desired.

Traditional Psychotherapy
The lack of both validation and logistics are concerns when considering the use of psychotherapy for managing rule breaking. Typically, traditional psychotherapy is a long process in which a client or group of clients and therapists spend a considerable amount of time reexperiencing past events and discussing current feelings. Psychotherapy is widely practiced in a variety of forms (e.g., psychoanalysis, nondirective psychotherapy, psychodrama, play therapy), but none of these variations has demonstrated consistent positive behavioral change with delinquents

(Mulvey et al., 1993). Van Evra (1983) has attributed this ineffectiveness to a mismatch between the central aspects of psychotherapy and the entry-level characteristics of rule breakers and delinquents. Specifically, psychotherapy typically relies on reflective thought, verbalization, the capacity to develop a meaningful relationship, and a motivation to change one's behavior. Since a large subgroup of delinquents and rule breakers do not possess these psychotherapeutic prerequisites, attempts to treat them with psychotherapy fail.

When combined with other program features such as vocational training and remedial education, however, psychotherapy may be beneficial. For example, Shore and Massimo (1979) found that male adolescent delinquents who received a combination of education, job placement, and psychotherapy achieved better overall adjustment than untreated control subjects. This adjustment, consisting of personality factors, cognitive functioning, and various overt behavioral measures, was reported to maintain up to fifteen years past initial treatment.

Transactional Analysis

Transactional analysis (Berne, 1961; Trojanowicz & Morash, 1992) is a psychodynamic technique that has been adapted for use with delinquents. Transactional analysis is based on the assumption that all people engage in "games" in order to defend against ego damage and to secure gratification. To maximize their potential gains from these social "games," individuals pick and choose among different roles or ego states. The three primary ego states are: (1) the child, a reflection of an individual's immature and prelogical youth; (2) the parent, a reflection of normative values and frequently judgmental; and (3) the adult, one who behaves in a mature and responsible manner. Since each of these ego state perceives and acts upon reality differently, an individual can easily employ the various ego roles in a manipulative fashion.

With delinquency, the major goal of transactional analysis is to teach the rule breaker the three major ego states and how they are used during instances of inappropriate behavior. As with traditional psychotherapy, the rule breaker is assumed to possess the motivation to change his or her overt behavior. Typically, the therapist presents the rule breaker with activities and exercises that are designed to strengthen the adult ego state while reducing the ego states representing the immature child and judgmental parents.

Haskell and Yablonski (1974) have reported that transactional analysis has been "helpful in improving life positions, vocations, recreations, and interpersonal relationships" (p. 491), as well as in assisting some youngsters to accept responsibility for their own futures. The authors cited as an example the case of a former parole violator who went on to study to become an IBM computer programmer. Unfortunately, they provide no empirical efficacy data. Transactional analysis was also employed with incarcerated delinquents in a California detention facility (Jesness,1976). All staff members received intensive training in transactional analysis, and the guiding principles of the therapy were applied in all facets of the rule breaker's institutional life. Improvement was observed in delinquents' attitudes toward the staff, in their psychological adjustment, and in the general climate of the institution. Even more compelling were data indicating a decrease in parole violation rates upon release from the facility.

Behavioral Approaches

The behavioral approach to managing delinquency views rule breaking behavior as a series of learned maladaptive behaviors. Unlike the psychodynamic model, the behavioral model does not consider rule breaking to be a symptom of underlying psychological disorders; rather, it sees each kind of rule violation as an individual behavior target in need of modification. As it does with the other patterns of disturbed behavior, the behavioral model conceptualizes both the antecedents and the consequences of a rule breaker's behavior as significant influencers of future occurrences of behavior. Thus, the major emphasis is on modifying environmental events so that inappropriate behaviors decrease and appropriate behaviors increase.

The application of behavioral procedures to rule breaking and delinquency is very much like the application of behavioral procedures to other behavior problems (e.g., hyperactivity and aggression). First, the teacher or clinician is to pinpoint or target the specific behaviors in need of intervention. Behaviors to be increased or decreased must be clearly specified and documented, and the definitions of each behavior must be stated in objective terms. Second, the individual initiating the behavior-change procedure must communicate the behavioral expectations to the rule breaker. Such communication is accomplished through the use of rules and procedures, since these cues identify behavioral expectations for specific activities (Rosenberg, 1986). Behavioral contracts (see Chapter 7), written agreements that solidify relationships between student behaviors and positive consequences, facilitate this process. Goldstein, Apter, and Harootunian (1984) have reviewed the literature on rule setting and developed "rules for rules." Their suggestions for clearly communicating behavioral expectations in a classroom can be found in Table 10.1.

The third step in applying behavioral procedures to rule breaking is to assess the pretreatment or baseline rates of the pinpointed or targeted behaviors. As discussed in Chapter 5, a variety of strategies exist to observe and record behavior. While teachers and clinicians often choose from discrete event-recording methods or continuous-recording strategies, time-efficient sampling procedures are frequently appropriate. The selection of a particular observation and recording system need not be a difficult task; oftentimes, specific recording strategies match up well to problem behaviors, as is the case with truancy, noncompliance, and physical/verbal aggression. On the other hand, direct-observation systems may not fully reflect the rate and intensity of certain hidden rule breaking behaviors such as stealing and cheating. Teachers and parents commonly learn about such rule violations from second parties or, in the case of stealing, by observing a stolen object in a youngster's possession. Because they cannot expect to witness the act, behavior modifiers must establish strict definitions of behavior or institute creative

TABLE 10.1　**Rules for the Development of Classroom Rules**

1. Define and communicate rules for student behavior in clear, specific, and, especially, behavioral terms. It is better (i.e., more concrete and behavioral) to say "Raise your hand before asking a question" than "Be considerate of others." Similarly, "Listen carefully to teacher instructions" or "Pay attention to the assignment and complete your work" are more likely to serve as rules that actually find expression in student behavior than the more ambiguous "Behave in class" or "Do what you are told."

2. It is more effective to tell students what to do rather than what not to do. This accenting of the positive would, for example, find expression in rules about taking turns or talking over disagreements or working quietly, rather than in rules directing students not to jump in or not to fight or not to speak.

3. Rules should be communicated in a way that aids students to memorize them. Depending on the age of the students, and the complexity and difficulty of the rules the teacher is presenting, such memorization aides may include: (1) keeping the rules short; (b) keeping them few in number; (c) repeating your presentation of the rules several times; and (d) posting the rules in written form where they can readily be seen.

4. Rule adherence is likely to be more effective when students have had a substantial role in their development, modification, and implementation. This sense of participation may be brought about by: (a) explicit student involvement in rule development; (b) thorough discussion of rules with the entire class; (c) having selected students explain to the class the specific meaning of each rule and (d) student role play of the behaviors identified by the rule.

5. Additional effective rules for rules are that they be developed at the start of the school year, before other less useful and less explicit rules emerge; that they be fair, reasonable, and within the students' capacity to follow; that all members of the class understand them; and that they be applied equally and evenly to all class members.

Source: Adapted from Goldstein et al. (1984).

measurement strategies. In an example of a strict behavioral definition, Patterson, Reid, Jones, and Conger (1975) advised parents to define stealing as the youngster's possession of anything not belonging to him or her. Thus, even if the youngster claimed to be "holding" something for a friend, the event would still be considered stealing. In an example of a creative measurement technique, Switzer, Deal, and Bailey (1977) placed highly desirable items around a classroom suffering from a high rate of theft and counted how many of those things "disappeared" every day. While it was impossible to attribute stealing to any individual student, the observation and recording technique was appropriate for a group contingency program implemented to reduce theft in the classroom.

　　The fourth step in applying behavioral procedures to rule breaking is to deliver the necessary consequences to the targeted or pinpointed behaviors. As with the modification of other problematic behaviors, a variety of strategies exists to achieve the goal of appropriate social functioning. First, the behavior modifier can apply one of several punishment techniques (response-cost, time-out, overcorrection) to specific instances of rule breaking. Second, a program can be designed in which appropriate behavior is strengthened or reinforced, and rule compliance is programmed to replace rule violation. Several types of reinforcers can be used in such cases, including attention and praise, specific activities or items, and tokens. The most successful behavioral treatment programs for controlling maladaptive behavior involve *both* the strengthening of appropriate behaviors *and* the weakening of inappropriate behaviors. Many programs are designed only to reduce or eliminate rule breaking behavior. All too often, the result is that a reduction in the violation of one rule is followed by a rise in the violation of another because the individual is unaware either of *how* to correctly behave or of the rewards for engaging in correct behavior.

The final step in applying behavioral procedures to rule breaking and delinquency is to evaluate the effects of the treatment program. Since every rule breaker differs in entry-level behaviors, varying combinations of reinforcers and punishers may have to be considered before a desirable outcome is achieved. In effect, each combination of techniques is a hypothesis, with the behavior modifier experimentally searching for the most efficacious treatment alternative.

Obviously, the most frequently cited behavioral targets for rule breakers and delinquents are their actual rule violations. However, several researchers (Keilitz, Zaremba, & Broder, 1979; Mulligan, 1972; Murray, 1976) have observed that specific learning or educational problems are related to the delinquent's repertoire of behavior. Data indicating that underachievement, a poor school record, impulsivity, and boredom are more predictive of rule breaking than race, ethnic background, or socioeconomic status (e.g., Zigler, Taussig, & Black, 1992) have led to a great advocacy for treatment programs that include academic skill remediation. For example, Feldman, Rosenberg, and Peer (1984) have observed that the therapeutic value of well-structured and behaviorally based educational activities can no longer be overlooked or relegated to a subordinate role if positive changes in delinquent behavior are to be attained. Such "educational therapy" can be easily incorporated into the total treatment program by (1) employing a series of well-stated sequential academic pinpoints as the overall educational plan, (2) using continuous-observation and recording methods for the pinpoints, and (3) utilizing effective instructional procedures and appropriate consequences for either the demonstration or nondemonstration of the pin-pointed skill. In essence, the successful treatment of rule breakers may depend on the application of behavioral procedures to both inappropriate delinquent behaviors and academic deficiencies.

Cognitive-Behavioral Approaches

From the cognitive-behavioral perspective, delinquency and rule breaking result from a deficiency in the social skills necessary to resolve conflict situations in an adaptive and nonaggressive manner (Kennedy, 1984). Although behaviorally based programs have produced positive outcomes such as higher rates of rule following behavior, increased academic achievement, and improved competence in vocational training, the evidence to date is that these initial outcomes do not maintain or generalize. Thus, the emphasis in cognitive-behavioral interventions with rule breakers is to program for more durable and expansive changes in behavior.

The overall strategy has been to focus on self-regulatory skills and adaptive think-ing processes, since it is believed that increased competence in such areas promotes generalization to nontreatment settings as well as post-treatment maintenance.

In order to attain these powerful outcomes, proponents of the cognitive-behavioral approach believe that the target behaviors of an intervention must be more encompassing than mere conformity to rules or the acquisition of specific academic skills. To achieve this wider range of skills, cognitive-behavioral tech-niques attempt to influence mediational responses that can help the delinquent in a variety of situations. These include moral reasoning, interpersonal problem solv-ing, self-instructional control of impulsive behavior, self-management skills, and perspective taking.

Moral Reasoning

The literature suggests that there is a relationship between an individual's level of moral reasoning and that person's levels of prosocial and antisocial behavior (e.g., Blasi, 1980; Campagna & Harter, 1975). Moral reasoning encompasses: (1) how one's sociomoral view reflects one's logical reasoning skills; (2) one's proficiency in social perspective-taking skills; (3) one's capacity to evaluate factual and value-laden claims; and (4) one's ability and disposition to weigh consequences of moral decisions across situations and time (Arbuthnot & Gordon, 1986; Maag, 1989). In an effort to increase the level of prosocial behaviors among rule breakers and delin-quents, programs stressing moral reasoning and behavior have been developed. Goldstein (1988) has advocated the use of "dilemma discussion groups" to teach children and adolescents to think about moral issues, to deal with moral situations that do not have clear–cut resolutions, and to use principles of fairness and justice in interactions with others. In these groups, students are required to defend their positions in relation to their principles of fairness; no attempts are made to indoc-trinate or teach any specific values or beliefs. Dilemma discussion groups are de-signed to remain focused on the issues at hand; they are not meant to become sessions of dynamic or behavioral therapy in which emotional conflicts are uncov-ered or pinpointed behaviors altered.

In preparing to run a dilemma discussion group, facilitators are to review the theoretical concepts of morality, justice, fairness, equality, and respect; learn how to identify the various stages of moral reasoning (e.g., Kohlberg, 1969); develop strategies for eliciting the information necessary to make accurate stage assess-ments (e.g., asking open-ended questions); and practice the assessment process. The six general steps involved in running a dilemma discussion group and a sam-ple dilemma recommended by Goldstein (1988) can be found in the accompany-ing box.

Unfortunately, the efficacy of moral reasoning in producing behavior changes in rule breaking behaviorally disordered students remains unclear. In a compre-hensive review of the literature on moral discussion groups, Maag (1989) attrib-uted the lack of demonstrated behavior change to this technique's inability to produce sufficient amounts of stage growth, to its reliance on dilemmas that do not reflect real-life situations, and to its failure to include complementary behavioral

Implementing a "Dilemma Discussion Group"

Goldstein (1988) has identified six steps involved in running a dilemma discussion group. What follows is a brief listing of these steps and two sample dilemmas taken from his moral reasoning training program.

Step 1: Form small groups of trainees at two to three consecutive stages of moral reasoning.

Step 2: Choose and prepare moral dilemma situations that will induce cognitive conflicts and that are relevant to the trainees.

Step 3: Create the proper set by explaining to the trainees the rationale for dilemma discussion groups, what they will be doing, what the trainer's role is in the group, and what guidelines will be followed in the group discussion.

Step 4: Begin the discussion by presenting the dilemma and getting initial opinions and rationales from the trainees. Then create a debate between the lowest reasoners and those one stage higher (noted as +1 stage).

Step 5: Guide discussion through all the stages represented by group members (e.g., start with a debate between Stage 1 and Stage 2 reasoners, then structure a debate between Stage 2 and Stage 3 reasoners, and so on if more than three levels of reasoning are represented), creating cognitive conflict for as many trainees as possible. Then present a +1 stage argument for the group to discuss (e.g., if the highest stage represented in the group is Stage 3, then present a Stage 4 argument).

Step 6: End discussion following the debate of the highest-stage argument or when all the major issues and important differences of opinion have been addressed.

Sharon's Problem Situation

Sharon and her friend Jill are shopping in a clothing store. Sharon has driven them to the store. Jill picks up a blouse she really likes and takes it into the dressing room to try on. When Jill comes out of the dressing room, Sharon sees that she is wearing the blouse under her coat. Jill then walks out of the store. Moments later, the security officer and the store owner come up to Sharon. The store owner says to the officer, "That's one of the girls who took the blouse!" The security officer checks Sharon's bag but doesn't find the blouse. "Okay, you're off the hook, but what's the name of the girl who was with you?" the officer asks Sharon. "I'm almost broke because of shoplifting," the owner says. "I can't let her get away with it."

What should Sharon say or do?

1. Should Sharon keep quiet and refuse to tell the security officer Jill's name?
   should keep quiet/should tell/can't decide
2. From the store owner's point of view, should Sharon:
   keep quiet/tell/can't decide
3. What if the store owner is a nice guy who sometimes lets kids buy an item even if they don't have quiet enough money for it. Then should Sharon:
   keep quiet/tell/can't decide
4. What if the store owner is Sharon's father? Then should Sharon:
   keep quiet/tell/can't decide
5. Is it ever right to tell on someone?
   yes/no/can't decide
6. Who's to blame in this situation?
   Sharon/Jill/the store owner/other/can't decide
7. How important is it not to shoplift?
   very important/important/not important
8. How important is it for store owners to prosecute shoplifters?
   very important/important/not important

Sarah's Problem Situation

Sarah works as a clerk in a grocery store. The store isn't too busy. George, a friend of Sarah's at school, comes over to her cash register and says, "Hey, I've only got a dollar with me. Ring up these cigarettes and a six-pack for a dollar,

---

Implementing a "Dilemma Discussion Group"   *Continued*

won't you? The manager's in the back of the store—he'll never know." Sarah likes George a lot, and George has done some favors for her. But Sarah also feels trusted by the manager.

What should Sarah say or do?

1. Should Sarah refuse George, or should Sarah say yes to George's suggestion?
   yes/no/can't decide
2. Was it right for George to put Sarah on the spot with his request?
   yes, right/no, not right/ can't decide
3. What if Sarah feels that other employees at the store do this for their friends? Then what should Sarah do?
   should refuse/should say yes/can't decide
4. What if Sarah feels that the store is making a profit and wouldn't miss a little money? then what should Sarah do?
   should refuse/should say yes/can't decide

5. What if the store owner is a good friend of Sarah's family? Then what should Sarah do?
   should refuse/should say yes/can't decide
6. What if *you* are the owner of the store where Sarah works? Then what should Sarah do?
   should refuse/should say yes/can't decide
7. How important is it to be honest at a store where you work:
   very important/important/not important
8. Let's say after Sarah says no, George just walks out of the store with the cigarettes and six-pack. Should Sarah tell the manager?
   yes, tell manager/no, keep quiet/can't decide

---

procedures that would promote generalization. Maag suggested that moral reasoning be incorporated into other intervention programs rather than being implemented in isolation.

Interpersonal Problem Solving

Many delinquents and rule breakers are believed to be deficient in the ability to generate alternative responses to interpersonal problems. Some simply fail to produce an appropriately large number of alternatives from which a successful solution can be chosen (D'Zurilla & Nezu, 1980), while others fail to make the causal connection between their behavior and its consequences for others in their environment (Spivack, Platt, & Shure, 1976). The goal of interpersonal problem solving with rule breakers and delinquents is to teach them generic problem-solving strategies that will enable them to solve problems as they arise; it is not to focus on isolated and specific socialization problems. Goldstein (1988), for example, has identified fifty generic skills (see Table 10.2) that form the foundation of an Interpersonal Skills Curriculum. No matter what the program employed, intervention usually involves the behavioral shaping of a problem-solving regimen involving modeling by the teacher or therapist, subsequent rehearsal by the student, and performance feedback. (See the accompanying box, entitled Defining and Promoting Interpersonal Problem-Solving, for a description of the problem-solving process.)

Interpersonal problem solving shows promise of efficacy with rule breakers and delinquents. Programs using a problem-solving training procedure have been

TABLE 10.2   Fifty Specific Skills Taught in the Interpersonal Skills Training Program

Group I: Beginning Social Skills
1. Listening
2. Starting a conversation
3. Having a conversation
4. Asking a question
5. Saying thank you
6. Introducing yourself
7. Introducing other people
8. Giving a compliment

Group II: Advanced Social Skills
9. Asking for help
10. Joining in
11. Giving instructions
12. Following instructions
13. Apologizing
14. Convincing others

Group III: Skills for Dealing with Feelings
15. Knowing your feelings
16. Expressing your feelings
17. Understanding the feelings of others
18. Dealing with some else's anger
19. Expression affection
20. Dealing with fear
21. Rewarding yourself

Group IV: Skill Alternatives to Aggression
22. Asking permission
23. Sharing something
24. Helping others
25. Negotiating
26. Using self-control
27. Standing up for your rights
28. Responding to teasing
29. Avoiding trouble with others
30. Keeping out of fights

Group V: Skills for Dealing with Stress
31. Making a complaint
32. Answering a complaint
33. Sportsmanship after the game
34. Dealing with embarrassment
35. Dealing with being left out
36. Standing up for a friend
37. Responding to persuasion
38. Responding to failure
39. Dealing with contradictory messages
40. Dealing with an accusation
41. Getting ready for a difficult conversation
42. Dealing with group pressure

Group VI: Planning Skills
43. Deciding on something to do
44. Deciding what caused a problem
45. Setting a goal
46. Deciding on your abilities
47. Gathering information
48. Arranging problems by importance
49. Making a decision
50. Concentrating on a task

responsible for lower recidivism rates of known delinquents. For example, Sarason and Ganzer (1973) found that modeling and group discussions centering on desirable and undesirable ways of coping with problem situations in social, vocational, and educational settings produced greater positive effects on counselor ratings than no-treatment controls. Moreover, two- to three-year follow-up data also showed decreased recidivism. Nonetheless, the majority of interpersonal cognitive problem-solving interventions have demonstrated only short-term improvements in specific targeted areas (Mulvey et al., 1993) and more work needs to be done in this critical area (Neel, Jenkins, & Meadows, 1990). It has been found, however, that the programming of "booster" follow-up interventions can influence the maintenance of certain classroom behaviors such as attention to task (Lochman, 1992).

Self-Instructional Control

The rule breaking behavior of some delinquents is considered to be the result of deficiencies in self-control. Like certain subgroups of hyperactive youngsters, rule breakers may lack the necessary self-instructions to refrain from impulse-laden norm violations. Those attempting to teach delinquents self-control have frequently adapted Meichenbaum and Goodman's (1971) regimen of "talking to oneself." For example, Kennedy (1984) cited Snyder and White's (1979) usage of modeling and rehearsal to replace inappropriate self-defeating self-verbalizations (e.g., when told it is time to get up, responding with "The hell with that, this feels good") with more appropriate and adaptive self-verbalizations (e.g., "Already,

---

Defining and Promoting Interpersonal Problem-Solving

One common approach to the teaching of rule-compliant behavior in recent years has been the formal and informal training programs in Interpersonal cognitive Problem-Solving Skills (ICPS). According to Spivak and Shure (1982), the theoretical foundation of ICPS rests on seven major assumptions:

1. Interpersonal problems are a natural consequence of being human and the ability to cope with such problems is a critical life skill.
2. To fully understand the efficiency with which an individual solves a problem, it is necessary to determine how that person recognizes and thinks through the presenting situation.
3. There is a distinct grouping of ICPS skills that mediates quality of social adjustment. These skills may be related, but are not identical, to intelligence.
4. The focus in ICPS is not on *what* someone thinks, but on *how* that individual thinks and puts his or her belief system to use.
5. The significance of the different ICPS skills to the process of adjustment may vary as a function of an individual's age.
6. Inadequacy in one or more ICPS skills may be the result of a failure to learn such skills,

interfering emotions, and consequent non-ICPS thinking, or it may be that once-learned ICPS processes have deteriorated.

7. Any program that enhances the exercise of ICPS skills will enhance the social adjustment of those involved.

Researchers (D'Zurilla & Goldfried, 1971; Spivak et al., 1976) have proposed the following sequence for teaching ICPS to children and adolescents. While this sequence should not be regarded as exhaustive, it does cover the major components of the problem-solving process.

1. Develop a general orientation or set to recognize the problem.
2. Define the specifics of the problem and determine what needs to be accomplished.
3. Stop and think prior to acting. Generate a series of problem-solving alternatives that may be used to accomplish goals.
4. Decide which of the alternatives would be the best choice by evaluating the possible consequences of each alternative.
5. Verify the decision process by assessing whether the selected alternative achieved the desired outcome.

damn. It feels good to stay in bed, but if I get up, I'll get the points I need for a home visit.") in a residential setting for delinquents. Such self-instruction resulted in a 50 percent greater reduction in academic class absences, in failures to complete responsibilities, and in impulsive behaviors than did control conditions. Similarly, Bowman and Auerbach (1982) reported that self-statement modification paired with problem-solving and relaxation training successfully reduced instances of impulsive antisocial behavior in adolescent youthful offenders. While such data are promising, more work is needed to assess how well self-instructional impulse-control procedures generalize outside of treatment facilities and maintain over time.

Self-Management Skills

Self-management is the ability to regulate one's own behavior. Interventions designed to improve the self-management skills of rule breakers or delinquents typically involve three steps. First, they are taught to set reasonable standards for their own behavior. Second, they acquire and practice methods to observe and evaluate their own behavior. Finally, they learn to reinforce their own behavior and to practice this self-reinforcement. Typically, this training in self-reinforcement depends on the acquisition of a repertoire of covert verbal reinforcers that reflect the individual's newly developed self-control (e.g., "I did it! I made it to school today without stealing anything from anyone. I'm proud of myself; it sure took a lot of self-control.").

Unfortunately, little is known about the relative strength of self-management training procedures. Although it has been determined that such skills can be taught to delinquents (Marshall & Heward, 1979), the small number of self-management efforts undertaken makes it difficult to adequately assess the relative efficacy of this procedure (Kennedy, 1984).

Perspective Taking

Perspective taking means considering other people's opinions, attitudes, or feelings. It has been long argued that some forms of rule breaking behavior result from the delinquent's inability to assume the perspective of the victim whose safety, rights, or property are being violated. While there is some evidence linking rule breaking to perspective-taking deficiencies (Rotenberg, 1973), there is a shortage of successful treatment packages in this area. Role-reversal play-acting activities have shown promising results (Chandler, 1973), but more research is needed to identify these specific processes (e.g., empathy, moral judgment) that should be emphasized during perspective-taking interventions.

A Combined Approach: Aggression Replacement Training

Goldstein and his colleagues (Goldstein, 1988; Goldstein & Glick, 1987; 1994) have developed Aggression Replacement Training (ART), a comprehensive curriculum that combines a number of the cognitive-behavioral approaches. In ART, the focus is on the (1) development of social skills through interpersonal skills training, (2) promotion of anger control, and (3) practice of moral reasoning. Previously, we described how moral reasoning and interpersonal social skills are taught within the cognitive-behavioral approach. Anger control training emphasizes how youngsters can control their level of anger arousal through procedures similar to those used in interpersonal skills training (i.e., modeling, role-playing, and group performance feedback). To tie the training to real world events, students employ Hassle Logs to monitor actual provocations experienced and to self-manage their responses.

Data-based evaluations of ART appear promising. Goldstein and Glick (1987; 1994) found the intervention to enhance prosocial skill competency, improve overt prosocial behavior, and reduce impulsivity among incarcerated juvenile delinquents in two youth centers. Such promising outcomes prompted Coleman, Pfeiffer, and Oakland (1991) to assess the effects of the approach on adolescents in a residential treatment facility. In contrast to Goldstein and Glick's findings, it was found that the adolescents improved, over controls, in only knowledge of social skills—not in actual overt skill behaviors. These lack of direct effects on overt behaviors may be the result of the limited ten-week intervention period and inconsistencies in how the adolescents were encouraged and reinforced for doing their homework (i.e., generalization) assignments. Coleman and colleagues concluded that to maximize treatment effects, it is essential that all staff involved in educational and habilitation efforts treat ART training as central to the clients' treatment, rather than just an adjunct to the regular program.

Ecological Approaches

As it does all forms of disturbed behavior, the ecological model views rule breaking and delinquency as disturbances in the reciprocal interactions between the child or adolescent and his or her environment. Since the locus of the problem is the discordant transactions between the rule breaker and significant others in the rule breaker's life, intervention is not directed solely to the observed offender. While the rule breaker is taught appropriate alternatives to delinquent behavior, members of the rule breaker's ecosystem (e.g., family, teachers, friends) also receive instruction in how to promote and maintain prosocial behavior. Strategies used to restore an appropriate balance to an ecosystem are quite diverse; since there are no "pure" ecological intervention techniques, treatment programs tend to use procedures from a variety of conceptual models. Thus, ecological interventions for delinquents and rule breakers can accommodate a wide range of techniques (Apter & Conoley, 1984; Zigler et al., 1992). The only requirement is that the application of such techniques deemphasize individual deficits and aim to restore balance to an obviously disturbed ecosystem.

The efficacy of ecological interventions for managing and treating delinquency and rule breaking is best illustrated by Lewis's (1982) review of residential-care follow-up studies and Zigler and co-workers' (1992) description of several early childhood programs designed to prevent delinquency. Analyzing both treatment and follow-up data from a variety of investigations, Lewis (1982) observed that the amount of improvement made by a resident during the period of treatment was not itself predictive of later adjustment in the home and community. However, when residential treatment was supplemented by a form of environmentally based outreach programming (e.g., working with parents and relevant members of the community), the degree of residential gain was related to later adjustment. Thus, the ecological notion of teaching appropriate behavior patterns to everyone in the delinquent's ecosystem may be a necessary prerequisite for the generalization and maintenance of successful residential programming—that is, if treatment is to be successful, change must occur in both the student and the ecology.

Zigler and co-workers (1992) found that ecologically based early intervention programs serve to alleviate many of the risk factors associated with later delinquency and rule breaking. Reviewing longitudinal evidence from a number of programs the authors posited that the effects of successful experiences early in childhood snowballed to generate further success in school and other social contexts. Specifically, the programs "enhanced physical health and aspects of personality such as motivations and sociability, helping the child to adapt better to later social expectations" (p. 1002). Similarly, O'Donnell, Hawkins, Catalano, Abbott, and Day (1995) found that an extensive six-year multifaceted school-based prevention program that enhanced classroom teaching practices, offered parent training, and provided interpersonal problem-solving training for social skills enhanced the school and social skills of boys. The boys also initiated delinquent behaviors at lower rates than control students and girls were found to abuse substances at lower rates than matched controls. Thus, broad-based, ecologically minded prevention efforts can serve multiple functions: Not only do they reduce the occurrence of school-based problems, they also serve to strengthen measures of social competence necessary for success in a number of family and community-based social situations.

Intervention Strategies for Specific Rule Breaking Behaviors

In the following pages, we will describe programs and techniques for managing and/or remediating several rule breaking behaviors typically encountered by those who work with children and adolescents. First, we will investigate several methods for reducing instances of theft. Then we will turn our attention to the costly phenomenon of school vandalism and the frightening enigma of substance abuse. We will conclude with a series of alternatives for the reduction of truancy.

Reducing Instances of Theft

Although stealing is a chronic problem in many classrooms, disproportionately little in the way of applied research and intervention guidelines can be found on the subject in the literature. This lack of data-based prescriptive advice can be attributed to the fact that stealing is such a difficult behavior to modify. Four major reasons militate against the quick and easy management of theft. First, theft delivers its own reinforcement in that a stolen object possesses value. Second, successful theft is almost by definition unobserved theft, and it is a ticklish task to determine who is responsible for it. Third, the consequences from authority figures are variable, delayed, and often inconsistent. Finally, theft is a relatively low-frequency behavior compared to other maladaptive classroom behaviors and there are no clear diagnostic criteria for judging the seriousness of the behavior at varying age and developmental levels (Miller & Klungness, 1989; Rosen & Rosen, 1983; Stumphauzer, 1979).

The first task in designing an intervention procedure for theft is to develop a system to detect if the act has taken place. One frequently recommended method is to consider any item in the individual's possession stolen unless ownership can be verified (Patterson et al., 1975). While such a system may violate an individual's right to "hold something for a friend," high rates of theft often call for the use of strict behavioral definitions.

Initial or infrequent acts of theft may not require protracted intervention procedures. Nonetheless, an effort must be made to ensure that an act of stealing does not acquire reinforcing properties. To that end, Blackham and Silberman (1975) have recommended that first offenses be handled by having the child or adolescent return the stolen object or reimburse the victim for its monetary value. Subsequent thefts would be handled by requiring the individual to both return the stolen object and be charged a fine equal in value to the stolen object.

Unfortunately, some residences and classrooms experience such high rates of theft that more involved intervention procedures are necessary. Switzer and colleagues (1977) described a case in which a school psychologist was asked to design a program to stop episodes of theft in several primary-level classrooms. While the items being stolen were not of great value (coins, pencils, toys, etc.), the rate of theft (almost daily) was alarming. The procedure aimed at reducing the instances of theft was an interdependent group contingency program. First, items common to a typical primary classroom, such as coins, markers, pens, pencils, and gum, were placed in various locations around the classrooms. After documenting pretreatment levels of stealing through direct observation for two weeks, each classroom teacher implemented the group contingency. If none of the items were stolen, each class was awarded ten extra minutes of free time after their usual snack period. When an item was missing, the teacher acknowledged the theft and provided an opportunity for the individual responsible to return the item to the teacher's desk while he or she briefly left the room. If the item was returned, the students were able to talk during the snack time; if not, they had to sit quietly while eating and, upon finishing their snack, fold their hands on their desk.

The administration of this group contingency resulted in a rapid reduction of stealing to zero or near-zero levels. In contrast, control conditions that employed lectures on dishonesty had no effect on the behavior. One caution is in order here: Group contingency programs can have the deleterious side effects of coercion, bullying, and scapegoating. Switzer and associates noted that while their group contingency achieved the desired reductions in theft without any observed social pressures on any individual students, the danger of coercive peer pressure may increase with age.

A group contingency program was also employed by Brooks and Snow (1972) to reduce the instances of theft of a known rule breaker. The 10-year-old subject had a tendency to disappear when the class left the room for special activities. Upon returning to class, he traded stolen objects for property owned by his peers. When in class, the student was frequently disruptive and off-task. The group contingency was designed to enlist the help of the target student's classmates. The entire class either earned or lost free time as a function of the single student's compliance to the present contingencies (i.e., completion of work, remaining in class for each period, and staying with the class when they left the room). The target student was also operating under an individual contingency in which a small amount of money was awarded for continued compliance. As with the program described by Switzer and colleagues (1977), instances of theft rapidly dropped to

Considerations in Designing Theft-Reduction Programs for Young Children

In a comprehensive review of theft-control procedures that can be used by parents and teachers, Williams (1985) concluded that while behavioral procedures will not "cure" all instances of stealing, several interventions can eliminate this behavior in young children. The following guidelines are recommended:

Use a variety of verbal and visual cues to help the young child understand the concept of personal property.

Treat the child's possession of items that he or she doesn't own as stealing.

Clearly specify rules and procedures regarding the borrowing of items belonging to others.

Consistently apply appropriate consequences after each and every instance of adult-defined theft.

At a later time, discuss the theft and its possible consequences for the offender and victims.

Do not differentially reinforce periods of not stealing, yet do reinforce the child for specific prosocial behaviors.

Williams cautions adults in authority to be aware of the rights of all involved. Rather than becoming amateur detectives who engage in elaborate searches, parents and teachers are advised to keep their eyes open, monitor children's activities, and ask about questionable items in the target child's possession (Patterson, 1982). Although early detection and intervention are critical for the elimination of stealing before the behavior becomes firmly established, young children should not be coerced into confessing or set up for denying involvement.

Finally, educational programs should be instituted that focus on the changing of accepting attitudes of criminal behavior. This can be accomplished by highlighting the negative consequences of theft, the available prosocial substitutes, and positive role models who do not engage in such activities (Miller & Klungness, 1989).

zero. In addition, as a result of spending more time with his class, the target student completed a greater amount of assigned work. In terms of follow-up and generalization, effects of the group contingency maintained for the entire school year and the target student was anecdotally observed to appear more motivated during school activities.

With adolescents, it may be more appropriate to develop an individual program for reducing theft. Stumphauzer (1976) employed a combination of family contracting and self-control training to reduce the high incidence of theft by a 12-year-old girl. According to both her parents and school officials, the subject had displayed such high rates of uncontrollable stealing that her attendance in her regular sixth-grade classroom was in jeopardy, despite her above-average academic performance. Treatment was initiated after the collection of baseline data. Family contracts involved the delivery of praise and money for periods of no stealing, while the self-control training focused on developing the target's self-monitoring, self-evaluation, and self-reinforcement. The combination of family contracting and self-control training resulted in a significant drop in the known rate of stealing (from four or five times a week to only two instances in a five-week period). Of even greater significance, Stumphauzer noted that after one and a half years, the effects of the treatment program had maintained and the positive outcomes had seemingly generalized. The girl's stealing stopped, and she had become an active and popular member of several school clubs.

No discussion of rule breaking management techniques can ignore the need to *prevent* acts of antisocial behavior in the first place. In terms of theft, Dreikurs, Grunwalk, and Pepper (1971) remind us that respect for property is learned and occurs through the building of proper attitudes and an appreciation of others' rights. In many cases, these attitudes and appreciation are acquired through the incidental processes of observational learning rather than from direct instruction—in other words, many youngsters learn their ethical standards by observing the significant adults in their environments. Some less-than-virtuous adults may think they can rely on the old maxim "Do as I say, not as I do," but, in fact, youngsters are apt to copy the dishonest behaviors of those around them. The implication is clear: Adults must both highlight and model honest behaviors if they wish to positively influence the prosocial development of children and youth.

Reducing School Vandalism

According to Zwier and Vaughan (1984), strategies designed to reduce school vandalism can be classified into three major orientations: conservative, liberal, and radical. The *conservative* position views the school vandal as a deviant who must be either deterred or caught and punished. The major emphasis of schools adopting this conservative stance has been the "vandal-proofing" of the school environment through such high-tech equipment as microwave sensors, infrared alarms, and closed-circuit television, as well as the more conventional strategies of increased illumination and alarms. While the initial cost of such systems is admittedly high, the immediate reduction in vandalism typically noted makes the expense seem worthwhile. For example, Epstein, Rothman, and Sabatino (1978) reported that the installation of a sixteen-camera closed-circuit surveillance system in Texas resulted in an 80 percent reduction in school-hour vandalism. Similarly, an intercom system designed to identify unusual noises (e.g., shattering glass) saved a Kentucky school corporation more than $110,000 in vandalism-related expenses.

The *liberal* orientation views vandalism as the result of a malfunctioning school system. Aspects of the educational establishment believed to be problematic include the design and layout of the physical plant, school administration, curriculum, and level of community involvement with the school. In terms of physical design, correlational data suggest that landscape, lighting, and overall aesthetic quality of the school may be negatively related to vandalism (Pablant & Baxter, 1975). Regarding school administration, the available research has not determined whether a principal's individual style (authoritarian versus democratic) affects the rate and frequency of vandalism, but has reported that the consistency with which administrators enforce rules and policies is related to the frequency of vandalism and a host of other disruptive behaviors (Zwier & Vaughan, 1984).

Reductions in vandalism have also been accomplished by a variety of creative curricular activities. Epstein and associates (1978) described the experiences of two school districts, one in California and the other in Washington, D.C. Two schools in South San Francisco implemented an incentive program called "1 per ADA." At the beginning of the year, a special fund was set up for end-of-year student activities; if any acts of vandalism occurred, the cost of those acts was subtracted from the fund. The program, designed to provide students with concrete knowledge of the debilitating costs of vandalism, reduced the district's vandalism-related expenses by 82.5 percent. In the Washington school, students were directly taught the importance of conservation and beautification for their school and community. By emphasizing school pride, the program increased student willingness to work on both school and community beautification projects. A more discrete measure of the program's effectiveness was the reduction noted in the incidence of broken windows.

Focusing on the personnel within a school system, Mayer, Butterworth, Nafpaktitis, and Sulzer-Azaroff (1983) observed that vandalism costs declined as teachers, administrators, and counselors received in-service training in alternative teaching and management techniques. Teams of educators were in-serviced in a variety of behaviorally based strategies, including the recognition and reinforcement of positive behaviors, the use of alternatives to conventional punishment techniques, and the appropriate utilization of high-interest academic materials. Not surprisingly, the three-year in-service treatment program also reduced frequency of other discipline problems (e.g., yelling, swearing, the throwing of objects) as well as the acts of vandalism.

From more *radical* orientations, school vandalism is a normal reaction to the debilitating conditions that exist within the educational establishment. The argument is that the anonymity and competitiveness of most large schools breed a natural frustration and hatred of the educational system, which is expressed as vandalism of the school building or its resources. Attempts to deter vandals or to alter the superficial appearance of the school are viewed as useless by radical theorists. Instead, they believe that significant changes in the educational system must be made. Frequent recommendations are the abandonment of large and impersonal schools and a moratorium on the use of competitive assessment procedures (Zwier & Vaughan, 1984). While such radical transformations might indeed reduce the incidence of school vandalism and other rule breaking behaviors, they are at this point more idealistic than practical.

Managing Substance Abuse

The use and misuse of drugs, alcohol, and tobacco products have been repeatedly discussed and analyzed in all the media. While substance abuse is generally regarded as a societal problem encompassing all age groups, no subject seems to spark the fears and heighten the emotions of parents and teachers more than the child or adolescent drug abuser. Still, the seriousness of substance abuse cannot be overstated. As observed by Cohen and Fish (1993), the statistics are grim reminders of this epidemic. Over 3 million teenagers in the United States are alcoholics, and nearly 30 percent of all adolescents have tried at least one illicit drug or controlled substance. It has also been estimated that one in every six 13-year-olds has used marijuana and that 75 percent of drugs used are purchased on school grounds (Irwin & Maag, 1993; Sabatino & Smith, 1989).

Sociologists, psychologists, and even biologists have presented a plethora of theoretical models (e.g., Maisto & Carey, 1985) that attempt to explain substance abuse among school-aged populations. While individual theories may each account for a small minority of abusers, it is generally believed that a variety of forces interact to cause the widespread substance abuse in our society. Still, no matter what the cause or causes of the problem, school personnel are being asked to assist and sometimes spearhead management and remedial efforts.

Involvement with Drugs and Alcohol

Severe substance abuse typically requires interventions that are beyond the available resources of most school districts. Children and adolescents in this category often need the intensive and costly services of withdrawal or detoxification centers as well as regularly scheduled psychological or psychiatric therapy. However, the local school can be the setting for preventive drug and alcohol programs. As Davis and Lanning-Ventura (1983) have observed, prevention programs can "nip the problem in the bud," thus sparing society the time and expense of rehabilitative efforts. Since they are familiar with their students and in a good position to observe behavioral change, teachers can intervene before the situation requires intensive therapeutic action. The necessary prerequisites for reliable observation are knowledge and understanding of the types of substances abused and their commonly observed effects.

Generic strategies used in educational settings to prevent substance abuse include self-esteem building, social competence skill training, academic achievement promotion, the development of effective communication skills, values clarification, problem solving, and peer tutoring and counseling, as well as the initiation of a wide range of recreational activities designed to combat boredom (Cohen & Fish 1993; Davis & Lanning-Ventura, 1983; Hawkins, Catalano, & Miller, 1992). Interestingly, drug and alcohol education is not in and of itself a highly effective deterrent to abuse. Once viewed as potentially a great preventive force, educational intervention failed largely because of the preponderance of scare tactics and factually incorrect information incorporated into the early curriculums. In addition, teachers were put in the uncomfortable position of having to teach content with which they were only vaguely familiar (Wong, 1979). The philosophy underlying the management, remediation, and prevention of substance abuse has changed quite a bit from the early days. Although unbiased awareness of the bad effects of drugs and alcohol is still believed to be important, today we focus more attention on the individual abuser's personal needs, pressures, and environmental situation. Effective programs assist abusers to recognize their basic psychological and social needs and the various methods for satisfying those needs, the ultimate goal being to get them to discover socially acceptable and productive means of satisfaction (Hawkins, et al., 1992; Lotsof, 1978; Millman, Khuri, & Hammond, 1981).

Few teacher-initiated programs to prevent or to reduce drug and alcohol abuse are found in the professional literature, in contrast to the case with other problems of childhood and adolescence such as inattention or disruptiveness. The reason is that it would be extremely difficult for any educator to implement an individual management program that could compete with the powerful secondary gains associated with substance abuse. Still it is generally recognized that school-based programs can be influential in the prevention as well as in the identification and early treatment of substance abuse. As noted by Millman and colleagues (1981), teachers are often the first to recognize behaviors associated with drug use and are in a position to teach students about the dangers of drugs. In addition, school counselors can implement peer group sessions that assist students to live a productive life and help them to deal with strains without resorting to drugs. Unfortunately, little is being done to provide students with behavior disorders with substance abuse prevention programming. Genaux, Morgan, and Friedman (1995), in a nationwide survey of teachers of students with behavioral disorders, found that lack of time and curriculum materials were among the greatest impediments to prevention programming. As students with disabilities are at high risk for substance abuse (Fox & Forbing, 1991; Irwin & Maag, 1993) it is essential that greater efforts be made to address factors associated with vulnerability. Fox and Forbing (1991) have recommended that preventative measures be taken in the following areas: (1) education about drugs and their effects; (2) affective skill building; (3) development of recreational skills; (4) appropriate modeling by adults; and (5) enhanced communication and support systems.

Management of Smoking

Despite the overwhelming evidence about the hazards of smoking, Americans of all ages and socioeconomic conditions continue to engage in this habit-forming activity. Many children and adolescents first experiment with cigarettes and other tobacco products in the school setting. The smoke-filled lavatory is a familiar sight for school administrators, teachers, and students. Traditionally, schools used mostly punitive measures to deal with smokers unfortunate enough to get caught. Depending upon how often they were apprehended and on the individual school's code of discipline, smokers could expect to be punished by detention, in-school suspension, parental notification, or out-of-school suspension. Recently, many schools have supplemented disciplinary measures with the presentation of the many hazards and disadvantages of smoking. Using materials provided by health agencies such as the American Cancer Society and the American Heart Association, teachers have actively attempted to prevent smoking by directly teaching students about the deleterious effects of tobacco. They have supplemented factual material with programs designed to give students the skills to resist peer pressure—often thought of as a major cause of adolescent and preadolescent smoking (Davis & Lanning-Ventura, 1983). A short-term cognitive-developmental program designed to prevent the progression from experimental to establishing smoking was successful with middle school students. Specifically, Hirschman and Leventhal (1989) found that students who attended only three thirty-minute sessions consisting of role-playing, slides, and discussions demonstrated reduced progression of smoking eighteen months later.

Truancy

Truancy, the unapproved absence from school, is a major problem in many school districts. Truancy disrupts the continuity of academic and social-emotional programming and is associated with poor school performance, low self-esteem, and low grades. There are many possible causes, with failure in school, peer pressure, and lack of parental support and encouragement for school activities being the most prominent. Researchers have also found that several classroom variables are related to high rates of absenteeism, including a competitive and teacher-controlled classroom climate, critical rather than positive or constructive feedback, and a preponderance of passive rather than active classroom activities (Moos & Moos, 1978; Needles & Stallings, 1975).

Several strategies have been tried to both prevent and remediate truancy. In terms of prevention, it is important for the teacher and school administration to demonstrate that regular attendance is necessary and valued. Some of the more successful techniques for recognizing and reinforcing attendance are certificates for perfect or outstanding attendance, verbal praise for attendance, and the honoring of good attenders with desirable student jobs (such as hall monitor and class president). Truancy can be prevented if school is a stimulating place where all students are given opportunities to succeed.

In terms of remediation, successful strategies include individual and group contingency management programs, counseling regimens, and cooperative home-school projects. Individual management programs (Bizzis & Bradley-Johnson, 1981; Brooks, 1974; Neel & DeBruler, 1979) have typically employed some form of contingency contract in which the truant earned privileges for increased school attendance. Group management programs (Barber & Kagey, 1977) and cross-age tutoring (e.g., Maher, 1986) have been both practical and beneficial in settings that have had large numbers of truants. A common technique to increase attendance is for the school to provide highly desirable group activities (e.g., parties, play, movies) if the entire class reaches the attendance criterion. Contacting the student's home upon each instance of absenteeism is one strategy that has been successfully employed by many local school districts to prevent truancy. Another, used to maintain high rates of attendance among identified truants, is for the school administrator or an appointee to praise parents for encouraging their child to go to school (Copeland, Brown, Axelrod, & Hall, 1972; Sheats & Dunkleberger, 1979).

In some extreme cases, it may be worthwhile for the school and parents to identify the factors that make school attendance so aversive and staying at home so pleasant, then to use that information to design an individual program to reverse this state of affairs. For instance, Schloss, Kane, and Miller (1981) designed an intervention program that sought to increase the amount of satisfaction adolescents gained from going to school, sought to decrease the amount of satisfaction they gained from staying home, and actively taught truants the social skills needed to benefit from school-based instruction. As a result of this cooperative home-school intervention, attendance dramatically increased to near-perfect levels.

In a comprehensive review of the literature, Schultz (1987) found that the large majority of studies reported failed to include assessments of treatment maintenance once the experimental variables were removed. Responding to this need, Hess, Rosenberg, and Levy (1990) investigated the effects of an intervention that combined contingency contracting with group counseling on rates of unexcused absences, academic grade point averages, and rates of grade retention with twenty-six middle-school students who had mild to moderate handicaps. The counseling component incorporated aspects of both rational emotive (Ellis, 1979) and theme-centered interaction (Cohn, 1970) techniques and was designed to promote the maintenance of the contingency contracts. Rates of truancy for students receiving the experimental condition were reduced significantly at follow-up; unfortunately, these gains in attendance did not maintain at post-treatment levels when assessed at an eight-week follow-up. Still, the experimental group's rates of truancy at follow-up did not approach the levels demonstrated by the students assigned to the control condition.

Large-Scale Programs to Manage and Remediate Rule Breaking and Delinquency

Most school systems have well-developed policies and procedures to deal with student misconduct. As we have noted, teachers are able to apply a variety of management and remedial procedures in a majority of cases. Extreme or repetitive infractions, however, typically require the assistance of a school administrator or the person responsible for implementing districtwide disciplinary and remedial procedures. In certain cases, it may be necessary to consider day-school programs housed outside the regular school environment or residential alternatives. What follows are descriptions of several large-scale interventions for dealing with extreme and repetitive acts of rule violation and delinquency. Obviously, some of the program alternatives described here are not appropriate for some rule breakers and school systems. Individual rule breakers have individual program needs, and it is sometimes necessary to devise a unique program of educational standards and disciplinary policies to fill these needs.

Suspension from School

An extremely common method of dealing with both rule breaking and unruly behavior is out-of-school suspension. Suspension has been defined as the removal of a student from school for ten days or less. Suspensions do not require full due process hearings because they do not constitute changes in placement. However, recent court decisions have resulted in several guidelines regarding the appropriate implementation of suspensions for students with handicaps. Table 10.3 summarizes these guidelines.

Despite the apparent popularity of this disciplinary procedure, the desirability and effectiveness of out-of-school suspension have been questioned. By being excluded from school, students lose valuable instructional time and rarely receive the opportunity to make up the missed work. Furthermore, suspended students are often unsupervised and thus free to engage in behavior that is anything but aversive to them. The local school district is also penalized by suspending students since funding is based on a formula that uses average daily attendance. It has also been speculated that expulsion may promote a sense of failure and ultimately lead to dropping out of school Most critically, out-of-school suspension does not result in a decrease in the behavior problem that caused the suspension (Garabaldi, 1982; Sabatino et al., 1983).

Because of the shortcomings of this exclusionary approach to discipline, many school districts have adopted in-school suspension. In-school suspension is generally defined as the removal of a student from the usual classroom to a special discipline setting. The obvious advantage of the in-school approach is that it allows the implementation of intervention procedures to reduce instances of rule breaking, disruptive behavior, and delinquency. Moreover, formal due process procedures are usually not necessary (Underwood & Mead, 1995), and they keep the suspended student from roaming the community without supervision (Yell, 1990). There are different ways to use this disciplinary regimen. Some school districts have capitalized on the confinement aspect of in-school suspension, in the belief that the isolation and boredom of the experience will deter future instances of misbehavior (Garabaldi, 1982). Other districts have used the suspension period to offer students support in both academic and social-emotional areas of deficiency, though they must work alone and are not permitted to interact with other students (Charbot & Garabaldi, 1982).

TABLE 10.3   Using Suspensions and Expulsions with Students with Handicaps: Court-Mandated Guidelines

Suspensions

1. The suspension of handicapped students requires a review of the individual education plan (IEP). The IEP review team must develop a plan of action dealing with the discipline of the student. The plan may include suspension (*Philip Pratt v. Board of Education of Frederick County*, 1980).

2. Suspension of handicapped students can be used as a disciplinary measure (*Board of Education of the City of Peoria v. Illinois State Board of Education*, 1982).

3. The suspension of a student for less than ten days is not a change in program placement. Suspensions do not require parent notification or an opportunity for a hearing (*Board of Education of the City of Peoria v. Illinois State Board of Education*, 1982).

4. Short-term consecutive suspensions cannot be for more than a total of ten days (*Blue v. New Haven Board of Education*, 1981).

Expulsions

1. If a student exhibits a behavior or action that is a clear danger to himself, herself, or others, immediate removal of that student from the educational setting is permissible for up to ten days (*Hong v. Doe*, 1988; *Jackson v. Franklin County School Board*, 1985).

2. The act of expelling a handicapped student is a change in placement (*Honig v. Doe*, 1988) and, therefore, the due process requirements stipulated by PL 94-142 must be utilized. These include the notification of the student's parents that a change of placement may occur and that the parents and student have the right to a hearing (*S-1 v. Turlington*, 1981; *Stuart v. Nappi*, 1978).

3. If the student's behavior is directly related to the handicapping condition, the student may not be expelled. A group of professionals and experts, and not the local school board, must be utilized to determine if a relationship exists between the behavior and the handicapping conditions (*S-1 v. Turlington*, 1981).

4. Students expelled from an educational setting must continue to be taught using alternative education procedures. An expelled student may not be denied instructional services (*Lopez v. Salida School District*, 1978; *Stuart v. Nappi*, 1978).

The ultimate measure of any in-school suspension program is how much it discourages problem behavior. Unfortunately, formal evaluation data for in-school suspension programs are sparse, and those that are available tend to be difficult to interpret because of the varying philosophies, disciplinary goals, and educational standards of the districts implementing such programs. Still, the current thinking is that in-school suspension can be effective when counseling, remediation, and strict rule adherence are integral components of the program (Sabatino et al., 1983).

It must be cautioned, however, that in-school suspension programs are not appropriate for all school situations or conducive to all administrative styles. As with any punishment technique, the program must be well conceived, logistically sound, realistic, and justifiable. Administrators must realize that most in-school alternatives require additional personnel, which often means extra funding. For the program to be successful, it is critical that administration, faculty, and parents cooperate in the development of clearly stated policies and procedures regarding its operation. In some cases, the use of in-school suspension should be included in a student's individual education plan. Equally important are consistency and impartiality. Students assigned to an in-school suspension program should be treated neither harshly nor leniently: Extremely stern adult behavior could promote negative attitudes toward school, while an agreeable experience could result in the student not wanting to return to the regular classroom (Garabaldi, 1982; Sabatino et al., 1983).

Expulsion

Students who display highly disruptive, aggressive, or dangerous behaviors may be expelled. Expulsion, generally defined as the exclusion from school for a specified period of time, is usually undesirable because it deprives students of their right to an appropriate education (Yell, 1990). Case law (*Blue v. New Haven Board of Education,* 1984; *Board of Education of the City of Peoria v. Illinois State Board of Education,* 1982; *Goss v. Lopez,* 1975) supports federal court rulings that have defined expulsion as the disciplinary removal from school of a student for more than ten days. Some states have tightened the definition of expulsion to mean the disciplinary removal of a student from the school setting for more than five days (McAfee, 1985).

The U.S. Supreme Court has ruled that a student who faces expulsion has certain minimal rights that are protected by the Fifth and Fourteenth Amendments (*Goss v. Lopez,* 1975). These rights are:

1. Notification of the pending expulsion.
2. A due process hearing.
3. A list of the acts the student is charged with committing.
4. The opportunity for the student to recount his or her side of the situations and events resulting in possible expulsion from an educational setting.

Based on the court rulings and guidelines, teachers of emotionally handicapped and behaviorally disordered students should remember that (1) students cannot be expelled without first having a change in placement meeting, and (2) aggressive and disruptive students may be removed for up to ten days even if the behavior is linked to the handicap. During this time period teachers may seek a change in placement for the student by adhering to the due process rights of the parents and the student, and if parents do not agree with the proposed change in placement, it cannot be made without a court order permitting its implementation.

Day-School Alternatives

Unfortunately, a school district's regular in-school alternatives do not always result in decreases of rule breaking and delinquency. In such cases, schools often rely on more intensive and restrictive programmatic alternatives. A variety of self-contained day-school alternatives have been implemented and, not surprisingly, the relative emphases of such programs have been varied. Some have focused on survival, adaptive, and academic skills while others have adopted therapeutic counseling and even outdoor adventure education approaches.

The most common emphases of day school programs for rule breakers, unruly students, and delinquents are behavior management and vocational training. For example, Safer and associates (Heaton, Safer, & Allen, 1982; Safer, Heaton, & Parker, 1982) implemented a multidimensional self-contained classroom program that used a token economy, individualized and small-group instruction, mainstreaming incentives, and a joint home–school reinforcement system. Although the program encountered a variety of logistical problems, a significantly lower number of suspensions and expulsions were noted in the experimental group of disruptive and delinquent junior high students. Also, on measures of academic achievement, the experimental students were superior to the control students. A large-scale vocational training program was far less successful. Ahlstrom and Havighurst (1971) implemented a longitudinal study of the effects of a work experience program and modified academic programming on the adaptive behavior of delinquent and predelinquent students. While many of these students did have positive experiences with the program, the program did little to reduce their rate of delinquency. In fact, there was some evidence that grouping predelinquent with already delinquent students actually increased delinquency—a condition not observed with the control students. The authors concluded that stronger interventions are needed to produce success with students from disorganized social environments.

In an attempt to evaluate the effectiveness of alternative education programs on delinquency-related outcomes, Cox, Davidson, and Bynum (1995) performed a meta-analysis on the relevant empirical literature. To be included in the analysis, alternative education programs had to use a separate curriculum, be housed outside of the conventional school, and assess at least one type of relevant outcome variable. In all, fifty-seven empirical studies that referenced statistical results were included in the analysis. The researchers concluded that alternative education programs can have a small positive effect on school performance, attitude toward school, and self-esteem. However, current efforts have been unable to affect delinquent behavior. Interestingly, it was found that those alternative programs that selected specific target populations (e.g., low school achievers, identified delinquents) had greater effects than undefined alternative schools. It was suggested that defined programs have a greater tendency to develop both a curriculum and structure around the needs of a specific population, whereas undefined programs, with a wide heterogeneity of presenting problems, are more prone to a less focused educational approach or curriculum. Still, the relative small number of methodologically sound studies continue to plague the alternative school literature and we need to know more as to why some programs succeed and others fail (Cox et al., 1995).

Residential Alternatives

Several approaches have been implemented for student rule breakers and delinquents deemed to need residential programming. As noted in Chapter 8, Redl and Wineman (1957) structured the environment of Pioneer House to serve as a therapeutic milieu. Psychodynamic techniques were employed to manage inappropriate surface behavior through the delivery of ego support, and life-space interviewing was used to promote long-term therapeutic growth and development. Project ReED (Rhodes, 1967), while not specifically designed for rule breakers and delinquents, demonstrated that an ecologically based short-term residential program for disturbed children can be successful. As we reported in Chapter 8, the program was designed as a temporary buffer between disturbed children (ages 6–12) and their environments (i.e., home, school, community) so that treatment could begin along a number of avenues. While ReED students were being taught strategies for successfully reentering their environments, key individuals in the students' communities were being instructed by a liaison teacher-counselor in the skills they needed to facilitate reintegration. Students were to be in residence for only three to six months, and during this time they were to return home every weekend. In effect, the perception of finality often associated with institutionalization was avoided. The results of ReED interventions have been favorable; academic and social gains made during the period of residence have been reported to maintain (Weinstein, 1969). Moreover, the ReED principles have been expanded to programs that concentrate on the development of skills necessary for the successful transition to the world of work. The Career Ladder Program (Siegal, 1988), for example, utilized team building, affective education, ecosystem intervention, and long-range enablement planning to address the issues students with behavior disorders face when they are ready to enter the workplace.

Achievement Place, a behaviorally based program, continues to have considerable success in modifying a variety of troublesome delinquent and predelinquent behaviors through the use of its teaching-family treatment model (Phillips, 1968; Phillips, Fixen, Phillips, & Wolf, 1979). A married couple, known as teaching parents, is responsible for managing an extensive program designed to teach small groups of boys the social, behavioral, and adaptive skills necessary for adjustment and success in the home and community. A highly comprehensive token economy and a standardized daily routine are central to the program. Unlike other intervention programs, which have general definitions of delinquency and global treatment objectives, Achievement Place is highly specific as to the behaviors it seeks to promote. For example, upon waking each day at 7 A.M., the boys are required to take care of their personal needs (showering, dressing, etc.) and clean their bedrooms and bathrooms. After breakfast and cleanup, the boys attend public school. School behavior and academic performance are monitored through daily report cards completed by the students' teachers. On returning from school, the boys complete their homework and then are permitted to engage in recreational activities if they have earned such privileges. After dinner, a family conference is held to discuss the events of the day and to provide feedback regarding home and school performance. Prior to bedtime at 9:30 P.M., the boys calculate the points they earned during the day.

Points are awarded for specific appropriate behaviors and lost for clearly specified inappropriate behaviors. The weighting of the points reflects the relative importance of the individual behaviors. Points are usually exchanged for privileges on a weekly basis, and the boys retain their privileges for a week. Most of the privileges are not special toys or treats, but items and events that are naturally available in most home situations. Occasionally, "one-of-a-kind" privileges are available and are awarded auction style. Eventually, an Achievement Place resident can advance to a merit system in which the comprehensive token economy is faded. If after four consecutive weeks of the token system the individual has engaged in desirable behavior, all privileges become free. At this time, behavior is carefully assessed to ensure that the appropriate behaviors are maintained in the absence of the more immediate reinforcers. If a boy maintains success during the merit system, he progresses to the homeward-bound system: Longer periods of time are spent at home until he is judged ready for a full-time return to his natural family environment.

A wide range of evaluation data has been collected on the efficacy of the Achievement Place teaching-family model. Early investigations (Phillips, 1968) found that the comprehensive token economy and its response-cost "fine" component were successful in reducing the frequency of aggressive statements and instances of poor grammar, particularly the use of the slang expression "ain't"; increases in punctuality and the completion of homework assignments were noted as well. In subsequent experiments (Phillips, Phillips, Fixen & Wolf, 1971), it was observed that promptness at meals, room cleaning, and current events knowledge could be significantly increased by the contingency management program. Perhaps most importantly, follow-up data comparing Achievement Place students and control students residing in state institutions indicated that the former were better prepared for community reintegration (Kirigin, Wolf, Braukmann, Fixen, & Phillips, 1979).

Because of the demonstrated efficacy of the Achievement Place model and its easily replicated procedural details, many communities have adopted their own versions of the teaching-family model for treating delinquent and predelinquent behavior. Communities have been especially attracted to the low cost of the Achievement Place treatment program compared to incarceration in state institutions for boys. The fact that Achievement Place espouses a community orientation greatly enhances the generalization and maintenance of treatment gains. In essence, as treatment occurs in and involves the natural environment, there is a high probability that the Achievement Place resident will successfully adjust to his home surroundings.

Summary

This chapter described several strategies and procedures for managing or preventing rule breaking or delinquent behavior. First, major model approaches (e.g., psychodynamic, behavioral, cognitive-behavioral, and ecological) were surveyed and critiqued. Then model programs dealing with specific rule infractions such as theft, substance abuse, vandalism, and truancy were discussed. The chapter concluded with an investigation of those large-scale and system-wide management alternatives that often become necessary when the intensity of a student's rule breaking dictates more restrictive programming.

Discussion Questions

1. How have both the quality and quantity of rule violations exhibited by students with behavior disorders changed over the past few decades?

2. Comment on the efficacy of psychodynamic intervention programs for rule breaking and delinquency. Why would these programmatic effects be difficult to document?

3. Identify the advantages and disadvantages of behavioral intervention programs for rule breaking and delinquency.

4. List and describe three major cognitive-behavioral intervention techniques designed to reduce instances of rule breaking behavior. How do cognitive-behavioral techniques address the issue of generalization across situations and behaviors?

5. Why is it difficult to implement behavior-reduction programs for such rule breaking behaviors as theft, vandalism, and substance abuse?

6. Drawing upon the available literature, name some of the more promising methods for reducing instances of (a) theft, (b) school vandalism, and (c) truancy.

7. In your opinion, what are the roles of the school and the individual teacher in dealing with substance abuse? Can schools mount effective programs for the prevention and/or reduction of drug and tobacco use?

8. Comment on the relative strengths and weaknesses of the following techniques used to manage rule breaking and delinquency: (a) out-of school suspension, (b) in-school suspension, and (c) expulsion.

9. When is it appropriate for rule breaking and delinquent students to be served in day school and residential alternatives? Comment on the efficacy of these settings in the management of problematic behaviors.

References

Ahlstrom, W. M., & Havighurst, R. J. (1971). *400 losers: Delinquent boys in high school.* San Francisco: Jossey-Bass.

Apter, S. J., & Conoley, J. C. (1984). *Childhood behavior disorders and emotional disturbance.* Englewood Cliffs, NJ: Prentice-Hall.

Arbuthnot, J., & Gordon, D. A. (1986). Behavioral and cognitive effects of a moral reasoning development intervention for high-risk behaviorally disordered adolescents. *Journal of Consulting and Clinical Psychology, 54,* 208–216.

Barber, R. M., & Kagey, J. R. (1977). Modification of school attendance for an elementary population. *Journal of Applied Behavior Analysis, 10,* 41–48.

Berne, E. (1961). *Transactional analysis in psychotherapy.* New York: Grove Press.

Bizzis, J., & Bradley-Johnson, S. (1981). Increasing the school attendance of a truant adolescent. *Education and Treatment of Children, 45,* 149–155.

Blackham, G. J., & Silberman, A. (1975). *Modification of child and adolescent behavior.* 2nd ed. Belmont, CA: Wadsworth.

Blasi, A. (1980). Bridging moral cognitive and moral action: A critical review of the literature. *Psychological Bulletin, 88,* 1–45.

Blue v. New Haven Board of Education, No. 81–41 (D. Conn, Mar. 23, 1981).

Board of Education of the City of Peoria v. Illinois State Board of Education, No. 81-1125 (C. C. II, Feb. 4, 1982).

Bowman, P. C., & Auerbach, S. M. (1982). Impulsive youthful offenders: A multimodel cognitive behavioral treatment program. *Criminal Justice and Behavior, 9,* 432–454.

Brooks, B. D. (1974). Contingency contracts with truants. *Personnel and Guidance Journal, 52,* 316–320.

Brooks, R. B., & Snow, D. L. (1972). Two case histories of the use of behavior modification techniques in the school setting. *Behavior Therapy, 3,* 100–103.

Campagna, A. F., & Harter, S. (1975). Moral judgment in sociopathic and normal children. *Journal of Personality and Social Psychology, 31,* 199–205.

Chandler, M. J. (1973). Egocentrism and anti-social behavior: The assessment and training of social perspective-taking skills. *Developmental Psychology, 9,* 326–332.

Charbot, R. B., & Garabaldi, A. (1982). In-school alternatives to suspension: A description of ten school district programs. *Urban Review, 14,* 317–336.

Cohen, J. J., & Fish, M. C. (1993). *Handbook of school-based interventions.* San Francisco: Jossey-Bass.

Cohn, R. (1970). The theme-centered interaction method: Group therapists as group educators. *The Journal of Group Psychoanalysis and Process, 2,* 19–36.

Coleman, M., Pfeiffer, S., & Oakland, T. (1991). Aggression replacement training with behaviorally disordered youth. *Behavioral Disorders, 18*(1), 54–66.

Copeland, R. E., Brown, R., Axelrod, S., & Hall, R. V. (1972). Effects of a school principal praising parents for school attendance. *Educational Technology, 12,* 56–59.

Cox, S. M., Davidson, W. S., & Bynum, T. S. (1995). A meta-analytic assessment of delinquency-related outcomes of alternative education programs. *Crime and Delinquency, 41,* 219–234.

Davis, S. L., & Lanning-Ventura, S. (1983). Substance misuse: Drugs, alcohol, and tobacco. In D. A. Sabatino, A. C. Sabatino, & L. Mann (Eds.), *Discipline and behavioral management.* Pp. 281–320. Rockville, MD: Aspen.

Dreikurs, R., Grunwald, B. B., & Pepper, F. C. (1971). *Maintaining sanity in the classroom: Illustrated teaching techniques.* New York: Harper & Row.

D'Zurilla, T. J., & Goldfried, N. (1971). Problem solving and behavior modification. *Journal of Abnormal Psychology, 78,* 107–126.

D'Zurilla, T. J., & Nezu, A. (1980). A study of the generation of alternatives process in problem solving. *Cognitive Therapy and Research, 4,* 67–72.

Ellis, A. (1979). *Theoretical and empirical foundations of rational emotive therapy.* Monterey, CA: Brooks/Cole.

Epstein, M. H., Rothman, S. G., & Sabatino, D. A. (1978). Programs for youth in trouble. In D. A. Sabatino and A. J. Mauser (Eds.), *Intervention strategies for specialized secondary education* (pp. 1–43). Boston: Allyn & Bacon.

Feldman, D., Rosenberg, M. S., & Peer, G. G. (1984). Educational therapy: A behavior change strategy for predelinquent and delinquent youth. *Journal of Child and Adolescent Psychotherapy, 1,* 34–38.

Fox, C. L., & Forbing, S. E. (1991). Overlapping symptoms of substance abuse and learning handicaps: Implications for educators. *Journal of Learning Disabilities, 24,* 24–31.

Garabaldi, A. (1982). In-school suspension. In D. J. Safer (Ed.), *School programs for disruptive youth.* Pp. 301–314. Baltimore: University Park Press.

Genaux, M., Morgan, D. P., & Friedman, S. G. (1995). Substance use and its prevention: A survey of classroom practices. *Behavioral Disorders, 20*(4), 279–289.

Goldstein, A. P. (1988). *The Prepare curriculum: Teaching prosocial competencies.* Champaign, IL: Research Press.

Goldstein, A. P., Apter, S. J., & Harootunian, B. (1984). *School Violence.* Englewood Cliffs, NJ: Prentice-Hall.

Goldstein, A. P., & Glick, B. (1987). *Aggression replacement training: A comprehensive intervention for aggressive youth.* Champaign, IL: Research Press.

Goldstein, A. P., & Glick, B. (1994). *The prosocial gang: Implementing aggression replacement training.* Thousand Oaks, CA: Sage.

Gross v. Lopez, 95 S. Ct., 729 (1975).

Haskell, M. R., & Yablonski, L. (1974). *Juvenile delinquency.* Chicago: Rand McNally.

Hawkins, J. D., Catalano, R. E., & Miller, J. Y. (1992). Risk and protective factors for alcohol and other drug problems in adolescence and early childhood: Implications for substance abuse prevention. *Psychological Bulletin, 112,* 64–105.

Heaton, R. C., Safer, D. J., & Allen, R. P. (1982). A contingency management program for disruptive junior high school students. I: A detailed description. In D. J. Safer (Ed.), *School programs for disruptive adolescents* (pp. 217–240). Baltimore: University Park Press.

Hess, A. M., Rosenberg, M. S., & Levy, G. K. (1990). Reducing truancy in students with mild handicaps. *Remedial and Special Education, 11,* 14–19.

Hirschman, R. S., & Leventhal, H. (1989). Preventing smoking behavior in school children: An initial test of a cognitive-development program. *Journal of Applied Social Psychology, 19,* 559–583.

Honig v. Doe, 56 S. Ct. 27 U.S. Supreme Court, January 1988.

Irwin, D. M., & Maag, J. W. (1993). Substance abuse among adolescents: Implications for at-risk youth. *Special Services in the Schools, 7*(1), 39–64.

Jackson v. Franklin County School Board, 606 F. Supp. 152 (S.D. Miss., 1985).

Jesness, C. F. (1976). The youth center project: Transactional analysis and behavior modification programs for delinquents. *Behavioral Disorders, 1,* 27–36.

Keilitz, I., Zaremba, B. A., & Broder, P. K. (1979). The link between learning disabilities and juvenile delinquency: Some issues and answers. *Learning Disability Quarterly, 2,* 2—11.

Kennedy, R. E. (1984). Cognitive behavioral interventions with delinquents. In A. W. Meyers & W. E. Craighead (Eds.), *Cognitive behavior therapy with children* (pp. 351–376). New York: Plenum.

Kirigin, K. A., Wolf, M. M., Braukmann, C. J., Fixen, D. L., & Phillips, E. L. (1979). Achievement Place: A preliminary outcome evaluation. In J. S. Stumphauzer (Ed.), *Progress in behavior therapy with delinquents* (pp. 118–145). Springfield, IL: Charles C. Thomas.

Kohlberg, L. (1969). Stage and sequence: The cognitive developmental approach to socialization. In D. Goslin (Ed.), *Handbook of special-ization theory* (pp. 347–479). New York: Rand McNally.

Lantieri, L. (1995). Waging peace in our schools beginning with the children. *Phi Delta Kappan,* January 1995, 386–392.

Lewis, W. W.. (1982). Ecological factors in successful residential treatment. *Behavioral Disorders, 7,* 149–156.

Lochman, J. E. (1992). Cognitive-behavioral intervention with aggressive boys: Three years follow-up and preventive effects. *Journal of Consulting and Clinical Psychology, 69,* 426–432.

Lopez v. Salida School District, CA No. C-73078, Dist. County Ct. of Denver (January 20, 1978).

Lotsof, A. B. (1978). Behavior related to suicides, runaways, alcoholism, and drug abuse. In D. A. Sabatino & A. J. Mauser (Eds.), *Intervention strategies for specialized secondary education* (pp. 157–198). Boston: Allyn & Bacon.

Maag, J. W. (1989). Moral discussion group interventions: Promising technique or wishful thinking? *Behavioral Disorders, 14,* 99–106.

Maher, C. (1986). Direct replication of a cross-age tutoring program involving handicapped adolescents and children. *School Psychology Review, 15,* 100–118.

Maisto, S. A., & Carey, K. B. (1985). Origins of alcohol abuse in children and adolescents. In B. B. Lahey & A. E. Kazdin (Eds.), *Advances in clinical child psychology,* Vol. 8 (pp. 149–193). New York: Plenum.

Marshall, A. E., & Heward, W. L. (1979). Teaching self-management to incarcerated youth. *Behavioral Disorders, 4,* 215–226.

Mayer, G. R., Butterworth, T., Nafpaktitis, M., & Sulzer-Azaroff, B. (1983). Preventing school vandalism and improving discipline: A three year study. *Journal of Applied Behavior Analysis, 16,* 355–369.

McAfee, J. K. (1985). Discipline, special education and students rights. *Information Edge, 1,* 1, 4.

Meichenbaum, D., & Goodman, J. (1971). Training impulsive children to talk to themselves: A means of developing self-control. *Journal of Abnormal Psychology, 77,* 115–126.

Miller, G. E., & Klungness, L. (1989). Childhood theft: A comprehensive review of assessment and treatment. *School Psychology Review, 18,* 82–89.

Millman, R. B., Khuri, E. T., Hammond, D. (1981). Perspectives on drug use and abuse. In C. F. Wells & I. R. Stuart (Eds.), *Self-destructive behavior in children and adolescents* (pp. 122–149). New York: Van Nostrand Reinhold.

Moos, R. H., & Moos, B. S. (1978). Classroom social climate and student absences and grades. *Journal of Educational Psychology, 70,* 263–269.

Mulligan, W. (1972). Dyslexia, specific learning disability, and delinquency. *Juvenile Justice, 23,* 20–25.

Mulvey, E. P., Arthur, M. W., & Reppucci, N. D. (1993). The prevention and treatment of juvenile delinquency: A review of the research. *Clinical Psychology Review, 13,* 133–167.

Murray, C. A. (1976). *The link between learning disabilities and juvenile delinquency.* Washington, DC: American Institute for Research.

Needles, M., & Stallings, J. (1975) Classroom processes related to absence rate. Paper presented at the annual meeting of the American Educational Research Association, Washington, DC.

Neel, R. A., & DeBruler, L. (1979). The effects of self-management of school attendance by problem adolescents. *Adolescence, 14,* 175–184.

Neel, R. A., Jenkins, Z. N., & Meadows, N. (1990). Social problem-solving behaviors and aggression in young children: A descriptive observational study. *Behavioral Disorders, 16,* 39–51.

O'Donnell, J., Hawkins, J. D., Catalano, R. F., Abbott, R. D., & Day, L. E. (1995). Preventing school failure, drug use, and delinquency among low-income children: Long-term intervention in elementary schools. *The American Journal of Orthopsychiatry, 65*(1), 87–100.

Pablant, P., & Baxter, J. C. (1975). Environmental correlates of school vandalism. *American Institute of Planners Journal, 21,* 270–279.

Patterson, G. R. (1982). *Coercive family processes.* Eugene, OR: Castalia Press.

Patterson, G. R., Reid, J. B., Jones, J. J., & Conger, R. E. (1975). *A social learning approach to family intervention.* Vol. 1: *Families with aggressive children.* Eugene, OR: Casklix.

Phillip Pratt v. Board of Education of Frederick County, 501 F. Suppl. 232, (D.D.M., 1980).

Phillips, E. L. (1968). Achievement Place: Token reinforcement procedures in a homestyle reha-

bilitation setting for "predelinquent" boys. *Journal of Applied Behavior Analysis, 1,* 213–223.

Phillips, E. L., Fixen, D. L., Phillips, E. A., & Wolf, M. M. (1979). The teaching family model: A comprehensive approach to residential treatment of youth. In D. Cullinan & M. H. Epstein (Eds.), *Special education for adolescents: Issues and perspectives.* Columbus, OH: Merrill.

Phillips, E. L., Phillips, E. A., Fixen, D. L., & Wolf, M. M. (1971). Achievement Place: The modification of pre-delinquent behaviors with token reinforcement. *Journal of Applied Behavior Analysis, 4,* 45–59.

Redl, F., & Wineman, D. (1957). *The aggressive child.* New York: The Free Press.

Rhodes, W. C. (1967). The disturbed child: A problem of ecological management. *Exceptional Children, 33,* 449–455.

Rosen, H. S., & Rosen, L. A. (1983). Eliminating stealing: Use of stimulus control with an elementary student. *Behavior Modification, 7,* 56–63.

Rosenberg, M. S. (1986). Maximizing the effectiveness of structured classroom management systems: Implementing rule-review procedures with disruptive and distractible students. *Behavioral Disorders, 11,* 239–248.

Rotenberg, M. (1973). Conceptual and methodological notes on effective and cognitive role taking (sympathy and empathy): An illustrative experiment with delinquent and nondelinquent boys. *Journal of Genetic Psychology, 125,* 177–185.

S-1 v. Turlington, 635 F. 2nd 342 (5th Cir. 1981).

Sabatino, D. A., Sabatino, A. C., & Mann, L. (1983). *Discipline and behavioral management: A handbook of tactics, strategies, and programs.* Rockville, MD: Aspen.

Sabatino, D. A., & Smith, R. R. (1989). Diagnosis of youth at risk for suicide, pregnancy, and drug and alcohol abuse. *Special Services in the Schools, 5,* 25–41.

Safer, D. J., Heaton, R. C., & Parker, F. C. (1982). A contingency management program for disruptive junior high school students. II: Results and follow-up. In D. J. Safer (Ed.), *School programs for disruptive adolescents* (pp. 241–254). Baltimore: University Park Press.

Sarason, I. G., & Ganzer, V. J. (1973). Modeling and group discussion in the rehabilitation of juvenile delinquents. *Journal of Counseling Psychology, 20,* 442–449.

Sautter, R. C. (1995). Standing up to violence. *Phi Delta Kappan,* January 1995, 1–12.

Schloss, P. J., Kane, M. S., & Miller, S. (1981). Truancy intervention with behavior disordered adolescents. *Behavioral Disorders, 6,* 175–179.

Schultz, R. M. (1987). Truancy: Issues and interventions. *Behavioral Disorders, 12,* 117–129.

Sheats, D. W., & Dunkleberger, G. E. (1979). A determination of the principal's effect in school-initiated home contacts concerning attendance of elementary school students. *Journal of Educational Research, 72,* 310–312.

Sheldon, W. H. (1949). *The varieties of delinquent youth.* New York: Harper.

Shore, M. F., & Massimo, J. L. (1979). Fifteen years after treatment: A follow-up study of comprehensive vocationally oriented psychotherapy. *American Journal of Orthopsychiatry, 49,* 240–245.

Siegel, S. (1988). The Career Ladder Program: Implementing Re-ED principles in vocational settings. *Behavioral Disorders, 13,* 16–26.

Spivack, G., Platt, J., & Shure, M. (1976). *The problem-solving approach to adjustment.* San Francisco: Jossey-Bass.

Spivack, G., & Shure, M. B. (1982). The cognition of social adjustment: Interpersonal cognitive problem-solving thinking. In B. B. Lahey & A. E. Kazdin (Eds.), *Advances in clinical child psychology,* Vol. 5 (pp. 323–372). New York: Plenum.

Stuart v. Nappi, 443 F. Supp. 1235 (D. Conn. 1978).

Stumphauzer, J. S. (1976). Elimination of stealing by self-reinforcement of alternative behavior and family self-reinforcement of alternative behavior and family contracting. *Journal of Behavior Therapy and Experimental Psychiatry, 7,* 265–268.

Switzer, E. B., Deal, T. E., & Bailey, J. S. (1977). The reduction of stealing in second graders using a group contingency. *Journal of Applied Behavior Analysis, 10,* 267–272.

Trojanowicz, R. C., & Morash, M. (1992). *Juvenile delinquency: Concepts and control.* Englewood Cliffs, NJ: Prentice Hall.

Underwood, J. K., & Mead, J. F. (1995). *Legal aspects of special education and pupil services.* Boston: Allyn & Bacon.

Uniform Crime Report. (1994). *Crime in the United States.* Washington, DC: Government Printing Office.

Van Evra, J. P. (1983). *Psychological disorders of children and adolescents.* Boston: Little, Brown.

Weinstein, L. (1969). Project ReED schools for emotionally disturbed children: Effectiveness as viewed by referring agencies, parents, and teachers. *Exceptional Children, 35,* 703–711.

Williams, R. L. (1985). Children's stealing: A review of theft-control procedures for parents and teachers. *Remedial and Special Education, 6,* 17–23.

Wong, M. R. (1979). Drug abuse prevention and the special education student. In D. Cullinan & M. H. Epstein (Eds.), *Special education for adolescents: Issues and perspectives* (pp. 185–202). Columbus, OH: Merrill.

Yell, M. L. (1990). The use of corporal punishment, suspension, expulsion, and timeout with behaviorally disordered students in public schools: Legal considerations. *Behavioral Disorders, 15,* 100–109.

Zigler, E., Taussig, C., & Black, K. (1992). Early childhood intervention: A promising preventative for early childhood education. *American Psychologist, 47,* 997–1006.

Zirkel, P. (1980. A quiz on recent court decisions concerning student conduct. *Phi Delta Kappan, 6,* 206.

Zwier, G., & Vaughan, G. M. (1984). Three ideological orientations in school vandalism research. *Review of Educational Research, 54,* 263–292.

Chapter *11*

Teaching Students with Mild and Moderate Behavior Disorders

Advance Organizer

As you read this chapter, prepare to identify and discuss:

- Why effective teaching of academic skills and strategies is often overlooked in programming for students with behavior disorders.
- The four distinct levels of instructional time.
- Strategies for making effective use of instructional time.
- Differences between one-to-one instruction and individualized instruction.
- How to best implement small-group instruction.
- The advantages of curriculum-based assessment in the assessment of academic deficiencies.
- How teachers can create a positive classroom climate.
- Generic instructional presentation techniques that typically result in increased student achievement.
- Strategies for maximizing the effectiveness of (1) lesson introductions, (2) direct presentations of new skills, (3) error-correction procedures, and (4) independent practice activities.
- The major characteristics of effective and efficient learning strategies.

Sometimes overlooked in the zeal to develop and implement successful management programs for students engaging in high rates of inappropriate behaviors is the need to provide effective instruction in the many content areas of the academic curriculum. It is easy to understand why this happens. First, these students' behavior problems tend to be more pronounced than their academic deficiencies. When they finally come to the attention of school officials concerned with the development of individualized educational plans (IEPs), their legacy of misbehavior makes behavior management a top priority. Second, most teachers at the beginning of their careers are apprehensive about classroom management. For example, in a review of studies concerned with the perceived problems of beginning elementary and secondary teachers, Veenman (1984) found that classroom discipline and student motivation were by far the most serious of perceived problems (ranked one and two, respectively). Instructional concerns such as lesson planning and effective use of different teaching methods did not even enter the list of top ten concerns.

This apprehension about classroom management on the part of beginning teachers may be warranted—after all, parents and school administrators often evaluate teachers by their ability to manage the behavior of their students. The need for competence in administering classroom management procedures is underscored by researchers' findings that measures of teacher control correlate with student achievement (e.g., Soar & Soar, 1979). But while obviously critical to teaching, classroom management should not be viewed as a concern that is independent of academics. Children identified as having behavior problems typically possess a wide range of academic deficiencies. Rubin and Balow (1978), for instance, found that students whom teachers regularly identified as having behavior problems scored lower on achievement test measures of reading, math, spelling, and language than those who were either inconsistently or never so identified. Scruggs and Mastropieri (1986) found few differences in academic performance between large samples of primary-aged students identified as behaviorally disordered and those assessed as learning disabled: All of these students scored below the twenty-fifth percentile on each of the eight subtests of the Stanford Achievement Test. In a comprehensive review of the literature, Rock, Fessler, & Church (1996) found that many children served in both school and clinical settings have overlapping learning disabilities and behavioral disorders and that this concomitance warrants comprehensive intervention and programming.

Thus, teachers of students with behavior disorders must provide effective instruction in academic skills as well as manage problem behavior. What follows is a description of teacher-based instructional variables that have been found to contribute to the successful teaching of academic skills to students with behavior problems. Although it is beyond the scope of this text to provide an overview of the myriad methods and procedures available for specific content areas, this chapter provides an overall framework for developing and delivering effective instructional sequences across a majority of content areas.

Effective Teaching

Ironically, those teachers who are most likely to engage in effective teaching (and correspondingly maximize student achievement) are the very ones who are most likely to resist having problematic students placed in their classrooms. Thus, as Gernsten, Walker, & Darch (1988) noted, students who have intensive instructional and management needs find it hard to access the most skilled teachers.

For the last twenty-five years, both special and regular educators have attempted to identify factors that contribute to effective teaching. In particular, researchers and practitioners have tried to isolate specific teacher behaviors that correlate with student achievement. These efforts have revealed a series of generic classroom and school leadership practices that can enhance students' academic performances. Each of these practices emerged from solid empirical data gleaned from a number of large-scale studies, including the Texas First Grade Reading Group Study (Anderson, Evertson, & Brophy, 1979), the Beginning Teacher Evaluation Study (Fisher et al., 1980), and the Direct Instruction Follow Through Program (Becker, 1977). A major theme of these and similar research efforts is that instructional efforts are most effective when teachers employ well-planned and structured methods of instruction.

The active components of a *structured method of instruction* (hereafter referred to as *structured instruction*) have been difficult to define because the variables of interest cut across all strands of education. In the elementary and secondary school literature, investigations into effective teacher behaviors are classified under the rubric "effective or exemplar schools movement." Central to this movement is the assumption that change in alterable classroom variables is a necessary condition for developing exemplary schools and improving the quality of education (Berliner, 1985). In the area of behavior analysis, structured instruction is conceptualized as the complete utilization of the operant paradigm. All too often, the use of behavioral consequences has dominated operant approaches to academic instruction; structured instruction techniques highlight the antecedent stimuli of instructional sequences, with special attention given to how teachers can structure their own unique learning environment, present academic content, select instructional materials, and provide quality opportunities to respond (Gersten, Carnine, & White, 1984). Finally, in the special education literature, structured instruction is defined as the constantly changing, yet carefully organized, classroom events and teacher behaviors designed to elicit preplanned changes in a learner's performance—changes involving the learning of concepts, skills, operations, and adaptive behaviors (Lloyd & Carnine, 1981).

Whatever the nomenclature, structured instruction techniques are critical in special education classrooms serving students with behavior problems. Just as they need clear and consistent management and teaching of social-emotional behaviors, students with behavior disorders require structured step-by-step procedures to acquire academic skills. Furthermore, effective and efficient instruction are necessities for students who must acquire new concepts and skills at a rapid rate if they are ever to reach the levels of performance expected in least restrictive or inclusive educational settings. We consider the "how to" of structuring academic instruction under these major categories: those related to organizing for instruction, those related to the delivery of instructional content, and those related to instruction in learning strategies.

Organizing for Successful Instruction

The ability to effectively organize an instructional environment before actually teaching gives teachers of students with behavior disorders confidence, security, and direction. Organizational skills allow them to prepare for and respond thoughtfully to the many rapidly occurring events typical of special education environments. The categories of organizational decision making most useful for the coordination of instructional efforts are management of instructional time, group-size considerations, task targeting, and climate setting.

Management of Instructional Time

The importance currently given to instructional time as a variable related to academic success can be attributed to Carroll's (1963) model of school learning. In that model, degree of learning was conceptualized as a function of time actually spent learning divided by the amount of time needed to learn. This somewhat revolutionary concept redefined learning: The only limitation on ability to learn was the amount of time available for learning. Acceptance of this view clarified the need for planning effective time utilization. Efficient use of instructional time is especially critical for teachers of students with learning and behavior problems if these students' opportunities to learn are to be maximized.

Instructional time can be viewed as existing at four distinct levels: allocated time, actual instructional time, engaged time, and academic learning time. *Allocated time* is the proportion of time a school system or individual teacher plans to teach a particular subject area. In most cases, it is the individual teacher who makes the final decisions about how much time to allocate to academic content. *Actual instructional time*, a subset of allocated time, is the amount of instructional time actually delivered to students. Intentions do not always translate into action; just because a teacher plans to teach a particular subject area for a particular amount of time does not necessarily mean that all of the planned instruction will occur. A variety of events ranging from fire drills to student misbehavior can preclude delivery of valuable minutes of the planned instruction. Typically, teachers deliver approximately 80 percent of the instructional time they allocate (Fisher et al., 1980).

Engaged time is the amount of time a student attends to delivered instruction. This is a more sensitive measure of instructional time in that it accounts for the reality that students can only learn when they are paying attention to classroom activities. Finally, *academic learning time* is the amount of time that students attend to work that is assigned at the correct level of task difficulty. This is arguably the most meaningful measure of instructional time in that teacher diagnostic ability, the quality of the work assigned, and student success rate are all factored into the analysis of time utilization.

Figure 11.1 illustrates the elusive nature of instructional time in a typical six-hour school day. The sequence of circle graphs shows the diminishing academic value of time allocated to instruction as one runs down the different levels of precision in the instructional time hierarchy.

A number of methods for making effective use of instructional time are available for teachers of students with learning and behavior problems. These methods can be conceptualized as addressing overall programming concerns (Rosenberg & Baker, 1985) and lesson-specific issues (Wilson & Wesson, 1986). Five categories of suggestions are presented for increasing time available for learning: (1) the allocation of more time to academic activities; (2) rewarding school attendance and punctuality; (3) programming for fluid transitions between activities; (4) minimizing classroom interruptions; and (5) increasing on-task rates during lessons.

More Time to Academic Activities

Teachers can become aware of those classroom activities that do not directly contribute to learning through an analysis of their own instructional patterns. It has frequently been observed (e.g., Rosenshine, 1980) that noninstructional activities account for well over 50 percent of the school day in classrooms where academic performance is faltering. Not that all noninstructional activities were the result of discipline problems; often they were seemingly harmless discussions of popular television shows or mundane and repetitive record-keeping chores. In contrast, in classrooms where students showed moderate to rapid gains in achievement, teachers maintained a strong academic focus throughout most of the school day; less time was spent on nonacademic activities such as arts and crafts or open-ended questions about personal feelings and beliefs. These teachers mastered instructional procedures ahead of time and covered academic subject matter during both morning and afternoon sessions. Relatedly, effective teachers kept recess and free-time activities within reasonable limits, with the awarding of such privileges being contingent on task completion.

Rewarding Attendance and Punctuality

Truancy, absenteeism, and tardiness significantly reduce time for learning. When students are absent or late, teachers often repeat certain activities to allow them to catch up. Although some teachers believe that absenteeism and tardiness are beyond their management or control, strategies do exist to prevent this potentially critical loss of time. First and foremost, teachers can structure their classroom routine so that attendance and punctuality are expected, valued, and rewarded on a regular basis. Rewards need not be overly intrusive; they can range from simple verbal praise to the awarding of points and certificates within the framework of a formal classroom management system (detailed descriptions of program alternatives for truancy can be found in Chapter 10).

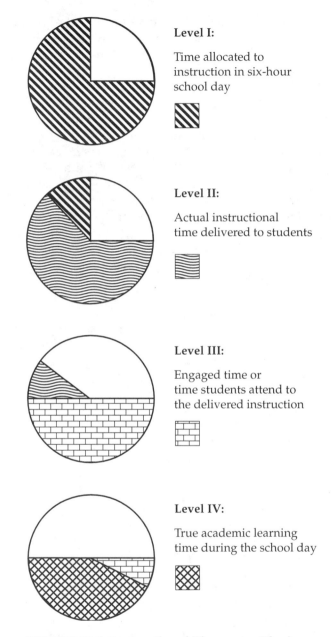

Level I:

Time allocated to
instruction in six-hour
school day

Level II:

Actual instructional
time delivered to students

Level III:

Engaged time or
time students attend to
the delivered instruction

Level IV:

True academic learning
time during the school day

**FIGURE 11.1 Instructional Time as an Elusive
Resource**

Programming for Fluid Transitions Between Activities
Generally, special education settings serving students with behavior disorders
have many activity shifts requiring movement either from one area of the classroom to another or, in cases of resource room programming and mainstreaming,
from one part of the building to another. Although these transitions are necessary

for a comprehensive educational program, they tend to be problematic because they reduce instructional time and often lead to instances of disruptive behavior. To reduce transition time, teachers need to establish and enforce class rules that encourage rapid transitions, arrange the physical environment to facilitate movement within the classroom, and use signals to clearly indicate transitions from one activity to the next.

Minimizing Classroom Interruptions

Two of the most common interruptions of instructional activities have little to do with students: social disruptions from colleagues and messages emanating from the school intercom. Unfortunately, some school personnel feel there is little harm in interrupting classroom activities if they need to speak with a teacher. Similarly, some school administrators have a tendency to make public address announcements whenever something of interest arises, rather than waiting for a pre-arranged scheduled part of the day. When added up over the course of a school year, these disruptions significantly reduce the amount of instructional time. Both principals and teachers can minimize the loss of such time by planning specific times for noninstructional interruptions.

Increasing On-Task Rates During Lessons

Wilson and Wesson (1986) suggest several lesson-specific guidelines for increasing the engaged time of students in special education settings. During teacher-directed instruction, teachers should teach more and test less, increase the number of opportunities to respond during demonstrations, use signals to prompt attention and responses, and teach with animation and enthusiasm. To increase engagement rates during controlled and independent practice—activities typically accompanied by low rates of on-task behavior among students with disabilities—teachers should structure seatwork time, clearly specify instructions, use varied and motivating practice activities, creatively reward correct student responses, employ reinforcing error-correction procedures, and periodically place highly distractible students in study areas or cubicles.

Group-Size Considerations

Issues concerning group size are unavoidably associated with the concept of individualization and the controversial matter of class size. *Individualization*, a term deeply rooted in the lexicon of special education, is based on the assumption that adapting instruction to the unique characteristics of learners will result in higher levels of achievement. While knowledge of specific traits or labels of special education students has not, for the most part, been valuable for differentiating instructional needs (i.e., aptitude treatment interactions), individualization on the basis of skills students need to be taught has been promising (Lloyd, 1984). Note that individualization is not synonymous with one-to-one instruction; rather, individualization refers to instruction that is geared to the current needs of the individual child regardless of the size of the group in which such instruction is delivered (Polloway, Cronin, & Patton, 1986).

The controversial nature of *class size* is evident when one considers the number of school districts and teacher organizations that negotiate class enrollment figures as part of their collective bargaining agreements. Unfortunately, the research dealing with class size is rather confusing. Although reviewers of the literature (e.g., Glass & Smith, 1979) have concluded that, all other things being equal, more is learned in smaller classes, the effects of reduced class size appear to be pronounced only when the number of students is below eighteen. In fact, the most rapid increases in student achievement occur when group size decreases from ten to one. We can conclude from these findings that in classrooms for students with mild learning and behavior problems, the size of groups during periods of small-group instruction may be a more important achievement-related variable than overall class size.

Although *one-to-one instruction* appears to lead to the greatest amount of short-term learning for individual students, some data suggest that teacher-led group instruction may be a more effective and efficient instructional arrangement for students with mild disabilities. In contrast to one-to-one instruction, *small-group instruction* provides students with increased opportunities for incidental or observational learning and appropriate peer interaction (Polloway et al., 1986). For students with behavior problems, small-group instruction allows for the teaching and practicing of appropriate classroom behaviors such as turn taking and listening to others. It also permits teachers to employ differential reinforcement techniques (e.g., reinforcing an appropriate behavior in one child in order to get another child to comply with group or classroom rules). Finally, in terms of efficiency, small-group instruction allows for a greater number of students to receive teacher-directed lessons. If, for example, a teacher had ten children in a class for students with learning and behavior problems and gave each of them one-to-one instruction, each student would receive only six minutes of direct teacher-led instruction per hour and would have to work independently for the remaining fifty-four minutes. Such a state of affairs would be highly undesirable since low-achieving students tend to be less engaged during periods when independent work is assigned.

When grouping students with learning and behavior problems for instruction, teachers should ensure that the process of group assignment does not result in an academic "pecking order" (Barnes & Rosenberg, 1986) and, consequently, contribute to the low self-esteem of these poorly performing students. One method to facilitate maximum student achievement and minimal risk to self-concept is specific-skill grouping, a procedure based on two assumptions: (1) that students possess a variety of strengths and weaknesses and (2) that placement in instructional groups must not remain static throughout the school year. In specific-skill grouping, teachers place students according to similar skill needs; regrouping is done when deficient skills are acquired or when varying rates of content acquisition upset group homogeneity.

The size of instructional groups should be based on levels of student performance and projected rates of skill acquisition. Paine (1982) recommends that groups of six to ten students be used for average and high performers and groups of three to five students for low performers. For tutorial and "firm-up" activities (often needed by very low performers), a group size of one to three is recommended. Before assigning students to small groups for instruction, however, the teacher should examine the nature of the content to be presented. In self-contained classroom settings, it is best to limit the use of small groups to those subject areas that have a "building-block" or task-analytic character. Many basic math and reading skills build systematically on one another and facilitate a flexible skill-grouping classroom regimen. In contrast, subjects such as science and social studies are not easily objectified into specific-skill sequences and are probably best presented in large- or whole-group formats.

Task Targeting

A major component of effective teaching is the careful selection of what to teach. While most of what is to be taught is suggested or mandated by state departments of education and district-wide curriculum committees, special education teachers face two major challenges: assessing for specific skill deficiencies and making assessed skill deficiencies teachable.

Assessing Skill Deficiencies

The assessment of students with learning and behavior disorders continues to grow more sophisticated. Consequently, assessment has become to many teachers and practitioners a complex, jargon-filled activity of standardized tests administered by psychometric experts. However, as noted by Wallace and Kauffman (1986), procedures to assess students' skill deficiencies need not be so specialized or mysterious that teachers are excluded from the diagnostic process. The teaching-learning process depends on teachers continually assessing and making use of vital assessment data.

Curriculum-based assessment (CBA), a method in which student needs are defined and subsequently evaluated in terms of a local curriculum, has been proposed as a sensitive teacher-based method of determining skill deficiencies (Deno, 1985; King-Sears, Cummings, & Hullihen, 1994). CBA involves the collection of direct and frequent measures of student performance on a series of sequentially arranged objectives within a local school's curriculum. To implement effective CBAs, Blankenship (1985) recommends the following steps:

1. List skills presented in the material to be assessed.
2. Examine the list to determine if all necessary skills are included.
3. Sequence edited list into a logical order.
4. Write an objective for each skill on list.
5. Prepare test items for each listed objective.
6. Prepare testing materials and plan how CBA will be administered.
7. Administer CBA prior to instruction on topic to determine student need and readiness for instruction.
8. Readminister CBA after instruction to assess student performance.
9. Periodically administer CBA to probe for long-term retention.

Using these CBA procedures to assess for skill deficiencies minimizes the separation between measurement and instruction: Student performance data are routinely collected and directly applied to the planning of instruction. CBA has greater relevance to instructional planning than many standardized assessment procedures; rather than diagnosing primarily for special educational placement concerns, CBA identifies specific skills students need to learn to make progress in a local school's curriculum.

Curriculum-Based Assessment: Why Should It Be Used?

There is little new or revolutionary about CBA. As a concept, it is as old as education itself (Tucker, 1985). However, in *use*, CBA—which is the measurement of students' academic or social-emotional performance in terms of expected curricular outcomes for a particular school or local education agency—departs considerably from the traditional standardized and norm-referenced measures of student achievement and skill attainment.

Breaking away from any conventional practice for students with disabilities, be it related to instruction or assessment, requires evidence that the new approach will improve the quality of educational services delivered. In the case of educational assessment, Poteet (1987) has described several persuasive reasons for using CBA when organizing and planning instruction. First, CBA assists teachers in determining the content that needs to be taught. A curriculum is the blueprint that guides any educational program, and it is the teacher's job to ensure that as many students as possible acquire the stated curricular content. By assessing what the student doesn't know within an appropriate age-graded curriculum, relevant individual educational plans can be constructed.

Second, CBA is an efficient means for evaluating both student progress and program effectiveness. It is easily implemented, reliable, valid, and readily understood by both service professionals and parents. The frequent monitoring of student progress provides the data necessary for quick changes in student programs when such changes are warranted. Since teachers are able to regularly evaluate the effec-tiveness of instructional methods or materials, the use of ineffective instructional strategies and procedures for long periods of time is avoided.

Third, CBA complies with the requirements of IDEA for assessment and can be used to make referral decisions. CBA is an objective procedure for specifying a student's present level of educational performance; it avoids many of the validation and bias issues that have surrounded traditional psychometric and projective testing. The relatively objective discrimination of either "knowing or not knowing" components of a set curriculum also helps identify students who may be in need of special assistance. Low achievement, or a large discrepancy between expected and actual progress in a curriculum, would be an initial, yet critical, signal that some type of special education arrangement may be necessary.

Finally, CBA has been shown to increase student achievement (e.g., Fuchs, Fuchs, Hamlett, & Allinder, 1991). As with data-based assessment (Rosenberg & Sindelar, 1982), CBA, when used as a precursor to curriculum-matched instructional sequences, can account for rapid gains in academic and social-emotional performance for two reasons. First, students are motivated to acquire skills in the curriculum by the regular feedback inherent in the data-based CBA process. Second, teachers have the opportunity to rapidly change instructional programs that are ineffective or inefficient. By changing methods and procedures during the course of an instructional unit, valuable instructional time is saved and greater amounts of learning and skill acquisition are possible.

Making Assessed Skills Teachable

Once assessed skill deficiencies are identified, teachers of students with learning and behavior problems face the challenge of presenting skills in a teachable format. Effective teachers meet this challenge by task-analyzing the content to be taught. *Task analysis,* defined as the breaking down of large, complex learning tasks into small, manageable, sequenced subtasks, is frequently applied to subject areas that have component subskills that build systematically upon one another. According to McLoughlin and Lewis (1981), two types of task analyses are typical of special education classrooms: functional and structural. A *functional task analysis* is the actual breaking down of a complex skill into teachable component subtasks. For example, a teacher would teach sequentially the component skills necessary to solve a long-division problem. In contrast, a *structural task analysis* is the breaking down of activities within an individual lesson designed to teach a specific subskill. An effective teacher may, for example, first demonstrate the successful completion of a problem, then provide opportunities for controlled practice, and finally assign independent seatwork. In short, to facilitate instruction of complex tasks, teachers first complete a functional task analysis and then develop a structural task analysis for each component subtask. (Alternatives to be considered in the structural task analysis will be detailed in later sections of this chapter that deal with strategies for effectively delivering instruction.)

Climate Setting

The term *climate* refers to the tone, character, or ambiance of an environment. Although it is difficult to define formally, few would argue that a positive classroom environment contributes to higher student motivation and achievement. Like the organizational variables discussed thus far, many variables related to classroom climate are under the direct control of teachers. Three such variables, communicating academic expectations for achievement, programming for high rates of student success, and developing of a convivial atmosphere, have been identified by Berliner (1985).

Communicating Academic Expectations

Achievement is maximized in both regular and special education settings when academic instruction is emphasized as the major activity of school. Successful teachers select and direct academic activities, approach their subject matter in a businesslike fashion, maintain attention, and perhaps most importantly, expect their students to master the material they present (Brophy & Good, 1986; Sindelar, Espin, Smith, & Harrison, 1990). In situations where expectations of student performance are less than positive, several deleterious environmental factors can develop. Naturalistic classroom researchers (e.g., Good, 1983) have found that students for whom teachers hold low expectations tend to be treated as second-class citizens. In comparison to those students expected by teachers to succeed, they are (1) seated farther away from the teacher, (2) called upon less to respond to questions, (3) given less time to answer questions, (4) smiled at less by the teacher, and (5) given praise at a less frequent rate. Obviously, such differential treatment of those perceived as high and low achievers influences the environmental climate of a classroom.

In order to create a classroom environment where academic success is expected for all students, teacher can do several things. First, an active and directed posture should be adopted: Teachers should select and direct learning activities, make themselves the center of attention, and teach content in a firm and businesslike way. Second, to minimize the negative effects of differential treatment that can result from varying expectations, teachers should regularly examine their organizational efforts. For example, careful monitoring of student performance should ensure that assigned tasks are at appropriate instructional levels. Also, during group activities, the teacher should try to ensure that all students participate and receive praise for their efforts, performances, and products.

Programming for High Rates of Success

When students experience success in their learning environments, their feelings of self-esteem and their measured academic performance both increase. Unfortunately, in environments providing few opportunities for success, the opposite holds true: Students feel like failures and do not show large gains in achievement (Fisher et al., 1980). The need for high rates of success for students with learning and behavior problems is obvious. These students have experienced early and repeated failure in classrooms and seem unmotivated in learning situations. Once it was argued that a strong self-concept was a prerequisite for learning in such students—that they had to develop a good self-image and confidence before they could achieve success in school. However, the reverse has been found to be true (e.g., Becker, 1977): Success on academic tasks actually precedes and contributes to the chain of events that enhances a learner's self-concept. In short, nothing succeeds like success.

There are three recognized levels of success: high success, in which 80 percent or more of student responses are correct; moderate success, in which 20 to 80 percent of responses are correct; and low success, in which students achieve only 20 percent or fewer correct responses. Effective instruction demands that success rates vary upward from 70 percent, depending upon the type of instruction being presented. For example, during initial phases of teaching in small-group situations, the success rate should range from 70 to 80 percent; but during review or independent practice session, the success rate should approach 100 percent (Rosenshine, 1983).

Fortunately, success rate can be controlled by well-planned and well-organized teaching. Marliave and Filby (1985) have outlined three categories of strategies to increase student success rate. First is *selection and sequencing of instructional objectives*. As mentioned in our previous discussion of task targeting, success on learning tasks is highly dependent on assigning work at an appropriate instructional level. Curriculum-based and criterion-referenced measures can facilitate accurate diagnoses of students' entry-level skills, since such measures are based on clearly defined and sequenced tasks within a curriculum. The second method for facilitating success rate is *instructional grouping*. By homogeneously grouping students according to their entry-level skills within the curriculum, teachers can adapt the content of their presentations to the specific needs of an instructional group. The chances for high levels of success go up if all the learners in a group have the prerequisites to acquire the new skill being presented. Finally, student success rates are enhanced when *clear and concise instructions* are given for task completion. To increase this attention to instructions, teachers should teach students to follow directions and require them to paraphrase or write down task-completion directions after assignments are given (Wilson & Wesson, 1986).

Developing a Convivial Atmosphere

Critics of structured approaches to instruction often contend that these approaches are inflexible, harsh, and manipulative. This need not be the case. In fact, structure works best when it is not viewed as synonymous with rigidity. If incorporated with warmth, enthusiasm, and flexibility, structured approaches to teaching can be more personalized, more rewarding, and more likely to lead to student success and satisfaction than other, less carefully crafted instructional methodologies (Barnes & Rosenberg, 1986).

Certainly, the development of a convivial atmosphere depends on a number of complex and interacting variables. First of all, teachers can facilitate the growth of warmth and enthusiasm in classrooms by planning for and securing student cooperation. Cooperation can be promoted on the first day of the school year, when classroom rules and procedures and student and teacher responsibilities are initially discussed, and by encouraging student input and putting it to use in the overall classroom management scheme. Furthermore, teachers should give respectful feedback to student efforts; instances of appropriate academic responding should be followed by directed praise and reinforcement, while incorrect responses should receive nonpunitive corrective feedback. Finally, a convivial classroom environment requires enthusiasm on the part of both students and teachers. Enthusiasm can be easily developed by employing exciting instructional techniques. As noted by Rosenshine and Stevens (1986), when instruction is done well, it is an exciting thing to watch and be a part of; both teachers and students confidently interact and feel the mutual satisfaction of learning new skills.

Delivering Instructional Content

After organizing for instruction, it is time to deliver the planned academic content. In this section, we describe several generic presentation techniques that typically result in increased student achievement. Like the teacher-based behaviors discussed under the heading "Organizing for Successful Instruction," each of the variables related to instructional delivery possesses a solid empirical framework, particularly for students characterized as low achievers. Rosenshine and Stevens (1986) have integrated the available research into a general model of effective instruction (see Table 11.1), and we have adapted the major components of this model to guide our discussion of how to best deliver academic lessons to students with learning and behavior problems.

TABLE 11.1   A General Model of Effective Instructional Functions

I. *Lesson Introduction and Review*
Check homework (routines for
students to check each other's
papers).
Reteach when necessary.
Review relevant past learning.
Review prerequisite skills.
Use advance organizers.
Review rules and procedures.

II. *Presentation of New Material*
Provide short statement of objectives.
Proceed in small steps, but at a rapid
pace.
Intersperse questions with the demon-
stration to check for understanding.
Highlight main points.
Provide sufficient illustrations and
concrete examples.
Provide demonstrations and models.
When necessary, give detailed and re-
dundant instructions and examples.
When necessary, use prompts and cues
cautiously.

III. *Guided or Controlled Practice*
Guide initial student practice.
Provide many opportunities for
students to respond and overtly
practice.
Ensure that questions are directly relevant to the new content or skill.
Check for understanding by evaluating
student responses.
Give all students a chance to respond
and receive feedback; ensure that
all students participate.
Make sure that initial student practice
is sufficient so that students can
work independently.
Continue guided practice (usually)
until a success rate of 80 percent is
achieved.

IV. *Academic Feedback and Error*
Correction
Follow quick, firm, correct responses
by another question or short
acknowledgment of correctness.
Follow hesitant correct answers by
process feedback (i.e., "Yes, Linda,
that's right because . . .").
Assume that student errors indicate
a need for more practice.
Monitor students for systematic
errors.
Try to obtain a substantive response
to each question.
Elicit an improved response when the
first one is incorrect.
Use praise in moderation, and remember that specific praise is more
effective than general praise.

V. *Independent Practice*
Make sure that practice is directly
relevant to skills/content taught.
Have students practice until their
responses are firm, quick, and
automatic.
Aim for a 95 percent correct rate
during independent practice.
Alert students that seatwork will
be checked.
Hold students accountable for their
seatwork.
Actively supervise students.
Utilize a variety of independent
practice activities.

VI. *Reviewing Subject Matter*
Use within-lesson summaries.
Use lesson-ending reviews.
Use weekly and monthly reviews.
Test frequently.
Reteach material missed on tests.

Source: Adapted from Rosenshine & Stevens (1986).

Lesson Introduction and Review

"Tell them what they are going to get, give it to them, and tell them what they got"!
While such a colloquial view of the teaching process is naive, simplistic, and forever
doomed to fail, it does highlight a step in the instructional process often overlooked

by teachers: lesson introduction or set induction. Three lesson-introduction activities are critical to the successful outcome of planned activities, particularly with students who have experienced repeated learning and behavior problems: advance organizers, lesson- or group-specific rules, and reviews of prerequisite skills.

Advance Organizers

Advance organizers are brief statements that bridge the information to be presented with knowledge already acquired; the statements provide the information students need to make sense of a lesson and assist them to recall already-learned information that can contribute to the successful completion of lesson activities (Ausubel, 1960). For students with learning and behavior problems, advance organizers are particularly important because they signal to students that a shift in attention will be necessary, direct students' attention to those academic areas critical to understanding the lesson, and refresh students' memories of material previously covered. Advance organizers can be verbal or visual (Darch & Carnine, 1986) and can take a number of forms ranging from a brief statement of the lesson's objectives to complex analogies comparing the new material to concepts previously covered or things and events within the student's environment. Whatever the form used, it is imperative that the organizer set the stage for the lesson, allow for smooth transitions between activities, and provide the structure or scaffolding (Slavin, 1986) that students need to acquire the new material. Students must also be taught to recognize advance organizers and know what to do with them once they are recognized (Lenz, Alley, & Schumaker, 1987).

Lesson- and Group-Specific Rules

Clearly and explicitly stated rules and procedures are intricate parts of most classroom management systems. Rules identify and operationalize the general standards of acceptable classroom behavior, and procedures define the steps needed to accomplish a task or activity. While few veteran teachers would argue against the need for *overall* classroom rules and procedures, only recently has the value of lesson- or group-specific rules been recognized. In a study done with highly distractible students, Rosenberg (1986a) found that daily lessons preceded by a brief review of rules were more effective than lessons that did not receive such a review. Daily review activities lasted less than two minutes and involved students repeating, both individually and in unison, the lesson-specific rules and procedures to be followed in order to earn token economy points. As noted in Figures 11.2 and 11.3, on days when the rules were reviewed, increased rates of time on-task and opportunities to respond were observed; on days without review, on-task rates dropped and students had fewer opportunities to respond.

Reviews of Prerequisite Skills

According to Rosenshine and Stevens (1986), there are two reasons for beginning lessons with brief reviews of prerequisite skills: to provide additional practice of previously learned material and to correct or reteach those prerequisites that remain difficult for students to acquire. One might assume that daily lesson-initiating reviews are common practice among educators, but they are not; naturalistic

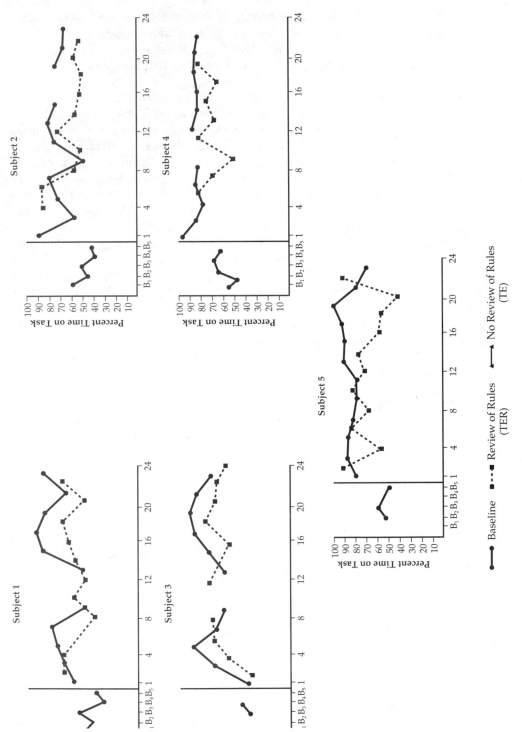

FIGURE 11.2 Different Rates of Time On-Task as a Function of Either Reviewing or Not Reviewing the Rules of a Token Economy

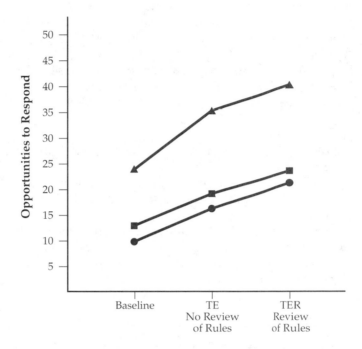

**FIGURE 11.3 Opportunities to Respond as a Function
of Three Conditions: Baseline, Token
Economy, and Token Economy Paired
with a Review of Rules**

Source: From Rosenberg (1986a)

classroom observations (e.g., Good & Grouws, 1979) have indicated that classroom
teachers use as little as 50 percent of available opportunities to provide introductory
reviews. A review of prerequisite skills can take many forms, but must be more
than a mere listing of previously covered concepts. Appropriate activities for lesson-initiating reviews include discussions and questions about material covered in
previous lessons, homework checks, brief quizzes, and students' preparation of
written or oral summaries of the previous day's lessons.

Presentation of New Material

The most effective and efficient method of presenting academic content is the three-step process of demonstrating, prompting, and practicing. The process of explicitly demonstrating or modeling skills, concepts, or operations to be learned is one of the hallmarks of the structured approach to teaching. Each step in the process of learning basic skills or solving problems is overtly demonstrated; thought processes believed private or covert are made overt and observable for instruction. The many steps involved in solving long-division problems, for example, would be taught through an appropriately sequenced set of overt rules and illustrations. Rosenshine and Stevens (1986) have presented several guidelines for making clear presentations of academic content:

1. Present material in small steps.
2. Organize and sequence material so that one point can be mastered prior to the presentation of the next.
3. Model the skill, concept, or operation being presented.
4. Use a large number and variety of examples and illustrations; question students frequently.
5. Provide detailed and redundant explanations of difficult points.
6. Test for understanding of one point before moving on to the next.
7. Have students summarize the lesson in their own words.
8. Avoid digressions and minimize the use of ambiguous terms, phrases, and pronouns.

Unfortunately, even when teachers follow these guidelines, their initial demonstration of academic material may not be enough to ensure that students with learning and behavior problems will succeed on practice activities. It is at these times that effective teachers should use prompts and cues to facilitate the initial acquisition of the instructional material. Prompts and cues can range from oral and written reminders to complex visual aids, but should be used with four general guidelines (Alberto & Troutman, 1986) in mind. First, prompts should not be so appealing or effective that they seduce students' attention from the lesson's prime objective, which is to learn the assigned skill. Second, prompts and cues should be designed to be as weak as possible, because if they are too strong, they can be intrusive and ultimately slow the learning process. Third, plans to fade prompts and cues should be made before their implementation, and fading procedures should begin as soon as possible. As with any crutch, prompts and cues will have to be abandoned eventually, since the ultimate goal of instruction is for students to be independent and automatic in their application of the new learning. Finally, unplanned or accidental prompts and cues should be avoided. Some students, particularly those with skill deficiencies, watch teachers for clues to the correct response. Teachers should make sure that their facial gestures and vocal inflections do not unintentionally prompt correct responding.

Guided or Controlled Practice

Once the demonstration and prompting of a skill or concept are completed, practice on that newly acquired material should follow. Guided or controlled practice should be directed by the teacher in a firm, active, and businesslike fashion. Prompts, leading questions, frequent repetition, and feedback are all key ingredients to successful controlled practice. Typically, teachers who use controlled practice activities have a prepared set of oral questions, ask many brief questions on the points being taught, have students answer questions frequently both in unison and individually, require written responses either at the board or on paper, have students check their answers, and provide summaries of the practice activities.

According to Rosenshine and Stevens (1986), four factors influence the success of guided or controlled practice activities: frequency of practice, percentage of correct responding, teacher-initiated checking for understanding, and the organization of practice. With regard to frequency of practice, a number of researchers (e.g., Anderson et al., 1979) have documented the need for high rates of opportunities to respond during controlled practice activities if these activities are to be successful. Clearly, the more times that students have to respond to questions regarding a particular skill or concept, the greater the probability of higher rates of achievement.

One strategy particularly successful in increasing opportunities to respond—and, correspondingly, the academic performance of elementary students with mild disabilities—is unison or choral responding. For example, Sindelar, Bursuck, and Halle (1986) found that children learned a set of sight words practiced with unison responding at a faster rate than words practiced through traditional ordered responding. They demonstrated the feasibility and usefulness of unison responding as well as the ease with which teachers can learn to incorporate this technique into lessons.

Closely related to the need for frequent opportunities to respond during guided or controlled practice is the need for a high percentage of correct student responses. As noted in our previous discussion of success rate, academic performance on assigned tasks increases when students experience frequent success in their learning environments. To facilitate a high percentage of correct student responses during controlled practice activities, the following general guidelines, adapted from Rosenshine and Stevens (1986), are recommended:

1. Ensure that instruction is broken down into small steps and that prerequisite skills are mastered prior to teaching and practicing a new skill.
2. Provide explicit demonstrations of new or difficult concepts and skills.
3. Intersperse all teacher-led demonstrations with frequent questions to maintain students' attention and to check for understanding.
4. Closely monitor initial practice activities and correct student errors immediately.
5. Provide additional guidance when leading practice activities on especially difficult or confusing material.
6. Reteach material when necessary.

Successful guided practice also includes frequent monitoring of whether students understand the skills they are practicing. These checks allow for any necessary reteaching at the earliest possible instructional opportunity and prevent the risk that students will make repeated errors on either independent practice activities or tests. It is not enough to check on only those students who volunteer to respond—these students usually know the content being practiced. To get a complete indicator of understanding, teachers should call upon students who do not raise their hands.

Academic Feedback and Error Correction

An important consideration both during the presentation and guided practice of lessons is the delivery of academic feedback. As defined by Barnes and Rosenberg (1986), academic feedback is any form of expression that gives a student information regarding his or her adequacy of performance. It can range from the simple acknowledgment of correctness to elaborate error-correction procedures. A necessary prerequisite for successful academic feedback is the continual and careful monitoring of student responses. In general, the sooner a teacher discovers a student's pattern of incorrect responding, the easier it is to remedy the errors.

Researchers have repeatedly demonstrated a positive relationship between the correcting of student errors and enhanced student performance across a number of content areas, including math (e.g., Carnine, 1977) and reading (e.g., Rosenberg, 1986b). Correspondingly, most educators agree that the correction of student errors is an important component of any effective instructional sequence. Unfortunately, many teachers remain unaware of the best methods of correcting academic mistakes. The common practice of merely supplying the student with the correct answer and then moving on is not related to increased achievement.

In order to correct student errors effectively, Paine (1982) recommends that teachers diagnose student mistakes to determine whether they are a function of inattentiveness or skill deficiency. Errors resulting from inattentiveness can be easily remedied by prompting, cuing, repeating instructions, and increasing motivation. Skill-deficiency errors can be corrected within the confines of the planned lesson activity by using the following steps:

1. Stop the student immediately.
2. Recognize those students who responded correctly.
3. Model the correct response for the student who made the error and lead the student through the correct response sequence.
4. Test the student again on the missed item.
5. Intersperse practice on the missed item with other items presented or practiced.
6. Provide delayed testing after several other tasks or minutes have intervened.
7. Review errors at the start of the next day's lesson.

Independent Practice

The major goal of appropriately conceptualized independent practice activities is fluency or automaticity in the skill being taught. To have the opportunity to attain this goal, however, students must first demonstrate proficiency in that skill. To ensure that students possess this proficiency, Rosenshine (1979) advocates that teachers spend both time and effort in preparing their students for independent practice activities. First, they should ensure that acquisition has reached a stage that makes automaticity and fluency goals attainable; typically, a correct response rate of 80 percent or higher during controlled or guided practice indicates a readiness for such activities. Second, independent activities should directly follow guided practice activities, with the independent exercises being relevant to the skills covered during the earlier parts of the lessons. Finally, teachers should direct the first few instances of the independent activity; active modeling of the correct mode of responding decreases the probability that students will make errors because they have misunderstood directions.

Independent Seatwork

The most frequently used form of independent practice is seatwork. Seatwork typically involves independent reading and writing tasks that can be performed without direct and immediate teacher supervision. Researchers (e.g., Fisher et al., 1980; Sindelar, Smith, Harriman, Hale, & Wilson, 1986) have found that samples of elementary students, both with and without mild disabilities, spend up to 70 percent of their instructional day at assigned seatwork activities. One advantage of seatwork is that it allows teachers to present direct instruction to small groups or individual students while the remainder of the class is oriented to a relevant instructional task. Unfortunately, rates of student on-task behavior tend to be lower for seatwork activities than for teacher-led activities.

As observed by Anderson (1985), a major management concern involves keeping "seatwork students" on-task so they can benefit from the independent work and not interrupt the other students who are receiving direct teacher instruction. To effectively manage students involved in independent seatwork activities, Rosenshine and Stevens (1986) make the following recommendations:

1. Whenever possible, the teacher should circulate during seatwork and provide feedback and reinforcement for appropriate seatwork behavior.
2. When teaching another group, the teacher should arrange the desks so that she can face both the group and those students assigned independent tasks.
3. The teacher should develop a seatwork routine so that all students understand the rules regarding seatwork and the procedures for obtaining assistance.

Two common problems that occur with seatwork are that teachers do not always (1) prepare students to be successful in independent practice and (2) manage work sessions to ensure high rates of engagement (McKee & Witt, 1990). To make sure that seatwork serves its function as an effective independent practice activity, teachers should assign exercises that are directly related to the objectives being taught. Sindelar, Wilson and Rosenberg (1991) found that seatwork tasks related only indirectly to an instructional objective (e.g., coloring activities or word-search puzzles used to teach oral reading objectives) had little impact on academic performance. In contrast, seatwork that directly matched the initial instructional objectives did provide the opportunities for practice necessary for students to attain automaticity and fluency.

Other Practice Activities

Other ways in which independent practice activities can be programmed for students with learning and behavior problems are cooperative group activities, peer tutoring, and computer-assisted instruction. In *cooperative practice activities*, students typically work together to prepare a common product or help one another on individually assigned tasks. Slavin and associates (e.g., Slavin, 1986; Slavin, Madden, & Leavey, 1984) have designed a program called *Team Assisted Individualization* (TAI) in which students work on individualized self-instructional materials in four-member mixed-ability teams. Members of the team assist one another when difficulty arises, check one another's work against prepared answer sheets, and encourage one another to work accurately and rapidly. Teams are rewarded for the quality of the work completed by each member of the team. Yet rewards are provided to teams rather than individuals. In reviewing the preliminary research on this recently developed technique, Slavin (1986) found that elementary students in classes that used TAI for mathematics computations gained an average of twice as many grade equivalents as those who received more traditional forms of practice. Strong TAI effects were also noted on the achievement of mainstreamed students with learning disabilities, although positive effects took longer to develop.

It should be noted that cooperative learning methods were developed for use in general education settings with little consideration for the special behavioral needs of students with challenging behaviors. Dettmer, Dyck, and Thurston (1996) and Topper, Williams, Leo, Hamilton, and Fox (1994) have identified a number of common problems and possible solutions that can be used during cooperative learning lessons. These strategies and other supports are found in Table 11.2.

A number of peer tutoring programs have considerable success in promoting academic success. Classwide peer tutoring (CWPT) designed by Greenwood and colleagues (e.g., Delquadri, Greenwood, Whorton, Carta, & Hall, 1986; Greenwood, Carta, & Hall, 1988) is a structured peer tutoring protocol that combines peer-mediated practice, teacher orchestrated procedures, and whole class participation. Each student in the class is paired with a partner and pairs are assigned to teams. Compared to teacher-initiated practice activities, these peer-mediated activities result in increased opportunities to respond on relevant practice activities. Variations of CWPT have been developed by other researchers (e.g., Maheady, Sacca, & Harper, 1988; Mathes, Fuchs, Fuchs, Henley, & Sanders, 1994) to address performance deficits in a number of content areas including reading, spelling, and mathematics.

TABLE 11.2 Cooperative Learning Activities—Some Common Behavioral Problems and Possible Solutions

Problem	Student does not get along with other team members.
	Give entire team additional reinforcement contingent upon team cooperation. Differentially reinforce those teams that exhibit appropriate behavior. Allow challenging student to provide mentoring to others. Provide specific feedback as to how to negotiate conflicts. Arrange grouping so there is limited access to those who set student off.
Problem	Student is ostracized by team members.
	Provide direct reinforcement for instances of equal opportunity. Select team for that student with care. Provide specific instruction in group cooperative processes.
Problem	Student refuses to participate in group activities.
	Highlight desirable components of the activity. Provide specific reinforcers for participation in activity. Allow student to work alone for certain components of the activity.

Source: Adapted from Dettmer, Dyck, & Thurston, 1996; Topper, Williams, Leo, Hamilton, & Fox, 1994.

Computer-assisted instruction is another useful alternative for providing practice activities to students with learning and behavior problems. As noted by Schiffman, Tobin, and Buchanan (1984), the microcomputer is both user friendly and non-judgmental. It can give a child who needs additional opportunities to respond the undivided attention that most teachers cannot physically deliver to individual students. Furthermore, the computer can be programmed to immediately reinforce correct student responses and to recognize errors as soon as they are made. Finally, for students who tend to be easily distracted from traditional task formats, micro-computer drill and practice activities can be designed with colorful graphics, animation, and sound effects.

Reviewing Subject Matter

The review of subject matter can be operationally defined as the teacher-directed rehearsal of previously presented, and presumably learned, topics, problems, or lessons. As with lesson-initiating reviews, three types of subject matter review activities have received empirical support from experimental and correlational research: within-lesson summaries, lesson-ending reviews, and weekly and monthly reviews.

Within-lesson summaries are recapitulations of significant facts or concepts presented at various intervals throughout a lesson. These summaries, typically delivered in the form of discussions or crisp restatements of content, serve to recap, "tie up," or condense a chunk of material before the teacher progresses to a new aspect of the lesson or demonstration. Similarly, lesson-end reviews summarize the major points covered throughout an instructional period. These teacher-directed summaries provide closure to the many activities provided during a lesson and serve to redirect students' attention to the main points presented. Restatement, summarization, and review should not, however, end at the conclusion of a lesson. To maximize the retention of newly acquired material, it is critical that teachers deliver both weekly and monthly review activities. For weekly reviews, it is recommended that teachers allocate approximately twenty minutes of each Monday's lesson to the skills and concepts covered during the previous week (Good & Grouws, 1979). Every fourth Monday should be devoted to a review of material presented during the previous month. These periodic weekly and monthly reviews serve two major purposes: (1) they provide the frequent checks necessary to ensure that students are learning the assigned material, and (2) they assist in promoting the maintenance and generalization of the newly acquired material.

Instruction in Learning Strategies

Although some (e.g., Wang, Reynolds, & Walberg, 1988) would contend that the above discussed elements of generic teaching will be effective regardless of a student's characteristics, it is clear that many students with behavior disorders require additional instructional adaptations if they are to achieve academic success. Reviewing the available literature, Kauffman and Wong (1991) have observed that different or additional technical skills are critical for teaching students who continue to fail, even when presented with exemplary structured or direct instruction procedures.

Students who succeed regularly in direct instruction situations tend to be efficient learners who use internal speech mechanisms to guide the development of individualized strategies for learning. These students are reflective learners who monitor and alter how they organize content material. In short, they know how to organize and think about the content being presented in instructional situations. In sharp contrast, many students with disabilities remain unaware of how to regulate their own learning and do not have a series of strategies to address academic problems. Deshler and associates (e.g., Deshler & Schumaker, 1986; Deshler et al., 1996) have developed a series of intervention strategies designed to teach students "how to learn." In effect, students acquire a specific set of explicit techniques, principles, and rules that enable them to solve problems and complete work independently.

According to Deshler and colleagues (1996), the strategies instruction approach is based on the idea that teachers are to develop three instructional areas for effective instruction. First, teachers must be able to articulate to students the range of general strategies that can be applied to all content areas. To do this, the teacher must be able to identify those strategies that are most related to academic success and how they can be adapted for specific content areas. Second, the teacher must be able to present content information in a way that will promote acquisition of content even though students do not have effective or efficient means for acquiring the content. In effect, the strategy compensates for the cognitive deficits of the students. Such compensation requires a repertoire of skills in which teachers provide explicit instruction on how to "think about" and process the content material. Finally, the environment in which learning and instruction take place must facilitate and enhance strategic learning, performance, and competence. This involves the recognition that strategic thinking and instruction to promote such thinking are important and that they be applied across settings and interactions. Thus, the ultimate goal of the strategy instruction approach is to identify strategies that are optimally effective in assisting students meet the demands of current and future tasks.

Effective and efficient learning strategies share characteristics that fall into three major domains: Content, design, and usefulness (Deshler et al., 1996; Ellis & Lenz, 1987). In terms of content, effective and efficient strategies (1) lead to specific and successful outcomes; (2) are sequenced in an efficient manner; (3) cue students to use metacognition as well as appropriate procedures, skills, and rules; and (4) are succinct and can be performed in a limited amount of time. In terms of design, effective and efficient strategies use fewer than seven steps, begin with action words, and contain a remembering system, such as a relevant mnemonic. Finally, strategies are useful when they can be applied across a variety of settings and situations to address common but important and enduring problems faced by students.

It is critical that strategies be taught using an effective sequence of instructional stages (Deshler et al., 1996). It is important that these stages be followed if students are to acquire and generalize the use of the strategy. Table 11.3 highlights the major states in the instructional sequence.

Specific strategies have been developed to address a number of academic and affective content areas including reading (e.g., Lenz, Schumaker, Deshler, & Beals, 1984), writing (e.g., Harris & Graham, 1992), mathematics (e.g., Montague, 1992), and social skills (Scanlon, 1995). A number of approaches have also been developed to assist teachers to alter their presentations of content material for students with cognitive deficits. These approaches have included specific details on how to best use content enhancements (e.g., Hudson, Lignugaris-Kraft, & Miller, 1993) such as advance organizers, visual or graphic organizers, study guides, mnemonic devices, and peer-mediated activities. Specific devices to assist teachers plan strategic presentations of concepts, units, and courses are also available (Bulgren & Lenz, 1995; Schumm, Vaughn, & Leavell, 1994).

Applied data-based investigations employing strategy-based interventions with students identified as having learning disabilities have generally been positive, although lingering issues regarding generalization and maintenance remain (Research Triangle Institute, 1993). Two recent studies investigating the effectiveness of strategy instruction with students having behavior disorders also yielded positive outcomes. Kinder and Bursuck (1993) developed a strategic problem-solution-effect model for teaching history that included instruction in note taking, reciprocal questioning, and the use of graphic timelines. Immediate and educationally significant improvements over baseline were found on unit section tests. Skinner, Bamberg, Smith, and Powell (1993) reported similar positive results in the area of math. Using a cognitive cover, copy, and compare subvocalization strategy, intermediate students with behavior disorders demonstrated and maintained increased rates of correct responding on division fact problems.

TABLE 11.3   Instructional Stages for Teaching Learning Strategies

Determine student's current level of strategy competence and make commitments.	Orientation to instruction and pretesting of current performance. Assessment of current strategy usage. Discussion of why academic problems are occurring in school. Development of a signed goal statement.
Describe the strategy.	Awareness of the overt and covert processes necessary for performing strategy. Articulation of a system for remembering the strategy. Comparison of new approach with previously used approaches. Development of timeline for meeting goals.
Model strategy usage.	Strategy is personalized so student sees benefit of use. Strategy is modeled while teacher explicitly "thinks aloud." Self-instructions in strategy use are emphasized. Student is prompted to use own words in self-talk. Corrective feedback is provided.
Provide opportunities for verbal elaboration and rehearsal.	Student reviews each of the steps in the strategy. Rapid-fire practice exercises are provided. Steps are memorized to 100 percent mastery levels.
Provide opportunities for guided and independent practice in controlled situations.	Ample opportunities for practice with familiar content and materials are provided. Prompts and cues are provided to ensure appropriate use of strategy. Elaborated feedback on how the student is using the strategy is delivered.
Provide opportunities for advance practice and feedback in real-life situations.	Practice and feedback procedures are repeated using materials from current coursework. Prompts and cues are faded so students assume responsibility for using strategy in a variety of contexts.
Confirm acquisition and make generalization commitments.	Strategy use is confirmed and accomplishment is celebrated. Plans for generalization are made and a commitment is made to put forth maximum effort.
Generalize strategy use across situations and over time.	How strategy can be used in varying situations is discussed. Application of strategy in a variety of settings is monitored. Students are provided with ways in which they might monitor long-term application of the strategy. Self-reinforcers for successful maintenance are articulated.

Source: Adapted from Bursuck, 1990; Deshler et al., 1996.

Summary

This chapter identified and described a number of factors associated with successful teaching, regardless of the type or label of student being taught. Structured forms of academic instruction are especially critical for students with behavior problems, though, because they require structured and appropriately sequenced procedures in order to benefit from an educational program. We noted that specific teacher behaviors, both organizational and instructional, have a direct impact on how much such students will achieve in school. Effective teachers of students with behavior problems are well organized and assume the role of instructional leader by setting tasks, maintaining attention, and pacing lessons carefully. They demonstrate or model skills, provide numerous examples, prompt correct responses, provide quality corrective feedback, and review skills and concepts frequently. Effective teachers also manage their instructional time carefully, valuing and rewarding punctuality and attendance, making specific provisions for fluid transitions among activities, and devoting significant amounts of time to academic instruction. In addition, they are excellent diagnosticians and planners who develop clearly defined instructional objectives through diagnostic procedures such as curriculum-based measurement and task analysis of content to be taught. Furthermore, these teachers are skilled in grouping. Finally, successful teachers of students with behavior problems recognize that teaching activities succeed most when they are functionally related to the preplanned goals of instruction; their major focus is on the actual assessed skills and strategies students lack rather than on the training of abilities or underlying processes believed to be related to academic skill development.

Discussion Questions

1. Why is effective teaching of academics often overlooked in programs that serve students with behavior disorders?

2. How does valuable instructional time seemingly vanish on a typical school day? What strategies are available for making better use of available instructional time?

3. Discuss the differences between one-to-one instruction and individualized instruction. How can teachers promote effective small-group instruction?

4. Identify the advantages and disadvantages of curriculum-based assessment. Illustrate how CBA could be implemented for students who have academic skill deficiencies.

5. List and describe several tangible suggestions for improving the climate of classrooms serving students with behavior disorders.

6. Identify and describe the generic instructional presentation techniques that result in increased student achievement.

7. Describe three techniques that can be used to improve the introductions of lessons.

8. What guidelines should be followed for the delivery of clear presentations of academic content?

9. What factors influence the success of (a) guided or controlled practice, (b) error-correction procedures, and (c) independent practice activities?

10. How can instruction in learning strategies improve the academic performance of students with disabilities?

11. In your opinion, why do many effective teachers resist the placement of problematic students in their classrooms?

References

Alberto, P. A., & Troutman, A. C. (1986) *Applied behavior analysis for teachers.* 2nd ed. Columbus, OH: Merrill.

Anderson, L. M. (1985). What are students doing when they do all that seatwork? In C. W. Fisher & D. C. Berliner (Eds.), *Perspectives on instructional time* (pp. 189–202). New York: Longman.

Anderson, L. M., Evertson, C. M., & Brophy, J. E. (1979). An experimental study of effective teaching in first-grade reading groups. *Elementary School Journal, 79,* 193–222.

Ausubel, D. P. (1960). The use of advance organizers in the learning and retention of meaningful verbal material. *Journal of Educational Psychology, 51,* 267–272.

Barnes, D. L., & Rosenberg, M. S. (1986). Increasing pupil achievement: Good teachers make the difference. In R. Weaver (Ed.), *Toward excellence in education: Three papers* (pp. 1–20). Muncie, IN: Ball State University.

Becker, W. C. (1977). Teaching reading and language to the disadvantaged—what we have learned from field research. *Harvard Educational Review, 47,* 518–543.

Berliner, D. C. (1985). Effective classroom teaching: The necessary but not sufficient condition for developing exemplary schools. In G. R. Austin & H. Garber (Eds.), *Research on exemplary schools* (pp. 127–154). New York: Academic Press.

Blankenship, C. S. (1985). Using curriculum-based assessment data to make instructional decisions. *Exceptional Children, 52,* 233–238.

Brophy, J., & Good, T. L. (1986). Teacher behavior and student achievement. In M. Wittrock (Ed.), *Handbook of research on teaching,* 3rd ed. (pp. 328–375). New York: Macmillan.

Bulgren, J., & Lenz, B. K. (1995). Strategic instruction in the content areas. In D. D. Deshler, E. S. Ellis, & B. K. Lenz (Eds.), *Teaching adolescents with learning disabilities* (pp. 409–473). Denver: Love Publishing Co.

Bursuck, W. D. (1990). *Postsecondary education transition planning and programming for students with learning disabilities.* Paper presented at Council for Learning Disabilities Spring Regional Conference, Williamsburg, VA.

Carnine, D. (1977). Frequency of corrections in beginning instruction. Unpublished manuscript, University of Oregon, Follow Through Project.

Carroll, J. B. (1963). A model of school learning. *Teachers College Record, 64,* 723–733.

Darch, C., & Carnine, D. (1986). Teaching content area material to learning disabled children. *Exceptional Children, 53,* 240–246.

Delquadri, J., Greenwood, C. R., Whorton, D., Carta, J. J., & Hall, R. V. (1986). Classwide peer tutoring. *Exceptional Children, 52,* 535–542.

Deno, S. L. (1985). Curriculum-based measurement: The emerging alternative. *Exceptional Children, 52,* 219–232.

Deshler, D. D., Ellis, E. S., Lenz, B. K. (1996). *Teaching adolescents with learning disabilities: Strategies and methods,* 2nd ed. Denver, CO: Love Publishing Co.

Deshler, D. D., & Schumaker, J. B. (1986). Learning Strategies: An instructional alternative for low-achieving adolescents. *Exceptional Children, 52,* 583–590.

Dettmer, P. A., Dyck, N.T., & Thurston, L. P. (1996). *Consultation, collaboration, and teamwork for children with special needs.* Boston: Allyn & Bacon.

Ellis, E. S., & Lenz, B. K. (1987). A component analysis of effective learning strategies for LD students. *Learning Disabilities Focus, 2*(2), 94–107.

Fisher, C. W., Berliner, D. C., Filby, N. N., Marliave, R., Cahen, L. S., & Dishaw, M. M. (1980). Teaching behaviors, academic learning time, and student achievement: An overview. In C. Denham & A. Liberman (Eds.), *Time to learn* (pp. 7–32). Washington, DC: National Institute of Education.

Fuchs, L. S., Fuchs, D., Hamlett, C. L., & Allinder, R. M. (1991). Effects of expert system advice with curriculum-based measurement on teacher planning and student achievement in spelling. *School Psychology Review, 20,* 49–66.

Gersten, R., Carnine, D., & White, W. A. T. (1984). The pursuit of clarity: Direct instruction and applied behavior analysis. In W. L. Heward, T. E. Heron, D. S. Hill, & J. Trapp-Porter (Eds.), *Focus on behavior analysis in education* (pp. 38–57). Columbus, OH: Merrill.

Gersten, R., Walker, H., & Darch, C. (1988). Relationship between teacher's effectiveness and their tolerance for handicapped students. *Exceptional Children, 54,* 433–438.

Glass, G. V., & Smith, M. L. (1979). Meta-analysis of research on class size and achievement. *Educational Evaluation and Policy Analysis, 1,* 2–16.

Good, T. L. (1983). Classroom research: A decade of progress. *Educational Psychologist, 18,* 127–144.

Good, T. L., & Grouws, D. A. (1979). The Missouri mathematics effectiveness project. *Journal of Educational Psychology, 71,* 355–362.

Greenwood, C. R., Carta, J. J., & Hall, R. V. (1988). The use of peer tutoring strategies in classroom management and educational instruction. *School Psychology Review, 17,* 258–275.

Harris, K. R., & Graham, S. (1992). *Helping young writers master the craft: Strategy instruction and self-regulation in the writing process.* Cambridge, MA: Brookline Books.

Hudson, P., Lignugaris-Kraft, B., & Miller, T. (1993). Using content enhancements to improve the performance of adolescents with learning disabilities in content classes. *Learning Disabilities Research and Practice, 8*(2), 106–126.

Kauffman, J. M., & Wong, K. L. H. (1991). Effective teachers of students with behavioral disorders: Are generic teaching skills enough? *Behavioral Disorders, 16,* 225–237.

Kinder, D., & Bursuck, W. (1993). History strategy instruction: Problem-solution-effect analysis, timeline, and vocabulary instruction. *Exceptional Children, 59,* 324–335.

King-Sears, M. E., Cummings, C. S., & Hullihen, S. P. (1994). *Curriculum-based assessment in special education.* San Diego, CA: Singular Publishing Group.

Lenz, B. K., Alley, G., Schumaker, J. (1987). Activating the inactive learner: Advance organizers in the secondary content classroom. *Learning Disability Quarterly, 10,* 53–67.

Lenz, B. K., Schumaker, J. B., Deshler, D. D., & Beals, V. L. (1984). *The word identification strategy.* Lawrence: University of Kansas.

Lloyd, J. W. (1984). How should we individualize instruction—or should we? *Remedial and Special Education, 5,* 7–15.

Lloyd, J. W., & Carnine, D. W. (1981). Forword. *Exceptional Education Quarterly, 2,* viii–xi.

Maheady, L., Sacca, M. K., & Harper, G. G. (1988). Classwide peer tutoring with mildly handicapped high school students. *Exceptional Children, 55,* 52–59.

Marliave, R., & Filby, N. N. (1985). Success rate: A measure of task appropriateness. In C. W. Fisher & D. C. Berliner (Eds.), *Perspectives on instructional time* (pp. 217–235). New York: Longman.

Mathes, P. G., Fuchs, D., Fuchs, L. S., Henley, A. M., & Sanders, A. (1994). Increasing strategic reading practice with Peabody classwide peer tutoring. *Learning Disabilities Research and Practice, 9*(1), 44–48.

McKee, W. T., & Witt, J. C. (1990). Effective teaching: A review of instructional and environmental variables. In T. B. Gutkin & C. R. Reynolds (Eds.), *The Handbook of School Psychology* (pp. 823–848). New York: Wiley.

McLoughlin, J. A., & Lewis, R. B. (1981). *Assessing special students.* Columbus, OH: Merrill.

Montague, M. (1992). The effects of cognitive and metacognitive strategy instruction on the mathematical problem solving of middle school students with learning disabilities. *Journal of Learning Disabilities, 25,* 230–248.

Paine, S. (1982). Setting up for instruction. *Association for direct instruction news, 2,* 8–9.

Polloway, E. A., Cronin, M. E., & Patton, J. R. (1986). The efficacy of group versus one-to-one instruction: A review. *Remedial and Special Education, 7,* 22–30.

Poteet, J. A. (1987). Educational assessment. In J. S. Choate, T. Z. Bennett, B. E. Enright, L. J. Miller, J. A. Poteet, & T. A. Rakes (Eds.), *Assessing and programming basic curriculum skills* (pp. 3–20). Boston: Allyn & Bacon.

Research Triangle Institute (1993). *Approaches and options for integrating students with disabilities: A decision tool.* Longmont, CO: Sopris West.

Rock, E., Fessler, M., & Church, R. (1996). The concomitance of learning disabilities and emotional/behavioral disorders: A model for conceptualization, assessment, and intervention. *Journal of Learning Disabilities.*

Rosenberg, M. S. (1986a). Maximizing the effectiveness of structured management programs: Implementing rule-review procedures with disruptive and distractible students. *Behavioral Disorders, 11,* 239–248.

Rosenberg, M. S. (1986b). Error-correction during oral reading: A comparison of three techniques. *Learning Disability Quarterly, 9,* 182–192.

Rosenberg, M. S., & Baker, K. (1985). Instructional time and the teacher educator: Training preservice and beginning teachers to use time effectively. *The Teacher Educator, 20,* 12–17.

Rosenberg, M. S., & Sindelar, P. T. (1982). Educational assessment using direct, continuous data. In J. T. Neisworth (Ed.), *Assessment in special education* (pp. 83–92). Rockville, MD: Aspen.

Rosenshine, B. (1979). Content, time, and direct instruction. In P. Peterson & H. Walberg (Eds.), *Research on teaching* (pp. 28–56). Berkeley, CA: McCutchan.

Rosenshine, B. (1980). How time is spent in elementary classrooms. In C. Denham & A. Lieberman (Eds.), *Time to learn* (pp. 107–124). Washington, DC: National Institute of Education.

Rosenshine, B. (1983). Teaching functions in instructional programs. *Elementary School Journal, 83,* 335–351.

Rosenshine, B., & Stevens, R. (1986). Teaching functions. In M. C. Wittrock (Ed.), *Handbook of research on teaching,* 3rd ed. (pp. 376–391). New York: Macmillan.

Rubin, R., & Balow, B. (1978). Prevalence of teacher identified behavior problems: A longitudinal study. *Exceptional Children, 45,* 102–111.

Scanlon, D. (1995). Social skills strategy instruction. In D. D. Deshler, E. S. Ellis, & B. K. Lenz (Eds.), *Teaching adolescents with learning disabilities* (pp. 369–407). Denver: Love Publishing Co.

Schiffman, G., Tobin, D., & Buchanan, B. (1984). Microcomputer instruction for the learning disabled. *Annual Review of Learning Disabilities, 2,* 134–136.

Schumm, J. S., Vaughn, S., & Leavell, A. G. (1994). Planning pyramid: A framework for planning for diverse student needs during content area instruction. *Reading Teacher, 47*(8).

Scruggs, T. E., & Mastropieri, M. A. (1986). Academic characteristics of behaviorally disordered and learning disabled students. *Behavioral Disorders, 11,* 184–190.

Sindelar, P. T., Bursuck, W. D., & Halle, J. W. (1986). The effects of two variations of teacher questioning on student performance. *Education and Treatment of Children, 9,* 56–66.

Sindelar, P. T., Espin, C. A., Smith, M., & Harrison, N. E. (1990). A comparison of more and less effective special education teachers in elementary programs. *Teacher Education and Special Education, 13,* 9–16.

Sindelar, P. T., Smith, M., Harriman, N. E., Hale, R. L., & Wilson, R. J. (1986). Teacher effectiveness in special education programs. *Journal of Special Education, 20,* 195–207.

Sindelar, P. T., Wilson, R. J., & Rosenberg, M. S. (1991). Comparisons of direct instruction and direct instruction with supplemental seatwork. Manuscript submitted for publication.

Skinner, C. H., Bamberg, H. W., Smith, E. S., & Powell, S. S. (1993). Cognitive cover, copy, and compare: Subvocal responding to increase rates of accurate division responding. *Remedial and Special Education, 14,* 49–46.

Slavin, R. E. (1986). *Education psychology: Theory into practice.* Englewood Cliffs, NJ: Prentice-Hall.

Slavin, R. E., Madden, N. A., & Leavey, M. (1984). Effects of cooperative learning and individualized instruction on mainstreamed students. *Exceptional Children, 50,* 434–443.

Soar, R. S., & Soar, R. M. (1979). Emotional climate and management. In P. Peterson & H. Walberg (Eds.), *Research on teaching: Concepts, findings, and implications.* Berkeley, CA: McCutchan.

Topper, K., Williams, W., Leo, K., Hamilton, R., & Fox, T. (1994). *A positive approach to understanding and addressing challenging behaviors.* Burlington, VT: University of Vermont.

Tucker, J. A. (1985). Curriculum-based assessment: An introduction. *Exceptional Children, 52,* 199–204.

Veenman, S. (1984). Perceived problems of beginning teachers. *Review of Educational Research, 54,* 143–178.

Wallace, G., & Kauffman, J. M. (1986). *Teaching students with learning and behavior problems.* 3rd ed. Columbus, OH: Merrill.

Wang, M. C., Reynolds, M. C., & Walberg, H. J. (1988). Integrating the children of the second system. *Phi Delta Kappan, 70,* 248–251.

Wilson, R., & Wesson, C. (1986). Making every minute count. Academic time in LD classrooms. *Learning Disabilities Focus, 2,* 13–19.

Chapter *12*

Teaching and Managing Students with Severe Behavior Disorders

Advance Organizer

As you read this chapter, prepare to identify and discuss:

- The characteristics and efficacy of operant procedures used in language interventions for students with autism.
- The major limitations of traditional behaviorally based language-intervention programs.
- How naturalistic behavioral teaching methods can promote social interactions among students with severe behavior disorders.
- Task characteristics that have been shown to enhance the social development of students with severe behavior problems.
- Major differences between naturalistic teaching techniques and directive methods of instruction.
- The three types of peer-mediated approaches for building the social skills of students with severe behavior disorders.
- The possible functions of seemingly purposeless self-stimulatory behavior and self-injurious behavior.
- Three alternative approaches for managing self-stimulatory behavior.
- Two approaches that have proved effective in managing self-injurious behavior.

Contributed by Cynthia O. Vail.

In Chapter 3, we described the patterns of behavior that are typical of students with severe behavior disorders. Our discussion of the early perspectives on the psychoses of childhood and youth was followed by an examination of the major characteristics and etiological formulations for the pervasive developmental disorders. In this chapter, we will describe teaching methods and management strategies for these severe but low-incidence behavior disorders. We will focus particularly on language-intervention strategies for children with autism, naturalistic teaching techniques for promoting social competence, and the management of self-stimulatory and self-injurious behaviors.

Language-Intervention Strategies for Children with Autism

The abilities to communicate and to develop and maintain social relationships are prerequisites for autonomy in society. Individuals must convey their needs and ideas to others and have the capacity to understand communications from others. Because children with autism commonly exhibit language deficits, language training is a central component of their special education. Useful speech by 5 years of age has long been recognized as one of the best predictors of good adjustment for individuals with autism (Eisenberg & Kanner, 1956). Given the importance of language and social skills, special educators must be prepared to provide effective language and social-skill training for children with autism.

Language-intervention strategies for children with autism have been based primarily on the behavioral account of language acquisition. Early researchers—Hewett, Lovaas, Risley, and Wolf—concentrated on speech training. Hewett (1965), for example, used behavioral procedures to train Peter, a nonverbal preschool child with autism, to speak. The training was conducted in a special training booth that seems quite restrictive and artificial by today's standards. Peter received edible reinforcers and social praise for correct responding. The edibles were gradually and systematically faded as social contact grew increasingly effective with Peter. When necessary, responses were prompted and shaped, both verbally and physically (by shaping Peter's mouth to produce sounds). Prompts were also faded as rapidly as Peter's progress would allow. Instruction involved many repetitions of each item, the gradual introduction of new items, and systematic review of previously learned items. The trainers withheld their attention from Peter when he was inattentive or behaving otherwise inappropriately, and this brief time-out intervention proved effective.

Hewett's procedures typify the operant training model used in the 1960s and 1970s. The teacher first trained Peter to make eye contact, then to imitate body movements and vocalizations. Peter's first word ("go") was shaped from "e-oo," a sound that he made before training began. After six months of training, Peter had developed a vocabulary of thirty words, some of which he transferred from the training context to natural settings. This study was quite remarkable for its time; in the 1960s, children with autism were typically institutionalized and often regarded as untrainable. Hewett demonstrated that a nonverbal child with autism could be taught to speak through behavioral technology, and that "his conditioned speech began to take on properties of meaningful language" (1965, p. 934).

Since the 1960s, numerous studies have validated the effectiveness of behavioral techniques in training speech and language (Frish & Schumaker, 1974; Guess, Sailor, & Baer, 1978; Lovaas, 1987; Sailor & Taman, 1972; Snyder, Lovitt, & Smith, 1975). Likewise, behavioral techniques have been used successfully to train specific social skills (Lovaas, 1987; Odom & Strain, 1984). However, despite the demonstrated success of behavioral techniques, professionals from cognitive, developmental, and traditional behavioral backgrounds have criticized the strict operant approach to both language and social-skills training.

Behavioral principles are not the issue but rather how they are applied in practice (Bricker & Cripe, 1992). This criticism stems primarily from the failure of individuals with autism to generalize skills from training contexts to natural settings (Bryen & Joyce, 1985; Carr, 1985a; Garcia & DeHaven, 1974; Halle, 1987; Spradlin & Siegal, 1982; Woods, 1984). Skills acquired and performed in classrooms or therapy rooms seldom occurred spontaneously outside of these environments. Researchers noted such difficulties in the earliest applications of the operant approach (Hartung, 1970). Among the strategies for increasing the likelihood of generalization are using multiple examples in training, teaching in the environment in which the behavior must ultimately occur, employing natural and logical reinforcers (Stokes & Baer, 1977; Stokes & Osnes, 1988), and utilizing training content that is functional and developmentally appropriate (Bricker & Cripe, 1992; Carr, 1985b; Dyer & Peck, 1987; Dyer, Santarcangelo, & Luce, 1987; Light, 1983).

These strategies, along with some other techniques to promote communication and social competence for children with autism, are explored in this section. One approach integrates developmental, operant, and ecological factors (Donnellan & Kilman, 1986; Dyer & Peck, 1987). We advocate basing curricular decisions on the *whole* communicative profile of the child rather than targeting specific skills in isolation. For example, an idiosyncratic behavior such as echolalia may seem noncommunicative—even aberrant—when viewed in isolation, but when analyzed in the context of social interaction, its meaning may become clear.

Traditional Behavioral Language and Social-Skill Intervention

Traditional behavioral intervention is based on manipulating such variables as the setting, materials, teacher, and teaching techniques on the theory that otherwise the child's role in acquiring language will be passive. *Input* is the crucial element of behavioral intervention (Carr, 1985a). Teachers are directive; they control interactions using specific verbal prompts (such as asking "What is this?" while pointing to a picture). Generally, specific responses are modeled and reinforced. This type of intervention when conducted as isolated drill, out of context, has not promoted spontaneous initiation of interactions by persons with autism. In addition, these methods may promote individuals to become prompt-dependent, interacting only after specific prompts are given. Therefore, directive techniques may not result in building functional language and social skills.

Traditional behavioral language interventions that are not considered to be naturalistic frequently involve what is called a *discrete trial format,* or DTF (Carr, 1985a). Instruction typically occurs in a room free of distractions. Many repeated trials are conducted, with correct responding followed by reinforcement (according to a preset schedule of delivery). Reinforcers are often arbitrary in that they are unrelated to the verbal response. For example, a correct response to the question "What is your name?" might be reinforced with an edible.

Numerous behaviorally based intervention studies of the 1960s and 1970s illustrated that some children with autism can be taught to use some language skills and specific social skills in training settings. However, the lack of generalized use of trained skills in nontraining contexts is a major limitation of this approach (Bricker & Cripe, 1992; Carr, 1985a; Garcia & DeHaven, 1974; Harris, 1975). Behaviorally oriented researchers have admitted that generalization is a problem. Their critics have concluded that the problem is inherent in the behavioral approach itself (Carr, 1985a), though it must be said that failures in generalization have plagued virtually all language-training approaches. Perhaps the reason behaviorally oriented interventions have been linked with this problem more frequently is that "the issue of generalization comes up only when treatment effects can be demonstrated; in absence of treatment effects, there is nothing to be generalized" (Carr, 1985a, p. 43).

Closely aligned with problems in generalization is the criticism that the language taught to subjects with autism via behavioral approaches frequently does not generate functional communication (Bryen & Joyce, 1985; Carr, 1985a; Hartung, 1970; Light, 1983; Lord, 1985). This problem may result either from the failure to generalize or from the use of nonfunctional content for individual children. For example, teaching a 3-year-old child with autism to request a favorite toy in a conventional manner is likely to be more functional than teaching the child to say "cow" when a picture card is presented. In general, behavioral language interventions are not associated with systematic guidelines for choosing curricular items (Bricker & Cripe, 1992; Brinker & Bricker, 1980; Carr, 1985a; Dyer & Peck, 1987; Yoder & Calculator, 1981).

Children with autism who receive traditional behaviorally based language training may become prompt-dependent, meaning their language is controlled by the verbal and physical stimuli used in training. Prompt-dependent children do not respond to untrained stimuli, however appropriate such responding might be, so their communications are seldom spontaneous and functional. For example, a child may be thirsty, yet may not request a drink unless prompted by a question. This problem is especially linked to traditional behavioral interventions because they are directive rather than facilitative in nature. The passive child-active environment model may actually promote prompt dependency (Donnellan, Mesaro, & Anderson, 1984).

Finally, some traditional behaviorally oriented methods used with persons with autism have been criticized for eliminating what seems to be aberrant behavior when the behavior is actually serving as a means of communication. For example, echolalia was considered deviant by early behavioral researchers (Lovaas, Schreibman, & Koegal, 1984), but recent research has illustrated that both immediate and delayed echolalia may serve various communicative functions (Prizant, 1983; Prizant & Duchan, 1981; Prizant & Rydell, 1984). It is interesting to note here that even though aggressive tantrumming was conceptualized early on as a possible means of communication for children with autism (Ferster, 1961), only recently have behavioral researchers (Carr & Durand, 1985; Durand & Carr, 1991) empirically examined this particular functional relationship.

Many of the criticisms just outlined have been addressed by behavioral researchers since the early 1970s. The following four techniques have been proposed to promote skill acquisition and generalization: (1) training multiple exemplars—across settings, objects, and trainers (Carr, 1985a; Carr & Darcy, 1990; Harris, 1975; Hartung, 1970; Stokes & Baer, 1977; Stokes & Osnes, 1988); (2) training in natural environments (Bricker & Cripe, 1992; Halle, 1987; Harris, 1975; McGee, Daly, Izeman, Mann, & Risley, 1991); (3) training responses that are functional and that meet a personal or social goal (Bricker & Cripe, 1992; Guess, Sailor, & Baer, 1978; Halle, 1987; Light, 1983; McGee, Krantz, & McClannahan, 1984; Stokes & Osnes, 1988); and (4) looking to the other disciplines for instructional content (Bricker & Cripe, 1992; Carr, 1985b; Dyer & Peck, 1987; Dyer, Santarcangelo, & Luce, 1987; Garcia & DeHaven, 1974; Prizant & Wetherby, 1989).

In the following section, we describe intervention techniques to promote social and communication competence in children with autism. These techniques either have been demonstrated to be effective or are based on tactics that promote skill generalization.

Naturalistic Teaching Methods

Many of the problems that children with autism face stem from their inability either to express themselves in conventional ways or to understand others' communications to them. Children with autism lack the two qualities that appear to be essential for building peer relations: the ability to relate in a positive reciprocal manner and the ability to adapt interaction skills to an ever-changing social situation (Howlin, 1986). Social interactions are built on subtle signals such as eye gaze, facial expression, posture, and other nonverbal behaviors. Although these skills can be trained in isolation through traditional behavioral techniques, the results are generally not functional because the training does not occur in changing social contexts (Frankel, Leary, & Kilman, 1987). Naturalistic teaching methods, on the other hand, including naturalistic behavioral techniques such as incidental teaching (McGee, Almeida, Sulzer-Azaroff, & Feldman, 1992; McGee, Krantz, Mason, & McClannahan, 1983; McGee, Krantz, & McClannahan, 1985), promote social and communicative competence. Developmentally appropriate skills are taught in natural environments, using functional materials in the context of naturally occurring routines and interactions. Training skills in their naturally occurring context may reduce the need for extensive generalization training.

In one study (Peck, 1985), teachers with directive teaching styles were trained to use facilitative techniques to promote social interactions among their students with autism and severe handicaps. Specifically, the teachers were trained to (1) provide their students with more choices and more opportunities to communicate, (2) increase their own responsiveness to student-initiated social and communicative behavior, and (3) imitate and elaborate student social and communicative behavior. As a result of the teachers' learned style, students evidenced increased spontaneous social and communicative behavior.

Naturalisic teaching techniques are not the only means for promoting social competence. These three task characteristics are believed to enhance social development (Donnellan & Kilman, 1986):

1. Tasks should be both *age appropriate* and *developmentally relevant*. For example, a popular age-appropriate card game could be adapted to meet an individual's developmental level.
2. The task should ensure *proximity to other persons*. It is not likely that social interaction will occur if students are involved in various activities at separate desks. Games such as Twister increase the likelihood of interactions.
3. The task should involve and require *more than one person*. For example, making sandwiches could be structured to require interaction: One person may be in charge of the bread and another in charge of the peanut butter. Students would then need to cooperate in order to make sandwiches for themselves.

A related set of techniques for facilitating social development is based on research conducted in Great Britain by Howlin and her colleagues (1987). First, parents deliberately intrude into their child's solitary play. Social interaction can be increased through such structured interference. For example, if a child is actively involved in putting together a puzzle and a parent withholds pieces, the child is required to interact to complete the task. Siblings can be involved in a similar manner: Puzzle or game pieces can be split among siblings to promote turn taking. Finally, family members can teach creative play through modeling. For example, if a child likes to spin the wheels of a car, the family member can join the child in playing with cars and model and encourage creative play in the process.

The procedures described above have components similar to incidental teaching, a naturalistic behavioral technique first described by Hart & Risley (1968). Research suggests that incidental teaching enhances generalization and maximizes learning for children with autism (McGee, Krantz, Mason, & McClannahan, 1983; McGee, Krantz, & McClannahan, 1984, 1985). Model programs for young children with autism use the following systematic components (McGee, Daly, & Jacobs, 1994).

> *(a) a natural environment is arranged to attract children to desired materials and activities (e.g., preferred toys are displayed in activity areas and teachers circulate continuously among children to promote high levels of engagement); (b) the child "initiates" the teaching process by indicating an interest in an item or topic, either gesturally or verbally (e.g., the child points to a block or says "I want the block"); (c) the teacher uses the child's initiation as an opportunity to*

prompt an elaboration related to the child's topic of interest (the teacher asks "What shape block?"); and (d) the child's correct response to the teacher's prompt results in a confirming response, then contingent access to the item/ topic of interest (e.g., the child says "I want a square block" and the teacher immediately provides it, saying "Terrific, here's a square block, let's build a tower with it"). (p. 137).

Imitation

Researchers (Tiegerman & Primavera, 1981, 1984) have investigated imitation as a means of facilitating social responsiveness in children with autism. Imitating the child's actions with a duplicate toy produced greater effects than manipulating the duplicate toy in a different way or playing with a different toy in a different way. That is, the children played longer with the toys and sustained eye contact longer when the teacher followed the child's lead. The developmental status of the child is an important variable to consider when deciding on an imitation strategy. In one study (Dawson & Adams, 1984), children with autism who have low imitative abilities exhibited more socially responsive behavior when an adult imitated their behavior with a duplicate toy than when the adult modeled either familiar or novel actions. In contrast, children with autism of the same age (4–6 years) with more highly developed imitation skills responded similarly to all three circumstances.

Duplicate sets of toys or functional items may be useful when teaching children with autism who have low imitative abilities. For example, if a student frequently spins a brush on the floor in a stereotypical fashion, the teacher may first imitate the spinning with a second brush. If the student responds socially to the teacher's imitative behavior, the teacher should begin to use the brush in a more functional manner. The student is more likely to imitate the behavior if he or she is socially engaged.

Arranging the Environment

Teachers can arrange their classrooms to facilitate communication and social interaction (Halle, 1984; McGee et al., 1991). First, materials and activities should be (1) reinforcing for the child; (2) easy to complete, so that frequent opportunities for functional language are provided; (3) composed of multiple components, each giving an opportunity for communication; (4) repetitive, giving repeated opportunities for language use; and (5) novel, to increase the likelihood that children will request information. Functional daily living activities satisfy many of these criteria. Snack time, for example, is usually reinforcing and comprises multiple components, some of which are repetitive (e.g., passing out cups) and some of which are novel (e.g., introducing a new vegetable like an artichoke).

Next, the physical environment should be arranged to promote communication. Some preferred that materials should be stored so that the students can see them, but cannot reach them. This forces them to ask their teachers or other adults for desired objects stored out of reach. McGee and colleagues (1991) suggest "hobby boxes" containing highly preferred materials. When materials can be accessed freely, opportunities for communication and social interaction are lost.

Daily routines may be analyzed for occasions that will promote communication. Nothing should be given to students without first providing ample opportunity for them to make a request (Charlop, Schreibman, & Thibodeau, 1985). Naturalistic time-delay procedures can be implemented, whereby the teacher systematically delays giving an item, assistance, or access to a preferred event in order to create an occasion for the child to communicate in a natural context for a functional purpose. Say a student needs assistance putting on his coat. Rather than providing unrequested aid, the teacher should look at the student with an expectant facial expression and say, "Need help?" Then, wait for him to initiate a verbal request or gesture for help. If after a prespecified time delay, such as five seconds, the student does not request assistance, the teacher should provide a verbal or gestural prompt, followed by assistance. With time delay, the latency between the request and prompt or assistance may be kept constant or systematically lengthened in a progressive manner (Schuster & Griffen, 1990).

Naturalistic versus Directive Teaching Methods

In recent years, researchers have compared the effectiveness of naturalistic teaching techniques to that of more traditional directive methods for promoting language skills in children with autism. In one study (Neef, Walters, & Egel, 1984), young children with autism were trained to respond appropriately to yes/no questions through two procedures: tutoring and embedded instruction. In embedded instruction, yes/no questions were incorporated naturally into the classroom routine. Embedded instruction was found to result in more correct responding than tutoring.

Nonverbal children with autism have been shown to increase their verbal responding in a language-intervention program that used natural teaching methods (Koegel, Koegel, & Surratt, 1992; Koegel, O'Dell, & Koegel, 1987). The Natural Language Teaching Paradigm included stimulus items chosen by the child and presented according to the child's interest. Rather than commanding the child to "say ball," the teacher manipulated the object and modeled the desired response. Any clear verbal attempt was reinforced with the opportunity to play with the object.

The major difference between directive methods and natural teaching methods such as embedded instruction, the Natural Language Teaching Paradigm, and incidental teaching (Hart & Risley, 1980; McGee et al., 1983; McGee et al., 1994; Warren & Kaiser, 1986) is the context of instruction. Directive methods require the teacher to initiate and prompt trials, whereas facilitative methods rrequire the child to initiate the teaching episode. Child initiation is encouraged by arranging the environment so that children must communicate in order to access certain items. With this technique, communication (e.g., requesting an object) occurs in context. For example, if a student says "Ball," in requesting to play with a specific ball, the teacher might hold the ball and ask, "Do you want the ball?" By doing so, a yes/no response is prompted in a natural context.

Proponents of directive methods may be more concerned with teaching methods than content, and as a result, what they teach may be unrelated to their students' everyday lives. For example, inner-city students might be taught to label pictures of barnyard animals as part of their language-training program. By contrast, proponents of natural facilitative methods attend more carefully to the content of training. They advocate the use of stimulus materials from their students' environments. They are more likely to teach labels for favorite toys, for example, or even requests for favorite toys, because a request is also functional. For example, in embedded instruction, after the child asks for an item (e.g., ball), the teacher is encouraged to ask, "Do you want a ball?" (Neef et al., 1984).

Another distinction between directive and naturalistic teaching methods is in means of reinforcing subjects. Reinforcement may be arbitrary and out of context in the directive model. Naturalistic methods, in contrast, incorporate reinforcers that are contextually related to the response. For example, correct labeling in the Natural Language Training Paradigm is reinforced through playtime with the item (Koegel et al., 1992; Koegel et al., 1987). Reinforcers should be logically linked to the task (e.g., labeling "cookie" is reinforced with a cookie).

Echolalia

Like instructional content, echolalia is understood differently today than it was originally. For years, echolalia was considered an aberrant behavior (Lovaas et al., 1974); researchers studied techniques to eliminate it and replace it with more functional phrases (Screibman & Carr, 1978). More recently, however, descriptive research has shown that echolalia, both immediate and delayed, is used by many children with autism to communicate (McEvoy, Loveland, & Landry, 1988; Prizant, 1983; Prizant & Duchan, 1981; Prizant & Rydell, 1984; Rydell & Mirenda, 1991; Rydell & Mirenda, 1994). Echolalia may serve many communicative functions, including turn taking, requesting, and affirming prior statements. Teachers must accept immediate echolalia, especially in young children with autism, and make use of the opportunities it provides (Prizant & Duchan, 1981). In a natural context, echolalia can be modified and expanded to become increasingly conventional. Echolalia may also facilitate the acquisition or performance of other skills. For example, echolalic children have been shown to correctly identify more objects after hearing (and echoing) the object name than after hearing (and echoing) an unrelated word (Charlop, 1983). Perhaps the echolalia serves as a self-generated signal for the students.

Finally, it appears that the verbal interaction style of the partner communicating with the child with autism influences the functional usage of echolalia. Rydell and Mirenda (1994) found that high constraint or directive utterances on the part of adults led to children using more immediate echolalia, functioning as an organizational or turn taking strategy. In contrast, low constraint utterances (e.g. reflective comments following child's interest) were followed by more delayed echolalia, functioning as requests or assertives. It appears that if a goal is to increase verbal turn taking, teachers may choose to use more directive utterances requiring specific responses. On the other hand, if the goal is to increase initiations for requesting information, providing information and regulating other's actions, then the use of a more responsive style should be used by the adult (Rydell & Mirenda, 1994).

Facilitated Communication

Facilitated communication is a method used with individuals with autism that has come to the forefront over the past five years. Whether facilitated communication is a valid technique for many individuals with autism is hotly debated. The popular media as well as the professional literature is quite involved in covering this topic. On both sides of the issue, many professionals are staunch in their opinions of facilitated communication as an effective or noneffective method of communication for otherwise noncommunicative students.

Myles and Simpson (1994) describe facilitated communication as "an augmentative communication procedure whereby literacy skills among nonspeaking people, especially those with autism, are promoted" (p. 208). Biklen, Morton, Gold, Berrigan, & Swaminathan (1992) elaborates on facilitated communication as

> *a means by which many people with major speech difficulties type or point at letters on an alphabet board or typing device to convey their thoughts. It involves a facilitator who provides physical support to help stabilize the arm, to isolate the index finger if necessary, to pull back the arm after each selection, to remind the individual to maintain focus, and to offer emotional support and encouragement; the facilitator progressively phases out the physical support (p. 243).*

Proponents of facilitated communication typically do not use empirically based studies to validate their stance on this issue. Instead, these researchers use anecdotal recording, observations, and case studies to evaluate facilitated communication. Indeed, many in the field regard facilitated communication as a promising means of augmentative communication for students with autism as well as other severe disabilities (Myles & Simpson, 1994).

For instance, Biklen and colleagues (1992) describe the method of facilitated communication with a 7-year-old student: "Without facilitation, Mark has no effective means of communicating. . . . With facilitation, he can say what is on his mind, he can converse with other students, and he is doing school work at and above the grade level norm for his age" (p. 15).

Kaiser (1994) focuses on common reports that the facilitator's view of students changes after facilitation. Facilitators tend to view the students with disabilities as "more human, more competent, and more like themselves" (p. 189). Furthermore, by this renewed viewpoint by the facilitators, the quality of life of these students will improve and the "interactional context of that individual's life may be changed fundamentally in the direction of normalization" (p. 189).

Conversely, opponents of facilitated communication cite the lack of empirical data to support this method as an alternative way of communication as a primary problem. These professionals generally agree that the facilitators control the situation. For example, Green and Shane (1994), write that "a reasonably large body of controlled evaluations using objective measure shows that facilitated communication does not enable people with disabilities to communicate at unexpected levels, but that facilitators control the overwhelming majority of facilitated communication productions" (p. 152). Additionally, Cabay (1994), agrees that "currently, there is no substantial evidence that facilitated communication is truly authentic communication from the child" (p. 524).

Other researchers advocate using facilitated communication only under certain conditions. Eberlin, McConnachie, Ibel, & Volpe (1993) state that "facilitated communication at this point seems only justified if done with scientifically adequate controls to ensure validation of the source of 'communication' " (p. 528).

There is clearly a difference of opinion among professionals regarding the validity of facilitated communication. Professionals teaching individuals with autism should view this subject objectively per individual. For some students with autism who are functionally noncommunicative, facilitated communication may be a method to be evaluated. We may want to approach this topic keeping the least dangerous assumption in mind.

Peer-Mediated Interventions

Numerous researchers have explored the use of nonhandicapped or mildly handicapped peers in interventions to influence the social behavior of children with autism. In peer-mediated behavioral interventions, children of similar age or developmental functioning are used to promote interaction through formal and informal methods. There are three types of peer-mediated approaches for building social skills (Odom & Strin, 1984):

1. *Proximity interventions* involve no specific training for the peers. The success of these interventions depends on the natural transmission of social skills to the child with autism through modeling and imitation in social contexts.
2. *Prompting and reinforcement* require that peers be trained to prompt the autistic child's participation in an activity and to reinforce any desired responses.
3. In *peer-initiated interventions,* peers are instructed to make social overtures to the child with autism. They set the stage for social responses by asking the child to play, providing assistance, or giving a toy to the child.

Peers can serve as effective change agents without specific training. Typical children have been shown to elicit and sustain play and interaction with peers who have autism (McHale, 1983; Meyer et al., 1987), simply after being instructed to help teach children with autism to play. The children without disabilities were persistent; once they found a successful game, they repeated it often. In a similar way, children with autism and their typical peers can interact positively with minimal adult supervision. Whether teachers gave frequent or infrequent directives and reinforcement to the children had little impact on the play behavior of disabled-nondisabled pairs (Meyer et al., 1987).

A proximity intervention involving group affection activities increased reciprocal peer interactions between young children with autism and their typical peers (McEvoy et al., 1988). Group affection activities were games that incorporated affectionate interactions (e.g., "If you're happy and you know it, hug a friend"). The target children interacted with their peers without disabilities more often during and after affection activities than they did with typical activities. Moreover, the increased interaction generalized to free-play periods—both children with autism and their typical peers initiated reciprocal interactions.

The success of proximity interventions may depend on the match between the children with autism and their typical peers. Playmates who are younger but developmentally similar to children with autism have been found to promote more spontaneous play than same-age typical peers (Bednersh & Peck, 1986) because the same-age peers were too directive in their play styles. However, too large an age difference between children with autism and their typical peers should be avoided because the type of play, toys, and activities may be chronologically inappropriate and stigmatizing. It is interesting that virtually no interaction occurred *between* children with disabilities—which highlights the need for integrated school and social settings for children with autism and other severe disabilities. More recently, McGee, Paradis, & Feldman (1993), found that young children with autism displayed significantly decreased levels of "autistic behaviors" when in close proximity to typical peers compared to when in close proximity to other children with autism.

Peer-mediated interventions using prompting and reinforcement or peer-initiated methods are more complicated at first, but in the long term are more effective in promoting prosocial behavior than proximity interventions (Odom and Strain, 1984). Less is left to chance. In a study of the relative effectiveness of prompt and reinforce versus peer-initiated interventions (Strain, Kerr, & Ragland, 1979), the treatments were found to be equally effective. Other studies have confirmed that peer-initiated interventions can be successful in increasing social interactions between trained typical peers and children with autism. In addition, increased interactions frequently generalized to typical peers not specifically trained (Brady, Shores, McEvoy, Ellis, & Fox, 1987; Schafer, Egel, & Neef, 1984).

Finally, Carr and Darcy (1990) demonstrated that children with autism can acquire a common preschool activity, such as follow the leader, through modeling specifically trained typical peers. Proximity coupled with verbal prompts alone were not sufficient for inducing behavior change. However, when peers used a combination of verbal and physical prompts in context, their peers with autism imitated at high levels. Further, these behaviors generalized across settings.

Prognosis for Communication with Children with Autism

Much of the research conducted to date that generate the techniques described so far in this chapter involve young children with autism. Intensive early intervention is vital with intensity being the key. Early intervention programs (Lovaas, 1987; Odom, Hoyson, Jamieson, & Strain, 1985) support the notion that important developmental progress can be promoted in some young children with autism. Clearly, the earlier that quality programs for children with autism are implemented, the better the prognosis.

Special educators are charged with the responsibility of preparing students to function as independently as possible in society. The key to this goal is functional communication and social competence. It is clear that language per se can be trained in controlled contexts, but research (Koegel et al., 1987; Neef et al., 1984) supports the effectiveness of naturalistic, behavioral methods for training language in children with autism. Moreover, these natural training methods incorporate tactics that have been identified as promoting generalization.

Finally, it is important to base social-skill and communication interventions on behaviors currently in the child's repertoire. Rather than eliminating seemingly aberrant behaviors, special educators must examine them for possible communicative function. They must determine the functional equivalence of unconventional behaviors, such as leading, and conventional communicative means, such as pointing. As the conventional response is trained and reinforced, the functionally equivalent but unconventional behavior should decrease. If behavior-reduction interventions must be implemented, it is vital to coordinate them with instructional methods that promote prosocial behaviors. It is important to remember that even the most atypical behaviors associated with autism—self-stimulatory and self-injurious behaviors—have proved amenable to treatments conceptualized through this framework.

Managing Self-Stimulatory and Self-Injurious Behavior

In Chapter 3, self-stimulatory (SSB) and self-injurious (SIB) behaviors were defined and described. You will recall that SSB (or stereotyped behaviors) are chronic, repetitive, unvarying, and seemingly purposeless acts that may occur so often as to preempt the occurrence of all other behaviors. SSB seems "purposeless" in that it does not generate any obvious, socially mediated reinforcement (Lovaas, Newsom, & Hickman, 1987). It is unvarying in that each instance of the stereotyped behavior looks like every other instance; in technical terms, the *topography* of the response varies little from occurrence to occurrence. Common examples of SSB are body rocking, mouthing objects, and hand and finger flapping. SSB occurs among severely and profoundly disabled persons and persons with autism, and is more common among individuals who are institutionalized than among those who live in integrated settings (LaGrow & Repp, 1984). These stigmatizing behaviors can make integration into the community difficult (Koegel & Koegel, 1989).

Although we may see these stereotyped behaviors as bizarre, almost all of us engage in some form of self-stimulatory behavior. If you doubt it, look around the library reading room during finals. You are certain to find some hair twirling, beard stroking, or nail biting going on, and although these topographies are more familiar and socially acceptable than body rocking, they have many of the same characteristics: They are repetitive, unvarying, and seemingly purposeless. Furthermore, normally developing infants and young children engage in stereotyped behaviors (Kravitz & Boehm, 1971; Thelen, 1971), although seldom frequently and persistently enough to be labeled abnormal (Lovaas et al., 1987).

Some researchers regard self-injurious behaviors (SIB) as a subset of SSB (Cataldo & Harris, 1982) because they, too, are highly repetitive, topographically unvarying, and without apparent purpose. Furthermore, both classes of behaviors may serve the same communicative (Carr & Durand, 1985; Durand & Carr, 1987; 1991) or reinforcing (Rincover, Cook, Peoples, & Packard, 1979; Rincover & Devany, 1982) functions, and both may have a common physiological basis (Cataldo & Harris, 1982; Lewis, Baumeister, & Mailman, 1987). But SIB differs from SSB in one important regard: It can happen with sufficient frequency, intensity, and persistence to create physical injury and to jeopardize the well-being of the behaver. SIB takes many forms, including head banging, biting, hair pulling, scratching, punching, slapping, and gouging. It can be expected to occur in roughly 15 percent of persons with severe developmental disabilities (Eyman & Call, 1977). More surprising is the fact that SIB occurs as commonly among normally developing youngsters (Gast & Wolery, 1987), although in this group, the behavior disappears by age 3. The most common topography of SIB in young normally developing children is head banging.

Although we described SIB and SSB as "seemingly purposeless," researchers have begun to identify their functions. These differ from individual to individual, and for most individuals, from time to time or situation to situation (Iwata et al., 1982). Because of the variety of functions they may serve, SSB and SIB are said to be "multiply motivated" (Durand & Carr, 1985, p. 172). Before we consider these functions individually, it is important to recognize that the notion of functional SSB (or functional SIB) is inconsistent with a strict biological interpretation. According to the biological point of view (Cataldo & Harris, 1982; Lewis et al., 1987), SSB and SIB result from impaired neurological functioning that, in turn, results from a lack of neurotransmitters (chemicals that transmit signals in the brain). SSB and SIB are the overt manifestation of this underlying brain pathology, so there is nothing adaptive or functional about them. Nevertheless, the best evidence suggests that even if SSB and SIB have an organic source, they are maintained by social consequences, as we shall see.

One hypothesis about the function of SSB and SIB is that each comprises learned behaviors that are maintained by the internal and external perceptual stimuli they generate (Lovaas et al., 1987). Indeed, research (Egel, 1981; Ferrari & Harris, 1981; Iwata et al., 1994) has shown that sensory stimulation alone can serve as a reinforcer for young children with autism and other developmental disabilities. SSB (Durand & Carr, 1987) and SIB (Carr & Durand, 1985; Durand & Carr, 1991; Iwata et al., 1994) are also thought to serve a communicative function: These behaviors substitute for other more typical communicative responses when children are confronted with a difficult task or demand or when they seek attention from others in their environment. When SSB and SIB result in the termination of a demand situation, their occurrence is negatively reinforced in an escape learning model; when these behaviors generate adult attention, their occurrence is positively reinforced. Finally, SSB and SIB may fulfill a regulatory or play function (Meyer & Evans, 1986) such that engaging in them allows behavers to adjust their levels of psychological arousal.

Each of these hypotheses has implications for managing SSB and SIB, and the implications will be discussed in a later section of this chapter. Before we turn to intervention, however, we must consider the justification for intervening—sometimes quite intrusively—into the lives of people who exhibit these disruptive behaviors. Do interventionists have the right to treat SSB and SIB, and if so, why?

First, high frequencies of SSB and SIB are associated with weak behavioral repertoires in general (Lovaas et al., 1987) and low levels of communicative ability in particular (Carr & Durand, 1985). That is to say, when disruptive behaviors dominate an individual's repertoire, that individual is unlikely to engage in other, more functional behaviors, including communication. Those so dominated by SSB and SIB are also unlikely to acquire new behaviors (Koegel & Covert, 1972; Varni, Lovaas, Koegel, & Everett, 1979). In the case of SSB, the perceptual stimuli that are generated may be far more reinforcing than any reinforcer the teacher controls (Lovaas, Litrownik, & Mann, 1971).

Second, these disruptive behaviors can impede the successful integration of severely disabled persons into more normal environments (Koegel & Koegel, 1989; Meyer & Evans, 1986). For one thing, they interfere with the acquisition of new skills prerequisite for successful community functioning. For another, their bizarre topographies may stigmatize the behavers (Durand & Carr, 1987) and create discomfort for members of the community unfamiliar with the behavior of severely disabled persons. Persons who exhibit SSB or SIB are typically the last to be included in, and the first to be excluded from, normalized environments (Meyer & Evans, 1986). Thus, the goal of full integration requires that SSB and SIB be successfully managed.

Finally, in the case of self-injurious behavior, intervention is justified because the behavior presents a physical threat to the well being of the behaver. Behaviors this dangerous warrant immediate intervention, with simultaneous programming to strengthen positive behaviors and weaken disruptive ones (Meyer & Evans, 1986; Meyer & Evans, 1989).

In the case of dangerous and destructive SIB, a second question must be asked: Is the behavior problem sufficiently serious to warrant the application of aversive procedures? Punishment has been demonstrated to be an effective way to manage both SSB and SIB (Durand & Carr, 1985; LaGrow & Repp, 1984); in fact, some researchers have concluded that aversive procedures are the most consistently effective way to eliminate SSB and SIB (cf. Iwata, Dorsey, Slifer, Bauman, & Richman, 1982). Several successful procedures involve relatively innocuous aversive stimuli: facial screening—pulling a bib over a young man's face (Lutzker, 1978); positive practice overcorrection—a procedure designed to strengthen appropriate responding by conducting training contingent upon the occurrence of SIB (Wells, Forehand, Hickey, & Green, 1977); time-out from positive reinforcement—particularly with initial low-rate SSB (LaGrow & Repp, 1984); and response-cost—in which treat tickets are lost contingent upon SIB (Woods, 1982). But more intrusive and pernicious aversive procedures have also been used, among them electric shock (Baumeister & Forehand, 1972; Prochaska, Smith, Marzilli, Colby, & Donova, 1974), corporal punishment (Koegel & Covert, 1972; Koegel, Firestone, Kramme, & Dunlap, 1974), forced contact with aromatic ammonia (Tanner & Zeiler, 1975), squirts of citric acid (Mayhew & Harris, 1979), and water mists (Dorsey, Iwata, Ong, & McSween, 1980).

Although punishment procedures may be successful in eliminating disruptive behaviors in the settings in which training occurs, their effects have not proved durable over time or settings (Frankel & Simmons, 1976; Harris & Ersner-Hershfield, 1978). The fact that the effects of punishment neither last nor generalize is enough to suggest that we avoid the use of aversive procedure whenever possible. But there are even more fundamental reasons for doing so. For one thing, nonaversive methods for managing SSB and SIB have proved effective and manageable for practitioners (LaVigna, 1987; Horner et al., 1990), and there can be no argument that when two procedures are equally effective, the less aversive is clearly preferred. Second, given the availability of nonaversive alternatives, the use of aversive procedures may represent a violation of the rights of the individuals being treated to freedom from harm and dehumanization (Association for Persons with Severe Handicaps, 1981). Just as the bizarre topographies of SIB and SSB may stigmatize disabled people, so may topographies of intervention, particularly when these exceed a community's standards for propriety in personal interaction. Of course, when aversive procedures are necessary, guidelines for their appropriate use must be established and followed strictly (cf. Lovaas & Favell, 1987; Repp & Dietz, 1978).

Finally, from a personal point of view, I would argue that aversive treatments are inappropriate for SSB under any circumstances—not only because these behaviors are amenable to nonaversive treatment, but also because they do not jeopardize the well-being of individuals and are apparently very reinforcing to them. I am concerned about the use of punishment procedures in schools and regard the application of aversive stimuli as inappropriate there. For one thing, teachers must be concerned about the legal and ethical implications of the ways they manage children (McAfee, 1987). For another, schools ought to be reinforcing and non-threatening places for all students, including students with disabilities, regardless of the severity.

Managing Self-Stimulatory Behavior

Three approaches to managing SSB are described: (1) differential reinforcement of other behavior (DRO) and its offshoot, differential reinforcement of incompatible behavior (DRI); (2) sensory extinction, and (3) functional communication training (FCG) (Durand & Carr, 1992). FCT and sensory extinction derive from hypotheses about the function of SSB, the former viewing SSB as communication and the latter viewing it as generator of reinforcing sensory stimulation. We will consider each approach in turn and carefully examine one successful application of each. However, before we do so, we must emphasize that every treatment program for SSB should begin with enriching the instructional environment. Increased opportunity for social interaction has been shown to reduce the frequency of SSB independent of any other intervention (LaGrow & Repp, 1984). Although environmental enrichment is not likely to eliminate a serious SSB problem (Horner, 1980), it is easy, it does help, and it ought to be done.

DRO and DRI

Differential reinforcement of other behavior has been defined as a "reductive schedule of reinforcement in which the omission of a target response for a specified period of time is reinforced" (LaGrow & Repp, 1984, p. 604). That is, students are reinforced for engaging in any other behavior *except* "self-stimming" during a pre-set period of time. DRO is often used in combination with other strategies, as was the case in a study reported by Horner (1980). This study is a particularly apt example because the treatment with which DRO was coupled was environmental enrichment. Participants in the student included five adolescent girls with profound disabilities, whose inappropriate behaviors included both SSB and SIB and whose adaptive behaviors were severely restricted. The initial treatment involved enriching the institutional environment by introducing toys and objects into the children's day room. After the enriched environment was introduced, removed, and introduced again, differential reinforcement of adaptive behaviors was added to the program. During these DRO phases of the experiment, the girls could earn reinforcement for any one of many adaptive behaviors, conceptualized as either adult-directed (seeks an adult), child-directed (hugs another child), self-directed (puts clothing on correct body part), or object-directed (rolls a ball).

The enriched environment produced increased frequencies of object-directed behaviors, as one might expect, but among all object-directed behaviors, increases in adaptive behavior were no larger than increases in maladaptive behavior. The increase in object-directed behaviors was also associated with decreases in maladaptive self-directed behaviors (SSB and SIB, among others), suggesting that object- and self-directed behaviors were incompatible. With the addition of differential reinforcement, greater increases in adaptive behaviors (30–40 percent) and greater decreases in maladaptive behaviors (20–30 percent) occurred.

These findings illustrate two important points about the use of DRO: first, it may be embedded in a broad treatment program in which several behaviors are targeted for reduction; and second, the treatment with which DRO is combined need not be an aversive contingency for disruptive behaviors. In this case, DRO was combined with environmental enrichment, and the effects of enrichment were significantly enhanced.

One potential unfortunate outcome of DRO is that inappropriate behaviors (other than the target response) may be reinforced and strengthened inadvertently. This problem may be avoided by specifying the "other" behaviors and making reinforcement contingent upon adaptive responding only (Horner, 1980). When the behaviors chosen for reinforcement are incompatible with a self-stimulatory response, the procedure is called *differential reinforcement of incompatible behaviors* (DRI). Behaviors are considered incompatible if they cannot occur at the same time—doing one makes doing the other impossible. Thus, in using DRI to manage hand flapping, behaviors such as coloring, toy play, and object manipulation may be selected for reinforcement because they cannot occur at the same time as the target response. Similarly, standing erect, walking, and running are incompatible with body rocking.

Like DRO, DRI combats SSB by strengthening other behaviors; it differs from DRO in that a limited number of behaviors are chosen for reinforcement and these behaviors are both adaptive and incompatible with the SSB. Although incompatible responses may be acquired without effect on the frequency of SSB (Klier & Harris, 1977), DRI still may be preferred to DRO. DRO involves weak consequences for the target response; to engage in it only delays the delivery of reinforcement (La-Grow & Repp, 1984). DRI, on the other hands, promotes the development of responses that are chosen in part because of their adaptiveness to the setting in which training occurs. Thus, students may be far more likely to come into contact with the DRI contingency.

In preparing to use DRO or DRI, there are two important considerations to keep in mind. First, DRO and DRI are most often and most effectively used in combination with other techniques, particularly when SSB occurs with high frequency. Individuals who exhibit high rates of SSB may not come into contact with the DRO (or DRI) contingency. Because SSB occurs so frequently and because reinforcement is contingent upon its nonoccurrence, other behaviors may not be reinforced and strengthened. Thus, a strategy that involves some consequence for the occurrence of SSB is a common complement to DRO and DRI. A second, related concern has to do with the length of time during which the behavior may not occur. Obviously, the shorter the interval, the greater will be the probability of reinforcement. It is critical to choose an interval length that allows individuals to earn frequent reinforcement (Repp, Dietz, & Dietz, 1976). As they progress, the interval may be gradually lengthened. Choosing an appropriate initial duration is one way to address the problem of high-frequency SSB without resorting to aversive consequences.

Haring and Kennedy (1990) found that the context in which intervention occurred controlled the relative effectiveness of DRO and time-out procedures. DRO was effective in reducing stereotypy in instructional contexts, but not during leisure activities. In contrast, time-out, defined as task withdrawal, was effective in decreasing stereotypy in the leisure context, but not during instruction. In this study, the DRO procedure was designed so that reinforcement (a token) was only given if the student omitted the stereotypic behavior for fifteen seconds and performed a task correctly. After ten tokens were earned, the student received an edible and the session was ended. It is likely the DRO was ineffective in the leisure context because the students did not want the session to end. This study illustrates how vital it is for practitioners to examine the relative effectiveness of interventions across various environments. The effectiveness of an intervention such as DRO for reducing aberrant behavior in one context does not mean that it will be equally effective in other environments.

Sensory Extinction

Recall that SSB is thought to generate stimulation that may be reinforcing for some persons. Thus, it may be possible to weaken and eliminate SSB by reducing or eliminating the sensory consequences it produces. When reinforcement that has maintained a behavior is removed, behavior will cease to occur, or extinguish. When the reinforcement in question is sensory stimulation, the process is known as *sensory extinction*. Sensory extinction has been applied to the treatment of SSB with considerable success (Maag, Rutherford, Wolchik, & Parks, 1986; Rincover, 1978; Rincover et al., 1979). The first step in the process is to identify the sensory consequences that may be maintaining the behavior. Then a means for masking or eliminating these consequences must be devised.

In one study (Rincover et al., 1979), four children, each diagnosed as autistic and chosen on the basis of their high rates of SSB and low rates of appropriate play, were selected for analysis. One boy flapped his hands in a stereotyped fashion; he "usually held his arms out to his sides, with his fingers, wrists, and arms in constant motion" (Rincover et al., 1979, p. 223). Another boy twirled objects, often a plate, on a hard surface such as a table top. One girl compulsively picked lint from her clothing, threw it in the air, and attempted to keep it afloat. A second girl flicked her fingers in front of her eyes.

It was determined that the boy's hand flapping was maintained by its proprioceptive consequences (the sensations generated by the movement of the body). To mask this stimulation, small battery-operated vibrators were taped to the backs of the boy's hands. The vibrators generated a high-frequence nonaversive impulse. The sensory extinction procedure resulted in the immediate and total suppression of hand flapping. Proprioceptive stimulation was one of two sensory reinforcers that maintained the finger flicking of the second girl. Although the use of the vibrators weakened the behavior, suppression was far from complete. Suppression was also incomplete when a blindfold was used to eliminate the visual stimulation that hand flapping produced. Only when the two sensory extinction procedures were used in combination was the behavior weakened sufficiently to consider the procedure a clinical success. This case illustrated that multiple control may succeed even when SSB is maintained by its sensory consequences.

Plate spinning was shown to be maintained by its auditory consequences, and the behavior was treated by carpeting the table on which the boy spun the plate. The carpeting masked the noise created by the spinning plate and the behavior extinguished. Finally, the compulsive lint play was greatly reduced by turning off the room lights contingent upon its occurrence. With the lights off, the room was so dark that the girl could not see the lint.

It is interesting that the children also preferred to play with toys that generated the same stimuli as their SSB. Thus, the children who hand flapped and finger flicked preferred blocks and beads to a music box, the boy who spun plates preferred the music box (and later an Autoharp), and the girl who picked lint liked blowing bubbles best of all. Perhaps sensory masking to reduce SSB can be combined with a more appropriate activity, such as block play, that provides similar sensory reinforcement in a more conventional way. When using sensory extinction, it is important to employ procedures that are least stigmatizing and intrusive. Of the examples described above, using carpet to mask auditory stimulation is less intrusive than blindfolding a student to suppress visual stimulation.

Sensory extinction is an effective and appealing intervention for several reasons. First, although it involves no aversive consequences, it may produce immediate and total response suppression. Second, it requires the introduction of no new arbitrary or artificial reinforcement contingencies; the existing (and natural) contingencies are exploited for the purpose of treatment. But sensory extinction can be expected to work effectively for only those children whose SSB is maintained primarily by its sensory consequences. Other strategies are necessary for contingencies in which the reinforcers are socially mediated, as we shall now see.

FCT

Recall that one current and significant hypothesis about the function of SSB is that it may substitute for more conventional forms of communication for persons who lack conventional communicative skills (Durand & Carr, 1987). If the communicative function of the SSB can be determined, then a socially acceptable alternative can be taught. As this alternative response is strengthened, SSB should weaken because it is no longer the individual's only means for communicating the need. The notion is that a trained conventional response is more efficient in obtaining a goal than an inappropriate response (e.g., SSB and SIB). Thus, the student should quickly choose to obtain the goal with the new response (Durand & Carr, 1991). This intervention strategy using communication as the functionally equivalent response has been called functional communication training (Durand, 1990; Durand & Carr, 1992).

Four boys with developmental disabilities, two of whom had autism also were the subjects of a FCT study (Durand & Carr, 1987). The boys engaged in either body rocking or hand flapping, and these responses were thought to be socially mediated in that they occurred reliably when the boys were faced with tasks they could not complete without assistance. When adult attention was reduced, the boys' SSB was largely unaffected. Thus, the SSB did not seem to function as a way to attract adult attention; rather, the body rocking and hand flapping seemed to communicate the boys' inability to complete the task. When the boys engaged in SSB, the behavior was negatively reinforced by the termination of the demand situation.

If self-stimulatory responding allowed the boys to escape from difficult tasks, then teaching an alternative means for reducing task difficulty ought to weaken SSB by rendering it unnecessary. So the boys were taught to say "help me" when faced with a task they could not complete. The boys used their "help me" response after training and, indeed, the increased use of this response was associated with decreased SSB. For all four of the boys, response suppression was nearly complete.

One key to the successful implementation of DRC is the notion of functional equivalence (Carr & Durand, 1985). The response alternative must be functionally equivalent to the self-stimulatory behavior it is meant to replace. If it is not, then teaching the alternative will not eliminate the SSB. Carr and Durand (1985) demonstrated this point by teaching verbalizations that were unrelated to the function of SSB. For example, children whose behavior was motivated by the escape it allowed from difficult tasks were taught to seek adult attention by asking, "Am I doing good work?" Of course, the acquisition of this new response had little effect on their disruptive behavior. In the same way, children whose disruptive behavior was motivated by the adult attention it solicited were taught to seek help with difficult tasks by saying, "I don't understand." There was no collateral effect on disruptive behavior.

The success of these last two treatment approaches highlights the importance of assessing the underlying motivating conditions as a first step in treating SSB. Treating an individual for whom SSB produces powerful sensory reinforcement is quite different from treating an individual whose SSB is an attempt at communication. Even among persons whose SSB serves a communicative function, assessment must be made of the circumstances under which the behavior occurs and the reinforcers it generates. As we know, the acquisition of some communicative alternatives will have little effect on self-stimulation. To eliminate SSB, the alternative communicative response must be its functional equivalent. To determine the functional equivalence of two responses, teachers must respond differentially to SSB and observe which of their actions halts the behavior. If a specific teacher response consistently stops SSB, then students may be taught more conventional means for eliciting the same response from their teacher. Finally, we have emphasized that SSB may be multiply motivated. In these cases, a single treatment may fail to eliminate the SSB, but assessment should reveal all possible motivating conditions.

Managing Self-Injurious Behavior

In this section, two approaches that have proved effective in managing SIB are considered: sensory extinction, and functional communication training. Since we have already discussed sensory extinction and FCT, we will present only case studies of the procedures applied to the more threatening problem of SIB.

Some more familiar treatment approaches are not included in this section on self-injurious behavior because of the serious problems associated with their use in schools. For example, time-out from reinforcement has been only moderately successful with SIB (Harris & Ersner-Hershfield, 1978); in fact, for students who find the classroom unreinforcing, time-out involves no functional consequence whatsoever. Extinction is not recommended for SIB because it induces an initial increase in the rate of responding and because of the total number of responses that will occur in the process (Zirpoli & Lloyd, 1987). Does the same concern apply to sensory extinction?

Sensory Extinction

Sensory extinction may not be extinction at all. Recall that the sensory extinction procedure produced immediate and nearly total suppression of self-stimulatory responding (Rincover et al., 1979). This effect is quite different from the effect of a more typical extinction process, which produces a temporary increase in responses, followed by a gradual reduction in the rate of responding. The effect of sensory extinction on self-injurious responding is far more like its effect on self-stimulatory responding (Rincover & Devany, 1982); hence, we can advocate its use in treating SIB without qualification.

In one study (Rincover & Devany, 1982), three young children with developmental delay exhibited self-injurious behaviors that seemed to be maintained by sensory, not social, consequences. (You may wonder how SIB can be reinforcing when its defining effect is physical injury. SIB can be understood as self-stimulatory behavior [Carr, 1977], with some topographies that relieve pain from other physical disorders. Alternatively, SIB itself may become a conditioned reinforcer through its association with other reinforcers [Frankel & Simmons, 1976].) Two of these children engaged in head banging, and the third in scratching her face with her fingernails.

To eliminate the sensory stimulation that head banging might produce, the walls, floors, and furniture in the first boy's environment were padded. The second boy was fitted with a helmet that masked the tactile stimulation his head banging was thought to create. The girl was required to wear thin rubber gloves that prevented her from damaging her skin, but not from scratching it. These sensory extinction procedures produced large and immediate decreases in SIB for all three children. With a simple stimulus-fading procedure, these gains were maintained for periods of three to seven months. Further, treatments were easily learned and implemented by the staff. After conducting functional analyses on 152 subjects Iwata and colleagues (1994) found that sensory reinforcement maintained SIB for 25.7 percent of the sample. This highlights the notion that sensory extinction may be an appropriate intervention for many students who exhibit SIB. However, this, as other interventions, should be based on systematic functional analyses.

FCT

It may seem surprising to us that children with disabilities would resort to self-injury in order to communicate their needs and desires, yet that is precisely what was found for two students with severe disabilities (Carr & Durand, 1985). In this study, two communicative functions for SIB were observed: terminating a demand situation (as was true for SSB) and soliciting adult attention. Self-injury increased for two of the students in a difficult task situation in which the behavior of the other two students was unaffected. When the four were assessed under conditions of reduced adult attention, the two who were unaffected by task difficulty engaged in more SIB, while the two who were affected by task difficulty were unaffected by adult attention. Clearly, SIB served two different functions.

The students were taught appropriate responses for the circumstances that had set the occasion for increased self-injury. Two were taught to solicit assistance when working on difficult tasks by saying, "I don't understand." Two were taught to solicit adult attention by asking, "Am I doing good work?" The students used the relevant responses they were taught, and when they did, their SIB was reduced to near-zero levels.

Durand and Carr (1992) note that teaching students to recruit the stimuli maintaining their behavior in a more conventional manner is likely not only to reduce challenging behavior, but may also facilitate maintenance. Once again a functional analysis is critical in determining what is producing or maintaining SIB. Iwata and colleagues (1994) found that social-negative reinforcement (i.e., escape) accounted for SIB in 38.1 percent of their sample, while social-positive reinforcement (i.e., attention or access to food or materials) accounted for SIB in 26.3 percent of their subjects.

To sum up, self-stimulation and self-injury, the two disruptive behaviors most commonly associated with severe behavior problems, are amenable to treatments that do not require any punishment procedure. Differential reinforcement of other behavior and differential reinforcement of incompatible behavior are two closely related reinforcement procedures that involve strengthening behaviors that compete with SSB. Sensory extinction requires that the sensory stimulation generated by SSB or SIB be identified and eliminated. FCT is based on the idea that some self-stimulatory and self-injurious behaviors serve a communicative function. This function must be identified and an equivalent, socially appropriate communicative response substituted for it.

Summary

This chapter described methods for teaching and managing severe problem behaviors. First, naturalistic teaching procedures to promote communication and language in children with autism were presented. Although numerous studies validate the effectiveness of traditional behavioral techniques for the development of language competence, the lack of generalization to nontraining contexts continues to be a major limitation of the existing research base. Next, a variety of teaching methods for the development of social interaction skills, including naturalistic teaching, incidental instruction, and peer-mediated instruction were presented. The chapter concluded with a description of the topography of self-stimulatory and self-injurious behaviors and a review of alternative approaches that have proved successful in the management of these severe behavior problems. The approaches highlighted were differential reinforcement of incompatible behavior, functional communication training, and sensory extinction. The need for conducting a functional analysis to determine what variables are generating and maintaining SSB and SIB is stressed.

Discussion Questions

1. List and describe the major limitations and criticisms of traditional behaviorally based language-intervention programs for students with autism.

2. How do naturalistic behavioral teaching methods differ from more traditional directive teaching styles? How would you characterize the efficacy of naturalistic teaching techniques?

3. Identify three types of peer-mediated interventions that are used to influence the social behavior of students with severe behavior problems.

4. Describe specific task characteristics that have been shown to enhance the social development of students with severe behavior problems.

5. How have theorists explained the development and maintenance of "seemingly purposeless" SSB and SIB?

6. In your opinion, are aversive intervention techniques appropriate for the treatment of
SSB and/or SIB? Prepare to defend your response.

7. Compare and contrast the efficacy of (1) differential reinforcement of other
behavior/differential reinforcement of incompatible behavior, (b) functional communication training, and (c) sensory extinction in the management of self-stimulatory behavior.

8. What is sensory extinction? How has it been used to reduce self-injurious behavior?

References

Association for Persons with Severe Handicaps.
(1981). Resolution on intrusive interventions.
TSH Newsletter, 7, 1–2.

Baumeister, A. A., & Forehand, R. (1972). Effects of
contingent shock and verbal command on
body rocking of retardates. *Journal of Clinical
Psychology, 28,* 586–590.

Bednersh, F., & Peck, C. A. (1986). Assessing social
environments: Effects of peer characteristics
on the social behavior of children with severe
handicaps. *Child Study Journal, 16,* 315–329.

Biklen, D., Morton, M. W., Gold, D., Berrigna, C., &
Swaminathan, S. (1992). Facilitated communication: Implications for individuals with
autism. *Topics in Language Disorders, 12*(4), 1–28.

Brady, M. P., Shores, R. E., McEvoy, M. A., Ellis, D.,
& Fox, J. J. (1987). Increasing social interactions of severely handicapped autistic children. *Journal of Autism and Developmental
Disorders, 17,* 375–391.

Bricker, D., & Cripe, J. J. W. (1992). *An activity-based
approach to early intervention.* Baltimore: Paul
H. Brookes.

Brinker, R. P., & Bricker, D. (1980). Teaching a first
language: Building complex structures from
simpler components. In D. Hogg & P. Mittler
(Eds.), *Advances in mental handicap research*
(pp. 197–223). London: Wiley.

Bryen, D. N., & Joyce, D. G. (1985). Language intervention with the severely handicapped: A
decade of research. *The Journal of Special Education, 19,* 7–39.

Cabay, M. (1994). Brief Report: A controlled evaluation of facilitated communication using

open-ended and fill-in questions. *Journal of
Autism and Developmental disorders, 24*(4), 517–
527.

Carr, E. G. (1977). The motivation of self-injurious
behavior: A review of some hypotheses. *Psychological Bulletin, 84,* 800–816.

Carr, E. G. (1985a). Behavioral approaches to language and communication. In E. Schopler &
G. B. Meisbov (Eds.), *Communication problems
in autism* (pp. 37–57). New York: Plenum.

Carr, E. G. (1985b). Converging perspectives in
psycho-linguistics and behaviorism. In E.
Schopler & G. B. Mesibov (Eds.), *Communication problems in autism* (pp. 89–92). New York:
Plenum.

Carr, E. G., & Darcy, M., (1990). Setting generality
of peer modeling in children with autism.
*Journal of Autism and Developmental Disorders,
20,* 45–59.

Carr, E. G., & Durand, V. M. (1985). Reducing behavior problems through functional communication training. *Journal of Applied Behavior
Analysis, 18,* 111–126.

Cataldo, M. F., & Harris, J. (1982). The biological
basis for self-injury in the mentally retarded.
*Analysis and Intervention in Developmental Dis-
abilities, 2,* 21–39.

Charlop, M. H. (1983). The effects of echolalia on
acquisition and generalization of receptive labeling on autistic children. *Journal of Applied
Behavior Analysis, 16,* 11–126.

Charlop, M. H., Schreibman, L., & Thibodeau,
M. G. (1985). Increasing spontaneous verbal
responding in autistic children using a time

delay procedure. *Journal of Applied Behavior Analysis, 18,* 155–166.

Dawson, G., & Adams, A. (1984). Imitation and social responsiveness in autistic children. *Journal of Abnormal Child Psychology, 12,* 209–226.

Donnellan, A. M., & Kilman, B. A. (1986). Behavioral approaches to social skill development in autism. In E. Schopler & G. B. Mesibov (Eds.), *Social behavior in autism* (pp. 213–236). New York: Plenum.

Donnellan, A. M., Mesaro, R. A., & Anderson, J. L. (1984). Teaching students with autism in natural environments: What educators need from researchers. *Journal of Special Education, 18,* 505–522.

Dorsey, M. F., Iwata, B. A., Ong, P., & McSween, T. E. (1980). Treatment of self-injurious behavior using a water mist: Initial response suppression and generalization. *Journal of Applied Behavior Analysis, 13,* 343–353.

Duchan, J. F. (1993). Issues raised by facilitated communication for theorizing and research on autism. *Journal of Speech and Hearing Research, 16,* 1108–1119.

Durand, V. M. (1990). *Severe behavior problems: A functional communication training approach.* New York: Guilford.

Durand, V. M., & Carr, E. G. (1985). Self-injurious behavior: Motivating conditions and guidelines for treatment. *School Psychology Review, 14,* 171–176.

Durand, V. M., & Carr, E. G. (1987). Social influences on "self-stimulatory" behavior: Analysis and treatment application. *Journal of Applied Behavior Analysis, 20,* 119–132.

Durand, V. M., & Carr, E. G. (1991). Functional communication training to reduce challenging behavior: Maintenance and application in new settings. *Journal of Applied Behavior Analysis, 24,* 251–264.

Durand, V. M., & Carr, E. G. (1992). An analysis of maintenance following functional communication training. *Journal of Applied Behavior Analysis, 25,* 777–794.

Dyer, K., & Peck, C. A. (1987). Current perspectives on social/communication curricula for students with autism and severe handicaps. *Education and Treatment of Children, 10,* 338–351.

Dyer, K., Santarcangelo, S., & Luce, S. C. (1987). Developmental influence in teaching language forms to individuals with developmental disabilities. *Journal of Speech and Hearing Disorders, 52,* 335–347.

Eberlin, M., McConnachie, G., Ibel, S., & Volpe, L. (1993). Facilitated communication: A failure to replicate the phenomenon. *Journal of Autism and Developmental Disorders 23*(3), 507–530.

Egel, A. L. (1981). Reinforcer variation: Implications for motivating developmentally disabled children. *Journal of Applied Behavior Analysis, 14,* 345–350.

Eisenburg, L., & Kanner, L. (1956). Early infantile autism. *American Journal of Orthopsychiatry, 26,* 556–566.

Eyman, R. K., & Call, T. (1977). Maladaptive behavior and community placement of mentally retarded persons. *American Journal of Mental Deficiency, 82,* 137–144.

Ferrari, M., & Harris, S. L. (1981). The limits and motivating potential of sensory stimuli as reinforcers for autistic children. *Journal of Applied Behavior Analysis, 14,* 339–343.

Ferster, C. B. (1961). Positive reinforcement and behavioral deficits of autistic children. *Child Development, 32,* 434–456.

Frankel, F., & Simmons, J. Q. (1976). Self-injurious behavior in schizophrenic and retarded children. *American Journal of Mental Deficiency, 80,* 512–522.

Frankel, R. M., Leary, M., & Kilman, B. (1987). Building social skills through pragmatic analysis: Assessment and treatment implications for children with autism. In D. J. Cohen & A. M. Donnellan (Eds.), *Handbook of autism and pervasive developmental disorders* (pp. 33–359). New York: Wiley.

Frish, S. A., & Schumaker, J. B. (1974). Training generalized receptive prepositions in retarded children. *Journal of Applied Behavior Analysis, 7,* 611–621.

Garcia, E. E., & DeHaven, E. D. (1974). Use of operant techniques in the establishment and generalization of language: A review and analysis. *American Journal on Mental Deficiency, 79,* 169–178.

Gast, D. L., & Wolery, M. (1987). Severe maladaptive behavior. In M. E. Snell (Ed.), *Systematic* instruction of persons with severe handicaps. Pp. 300–332. Columbus, OH: Merrill.

Green, G., & Shane, N. (1994). Science, reason, and facilitated communication. *Journal of the Association for Persons with Severe Handicaps, 19*(3), 151–172.

Guess, D., Sailor, W., & Baer, D. M. (1978). Children with limited language. In R. L. Schiefelbusch (Ed.), *Language intervention strategies.* Pp. 101–144. Baltimore: University Park Press.

Halle, J. W. (1984). Arranging the natural environment to occasion language. Giving severely language delayed children reasons to communicate. *Seminars in Speech and Language, 5,* 185–197.

Halle, J. W. (1987). Teaching language in the natural environment: An analysis of spontaneity. *The Journal of the Association for Persons with Severe Handicaps, 12,* 28–37.

Haring, T. G., & Kennedy, C. H. (1990). Contextual control of problem behavior in students with severe disabilities. *Journal of Applied Behavior Analysis, 23,* 235–243.

Harris, S. (1975). Teaching language to nonverbal children—with emphasis on problems of generalization. *Psychological Bulletin, 82,* 565–580.

Harris, S. L., & Ersner-Hershfield, R. (1978). Behavioral suppression of seriously disruptive behavior in psychotic and retarded patients: A review of punishment and its alternatives. *Psychological Bulletin, 85,* 1352–1375.

Hart, B. M., & Risley, T. R. (1986). Establishing the use of descriptive adjectives in the spontaneous speech of disadvantaged children. *Journal of Applied Behavior Analysis, 1,* 109–120.

Hart, B., & Risley, T. R. (1980). In vivo language intervention: Unanticipated general effects. *Journal of Applied Behavior Analysis, 13,* 407–432.

Hartung, J.R. (1970). A review of procedures to increase verbal imitation skills and functional speech in autistic children. *Journal of Speech and Hearing Disorders, 35,* 203–217.

Hewett, F. M. (1965). Teaching speech to an autistic child through operant conditioning. *American Journal of Orthopsychiatry, 35,* 927–936.

Horner, R. D. (1980). The effects of an environmental "enrichment" program on the behavior of institutionalized profoundly retarded children. *Journal of Applied Behavior Analysis, 13,* 473–491.

Horner, R. H., Dunlap, G., Koegel, R. L., Carr, E. G., Sailor, W. Anderson, J., Albin, R. W., & O'Neill, R. E. (1990). Toward a technology of "nonaversive" behavioral support. *Journal of the Association for Persons with Severe Handicaps, 15,* 125–132.

Howlin, P. (1986). An overview of social behavior in autism. In E. Schopler & G. B. Mesibov (Eds.), *Social behavior in autism* (pp. 103–131). New York: Plenum.

Howlin, P., Rutter, M., Berger, M., Hemsley, R., Hersov, L., & Yule, W. (1987). *Treatment of autistic children.* New York: Wiley.

Iwata, B. A., Dorsey, M. F., Slifer, K. J., Bauman, K. E., & Richman, G. S. (1982). Toward a functional analysis of self-injury. *Analysis and Intervention in Developmental Disabilities, 2,* 3–20.

Iwata, B. A., Pace, G. M., Dorsey, M. F., Zarcone, J. R., Vollmer, T. R., Smith, R. G., Rodgers, T. A., Levman, D. C., Shore, B. A., Mazaleski, J. L., Goh, H., Cowdery, G. E., Kalsher, M. J., McCosh, K. C., & Willis, K. D. (1994). The functions of self-injurious behavior: An experimental-epidemiological analysis. *Journal of Applied Behavior Analysis, 27,* 215–240.

Kaiser, A. P. (1994). The controversy surrounding facilitated communication: Some alternative meanings. *Journal for the Association for Persons with Severe Handicaps, 19*(3), 187–190.

Klier, J., & Harris, S. L. (1977). Self-stimulation and learning in autistic children: Physical or functional incompatibility? *Journal of Applied Behavior Analysis, 10,* 311.

Koegel, R. L., & Covert, A. (1972). The relationship of self-stimulation to learning in autistic children. *Journal of Applied Behavior Analysis, 5,* 381–387.

Koegel, R. L., Firestone, P. B., Kramme, K. W., & Dunlap, G. (1974). Increasing spontaneous play by suppressing self-stimulation in autistic children. *Journal of Applied Behavior Analysis, 7,* 521–528.

Koegel, R. L., & Koegel, L. K. (1989). Community referenced research on self-stimulation. In M. J. Begab (Series Ed.) & E. Cipani (Vol. Ed.), *Monographs of the American Association on Mental Retardation, 12. The Treatment of Severe*

Behavior Disorders (pp. 129–150). Washington, DC: American Association on Mental Retardation.

Koegel, R. L., Koegel, L. K., & Surratt, A. (1992). Language intervention and disruptive behavior in preschool children with autism. *Journal of Autism and Developmental Disorders, 22,* 141–153.

Koegel, R. L., O'Dell, M. C., & Koegel, L. K. (1987). A natural language teaching paradigm for nonverbal autistic children. *Journal of Autism and Development Disabilities, 17,* 187–200.

Kravitz, H., & Boehm, J. J. (1971). Rhythmic habit patterns in infancy: Their sequence, age of onset, and frequency. *Child Development, 42,* 399–413.

LaGrow, S. J., & Repp, A. C. (1984). Stereotypic responding: A review of intervention research. *American Journal of Mental Deficiency, 88,* 594–609.

LaVigna, G. W. (1987). Non-aversive strategies for managing behavior problems. In D. J. Cohen, A. M. Donnellan, & R. Paul (Eds.), *Handbook of autism and pervasive developmental disorders* (pp. 418–429). Silver Spring, MD: V. H. Winston & Sons.

Lewis, M. H., Baumeister, A. A., & Mailman, R. B. (1987). A neurobiological alternative to the perceptual reinforcement hypothesis of stereotyped behavior: A commentary on "Self-stimulatory behavior and perceptual reinforcement." *Journal of Applied Behavior Analysis, 20,* 253–258.

Light, J. C. (1983). Language intervention programs for autistic children. *Special Education in Canada, 57,* 11–16.

Lord, C. (1985). Contribution of behavioral approaches to the language and communication of persons with autism. In E. Schopler & G. B. Mesibov (Eds.), *Communication problems in autism* (pp. 59–68). New York: Plenum.

Lovaas, O. I. (1987). Behavioral treatment and normal educational and intellectual functioning in young autistic children. *Journal of Consulting and Clinical Psychology, 55,* 3–9.

Lovaas, I., Litrownik, A., & Mann, R. (1971). Response latencies to auditory stimuli in autistic children engaged in self-stimulatory behavior. *Behavior Research and Therapy, 9,* 305–310.

Lovaas, I., Newsom, C., & Hickman, C. (1987). Self-stimulatory behavior and perceptual reinforcement. *Journal of Applied Behavior Analysis, 20,* 45–68.

Lovaas, O. I., & Favell, J. E. (1987). Protection for clients undergoing aversive/restrictive interventions. *Education and Treatment of Children, 10,* 311–325.

Lovaas, O. I., Schreibman, L., & Koegel, R. L. (1974). A behavioral modification approach to the treatment of autistic children. *Journal of Autism and Childhood Schizophrenia, 4,* 111–129.

Lutzker, J. R. (1978). Reducing self-injurious behavior by facial screening. *American Journal of Mental Deficiency, 82,* 510–513.

Maag, J. W., Rutherford, R. B., Jr., Wolchik, S. A., & Parks, B. T. (1986). Sensory extinction and overcorrection in suppressing self-stimulation: A preliminary comparison of efficacy and generalization. *Education and Treatment of Children, 9,* 189–201.

Mayhew, G., & Harris, F. (1979). Decreasing self-injurious behavior: Punishment with citric acid and reinforcement of alternative behavior. *Behavior Modification, 3,* 322–336.

McAfee, J. K. (1987). Emerging issues in special education tort liability: Implications for special educators and teacher trainers. *Teacher Education and Special Education, 10,* 47–57.

McCormick, L., & Schiefelbusch, R. L. (1984). *Early language intervention: An introduction.* Columbus, OH: Merrill.

McEvoy, M. A., Nordquist, V. M., Twardosz, S., Heckaman, K. A., Wehby, J. H., & Denny, R. K. (1988). Promoting autistic children's peer interaction in an integrated early childhood setting using affection activities. *Journal of Applied Behavior Analysis, 21,* 193–200.

McEvoy, R. E., Loveland, K. A., & Landry, S. H. (1988). The functions of immediate echolalia in autistic children: A developmental perspective. *journal of Autism and Developmental Disorders, 18,* 657–668.

McGee, G. G., Almeida, M. C., Sulzer-Azaroff, B., & Feldman, R. S. (1992). Promoting reciprocal interactions via peer incidental teaching. *Journal of Applied Behavior Analysis, 25,* 117–126.

McGee, G. G., Daly, T., Izeman, S. G., Mann, L. H., & Risely, T. R. (1991). Use of classroom materials to promote preschool engagement. *Teaching Exceptional Children, 23*(4), 43–47.

McGee, G. G., Daly, T., & Jacobs, H. A. (1994). The walden preschool. In S. L. Harris & J. S. Handleman (Eds.). *Preschool education programs for children with autism* (pp. 127–162). Austin, TX: Pro-Ed.

McGee, G. G., Krantz, P. J., Mason, D., & McClannahan, L. E. (1983). A modified incidental-teaching procedure for autistic youth: Acquisition and generalization of receptive object labels. *Journal of Applied Behavior Analysis, 16,* 329–338.

McGee, G. G., Krantz, P. J., & McClannahan, L. E. (1984). Conversational skills for autistic adolescents: Training assertiveness in naturalistic game settings. *Journal of Autism and Developmental Disorders, 14,* 319–330.

McGee, G. G., Krantz, P. J., & McClannahan, L. E. (1985). The facilitative effects of incidental teaching on preposition use by autistic children. *Journal of Applied Behavior Analysis, 18,* 17–31.

McGee, G. G., Paradis, T., & Feldman, R. S. (1993). Free effects of integration on levels of autistic behavior. *Topics in Early Childhood Special Education, 13,* 57–67.

McHale, S. (1983). Changes in autistic children's social behavior as a function of interaction with nonhandicapped children. *American Journal of Orthopsychiatry, 53,* 81–91.

Meyer, L. H., & Evans, I. M. (1986). Modification of excess behavior: An adaptive and functional approach for educational and community contexts. In R. H. Horner, L. H. Meyer, & H. D. B. Fredericks (Eds.), *Education of learners with severe handicaps. Exemplary service strategies.* Baltimore: Paul H. Brookes.

Meyer, L. H., & Evans, I. M. (1989). *Nonaversive intervention for behavior problems: A manual for home and community.* Baltimore: Paul H. Brookes.

Meyer, L. H., Fox, A., Schermer, A., Ketelson, D., Montan, N., Maley, K., & Cole, D. (1987). The effects of teacher intrusion on social play interactions between children with autism and their nonhandicapped peers. *Journal of Autism and Developmental Disabilities, 17,* 315–332.

Myles, B. S., & Simpson, R. L. (1994). Facilitated communication with children diagnosed as autistic in public school settings. *Psychology in the Schools, 31,* 208–220.

Neef, N. A., Walters, J., & Egel, A. L. (1984). Establishing generative yes/no responses in developmentally disabled children. *Journal of Applied Behavior Analysis, 17,* 453–460.

Odom, S., Hoyson, M., Jamieson, B., & Strain, P. S. (1985). Increasing handicapped preschoolers' peer social interactions. Cross-setting and component analysis. *Journal of Applied Behavior Analysis, 18,* 3–16.

Odom, S. L., & Strain, P. S. (1984). Peer-mediated approaches to promoting children's social interaction: A review. *American Journal of Orthopsychiatry, 54,* 544–557.

Peck, C. A. (1985). Increasing opportunities for social control by children with autism and severe handicaps: Effects on student behavior and perceived classroom climate. *Journal of the Association for Persons with Severe Handicaps, 10,* 183–193.

Prizant, B. M. (1983). Language acquisition and communicative behavior in autism: Toward an understanding of the "whole" of it. *Journal of Speech and Hearing Disorders, 48,* 296–307.

Prizant, B. M., & Duchan, J. F. (1981). The functions of immediate echolalia in autistic children. *Journal of Speech and Hearing Disorders, 24,* 241–249.

Prizant, B. M., & Rydell, P. J. (1984). Analysis of functions of delayed echolalia in autistic children. *Journal of Speech and Hearing Disorders, 27,* 183–192.

Prizant, B. M., & Wetherby, A. M. (1989). Enhancing language and communication in autism. In G. Dawson (Ed.), *Autism: New perspectives on diagnosis, nature, and treatment* (pp. 282–309). New York: Guilford.

Prochaska, J., Smith, N., Marzilli, R., Colby, J., & Donovan, W. (1974). Remote-control aversive stimulation in the treatment of head-banging in a retarded child. *Journal of Behavior Therapy and Experimental Psychiatry, 5,* 285–289.

Repp, A. C., & Dietz, D. E. D. (1978). On the selective use of punishment: Suggested guidelines for administrators. *Mental Retardation, 16,* 250–254.

Repp, A. C., Dietz, S. M., & Dietz, D. E. D. (1976). Reducing inappropriate behaviors in classrooms and in individual sessions through DRO schedules of reinforcement. *Mental Retardation, 14,* 11–15.

Rincover, A. (1978). A procedure for eliminating self-stimulatory behavior in psychotic children. *Journal of Abnormal Child Psychology, 6,* 299–310.

Rincover, A., Cook, R., Peoples, A., & Packard, D. (1979). Sensory extinction and sensory reinforcement principles for programming multiple adaptive behavior change. *Journal of Applied Behavior Analysis, 12,* 221–233.

Rincover, A., & Devany, J. (1982). The application of sensory extinction procedures to self-injury. *Analysis and Intervention in Developmental Disabilities, 2,* 67–81.

Rydell, P. J., & Mirenda, P. (1991). The effects of two levels of linguistic constraint on echolalia and generative language production in children with autism. *Journal of Autism and Developmental Disorders, 21,* 131–157.

Rydell, P. J., & Mirenda, P. (1994). Effects of high and low constraint utterances on the production of immediate and delayed echolalia in young children with autism. *Journal of Autism and Developmental Disorders, 24,* 719–735.

Sabin, L. A. & Donnellan, A. M. (1993). A qualitative study of the process of facilitated communication. *Journal of the Association for Persons with Severe Handicaps, 18*(3), 200–211.

Sailor, W., & Taman, T. (1972). Stimulus factors in the training of prepositional usage in three autistic children. *Journal of Applied Behavior Analysis, 5,* 183–190.

Schafer, M. S., Egel, A. L., & Neef, N. A. (1984). Training mildly handicapped peers to facilitate changes in the social interaction skills of autistic children. *Journal of Applied Behavior Analysis, 17,* 461–476.

Schreibman, L., & Carr, E. G. (1978). Elimination of echolalic responding to questions through the training of a generalized verbal response. *Journal of Applied Behavior Analysis, 11,* 453–463.

Schuster, J. W., & Griffen, A. K. (1990). Using time-delay with task analyses. *Teaching Exceptional Children, 22,* 49–53.

Snyder, L. K., Lovitt, T. C., & Smith, J. O. (1975). Language training for the severely retarded: Five years of behavioral analysis research. *Exceptional Children, 42,* 7–15.

Spradlin, J. E., & Siegal, G. M. (1982). Language training in natural and clinical environments. *Journal of Speech and Hearing Disorders, 47,* 2–6.

Stokes, T. F., & Baer, D. M. (1977). An implicit technology of generalization. *Journal of Applied Behavior Analysis, 10,* 349–367.

Stokes, T. F., & Osnes, P. G. (1988). The developing applied technology of generalization and maintenance. In R. H. Horner, G. Dunlap, & R. L. Koegel (Eds.), *Generalization and maintenance: Life-style changes in applied settings* (pp. 5–20). Baltimore: Paul H. Brookes.

Strain, P. S., Kerr, M., & Ragland, E. (1979). Effects of peer-mediated social initiations and prompting/reinforcement procedures in the social behavior of autistic children. *Journal of Autism and Developmental Disabilities, 9,* 41–54.

Tanner, B. A., & Zeiler, M. (1975). Punishment of self-injurious behavior using aromatic ammonia as the aversive stimulus. *Journal of Applied Behavior Analysis, 8,* 53–57.

Thelen, E. (1979). Rhythmical stereotypes in normal human infants. *Animal Behavior, 27,* 699–715.

Tiegerman, E., & Primavera, L. (1981). Object manipulation: An interactional strategy with autistic children. *Journal of Autism and Developmental Disabilities, 11,* 427–438.

Tiegerman, E., & Primavera, L. H. (1984). Imitating the autistic child: Facilitating communicative gaze behavior. *Journal of Autism and Developmental Disabilities, 14,* 27–38.

Varni, J. W., Lovaas, O. I., Koegel, R. L., & Everett, N. L. (1979). An analysis of observational learning in autistic and normal children. *Journal of Abnormal Child Psychology, 7,* 31–43.

Warren, S. F., & Kaiser, A. P. (1986). Incidental language training: A critical review. *Journal of Speech and Hearing Disorders, 51,* 291–299.

Wells, K. C., Forehand, R., Hickey, K., & Green, R. (1977). Effects of a procedure derived from the overcorrection principle and nonmanipulated behavior. *Journal of Applied Behavior Analysis, 10,* 679–687.

Williams, D. (1994). In the real world. *Journal of the Association for Persons with Severe Handicaps, 19*(3), 196–199.

Woods, T. S. (1982). Reducing severe aggressive and self-injurious behavior: A nonintrusive, home based approach. *Behavioral Disorders, 7,* 180–188.

Woods, T. S. (1984). Generality in the verbal tacting of autistic children as a function of "natural-ness" in antecedent control. *Journal of Behavior Therapy and Experimental Psychiatry, 15,* 27–32.

Yoder, D. E., & Calculator, S. (1981). Some perspectives on intervention strategies for persons with developmental disorders. *Journal of Autism and Developmental Disorders, 11,* 107–123.

Zirpoli, T. J., & Lloyd, J. W. (1987). Understanding and managing self-injurious behavior. *Remedial and Special Education, 8,* 46–57.

Chapter *13*

Educating Students with Behavior Disorders: Prevailing Issues and Future Challenges

Advance Organizer

As you read this chapter, prepare to identify and discuss:

- Why students with behavior problems remain both underidentified and underserved.
- The National Agenda for Achieving Better Results with Students with Behavior Problems
- How the controversies surrounding service delivery alternatives are influencing professionals' thoughts about placement options for students with behavior problems.
- Methods by which bias in assessment could be reduced for culturally diverse students.
- The limitations in our knowledge base regarding the needs of drug- and alcohol-exposed children.
- Alternative solutions for facilitating the transition from school to work of students with behavior problems.
- The factors that contribute to feelings of stress by teachers of students with behavior problems.
- Signs that the profession of educating students with behavior disorders is growing out of its adolescence.

Prevailing Issues and Future Challenges

In the preceding twelve chapters, we addressed a number of critical areas in the education of students with behavior disorders. Our goal was to provide an even-handed, *data-based* presentation of what is currently regarded as best practice in the education of students with behavior disorders. For each chapter, we had one key assumption: An effective educational program is the most important variable that teachers can provide to students with behavior disorders. Consequently, most of the content presented in this text focused on critical teacher-directed educational activities such as the assessment, management, and remediation of specific problem behaviors and the teaching of academic and prosocial skills. Educational events were highlighted because they occur in an environment—the classroom—that is alterable by specific teacher actions. Active and dedicated teachers who have a repertoire of effective strategies at their disposal will have greater success with students than those who cling passively to any single approach.

In the preceding twelve chapters, many promising alternatives for educating students with behavior disorders were reported. It is evident from the professional literature that we have made great strides in developing methods and tools for assessing problem behavior and in designing techniques to remediate the identified problems. As Paul (1985) observed, these strides reflect the dynamic nature of our profession and the quality of leadership this challenging field has enjoyed.

Still, we are far from fulfilling the goal of providing effective educational services to all students with behavior disorders. They remain both underidentified and underserved. As noted in earlier chapters, the major factors believed to be related to underidentification are: (1) attitudes toward the label "emotional disturbance" (Huntze, 1985; Long, 1983); (2) issues surrounding the interpretation of the definition of emotional disturbance and the use of such interpretations at times to stop the delivery of services to students in need (Center, 1989); (3) the lack of commonly accepted standardized assessment instruments directly related to the identification of emotional disturbance; and (4) underfunded school districts with high minority enrollments (Long, 1983). Obviously, more needs to be done to ensure that all students with behavior problems are identified so that educators can provide them with appropriate educational activities to meet their assessed deficiencies.

Currently, students with identified emotional disturbance earn lower grades, fail more courses, and are retained at grade level more than any other group of students with disabilities (Chesapeake Institute, 1994). They also miss more days of school per year (approximately eighteen) than the others and tend to have a high rate of encounters with the juvenile justice system. In fact, the Chesapeake Institute (1994) reports that 20 percent of students with emotional disturbance are arrested at least once before they leave school (compared with 6 percent of all students) and 58 percent are arrested within five years of leaving school. This figure increases to 73 percent if only those students who drop-out of school are considered. Finally, a mere 42 percent earn a high school diploma, a most unacceptable rate when one views the data on all students with disabilities (50 percent) and peers in general education (76 percent).

Clearly, how to best educate students with behavior problems continues to be a critical concern. We need to ensure that once students with behavior problems are identified, they are served in a fashion that is appropriate, ethical, and efficacious. To those who work or are planning to work with these students, advocacy for appropriate services will remain a difficult task because the antisocial and often destructive behaviors displayed by students with behavior disorders do not exactly spark the nurturing instincts of most educators and educational policymakers. That is why it is so crucial for special education professionals to be effective change agents.

In the sections that follow, several critical issues related to the delivery of educational services to students with behavior disorders are presented. These issues demand to be addressed if we are to squarely meet the challenges that difficult-to-manage students present to our system of public education.

A National Agenda for Achieving Better Results

A number of recent national reports (e.g., National Mental Health Association, 1993; Valdes, Williamson, & Wagner, 1992) have continued to document the critical needs of students with behavior problems and how the collective "we" in the educational and service systems arenas have failed to adequately address these needs. In response to these reports, the Department of Education (Chesapeake Institute, 1994) has developed a comprehensive national agenda for achieving better results for children and youth with serious emotional disturbance. In this document specific mission and vision statements are articulated and seven interdependent strategic targets are enumerated. The mission of the agenda is simple and straightforward: Achieving better results for students with severe emotional disturbance. The vision is a "reorientation and national preparedness to foster the emotional development and adjustment of children and youth with or at risk of developing serious emotional disturbance, as the critical foundation for realizing their potential at school, work, and in the community" (p. 3).

The interdependent reorientation of the National Agenda is reflected in Figure 13.1, and a brief description of each of the seven strategic targets is provided in Figure 13.2. Underlying the conceptual framework and the strategic targets are three critical assumptions. First, collaborative efforts must extend to initiatives that prevent emotional and behavioral problems from developing or escalating. Second, all services must be delivered in a culturally sensitive and respectful manner. Finally, delivered services must empower all stakeholders and maintain a climate of possibility and accountability (Chesapeake Institute, 1994).

By addressing the strategic targets within the context of a unified and adequately funded national effort, it is hoped that our states, institutions of higher education, local governments, mental health and juvenile justice agencies, in concert with local school district personnel can (1) provide and maintain an adequate number of qualified personnel to serve students with severe emotional disturbance;

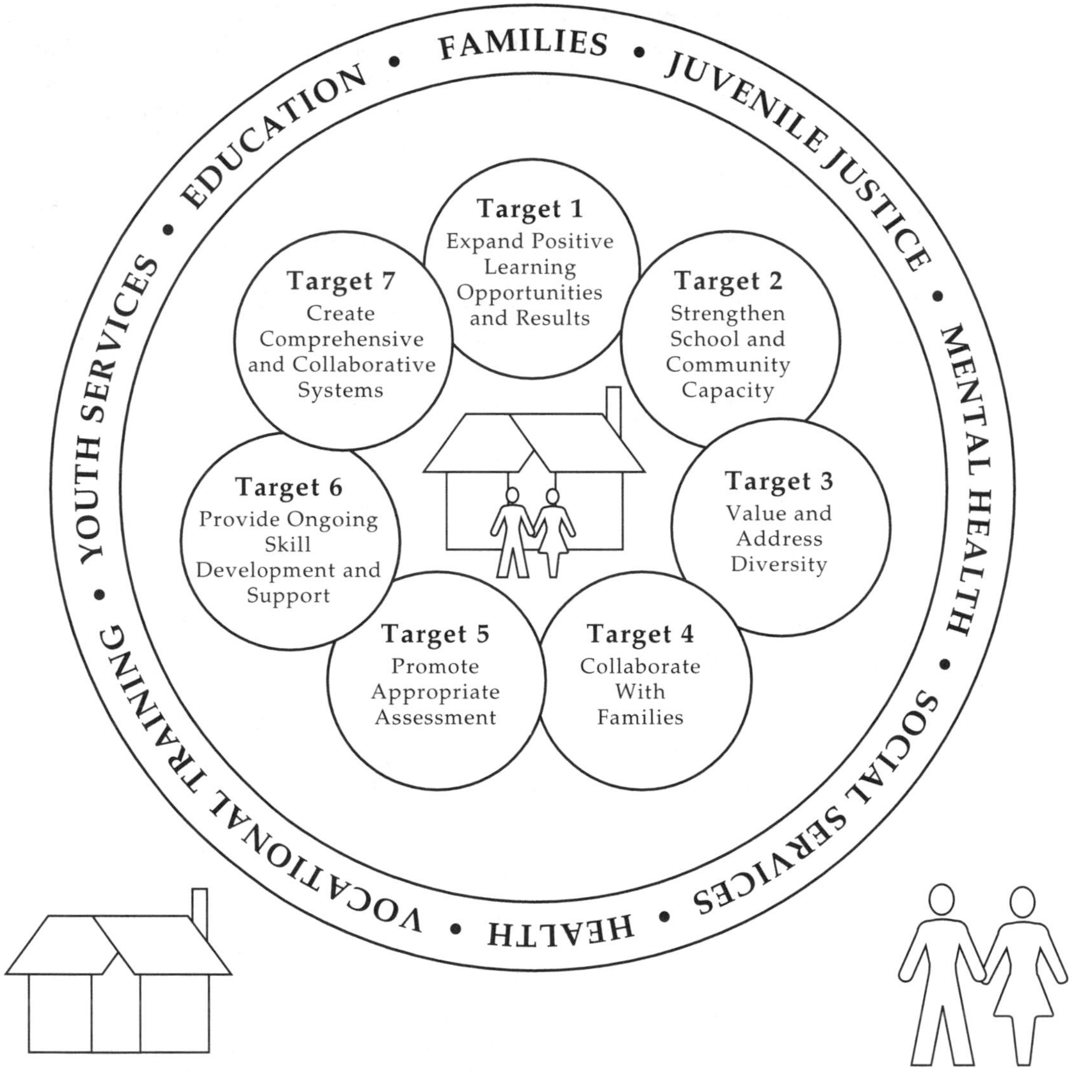
FAMILIES • JUVENILE JUSTICE • MENTAL HEALTH • SOCIAL SERVICES • HEALTH • VOCATIONAL TRAINING • YOUTH SERVICES • EDUCATION •
Target 1
Expand Positive Learning Opportunities and Results
Target 2
Strengthen School and Community Capacity
Target 3
Value and Address Diversity
Target 4
Collaborate With Families
Target 5
Promote Appropriate Assessment
Target 6
Provide Ongoing Skill Development and Support
Target 7
Create Comprehensive and Collaborative Systems

School and Community Results
- Community Strength
- Family Preservation
- Fiscal Efficiency
- Teacher Retention
- School Effectiveness

Student Results
- Improved Grades
- Enhanced Learning
- Higher Graduation Rates
- Increased Equity
- Successful Transition to Adult Roles

Collaborate ⟶ Implement Targets ⟶ Achieve Results

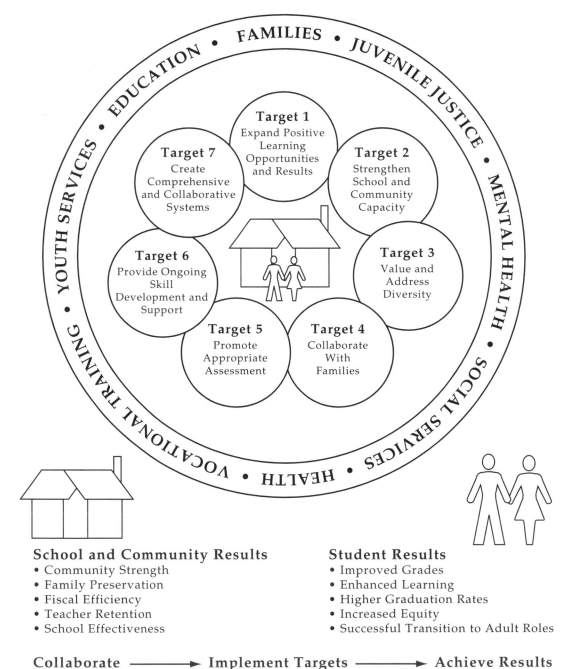

FIGURE 13.1 An Interdependent Reorientation to Achieve Better Results

TARGET #1: EXPAND POSITIVE LEARNING OPPORTUNITIES AND RESULTS

To foster the provision of engaging, useful, and positive learning opportunities. These opportunities should be result-driven and should acknowledge as well as respond to the experiences and needs of children and youth with serious emotional disturbance.

TARGET #2: STRENGTHEN SCHOOL AND COMMUNITY CAPACITY

To foster initiatives that strengthen the capacity of schools and communities to serve students with serious emotional disturbance in the least restrictive environments appropriate.

TARGET #3: VALUE AND ADDRESS DIVERSITY

To encourage culturally competent and linguistically appropriate exchanges and collaborations among families, professionals, students, and communities. These collaborations should foster equitable outcomes for all students and result in the identification and provision of services that are responsive to issues of race, culture, gender, and social and economic status.

TARGET #4: COLLABORATE WITH FAMILIES

To foster collaborations that fully include family members on the team of service providers that implements family focused services to improve educational outcomes. Services should be open, helpful, culturally competent, accessible to families, and school- as well as community-based.

TARGET #5: PROMOTE APPROPRIATE ASSESSMENT

To promote practices ensuring that assessment is integral to the identification, design, and delivery of services for children and youth with serious emotional disturbance. These practices should be culturally appropriate, ethical, and functional.

TARGET #6: PROVIDE ONGOING SKILL DEVELOPMENT AND SUPPORT

To foster the enhancement of knowledge, understanding, and sensitivity among all who work with children and youth with and at risk of developing serious emotional disturbance. Support and development should be ongoing and aim at strengthening the capacity of families, teachers, service providers, and other stakeholders to collaborate, persevere, and improve outcomes for children and youth with serious emotional disturbance.

TARGET #7: CREATE COMPREHENSIVE AND COLLABORATIVE SYSTEMS

To promote systems change resulting in the development of coherent services built around the individual needs of children and youth with and at risk of developing serious emotional disturbance. These services should be family-centered, community-based, and appropriately funded.

FIGURE 13.2   National Agenda for Achieving Better Results for Children and Youth with Serious Emotional Disturbance

(2) develop the capacity to ready systems to meet the needs of changing populations of students in need; (3) secure and expand access and inclusion for those with emotional and behavioral problems, and ultimately (4) improve academic and "real-life" outcomes for those with behavioral problems.

Service Delivery Alternatives

Educators have long debated how best to deliver services to children identified as having special education needs. This debate is the result of tension between the desire to provide an appropriate education to students identified as having handicaps and the need to maintain these students in least restrictive environments. An increasing number of professionals (Biklen & Zollers, 1986; Gartner & Lipsky, 1987; Giangreco, Baumgart, & Doyle, 1995; Stainback & Stainback, 1984; Wang, Reynolds, & Walberg, 1988; and Will, 1986) have questioned—some with and many without data—the efficacy and efficiency of special education as it is presently delivered. The tension between educational need and the need for normalization has led many to explore alternative administrative structures for delivering special education services. Advocates of this restructuring, originally termed the regular (or general) education initiative (REI) and more recently referred to as inclusion, propose that the general education system assume unequivocal primary responsibility for all students in public schools, including all those identified as handicapped. Arguments for inclusion stem from dissatisfaction with existing service delivery and frustration that such practices result in: (1) too many students being identified as disabled; (2) fragmentation of educational services for students who are "pulled out" of general education settings; and (3) an overemphasis on the identification of students' problems at the expense of developing effective strategies for combating those problems (Maheady, 1988).

The rationale for inclusive education is quite compelling, particularly on philosophical and social grounds. Clearly, it is difficult to argue against the position that all children should reap the potential benefits of inclusive programming (e.g., attending one's neighborhood school in classrooms where there is a climate of acceptance, ending the segregation of large numbers of students, all students participating in shared educational experiences with individualized outcomes). However, most of the discussions on inclusion have (1) ignored the barriers and conditions within our schools that preclude successful inclusive efforts and (2) minimized the real life day-to-day demands on teachers who are expected to teach an ever increasing diversity of students with and without disabilities (Joint Committee on Teaching Planning for Students with Disabilities, 1995). Based upon the results of four large scale studies, the Joint Committee found that for students with disabilities to be successfully included in the general education classroom, educators need to think in terms of "supported inclusion" not simply inclusion.

Supported inclusion was defined as a set of instructional conditions in which classroom teachers:

- Are philosophically committed to meeting the needs of all students in the general education classroom, including those with mild disabilities
- Have sufficient time to think about and plan for the diverse needs of students in their class(es)

- Incorporate teaching practices that enable them to better meet the needs of all students in their class(es)
- Collaboratively work with special education teachers to assess, teach, and monitor student progress
- Have the option for their students to receive short-term, intensive instructional support from a special education teacher
- Have the option for their students to receive sustained instruction in basic skills or learning strategies that cannot be provided in the general education classroom (Joint Committee on Teacher Planning for Students with Disabilities, 1995, p. 3–4)

Although few have disputed the desirability of the inclusion movement's goals, many (e.g., Hallahan, Keller, McKinney, Lloyd, & Bryan, 1988; Kauffman, Lloyd, Baker, & Riedel, 1995) have questioned the feasibility of restructuring given the lack of data indicating that restructuring will work and evidence that general educators are far from eager to serve students with disabilities in regular classes, particularly those with behavior disorders. In fact, reform efforts demanding higher academic standards and increased teacher accountability may actually lower general educators' willingness to accept difficult to teach students in their classrooms. Although general educators can acquire structured management skills, it may be unreasonable to expect them to develop expertise to manage and resolve the unusually deviant behaviors of students with behavior disorders (Council for Children with Behavior Disorders, 1989).

Moreover, many general education settings lack the preconditions to successfully serve students with challenging behaviors. As observed by Kauffman and colleagues (1995), very few schools have (1) a critical mass of trained, experienced, and mutually supportive personnel located in physical proximity to each other and (2) very low pupil professional staff ratios. Clearly, the inclusion of students with behavior disorders requires an intensity of resources that are not typically found in general education settings. Still, legal requirements necessitate that schools make good faith efforts to include students with behavior disorders. Yell (1995) has observed that the courts have been clear that educators must provide supplementary aids and services, such as behavior management plans, consultation, and behavioral supports to enhance inclusive efforts. Yet, when an appropriate education cannot be achieved in the general education setting with these supplements, the presumption for an integrated placement is overcome and placement in a more restrictive setting may occur.

Although many of the arguments surrounding the move toward more inclusive programming have tended to be polemic, much good has come from the debate they have sparked. At least now all agree that improvements are needed in the delivery of special education services to those students who violate the implicit and explicit norms of schools. As Maheady (1988) noted, such controversy may prove to be a golden opportunity for stimulating and systematically evaluating creative alternatives for these underidentified and underserved students.

Assessment Practices with Culturally Diverse Students

One of the major influences on education in general, and on special education in particular, is the changing demographics of students served in U.S. public schools. As the population of the United States ages, the numbers of traditionally under-represented minorities (black, brown, and Asian Americans) are increasing dramatically, with Hispanics now the fastest-growing group in the United States (Yates, 1988). The obvious conclusion is that we will see a rise in the numbers of students from these groups who are referred for special education services. Unfortunately, the available data (e.g., Artiles, 1994; Jones, Sacks & Bennent, 1985) suggest that some minority groups are overrepresented in special education programs today, while other groups are underrepresented. In terms of behavior disorders, African Americans and Hispanics tend to be overrepresented, while Asians tend to be underrepresented (Sugai, 1988).

According to the Council for Children with Behavioral Disorders (1989), three factors contribute to the misclassification of culturally diverse children referred for possible behavior problems. First, linguistic competence often influences how others in the environment perceive and interact with a student. Successful interpersonal interactions are reciprocal processes that are impeded when there is no common mode of communication. Consequently, language differences between a student and the majority in the educational environment increase the probability that that student will have social-behavioral problems. Second, teachers may have preconceived perceptions of, and lower expectations for, culturally different students, and therefore interact less frequently and less favorably with these students. This can start a chain of self-fulfilling events in which low expectations translate into poor academic performance and social behavior and, ultimately, result in higher rates of referral for behavior problems. Finally, culturally diverse students may be at great risk for misidentification merely because they are referred for special education at higher rates than the majority of students (e.g., Bickel, 1982). Once a student is referred for special assistance, there is a high probability that he or she will be placed in special education.

Clearly, we need assessment practices that reduce test bias and improve our ability to identify and intervene to correct those behaviors that are associated with behavioral disorders. The CCBD (1989) believes that the needs of culturally diverse students would be best served through a functional assessment approach that examines student performance under existing teaching conditions, alters instructional practices to improve student performance, and monitors student performance on a continuous basis to assess the effects of the alterations in practices. Since assessment would be both direct and continuous, bias due to cultural differences should be minimized. Assessors would rely more on large numbers of direct observations in natural settings, and thus would be able to observe the behaviors of nonreferred peers to determine if problem identification is the result of quantifiable behavioral differences or intolerance of cultural diversity.

Although the functional assessment approach is becoming more and more prevalent, particularly in districts that have adopted prereferral intervention programs (e.g., Graden, Casey, & Christensen, 1985), far too much non-data-based decision making and *inappropriate* norm-referenced identification are resulting in poor educational placements for culturally diverse students. Educators are challenged to develop a greater awareness of functional assessment procedures for all students and to recognize that the identification and assessment of problem behavior is a means to an end, not an end in itself (CCBD, 1989).

Addressing the Needs of Drug- and Alcohol-Exposed Children

It is estimated that by the year 2000 there will be over 4 million drug exposed children in the United States (Sautter, 1992). Those who teach children with learning and behavioral problems continue to express a need for clear and accurate information regarding the characteristics, expected behavioral outcomes, and possible interventions for young children who have been prenatally exposed to illicit drugs and alcohol. Although there is an increasing knowledge base indicating that alcohol and illicit substances such as cocaine, phenylcycidine hydrochloride (PCP), and other central nervous system active drugs result in infants and children with abnormal brain wave patterns, short-term neurological signs, depression of interactive behavior, and poor organizational responses to environmental stimuli (Van Dyke & Fox, 1990), recent reviews (e.g., Carta et al., 1994; Shriver & Piersal, 1994) have concluded that with the exception of fetal alcohol syndrome (FAS), it is not yet possible to predict the outcomes for individual children exposed prenatally to drugs.

While there is much written in the popular press about "drug-exposed babies," there are a relatively small number of methodologically sound empirical studies concerned with the developmental, behavioral, and academic outcomes of children prenatally exposed to drugs. Such research is difficult because of the inherent difficulty in separating out the multitude of risk factors experienced by many children of drug abusers. The environments in which drug exposed children grow up are often characterized by poverty, poor nutrition, community violence, and unstable family dynamics—multiple environmental factors that impact on, and mediate, the possible direct effects of intrauterine drug exposure on developmental, social, and academic outcomes (Austin & Prendergast, 1991; Shriver & Piersal, 1994). Thus, while we are unsure as to the specific behavioral profiles and available intervention strategies, it is clear that recent increases in alcohol and drug abuse among young females of childbearing age will result in a significant increase in the numbers of children who will require special attention for learning and behavioral problems (Van Dyke & Fox, 1990).

What then should be done? It is likely that the primary characteristics of drug-exposed children will make them candidates for early intervention special education programs that specialize in behavior problems (Bauer, 1991; Sautter, 1992). As with other children with behavioral problems, a number of pilot programs (e.g., Chasnoff, 1992; Howard, 1992) have demonstrated that drug-exposed children can and will improve in their academic and behavioral functioning if early intervention efforts are provided. If no early intervention is provided, these students may be referred to special programs for students with behavior disorders. However, children with behavior problems are underserved, sometimes unidentified, and often placed in programs that are inadequate and lacking in appropriately trained personnel. Greer (1990) has observed that no single human service agency, including the schools, has the human and fiscal resources to meet the needs of drug-exposed children and their families. Perhaps the coordinated efforts of social service agencies, public health and medical organizations, and the schools can assist in designing a comprehensive approach for addressing the multitude of challenges presented by drug-exposed children.

Transition to Postsecondary Alternatives

The transition from high school to work or postsecondary education is a difficult road for many high school students. The first step in this transition is graduation from secondary school and the graduation data for students with disabilities are discouraging, at best. For students with mild and moderate disabilities, less than 70% will graduate with their chronological classmates (Cohen & deBettencourt, 1991). Graduation rates for students with emotional and behavioral disorders are the second lowest for all categories of students with disabilities (only students with multiple and severe disabilities graduate at lower rates) and the dropout rates for students with emotional and behavioral disorders are the highest of all student groups (Wagner, 1991). The data in Table 13.1 illustrate dropout and graduation rates for students without disabilities and for selected groups of students with disabilities. Low graduation and high drop-out rates for students with emotional and behavioral disorders remain one of the most serious concerns for practitioners in the field. Promising and successful interventions, however, have appeared in recent years. Mayer and colleagues (1993), for example, trained high school students with emotional and behavioral disorders (and others) to deliver consulting and tu-

TABLE 13.1   High School Exit Rates for Students with and without Disabilities

	Diploma	Certificate or Maximum Age	Drop-out
All students	74%	2%	24%
Students with disabilities	46%	15%	39%
Students with EBD	31%	9%	60%
Students with LD	52%	12%	36%
Students with MR	39%	30%	31%

toring services and found that dropout rates decreased substantially and positive ratings of classroom environments increased.

It has been suggested that approximately 20 million noncollege-bound youths between the ages of 16 and 24 will have a difficult time finding and keeping a job that offers the possibility of career advancement (Olson, 1990). The data for graduates of special education programs are even more disconcerting. According to Edgar and associates (e.g., Edgar, 1988, 1990; Neel, Meadows, Levine, & Edgar, 1988), only 60 percent of students with mild disabilities find employment within a year of leaving school. For students with emotional and behavior disorders, 57 percent are employed at six months and 59 percent at two years after leaving school. Most disheartening are the data concerning the types of jobs these students have: For the total group of students with emotional and behavior disorders, only 20 percent earn above the minimum wage two years after graduation. Furthermore, only 32 percent of graduates with behavior disorders were found to be living independently compared with 52 percent of the graduates without disabilities. Edgar (1990) estimated that no more than 30 percent of all graduates with mild disabilities ever match the portrait of productive adulthood.

These data on employment outcomes signal a need to consider alternative solutions for facilitating the transition to the work world of students with mild disabilities, particularly those with behavior problems. Edgar (1988) has suggested that service providers "beef up" vocational training opportunities, include problem solving and independent life skills into the training curricula, and incorporate mentoring activities into vocational-skills training programs. Along with these content variables, several processes are also recommended:

1. Cooperative transition planning and orientation.
2. A comprehensive assessment of instructional and training variables to guide the development and delivery of interventions.
3. The individualization of training goals.
4. The incorporation of training in the psychosocial and independent living skills that are prerequisites for successful vocational adjustment.
5. Skills development methodologies that promote generalization outside the training environment.
6. The development of self-advocacy skills.

Disappointing outcome data have also led some people to question the efficacy of the incremental educational paradigm that guides special education. Edgar (1990), for example, believes that we need to move from the present person-centered "fix-it" environmental manipulation paradigm to one that incorporates skill building with ongoing support services. With this new model,

> *we no longer only ask what to teach or how to teach. We now ask global questions such as: what is needed for this individual to be a productive part of the community; what skills, information, or attitudes does the person need, what support do*

they need, what skills, information or attitudes does the community need and what supports does the community need. (p. 13).

The transition to adult life is a difficult process for all adolescents. It is especially so for adolescents with mild disabilities because leaving school means the end of special entitlements. Beyond family networks and connections, these young adults receive little assistance, and many of them slip into the ranks of the unemployed. The available outcome data on students with behavior problems tell us quite clearly that we need to do more both to ensure high school graduation and to promote a successful adjustment to life after school. The challenge is to develop successful alternatives that will improve upon our current methods of delivering secondary education and transition services. Whether such changes can occur within the context of our current educational system or whether we need to make a revolutionary shift in how we prepare students to meet the postschool world remains to be seen.

Concern for Self: Reducing Stress and Burnout

Teaching is a stressful profession. Of those who have left teaching, 27 percent cite emotional aspects such as stress, frustration, boredom, and burnout as the primary reasons for making a career change. All classrooms, whether they house special or normally achieving students, are active settings that contain a variety of organizational pressures that affect teachers' levels of stress and anxiety. As noted by Doyle (1980), classrooms are public forums that require frequent and immediate teacher action in the face of often overwhelming, and sometimes unpredictable, environmental variables. Six of these variables—immediacy, publicness, multidimensionality, unpredictability, history, and simultaneity—are described in Figure 13.3. Their range and intensity can vary according to the time of year (i.e., proximity to holidays), the time of day (*that* seventh-period English class), the management style of the building administrator, and the experience level, dedication, and competence of the individual teacher.

For special education teachers, the organizational pressures of classrooms are even more intense. Besides being charged with the usual array of diagnostic and instructional responsibilities, teachers of students with handicaps are typically called upon to complete and interpret full-scale educational evaluations, coordinate mainstreaming activities, initiate and maintain collaborative working relationships with related service personnel, and develop outreach programs with parents, teachers, and significant others in students' ecosystems (Rosenberg, O'Shea, & O'Shea, 1991). With all these demands, it is no wonder that special education teachers show higher levels of stress and burnout than other teachers.

The increased demands associated with the peculiar needs of special education students often place teachers in roles that lack clarity. Although they are trained to assume a range of responsibilities, conflicts can arise when the role def-

Immediacy	→	Large numbers of events require immediate attention or action
Publicness	→	Teacher is always onstage
Multidimensionality	→	Classrooms are crowded and busy places in which limited resources are used to achieve a wide range of goals
Unpredictability	→	Events in classrooms change daily and many occurrences are difficult to predict
History	→	Events that occur early in the school year set the tone for later happenings.
Simultaneity	→	Many things happen at the same time in the classrooms

FIGURE 13.3   Organizational Pressures of Classrooms

Source: Adapted from Doyle (1980).

inition they assume for themselves does not match the role expectations of principals, colleagues, or the community school board. For example, as advocates for the handicapped, special educators often find themselves "battling" school administrators for dwindling resources, mainstreaming, and equal status within the school building—an experience that can be enormously stressful if principals and school districts view these activities as outside the teacher's responsibilities. Also, special educators are often called upon to act as "specialists" in problems that other teachers feel ill prepared to resolve—a time-consuming role that often causes stress because it interferes with their ability to serve the students in their direct charge. In addition, special education teachers often deal with parents who are, at best, ambivalent about their children's placement and performance in school—a difficult role that often causes them to question just how far they should go in trying to involve parents in their children's educational programs.

On top of the stress caused by all these potential role conflicts, special education teachers are particularly vulnerable to burnout because students with behavior problems present a wide range of behavioral excesses and deficits, arouse strong emotional reactions in others, and are unwelcome to most educators (Zabel, Boomer, & King, 1984). Fortunately, models (e.g., Cook & Leffingwell, 1982; Zabel, Boomer, & King, 1984) and descriptive research efforts (e.g., Crane & Iwanicki, 1986; Fimian & Blanton, 1986) have identified a series of intervention targets (role conflict, role ambiguity, and lack of time and resources) associated with stress and burnout. The suggested solutions center on four general needs. First, there is a need for more effective preservice and in-service opportunities for special education teachers to identify and cope with sources of stress. Second, special educators need support groups so they can share their successes and failure with understanding peers. Third, they need to be able to schedule enough time to deal with the additional paperwork and planning associated with working with students with disabilities.

Fourth, and far from least, teachers of challenging students need to be recognized as dedicated people who are performing services above and beyond what is typical for regular educators.

So far, unfortunately, we have produced little data concerning the efficacy of *specific strategies* for assisting teachers of challenging students to combat the factors that lead to stress and burnout. If we are to maintain a high quality of educational services for students with behavior disorders, school districts and researchers must make much greater effort to design, implement, evaluate, and disseminate programs that promote the "wellness" of those who teach difficult students.

The Maturation of the Profession

As we mentioned earlier in this chapter, there is much room for improvement in the delivery of services to students with behavior disorders. We identified several areas of current concern to professionals and briefly described the issues involved. These issues will not be easily or quickly resolved, for they are complex and deeply rooted in differences among professionals.

As professionals interested in the education of students with behavior disorders, we should be proud of the high levels of commitment and activity devoted to the search for new and innovative instructional alternatives. We must, however, be aware of our own professional behavior as we seek to improve upon the educational status quo. Kauffman (1986) aptly characterized the education of students with behavior disorders as a field just emerging from the adolescent stage of development. Like a confused adolescent, the profession searched for identity, conceptual roots, security, support, and reality in the recent past. We tended to overestimate our abilities and importance and underestimate our needs; to overly rely on legal constructions rather than on our parent professions of education and psychology; to have a low tolerance for ambiguity; to be uncertain of our identity; to cling to a belief in magical solutions rather than facing reality; and to desire immediate gratification.

But we are definitely growing out of our adolescence. Whereas once, because we overestimated our own abilities, we believed that our compensatory special education efforts could address and ultimately *solve* any and all educational ills, we are now aware of the limits of special education and the value of preventative efforts. We are fast becoming cognizant of the fact that special education alone cannot address the ills of our educational system (Kauffman, 1986). Although we may want to influence the total lives of troubled students, a complete cure of society's problems exceeds our well-intentioned reach. Special educators must work collaboratively with a host of other social service professionals if we are to maximize our impact.

One of the emerging positive trends is the collaborative provision of comprehensive services to students with behavioral disorders (Epstein et al., 1993; Lowenthal, 1996). In its simplest form this collaboration is evidenced as cooperation between educators and mental health professionals. In the past students with behavioral disorders often received educational services at school and mental health services at community mental health centers (and other outpatient agencies) with little communication occurring among various service providers. Recently, interdisciplinary initiatives have generated promising collaborative treatment programs. The National Special Education and Mental Health Coalition (Forness, 1988) is an excellent example of such an initiative.

Now that the need for integrated services appears obvious, descriptions of exploratory, demonstration, and exemplary programs are appearing in the professional literature (Fredericks, 1994; Nelson & Person, 1991). The central premise underlying these practices is that students with emotional and behavioral disorders require community-based, integrated, and comprehensive services that involve education, mental health, foster care, social work, and other human service professionals communicating and acting in concert to meet all of the needs of students with emotional and behavioral disorders and their families. Interested readers are referred to the special edition of the *Journal of Emotional and Behavioral Disorders* (Epstein & Douglas, 1994) devoted solely to this topic.

One of the interesting and exciting cross-over trends in special education is the emergence of analogous concerns in both learning disabilities and emotional and behavior disorders. In the field of learning disabilities practitioners have agreed that the provision of academic services is insufficient for many students with learning disabilities, who often experience psychological and behavior problems (Price, Johnson, & Evelo, 1994; Rosenthal, 1992). In a similar fashion in the field of emotional and behavioral disorders researchers have demonstrated that good instructional programming can also be effective behavior management (Clarke et al., 1995) and the state of Colorado has undertaken an initiative to remediate behavior disorders through instructional programming (Cessna, Adams, Borock, Neel, & Swize, 1993).

It is our hope that special education will continue to emerge from this difficult stage of development with a greater sense of purpose and an enlightened sense of self and society. The years of experience should enable us to interpret our knowledge base with a greater feel for broadening the impact of our efforts and with a wiser sense of how to use what we have learned with care, humility, discretion, and dedication.

Discussion Questions

1. Why do students with behavior disorders remain both underidentified and underserved?

2. What are the seven strategic targets of the National Agenda for Achieving Better Results for students with behavior problems? How can these seven interdependent targets serve to coordinate how services are delivered to students with challenging behaviors?

3. What is inclusion? In your opinion, will the restructuring of service delivery systems benefit students with behavior disorders?

4. What factors contribute to the misclassification of culturally diverse children who are referred for special education services because of their behavior problems?

5. Why is it difficult to assess the extent of the need associated with drug- and alcohol-exposed children?

6. What factors need to be considered when designing programs to help facilitate the transition between school and work for students with behavior problems?

7. List and describe the pressures that can contribute to the stress associated with teaching students with behavior disorders. In your opinion, what can researchers and school administrators do to alleviate these stressors?

8. Are there any tangible signs that the profession of educating students with behavior disorders is growing out of its adolescence?

References

Artiles, A. (1994). Overrepresentation of minority students in special education: A continuing debate. *Journal of Special Education, 27*(4), 410–437.

Austin, G., & Prendergast, M. (1991). Young children of substance abusers. *Prevention Research Update, 8,* 1–31.

Bauer, A. M. (1991). Drug and alcohol exposed children: Implications for special education for students identified as behaviorally disordered. *Behavioral Disorders, 17*(1), 72–79.

Bickel, W. E. (1982). Classifying mentally retarded students: A review of placement procedures in special education. In K. A. Heller, W. H. Holtzman, & S. Messick (Eds.), *Placing children in special education: A strategy for equity* (pp. 182–229). Washington, DC: National Academy Press.

Biklen, D., & Zollers, N. (1986). The focus of advocacy in the LD field. *Journal of Learning Disabilities, 19,* 579–586.

Carta, J. J., Sideridis, G., Rinkel, P., Guimaraes, S., Greenwood, C., Baggestt, K., Peterson, P., Atwater, J., McEvoy, M., & McConnell, S. (1994). Behavioral outcomes of young children prenatally exposed to illicit drugs: Review and analysis of experimental literature. *Topics in Early Childhood Special Education, 14*(2), 184–216.

Center, D. B. (1989). *Curriculum and teaching strategies for students with behavioral disorders.* Englewood Cliffs, NJ: Prentice-Hall.

Cessna, K., Adams, L., Borock, J., Neel, R., & Swize, M. (1993). *Instructionally differentiated programming: A needs-based approach for students with behavior disorders.* Denver: Colorado Department of Education.

Chasnoff, I. J. (1992, Winter). Hope for a "lost generation". *School Safety,* 4–6.

Chesapeake Institute. (September 1994). National agenda for achieving better results for children and youth with serious emotional disturbance. Washington, DC: U.S. Department of Education.

Clarke, S., Dunlap, G., Foster-Johnson, L., Childs, K., Wilson, D., White, R., & Vera, A. (1995). Improving the conduct of students with behavioral disorders by incorporating student interests into curricular activities. *Behavioral Disorders 20*(4), 221–237.

Cohen, S., & deBettencourt, L. (1991). Dropout: Intervening with the reluctant learner. *Intervention in School and Clinic, 26,* 263–271.

Cook, J. M. E., & Leffingwell, R. J. (1982). Stressors and remediation techniques for special educators. *Exceptional Children, 49,* 54–59.

Council for Children with Behavioral Disorders (1989). Best assessment practices for students with behavioral disorders: Accommodation to cultural diversity and individual differences. *Behavioral Disorders, 14,* 263–278.

Crane, S. J., & Iwanicki, E. F. (1986). Perceived role conflict, role ambiguity, and burnout among special education teachers. *Remedial and Special Education, 7,* 24–31.

Doyle, W. (1980). *Classroom management.* West Lafayette, IN: Kappa Delta Pi.

Edgar, E. (1988). Employment as an outcome for mildly handicapped students: Current status and future directions. *Focus on Exceptional Children, 21,* 1–8.

Edgar, E. (1990). Is it time to change our view of the world? *Beyond Behavior, 1,* 9–13.

Epstein, M., & Douglas, C. (1994). Special series: Center for mental health services research projects. *Journal of Emotional and Behavior Disorders, 2*(4).

Epstein, M., Nelson, C., Polsgrove, L., Coutinho, M., Cumblad, C., & Quinn, K. (1993). A comprehensive community-based approach to serving students with emotional and behavior disorders. *Journal of Emotional and Behavior Disorders, 1*(2), 127–133.

Fimian, M. J., & Blanton, L. P. (1986). Variables related to stress and burnout in special education teacher trainees and first-year teachers. *Teacher Education and Special Education, 9,* 9–21.

Forness, S. R. (1988). Planning for the needs of children with serious emotional disturbance: The National Special Education and Mental Health Coalition. *Behavioral Disorders, 13,* 127–132.

Fredericks, B. (1994). Integrated service systems for troubled youth. *Education and Treatment of Children, 17*(3), 387–416.

Gartner, A., & Lipsky, D. (1987). Beyond special education: Toward a quality system for all students. *Harvard Educational Review, 57,* 367–395.

Giangreco, M. F., Baumgart, D. M., & Doyle, M. B. (1995). How inclusion can facilitate teaching and learning. *Intervention in School and Clinic, 30*(5), 273–278.

Graden, J. L., Casey, A., & Christensen, S. L. (1985). Implementing a prereferral intervention system. I: The model. *Exceptional Children, 52,* 244–265.

Greer, J. (1990). The drug babies. *Exceptional Children, 56*(5), 382–384.

Hallahan, D., Keller, C., McKinney, J., Lloyd, J., & Bryan, T. (1988). Examining the research base of the regular education initiative: Efficacy studies and the Adaptive Learning Environments Model. *Journal of Learning Disabilities, 21,* 29–35.

Howard, J. (1992, Winter). Developing strategies for educational success. *School Safety,* 14–17.

Huntze, S. L. (1985). A position paper of the Council for Children with Behavioral Disorders. *Behavioral Disorders, 10,* 167–173.

Joint Committee on Teacher Planning for Students with Disabilities. (1995). Planning for academic diversity in America's classrooms: Windows on reality, research, change, and practice. Lawrence: The University of Kansas Center for Research on Learning.

Jones, D. H., Sacks, J., & Bennent, R. E. (1985). A screening method for identifying racial overrepresentation in special education placement. *Educational Evaluation and Policy Analysis, 7,* 19–34.

Kauffman, J. M. (1986). Growing out of adolescence: Reflections on change in special education for the behaviorally disordered. *Behavioral Disorders, 11,* 290–296.

Kauffman, J. M., Lloyd, J. W., Baker, J., Riedel (1995). Inclusion of all students with emotional or behavioral disorders? Let's think again. *Phi Delta Kappan,* 542–546.

Long, K. (1983). Emotionally disturbed children as the underdetected and underserved public school population. *Behavioral Disorders, 9,* 46–54.

Lowenthal, B. (1996). Integrated school services for children at risk: Rationale, models, barriers, and recommendations for implementation. *Intervention in School and Clinic, 31*(3), 154–157.

Maheady, L. (1988). An opportunity for developing instructional diversity. *Service Systems Digest, 2,* 4–6.

Mayer, G. R., Mitchell, J. K., Clementi, T., Clement-Robertson, E., Myatt, R., & Bullara, D. J. (1993). A drop out prevention program for at-risk high school students: Emphasizing consulting to promote positive classroom climates. *Education and Treatment of Children, 16*(2), 135–146.

National Mental Health Association. (1993). All systems failure: An examination of the results of neglecting the needs of children with serious emotional disturbance. Washington, DC: Author:

Neel, R. S., Meadows, N., Levine, T., & Edgar, E. B. (1988). What happens after special education? A statewide follow-up study. *Behavioral Disorders, 13,* 209–216.

Nelson, M., & Pearson, C. (1991). Integrating services for children and youth with emotional and behavior disorders. Reston, VA: The Council for Exceptional Children.

Olson, L. (1990). Federal agencies sound the alarm over the "school to work transition." *Education Week, IX,* 1, 19.

Paul, J. (1985). Where are we in the education of emotionally disturbed children? *Behavioral Disorders, 10,* 145–151.

Price, L., Johnson, J., & Evelo, S. (1994). When academic assistance is not enough: Addressing the mental health issues of adolescents and adults with learning disabilities. *Journal of Learning Disabilities, 27*(2), 82–90.

Rosenberg, M. S., O'Shea, L., & O'Shea, D. J. (1991). *Student teacher to master teacher: A handbook for preservice and beginning teachers of students with mild and moderate handicaps.* New York: Macmillan.

Rosenthal, I. (1992). Counseling the LD late adolescent and adult: A self psychology perspective. *LD Research & Practice, 7,* 217–225.

Sautter, R. C. (1992, November). Crack: Healing the children. *Kappan Special Report,* K1–K12.

Shriver, M. D., & Piersel, W. (1994). The long-term effects of intrauterine drug exposure: Review of recent research and implications for early childhood special education. *Topics in Early Childhood Special Education, 14*(2), 161–183.

Stainback, W., & Stainback, S. (1984). A rationale for the merger of special and regular education. *Exceptional Children, 51,* 102–111.

Sugai, G. (1988). Educational assessment of the culturally diverse and behavior disordered student: An examination of critical effect. In A. A. Ortiz & B. A. Ramirez (Eds.), *Schools and the culturally diverse exceptional student: Promising practices and future directions* (pp. 63–75). Reston, VA: Council for Exceptional Children.

Valdes, K., Williamson, C., & Wagner, M. (1990). The national longitudinal study of special education students, statistical almanac. Vol. 3: Youth categorized as emotionally disturbed. Menlo Park, CA: SRI International.

Van Dyke, D. C., & Fox, A. A. (1990). Fetal drug exposure and its possible implications for learning in the preschool and school-age population. *Journal of Learning Disabilities, 23*(3), 160–163.

Wagner, M. (1991). Dropouts with disabilities: What do we know? What can we do? Menlo Park: SRI International.

Wang, M., Reynolds, M. C., & Walberg, H. (1988). Integrating the children of the second system. *Phi Delta Kappan, 70,* 134–138.

Will, M. C. (1986). Educating children with learning problems: A shared responsibility. *Exceptional Children, 52,* 411–415.

Yates, J. R. (1988). Demography as it affects special education. In A. A. Ortiz & B. A. Ramirez (Eds.), *Schools and the culturally diverse exceptional student: Promising practices and future directions* (pp. 1–5). Reston, VA: Council for Exceptional Children.

Yell, M. L. (1995). *Clyde K. and Sheila K. v. Puyallup School District:* The courts, inclusion, and students with behavioral disorders. *Behavioral Disorders, 20*(3), 179–189.

Zabel, R. H., Boomer, L. W., & King, T. R. (1984). A model of stress and burnout among teachers of behaviorally disordered students. *Behavioral Disorders, 9,* 215–221.

Index

Borgstedt, A.D., 202
Borkovec, T.D., 50, 230
Borkowski, J.G., 226
Bornstein, P., 226, 227
Borock, J., 419
Bostow, D.E., 222, 258, 261
Bott, D.A., 113
Bowen, C., 83, 99
Bower, E.M., 3, 68
Bowlby, J., 276
Bowman, P.C., 320
Boyle, M., 45
Braake, N.P., 276
Braaten, S., 262
Bradley, C., 83, 99
Bradley, D.F., 285
Bradley-Johnson, S., 329
Brady, M.P., 261, 386
Brakley, R.A., 201
Braud, L.W., 231
Braud, W.G., 231
Braukmann, C.J., 264, 336
Braunstein, P., 99
Brawley, E.R., 285
Breen, M., 211
Breidenbaugh, B., 247
Bremner, R.S., 93
Bricker, D., 377–379, 378
Brinker, R.P., 378
Broder, P.K., 58, 59, 314
Brooks, B.D., 329
Brooks, R., 11
Brooks, R.B., 324
Brophy, J.E., 225, 345, 353, 361
Brown, L., 126
Brown, R.T., 203, 230, 330
Brozovich, R., 247
Brulle, A.R., 66, 68
Brundage-Aguar, D., 212
Brunton, M., 9, 60
Bryan, T., 411
Bryen, D.N., 377, 378
Buchanen, B., 365
Buck, H., 123
Buckley, N.K., 221
Buell, J., 285
Bugenthal, D., 255
Buhrmester, D., 203
Buie, J., 262

Buisson, G,, 153
Bulgren, J., 367
Bullara, D.J., 413
Bullock, L.M., 26, 266
Burch, P.R., 260
Burchard, J., 256
Burks, H.F., 68, 126
Burland, S., 227
Burnett, J., 221
Bursuck, W.D., 45, 194, 361, 367, 368
Buss, A.H., 9, 101
Butterworth, T., 326
Buxbaum, E., 47, 48, 248
Bynum, T.S., 334

C
Caan, B., 213
Cabay, M., 384
Cahen, L.S., 162, 345, 346, 354, 363
Caine, E., 202
Cairns, R., 52
Calculator, S., 378
California Psychological Inventory, 123
Call, T., 388
Cammisa, K., 90, 91
Camp, B.W., 18, 44, 227, 259, 260
Campagna, A.F., 315
Campbell, R.A., 219
Canter, L., 162
Canter, M., 162
Cantrell, M.L., 284
Cantwell, D.P., 32, 33, 35, 36, 37, 40, 92, 198, 205, 207
Caplan, N.S., 58
Caplinger, T.E.53
Career Ladder Program, The, 335
Carey, K.B., 327
Carlson, G.A., 207
Carlson, P.M., 287
Carnine, D.W., 223, 225, 345, 357, 362
Carr, E.G., 150, 256, 377, 379, 379, 383, 386, 388, 389, 390, 394, 396
Carr, R.P., 205
Carran, D., 227
Carroll, J.B., 346
Carta, J.J., 283, 284, 297, 364, 413
Carter, J., 101, 231
Cartledge, G., 69
Casey, A., 4, 413

Street, A., 289
Strider, F., 231
Strider, M., 231
Strumphauzer, J.S., 323, 325
Stuart v. Nappi, 332
Stzelecki, E., 203, 204
Sugai, G.M., 101, 284, 412
Sulzer, B., 222
Sulzer-Azaroff, B., 153, 221, 326, 379
Sumberg, C., 263
Suratt, A., 382, 383, 387
Sutton, L.P., 59
Sutton, S., 202
Sverd, J., 38
Sverson, H.H., 281
Swaminathan, S., 384
Swanson, H.L., 226
Swanson, J.M., 198, 201, 202, 203, 205, 207, 209, 230
Swift, M.S., 26, 116, 126
Switzer, E.B., 313, 323, 324
Swize, M., 419
Sykes, D., 38
Sykes, E., 34
Symons, F.J., 89, 90
Szatmari, P., 93

T
Tager-Flusberg, H., 87
Talkington, K., 255
Talkington, L., 50
Taman, T., 377
Tamm, L., 209, 230
Tanner, B.A., 389
Tannhauser, M.T., 232
Tannock, R., 205
Tappan, P., 53
Tarpley, H., 258
Taussig, C., 65, 314, 321, 322
Tawney, J.W., 164
Taylor, E., 33
Taylor, F., 256, 262
Taylor, R.L., 118, 122, 123, 124, 125
Terdal, L., 127
Terrel, D., 119
Thelen, E., 387
Theraplay, 248, 249
Thibodeau, M.G., 382

Thies, A.P., 10
Thomas, A., 68
Thomas, C.B., 67
Thomas, C.C., 26
Thomas, D.R., 219, 222
Thomas, J.D., 229
Thomas, S.B., 260
Thorensen, C., 256, 264
Thorensen, K., 264
Thorley, G., 33
Thorne, J.M., 150
Thorpe, I., 123
Thurber, E., 58
Thurlow, M.L., 111, 112, 113, 225
Thurman, S.K., 114
Thurston, L.P., 364, 365
Tiegerman, E., 381
Tiegs, E., 123
Timm, M.A., 275, 286, 294
Timmons-Mitchell, J., 256
Tindal, G., 112
Tinsley, B.R., 277
Tobin, D., 365
Todd, D.D., 222
Todd, N.M., 66, 69, 120, 280–282
Todis, B., 289, 292
Topmasi, L., 213
Topper, K., 364, 365
Towbin, K.E., 97
Townsend, M.A., 216
Tracey, M.L., 8
Traisman, E., 213
Treffert, D., 83
Tremblay, A., 294
Trojanewicz, R.C., 61, 64, 311
Troutman, A.C., 16, 164, 216, 220, 360
Tsai, L.Y., 88, 90
Tucker, J.A., 352
Tucker, S.B., 211
Turkewitz, H., 42, 148, 173, 257, 259
Twardosz, S., 385
Twyman, J., 262

U
Ullman, R.K., 211
Ulrich, R.F., 50, 211, 222, 255
Underwood, J.K., 331
Ungere, J.A., 85